PITTSBURGH

by

Loriann Hoff Oberlin,

Jenn Phillips,

&

Evan M. Pattak

The Insiders' Guide®
An imprint of Falcon® Publishing, Inc.
A Landmark Communications company
P.O. Box 1718
Helena, MT 59624
(800) 582-2665
www.insiders.com

•

Sales and Marketing: Falcon Publishing, Inc.
P.O. Box 1718
Helena, MT 59624
(800) 582-2665
www.falcon.com

•

FIRST EDITION
1st printing

•

•

Printed in the United States of America

•

Front cover photo: Point State Park and Pittsburgh skyline, Commonwealth Media Services.
Back cover photos, clockwise from top left: Skyline at night, Andrew A. Wager;
Steelers fans, Michael F. Fabus; Mr. Rogers, Family Communications; Pittsburgh
neighborhood, Jeff Greenberg; Downtown architecture, M.G. Ellis;
University of Pittsburgh Cathedral of Learning, Jeff Greenberg.
Spine photo: The Kaufmann's clock, Kaufmann's Department Store.

•

Publications from *The Insiders' Guide®* series are available at special discounts for
bulk purchases for sales promotions, premiums, or fundraisings. Special editions,
including personalized covers, can be created in large quantities for special needs.
For more information, please contact Falcon Publishing.

ISBN 1-57380-070-8

Preface

When you arrive in Pittsburgh, what sort of folk will you find here? Southwestern Pennsylvania is diverse enough that generalizations about our residents can be tricky. Nevertheless, most people tote around an obsolete image of Pittsburghers that was forged in the furnaces of our steel mills. They envision us as a rough-hewn breed, square-shouldered, lantern-jawed men toughened by backbreaking labor in sweltering mills and subterranean mines.

This hardly dovetails with the reality of modern Pittsburgh, which you'll discover to be a sophisticated, diverse city with an economy driven by service and software industries and, to a lesser extent, manufacturing. Nor does this dated image allow for the increasingly important roles of women and minorities in the local economy and society. It's true that the "old boys" network that ran the mills and mines was a tad slow to provide opportunities for women and minorities. The dominance of steel and coal, however, is part of our history, fuller participation of women and minorities a thing of the present.

Shopworn as that traditional image of our residents may be, as most stereotypes, it still can tell us revealing things about Pittsburghers. First, it speaks of our friendliness, probably our defining characteristic. We are, after all, a people who built America's greatest industrial center, watched it collapse, then rolled up our sleeves and constructed a new, multifaceted economy. In accomplishing all that, we were a cradle of the American labor movement. We're veterans of collective action, and the cooperative spirit it requires.

Thus, Pittsburghers are above all a friendly, unpretentious people. Doesn't matter who you are or where you're from. Yinz—our peculiar version of the second person plural—will be accepted here. Nor is there a limit to our friendliness. The spirit of volunteerism is alive and well in Southwestern Pennsylvania, among individuals and corporations. We've developed a far-reaching network of civic and charitable organizations to keep our residents from falling through the cracks. We'll give you the shirts off our backs—skin, too, if that would help.

This uncommon friendliness, however, has its down side—a relentless focus on neighborhoods and the local scene. Our neighborhoods are charming, some even unique, and a considerable strength of our region. We are devoted to them. Allegheny County alone boasts 130 municipalities, while the region is carved into 100 school districts. Think of the duplicative costs for elections, for garbage collection, for street maintenance, for a hundred other services. Whatever its costs, we cherish our parochialism. Pity the poor politician who runs on a platform of municipal consolidation. He'll be tarred with the dreaded "M" word—Metropolitanism—and hooted back to the murky obscurity that produced him.

Those who relocate to this region become keenly sensitive to this duality. They are overwhelmed with Welcome Wagons of friendliness but never quite accepted as natives. Michelle Madoff, a native Canadian who for years was a Pittsburgh city councilwoman and one of our most prominent and high-profile public officials, never ceased to wonder at our attitude. "I've been here for 35 years," she was wont to say, "and I'm still not a Pittsburgher."

Can't be helped, Councilwoman. If you're not from this city, you're not of this city.

Cultural Riches, Sometimes Ignored

This engaging friendliness coupled with a tendency toward the insular marks our culture as well. We are a region of stunning and diverse cultural opportunities. These include Carnegie Museums of Pittsburgh, The Andy Warhol Museum, the Pittsburgh Symphony—world-class institutions each. Our Downtown boasts five halls for the performing arts, including two glittering temples, Heinz Hall and the Benedum Center for the Performing Arts. Our colleges and universities offer community theater, and we boast highly regarded opera and ballet companies. The region is rich in art galleries, well spaced through many communities.

Tap a Pittsburgher on the shoulder, though, and ask him what he thinks of these cultural jewels and he's likely to respond with a sheepish grin, "Never been there."

It's as if, once our cultural institutions attract national and international attention, they're too highfalutin' for us. This tendency to look elsewhere when the real riches are in your own backyard may be true in other cities, but it's especially evident here.

We're slow to pick up on cultural trends, slow to let them go once we finally get the hang of them. Consider "The Wave," that form of fan participation at sporting events that caught fire some years ago. For a time, you didn't see much of that newfangled thing at Three Rivers Stadium. Now, years after The Wave has waved good-bye to the national scene, you'll see it in force at Three Rivers, perhaps America's last bastion of this homely cheer.

We're hard to pin down culturally, perhaps a little schizoid. We have towns called Dubois and Versailles, and we pronounce them DOO-Boyce and Vur-SALES. It's not that we don't know about that palace with all the mirrors that King Louis built. It's just that local landmarks are more important to us.

In a 1991 survey, the *Pittsburgh Post-Gazette* asked its readers to rate its comic strips. Doonesbury, Garry Trudeau's satirical look at the contemporary world, was voted the second most popular strip, behind the soon-to-be-discontinued The Far Side. Pretty sophisticated tastes, right? Well, that same audience also voted Doonesbury the strip they would most like to see dropped. Go figure.

A Ready Sense of Humor

As we say, the typical image of Pittsburghers is accurate in some regards, off the mark in others. Perhaps its most glaring omission is that it doesn't begin to acknowledge our rich and ready sense of humor. Yes, we tend to be traditional, our focus tends to be local. We know it, though, and we're comfortable with it. If you want to poke fun at us, go right ahead—we'll laugh along with you.

For one of the best examples of our self-effacing humor, listen for a series of radio ads for Burgunder Dodge, a local car dealer. One doesn't usually turn to automobile advertisements for trenchant regional insight, but these commercials are different. In the series, hapless Pittsburgh motorists—we know they're from Pittsburgh because they say things like "yinz" and "dahntahn"—who are lost in endless traffic jams are rescued by the thunderous voice of God, as spoken by Pappy Long Himself.

Our favorite features a motorist named Sue, harried by her restless kids, who allows that the urchins should be kept in cages—you know, like in that movie, "The Science of Them Lambs." Sue is near despair when Pappy's voice cuts through the confusion.

"Take it easy an'at," He intones.

Sue's response: "Get aht!"

Here, in 60 priceless seconds, you find the essential Pittsburgh humor. We laugh at the hopeless traffic snarls we've created, at our tenuous grasp of popular culture ("The Science of Them Lambs"), at our reverence for local icons (Pappy Long). We laugh, too, at Sue's response to the presence of deity, pleased but hardly awed, as if we've known all along that God would be an okay guy from the neighborhood who could be counted on to lend a lawnmower.

Whether visitors to our region or new residents, you are cordially invited to laugh along with us. Yinz can poke fun at us an'at, but don't push too far!

About the Authors

Loriann Hoff Oberlin

Loriann Hoff Oberlin was born and raised in Pittsburgh. When she's not writing books or magazine articles, teaching workshops, or providing public relations support, she has great fun exploring this region she calls home with her two young sons.

While at Westminster College in New Wilmington, Pa., Loriann discovered the quiet towns and scenery north of Pittsburgh where tourists and residents now flock for shopping and a pleasant daytrip. Every summer (literally since birth!), she's also enjoyed a mountain escape in Western Maryland, home to Deep Creek Lake. And her writing has brought her in contact with many special people, including one of her favorite Pittsburghers, Fred Rogers and his dedicated staff.

Loriann is the author of several other books, including *Surviving Separation & Divorce: A Woman's Guide to Making It Through the First Year,* and *The Angry Child,* written with Timothy F. Murphy, Ph.D. She's also written *Writing For Money* and *Working At Home While The Kids Are There, Too.* Loriann has been the guest on numerous talk shows and news programs, including the CNN Morning News, and she's spoken at writer's conferences throughout the country.

Her feature articles have appeared in *The Saturday Evening Post, Attache, Bridal Guide, Family Circle, Woman's Day, Pittsburgh's Parent,* and *First for Women,* among other publications.

Loriann is active in community affairs, volunteering her time as a member of the East Suburban Task Force Against Domestic Abuse/Violence. She maintains a website regarding her books at members.aol.com/lhoberlin/author.html.

Jenn Phillips

Jenn Phillips is a writer and editor who works internationally from her office in Pittsburgh. She founded her consulting business, Writing Well Communications, six years ago. She writes articles and books, edits nearly anything she can get her hands on, coaches would-be authors, and designs and teaches workshops on writing. She's also a Kundalini yoga teacher, thus some of her favorite topics to write about include yoga and holistic health; she offers considerable expertise in these areas. She holds a bachelor's degree in professional and creative writing from Carnegie Mellon University, and she's currently completing her master's thesis, a nonfiction novel called *You Never Can Tell,* at the University of Pittsburgh.

Evan M. Pattak

Evan M. Pattak, a Pittsburgh native, is a writer, editor, publicist, and teacher, among other pursuits. His magazine writing has won Golden Quill and Women in Communications Matrix Awards and was anthologized in *Our Roots Grow Deeper Than We Know*, a collection featuring Pennsylvania writers.

He served as the last editor-in-chief of *Executive Report*, a former monthly business magazine in Pittsburgh, contributes regularly to local magazines T.E.Q. and Mfg., and operates a public relations agency serving such clients as the Urban Redevelopment Authority of Pittsburgh. He served for many years as public relations director for the cable television franchise in Pittsburgh. He began his career as a reporter for the Associated Press.

For nearly two decades he served on the adjunct writing faculty at Seton Hill College in Greensburg, PA., teaching journalism, magazine writing, and oral history.

He is an official scorer for Major League Baseball's National League and is proud to have scored a League Championship Series, an All-Star Game, and a no-hitter. He serves as part-time host and handicapper for the Ladbroke Racing Network and acknowledges that as a handicapper, he's a great editor.

He graduated from the University of Pittsburgh with a B.A. in political science. He resides in the Park Place neighborhood of Pittsburgh with his wife, Pohla Smith, horse racing writer for the *Pittsburgh Post-Gazette*, past president of the National Turf Writers Association, and author of several sports books for children and the biography *Citation*.

Acknowledgements

Loriann

Having loved and lived in this city all my life, it's hard to list all the influential people who have taught me about Western Pennsylvania without accidentally omitting someone.

On this project, in particular, I first have to thank family and friends. My parents introduced me to Pittsburgh long ago. I'll always have fond memories of discovering Downtown Pittsburgh, at a young age, even if it was to visit the dentist or get a new pair of glasses! Summer drives to Deep Creek and carting my stuff to and from Lawrence and Mercer Counties was especially memorable as well.

My sons, Andy and Alex, have shown me what it's like to rediscover old places and make new memories as we've enjoyed museums, parks, pumpkin patches, and more. They've endured my endless hours at the keyboard and telephone. Writing a book isn't easy. Neither is being a single mom. Combine the two, and someone here deserves a reward. Most definitely, it's my children.

This *Insiders' Guide to Pittsburgh* wouldn't have been possible without the research assistance of professionals all over the region. My thanks go out to Susan McGrane and Laura Robezzoli of the Greater Pittsburgh Convention & Visitors Bureau; Scott Henry at Bozell Kamstra in Pittsburgh; Linda Heacock of the Beaver County Tourist Promotion Agency; and the staff members of all other regional tourism departments who returned countless phone calls and sent numerous packages of material.

In addition, the folks at Carnegie Ready Reference, Child Care Partnerships, the Historic Review Commission, and the Pittsburgh History & Landmarks Foundation were also instrumental in completing research. Hedda Sharapan and Fred Rogers at Family Communications have exceptional knowledge of children and families and their needs and concerns, and I'd like to thank them for sharing those gifts with the rest of us. Mary Lou Rosemeyer, who represents Kennywood, Idlewild, and Sandcastle Parks, has been a wonderful resource, as was Ann Nemanic of Mountain View Inn, Donna Winner at Tara and the Buhl Mansion, Susan McCarthy at Nemacolin Woodlands, Marianne Lee at the Westin William Penn, and the staff of Hershey Entertainment & Resorts.

In addition, Bruce Randolph of Christian Associates of Southwest Pennsylvania, Martha Isler of The Early Childhood Initiative, and Bob Hoover, Lori Ling, and Liz Gray from the *Pittsburgh Post-Gazette* and others who contributed information and photographs.

My co-authors were great to work with. If you see any of us around town with a telephone permanently attached, please understand that there was a prodigious amount of research involved in this project. And while this book spent a good bit of time in the "to be done" pile, many people from Insiders' Guides and Falcon Publishing helped bring this book to the shelf, particularly John Harrington, our editor, who stuck with us and made this fun.

Finally, friends Cindy Etling, Jim Farwell, Dick Ollinger, Pam Price, and Tony Turo contributed insights to specific chapters. Linda Soldressen personally showed me around Beaver County and answered countless questions without complaint. Donna Israel and Michael Yarbrough added their insights and inspired me to finally get a nightlife! And Bob Laurenzano provided great companionship as I researched particular segments of this book.

Finally, if it weren't for my parents mentioned earlier—Elmer and Mary Jane Hoff—I would never have gotten to know this city and region as I have. So I dedicate this book to them. I'll always have roots in Pittsburgh because of them and the wonderful memories here. It's indeed been a beautiful day in my neighborhood!

Jenn

I would like to thank my friend Mary Beth Kelly, who has incredible administrative capacities and who assisted me with making phone calls throughout this project. I would also like to thank poets Lois Williams and Jennifer Dickie, who finished their own manuscripts in just enough time to help me wrap up the last few calls and stay on time with this project.

I offer love and gratitude to my wonderful parents, who stand beside me even though they're not sure I have a real job (wink), and to my dear friends (you know who you are) who never fail to cheer me on. I thank my spiritual teachers and my teachers of writing, who have helped prepare me for a good and happy life. And, of course, I offer my greatest thanks to God, without whom the simplest and most ineluctable thing, the breath of life itself, would not be.

Evan

Preparation of a work this dense inevitably depends on hundreds of collaborators. It's a measure of the legendary friendliness of Pittsburgh residents that our guide contains so much information. Wherever I went, whether Dahntahn or Sliberty, I found people eager to help. Allow me to extend my thanks to all of you while I cite those who went above and beyond the call.

Jan D'Arcangelo, formerly of the Pittsburgh Convention and Visitors Bureau, was a source of information and creativity throughout; many of our Insiders' Tips are based on Jan's contributions. Al Dettore, Jr., director of media relations for Westmoreland County, provided many valuable leads.

Pat Jurczak of The Hospital Council of Western Pennsylvania pointed me on the right path to Healthcare sources. Brad Magill, deputy chief of the division of Emergency Services for Allegheny County, was generous with his time in providing background on the 911 system.

For Parks, Mike Diehl, formerly with the Allegheny County Department of Parks, and Bob Gangewere, editor of Carnegie, provided useful research tools. For Getting Around, PennDot's Dick Skrinjar helped me avoid literary potholes. For Recreation, I shamelessly tapped the expertise of the *Post-Gazette* staff: Phil Axelrod, Mike Sajna, Larry Walsh, and the now-retired Danny Palmer all contributed.

Pat Crawford of Pittsburgh Public Schools, Herbert L. Morgan, Ph.D., learning research associate for the Steel Valley School District, and Paula A. Calabrese, Ph.D., assistant executive director of the Allegheny Intermediate Unit, guided me through education issues and developments. Dan Langan, press secretary for the Pennsylvania Department of Education, also provided important data.

Our Golf chapter is immeasurably stronger for the statistics provided by Judy Thompson of the National Golf Foundation. Mike Dudurich of the *Tribune-Review* and Marino Parascenzo, now retired from the *Post-Gazette*, suggested key contacts.

For Restaurants, I found it necessary to deploy all the troops—family and friends alike. Guillermo Cole of the Allegheny County Health Department and Charles E. Radle, now retired from the Pennsylvania Department of Agriculture, walked me through the regulatory apparatus. My sister-in-law, Kathy Pattak, recommended a number of South Hills restaurants, while my mother-in-law, Hazel Smith, served as field investigator for establishments in Armstrong and Butler counties. Sheila Goettmann and Kevin Decker did the same for Washington County.

Finally, special thanks to Bill Friedman, who started it all in the summer of 1997 by sending me an innocent-looking recruitment ad for writers. He since has been advised to focus on his law practice and restrict his clipping to manufacturers' coupons.

Table of Contents

Directory of Maps

Western Pennsylvania

Greater Pittsburgh

Downtown Pittsburgh

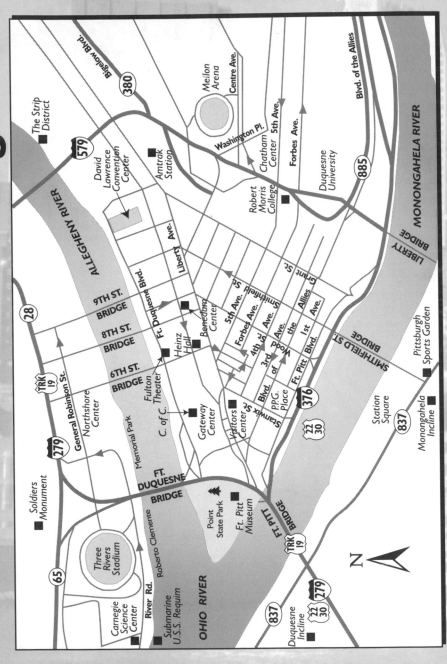

How to Use This Book

Many city guides languish on living room coffee tables. It is our fondest hope that the *Insiders' Guide to Pittsburgh* isn't one of them.

Rather, our purpose in producing this book is to provide you with the most complete, most dependable resource about Pittsburgh. We hope that you consult it often, that it will become your best source of information about the city, its people, and its amenities. While our guide does not strive to be exhaustive—it does not include every restaurant or hotel in the region, for example—we've tried to provide the best and the brightest of Pittsburgh.

We've researched and organized our guide so that it will serve as a valuable resource about Pittsburgh for those newly relocating to the city as well as for tourists and visitors. But we also believe that even longtime residents will find this an indispensable tool. If you're one of those veteran Pittsburghers, don't be embarrassed to refer to our book again and again. As we found out as we wrote this book, there is much more to this town than even natives could know.

Our guide includes useful information about restaurants, accommodations, shopping, nightlife, festivals, spectator sports, recreation, attractions, and daytrips. We also have compiled key information that should help you navigate the daily course of life. We've included a chapter about elementary and secondary schools, as well as a chapter about Pittsburgh's colleges and universities. A chapter details many of Pittsburgh's most interesting neighborhoods, while others outline services and opportunities for kids and senior citizens.

You'll also find chapters about art, architecture, healthcare, transportation, golf, media, and worship. In some cases, a Pittsburgh amenity or feature would fit comfortably in more than one chapter. For example, a description of the Pittsburgh Zoo would be at home in both the Kidstuff and Attractions chapters. In such cases, we've provided a full write-up in one chapter, with a shorter description—as well as a reference to the primary coverage—in the second chapter.

Any definition of Pittsburgh is bound to be somewhat arbitrary. Most would agree that Pittsburgh does not end with the city's limits, but just what should be included? Our guide goes beyond the city and Allegheny County to include Armstrong and Butler counties to the north, Westmoreland County to the east, parts of Washington County to the south, and Beaver County to the west.

In determining our geographic definition of Pittsburgh, we imagined you asking the question, "What shall we do today?" By including the additional counties, we've tried to provide as many answers to that question as possible.

To help you locate information quickly, we've followed a specific geographic rotation—Downtown, North, East, South, West—in all chapters where such organization is appropriate. In other chapters, material is organized in ways that make the most sense for readers. Where we've strayed from our geographic breakdown, we'll tell you in the chapter introduction.

In the Daytrips chapter, for example, we transcended our boundaries of Pittsburgh to include destinations within a three-hour drive of the city. In researching Senior Scene, we noticed that many municipal services are restricted to residents of the offering municipalities. Therefore, we have presented those services by county and reverted to our standard organization for unrestricted services and opportunities.

In all cases, you can quickly determine if an entity or service is included by checking the comprehensive index in the back of the book.

You'll find several special features that we've developed for your convenience and enjoyment. Frequently called phone numbers and sources of additional information are highlighted in gray boxes. New to town and need a physician? You'll find the phone numbers for physician referral agencies highlighted in a gray box in the Healthcare chapter.

We've captured many interesting quick-hitters about Pittsburgh; these "Insiders' Tips" are spaced throughout the book. You'll also find "Close-ups"—feature stories about the city, its residents, characteristics, and peculiarities. Both the "Tips" and "Close-ups" will pique your interest in Pittsburgh.

In our Restaurants and Accommodations chapters, each entry includes from one to four dollar signs to give you some idea of the price of a meal or an overnight stay. Prices represent comparisons within the Pittsburgh market only. Thus, a restaurant listed with "$$$$" would be among Pittsburgh's more expensive establishments, but the price should not be compared to those of restaurants in other cities.

Finally, a word about area codes. Phone numbers, of course, are an important feature of our guide, but the challenge of compiling accurate phone numbers was compounded by the introduction of the 724 area code in February 1997 to complement Pittsburgh's 412 area code. Remember that if you're dialing anywhere outside your area code—even if it's only across town—you'll need to dial 1 and the area code before the seven-digit phone number.

We hope you enjoy the *Insiders' Guide to Pittsburgh* and use it often. One of the recurring themes of the guide is the helpfulness and neighborliness of Pittsburgh residents. Being neighborly Pittsburgh residents ourselves, we may drop in on you one day. It's okay if we find our guide on your coffee table . . . so long as the book is well-thumbed.

Area Overview

Carved out of hilltops, nestled into valleys, and separated by the rivers, this region we call Greater Pittsburgh is a place people eagerly discover. In years gone by, if you told friends of an upcoming visit to Pittsburgh, they offered their immediate condolences. Images of the steel city translated into perceptions of smoke, soot, grime, and grunge.

The industrial age, sparked by the War of 1812, saw Pittsburgh capitalize on its bituminous coal resources. Mining, coupled with iron, steel, and glass production, flourished, with three convenient rivers to distribute the finished products to the rest of the country. With all that industry, it's no wonder Pittsburgh was called the Smoky City.

Early morning streets were darkened, and building exteriors were blanketed with the filthy remnants of heavy industry. In 1941, Pittsburgh had a higher rate of pneumonia than any other U.S. city. Pittsburgh pride and partnership took exception to the notion that it was simply a dirty city, knowing that if outsiders peered beneath the surface, they'd find a region with deep roots, bursting with life, strong traditions, positive aesthetic properties, and so much potential that's it's still being tapped today. Determination to transform the old Pittsburgh into the new paid off in ways even the best urban planners could not have predicted.

The city's first Renaissance was initiated in the 1950s, shortly after World War II, as then-mayor David L. Lawrence began a campaign called "Smoke Must Go." Railroad and shipping companies converted from coal-fired to diesel engines, and the steel and coal industries responded in kind with better technologies for eliminating airborne pollutants. Residents even switched from coal furnaces to much cleaner oil, electric, or natural gas.

That was just the first transformation. Renaissance II followed in the 1980s, under the tenure of the late Mayor Richard S. Caliguiri. Old buildings were razed and more modern towering structures were welcomed to the city skyline. This reformation occurred not only in Pittsburgh and in Allegheny County, but in outlying towns where mills and factories had forged the foundation of many Western Pennsylvania communities. Areas like Beaver, Butler, Armstrong, Westmoreland, and Washington counties had their share of coal mines, steel mills, and industrial sites.

When the wrecking ball demolished the last two blast furnaces at the Jones & Laughlin steel mill in the early 1980s, much of the region's industrial strength crumbled with them, as did thousands of jobs. Workers who knew everything about blast furnaces and organized labor knew little of service industries, re-engineering, and how their lives would be affected by Pittsburgh's continuing Renaissance.

One thing, however, sets Pittsburgh apart from its counterpart cities—the people who call it home. They are strong, proud, and particularly friendly, even amidst adversity.

LOOK FOR:
- **Vital Statistics**
- **Pittsburgh's Personality**
- **It's a 'Burgh Thing**
- **Famous Faces**
- **Economic Indicators**
- **Navigating Neighborhoods**
- **County Lines**
- **Pittsburgh Today**

AREA OVERVIEW

Pittsburgh's Vital Statistics

Founded: 1758
Incorporated: 1816
Size: 55.5 square miles
Elevation: 1,223 feet

Population:
City of Pittsburgh: 369,879
Allegheny County: 1,336,449

Pittsburgh Mayor: Tom Murphy
Pennsylvania Governor: Tom Ridge

Airport:
Pittsburgh International Airport

Average Temperatures:
July: 72 F
January: 26 F

Average Yearly Precipitation: 36 inches

Colleges and Universities:
29 in Western Pennsylvania, including the University of Pittsburgh,
Duquesne University, Carnegie Mellon University, Robert Morris College

Daily Newspapers:
Pittsburgh Post-Gazette, Pittsburgh Tribune-Review

Radio Stations: 12 AM, 20 FM
Television Stations: 11

Driving laws:
Driver's license at age 17; maximum speed limit 65 mph; seat belts
mandatory for driver and all front seat passengers; helmets mandatory for
motorcycle riders.

Famous Pittsburghers:
Christina Aguilera, Rachel Carson, Bill Cullen, John Davidson, Scott Glenn,
Martha Graham, Michael Keaton, Gene Kelly, Oscar Levant, Andrew Mellon,
Adolphe Menjou, William Powell, Fred Rogers, David O. Selznick, Gertrude
Stein, Joseph Wambaugh, Andy Warhol

Important dates in history:

1754: Captain William Trent begins construction of Fort Prince George for Virginia. French and Indians capture the fort soon thereafter.

1758: Brig. Gen. John Forbes in charge of an expedition to reclaim the fort, now known as Fort Duquesne. French desert the fort, and Forbes names his conquest "Pittsburgh" in honor of British leader William Pitt.

1787: Pennsylvania charters the Pittsburgh Academy, later to become the University of Pittsburgh.

1790: The first U.S. census shows Pittsburgh with a population of 376, while Allegheny County has 10,309 citizens.

1816: Pittsburgh is incorporated as a city.

1845: The Great Fire destroys 56 acres and 1,000 buildings in the heart of the city. Among the landmarks burned: Monongahela House, Bank of Pittsburgh, Western University, and the Monongahela Bridge.

1848: Andrew Carnegie, age 13, arrives from Scotland.

1856: Pittsburgh hosts the first Republican National Convention.

1858: The Sons of Vulcan, an association of iron puddlers and boilers and a predecessor to labor unions, is formed in Pittsburgh.

1859: Edwin L. Drake strikes oil in Titusville, and hour and a half northeast of Pittsburgh, marking the beginning of the U.S. petroleum industry.

1869: The first H.J. Heinz plant opens in Sharpsburg, just north of Pittsburgh.

1870: Mellon and Sons opens its banking business on Smithfield Street. Also, Monongahela Incline opens.

1880: Immigrants from southeastern Europe begin arriving in large numbers.

1886: George Westinghouse forms the Westinghouse Electric Co. Also formed in Pittsburgh is the Pittsburgh Reduction Co., later to become the Aluminum Company of America or Alcoa.

1892: Pittsburgh's National League baseball team becomes known as the Pirates for stealing a player from the Brooklyn Dodgers.

1905: The world's first all-motion picture theater, the Nickelodeon, opens in Pittsburgh.

1910: Robert L. Vann publishes the *Pittsburgh Courier,* one of the nation's finest black newspapers.

1950s: Renaissance I helps Pittsburgh begin its transformation into a modern city. Among the changes: reclamation of the point downtown.

1953: Jonas Salk announces success with the first polio vaccine.

1974: Point State Park is officially dedicated with the completion of the fountain.

1980s: Renaissance II revitalizes downtown yet again, with a new subway, convention center, and several prominent building's on the city's skyline.

Greater Pittsburgh Convention & Visitors Bureau:
Regional Enterprise Tower, 425 Sixth Ave., Pittsburgh, PA 15219.
Tourism information line: (800) 366-0093.

Pittsburgh's Personality

Pittsburghers stay put. It's not that we think there is no other comfortable place to live, it's just that we value our roots and traditions, our familiar routines, and even our minor frustrations. The occasional complaints about bridge repairs or tunnel traffic along the parkways are understandable, but take away the gorgeous view as we exit the Fort Pitt Tunnel entering the city, and we'd really have something to complain about. Sure, some neighborhoods have more parking problems than others, particularly in the winter, but as for the seasons, we revel in all four.

The Pittsburgh climate is not particularly harsh. Some winters we've been hard hit by snow and summers have occasionally been real scorchers, but by national standards, the region doesn't stand out significantly weather-wise. A Pittsburgher's only concern might be springtime flooding and a few too many rainy or overcast days. Such is our weather.

If it's a chilly day, you might see us skating in Schenley Park, and on a cold winter's eve it's a hockey night in Pittsburgh with fans packing the Mellon Arena to watch our Penguins. Spring urges us out among friends, visiting neighborhood parks, taking easy daytrips, and, of course, heading to the stadium to root for the Bucs. In summer, the big amusement parks open—Kennywood, Idlewild, and Sandcastle. Office workers take their lunches outdoors and enjoy the Three Rivers Arts Festival in conjunction with their meals. And who could forget Fourth of July fireworks at the Point or the Three Rivers Regatta each August? (See our Annual Events chapter for more detailed descriptions of these popular events.)

INSIDERS' TIP

For river recreation, there are more than 26,000 pleasure boats registered in Allegheny County, second only to Dade County, Florida.

As the leaves turn color, it's once again time for those glorious weekend getaways. We'll drive a distance just to pick our own pumpkin out of a patch on an outlying farm. In autumn, we're often back to school, cheering on our Steelers, taking in the fall flower show at Phipps Conservatory, and revisiting and enjoying a vast array of other indoor attractions.

The Monongahela Incline, built in 1870, is the oldest inclined plane in the country and provides visitors with a bird's-eye view of one of the country's most spectacular skylines.

Photo: Courtesy of Diane DaBaldo/Port Authority

Marconi Communications built its state-of-the-art headquarters in Warrendale.

Photo: Courtesy of Marconi Communications

Having such splendid seasons adds to Pittsburgh's appeal. It's no wonder that our pleasant city has often served as the on-screen double for much larger New York City. Film crews have camped out at Pittsburgh landmarks throughout the decades to make films like *Flashdance* and *Hoffa,* as well as more recent cinema picks likes *Striking Distance, Diabolique, Silence of the Lambs,* and *Inspector Gadget.*

It's A 'Burgh Thing

Just as the South has its drawl and New England its accent, Pittsburgh has its own dialect (see this chapter's Close-up). Beyond the spoken word, many other items foster familiarity among the locals. You haven't eaten deli fare unless you've actually experienced the fries and the slaw inside the sandwich, with Heinz ketchup of course. People all over the world enjoy ham sandwiches, but ours are chipped-chopped. Pittsburghers do take their food seriously. While many ethnic groups enjoy special cuisines and dishes, there's a certain kind of preparation that goes into native pierogies, kielbasa, stuffed cabbages, and Iron City Beer. Ice cream is standard, but Klondike Bars can't be beat. This, friends, is only a sampling of what's on the menu (see the Restaurants chapter and we'll whet your appetite even more).

Famous Faces

If you feel you've already experienced Pittsburgh's personality, it could be a direct result of a famous Pittsburgher. Indeed, this city has served as hometown for more than just Andrew Carnegie and H.J. Heinz, names easily associated with Pittsburgh. Did you know that Arnold Palmer grew up in Latrobe, not far from the origin of Mr. Rogers? The famous golfer still has a car dealership in Westmoreland County.

Other natives include actress Shirley Jones, artist Andy Warhol (whose surname was originally Warhola), playwright August Wilson, composer Stephen Foster, and actor Michael Keaton, who has returned home to make box-office hits such as *Gung Ho.*

Television producer Steven Bochco attended Carnegie

INSIDERS' TIP

Allegheny County has more than 1,700 bridges, with 720 inside the city limits and 15 major bridges crossing waterways in downtown Pittsburgh alone.

Talkin' Pittsburgh

While traveling, you've probably heard many unique versions of the English language, but if you had a college roommate from Western Pennsylvania, or if you've spent some time here yourself, then you know the version of English to which we refer. For the uninitiated, we call it Pittsburghese.

CLOSE-UP

Indeed, not all inhabitants reflect their Pittsburgh origin when they speak. Many disdain the dialect. Others, however, epitomize the vernacular.

Take the following fictitious conversation, for example:

"Jeet jet?"

"Nah, yunz gonna worsh yer hans?"

"Sure. I was just aht at the Jynt Igl. Brought us some jumbo, chipped-chopped ham, a couple of Klondikes—oh, and I stopped Dahntahn for an Arn."

"Then we better redd off this table. The Stillers game starts at one. Ats what the PG says."

And so it is—Pittsburghese. In our own defense, it's not that we Pittsburghers lack the knowledge of correct speech. It's merely that we're so excited, we can't wait to share what we have to say!

Slurred speech and shortened words aside, Pittsburghese bonds many of us. Above all else, we've learned to laugh at our native dialect. Witness the gift books created: Sam McCool's *New Pittsburghese*, Eric Schuman's *Are You A Real Pittsburgher?*, and *The Tongue-in-Cheek Guide to Pittsburgh*—written as much for our own humor as an out-of-towner's guide.

Here's a sampling of what's in store:

Ahia	state to the west of Pennsylvania that others spell with O's
Aht	out
Arn	short for Iron City Beer
Cahr Pahr	Cowher Power (it's a football thing!)
Chipped-chopped ham	our form of lunchmeat or deli ham
Crick	creek, as in a small body of water
Cleveland	the butt of many a Pittsburgher's jokes
Dahntahn	downtown
dill	no, not a pickle but a deal
dittent	did not
gumbans	elastic fasteners like rubber bands
high hills	not necessarily referring to mountain views, but a description of women's footwear
in regards to	a wordy expression that sounds a whole lot more impressive than it ever is
jeet jet?	an interrogatory meaning "did you eat yet?"
Jynt Igl	Giant Eagle, as in a supermarket, not a bird
jumbo	not a synonym for large, but merely bologna
Klondike	popular ice cream treats savored over the decades
Mon	short for Monongahela (well, hey, would you want to remember that spelling?)
needs	shortened form of "needs to be"
Parkway	trust us, this isn't where you park (unless you're driving at rush hour!)
PG	abbreviated nickname of *The Post-Gazette*

The Point	Point State Park (you know, where the fountain flows)
pop	carbonated beverage most of America calls "soda"
Presby	short for Presbyterian University Hospital
redd up	to clean, tidy, or make better than it is
Sahside	South Side
'Sliberty	East Liberty
spicket	the tap where water flows from
The Strip	no, not exactly a turn on, unless it's a Saturday morning and you're hot after fresh produce
Super Mario	not a video game, but truly our hockey hero who saved the team once by performance, again by owning it
The T	well, of course it follows "S," but in our town, it's the subway
whole 'nother	another whole item
worsh	to wash
Yock	the Youghiogheny River (try spelling that one, too!)
yunz	all of you, or more literally, "you ones"

Mellon University, and novelist Michael Chabon hit it big with *Mysteries In Pittsburgh,* inspired during his stint as an undergraduate student at the University of Pittsburgh. Chabon went on to write *Wonder Boys,* the movie version of which was filmed here as well.

Although it's technically outside our coverage area, we must point out that Jimmy Stewart was born and raised in Indiana, Pennsylvania, where his father held on to the family hardware store just in case Jimmy's film career didn't pan out. Well, Jimmy didn't need that contingency plan!

Jim Delligatti, a McDonald's franchisee in Western Pennsylvania, introduced the ingredients from his special sauce to a sesame seed bun, creating a sandwich better known today as the Big Mac. Other drive-through chains served double-decker burgers, and Delligatti wanted his creation to be big, so in 1967 the Big Mac was introduced for 49 cents. It took several improvements and lots of fun promotions to get to the Big Mac as we know it today.

In a town known for the industrial strength of men, women have made their marks. Among them, Nellie Bly, the famous newspaper reporter; Rachel Carson, a local biologist who took on the environmental movement; and Mary Cassatt, an artist who later found fame in France as the leading female impressionist painter.

Finally, just as appreciated is Mr. Yuk. That's right; the widely recognized safety symbol used to warn children away from dangerous substances was created at Pittsburgh's Children's Hospital.

Economic Indicators

As we've already mentioned, Pittsburgh's economic infrastructure has been transformed. Some companies and conglomerates, including Mellon Bank, USAirways, Pittsburgh National Bank, the University of Pittsburgh, and the University of Pittsburgh Medical Center (to name only a few)—the powerhouses of the local economy in decades past—continue to provide jobs for area residents. Some companies have, however, reduced their work forces during the years in an effort to stay competitive. U.S. Steel, now known as USX Corporation, may have laid off steel workers, but it continues to be one of the area's major employers as it has moved into oil and gas resources, real estate, transportation, and utility subsidiaries.

Though Westinghouse had its financial struggles throughout the '80s and '90s, becoming CBS and selling off different divisions, the Westinghouse name still exists. The nuclear business remains in Monroeville under American/British ownership that's once again growing the company.

Growth and change bring new partners to the economic front. Innovative players like the former FORE Systems (now known as Marconi Communications), the Pittsburgh

INSIDERS' TIP

In the first six months of 1999, there were more than 1.7 million hits at the website visitpittsburgh.com.

Technology Center, and the National Robotics Engineering Consortium add to the region's economic vitality. Small business and entrepreneurship abound here as well. One key word describing the area's employment and economic future would be diversification, as this region continues to be developed to its full potential.

Already a convenient airport from which business travelers can reach most other United States cities with only a two-hour flight, Pittsburgh International is built to accommodate more air carriers adding even more routes, destinations, and accessibility. City planners have begun the expansion of the David L. Lawrence Convention Center and have called for an increase in downtown hotel rooms. The O'Reilly Theater opened in 1999 as the fifth theater in Pittsburgh's Cultural District. Two new sports stadiums on Pittsburgh's North Side will be completed by 2001. And, new shopping districts and leading retailers are about to settle in Pittsburgh.

Navigating Neighborhoods

Within the city limits, our neighborhoods have names you'll hear on newscasts and in conversation. Some are easily definable, like Polish Hill, founded by Polish immigrants. From imbibing various beers and tasting the sauerbraten and schnitzel, you'd rightly guess that the influences at the Priory and nearby Penn Brewery on the city's North Side were of German descent. The Mexican War Streets neighborhood, however, doesn't get its name from Mexican Americans who live there—in fact, few do. The streets were named after Mexican battles and generals.

You'll soon associate Squirrel Hill with the foundations of Pittsburgh's Jewish community, the Hill District with the African-American community, and Shadyside with either old money or the new and trendy. The South Side (along the flats and slopes) maintains much of its Eastern European heritage, while Bloomfield revels in its Italian traditions. Nearby Lawrenceville is a blend of Italian, Irish and Polish pride. You'll quickly come to associate Oakland with top universities, but others know it as home. As you'll read in our History chapter, many German families still reside on the city's North Side. And as Pittsburgh has attracted very learned engineers, doctors, and other professionals, many of the surrounding suburbs have become much more multi-cultural than they were half a century ago.

Despite neighborhoods that are comprised of a certain folk, there's a good racial and ethnic mix in many areas. While you will find wealthy communities, the per capita income in 1997 (the most

Pittsburgh's Golden Triangle sits at the convergence of the Monongahela, Allegheny, and Ohio rivers.

Photo: Andrew A. Wagner

AREA OVERVIEW

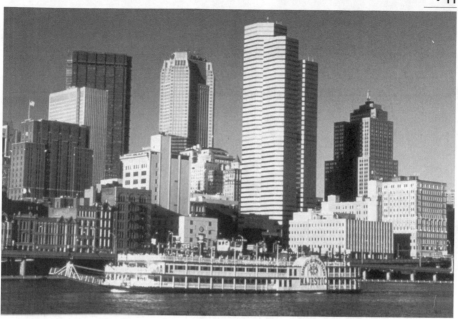

The Gateway Clipper ship sails along Pittsburgh's skyline.

Photo: Jeff Greenberg

current year reported) was $26,243, slightly above the national average of $25,288. And according to the Convention and Visitors' Bureau, the median family income as of 1997 was $38,200.

Allegheny County is the most populated of the Western Pennsylvania counties. It's interesting to note that this territory, which includes the City of Pittsburgh, encompasses the gamut of urban settings, as well as hundreds of outlying farms, many golf courses, and smaller neighborhoods that seem like little villages. That diversity, coupled with easy accessibility to the city's business district and sporting and cultural events, is the charm of living here. When families decide to live in Allegheny County, they realize their property taxes will be slightly higher than those in surrounding counties. It's a trade-off many people are willing to make for the conveniences, including a greater selection of school districts, hospitals, churches and synagogues, social services, access to many colleges and universities, and much more.

Don't let the neighborhood names in the region's outskirts confuse you. If you hear California or Indiana mentioned, don't automatically assume we mean "off in another state," for these are towns in Western Pennsylvania. Little Washington certainly isn't near the Pacific or our nation's capital. It's Washington, Pennsylvania, to the southwest of Pittsburgh. Indeed, Allegheny County is much more populated than Beaver, Butler, Armstrong, Westmoreland, or Washington counties (those we've defined as our coverage area for this book). As a result, most of the attractions, restaurants, and shopping emanate from this area.

Finally, Pittsburgh gained another distinction in 1999. It was named as one of America's most driveable cities by the Surface Transportation Policy Project. The group studied aggressive driving, and found that Pittsburghers drive at less risk than their counterparts in other metropolitan areas.

County Lines

Beyond Allegheny, there's Beaver County, just a few miles from Pittsburgh International Airport. Towns like Ambridge (another old steel town) sit along the Ohio River. You might

INSIDERS' TIP

Pittsburgh ranks as the 13th largest city in the nation. Pittsburgh ranked in the top five Most Livable Cities in the *Places Rated Almanac* in the 1993, 1989, and 1985 editions.

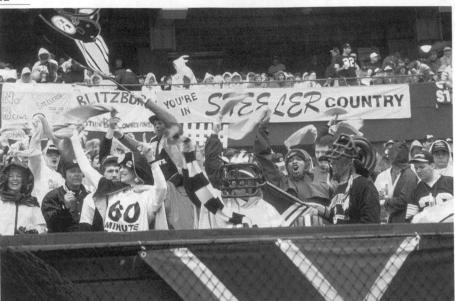

Pittsburghers take their football seriously, waving their Terrible Towels at Steelers games.

Photo: Michael F. Fabus

want to visit Old Economy Village, where the Harmonists, a German sect, built their final homestead. It is beautifully lit for candlelight tours during the holidays (see the Attractions chapter). Beaver is the county seat, and Beaver Falls sits at the northern end.

The Beaver River spills into the Ohio, and marinas abound in Beaver County river communities like New Brighton and Bridgewater. Parks are prevalent. You can visit Raccoon State Park, and the county parks of Brush Creek, Economy, and Brady's Run.

Butler County offers more history in Harmony, where German immigrants first settled in the early 1800s. The city of Butler is the seat of county government, but areas just north of suburban Pittsburgh such as Cranberry Township have seen tremendous growth in recent years. On a leisurely summer weekend, people often drive north to Lake Arthur and Moraine State Park, the state's fourth largest park. Cultural opportunities include the Butler County Symphony Orchestra, which celebrated its 50th season in 1998. (see the Arts chapter).

In Armstrong County, the Allegheny River runs southward. Towns here include Apollo, Kittanning, Freeport, and Ford City, where the first successful plate glass manufacturing venture in the United States operated as Pittsburgh Plate Glass Company, now named PPG Industries.

Greensburg is the center of action in Westmoreland County. There, you'll find the Westmoreland County Museum of American Art, the Westmoreland Symphony, and the Laurel Ballet. Fort Ligonier Days are popular for outings, as is the Westmoreland County Air Show and the Arts & Heritage Festival. Children can't wait each year for the opening of Idlewild Park, with its family setting in the wooded Laurel Highlands and the memorable trolley ride through Mister Rogers' Neighborhood of Make-Believe (check out our Attractions and Kidstuff chapters).

In Washington County, just off Interstates 79 and 70, Ladbroke at the Meadows brings out the equestrian enthusiasts who enjoy clubhouse dining and harness horse racing. Burgettstown's Post-Gazette Pavillion is the site of many summer concerts, with performers like John Tesh, Jimmy Buffett, and Alan Jackson appearing in past years.

The Pittsburgh Penguins hockey team, now under the ownership of former player and hero Mario Lemieux, practices at the Iceoplex in Southpointe, Washington County.

Also, Meadowcroft Village in Avella is a landmark in itself, a 200-acre facility offering a trip into the history of Native Americans, frontier settlers, farmers, coal miners, and conservationists. The Pennsylvania Trolley Museum offers a chance to climb aboard a streetcar and experience the sights and sounds of an earlier era when these vintage cars were the mainstay of transportation throughout Western Pennsylvania. Don't leave Washington County without photographing a few of the covered bridges you'll find in your travels.

Speaking of travels, some daytrips and sights make it worth driving into counties outside our coverage area. A trip to see Frank Lloyd Wright's Fallingwater is one of them. This masterpiece was constructed in Fayette County south of Pittsburgh in the 1930s for the Edgar Kaufmann family. Today it's maintained by the Western Pennsylvania Conservancy, which conducts guided tours of the house on the waterfall.

Shoppers also make several obligatory trips to Lawrence and Mercer counties (northwest of the city) for the Prime Outlets in Grove City, where more merchants than you can imagine are congregated in one spot. If your Mercer County daytrip becomes a weekend getaway, make Tara, a country inn, your romantic hideaway.

Finally, did you know that Indiana, Pennsylvania, bills itself as the Christmas tree capital of the world? Shopping, sightseeing, rekindling romance, and, yes, even chopping down our own Christmas trees are just a few of the reasons we venture beyond our own communities (see both the Daytrips/Weekend Getaways and Shopping chapters for further adventurous ideas).

Pittsburgh Today

We call the time period from 1980 to the present the Post-Industrial Era—and it's still evolving. Corporations continue the diversification of our economy begun in the late 1970s, furthering an infrastructure of finance, research and scientific concerns, high technology, healthcare advances, and educational excellence. You may be surprised to learn that there are more doctoral scientists and engineers per capita in Pittsburgh than in Boston, Los Angeles, or San Francisco.

Beyond all the accolades, a city is its people. Pittsburgh will remain prominent because it offers a high quality of life for the people who call it home. It maintains a relatively low crime rate, wonderful recreation, championship sports teams, a thriving cultural community, and tremendous warmth tied to its sense of family, ethnic heritages, and traditions. You'll enjoy it here. We just know it!

Downtown Pittsburgh.

Photo: Tim Barbano courtesy of Greater Pittsburgh Convention & Visitor's Bureau

Getting Here, Getting Around

Pittsburgh has a glorious transportation history, reaching back to its days as the "Gateway to the West" with bustling river and railway traffic. While the riverboats are gone and passenger trains have dwindled to a few, Southwestern Pennsylvania remains a busy inland region, within 500 miles of more than half the U.S. population. Because of its proximity to so many vital destinations, US Airways has designated Pittsburgh a hub, assuring a heavy volume of air traffic.

The region has developed a colorful and diversified transportation system to meet the demand. Pittsburgh International Airport is a sparkling facility with impressive room for expansion. Public transportation can take you just about anywhere you want to go, and the system features a variety of shared-ride services targeted to senior citizens and disabled patrons. As you move out from Pittsburgh and population density thins, public transportation options thin as well.

Highway travel is not always as gratifying, thanks to the double whammy of topography and weather. The region is hilly, the city itself squeezed between three rivers. These factors have contributed to the development of narrow urban streets; if you're looking for a town with broad, sweeping boulevards, you've probably come to the wrong place. Moreover, many of the older highways around town, once high-speed routes to and from the city, have seen neighborhoods and business districts spring up around them. As a result, some are ill-equipped to handle the unanticipated influx of traffic. Transportation planners labor to catch up, making highway development a dynamic, ongoing process here. Nevertheless, if you're from Washington, D.C. or New York, you'll think traffic during our rush hour is just breezing along. However, you will want to take note of two 'burgh things to avoid a potential pile-up: Pittsburghers slow down in tunnels and, at lights, they *often* let the person turning left have the right of way. That means some people turning left now *take* the right of way, so watch out.

Note also that weather does take its toll; winter's freeze-thaw cycles often lead to an annual spring fling of potholes. The good news about winter weather is that it seldom immobilizes the region. Between 1983 and 1997, Pittsburgh International Airport and its predecessor, Greater Pittsburgh Regional Airport, were closed by weather once . . . for 15 minutes.

We've divided our review of transportation in Southwestern Pennsylvania into two major segments—travel to and from Pittsburgh, and travel in Pittsburgh. We've paid particular at-

INSIDERS' TIP

A footnote to Pittsburgh's transportation history is the 77/54, a now-defunct bus route that, because of consolidations, wound an unusually lengthy and circuitous course. The route was affectionately known as "The Flying Fraction."

tention to three key areas of travel: Pittsburgh International Airport, public transportation, and parking in Pittsburgh's downtown and Oakland neighborhoods. One way or another, developments here likely will affect you, just about every day.

Travel to and from Pittsburgh

Air Travel

Pittsburgh International Airport
• **(412) 472-3526**

Pittsburgh International Airport is a marvel. It spans more than 10,000 acres, making it the fourth largest airport complex in the United States. To give you a better sense of its size, consider that Atlanta's Hartfield Airport and Chicago's O'Hare Airport—together—would fit comfortably within Pittsburgh International's borders. The airport routinely handles nearly 20 million passengers annually, making it the 27th busiest airport in the country, and by tapping unutilized acreage, it could accommodate more than twice that many.

INSIDERS' TIP
Don't even think about lighting up at Pittsburgh International Airport. It's a smoke-free facility.

One reason for its popularity is the airport's proximity to so many important locales. It's within one hour's flying time of such cities as New York, Detroit, and Washington, D.C., and within 90 minutes' flying time of 20 states and much of Canada. Yet another reason Pittsburgh International ranks so highly with travelers is the scope of its amenities and services for travelers. The facility debuted in 1992 following an $800 million construction project; you'd swear that its grand opening was yesterday. That's how new and inviting it looks.

Nor do you have to take our word for it. In 1999, when *Conde Nast Traveler* magazine released the results of its Readers' Choice Awards, the most prestigious distinction in the travel industry, Pittsburgh International Airport ranked first in the United States and third in the world. The magazine tabulated surveys from over 25,000 readers, making the prestigious poll also the largest private survey of consumer attitudes in the United States. Airports were rated on comfort/ambiance; customs/baggage claim; ease of connections; food/shops/amenities; and location/access. Only Singapore/Changi and Amsterdam Schipol airports received higher marks than Pittsburgh. You'll find the Pittsburgh International Airport in Findlay Township, about 16 miles west of downtown Pittsburgh. Let's take a tour through Pittsburgh International Airport. We'll call it PIT, as they do in air traffic controller circles, to get a real feel for the place.

Design

PIT features two main buildings: the Landside Terminal, with 25 commuter gates, and the Airside Terminal, which is shaped like a giant X and features 75 jet gates. When you arrive at the Landside Terminal, you'll be shuttled through a one-half-mile tunnel to the Airside Terminal by PIT's peoplemover system. The subway-like peoplemover can transport up to 13,200 passengers per hour at speeds of up to 32 miles per hour. You can't get from Landside to Airside except via the peoplemover, but don't worry about lengthy waits. No matter when you arrive, the peoplemover will be at your service in less than two minutes. Once you're at the Airside Terminal, you'll be at the center of the giant X, with the four concourses spoking off in each diagonal direction.

Because PIT is so large, it can be quite a hike from the most remote gates to the baggage claim area. PIT helps make it a more comfortable trip by providing moving walkways that will take you part of the way through each concourse. In addition, people with physical challenges who are flying on US Airways have the option of being transported through the airport in a large golf-cart-like conveyance. Wheelchairs are available for public use at the Traveler's Aid booth.

Airlines

To say that US Airways is PIT's dominant airline would be something of an understatement.

Of the facility's 75 jet gates, 50 are leased by US Airways. Of the 192,167 planes that landed at PIT in 1999, US Airways accounted for 46 percent of them; combined with landings by US Airways Express carriers, the airlines accounted for 86 percent of the commercial landings at PIT. Of the passengers who boarded at PIT in 1999, nearly 75 percent of them got on US Airways planes; combine US Airways and US Airways Express and that figure rises to nearly 87 percent.

PIT is a major hub for US Airways, which accounts for much of the airport's vitality, to say nothing of the positive impact on the local economy. Without US Airways' commitment to gate leasing and construction of an automated baggage handling system, PIT might still be on the drawing boards.

There is, however, another side to the coin. While PIT serves 114 locations with nonstop flights, to get to most of those cities, you won't find a choice of carriers. For travel to and from such major cities as Los Angeles, Baltimore, Charlotte, and Miami, you'll find that US Airways provides the only nonstop flights. That's the tradeoff at PIT: an airline vital to the well-being of the region, but one so dominant that potential competitors look elsewhere.

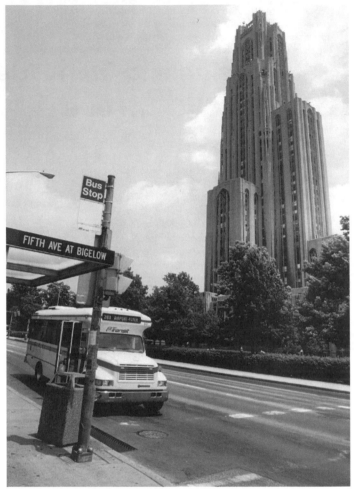

PAT introduced service to Pittsburgh International Airport via Oakland and Robinson Town Center in November 1996. Now, PAT has extended service to other suburban areas.

Photo: Fred P. Kenderson courtesy of Port Authority

Other airlines that serve PIT are Air Canada, American Airlines, Continental Airlines, Delta Airlines, Laker Airways, Northwest Airlines, Pan Am, Skyway Airlines, Trans World Airlines, United Airlines, and Vanguard. International travelers can take advantage of US Airways service to Frankfurt, Paris, and London.

Baggage

PIT likes to claim that its $32 million automated baggage handling system is reliable 98.9 percent of the time, and travelers seem to agree, considering the *Conde Nast* survey cited above. Among airlines that serve PIT, US Airways is the only authorized user of the automated system. That shouldn't hold you up if you're flying with another carrier; once US Airways passenger luggage is out of the equation, other carriers have relatively few bags to move.

You'll find the baggage claim area on the ground floor of the Landside Terminal, a pretty fair piece from some of the more remote jet gates. In many cases, since the automated system sorts 400 bags per minute, once you've walked and peoplemovered from your gate, you'll find your luggage waiting for you. Overhead neon signs will tell you which carousel has your baggage.

Ground Transportation

You'll find many ways to get from PIT to your ultimate Southwestern Pennsylvania destination. One of the most economical is the Port Authority Transit's express bus service called the Airport Flyer. The Airport Flyer links PIT, downtown Pittsburgh, and the Oakland university-medical complex with buses that run every 30 minutes between 5:30 AM and 12:30 AM. The bus also stops at Robinson Town Center, gateway to a rapidly expanding commercial and residential neighborhood near the airport. Perhaps the most attractive feature of the Airport Flyer is its price: $1.95 one way.

Airport Express, a privately run service, provides transportation to and from downtown hotels each 30 minutes by day, hourly by night. Rates are $12 one way, $20 for a round trip. Other options include taxi cabs, which typically charge about $30 for a trip to or from downtown. If your destination is east of downtown, expect to pay more.

Another private service, operated by Checker Cab, is Pittsburgh Air Bus, (412) 381-5600, which provides door-to-door bus service to and from PIT. Fares are based on zones traversed but typically range from $20 to $35. If you're traveling with a companion, the discount for the second fare can be as much as 75 percent.

Seven car rental agencies operate at PIT—all rental counters are located in the Landside Terminal. See this chapter's gray box for their names and phone numbers.

Be advised that if you're outside the terminal waiting for pick-up, you must be on the correct side of the terminal, since one side is dedicated exclusively to commercial ground transportation. If you look up and don't see a parking garage, we suggest you whistle a happy tune and head back through the terminal to the other side. (Where did we pick up this handy tip? Let's call it experience and leave it at that.)

Parking

PIT's tag line when promoting its service is "You Can't Park Any Closer." It would be hard to argue with that, as the airport offers a variety of parking options that can accommodate a total of

Pittsburgh International Airport is a hub for US Airways and serves many other airlines as well.

Photo: Courtesy of Greater Pittsburgh Convention & Visitor's Bureau

GETTING HERE,
GETTING AROUND

GETTING HERE,
GETTING AROUND

US Airways Boeing 737 jets are a common sight at Pittsburgh International.

Photo: Courtesy of Greater Pittsburgh Convention & Visitor's Bureau

9,528 vehicles. You'll find an indoor garage for short-term parking at $2.50 per hour to a maximum of $14 per day. For long-term parking, PIT maintains an outdoor lot with rates of $1.50 per hour to an $8.50 daily maximum. Both the short-term and long-term facilities provide access to an indoor moving walkway to facilitate your trip to the terminals.

For extended parking, PIT provides a 5,200-space lot, with a rate of $5.75 per day. Because these spaces are more distant from the terminals, PIT offers continuous shuttle service to and from the extended lot. No matter which option you choose, the parking areas are patrolled by Allegheny County Police. You'll enjoy complimentary emergency car-starting service, and you can pay for your parking with a credit card.

Convenient as airport parking may be, there are other options. A number of private carriers offer spacious parking lots and shuttle service to the airport. The shuttle services are easy to contact when you're at PIT—all their phone numbers are grouped on phones that enable you to access them by pushing a single button.

Prices for these services tend to be market driven; in considering them, be aware of the potential tradeoffs involved. For example, if you're paying more at the airport, is the convenience and security provided by the patrolling county police worth the extra price to you? Each traveler will answer that question differently. The shuttle services typically offer a number of discount programs, such as reduced prices for AAA West Penn/West Virginia members.

Amenities

The AirMall, a shopping mall contained within PIT, is so vast and attractive that if you're shopping there, you may have a hard time remembering to make your flight. It's described more fully in our Shopping chapter. While we're here, however, we should at least mention that all the shops and restaurants are PIT are required to charge the same prices inside the airport that they charge in other locations. You won't be paying $6 for a travel-sized bottle of aspirin here.

You'll find a food court with emporiums offering everything from pizza to deli fare, from baked goods to frozen yogurt. You also may enjoy several full-service restaurants, and you'll find food purveyors and lounges along the concourses as well as at the food court. You won't lack for nourishment here, but if there is a shortcoming at the food court, it's occasional congestion in the limited seating area.

If you're traveling with young children, you'll love Kidsport, a multifaceted play area for children designed to resemble a miniature amphitheater complete with tiered seating, padded floors, and ramps. When PIT's predecessor facility launched Kidsport in 1983, it was the first of its kind in the nation. It has grown substantially and today features displays from some of the region's cultural leaders, including Carnegie Science Center, The Pittsburgh Zoo, The National Aviary in Pittsburgh, and the Pittsburgh Children's Museum—all rotated every six months.

INSIDERS' TIP

You'll find America's shortest interstate highway in Pittsburgh. I-579, all 0.5 miles of it, connects the Liberty Bridge and I-376 (via the Boulevard of the Allies) to the Veterans Bridge across the Allegheny River and I-279. This mighty little highway often goes by an alternate name: the Crosstown Expressway.

Kidsport also offers continuously running videos that capture entertaining Western Pennsylvania scenes, a map of the United States designed into the floor, children's books, and a ticket counter designed to stimulate imaginative play. You'll find a baby-changing station and a gallery and seating area for sleeping children or nursing mothers. Kidsport is in Concourse C in the Airside Terminal, allowing convenient access to the food court and Airmall. One note: Kidsport is an unsupervised play area.

For adult recreation, PIT sports Airport Fitness, considered the nation's first health club located at an airport. The club features cardiovascular and strength-building equipment such as treadmills, stairsteppers, stationary bikes, and free weights. You can rent everything from clothing to shoes, and the club provides locker rooms, showers, a sauna, and secure storage areas for your luggage. An annual membership costs $420, while a daily workout costs $11.25.

Other Airports

Allegheny County Airport
12 Allegheny County Airport, West Mifflin
• (412) 461-4300

This airport, situated on a 432-acre plateau, once served as the region's chief commercial airport and continues to serve as a vital general aviation airport. Dozens of corporate and private aircraft are based at the facility, which functions as a gateway to the Mon Valley. It features three runways, a 23,500-square-foot terminal building, parking for 500 cars, and a range of aviation services. These include fueling, aircraft sales, rental and maintenance, parts and supplies, storage and tie-down services, and flight and mechanical instruction.

Beaver County Airport
Piper St., Beaver Falls
• (724) 847-4662

Since 1950, the Beaver County Airport has functioned as a general aviation facility, used primarily for business, training, and recreational flights. The facility is designated a "reliever" airport for Pittsburgh International Airport to provide additional capacity during times of congestion. Air Heritage of Western Pennsylvania, a working museum that restores aircraft of historical interest, is located on the premises. Beaver County Airport sponsors a popular airshow each August.

Butler County Airport
473 Airport Rd., Butler
• (724) 586-6665

Both corporate and private plane owners utilize Butler County Airport, which features an asphalt runway; The Runway restaurant; and a full-service fixed-base operator that provides fueling, maintenance, training, and charter service. The facility is a designated "reliever" for Pittsburgh International Airport.

Washington County Airport
205A Airport Rd., Washington
• (724) 228-5151

This facility offers a 5,000-foot runway used by corporate and private aircraft, as well as a fixed-base, aeronational operator to handle fueling and maintenance needs.

Arnold Palmer Regional Airport
200 Pleasant Unity Rd., Latrobe
• (724) 539-3110

Ground transportation from Pittsburgh International Airport to parts of Westmoreland County can be an exhausting three-hour journey. Another option is to land at Arnold Palmer Regional Airport, a convenient spot if your destination is Greensburg or points east. US Airways services the airport, as do several full-service air charter firms and car rental agencies. At the airport, you'll find a gift shop and Jimmy Monzo's Blue Angel, a full-service restaurant. Flight training is also available.

When you're traveling to or from the region via Pittsburgh International Airport, here's a directory of key phone numbers that can help things go more quickly.

Airlines

Air Canada	(888) 247-2262
American Airlines	(800) 443-7300
British Airways	(800) 247-9297
Continental Airlines	(800) 523-3273
Delta Airlines	(800) 221-1212
Northwest KLM Airlines	(800) 225-2525
Trans World Airlines	(800) 221-2000
Spirit Airlines	(800) 772-7117
United Airlines	(800) 241-6522
US Airways	(800) 428-4322

Commuter Airlines

Allegheny (US Airways Express)	(800) 428-4322
American Airlines	(800) 433-7300
Chautauqua (US Airways Express)	(800) 428-4322
ComAir (Delta Connections)	(800) 221-1212
Continental Express	(800) 523-3273
Mesa (US Airways Express)	(800) 428-4322
Mesaba Airlines (Northwest KLM Airlink)	(800) 225-2525
Piedmont (US Airways Express)	(800) 428-2322
PSA (US Airways Express)	(800) 428-2322
Trans States Airlines (TWA Express)	(800) 221-2000
United Express	(800) 241-6522

Car Rentals

Alamo Rent-A-Car	(412) 472-5060
Avis Rent-A-Car	(412) 472-5200
Budget Rent-A-Car	(412) 472-5471
Dollar Rent-A-Car	(412) 472-5100
Enterprise Rent-A-Car	(412) 391-7766
Hertz Corporation	(412) 472-5955
National Car Rental	(412) 472-5094
Thrifty Rent-A-Car	(412) 472-5288

Other Useful Numbers

Airport Information	(412) 472-3526
Airport Lost and Found	(412) 472-3500
Airport Parking Information	(412) 472-5050
Travelers Aid Society	(412) 472-3599
Police - General Information	(412) 472-5510

Train Travel

Amtrak
1100 Liberty Ave., Pittsburgh
• **(412) 471-6172, (800) 872-7245**

Amtrak's Pittsburgh station is located at the eastern edge of downtown, near the Greyhound bus terminal and Liberty Center. It's also convenient to many Port Authority of Allegheny County bus lines. Amtrak offers an automated reservation system that will provide you with schedules and fare information. You can also get that by visiting Amtrak's web site, amtrak.com.

Destinations for the two, reservations-only trains that service Pittsburgh currently include New York, Philadelphia, Harrisburg-Altoona, Johnstown-Pittsburgh, and Chicago. If you ride the Pennsylvanian or Three Rivers, you'll find

Port Authority's "T" links communities in the South Hills directly to the heart of downtown.

Photo: Courtesy of Port Authority of Allegheny County

sandwiches and snacks in the dinette and a lounge area where smoking is permitted during certain times of day. You also may utilize the Amtrak Express Shipping and Checked Baggage Service aboard the Three Rivers.

The Three Rivers offers connections to the Capitol Limited. No matter which train you ride to New York, you'll find buses to connect you to Kennedy and LaGuardia airports. Amtrak's Pittsburgh station is fully accessible to wheelchair users.

Bus Travel

Greyhound Bus Lines
11th & Liberty Ave., Pittsburgh
• **(412) 392-6513, (800) 231-2222**
Mall Circle Dr., Monroeville
• **(412) 856-3080**
• **www.greyhound.com**

Greyhound offers two area terminals, in downtown Pittsburgh and the eastern suburb of Monroeville. The company travels to 1,400 different destinations; you can reach most of them from Pittsburgh, although some involve bus changeovers. You'll find discount programs for advance bookings and kids, as well as a "companion fare" program offering reduced rates.

While the company's national fleet numbers about 2,400 buses, not all are wheelchair accessible. To find out if a bus can accommodate your needs, it's best to call in advance.

Car Travel—
Interstate Highways

The interstate highway system can make car travel to and from Pittsburgh a pretty easy and comfortable mission, although there is one unusual feature of interstate highway travel here. The Pennsylvania Department of Transportation (PennDOT) reports that, while trucks typically account for about 10 percent of all traffic on interstate highways, the percentage in our region is about 50 percent higher, or 15 percent of all vehicles on the road. Note the variability in speed limits from 55 to 65 mph throughout the region; if you're not paying attention, you could easily cross into a 55 mph zone while doing 65.

Interstate 76

This is the Pennsylvania Turnpike, which covers 506 miles and crosses the Commonwealth, linking the cities of Pittsburgh, Harrisburg, and

Philadelphia and connecting with the Ohio and New Jersey turnpikes. The turnpike also features a Northeast Extension that will take you to Scranton and other Northeastern Pennsylvania locations. Locally, you'll find access to the turnpike at Monroeville, Harmarville, Warrandale, Butler, and Beaver Valley.

The highway is administered by the Pennsylvania Turnpike Commission, which charges 4.1 cents per mile for passenger cars. You must pay your tolls in cash upon leaving the highway. PennDOT maintains a Welcome Center along the turnpike near Beaver Falls. One caution about turnpike driving: exits can be as far as 30 miles apart, so you don't want to miss yours.

Interstate 376

I-376, known locally as the Parkway East, connects the Pennsylvania Turnpike with downtown Pittsburgh and is the principal link between the city and its eastern suburbs. It's heavily traveled, carrying 93,000 vehicles each weekday, and you can expect routine rush hour delays that can make the road look like a genuine park way, but pile-ups usually don't last long. If you travel I-376, you'll course through the Squirrel Hill tunnels at the City of Pittsburgh's eastern edge. Watch out for delays here; remember, Pittsburgh drivers slow down as they drive through tunnels. Go figure...

Interstate 79

This is a major north-south highway that goes from Erie all the way to southern West Virginia. It also intersects with I-70 in Washington County. PennDOT maintains a Welcome Center along I-79 in Greene County.

Interstate 279

I-279 is a loop off I-79 and serves as a vital connection between the heavily populated North Hills, the City of Pittsburgh, and Pittsburgh International Airport. Local residents call I-279 either the Parkway West or the Parkway North, depending on which section they're talking about. The highway exits downtown Pittsburgh across the Fort Pitt Bridge and through the Fort Pitt Tunnels; here, it becomes the state's most heavily traveled highway, handling 148,000 vehicles per day. Rush hour traffic jams are common.

An important feature of I-279 is the region's only high occupancy vehicle (HOV) lane, which during morning and evening rush hour is restricted to vehicles with a minimum of two occupants. At all other times, the HOV lane functions as an express lane and is open to all drivers. You'll find the HOV lane between the North Side of Pittsburgh and the city's northern suburbs.

Interstate 70

I-70 is an important highway in Washington and Westmoreland counties, taking you through the Mon Valley or west into West Virginia, Ohio, and beyond. PennDOT maintains a Welcome Center along I-70 in Washington County.

Interstate 80

It's slightly north of our principal coverage area, but I-80—sometimes called the "Keystone Shortway"—is a road you should know about. It's a good route to central and eastern Pennsylvania points, and it will deposit you directly in New Jersey going east or Ohio going west. To reach I-80, take I-79 north to New Castle in Lawrence County.

Travel in Pittsburgh

Because public transportation in Southwestern Pennsylvania tends to be organized and administered by county, we'll begin our look at public transportation in the same way. That doesn't mean you can't get from, say, Westmoreland County to Allegheny County. You can, although the options are limited; county boundaries tend to shape the contours of the region's public transportation. That will be important to keep in mind if you're a public transportation user.

Allegheny County

In Allegheny County, public transportation is the domain of the Port Authority of Allegheny County, or PAT as it's popularly known. It's a massive job, as PAT provides service to 250,000 riders per weekday. It accomplishes this by deploying about 750 buses each day along with several nifty features—inclines and the "T" light rail and subway system—that we've described below.

INSIDERS' TIP

City, county, and state government all have responsibility for highway maintenance in Southwestern Pennsylvania.

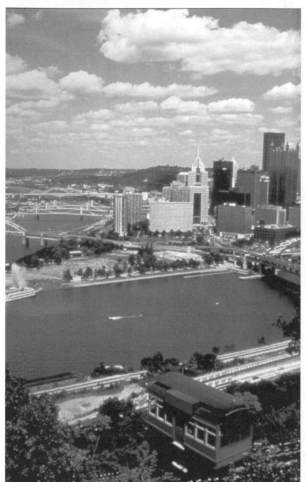

The Duquesne Incline is not only a tourist attraction, but a means for commuters to get down to the city from Mt. Washington.

Photo: Courtesy of Greater Pittsburgh Convention & Visitor's Bureau

nior citizens and those with disabilities. Many ACCESS riders enjoy discounts of up to 90 percent once eligibility has been established. It's a vital service in the county, providing more than 2 million passenger trips each year. For information about ACCESS, call PAT at (412) 562-5380.

The fare for a ride on a PAT bus is $1.25. If you need to transfer to another route, it's an extra 25 cents. Within downtown, all buses are free until 7 PM, when fares become 75 cents. If you're a frequent rider, PAT offers a number of discount opportunities, including: books of 10 discounted tickets; weekly, monthly, and annual subscription passes; a Weekend Day Pass; and a Summer Ride Pass.

Disabled patrons may ride for half price during off-peak hours, while senior citizens ride for free during off-peak hours on weekdays and all day on Saturdays, Sundays, and holidays. For certification to either program, call PAT at (412) 255-1356 or stop by the PATransit Downtown Service Center, 534 Smithfield Street. Applications for Senior Citizen Transit Cards also are available at senior centers throughout the county.

PAT modifies its routes and schedules several times per year to respond to changing conditions and customer needs. You can keep up with all routes, schedules, and changes by visiting PAT's web site, www.ridegold.com, or by calling PAT's Customer Service department, (412) 422-2000. They'll send you "The Ride Guide," which is a complete directory of routes, and other helpful information.

The bus system also features a number of exclusive bus lanes that serve most of the county and cut much of the time from your trip. These include the South Busway, the Martin Luther King, Jr. East Busway, and a High Occupancy Vehicle (HOV) Lane that's part of Interstate 279 in the North Hills. The HOV Lane is open to carpoolers as well.

PAT offers a number of programs for riders with special needs, including 228 bus routes that are accessible to wheelchairs each weekday; all PAT routes are wheelchair-accessible on Saturdays, Sundays, and holidays. In addition, PAT sponsors and administers ACCESS, a door-to-door, advanced reservation, shared-ride transportation service targeted primarily to se-

Inclines

Imagine a subway car rolling along a track. Now imagine the car and track tilted at about a 35-degree angle to carry you up a mountainside. You now have a mental picture of an unusual transportation mode known as an incline. In Pittsburgh, you don't have to imagine it, as the city is served by two inclines that function both as tourist attractions and as important daily conveyances for downtown commuters.

Between 1870 and 1901, transportation

pioneers in the city erected and operated 15 "inclined planes," as they were formally known, to carry folks up and down Pittsburgh's steep hills. Although most were passenger conveyances, at least one served as a freight incline to haul horses, buggies, furniture, and coal. As the city's roadway and public transportation systems improved, incline ridership declined. Today, only two inclines survive.

Both the Monongahela Incline and the Duquesne Incline link the Mt. Washington and Duquesne Heights neighborhoods to the South Side, more than 600 feet below. The cars traverse Mt. Washington at 6 miles per hour. They're popular with tourists, as a ride on the incline can be combined with a stop at the observation decks atop Mt. Washington, providing breathtaking views of the city and its three rivers. Mt. Washington and Duquesne Heights residents use them to reach the South Side; from there, a walk across the Smithfield Street Bridge gets them to work. Their total commuting costs: $1 each way for the incline ride.

The inclines operate from 5:30 AM to 12:45 AM Monday through Saturday, with reduced hours on Sundays and holidays. Both inclines run on demand; that means, after waiting only a few minutes, ostensibly, you could have the thing to yourself. For information about the Mon Incline, contact the Port Authority of Allegheny County, (412) 442-2000. The Duquesne Incline is operated by a nonprofit group called the Society for the Preservation of the Duquesne Heights Incline. You can reach them at (412) 381-1665.

Parking

Downtown Pittsburgh offers approximately 42,000 parking spaces, including metered on-street parking and downtown and downtown fringe lots and garages. That may seem like a pretty generous number, but if you consider that 148,000 vehicles whiz past downtown each day on I-279, it's pretty easy to see the peril here. If downtown is the destination for too many of those drivers, there won't be enough parking to go around.

Of course, it seldom is as bad as that. Many of those drivers aren't coming downtown, and those who do aren't necessarily parking all day, so there is some turnover. If you arrive early enough or late enough in the workday, chances are you'll find the space you desire, or one pretty close to it. You will encounter a crunch virtually every mid-day, when the all-day parkers

have yet to depart and downtown crowds are swollen by noon hour shoppers and diners.

Moreover, downtown won't pose the only parking challenges for you in the city. The Oakland neighborhood, with its phalanx of important hospitals and universities, is notoriously crowded when the colleges are in session. In some of Pittsburgh's residential neighborhoods, parking is at such a premium that the city has taken to providing permits to local residents for on-street parking: no permit, no park.

Public transportation and car-pooling may be your most reliable alternatives. If you must drive, however, we'll try to give you a wheel up by profiling the largest parking garages in downtown and Oakland, providing some information about PAT's "Park and Ride" program, and offering some insight into Pittsburgh's homegrown parking solution—a chair strategically placed in "your" parking space.

Parking—Downtown

Downtown proper offers about 26,000 parking spaces. With a little ingenuity and luck, you can find one. You may need to walk a little further than you had planned or grab the "T" to reach your destination, but with persistence, you'll find your space.

For each facility, we've provided the minimum and maximum hourly rates—in other words, what you'd pay to park from 0-30 minutes and the maximum that you'd pay to park all day. Included within the range is what you'd pay to park on a weekend or week night; the cost is often a lower hourly rate or flat fee then. If different pricing applies during special events, we've noted that. Phone numbers listed are those of garage operators and may ring at corporate offices rather than on site. Unless otherwise noted, all garages and lots offer security guards, handicapped-reserved spaces, and discounted evening rates. Downtown garages also provide escort service upon request. Where valet parking is offered, that usually means a charge and/or a tip over and above the standard hourly rate. The entries below are not comprehensive, as you'll find many other surface lots and indoor garages, but these are the largest parking sites, where open spaces are most likely.

Boulevard of the Allies Garage
Blvd. of the Allies, Pittsburgh
• (412) 261-0672

An indoor bridge connects this garage to three other sites: Oxford Centre, Forbes Av-

With its 908 buses and 55 light rail vehicles, PAT provides 250,000 rides daily.

Photo: Diane DaBaldo courtesy of Port Authority

enue Garage, and Kaufmann's department store. Thus, it's possible to do all your parking and shopping without ever setting foot outdoors. On raw or rainy days, that can be a big advantage. The garage offers 500 spaces, rates ranging from $2.50 to $10.50, and discounts with a purchase from a participating merchant. Monthly leases are priced at $165, but don't count on one of these—there's a two-year waiting list.

Convention Center Garage
1001 Penn Ave., Pittsburgh
• **(412) 344-6565**

Part of the David L. Lawrence Convention Center, this 535-space garage provides the closest possible parking for Convention Center events. It's also connected by an indoor bridge to Liberty Center and The DoubleTree Hotel. Rates range from $3 to $10.50. Monthly leases are priced at $175 by day, $85 by night.

Forbes Avenue Garage
Forbes Ave., Pittsburgh
• **(412) 261-0672**

Veteran Pittsburgh parkers often refer to this facility as "Cherry Way," since that's where you'll find its vehicular entrance. The garage is

connected by indoor bridges to both One Oxford Centre and Kaufmann's department store—a great advantage in foul or cold weather. You'll find 800 spaces and rates ranging from $2.50 to $11. The garage offers monthly night leases for $45 and discounts when you patronize certain downtown establishments.

Fort Duquesne & Sixth Street
120 Sixth St., Pittsburgh
• **(412) 765-1938**

You'll find this a convenient garage for events in the Cultural District. Rates for the 920 spaces range from $2.75 to $8, and you'll receive a discount when you patronize certain downtown establishments. Monthly lease rate is $190 by day, $45 by night.

Gateway Center Garage
400 Liberty Ave., Pittsburgh
• **(412) 531-5668**

You'll feel like you've discovered an underground grotto when you park here. The garage is connected by subterranean tunnels to the six buildings in the Gateway Center complex as well as the Hilton Hotel. Rates for the 650 spaces range from $3.50 to $17, and you can opt for valet parking. You can lease a space for $260 per month.

Liberty Center Garage
10th & Liberty, Pittsburgh
• (412) 261-6655

You'll be beneath Liberty Center and the DoubleTree Hotel when you park here. The garage offers 500 spaces, rates ranging from $5 to $15, and monthly leases for $220 to $245. You also may take advantage of valet parking.

The Manor Complex Garage
564 Forbes Ave., Pittsburgh
• (412) 323-4455

This garage is part of the Manor Building and a quick walk from Grant Street, the hub of the city's legal and political activity. Rates for the 750 spaces range from $4 to $9, with monthly leases available for $175.

Mellon Square Garage
Mellon Sq., Pittsburgh
• (412) 323-4455

One of the most popular garages because of its central location, Mellon Square Garage offers 1,000 spaces at rates ranging from $3 to $11. Monthly lease rate is $220, with a discounted monthly lease night rate available.

Mon Wharf Parking
Mon Wharf, Pittsburgh
• (412) 456-2770

If you plan to park on the Mon Wharf, you will enjoy a favorable rate—$6, no matter how long you stay—but you need to be aware of certain things. First, this surface lot is only a few paces from the Monongahela River, meaning you will have a bit of a walk to central downtown locations. Perhaps more importantly, the lot typically is flooded several times each year when the Mon rises, so you need to be aware of river conditions before you park here. The lot offers 850 spaces and security from 1 PM to 9 PM but no monthly leases.

Ninth & Penn Garage
130 Ninth St., Pittsburgh
• (412) 456-2770

When you're planning to enjoy a play or performance in Pittsburgh's Cultural District, you'll find this lot a short walk from your venue. It features 530 spaces and rates ranging from $2.75 to $8. Monthly leases are available for $190, and monthly night

leases are priced at $45. Your hourly rate will be discounted with a purchase from participating downtown merchants.

One Oxford Centre Garage
Smithfield & Third, Pittsburgh
• (412) 263-2180

If you're planning a shopping expedition at trendy Oxford Centre, you can't beat the convenience of this 850-space garage. Rates range from $3.50 to $12, with discounts when you patronize certain shops in Oxford Centre. Cost for monthly leases is $270—slightly less for Oxford Centre tenants.

The garage is connected by a series of bridges to both the Forbes Avenue Garage and the Boulevard of the Allies Garage.

PPG Place Garage
311 Market St., Pittsburgh
• (412) 434-1900

As the name suggests, this garage is part of the six-building PPG Place complex, headquarters to many important Pittsburgh companies and adjacent to the popular dining spots of Market Square. Rates for the 673 spaces range from $3 to $14, with monthly leases ranging from $210 for open parking to $275 for a reserved space.

Sixth & Penn Garage
Sixth St. & Penn Ave., Pittsburgh
• (412) 323-4455

On many nights, there's a palpable excitement around this garage—it's the closest parking garage to Heinz Hall, home of the Pittsburgh Symphony Orchestra and many touring troupes and plays. The garage offers 500 spaces, rates ranging from $2 to $11, and monthly leases for $215.

Smithfield Street & Liberty Avenue
629 Smithfield St., Pittsburgh
• (412) 765-1938

An indoor tunnel connects this 620-space garage to the Duquesne Club, making it a convenient parking site when you're dining at the club. Rates range from $2.75 to $11, with monthly leases priced at $230. Your fee will be discounted with a purchase at participating downtown establishments.

Stanwix Street Garage
625 Stanwix St., Pittsburgh
• (412) 391-0267

This garage near Gateway Center offers 738 spaces with rates ranging from $4 to $11. Monthly leases are priced at $200—$230 if you'd prefer valet parking. Hourly rates are discounted with purchases from participating merchants.

Third Avenue Garage
Third Ave. at Wood St., Pittsburgh
• (412) 323-4455

This centrally located garage offers 550 spaces, with rates ranging from $2.75 to $10 and monthly leases for $200.

USX Tower Garage
600 Grant St., Pittsburgh
• (412) 263-0440

When you have an appointment at USX Tower, one of the city's most important headquarters facilities, you can't beat the convenience of this 650-space garage. Rates range from $3 to $16, with monthly leases available for $275 and valet parking offered.

Westinghouse Garage
10 Stanwix St., Pittsburgh
• (412) 323-4455

When other downtown garages are full, you may find a space here. Perhaps the disappearance of Westinghouse from Pittsburgh's corporate scene has freed space in the lot. Whatever the reason, this garage is always worth a shot. Rates for its 341 spaces range from $4 to $12. Monthly leases are available for $200.

Wood Allies Garage
228 Blvd. of the Allies, Pittsburgh
• (412) 456-2770

This 536-space garage is convenient to PPG Place and Market Square, both of them just a few paces across the Boulevard of the Allies. Rates range from $2.75 to $8, with monthly leases priced at $175 by day, $30 by night. The garage offers discounts with a purchase from participating downtown merchants.

Downtown Fringe

Many commuters avoid high downtown parking rates by parking in lots that dot the fringes of downtown. These are among the largest parking sites in the city, offering about 16,000 spaces. From some sites, you'll need to walk a bit to reach your ultimate destination, while others provide complimentary shuttle bus service. Commuters on a budget put the fringe on top.

11h & Etna Lot
11th & Etna, Pittsburgh
• (412) 323-4455

This Strip District surface lot offers 1,450 spaces for a daily rate of $5. When you park here, you'll have a short walk to the David L. Lawrence Convention Center and Liberty Center.

Allegheny Center Parking Garage
Allegheny Center, Pittsburgh
• (412) 323-4455

You'll find 2,500 indoor parking spaces at this garage, which is just across the Seventh Street Bridge from downtown. Rates range from $2.50 to $8.50, with monthly leases priced at $90. You can enjoy discounts by purchasing the garage's coupons or parking stamps, or through purchases at participating merchants.

Boardwalk Lot
15th & Smallman, Pittsburgh
• (412) 323-4455

This 1,500-space surface lot is in the Strip District, a short walk from the David L. Lawrence Convention Center and Liberty Center. The lot provides complimentary shuttle service to and from several downtown locations. You'll pay by day-part. For example, you can park from 5 AM to 11:30 AM for $4.50. Parking from 11:30 AM to 1:30 PM is free Monday through Friday.

Chatham Center Garage
54 Chatham Center, Pittsburgh
• (412) 261-0809

Located in the uptown section near the Mellon Arena, Chatham Center offers 2,281 indoor spaces. The garage is about a five-minute walk from Grant Street in downtown. Rates range from $3.25 to $12.75, with monthly leases priced at $173.25. You can get a discounted "early bird" monthly lease, good Monday through Friday from 5:30 AM to 6:30 PM, for $147.

Mellon Arena Lots
Centre Ave., Pittsburgh
• (412) 642-4284
Washington Pl., Bedford Ave., Lemieux Pl., Crawford St.

You'll find 2,500 spaces to welcome you in the arena area—unless an event at the Mellon Arena causes a jam. The regular daily rates range from $5 to $6.50, 6 AM to 6 PM, Monday through

Several organizations in the region are dedicated to helping travelers. If you've ever needed emergency road service on a dark and lonely road, you well know the value of the American Automobile Association. The AAA member service center in Southwestern Pennsylvania is AAA West Penn/West Virginia, (412) 363-5100, located at 5900 Baum Boulevard in Pittsburgh's East Liberty neighborhood. AAA operates 49 branch offices in the tristate area, offering a variety of services that go well beyond emergency help.

Services include worldwide air, cruise, and rail tickets; hotel and rental car reservations; American Express travelers checques at no fee; credit cards, and maps, and individually tailored routings, otherwise known as the much-loved Triptiks. AAA also operates travel and insurance agencies. There is an annual membership fee.

Also available for wayward wayfarers is Travelers Aid Society of Pittsburgh, a nonprofit agency that helps travelers throughout the country. The agency assists people stranded here and without the means of reaching home or another destination. Among the group's beneficiaries are runaway youths, the homeless, and those in need of counseling or referral.

You'll find two Travelers Aid Society locations in Southwestern Pennsylvania: Pittsburgh International Airport, (412) 472-3599, and the Greyhound Bus Terminal in downtown Pittsburgh, 11th and Liberty Avenue, (412) 281-5466 or (412) 281-5474.

Friday. During Mellon Arena events, which usually take place on the weekends, rates are higher, varying with different events.

Expect to walk no longer than 10 minutes to reach downtown; the most distant Mellon Arena lot is only four blocks from Grant Street. If you work in USX Tower, park in the Mellon Arena lot nearby and sprint to work in five minutes or less; you may even be able to look down on your car from your office window.

Be sure to check out the Melody Tent lot above the Mellon Arena if you're a commuter. You won't find the Civic Light Opera crooning tunes there are you would have in the 1960s, but you might be interested in the shuttle bus that operates on weekdays from 6 to 9:45 AM and 3 to 6:30 PM. The other four Mellon Arena lots are named after the points on the compass in which you'll find them. Not nearly so groovy as the Melody Tent, but you'll know where you are.

Greyhound Garage
11th & Penn, Pittsburgh
• **(412) 765-1775**
Though not among the most spacious garages—it has 190 spaces—this facility is worth noting because it is adjacent to the Greyhound Bus Terminal. Rates range from $4 to $13, with monthly leases priced at $175.

Second Avenue Parking Plaza
Second Ave., Pittsburgh
• **(412) 323-4455**
This surface lot in the Uptown neighborhood offers 800 parking spaces for a daily rate of $3.50, monthly leases for $70, and free shuttle service to downtown points.

Station Square Parking
One Station Square, Pittsburgh
• **(412) 261-1993**
This popular shopping/office complex features two surface lots and a garage providing a total of 3,500 parking spaces. You will need to walk across the Smithfield Street Bridge to reach town. Indoor rates range from $2.35 to $12, with outdoor rates in the East lot ranging from $1.35 to $4.85. You also may park for a $4 daily rate in the West lot. During Steelers and Pirates games, expect a rate hike—up to almost twice the price for the day. Monthly lease prices range from $80 to $120.

Parking— Oakland

As the hub of the region's higher education and medical sectors, Oakland frequently has more would-be parkers than it

INSIDERS' TIP
The Pittsburgh Downtown Partnership, (412) 566-4190, provides a free guide to downtown parking with basic information about parking spaces, garages, and lots as well as a listing of retail establishments that participate in discount parking programs.

can comfortably accommodate. You'll find plenty of metered on-street parking, but you can't use most of those spaces during morning and evening rush hours. You'll also find plenty of garages, only to be frustrated by the "Permit Parking Only" warnings, indicating that the garages are reserved—often for University of Pittsburgh personnel. When classes are in session, there's no real remedy for the parking crunch. Here are some garages and lots that can help.

Forbes & Semple Garage
210 Meyran Ave., Pittsburgh
- **(412) 621-5922**

This 430-space garage is part of Oakland's commercial district. Rates range from $2 to $7, with monthly leases priced at $115 by day, $40 by night. Discounts are offered through participating professional and university offices.

University Parking
3915 O'Hara St., Pittsburgh
- **(412) 624-4034**

O'Hara Garage provides a convenient location between the University of Pittsburgh's lower and upper campuses. From here, you're within walking distance of most of Oakland's hospitals and medical offices. Rates for the 455 spaces range from $3 to $9, with discounts for Pitt personnel and students. Leases are available through the university for its faculty and staff only.

Schenley Plaza
Schenley Plaza, Pittsburgh
- **(412) 560-PARK**

This is a great location for a surface parking lot. It separates the Carnegie Library of Pittsburgh and the University of Pittsburgh's Hillman Library, and it can be considered part of the campus of both Pitt and Carnegie Mellon University. It features 250 spaces with rates ranging from $2 to $12. You won't find much turnover at this lot. Once people find spaces here, they tend to milk them for all they're worth. When the universities are in session, people actually line up to get in here.

Webster Hall Garage
101 N. Dithridge St., Pittsburgh
- **(412) 621-6751**

This garage provides 245 spaces at rates ranging from $3 to $7.25, with discounts for purchases at participating merchants. It also offers valet parking and monthly leases priced at $120—you also must provide a $50 security de-

posit for a lease. Webster Hall is a former elegant hotel now serving as an office and apartment building.

Park and Ride Lots

One way of avoiding downtown parking expenses is to utilize the Port Authority of Allegheny's Park and Ride lots. These 35 lots offer more than 5,000 parking spaces, most free or with a nominal charge. They're all located adjacent to public transportation routes, so you can park cheaply and ride the bus or T to town. If you call PAT at (412) 442-2000, they'll send you a free map of Park and Ride lots.

Pittsburgh Neighborhoods

As you tool through Pittsburgh's residential and commercial neighborhoods, you'll notice a chair standing unattended before the curb. Then another. Then another. These are not the products of some mass sheriff's evictions. Rather, Pittsburghers use chairs to stake their claims to parking spaces in front of their homes or businesses. They're especially prevalent on snowy days, when residents who have shoveled out their parking spaces feel particularly protective about them. The chairs are a colorful facet of Pittsburgh residential life, but don't take them lightly. Many a neighborhood brawl began when someone shoved aside a chair to trespass on a reserved parking space.

The need for such a home-grown strategy stems from the tightness of parking spaces in some city neighborhoods. Many Pittsburgh streets are narrow and can't accommodate parking on both sides of the street. In addition, neighborhoods with institutions such as hospitals draw many visitors in search of on-street parking to beat the prices of lots, garages, and meters.

The city has implemented a more rational approach to the problem through its Residential Parking Permit Program. Through RPPP, residents of 10 city neighborhoods—Beechview, Bloomfield, The Bluff, Garfield, Lawrenceville, Lower Hill District, Mt. Washington, North Squirrel Hill, Oakland, and Shadyside—enjoy exclusive on-street parking rights from 8:30 AM to 4 PM each weekday. To acquire a permit that admits you into the program, you'll need to provide proof of residency and car ownership, a driver's license, and an annual fee of $20 per vehicle. You'll also be entitled to one guest car per household for an annual fee of $10. For more information or an application, contact the Pittsburgh Department of City Planning, (412) 255-8996.

If you don't live in an eligible neighborhood, we advise that you pick up a couple of folding chairs.

Subway

Pittsburgh's subway system, known as the "T," is an unusual blend of subterranean and above-ground features. When it courses through the city's South Hills, the "T" is largely an above-ground conveyance that resembles a trolley line, although it's officially called a "light rail system." When it reaches downtown, the "T" dives beneath the service to provide riders with an unobstructed trip below city streets. Actually, three downtown stops—Gateway Center, Wood Street, Steel Plaza—are underground, while the "T" stops at Penn Park and Station Square are above ground. By combining these features, the "T" serves as both a convenient means of downtown-only travel as well as a key component of the region's commuting infrastructure.

For downtown travel, it would be hard to beat the price of the "T"— there's no charge for travel between the three underground stations. When you visit those stations, you'll enjoy the soothing strains of classical music provided by PAT. For longer "T" rides for which there is a charge, PAT encourages riders to purchase tickets and passes by imposing a surcharge, ranging from $1.25 to $2, on cash payments. For more information, call (412) 442-2000.

Armstrong County

In Armstrong County, the Mid-County Transit Authority, (724) 548-8696 or (800) 245-8588, provides three bus programs. The first features fixed-route service in the county's central communities—Applewold, Ford Cliff, Ford City, Kittanning, Manorville, and West Kittanning. The buses run about once every hour, Monday through Saturday, at a base fare of 75 cents plus additional charges for zones traversed. All buses are wheelchair accessible. As a bonus, MCTA provides service to hospitals and shopping malls in East Franklin.

The second service, called Armstrong Rural Public Transit, is a shared-ride program available to all Monday through Friday. You must reserve your transportation at least 24 hours in advance, with cost on a zones-traversed basis. The buses are primarily, though not exclusively, wheelchair accessible. While service normally runs from 8 AM to 5 PM, the program will transport you to doctors' office visits from 6 AM until 8 PM

The third MCTA service provides transportation for children in the county's Head Start program.

Beaver County

The Beaver County Transit Authority, (724) 728-8600, manages public bus transportation throughout the county. You'll find routes that operate exclusively within Beaver County as well as express and local routes between Beaver County and the City of Pittsburgh. Your fare will depend on the number of zones traversed; a one-way fare from Pittsburgh ranges from $2.10 to $3.75. Exact fare is required, unless you pay by tickets purchased at the BCTA Transportation Center in Rochester. Transfers are free. An important note to remember: BCTA buses do not operate on major holidays.

Senior citizens may ride BCTA's Beaver County routes free of charge during off-peak hours and all day Saturday. To get your senior citizen transit card, call BCTA at (724) 728-8600 or visit the transportation center. For riders who use wheelchairs, most routes are accessible. You may want to check with BCTA to determine which routes might be right for you. The county also provides a shared-ride service called Demand and Response Transit (DART) for people with disabilities. Call DART at (724) 728-4200 for more information or to schedule a ride.

INSIDERS' TIP

Here's a handy tip that can help you avoid a moment of embarrassment when riding a Port Authority of Allegheny County bus. On buses heading to downtown, you pay your fare when you board. On outbound buses, pay as you exit. You'll need the exact fare, as PAT drivers don't carry any change.

The county maintains several Park 'n Ride lots in close proximity to BCTA stops throughout the county. In addition, you'll find a convenience lot just outside the transportation center where you can park while conducting any short-term activity at the center. Beaver County officials call these lots "Kiss 'n Ride," but these activities are not mandatory when visiting the transportation center . . . at least we don't think they are.

Butler County

Bus service in Butler County is something of a mix-and-match affair. In the City of Butler and environs, bus service is provided by the Butler Township-City Joint Municipal Transit Authority, (724) 285-4124.

Travel between Butler County communities is handled by the Butler County Commissioners through a demonstration program supported by the Pennsylvania Department of Transportation and the Pennsylvania Lottery. This service links the communities of Butler, Connoquenessing, Harmony, Evans City, Zelienople, and Cranberry. Fares are based on zones traversed and range from $1.25 to $2. For an extra $1, however, the bus driver will go up to one-quarter mile "off route" to pick you up or drop you off. You must arrange off-route service in advance by calling (800) 950-1287.

Exact change is required. Senior citizens age 65 and older ride free during off-peak hours once they have acquired appropriate transit cards. Patrons with disabilities and wheelchair users can access the buses in this demo program.

The schedule varies from day to day. On Wednesdays, for example, the City of Butler is not part of the route. Call the county at (724) 283-0445, extension 217, for complete schedule and fare information.

Washington County

You'll have several options for bus service in Washington County, depending on your needs. For Pittsburgh or locations in or near the City of Washington, GG&C Bus Lines, (724) 222-2320, provides express service from Washington County to downtown Pittsburgh, connecting with the "T" at South Hills Village Station, as well as local service throughout the City of Washington.

For service in the Mon Valley and along the Route 88 corridor, Mid-Mon Valley Transit Authority, (724) 489-0880, provides local service as well as commuter service to downtown Pittsburgh.

Westmoreland County

Westmoreland County Transit Authority operates a far-reaching, sophisticated bus system that includes 19 routes and features service throughout the county as well as buses to Pittsburgh. For schedules, call WCTA at (724) 834-9282 or (800) 221-9282, or visit them at the Westmoreland Transit Center, 41 Bell Way, Greensburg. Please note that WCTA buses do not operate on major holidays.

As with many municipal transportation systems in the region, fares are based on the number of zones traversed; for travel within Westmoreland County, expect your fare to range from $1.25 to $4. Transfers are free when needed to complete one-way travel, but you must use your transfer on the next bus going your way. While exact fare is not required, drivers will change $1 bills only. You can avoid the need for cash by purchasing "Ten Trip Tickets" that offer a 5 percent discount off the total ticket price. Drivers carry the ticket books for your convenience.

Senior citizens age 65 and older ride free during off-peak hours on weekdays and on Saturdays and holidays. Patrons with disabilities ride for half fare at all times. Seniors should apply for their eligibility cards at the transit center, while those with disabilities may apply by calling the center at (800) 221-9282. If you're a wheelchair user, WCTA asks that you call them at (800) 221-9282 two days to one week before you need their service.

For disabled persons unable to utilize public transportation, the county operates a paratransit service in association with several local taxi cab companies. The paratransit service operates in the same communities, and during the same hours, as WCTA's bus routes. Fares, however, are twice the amount charged for a similar bus trip. To apply, call WCTA at (724) 832-2211.

Taxi Cabs

The first thing you must appreciate about travel by cab in Southwestern Pennsylvania—if you wave your arm for a cab here, you're likely to get a tired arm. Typically, you won't find cabs cruising city streets. The demand is relatively small for standard cab service, and companies size their fleets to match that demand. In fact, most of the cab companies here also provide paratransit and shared-ride service to complement their cab fleets.

You will find cabs aplenty at Pittsburgh International Airport and downtown Pittsburgh's major hotels. If you're not anywhere near the airport or a hotel, the best way to get a cab is to call and book one. All companies profiled here offer round-the-clock service each day of the year.

Also, a word about jitneys. You'll find these private operators, who transport customers at negotiated fees, in several Pittsburgh neighborhoods. Residents contend that, because licensed cab companies seldom ventured into these neighborhoods in years past, jitneys arose and thrived to meet a pressing need. Jitneys are unlicensed by the state and have no official standing, so you'll have very little recourse should something go awry. Patronize them at your discretion. Frequent jitney users often know their drivers.

Checker Cab
36 S. 6th St., Pittsburgh
• (412) 381-5600

These distinctive cabs, with their green checkerboard patterns accented by gold striping, operate in downtown Pittsburgh and the city's western suburbs. You'll find a fleet of 25 cabs that await you at major hotels and are authorized to transport you to and from Pittsburgh International Airport. Checker also operates shared-ride service as part of the Port Authority of Allegheny County's ACCESS program.

Peoples Cab Company
6100 Ellsworth Ave., Pittsburgh
• (412) 681-3131

To reserve your red and white Peoples Cab, you must call ahead. They can provide you with service to—but not from—Pittsburgh International Airport, although that may soon change. Peoples Cab provides vehicles and drivers to serve schools and school districts with established contracts.

S&S Transit
400 Eden Park Blvd., McKeesport
• (412) 751-6780

You won't see many S&S cabs around. They have a fleet of six green cabs that serves the Monongahela Valley. The company maintains a much larger fleet—70 vehicles—for its shared-ride programs in Allegheny and Westmoreland counties. Rented vans, complete with drivers, are available for rental on an hourly basis.

Yellow Cab Co.
5931 Ellsworth Ave., Pittsburgh
• (412) 665-8100

By far the largest provider in the region, Yellow Cab offers a fleet of about 360 vehicles. It serves corporate accounts, stands at major hotels, and deploys about 60 cabs at any given time at Pittsburgh International Airport. As a special service, Yellow Cab offers several regional phone numbers to spare residents of those areas toll calls. If you live in the South Hills, call the company at (412) 344-TAXI. In Monroeville, the number is (412) 374-TAXI.

Local Driving

Driving in and around Pittsburgh can be at once rewarding and frustrating. When you drive here, you'll travel along roads that take you through charming towns with attractive river views. The hills and mountains provide breathtaking vistas that attract international tourists. Those same hills, however, can become treacherous in bad weather. Even more maddening is the way many streets in the region are named.

Take the City of Pittsburgh, for example. In downtown Pittsburgh, you'll find avenues numbered from 1 to 7. At the same time, you'll encounter numbered streets that begin with 6 and go all the way to the 50s in the city's Lawrenceville neighborhood. If that weren't confusing enough, South Side cross streets begin at 1 and go into the 20s. Got it? Now, when someone says to meet him on 6th, what on earth do you do?

You'll get used to it soon enough, and the charm of Pittsburgh's streets will prevail. The following is a look at some of the principal state routes, city streets and bridges with which you'll become familiar.

State Routes

The primary state routes in the region are similar in a number of key respects. They pass through residential and commercial districts, offering only the occasional high-speed sections. They're great for local travel, but you'll probably prefer the interstate network for longer hauls.

Allegheny County also offers a beltway of five concentric rings—designated blue, green, yellow, orange, and red—with the City of Pittsburgh at the center. These were developed many years ago as alternatives to driving through the city. They may have been effective at one time, but with the growth of commercial and residential districts along the belts, and the concomitant increase in traffic and traffic signals, you frequently won't make good time if you use the belts. When you get to know them well—if you're one of the few who does—you'll find the belts can help you detour around local traffic snarls.

Route 8

This is an important connector between the City of Pittsburgh and Butler County, passing through the city's northern suburbs en route.

Route 19

Route 19 spans both the North Hills and the South Hills of Pittsburgh, reaching all the way to Washington County. The highway offers separate truck spurs in both the North Hills and South Hills.

Route 22

A major route from Pittsburgh to the east, Route 22 provides access to such communities as Indiana and Johnstown. Many folks traveling to Penn State University travel Route 22 to State College.

Route 28

Route 28 reaches from the City of Pittsburgh north to Kittanning in Armstrong County, pretty much paralleling the Allegheny River, which is intermittently visible along the way. You can follow Route 28 well into Northwestern Pennsylvania, though with the development of I-79, few would do that.

Route 30

This highway takes you east, through Westmoreland County and into the Laurel Highlands region. Route 30 is linked to Route 22 by a 14-mile high-speed highway called the Amos K. Hutchinson Bypass. It's a toll road maintained by the Pennsylvania Turnpike Commission.

Route 51

You can travel Route 51 from Pittsburgh southeast to Uniontown, passing through some

of the South Hills and the Mon Valley along the way.

Route 60

Route 60 links most of Beaver County's major towns and extends north all the way to I-80. A 17-mile stretch of the road between Beaver Falls and New Castle is a high-speed toll road, maintained by the Pennsylvania Turnpike Commission, called the Beaver Valley Expressway.

Route 65

Route 65 offers a scenic drive along the Ohio River as it carries you from Pittsburgh west to Beaver County.

Route 422

This Butler County road links Route 28 with I-79. It's an important highway for residents of Armstrong and Butler counties.

Pittsburgh Streets

Two of the city's most important streets are Fifth Avenue and Forbes Avenue, which run roughly parallel from downtown about 6 miles to the city's eastern neighborhoods. Forbes is one-way outbound through Oakland, while Fifth is one-way inbound from Oakland. When you drive these streets, you'll pass by five colleges or universities—Duquesne University, Carlow College, the University of Pittsburgh, Carnegie Mellon University, and Chatham College. You'll find it positively enlightening.

When you're looking to avoid traffic jams on the Parkway East, Second Avenue and the Boulevard of the Allies might help. The Boulevard of the Allies reaches from downtown to the Squirrel Hill neighborhood, providing a pleasant drive through Schenley Park. The Second Avenue trip also is interesting, paralleling the Monongahela River and passing the gleaming Pittsburgh Technology Center as it takes you to Hazelwood.

Penn Avenue and Liberty Avenue also are important routes to and from town, connecting the central business district and eastern neighborhoods. Penn is one-way inbound near downtown. Two steep streets, Perrysville Avenue and Mt. Troy Road, will take you from the Allegheny River to the city's northern neighborhoods.

One of the city's most interesting streets is Carson Street—it's East Carson Street or West Carson Street, depending on which side of the Fort Pitt Bridge you find yourself. The street provides you with views of the city's West End and the town of McKees Rocks, passes through the vital South Side and its brace of trendy restaurants and galleries, and continues through to West Homestead in the Mon Valley, offering glimpses of former industrial sites now being recycled as residential, office and entertainment complexes. Not a bad tour of the city . . . and you never have to leave Carson Street.

Bridges

If you like bridges, you'll love Pittsburgh. In Allegheny, Beaver, and Lawrence counties alone, you'll find an estimated 1,677 bridges, many of them beautiful and distinctive, sporting ornate metalwork and a vast variety of architectural approaches. Since you'll be using them every day, you'll probably think of them more as conveniences than art, but it's nice to appreciate their design every so often.

You'll become familiar with such Allegheny River bridges as the Fort Duquesne Bridge, Veterans Bridge, the Sixth Street Bridge, the Seventh Street Bridge, the Ninth Street Bridge, the 16th Street Bridge, the 31st Street Bridge, the 40th Street Bridge, and 62nd Street Bridge, the Highland Park Bridge, and the Hulton Bridge, with its lavender superstructure.

Across the Monongahela, you'll find the Fort Pitt Bridge, (although it could be argued that this bridge is above The Point and therefore crosses all three rivers) and the Liberty Bridge, a major artery—along with the companion Liberty Tunnels—between Pittsburgh and the South Hills. Other Monongahela River crossings include the 10th Street Bridge (Remember what we told you about street numbering here?), the Birmingham Bridge, and the Rankin Bridge.

Near Pittsburgh, you'll cross the Ohio River at the West End Bridge, the McKees Rocks Bridge, and the Sewickley Bridge.

The McKees Rocks Bridge is the longest at better than 1.5 miles, while Veterans Bridge covers the most deck area with its six lanes. Clearly, we've presented only a selection of the region's bridges, those that are most heavily used.

History

Boom, Bust, and Rebirth
Along the Three Rivers

When the first hardy 18th-century traders gazed upon the land that would come to be known as Pittsburgh, they saw a valley of verdant hillsides cut by a triangle of rivers, with majestic, unspoiled forests rising as sentinels above. The strengths they viewed were formidable. On the one hand, the flatter land between and along the rivers would serve for trading posts, forts, settlements. On the other hand, the rivers would provide convenient and economical transport routes—both to the settled cities of the East and the unexplored domains of the West—while the virgin woods would offer game as well as timber for building.

It's impossible, of course, to know what really went through the minds of those intrepid early traders as they surveyed for the first time the site of the future Pittsburgh. But it is clear that the assets they saw—and those that they couldn't see, such as abundant coal beneath the soil—would form the foundation of a city that would become the industrial giant of America, as well as a home to generations of immigrants. The story of Pittsburgh is a story of boom, bust, and rebirth, the rise and decline of a great manufacturing center recreated as a thriving, progressive metropolis based on economic and social diversity.

All who observed this land recognized its commercial and strategic importance as the Gateway to the West. Even before 1750, the French had successfully navigated the river network all the way from the Point, where the Allegheny and Monongahela rivers merge to form the Ohio River, to the Mississippi River. In fact, well before Pittsburgh was officially founded or named, the French and the British, each allied with different Indian nations of the region, extended their European battle for dominance to what was then known as the Ohio country. The struggle was protracted and bloody, the outcome far from certain.

In 1754, the French held dominion over the Ohio country from Fort Duquesne, the redoubt constructed at the Point. It was in that year that a young major named George Washington led a group of Virginians against the French, only to meet ignominious defeat. A 1755 expedition against the fort, this one led by Gen. Edward Braddock, suffered even worse consequences. Braddock and many of his officers were killed; Washington, miraculously, defied death in the Ohio country for the second time in two years.

It was only in 1758, as Britain began to gain the upper hand all across the New World, that the French occupation of the Ohio country ended. On November 24, as the British army prepared for its final assault on the fort, a scouting party delivered the news: the French had abandoned Fort Duquesne. Three days later, Gen. John Forbes, the British commander, solemnly renamed the fort in honor of British Prime Minister William Pitt.

The prolonged struggle for control of the Ohio Country may have been over, but the growth of the settlement continued at a measured pace. This, after all, was the wilderness. Beautiful as the land was, life remained harsh. Home very often was little more than a hut along the rivers that could be swept away by the fury of a spring flood. In 1760, two years after the final conquest of the French, the settlement that surrounded Fort Pitt numbered 151 people. Even at the close of the Revolutionary War, the population still numbered in the hundreds.

Slow though growth may have been, the late 18th century brought several important developments. The year 1787 marked the founding of the Pittsburgh Academy, forerunner of today's University of Pittsburgh. On April 22, 1794, the city became a borough and staged its first elections.

The Riverboat Era

As the century closed, the city began to fulfill its promise as the Gateway to the West. With the young nation expanding, Pittsburgh became an excellent launching point for traffic that could navigate the inland waterways all the way to New Orleans.

From the turn of the 19th century, Pittsburgh served as a significant center for flatboat traffic. The craft not only transported cargo, but were also a primary transportation mode for immigrants seeking to settle the West. Since Pittsburgh merchants often loaded flatboats with goods for sale at ports of call along the way, the colorful craft resembled nothing so much as floating department stores. Lacking a way to float the boats upstream, the owners typically disassembled the craft and sold them for their lumber at journey's end.

Upstream traffic required a different kind of vessel—the keel boat, long and narrow, pointed at the ends, propelled by human rowers or polers. The upstream journey was tedious and arduous for passengers, as the trip from Louisville to Pittsburgh might last a month. More difficult still was the work of the polers, a hard-drinking, hard-living breed.

The riverboat era produced one of the most colorful characters in Pittsburgh history—Mike Fink, self-proclaimed King of the Boatmen, whose brawls and benders took on mythic proportions.

Pittsburgh even became an early hub of shipbuilding, a natural given the volume of its river traffic. With the development of steam-powered vessels, however, shipbuilding died out in Pittsburgh, and the era of flatboats and keel boats lasted no more than a few decades. Mike Fink, frustrated by the advent of steam-powered vessels, took off for the badlands of the Rockies and departed Pittsburgh's history forever.

The city's future would not lie in shipbuilding. But the riverboat era proved conclusively that Pittsburgh and its waterways could serve the nation well as a transport center, a role the city would continue to play throughout the period of America's industrialization.

From Europe They Came... And Came... And Came

During the 19th century and the first part of the 20th century, Pittsburgh developed its modern identity as a melting pot for dozens of nationalities and cultures, and as the most important steel manufacturing center in America.

Blessed with the natural elements used for manufacturing, the city needed only the human component to complete the equation. In the 19th century, seemingly endless waves of immigration satisfied that need.

Early in the century, a steady stream of uprooted Europeans settled in Pittsburgh, drawn to the city for a number of reasons. Among that early group were Irish fleeing famine in their homeland and finding work in Pittsburgh's mining industry; Scotch-Irish, Scots, Welsh, and Dutch who were among the earliest settlers; and skilled Belgians who answered a call for help from a fledgling Pittsburgh glass manufacturer. Still others came as indentured servants or criminals, working off their contracts or sentences in the New World.

In the 1840s, the trickle of immigration grew to a flood, with the influx of new Pittsburghers primarily from Ger-

INSIDERS' TIP

Pittsburgh lost the "h" in its spelling in 1891. Twenty years later, bowing to popular pressure, the U.S. Board on Geographic Names approved restoration of the "h."

INSIDERS' TIP

If you'd like to read an in-depth account of regional history, complete with hundreds of photographs, get a copy of the comprehensive coffee table book *Pittsburgh: Story of an American City* by Stefan Lorant, now in its 5th edition.

many and Ireland. Yet another wave, in the 1890s, brought immigrants from Central and Southeastern Europe.

The contributions of these new residents can not be overestimated. The immigrants tended to settle with their fellow displaced countrymen in neighborhoods ringing the burgeoning downtown that reflected their distinct cultures and religions. Many Italians, for example, settled in Bloomfield, a few miles east of downtown Pittsburgh. Even today, Italian can be heard spoken on Bloomfield's streets.

The Irish gathered in downtown itself before fanning out to neighborhoods such as Garfield. Many German immigrants found new homes in the hilly area north of downtown that would become known as Troy Hill. European Jews congregated in the Hill District; later, this neighborhood adjacent to downtown would become the city's most important African American community with the 19th-century wave of migration from the American South. Polish immigrants settled in a number of new neighborhoods, including Lawrenceville along the Allegheny and South Side along the Monongahela.

Even relatively small immigrant groups made an impact. Scandinavians, for example, never settled in Pittsburgh in large numbers. Yet Swedish immigrants who came for work in the steel mills gathered in the working class suburb of McKeesport, where they erected churches that conducted services in their native tongue well into the 20th century. Finnish immigrants clustered in the Monongahela River towns of Glassport and Monessen, building schools, churches, and fraternal organizations.

These distinctive neighborhoods, insular in their way but steeped in the traditions and culture of the Old World, would provide Pittsburgh with a foundation of ethnicity that, to this day, is a defining characteristic of the city. Pittsburgh became the very embodiment of the "melting pot," and the effects continue to be profound. A mid-20th century study found that, years after the principal waves of European immigration had ended, 42 percent of the population of Allegheny County (of which Pittsburgh is the seat) were foreign born or children of those born outside America.

The Heart of Steel

With all the components in place, manufacturing in Pittsburgh was set for take off. As early as the 1820s, Pittsburgh boasted eight rolling mills driven by steam power. Between that period and the Civil War, several developments facilitated the transformation of the fledgling steel industry to a growing giant.

One such development was the discovery that bituminous coal, so plentiful in the region, could be used to create coke, an abundant and relatively cheap fuel to power the mills. A second was the almost simultaneous development, by England's Henry Bessemer and Pittsburgh's William Kelly, of air cooling the molten iron to strengthen and purify the product. With these refinements in the production process, and others that would follow, such as the creation of the open-hearth process in the early 20th century, Pittsburgh was poised to become the steelmaking heart of America.

It had the economic muscle, through such financiers as the Mellon family. It had the natural resources necessary for steel production and the river and railroad networks to ship products anywhere. It had a willing and skilled labor force. And it had the entrepreneurial talent.

Many of the giants of industrialism grew in Pittsburgh along with the city's manufacturing base. In 1881, a Scottish immigrant named Andrew Carnegie joined with his six brothers in a venture that later would become Carnegie Steel Company, itself a predecessor of the giant U.S. Steel Corp. (today known as USX). In one of those ironies of history, Carnegie located his first major mill, the Edgar Thomson Works, on the site where the ill-fated Gen. Braddock fell to the French.

Other early steel and coal magnates included Henry Phipps, an early Carnegie partner, Henry W. Oliver and Henry Clay Frick. Nor was entrepreneurship limited to the steel industry. In 1869, George Westinghouse invented the air brake in Pittsburgh, a development that advanced the continuing growth of the railroad industry. A protean figure, Westinghouse helped found or operate an estimated 60 companies, including the business that would become a 20th century giant—Pittsburgh-based Westinghouse Electric Corp.

These titans of industry left an indelible mark on the region, in a number of ways. Their impact on the area's economy, of course, was profound. But so, too, was their perpetuation—if not downright origination—of the concept of philanthropy. The Carnegie Museums of Pittsburgh, the Carnegie Library (a thriving institution in so many western Pennsylvania towns), The Frick Art & Historical Center, Phipps Conservatory and Botanical Gardens, Mellon Park, Mellon Square—all remain vital features of contemporary Pittsburgh, and all are living testament to the philanthropy of Pittsburgh's leading industrialists.

Aided by such corporate largesse as well as the traditions that the transplanted Europeans brought with them, culture and education in Pittsburgh flourished in this period. These years marked the founding of such foundation arts institutions as the Pittsburgh Symphony in 1895 and the Pittsburgh Opera in 1938.

In education, Carnegie Tech University—later to become Carnegie Mellon University with an infusion of Mellon family money—was founded in 1900, Duquesne University in 1878. The development of the University of Pittsburgh speaks volumes about the community partnership that was at the heart of Pittsburgh's growth.

To finance its landmark 42-story Cathedral of Learning, the University of Pittsburgh asked residents to participate by "buying" bricks for the edifice at a dime apiece. In the 11 years between 1926 and the Cathedral's completion in 1937, the University "sold" bricks to 114,000 people. The Cathedral of Learning still towers over the city as a symbol of Pittsburgh's commitment to education, and to the cohesiveness and community spirit of Pittsburghers.

The Rise of Labor

The impact of the leading industrialists of the 20th century was evident in yet another way—the rise of organized labor. As more and more men went to work in the mines and mills, they realized they would need representation to assure them of fair wages and safe working conditions. The nascent labor movement would not be readily accepted by the same men who had dotted the community with the libraries and museums that spoke of their generosity.

In 1858, as recorded by Arthur C. Bining in *Pennsylvania's Iron and Steel Industry*, a group of steelworkers formed a secret organization called the Iron City Forge of the Sons of Vulcan, the first permanent labor association in the iron industry. In 1876, the Sons of Vulcan merged with three other newly formed organizations to create the National Amalgamated Association of Iron and Steel Workers.

Forming a union was one thing; persuading management to recognize it was another. The growth of steel in Pittsburgh was marked by regular confrontations between management and labor, none more infamous or bloody than the Homestead strike of 1892. In a dispute over wages and the right to organize, workers at U.S. Steel's Homestead plant along the city's southeastern border seized the factory and captured 300 Pinkerton detectives sent in to quell the strike. The situation degenerated into a series of pitched battles along the Monongahela River and a failed assassination attempt against U.S. Steel Board Chairman Henry Clay Frick. By the time the Pennsylvania Militia restored order, 10 were dead.

Far from hastening management-labor accord, the Homestead strike served only to polarize the parties. It was 45 years after the strike that U.S. Steel officially recognized the steelworkers union, breaking the impasse in the industry. Finally, with labor and management at relative peace, the boom could roll on.

Pittsburgh's role as the industrial heart of American reached its full flower during World War II, when the Commonwealth of Pennsylvania produced one-sixth of the world's iron and steel.

The city's reputation reached international proportions. On his historic visit to the United States during the height

INSIDERS' TIP

Washington's Landing, an Allegheny River island home to manufacturing, office buildings, recreation, and residence life, is so named because George Washington found refuge there during a 1753 storm.

Take a ride into the past at the Pennsylvania Trolley Museum in Washington, Penn., where you'll see old-fashioned cars from all over Pennsylvania.

Photo: James Crough, Jr.

of the Cold War, Soviet Premier Nikita S. Khrushchev included Pittsburgh on his itinerary. While in the city, he was heard to remark that if the Soviets really wanted to cripple America, they would drop a bomb on the Duquesne Club, where Pittsburgh's leading industrialists gathered for lunch and hosted their guests overnight. It was thought to be a joke, but Khrushchev, perhaps mindful of his words, chose to spend the night at the Carlton House.

A Renaissance Drama, in Two Acts

The city in the Golden Triangle, as the land near the Point was called, was a stunning success. Yet as America settled into postwar normalcy, Pittsburgh was in danger of choking on that very success. The problems were twofold. First, the same plants that were the city's lifeblood also were spewing smoke into the air, creating deadly dark clouds that, at their worst, literally blocked the rays of the sun and created virtual 24-hour-a-day nights. Ask Pittsburghers of a certain age about that era, and what they remember most is the smoke, the gasping for air, the clothes that would turn pitch black when hung on the line to dry.

The second problem was the helter-skelter pattern of development that had left the Golden Triangle an unattractive warren of dirty warehouses and untended tracks to nowhere. If Pittsburgh were to continue its growth, both problems would have to be addressed.

Pittsburgh Mayor David L. Lawrence and leading industrialist and financier Richard K. Mellon had, independently, reached that conclusion. Lawrence was more than the city's top official and the future governor of Pennsylvania; he controlled the Democratic party, which in the labor-dominated city was the only party that mattered. Mellon was perhaps the city's most powerful industrialist, one who could lead others in important new directions. They joined forces in a new entity called the Allegheny Conference on Community

INSIDERS' TIP

He wrote "My Old Kentucky Home," but Stephen Collins Foster was a Pittsburgh native. The Stephen C. Foster Memorial stands at the University of Pittsburgh.

Development, an organization that, 50 years later, continues to play an important role in Pittsburgh's growth.

Their collaboration was historic, as government to that point had played little role in the city's development. John P. Robin, who worked for the Allegheny Conference and would be a pivotal player in Pittsburgh's growth for five decades, described that historic collaboration in a 1997 oral history.

"It was really a different climate than had existed," Robin said. "There was excitement and willingness. There never was a precise plan for development. The appetite, I usually say, grew with the eating. There was a contagion, a belief that nothing was impossible and we ought to try it."

The result was an unprecedented redevelopment that became known as the Renaissance. The partnership set out to improve their city on both key fronts. On smoke control, the city passed a series of abatement measures that, with the blessing of Mellon and other corporate leaders, industry implemented without complaint.

On the land use front, the partnership in 1947 persuaded the Pennsylvania Legislature to enact a new body, the Urban Redevelopment Authority of Pittsburgh, that would have sweeping powers to acquire and assemble land. With those new powers, the city went to work on its Golden Triangle. At the very point where the Allegheny and Monongahela rivers converge to form the Ohio River, the City and the Commonwealth of Pennsylvania created Point State Park, a 36-acre urban oasis with riverfront benches, a majestic fountain, and the Fort Pitt Blockhouse, the sole surviving section of the old Fort Pitt.

Adjacent to Point State Park, the partnership demolished the rat's nest of tracks and warehouses and created Gateway Center, a six-building office cluster that became a prestigious downtown address. It remains so today, with entities such as the United Steelworkers of America headquartered there.

Uptown from the Golden Triangle, the URA acquired properties and assembled them in a tract that in 1961 became the home of the Mellon Arena (formerly known as the Civic Arena), a pioneering sports and entertainment complex that features a retractable silver dome.

> **INSIDERS' TIP**
>
> Several Fortune 500 companies are headquartered in Pittsburgh: Alcoa, Consolidated Natural Gas, Heinz USA, Mellon Bank, PNC Bank, PPG Industries, and USX. Pittsburgh is the sixth-largest software center in the United States, in terms of number of employees.

This period of ongoing prosperity also marked the suburbanization of Pittsburgh. Decades of success had provided thousands of Pittsburghers with the wherewithal to seek larger homes in more pastoral settings. Not all abandoned the inner city, of course, as Pittsburgh's distinctive neighborhoods remain a compelling feature of the city. But people relocated in sufficient numbers that a new term—Greater Pittsburgh—entered the local lexicon. In 1960, the Greater Pittsburgh population soared to nearly 2.4 million.

With the city scrubbed clean of deadly smoke and the public-private development partnership both secure and experienced, Pittsburgh entered the second phase of its Renaissance in the 1970s and 1980s.

As visitors drive through the Fort Pitt Tunnel to enter the city for the first time, they typically are stunned by the unexpected beauty of Pittsburgh's skyline, defined by towering skyscrapers so architecturally and functionally diverse that, in aggregate, they defy quick or easy description. The most common response is a sharp intake of breath and a determination to explore them all.

Even more remarkable is that most of these signature buildings were created during Renaissance II. Their import is so great that they deserve to be mentioned at some length, and we've devoted an entire chapter of this book (Architecture) to doing just that.

During Renaissance II, these multiple downtown building projects generated about $2 billion in private and public investment while creating more than $21 million annually in new local tax revenues. While the redevelopment efforts of cities are difficult to quantify, let alone compare, it seems fair to say that few cities have accomplished so much over such a short period. Between the first and last of these developments, only about 15 years elapsed.

Once again the world took notice of Pittsburgh's remarkable achievements. It was during this period that the city reaped a number of prestigious honors. *Places Rated Almanac* judged Pittsburgh "America's Most Livable City" in 1985. *Health* magazine ranked Pittsburgh in its Top 10 American cities. *Savvy* called the city the sixth-best in the nation for raising kids. *Fortune* cited

Pittsburgh on two fronts: it had the eighth-best business climate and was the third Most-Conducive-To-Marriage City.

The two phases of Pittsburgh's Renaissance extended the unbroken record of prosperity in Pittsburgh and promised even more for the future. That promise, however, would not be fulfilled, at least not at once.

Decline, Then Diversification

At first, it was just a few troubling signs. In 1984, Chevron acquired Gulf Oil, a bulwark of Pittsburgh's economy, and relocated its functions and employees to California. By 1986, only seven Gulf staff remained in Pittsburgh. In 1989, Pittsburgh's Rockwell Manufacturing fell victim to a similar fate—acquisition and relocation to California.

A casual observer might have viewed these defections as aberrations, blips on an otherwise prosperous economic map. But such optimism would not survive the collapse of Big Steel.

The decline was precipitous. In the 1980s, Greater Pittsburgh lost an estimated 127,500 jobs in steel and related manufacturing industries. All the support industries that had grown up around steel also felt the blow.

Analysts differ in their assessment of steel's collapse. In his book *And The Wolf Finally Came,* labor writer and historian John Hoerr points to such factors as incursions by foreign manufacturers and "minimills," which could produce steel at lower cost. He also fingers the inability of Big Steel to adequately respond due to a cumbersome organizational structure and the age-old credibility gulf between management and labor.

Whatever the reasons, the impact on the region was severe. Without a healthy manufacturing industry to provide jobs for its young, the region—for the first time in its history—experienced significant out-migration. By 1990 the population of the city proper had plunged to just under 370,000, its lowest mark since 1900. The total for Greater Pittsburgh dipped below 2 million. During its economic heyday, Pittsburgh ranked as America's third-largest headquarters city, behind only New York and Chicago. Between 1984 and 1994, nine "Fortune 500" companies left Pittsburgh or vanished from the rankings.

Throughout its history, the hearty folk who had settled Pittsburgh proved themselves a can-do people; now, more than ever, they needed to do it again. With desperate determination, the city, led by the administration of Mayor Tom Murphy, in concert with the Commonwealth of Pennsylvania, the private sector, foundations and neighborhood-based development organizations, unveiled a two-pronged approach to revitalization. First, the partnership would reclaim abandoned industrial sites and develop in their wake a more diversified economy. Just as important, the partnership would exploit the city's rivers, just as Pittsburgh's original settlers had, with exciting new developments that would contribute to the region's emerging economic diversity.

In short order, the city and its partners made significant progress on both fronts. Along the Monongahela, the partnership constructed 300 attractive housing units, with as many as 1,000 more homes to follow. Along the Allegheny, the partnership developed 230 luxury apartments at a site adjacent to new headquarters for Alcoa, the giant aluminum company that renewed its commitment to the city.

In building economic diversity, the region had considerable help from its two largest research universities, Pitt and Carnegie Mellon, sources for dozens of technology-based spin-off companies. Today the city ranks sixth in the nation in software sector employment, while the broader technology sector employs more than 100,000.

Encouraged by Pittsburgh's emergence as a fertile bed for the growth of technology-based industries, the National Aeronautics and Space Administration in 1996 committed $50 million to help launch a national robotics consortium, along the banks of the Allegheny, to be operated in conjunction with Carnegie Mellon. That development has pushed Pittsburgh to the forefront of robotics.

So complete was Pittsburgh's transformation that in 1996 manufacturing, mining, and construction accounted for only 17.5 percent of Pittsburgh's jobs.

INSIDERS' TIP

The distinctive fountain at Point State Park, at the confluence of the Allegheny, Monongahela and Ohio rivers, is fed by a glacial formation and sprays 6,000 gallons per minute.

HISTORY

The New Pittsburgh

Throughout the city, there are compelling symbols of the region's transformation. Washington's Landing, an Allegheny River island two miles north of downtown, had long been used for industrial operations, including the rendering of animal byproducts; when industrial companies abandoned the island, they left a legacy of contaminated soil. In the 1990s, Pittsburgh's public-private development team entombed the tainted soil and readied the land for redevelopment. Today, Washington's Landing is the site for light manufacturing, office buildings, a marina, townhomes, and recreation.

In Hays, in the city's southeast corner, the U.S. Army Ammunition Plant served as an important cog in the nation's military machine but had been vacant since the Vietnam War. The city's Urban Redevelopment Authority acquired the site from the Army for $1 and prepared it for new uses. Now, it is the home of GalvTech, a technology-based company that zinc coats steel coils.

Perhaps the most persuasive symbol of the region's rebirth is the Pittsburgh Technology Center, a gleaming complex along the Monongahela near the Oakland cluster of universities and hospitals. The site just east of downtown was once home to J&L Steel's Hot Strip Mill; it glowed round the clock as one of the brightest lights of steelmaking.

When the site was abandoned in 1983, the city acquired it and began its conversion to a technology center. The complex currently is home to the University of Pittsburgh Center for Biotechnology and Bioengineering, the Carnegie Mellon Research Institute, Union Switch & Signal (a company founded by the ubiquitous Mr. Westinghouse), and a brace of support organizations for technology-based companies.

To stand on the campus of the Pittsburgh Technology Center is to see the city's history encapsulated. Gaze to the west and you see the gleaming skyscrapers that have defined the downtown since Renaissance II. Look toward the east and you notice the hot metal bridge spanning the Monongahela, still connecting the site to the mill's former coking operations across the river. And all of it wrapped by a latticework of highways, as if bound and determined to enclose and preserve the contrast for posterity.

In its roughly 250 years of settlement, Pittsburgh has experienced the booms and busts of an economic roller coaster, rising through most of its years to a position of prominence among the world's manufacturing centers, feeling the sting when that manufacturing declined, and emerging as a region of multiple strengths. Its impressive downtown, inviting suburbs and distinctive, close-knit neighborhoods are appealing for residents and visitors alike. It offers a rich mix of cultural and entertainment amenities, a reflection of the diverse heritage of its residents.

Above all, it retains the two most important characteristics of its spectacular, sometimes surprising development. Pittsburgh remains within 500 miles of more than half of America's population, making it a preferred site for business and residential location. By land, by water, by air, you can get there from Pittsburgh.

And it continues to boast a population imbued by the work ethic brought to America by its forebears, a population that epitomizes the ideals of America's melting pot, a population ready to roll up its sleeves and get the job done together.

Moving into the 21st Century

Amid protests and political controversy, several new initiatives and projects will be unveiled in this new century. Among them will be two new stadiums for the Pittsburgh Pirates and Pittsburgh Steelers sports teams. Already, Pitt Stadium has been razed to make room for a convocation and events center at the University of Pittsburgh.

The David L. Lawrence Convention Center will undergo expansion and revitalize the riverfront even further. The O'Reilly Theater attracts more patrons to the city's Cultural District.

A new form of government takes its place in Allegheny

HISTORY

INSIDERS' TIP

Pittsburgh's KDKA-AM delivered the nation's first regularly scheduled radio broadcast in 1920, coverage of the Harding-Cox presidential election. Because of their role as radio pioneers, KDKA and Pittsburgh's KQV-AM are among the three radio stations east of the Mississippi River permitted to begin their call letters with "K." (Philadelphia's KYW is the third.)

County with the newly created position of County Executive to work with the County Council. A champion of county concerns, former commissioner Tom Foerster passed away in January 2000, leaving his mark on the Community College of Allegheny County, the Kane Hospitals, and the Pittsburgh International Airport, which he worked tirelessly to see to completion.

Both major banks—Mellon and PNC—are moving ahead with new operations centers. The toppling of the LTV Steel stacks in Hazelwood makes way for additional riverfront revitalization in that area as well. With the purchase of Westinghouse's nuclear business in Monroeville, new owners are not only keeping the Westinghouse name but growing the business, adding jobs, and maintaining a vital part of that community's commercial base.

In the years ahead, there will be more abandoned rails made into bicycle and walking trails, and more worn-down properties converted to modern shops, restaurants and entertainment venues. Indeed the pages of Pittsburgh history will move into new chapters in the new millennium.

HISTORY

Accommodations

Price Code

The area of rates is not easily summarized. It might not appear so on the surface, but Pittsburgh is a community with peak seasons. The summer season is heaviest, fueled in part by convention business. Traveling in Pittsburgh also spikes around holidays and the skiing season. In light of all this, most operators maintain a range of rates rather than a set charge. Asked about her typical rates, one operator replied, "It depends on the day."

That kind of variability makes reporting on rates difficult. With each description, we've indicated rate categories with from one to four dollar signs. The rates are for standard rooms, double occupancy. Here's the key:

$	$30 to $65
$$	$66 to $100
$$$	$101 to $135
$$$$	$136 and over

Remember that when capacity is tight, your rate may be appreciably higher than the standard charge.

Looking to overnight in Pittsburgh? Well, have we got options for you. You can stay in a large, happening hotel in the heart of the city; repair to the suburbs for the quiet of a country inn; luxuriate in an all-seasons resort; grab a room near the airport so you'll be sure to catch that early flight; or join the international crowd at a youth hostel. All are attractive options in Pittsburgh and environs.

Accommodations in Pittsburgh are, in a word, accommodating. You'll find a setting, style, and price range to suit you. Note that we've separated one popular category of accommodation—the bed and breakfast inn—into its own chapter.

With so many options in Greater Pittsburgh, you might think that dropping in and finding the room of your choice would be no problem. In most cases, that's true. Keep in mind, though, that the city is a business center and a popular site for conventions. If we're hosting a major convention, or even several medium-sized gatherings, accommodations in the city are snapped up, forcing visitors to more distant sites. Even there, availability during these occasional crunch times is no guarantee.

Therefore, the wise traveler plans ahead when coming to Pittsburgh. Take the time to make a few phone calls and reservations where appropriate. You'll find the effort rewarded with a guaranteed room you're sure to like.

Most of the time, though, there's more than enough capacity, resulting in sometimes keen competition for business. This has brought some important benefits to customers. For example, virtually all places of lodging in Pittsburgh offer both smoking and nonsmoking rooms; any exceptions are noted in the individual write-ups below.

Policies on pets have changed as well. It was not too many years ago that, if you wanted to bring Bowser along with you, you needed to hide him in your picnic basket. With the boom in rooms, many hotels are accommodating pets as an added attraction for guests. You'll find pet policies detailed in the individual write-ups.

Accessibility for the disabled is another area of growing concern, for both operators and customers. Rare is the establishment in Pittsburgh that doesn't consider itself wheelchair-accessible. As anyone who requires such facilities knows, however, there can be quite a difference between compliance with the letter of the law and convenience and comfort for you. When you're making those phone calls, be sure to ask specific questions about facilities and amenities for disabled guests as well as guests with other special needs.

Most establishments offer discount programs, such as those available through AAA or AARP. Many also maintain frequent traveler programs that help you reduce the cost of your stay. Make sure you inquire about these as well as special packages and offers for which you may be eligible. In Allegheny County, be prepared to pay a 7 percent room tax; elsewhere, the room tax varies from county to county. All establishments described below accept major credit cards.

In our write-ups, we've tended in most instances to avoid facilities that are part of well-known national chains, many of which have a strong presence in our area. This is not meant as a slight. Our thinking here is that the chains are so prominent that you know pretty much what to expect when you stay with them. We have included such facilities, however, where their locations make them potentially important to you.

For example, we've tried to include most hotels and motels near Pittsburgh International Airport for the convenience of those traveling here by air. We've described all hotels and motels in the Oakland neighborhood's university-medical complex, which attracts many visitors in need of convenient lodging. For those occasions when downtown's finest are booked, we've featured a number of facilities on the perimeter of downtown that are good sites for overflow traffic.

After our section on Hotels & Motels, look for listings for Extended Stay Accommodations, Resorts, and Hostels. We've tried hard to include something for everyone.

Exploring Pittsburgh's lodgings will be a joy for you. Whatever your choice, you'll find your enjoyment enhanced by the legendary hospitality of Pittsburghers. If you don't mind our saying so, we'll make any room you choose seem like your home away from home.

Need help locating a hotel? Try the Greater Pittsburgh Convention & Visitors Bureau, (412) 281-7711, for information about hotels and other Pittsburgh attractions. The bureau offers two recorded phone messages detailing current activities: Tourism Information Line, (800) 366-0093, and Weekend Package Hot Line, (800) 927-8376.

Hotels & Motels

Downtown

Doubletree Hotel
$$$$ • 1000 Penn Ave., Pittsburgh
• (412) 281-3700
• www.doubletree.com

This is definitely one of the deluxe hotels in town, and very convenient to the David L. Lawrence Convention Center across the street. With 618 rooms and 42 suites, guests who want a little luxury while on business in the downtown area may opt to stay here. The banquet room seats approximately 960 people, and there are 24 meeting rooms. Guests enjoy two-line data ports with speaker phones, complimentary Doubletree cookies upon check-in, a minibar, and ironing supplies in each room. There are three restaurants, including the Fish Market. Parking is convenient underneath the hotel, but because parking is at a premium in downtown, it's $15 a day for guests. Patrons of the Fish Market can park for $5, and valet parking is available.

Duquesne Club
$$$ • 325 6th Ave., Pittsburgh
• (412) 391-1500

The Duquesne Club is one of the city's most prominent and traditional institutions. Since the turn of the century, business and civic leaders have gathered here to relax and forge plans for the city's growth. Less well known are the 30 overnight rooms that the club offers to visitors (provided they are guests of members). The experience here is Old World, with attentive staff and quiet surroundings. Many who stay here return each time they're in town, enamored of the ambiance.

You'll be in the heart of downtown Pittsburgh, within walking distance of virtually every center city attraction. The club does not permit pets. See our Architecture chapter for a few of the Duquesne Club's aesthetic details.

Pittsburgh Hilton and Towers
$$$$ • 600 Commonwealth Pl., Pittsburgh
• (412) 391-4600, (800) HILTONS
• www.hilton.com

If you arrive at the Hilton and wonder about that attractive greenery across the street, wonder no longer. That's Point State Park, the unusual urban park that's the site for many entertainment and cultural events, including the annual Three Rivers Arts Festival (see our Annual Events chapter). Stay at the Hilton and the park and its attractions will be at your doorstep—literally.

The hotel is the city's most capacious, offering 712 guest rooms that include a complement of Concierge Class rooms. In your room, you'll enjoy two phone lines with voice mail, a fully stocked mini-bar, a writing desk, in-room movies, a coffee maker and an iron set. Each guest room boasts a river or city view.

If business beckons, the Hilton is well equipped to meet your needs. Its Executive

Center is sequestered in a quiet corner of the first floor and offers boardrooms, computers, and secretarial service. If it's a meeting that you're planning, consider the Hilton's 18,200-square-foot ballroom, said to be the largest between New York and Chicago.

The health center includes Universal weights, treadmills, Stairmasters, rowing machines, and stationary bicycles. You'll enjoy both casual and more elegant dining in the hotel's two restaurants and two lounges.

The Hilton will allow small pets with management's prior approval.

Pittsburgh Marriott City Center
$$$ • 112 Washington Pl., Pittsburgh
• (412) 471-4000, (888) 456-6600
• www.marriott.com

While some urban hotels struggle to find space for exercise equipment, Pittsburgh Marriott City Center has no such problem. It offers a 40-foot indoor pool, a health club, and a sauna. Parking, another possible headache for urban hotels, also is hardly a problem here, as hotel guests have access to a 2,100-space indoor garage.

The hotel offers 401 guest rooms as well as five parlor suites and the deluxe Golden Suite, complete with Jacuzzi and wet bar. Small pets are welcome.

When you're ready to eat, you'll find fare that will match your mood. You'll want to try The Steelhead Grill, the on-premises seafood restaurant that has won national awards. In the mood for something lighter? Try Pizza Hut selections, available through room service for late night snacks.

While the hotel is only a few blocks from the center of downtown, it offers complimentary shuttle transportation to key downtown points.

Ramada Plaza Suites
$$$ • One Bigelow Sq., Pittsburgh
• (412) 281-5800, (800) 228-2828
• www.ramada.com

Life is suite at Ramada Plaza. That's because all accommodations here are suites. Your suite features a kitchen or kitchenette, microwave oven, coffee maker, utensils and dishware, dining and work areas, cable television, and recliners. Street-level retail shops provide a variety of valuable services. You'll find a hair stylist, a florist, a travel agency, and same-day laundry and valet services.

The health club is impressive, featuring 10,000 square feet including an indoor track, a free-weight room, aerobics classes, a pool, a sauna, a steam room, and a tanning bed. The hotel also offers meeting and banquet facilities.

For dining, the Ruddy Duck Restaurant and Lounge is popular with hotel guests and downtown visitors alike. The restaurant and hotel are just a few paces from Grant Street, the hub of Pittsburgh's professional activity.

Ramada Plaza Suites does not permit pets.

Sheraton Station Square Hotel
$$$ • 7 Station Square Dr., Pittsburgh
• (412) 261-2000, (800) 255-7488
• www.sheraton.com

Station Square is a vibrant urban riverfront shopping center with 60 upscale shops. It's actually situated on the city's South Side, but it's so close to downtown (right across the Smithfield Street Bridge) that we decided to include it here. Stay at the Sheraton Station Square and you'll be only a few excited paces from all that activity.

The hotel offers 293 guest rooms as well as a club level with special amenities. Many rooms provide dramatic views of Pittsburgh's rivers and skyline, while all guest rooms offer cable television, in-room movies, and coffee service. You'll enjoy an indoor pool, whirlpool, sauna, and fitness center, while massage therapists stand at the ready to soothe any aches and pains. Meeting and banquet facilities can accommodate up to 1,500 people.

The atrium lobby is a must stop, whether you're staying at the hotel or dropping by for refreshments. There, you'll see a waterfall that cascades seven stories into a charming lily pond. The water show makes the Waterfall Terrace Lounge and the Waterfall Terrace Restaurant particularly appealing. Reflections Dining Room serves a popular Sunday brunch.

The Sheraton is just across the Smithfield Street Bridge (see our Architecture chapter for more details and the start of a walking tour). The hotel welcomes pets.

The Westin William Penn
$$$ • 530 William Penn Way, Pittsburgh
• (412) 281-7100
• www.westin.com

Relaxing in the Palm Court Lobby of The Westin William Penn is one of the city's most civilized experiences. While you enjoy a beverage and bask beneath the ornate chandeliers, you can laugh with friends and watch the swells stroll through the lobby. It's such a comfortable experience that you might not want to leave.

Once you manage to get past the lobby, you'll find 595 guest rooms offering mahogany furnishings, plush carpeting, and marble baths. The hotel welcomes your pets. Ask about the special amenities at the Crown Service level.

In 1998, the hotel finished a three-year, $25 million renovation that gave facelifts to meeting rooms on the conference level, including new names that reflect Pittsburgh's industrial history—names like Frick, Heinz, Oliver, Phipps, and Vandergrift. Many of the luxury suites have also been updated. Each boasts multiple bedrooms, living and dining rooms, sitting areas, and full kitchens. Electronics throughout the hotel were improved as well, so guests now enjoy two phone lines and voice mail.

The hotel features more than 52,000 square feet of meeting space, capped by the two-story Grand Ballroom. For your dining pleasure, you'll choose from several restaurants, including the Terrace Room, one of the city's most popular spots for breakfast meetings. The Palm Court lobby is a grand space flanked by seven arches on each side.

The Westin William Penn sits in the center of the city, within walking distance of all the cultural amenities as well as Grant Street political happenings. Turn to our Architecture chapter, where this hotel, commissioned by Henry Clay Frick, appears as part of the walking tour of Downtown Pittsburgh. Don't miss afternoon tea in the Palm Court lobby, a simply splendid tradition (albeit borrowed from the British).

North

Comfort Inn Butler
$ • 1 Comfort Ln., Butler
• (724) 287-7177
• www.comfortinn.com

Guests in the 70 rooms at Comfort Inn, about 25 miles north of Pittsburgh, enjoy rooms with computer access and whirlpools. You also can take advantage of the complimentary breakfast buffet, indoor pool, and fitness center. The rooms are standard fare for this well-known national chain.

The big days at the hotel are Tuesday and Wednesday, when management throws a complimentary happy hour bash and awards a free

---

INSIDERS' TIP

A brothel once flourished near The Priory when that city inn was a home for Benedictine monks in the 1880s. When the bishop discovered the house of ill repute, he ordered the front curtains closed and relocated the priests to the back room.

---

upgrade to the VIP of the day. You're very important—give it a try.

Sign a pet waiver and pay with a credit card, and Rover can stay too.

Conley Resort Inn
$$ • 740 Pittsburgh Rd., Butler
• (724) 586-7711, (800) 344-7303
• www.conleyresort.com

While the designation "resort" may be a little highfalutin', Conley Resort Inn does offer a number of attractive amenities. It features an 18-hole golf course, a putting green, tennis courts, and an indoor pool. If the kids are along, dare them to try either the 100-foot water slide or the speed slide. Pets are not permitted.

When you stay in one of the 56 guest rooms, you'll receive complimentary breakfast. Ask about specially priced golf packages. Conley Resort Inn is located along Pa. Route 8, a major state highway that connects Pittsburgh and Butler.

Days Inn—Butler/Conference Center
$ • 139 Pittsburgh Rd., Butler
• (724) 287-6761, (800) 325-2525
• www.daysinnbutlercounty.com

As the name suggests, conferences are popular at Days Inn, which offers meeting and banquet space for up to 1,000 people. That's far from the only attraction, though. The 133 guest rooms feature cable television, and you also can enjoy the pool, Jacuzzi, Brentwood Café, and Frisco's Night Club. Bring your pet, but be prepared to pay a $50 refundable deposit.

The facility offers specially priced golf packages that allow you to test as many as four Butler-area courses. Days Inn is located along Pa. Route 8.

Clarion Hotel
$$ • 300 Tarentum Bridge Rd., New Kensington
• (724) 335-9171, (800) 329-7466
• www.clarioninn.com

Looking to hold a banquet or meeting in the New Kensington area? This may be your place, with facilities than can accommodate up to 900 and complete audio-visual equipment offered on site.

Stay in one of the 113 guest rooms and you'll

have access to an outdoor pool. If you're willing to sign for responsibility for any clean-up or damages, you're welcome to bring your pets.

Fairfield Inn Butler
$$ • 200 Fairfield Ln., Butler
• (724) 283-0009
• www.fairfield.com

Operated by Marriott, Fairfield Inn offers complimentary continental breakfast, in-room work areas, an indoor pool and a whirlpool. Feel free to use the hotel's fax service. Pets are not permitted in the 64 guest rooms.

While Fairfield Inn is about 25 miles from Pittsburgh, it is convenient to the many attractions of Butler, including Butler Memorial Hospital and the Big Butler Fairgrounds, host to the annual Butler County Fair in early July (see our Annual Events chapter).

Holiday Inn Allegheny Valley —RIDC Park
$$$ • 180 Gamma Dr., O'Hara
• (412) 963-0600
• www.holiday-inn.com

If you expect your stay to last longer than a day or two, consider this Holiday Inn's leasing opportunities. The hotel offers 40 apartment-style suites with kitchen facilities and patios. You can take advantage of short- and long-term rates. "RIDC" is short for Regional Industrial Development Corporation, which developed the business park in which the hotel is located. Many who are in town on business in the park take advantage of this Holiday Inn's long-term rates.

Guests can relax in the fitness room, game room, the Cabana Club bar (in the warmer months) and Accolade's Restaurant and Nitescape Lounge. Meeting space can accommodate up to 600 people. The hotel welcomes your pets.

Holiday Inn—Pittsburgh/McKnight
$$$ • 4895 McKnight Rd., Ross
• (412) 366-5200
• www.holiday-inn.com

Stay at this Holiday Inn and you'll hear the "Call of the Mall." It's located in the suburban North Hills on McKnight Road, an active strip of malls sure to satisfy your every shopping need.

The hotel offers 147 standard issue guest rooms with cable television, computer access, voice mail, coffee makers and iron sets, and you can dine at the on-premises restaurant. Holiday Inn welcomes pets.

Holiday Inn Pittsburgh North
$$ • 10 Landings Dr., Pittsburgh
• (412) 828-9300
• www.holiday-inn.com

One of the principal attractions of this hotel is a host of unusual entertainment opportunities nearby. Within a few minutes' walk are Blade Runners Ice Complex, featuring two regulation ice skating surfaces, and Ladbrokes, an off-track wagering facility where you can watch and wager on as many as 25 horse racing tracks per day.

Located just off Exit 5 of the Pennsylvania Turnpike, the hotel offers four suites in addition to its 63 standard rooms, as well as a small indoor pool. Sorry, but this Holiday Inn prefers no pooches.

The Priory—A City Inn
$$$ • 614 Pressley St., Pittsburgh
• (412) 231-3338
• www.thepriory.com

In the late 19th century, Benedictine priests traveling through Pittsburgh would take respite at The Priory. Current owners have restored the facility with Victorian-style furnishings in its 24 guest rooms. If you need an office-away-from-the-office, this probably isn't the place. If you're looking for an old-world experience in elegant surroundings, you'll find it at The Priory.

The inn is unobtrusive, located on a North Side residential street, but the appointments are splendid. You'll enjoy complimentary breakfast and evening wine around the fireplace. You can walk in the garden courtyard or to any of the city's nearby attractions, including Three Rivers Stadium and The National Aviary.

If you like, you can use complimentary limousine service for the half-mile trip across the Ninth Street Bridge into downtown Pittsburgh. Or you can sip your wine, gaze across the Allegheny River at the hustle and bustle of downtown, and contemplate how good life can be. Pets are not permitted.

INSIDERS' TIP

Where do celebrities stay when in Pittsburgh? Jodie Foster stopped at the Shadyside Inn, while Gregory Peck opted for the Duquesne Club. Jack Nicholson chose the Vista (predecessor of The DoubleTree) and had television coverage of his beloved Los Angeles Lakers piped in via special arrangement.

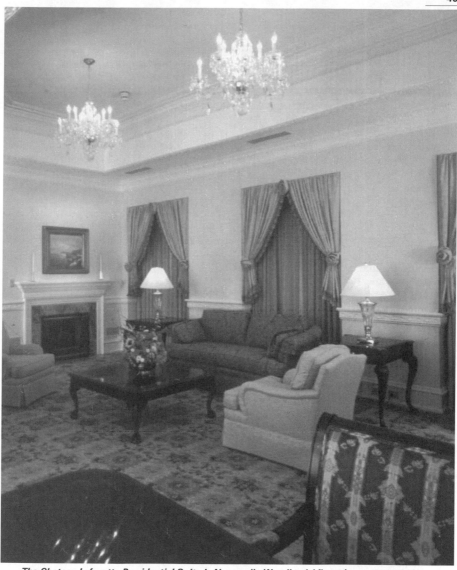

The Chateau Lafayette Presidential Suite is Nemacolin Woodlands' finest in accommodations.

Photo: Courtesy of Nemacolin Woodlands Resort & Spa

ACCOMMODATIONS

Rodeway Inn
$ • RD#6, Box 279G, Kittanning
• (724) 543-1100

Here's a quaint establishment with only 20 rooms; what it lacks in volume it makes up in dedicated customer service. The hotel keeps records on all its guests. When guests come for return visits, staff have their customers' favorite touches waiting for them. Everyone who stays here will enjoy the free continental breakfast and complimentary *USA Today*.

Guest rooms feature cable television, computer access, and coffee makers. Bring your small pets, but you must provide a $10 refundable deposit. This Rodeway Inn is in Armstrong County, about 30 miles north of Pittsburgh.

Sheraton Inn Pittsburgh North
$$$ • 910 Sheraton Dr., Mars
• (724) 776-6900
• www.sheraton.com

Don't worry about being on Mars. This

community is part of Pittsburgh's growing suburban North Hills, which means you'll be close to many attractions.

This Sheraton Inn offers 192 rooms with a number of compelling views. You can request a room with a balcony or one that faces the hotel's atrium. All rooms offer cable television, computer access, coffee makers, hair dryers, and iron sets. You'll also have access to fax and copier service.

For a workout, try the on-site health club, indoor/outdoor pool and Jacuzzi. You can slake the thirst you work up at the on-premises lounge, Legends Pub. Sheraton Inn does not permit pets.

East

Antiochian Village
$$ • R.R. #1, Box 307, Bolivar
• (724) 238-3677
• avcenter@westol.com

Antiochian Village specializes in lodging for groups and conferences; it offers 11 meeting rooms. The experience here is quiet and thought-provoking. There are no televisions or other distractions in any of the 100 guest rooms, but you will find televisions in two common areas.

Antiochian Village provides plenty of amenities for group activities, including a baseball diamond, a football field and basketball courts. For meals, a full-time chef is waiting to serve you. Antiochian Village does not permit pets.

Best Western University Hotel
$$ • 3401 Blvd. of the Allies, Pittsburgh
• (412) 683-6100, (800) 245-4444
• www.bestwestern.com

Stay at Best Western University Hotel and you'll be at the doorstep of Magee Woman's Hospital and the other healthcare providers that constitute Pittsburgh's most important medical center. The hotel provides free shuttle service throughout the Oakland university-medical complex. Pick up your shuttle schedule at the front desk.

The 119 guest rooms include cable television and private balconies, and you'll have access to fax service, meeting space, and an on-site restaurant. You also can request an execu-

tive room and enjoy such amenities as a hair dryer, coffee maker, and complimentary breakfast. Pets are welcome.

Comfort Inn of Greensburg
$$ • 1129 E. Pittsburgh St., Greensburg
• (724) 832-2600, (800) 228-5150
• www.comfortinn.com

This Comfort Inn offers 77 rooms, including 24 whirlpool mini-suites and two specialty suites. All rooms include cable television and complimentary continental breakfast, as well as access to fax and copier service. Staying here affords plenty of shopping opportunities, as the Westmoreland Mall is only a mile away, and there are plenty of other stores (Barnes & Noble, Toys R Us) and restaurants in the immediate area. When you're finished shopping, take a dip in the outdoor heated pool (if it's summer, that is!). No pets, please.

Days Inn—New Stanton
$ • 127 W. Byers Ave., New Stanton
• (724) 925-3591
• www.daysinn.com

If you're traveling the Pennsylvania Turnpike, Days Inn will be a welcome stop—it's close to the New Stanton exit where the Turnpike meets I-76. You'll find 137 guest rooms with many attractive features, including cable television, computer access, voice mail, hair dryers, and iron sets.

When you're ready to relax, try the outdoor pool, the weight room, the restaurant, and the lounge. Days Inn does not permit pets.

Four Points Hotel by Sheraton
$$ • Rt. 30 E., 100 Sheraton Dr., Greensburg • (724) 836-6060
• www.sheraton.com

Don't be surprised if you hear wedding bells ringing as you near Four Points. Not only does the hotel offer an old-fashioned bridal suite, but it also maintains a wedding coordinator to help you with the details of your nuptials.

Even if you're not in the matrimonial mood, you'll find the experience here pleasing. The hotel offers 140 rooms—six with Jacuzzis—that feature cable television, in-room movies, and computer access. You'll enjoy the indoor pool, but if you need a more vigorous workout, you can hit the weights at

INSIDERS' TIP
While in Pittsburgh with his orchestra in the 1940s, Lawrence Welk "discovered" his trademark bubble machine at the Westin William Penn. The original machine, devised by a staff chef, remains on the premises.

a nearby fitness center for a $10 fee. The hotel's fitness room is less equipped.

Relax at The Prospect Lounge and the Vista Plateau, both on site. Four Points does permit pets if you're willing to pay the $99 room rate.

Hampton Inn Monroeville
$$ • 3000 Mosside Blvd., Monroeville
• (412) 380-4000, (800) HAMPTON
• www.hamptoninn.com

The Hampton Inn is one of Monroeville's newest hotels, strategically located just off the Pennsylvania Turnpike, the Parkway East, and Route 22. There are 140 guest rooms and two meeting rooms for business or conferences. The banquet space seats 30. Enjoy the indoor pool, fitness room and complimentary continental breakfast. Guests can also enjoy the Outback Steakhouse attached to the Hampton Inn. Situated in Monroeville, you're close to shopping with the Miracle Mile Shopping Center right up the road and Monroeville Mall five minutes away. Just drive down Business Route 22 and you're never at a loss for a gas station or store! Boyce Park is approximately 10 minutes away in nearby Plum Borough. And that's a good thing since pets are indeed allowed at this Hampton Inn location.

Hampton Inn Westmoreland
$$ • 1000 Towne Square Dr., Greensburg
• (724) 838-8800, (800) HAMPTON
• www.hamptoninn.com

This Hampton Inn is much like any other location, only with a few differences. There's an outdoor pool, exercise facility, and 69 guest rooms at this location. You'll find restaurants within two miles, and this hotel is not far from the Westmoreland Mall. No pets allowed here, however. All Hampton Inns feature complimentary continental breakfast and free local telephone calling.

Hampton Inn Pittsburgh University Center
$$$ • 3315 Harriet St., Pittsburgh
• (412) 681-1000, (800) HAMPTON
• www.hamptoninn.com

The chief attraction here is the location in Oakland's university-medical complex. The hotel provides free shuttle service to the area's hospitals and universities, making it an attractive option for travelers visiting those institutions. If you arrive at the Pittsburgh International Airport, you can catch the free shuttle to the hotel, but a trip back for your departure flight will cost you $12.50 per person. Each guest

room features a hair dryer and iron set. Small pets are permitted.

Holiday Inn Parkway East
$$$ • 915 Brinton Rd., Wilkinsburg
• (412) 247-2700
• www.holiday-inn.com

This hotel offers 180 guest rooms, with suites also available. You'll enjoy the indoor pool as well as privileges at a local fitness center that offers tennis and racquetball courts. For on-site dining, try the 915 Cafe. The Collegiate Hall Ballroom can accommodate up to 300 for banquets and meetings. The hotel welcomes small pets.

Holiday Inn Pittsburgh-Monroeville
$$$ • 2750 Mosside Blvd., Monroeville
• (412) 372-1022
• www.holiday-inn.com

All 189 guest rooms at the hotel offer cable television and designated phone lines for modem connections. If you'd like a coffee maker, hair dryer, or iron set, ask for one of the facility's specialty rooms. No matter which room you choose, pets are permitted.

Amenities include an outdoor swimming pool and an on-premises restaurant called Finnegan's, which serves breakfast, lunch, and dinner, plus a Sunday brunch. Meeting and banquet facilities can accommodate up to 300 people.

The hotel is a quarter mile from Exit 6 of the Pennsylvania Turnpike.

Holiday Inn Select
$$$ • 100 Lytton Ave., Pittsburgh
• (412) 682-6200
• www.holiday-inn.com

When you stay here, you'll be smack-dab in the middle of the University of Pittsburgh campus. The historic Cathedral of Learning is several hundred yards away, and you'll enjoy the compelling sight of students on their way to class. You can reach all of Oakland's hospitals by walking or a short bus ride.

All 251 guest rooms feature cable television, in-room movies, coffee makers, hair dryers, iron sets and voice mail. Business travelers might prefer Executive Edition Rooms with refrigerators and a daily buffet. Small pets are permitted.

Recreational opportunities include an indoor pool, a sauna and exercise equipment. For dining, try the on-premises Foster's Grill, which features a popular Champagne Jazz Brunch each Sunday.

ACCOMMODATIONS

The hotel offers 7,000 square feet of meeting and banquet space. While you're here, treat yourself to a tour of the Cathedral of Learning's impressive Nationality Rooms. For more on those, see our Attractions chapter.

Mountain View Inn
$$ • Rt. 30 E., Greensburg
• **(724) 834-5300, (800) 537-8709**
• **www.mountainviewinn.com**

Built in 1924, Mountain View Inn has remained under continuous ownership of the Booher family since 1940. They have maintained the Early American setting, with guest rooms featuring antique furnishings as well as brass or canopied beds. You can opt for a suite or schedule a meeting for your group in the facility's spacious banquet rooms.

You'll enjoy the outdoor pool and take special pleasure in dining at the Mountain View Inn, acclaimed for its decor and excellent food. If you're looking for understated elegance, you'll find it at Mountain View Inn.

This inn also makes for the perfect romantic getaway with some suites featuring small fireplaces, spacious Jacuzzis, and the lavish touch of fresh floral arrangements.

Palace Inn
$ • Rts. 22 & 48, Monroeville
• **(412) 372-5500, (800) 545-6600**

This hotel offers the distinctive touch of owner Al Monzo, who stages such unusual and attractive events as boxing cards on site. Other entertainment options include indoor and outdoor swimming pools, a Jacuzzi, an exercise room, and a tanning salon. The Casa Di Monzo restaurant features weekend entertainment, and you also can sample lighter fare at Daisy's Coffee Shop.

Guest rooms include cable television and in-room movies, and suites are available. Pets are not permitted. Weekdays bring complimentary free breakfast. The facility is a popular site for meetings, offering a Grand Ballroom with seating for 2,000.

You can reach the Palace Inn via the Pennsylvania Turnpike or Interstate 376 (the Parkway East).

Radisson Hotel
$$$ • 101 Mall Blvd., Monroeville
• **(412) 373-7300, (800) 333-3333**
• **www.radisson.com**

A compelling attraction of the Radisson is its proximity to Pittsburgh ExpoMart, a popular venue for a wide variety of exhibits and trade shows. If you're participating in or visiting one of those events, you won't beat Radisson's convenience.

You can select from 322 guest rooms and penthouse suites that feature data ports, wet bars and whirlpools. All guests can swim in the pool, relax in the Jacuzzi, or drink and dine in the Grand Stand Bar and the Oxford Dining Room. You also will enjoy privileges at the nearby Oxford Athletic Club, a full-service fitness center.

If that doesn't tire you out, the 160-shop Monroeville Mall and Borders Books & Music are a quick walk from the hotel, which is accessible from both the Pennsylvania Turnpike and Interstate 376 (the Parkway East). The hotel does not permit pets.

Ramada Inn & Conference Center
$$ • 699 Rodi Rd., Wilkins
• **(412) 244-1600, (800) 321-2323**
• **www.ramada.com**

Travel up the long winding road that's the driveway, and you'll reach a scenic view of Pittsburgh's eastern communities. You'll also find such amenities as indoor and outdoor pools, saunas, a whirlpool, and lighted tennis courts. This hotel was newly remodeled in 1999.

In-room telephones are computer adaptable, and you may utilize the hotel's fax services. HBO and the Movie Channel are available in all rooms. Pets, however, are not permitted. Rivers Three Restaurant, located within the hotel, takes pride in its wine list.

This Ramada is accessible from the Pennsylvania Turnpike (by only a few miles) and Interstate 376 (the Parkway East).

Ramada Inn at Historic Ligonier
$$ • 216 W. Loyalhanna St., Ligonier
• **(724) 238-9545**
• **www.ramada.com**

You'll find 66 guest rooms with computer access, as well as deluxe rooms that feature a large work and sitting area. In addition, there are seven suites with Jacuzzis and mini-kitchens. All rooms have access to fax and copier service, and all guests can enjoy The Bistro, located on-site, as well as Cappy's Café which is a casual deli. In season, you can splash in the outdoor pool. The hotel does not permit pets.

At the Ramada, you'll be in the scenic Laurel Highlands recreation area, close to many attractions. Make sure you inquire about special guest packages featuring the Seven Springs Mountain Resort and Idlewild Park, a popular amusement park (see our Kidstuff chapter for details).

South

Days Inn Pittsburgh
$ • 1150 Banksville Rd., Pittsburgh
• (412) 531-8900, (800) 325-2525
• www.daysinn.com

This is a serviceable hotel with 70 rooms, an outdoor swimming pool and banquet facilities that can service up to 200 people. You also can request a room with a Jacuzzi. Fax service is available, and all rooms offer cable television.

The most important feature of this facility, however, is its central location, less than two miles from downtown Pittsburgh. When convention or holiday traffic causes congestion at downtown hotels, many travelers look to Days Inn as a convenient alternative.

The hotel does not permit pets.

Holiday Inn Pittsburgh South
$$ • 164 Fort Couch Rd., Bethel Park
• (412) 833-5300
• www.holiday-inn.com

The hotel offers 208 guest rooms featuring cable television, computer access, and iron sets. Fax and copier service are also available. For recreation, the hotel provides guests with complimentary passes to a nearby fitness center. Pets are welcome here.

Holiday Inn is located in Pittsburgh's busy suburban South Hills, near many shopping malls (within walking distance) and the border between Allegheny and Washington counties. Because of the hotel's convenient location, many organizations stage meetings and banquets here.

Holiday Inn Meadow Lands
$$$ • 340 Racetrack Rd., Meadow Lands
• (724) 222-6200
• www.holiday-inn.com

If horse racing is in your blood, then this Holiday Inn is in your future. It's about a furlong from Ladbroke at the Meadows, a harness racing facility that features both live and simulcast racing (see our Spectator Sports chaper). The hotel offers several Ladbroke packages that include box seats at the track and race programs.

Stay in one of the 138 guest rooms and you'll enjoy the pool, exercise equipment, Jacuzzi, and steam room. A lounge and restaurant are on the premises, and you can repair to your room to watch cable television. You also may take advantage of golf privileges at a nearby club. The hotel welcomes pets.

Because Racetrack Road is an important connector between Interstate 79 and Pennsylvania Route 19, the hotel is a popular and convenient site for banquets.

Perhaps you'll get lucky and pay for your stay with your Ladbroke winnings. Should you come up a loser, the hotel probably will expect you to pay your bill anyway.

INSIDERS' TIP
Pittsburgh's most elegant hotel during the 19th century was the Monongahela House, which stood next to the Monongahela Wharf. Six presidents, including Abraham Lincoln, stayed there during Pittsburgh's heyday as a river port.

Ramada Inn
$$ • 1170 W. Chestnut St., Washington
• (724) 225-9750
• www.ramada.com

This Ramada offers 92 guest rooms and one suite. You'll have computer access in your room, and the hotel also provides fax and copier service. Ask about business class rooms and full breakfast plans. On the rare occasion, pets are allowed for a $25 non-refundable deposit.

Relax in the outdoor pool or at the Gallery and the Oakwood Room, the on-premises restaurant and lounge. The establishment's banquet facilities can accommodate 300 people.

Ramada Inn Redwood
$$ • 2898 Banksville Rd., Pittsburgh
• (412) 343-3000
• www.ramada.com

With its 95 rooms conveniently situated only 2 miles from downtown Pittsburgh, Ramada Inn represents an attractive alternative when downtown hotels are booked. You can opt for suites with Jacuzzis and enjoy the outdoor pool. If you're planning an event, you'll appreciate the banquet facilities, which can accommodate up to 300 people. Enjoy the full-service restaurant The Forest Restaurant & Lounge. The hotel does not permit pets.

The "Redwood" in the name, incidentally, is a carry-over from the hotel's previous name and ownership several years ago.

Washington Motor Inn
$ • 1385 W. Chestnut St., Washington
• (724) 222-6500

If you're looking for economical, serviceable lodgings in Washington, this might be the place.

The 62 rooms offer cable television, and guests enjoy complimentary continental breakfast. Pets are not permitted. Find this motor inn at exit 4 off I-70.

West

Best Western Parkway Center Inn
$$ • 875 Greentree Rd., Green Tree
• (412) 922-7070
• www.bestwestern.com

Location is an important plus for this hotel. It's two miles west of downtown Pittsburgh along the Interstate 279 corridor. That means it's only a 15-minute drive or ride to Pittsburgh International Airport, and you can utilize the hotel's airport shuttle service. The hotel is adjacent to the 85-store Parkway Center Mall, which will provide you with such amenities as shopping, dining, a post office, a travel agency, and automobile rentals.

The hotel offers 138 rooms, a complimentary breakfast buffet, and complimentary cocktails—enjoy them around the indoor pool. You can take advantage of the fitness center while the kids invade the video arcade. Pets are not permitted.

As you drive along I-279 (the Parkway West), you'll spot the inn by the distinctive "P" on the building. Trouble is, it's a red "P" that looks suspiciously like the Philadelphia Phillies logo. In Pittsburgh? Nah, couldn't be.

INSIDERS' TIP
The Vista Hotel, predecessor of today's The DoubleTree Hotel, was built by modular design. Factory-constructed components such as the bathrooms came in a complete package with marble vanity, mirrors, wallpapering, and ceramic tiling already in place. The modules were simply unwrapped and set in place.

Crowne Plaza Hotel
$$$ • 1160 Thorn Run Ext., Coraopolis
• (412) 262-2400
• www.crowneplaza.com

The 193 guest rooms at the Crowne Plaza offer in-room work areas and telephones with modem ports. For a special treat, try the Concierge Level, where you'll enjoy complimentary breakfast and cocktails and a billiards table, or swim in the outdoor pool. There is a restaurant and lounge on property.

No matter which room you choose, feel free to bring your pets. The hotel's meeting space can accommodate up to 1,000 people. You also can access round-the-clock courtesy transportation to and from Pittsburgh International Airport, which is about 6 miles away.

Clubhouse Inn
$$ • 5311 Campbells Run Rd., Robinson
• (412) 788-8400, (800) CLUB INN
• www.clubhouseinn.com

Located 8 miles from Pittsburgh International Airport and 9 miles from downtown Pittsburgh, Clubhouse Inn is a convenient hotel if you need access to both downtown and the airport. The hotel offers 152 rooms and 26 suites as well as a complimentary breakfast buffet and evening cocktails. The Red Bull Inn restaurant is next door.

To relax, try the pool, the whirlpool spa, or a stroll in the garden courtyard. When you're ready for that business meeting, the hotel's space can accommodate groups of up to 50 people.

Pets are not permitted.

Comfort Inn Pittsburgh Airport
$$ • 7011 Old Steubenville Pike, Oakdale
• (412) 787-2600
• www.comfortinn.com

One of the neatest attractions of this hotel—it's adjacent to the Tonidale Restaurant, well known locally for its extensive menu and homemade fare. In fact, the hotel used to be known as The Tonidale.

It features 74 guest rooms, such business services as a fax and copier, a fitness center, and courtesy transportation to Pittsburgh International Airport, which is about 7 miles away. You can lodge your pet with you for an additional $8 per day, but if you're smart, you won't let Rover anywhere near your Tonidale pie.

Courtyard by Marriott
$$$ • 450 Cherrington Pkwy., Coraopolis
• (412) 264-5000, (800) 321-2211
• www.courtyard.com

At Courtyard by Marriott, you can relax while you work, or work while you relax. Either way, you'll find accommodating facilities here.

The 148 guest rooms offer large working areas as well as two telephones with modems, coffee makers, and cable television. When you're ready for a break, try the mini-gym, indoor pool, and whirlpool. Later, you can enjoy the on-site restaurant.

The facility can provide meeting rooms for up to 35 participants as well as fax and copier service. The establishment does not permit pets.

Embassy Suites Hotel
$$$$ • 550 Cherrington Pkwy., Coraopolis
• (412) 269-9070
• www.embassy-suites.com

As the name suggests, you'll find well-appointed suites here, each with a refrigerator, microwave, coffee maker, voice mail, and computer access. Take advantage of the pull-out sofa and meeting area within each suite. You'll enjoy cable television and in-room movies.

The hotel offers a health club and swimming pool as well as the Foggy Bottom Restaurant and Horsefeathers Bar, both on-site. You won't go hungry here, as you'll feast on a cooked-to-order breakfast and a complimentary everyday buffet.

Your pets are welcome here. Embassy Suites is several miles from Pittsburgh International Airport.

Fort Pitt Motel
$ • 7750 Steubenville Pike, Oakdale
• (412) 788-9960

Fort Pitt Motel is an unusual little budget-type establishment with only 19 rooms. The story here is the surprising amenities. Seven rooms offer heart-shaped whirlpools, while a number of rooms feature balconies, patios and working fireplaces. It's pretty Spartan otherwise, but the unusual features and location about 10 miles from Pittsburgh International Airport make this one worth checking out.

Hampton Inn Green Tree
$$ • 555 Trumbull Dr., Green Tree
• (412) 922-0100
• www.hamptoninn.com

The Hampton Inn is among a cluster of three hotels in the Pittsburgh suburb of Green Tree. All offer great locations, only 3 miles from downtown Pittsburgh and just a 15-minute ride from Pittsburgh International Airport. The hotel offers free airport shuttle service.

Its 133 rooms offer work tables and telecommunication ports. If you're getting in a little work during your visit, feel free to use the copier and fax machine as well as the hotel's meeting rooms. These can accommodate up to 35 people.

If you have a pet under 50 pounds, bring it along. Of course, you must sign a pet policy for any potential damages.

Hampton Inn Pittsburgh Airport
$$ • 1420 Beers School Rd., Coraopolis
• (412) 264-0020
• www.hamptoninn.com

Hampton Inn offers complimentary shuttle service to and from Pittsburgh International Airport, which is a convenient 6 miles away. If you're visiting Robert Morris College, the hotel is only a mile from campus. Bring your pets along for the visit—they're welcome here.

Accommodations include 129 guest rooms featuring cable television and a complimentary breakfast buffet. With Robinson Town Centre and The Pointe at North Fayette about five minutes east (toward the city), you'll have plenty of shopping and restaurants to keep you entertained and fed.

> ## INSIDERS' TIP
> When Prince Charles visited Pittsburgh for the 1988 "Remaking Cities" conference, he overnighted at the Vista Hotel, now The DoubleTree Hotel.

Holiday Inn Beaver Falls
$$ • 7195 Eastwood Rd., Beaver Falls
• (724) 846-3700
• www.holiday-inn.com

The fitness buffs in your party will love the hotel's Holidome, which features a pool, a sauna, a whirlpool, a miniature golf course, and a video arcade. When you're ready to eat and drink after your workout, you'll find a restaurant and a lounge on the premises.

The hotel offers 156 rooms with cable television, computer access, hair dryers, and iron sets, and it welcomes your pets. You can reach Holiday Inn easily—it's just off Exit 2 of the Pennsylvania Turnpike.

Holiday Inn Pittsburgh Airport
$$$ • 1406 Beers School Rd., Coraopolis
• (412) 262-3600, (800) 333-4835
• www.holiday-inn.com

You can almost see Pittsburgh International Airport from the Holiday Inn, and the courtesy transportation the hotel provides will get you to the Airport in a few moments. The hotel's 257 rooms include work areas and in-room movies; you also can opt for an executive room with a king-size bed and a recliner. Stuck with work on your trip? The hotel's computer ports, fax, copier and secretarial assistance will help you get it done more quickly.

The highlight of the hotel's recreational facilities is the indoor "aquacade," featuring a pool and whirlpool. You can dine at the on-site Beef and Burgundy restaurant or choose from the many restaurants along Beers School Road. For meetings and banquets, the hotel offers more than 12,000 square feet of conference space.

Your pets are welcome here.

Holiday Inn Pittsburgh Central
$$$ • 401 Holiday Dr., Green Tree
• (412) 922-8100
• www.holiday-inn.com

The Holiday Inn is part of the Green Tree cluster of hotels, with that great location convenient to both downtown Pittsburgh and Pittsburgh International Airport.

The hotel's 200 rooms offer phone modems, work areas and balconies, so you can work a little and relax a little. If you're looking for a workout, try the outdoor pool or fitness center. Afterwards, you can repair to Harlan's Saloon and Eatery, the in-house restaurant that stages a sumptuous Sunday brunch that's popular with hotel guests and others in search of a good meal. Bring your pets—they're welcome here.

For banquets, the hotel's Grand Ballroom can seat up to 1,000 guests. You can deploy the dozen breakout rooms as well.

LaQuinta Inn
$$ • 1433 Beers School Rd., Coraopolis
• (412) 269-0400

Stay at LaQuinta and you'll be treated to complimentary continental breakfast. You'll enjoy in-room movies and complimentary airport transportation.

For business purposes, each of the 129 rooms and three suites features dataport phones and access to voice mail and fax service. The hotel permits small dogs in rooms.

Pittsburgh Airport Marriott
$$$ • 777 Aten Rd., Coraopolis
• (412) 788-8800
• www.marriott.com

There are quite a few hotels in the Pittsburgh International Airport corridor, but the Pittsburgh Airport Marriott physically stands out, rising like a pastel palace of the Parkway West. Its lobby, grand and inviting, extends the palatial theme.

The hotel offers 314 guest rooms as well as a Concierge Level and five mini-suites. Your pets are welcome here. On-site recreational opportunities include indoor and outdoor pools, an exercise room, a whirlpool, and a sauna. Try Meritage Grill and The Quiet Bar for dining and drinking pleasure.

The hotel offers 12,000 square feet of meeting space (16 rooms) and free airport transportation.

Radisson Hotel
$$$ • 101 Marriott Dr., Green Tree
• (412) 922-8400, (800) 525-5902
• www.radisson.com

The hotel is conveniently located in the airport Parkway West corridor and only 3 miles from downtown Pittsburgh. While it might seem strange that a Radisson sits upon Marriott Drive, that's because this hotel used to be the Green Tree Marriott.

The Radisson offers 467 guest rooms, five suites, and nine parlors (meeting rooms with a Murphy bed). In your room, you'll find cable television, in-room movies, a minibar, heat lamp, and voice mail. If you're of a mind, check out the enhanced amenities (including free local calls, one free in-room movie, and a full breakfast) of the Concierge Level.

For a workout, try the health club, indoor pool, two outdoor pools, sauna, and gym. You can relax in the lounge and two restaurants, all located on site. One restaurant is full-service, and the other a small deli with Pizza Hut included. The hotel features 27,000 square feet of meeting and banquet space, highlighted by the grand ballroom.

Bring your pets along—they're welcome here.

Airport Plaza Hotel
$ • 1500 Beers School Rd., Coraopolis
• (412) 264-7900, (800) 542-8111

This is a serviceable hotel about as close as you can get to Pittsburgh International Airport. The hotel offers round-the-clock courtesy airport transportation.

Each of the 200 guest rooms features access to fax service, an exercise room, and complimentary continental breakfast and evening cocktails. You also can enjoy an on-site restaurant.

You're welcome to bring your pet, but you must provide a $50 deposit, all but $10 refundable.

Sewickley Country Inn
$$ • 801 Ohio River Blvd., Sewickley
• (412) 741-4300

For an experience that will take you back to a kinder, gentler era, try the Sewickley Country Inn. You'll be situated right along a scenic section of the Ohio River; the view alone will relax you.

The innkeepers have not ignored modern amenities. The 149 guest rooms feature cable television, and you'll have access to an outdoor swimming pool and fitness facilities at the nearby YMCA (which is co-ed), as well as a dining room and a lounge on premises. The inn is about equidistant from downtown Pittsburgh and Pittsburgh International Airport, with complimentary airport transportation offered. Meeting space can accommodate up to 300 people.

As you might expect in an establishment of such old-fashioned charm, small pets are welcome.

Wyndham Garden Hotel
Pittsburgh Airport
$$ • 1 Wyndham Cir., Coraopolis
• (412) 695-0002
• www.wyndham.com

Wyndham Garden is near Pittsburgh International Airport, but there's much more here than a convenient location. The hotel offers 140 guest rooms, featuring cable television, in-room movies, voice mail, computer accessibility, hair dryers, and iron sets. The fitness room and outdoor pool will beckon you, as will the on-site restaurant.

Ask about specially priced corporate packages. Pets are not permitted.

Extended Stay and Temporary Accommodations

One product of Pittsburgh's rich corporate history is a tradition of company teams traveling to headquarters here for extended assignments. While massive corporations no longer are the rule in Pittsburgh, they remain sufficiently numerous to provide a basis for a strong extended-stay and temporary accommodations sector.

Even as many corporations have downsized, the booming film production business has brought many actors, technicians and executives to town. They, too, require temporary accommodations, enhancing the presence of this hospitality sector.

If you're seeking such accommodations, keep

some key questions in mind: Do prospective providers offer accommodations in a variety of locations, so you can select one that's convenient for you? Can they provide for your family? Do their rate schedules dovetail with the projected length of your stay? If you get the right answers, you'll know you've found the right temporary digs.

Rather than list these places geographically, we've included the whole region in one listing and present your options in alphabetical order.

AmeriSuites Pittsburgh/Airport
6011 Campbells Run Rd., Pittsburgh
• (412) 494-0202, (800) 833-1516
AmeriSuites Pittsburgh/Cranberry
136 Emeryville Dr., Cranberry
• (724) 779-7900
• www.amerisuites.com

Billed as America's all-suite hotels, guests enjoy separate living and sleeping areas, a refrigerator, microwave, wet bar, and a coffee maker with complimentary coffee in every suite. There is also 26-inch cable TV, ironing supplies, voice mail, and dataport telephones in each suite. Do partake of the bountiful breakfast buffet, the indoor heated pool, fitness center and the MBE Business Express Center. If you need to do laundry there are both valet service and laundry facilities available. With a free *USA Today* thrown in, it's just like being at home—well, almost.

> ## INSIDERS' TIP
> Downtown Pittsburgh offers 2,300 "committable" hotel rooms. Hoteliers save a few beyond that for emergencies and their own needs.

Bridgestreet Accommodations
1501 Reedsdale St., Pittsburgh
• (412) 322-3999

You'll find a diverse selection here, as Bridgestreet offers 245 units at nine locations—by visiting them on the web at www.bridgestreet.com, you can take a virtual tour of each location. All units are in Allegheny County. You'll enjoy cable television, a complete kitchen, a washer and dryer, and housekeeping services. If you've been forced from your home for any reason, you'll find temporary housing options at Bridgestreet.

Daily rates range from $62 to $92, while the range for monthly rates is $1,860 to $2,010.

Corporate Accommodations
950 Greentree Rd., Suite 210, Green Tree
• (412) 921-2449, (800) 899-5456

Corporate Accommodations offers a broad

selection of units—105 in 16 complexes, primarily in Allegheny County, but fast-growing Butler County also is represented. Your apartment will feature cable television, housekeeping and linen service, and a furnished kitchen.

To assure that their rooms meet your needs, customer service personnel inspect the preparations of the housekeeping staff before turning the unit over to you. Corporate Accommodations also provides short-term housing options for those forced from their homes by catastrophes.

Daily rates range from approximately $56 to $91, while the range for monthly rates is $1,380 to $2,430. There are lower rates for longer stays.

Extended StayAmerica
520 N. Bell Ave., Carnegie
- **(412) 278-4001**
3851 Northern Pike, Monroeville
- **(412) 856-8400**
- **www.extstay.com**

Extended StayAmerica offers both daily rates, ranging from $54 to $74, and weekly rates, ranging from $269 to $380. As appropriate for an extended stay, you'll find your room equipped with a refrigerator, stove top, and microwave oven, and you can utilize the on-site laundry.

The Carnegie facility is located in the Pittsburgh International Airport corridor and is convenient to both downtown Pittsburgh and the airport. If you stay here, though, better give your pets a big good-bye hug—they're not permitted.

Studio Plus Pittsburgh Airport at the Pointe is affiliated with this extended-stay hotel group, and the accommodations are very similar but with studio apartments that have a full kitchen. The address is 200 Chauvet Drive (in North Fayette). Call them at (412) 490-0979.

Shadyside Inn
5405-5415 Fifth Ave., Pittsburgh
- **(412) 682-2300, (800) 767-8483**

You're more than welcome to stay at Shadyside Inn for one night only, but the facility also can meet your temporary housing needs for weeks or months. All accommodations are suites featuring cable television and a VCR, a telephone answering machine, and an equipped kitchen. You also may utilize the on-site laundry and a complimentary pass to a local fitness center. For business needs, optional amenities include fax, copier, and secretarial service. There are 100 guest suites here.

Daily rates range from $89 to $150, while the range for weekly rates is $463 to $880. If you prefer the monthly rate, the range there is $1,595 to $2,595.

Once here, you're within walking distance of the popular Shadyside shopping and dining district, and you're a short bus ride from Oakland's university-medical complex, making this an attractive option for those visiting Pittsburgh's colleges or hospitals for an extended period.

Bring your pets if they're under 25 pounds, but expect to pay a one-time fee of $60 for the privilege.

SpringHill Suites by Marriott
239 Summit Park Dr., Pittsburgh
- **(412) 494-9446**
- **www.springhillsuites.com**

Nestled among many other properties and retail establishments at the Pointe in North Fayette Township, you'll find SpringHill Suites with 102 guest rooms. Guests enjoy the continental breakfast provided. Each suite offers a microwave, refrigerator, in-room coffee maker, and hair dryer. See our Shopping chapter for more information about all that's offered at the Pointe, for there is much shopping and many restaurants to choose from. This property is also along the airport corridor, so you're not far from catching your flight.

> ## INSIDERS' TIP
> Even children can partake of afternoon tea at the Westin William Penn Hotel. Ask for the Mad Hatters Tea, a selection of tasty cookies and confections kids will love!

Resorts

When you start to discuss resort communities, Pittsburgh may not be the town that springs to your lips. Think about it, though. We have warm, beautiful summers that are just the ticket for golf. We have plenty of inland waterways, the ideal setting for a variety of water sports. We have mountains and snow; last time we checked, those were a couple of the key ingredients in skiing. So who needs a beach and boiling temperatures?

With all these elements, Pittsburgh offers a number of resorts that take full advantage of the four seasons to vary their offerings and assure year-round attractions. While each of the resorts is a bit outside our five-county geo-

Relaxing resorts dot the Western Pennsylvania countryside.

Photo: Courtesy of Nemacolin Woodlands Resort & Spa

graphic coverage area, we've included them here rather than in our Daytrips chapter, since each is no more than a 90-minute trip from Pittsburgh.

While we've adhered to our rate code for the resorts below, remember that seasonal swings in rates may be severe. Unless otherwise noted, the resorts offer smoking and non-smoking rooms but do not permit pets.

East

Hidden Valley Resort
$$$$ • One Craighead Dr., Hidden Valley
• (814) 443-8000, (800) 458-0175
• www.hiddenvalleyresort.com

Place a gorgeous community in the heart of the Laurel Highlands, sprinkle with beautiful fall foliage, crisp air and pure snow, and you have the recipe for Hidden Valley Resort. Located about 60 miles east of Pittsburgh in the Laurel Highlands, the resort is primarily a community of homes. You're welcome to stay for a night or weekend, however, as owners often rent out their homes. That means a treat for you.

You'll enjoy a golf course, tennis courts, four swimming pools, and a playground with basketball and volleyball. The resort stocks its freshwater lake seasonally with trout and bass, and you'll also enjoy canoeing, paddle boating,

kayaking and sailboating. The sports club in the conference center complex features racquetball courts and exercise equipment, as well as a whirlpool, sauna, suntan bed, massage room, hair salon and video arcade.

Skiing is particularly popular at the resort (see our Recreation and Golf chapters for fuller descriptions of these features), as are hiking and biking. You'll find more than 30 miles of trails, and you'll enjoy complimentary use of the resort's mountain bikes and helmets.

Hidden Valley offers no fewer than 10 restaurants and lounges; it's hard to imagine staying hungry very long. With so many attractions, it's no wonder that so many permanent residents became familiar with the resort as weekend guests.

Seven Springs Mountain Resort
$$$$ • RD #1, Champion
• (814) 352-7777, (800) 452-2223
• www.7springs.com

Seven Springs is justifiably known for its excellent skiing—more about that in our Recreation chapter. The resort offers so much more than that it's become one of the region's premier sites for conferences. If you're looking for a romantic getaway, you'll find that here as well.

The resort can accommodate 5,000 overnight guests in its lodges, 10-story high-rise, chalets, condominiums, and cabins. They need every bit of that capacity, as Seven Springs each year hosts more than 700 conferences and meetings that take advantage of exhibit and festival halls and the many indoor and outdoor recreational activities.

If a fresh snowfall calls to you, try the snow tubing park or the alpine slide. Indoors, you'll enjoy a swimming pool, massage, an exercise room with a whirlpool, a Universal gym and a sauna, miniature golf, bowling, racquetball, roller skating, and a variety of video games. Outdoor activities include golf, tennis, hiking, horseback riding, and volleyball.

You'll work up an appetite with such active participation; Seven Springs is prepared to satisfy the heartiest of appetites with 10 restaurants and six lounges, some of which feature live entertainment. Be sure to check out Helen's, the original home of the resort's founders that now serves as a slopeside restaurant serving intercontinental cuisine.

Seven Springs is about 60 miles east Pittsburgh, reachable from both Exit 9 and Exit 10 of the Pennsylvania Turnpike.

INSIDERS' TIP

The Pittsburgh Hilton Hotel and Towers claims the world's largest revolving door.

South

Linden Hall
$$ • R.D. #1, Dawson
• (724) 529-7543

This splendid mansion derives its name from the linden trees imported from Berlin by the original owner, Sarah Cochran, widow of coke and coal pioneer Philip Cochran. The estate has been transformed by its current owners, United Steelworkers of America, into a crackerjack resort and conference center with overnight facilities for up to 300 guests, all at working persons' rates.

Recreation is a key theme at Linden Hall. You'll enjoy golf, tennis, biking along the scenic Yough River Trails, and fishing in a 25-acre lake. The picnic pavilion features sand volleyball and boccie courts, softball and soccer fields, and a children's playground.

You can relax in the sports pub and the charming country restaurant. The Great Hall can host your reception, while the outdoor gazebo provides a splendid backdrop for photographs. Make sure you inspect the Great Hall's Aeolian pipe organ, said to be one of only three in the world.

The resort is near Uniontown, 37 miles from Pittsburgh via Pennsylvania Route 51 south.

Linden Hall is closed from mid-December through mid-March; the golf course remains open year round, weather permitting.

Nemacolin Woodlands Resort & Spa
$$$$ • 40 E., Farmington
• (724) 329-8555, (800) 422-2736
• www.nemacolin.com

Nemacolin was named for a Native American chief. His name does not translate even loosely into "lap of luxury." Perhaps it should, because when you arrive at Nemacolin, you'll think you've fallen there. The artwork alone is indicative of the ambiance. You'll encounter pieces by Tiffany, Audubon, Calder, and Remington, just to name a few.

Your experience in this 1,000-acre jewel begins with your accommodations, whether in the inn, the condominiums, or the 124-room The La Fayette, modeled after The Ritz in Paris. Rooms and suites are spacious and well lighted, with plush footstools and scenic views of the resort. Enjoy the view in your terrycloth robe—it will be hanging in your room for you.

You'll enjoy golf, skiing, an equestrian center and polo field (more about Nemacolin's golf, skiing, and equine activities in our Golf and Recreation chapters), tennis, hiking, biking, and a broad range of water activities including canoeing, fishing, and white-water rafting. Looking for less demanding activities? How about croquet and billiards—they're both available as well.

When you're ready to be pampered after your workout, attendants at the three-story spa await your bidding. The spa, of polished marble tiles, may be Nemacolin's piece de resistance. It offers a fitness center, cardiovascular equipment, an aerobics room, and a lap pool. You can try it all under the watchful eye of your personal trainer. The spa's salon offers more than 60 treatments. When you arrive at the spa, the scent of aromatherapy convinces you to try out additional pampering such as the eight different types of massages, nine body therapies, five hydrotherapies, and nine facials. The Woodlands Spa boasts a signature treatment in the Water Path, an adaptation of European thermal therapy that stimulates circulation and improves immune function. The Woodlands Vitamin Facial is also special, for it features vitamin repair and hydroxy exfoliation, improving skin tone and elasticity.

Seasons is the on-site restaurant for the Woodlands Spa, giving guests as healthy a cuisine as the treatments they've just enjoyed. Dining at other restaurants, too, is a rich experience at Nemacolin, especially if done at The Golden Trout. Don't worry about ordering an obscure wine. The wine cellar has a capacity of 10,000 bottles. Lautrec is the French restaurant featuring a Sunday brunch from 10:30 AM to 1:30 PM. Reservations are required. But dining here is a lovely experience any time.

In all, Nemacolin offers six restaurants, each with its own theme, as well as a '50s-style ice cream parlor. Nemacolin is accessible from the Pennsylvania Turnpike, about 60 miles from Pittsburgh. If you'd really like to make a grand entrance, taxi up the resort's 4,000-foot private air strip. Everything else about Nemacolin says class—why shouldn't your arrival?

West

Oglebay Resort and Conference Center
$$$$ • Rt. 88 N., Wheeling, W.Va.
• (304) 243-4000, (800) 624-6988
• www.oglebay-resort.com

This 1,500-acre resort was once the elegant summer estate of Cleveland industrialist Col. Earl W. Oglebay, but now is operated by the City of Wheeling, West Virginia. Oglebay is so fun filled that it will take you several days just to sample it all.

It features two golf courses, including the Speidel Championship Golf Course that has played host to a number of Ladies Professional Golf Association events, as well as a par 3 course. (For more on Oglebay's golf delights, see our Golf chapter.) You'll enjoy miles of jogging trails that crisscross the estate, as well as Waddington Gardens, which glows with such seasonal flowers as tulips, daffodils, and mums. Wedding parties travel for miles to Waddington Gardens to stage their nuptial pictures.

The Good Children's Zoo showcases such animals as bears, otters, bison, and rare red wolves in natural settings. The Crispin Center offers outdoor swimming and tennis courts, and you'll find a number of venues for shopping.

You'll work up quite an appetite with all that activity, and you'll satisfy it just as surely in the Ihlenfeld Dining Room in Wilson Lodge, the principal guest house. If you'd like to get a little more rustic than the lodge, Oglebay offers a number of cottages where you can snuggle by the fireplace—the resort provides the firewood, you provide the rest. Pets are permitted only in cottages.

The highlight of the year at Oglebay is the Winter Festival of Lights, featuring more than 1 million lights. Travelers come from miles around to enjoy the 6-mile driving tour. You can reach Oglebay from Pittsburgh by taking I-79 south, then I-70 west.

Hostels

Hostelling International—Pittsburgh
830 E. Warrington Ave., Pittsburgh
• (412) 431-1267

You know you've arrived at a popular spot for international travelers when the signs posted on walls and windows are in Norwegian and other languages. That's the case at Hostelling International—Pittsburgh, an important facility for travelers who use hostels as economical and convenient lodging.

This hostel is part of a quiet residential neighborhood called Allentown, a short bus ride from downtown. You'll be close to public transportation.

The facility features 50 beds and shared kitchen and laundry facilities. You'll find the dorms clean and inviting. You can rent linens and store your bike. Room rate is approximately $20 ($17 for HI members), and several family rooms with private baths are available.

HI local headquarters are housed in the same building, so you can use their brochures and maps to plan the balance of your trip while you're here.

The hostel's hours are 8 to 10 AM and 5 to 10 PM. Warning: when they post those as their hours, they mean it. If you arrive at other times, no one will be here to let you in. For such cases, management has provided rental lockers in the vestibule. You can stash your stuff, explore the city and return when the hostel reopens.

INSIDERS' TIP
A part of Westin William Penn lore is that Bob Hope proposed to his wife, Delores, while both were performing in Vaudeville at the hotel.

ACCOMMODATIONS

Bed and Breakfast Inns

Price Code

We've included with our listings a rate guide to help you pick the establishment that best fits your budget. With each write-up, you'll see from one to four dollar signs to help you place the inns within these categories:

$	$45 to $65
$$	$65 to $90
$$$	$90 to $135
$$$$	$135 to $200

Rates represent average charges for double occupancy. Keep in mind that rates will vary with season and availability, and that many establishments maintain discount programs through such organizations as AAA, AARP, or their own frequent guest programs. The room tax in Allegheny County is 7 percent; elsewhere, it varies from county to county. Except as noted, all bed and breakfast inns profiled here accept at least one major credit card.

Up until six or eight years ago, accommodations in Pittsburgh tended toward the traditional. And city ordinances weren't too friendly to the potential bed and breakfast industry. Nowadays, while within the city limits Pittsburgh still can offer only about 30 bed and breakfast rooms, these accommodations are first-class—some of them downright luxurious. (Check out the full-line of spa services available at Shadyside Bed and Breakfast or the 2,000-square-foot ballroom at Victoria House on the Northside.) You'll also find about 150 more rooms around the city in the surrounding county areas, some of which are quite convenient to the downtown business district.

In the rural county areas, several farms have jumped on the hay-wagon of the farm stay craze, generating extra revenue by converting underutilized space to guest accommodations. A number of these agrarian facilities are set on working farms, with guests invited to pitch in with chores. Your kids will love it!

It is important to remember, however, that as numerous as they are, bed and breakfast inns typically offer no more than five or six guest rooms. In addition, as small business owners, proprietors of bed and breakfast inns may take off for vacation or suspend their services for long periods of time for other reasons. Some accommodate guests by reservation only. Under these circumstances, it makes a lot of sense for you to reserve your room, rather than dropping by and hoping for the best.

Planning is also important in the area of amenities; some bed and breakfasts do not offer the conveniences we take for granted in hotels and motels, such as in-room baths, telephones, television, air conditioning, and computer accessibility. Some establishments welcome children, a few permit pets, and only a handful allow indoor smoking. With our write-ups, we've indicated policies on pets and children. Unless otherwise indicated, smoking is permitted only outdoors. If a particular amenity is important to you, check with the proprietors when you call to make your reservation.

In a number of cases where inns prohibit children and pets, owners have indicated that they try to be as accommodating as circumstances allow. If they're fully booked with adult parties, they'll probably enforce their prohibitions. If your party is the only guest, they may be more flexible about children and pets. The bottom line: always ask, and don't be afraid to negotiate.

In summary, it's important that you consider all your needs—even those you customarily take for granted—in selecting a bed and breakfast. Pick the right one and

Bed & breakfast inns tend to limit their advertising, so it can be tough to find out where they are and what they offer. In Pittsburgh, you can get current information from a trade group, the Western Pennsylvania Bed and Breakfast Association. You can reach them at (888) 400-6380. Their website address is www.westernpabandb.com.

You can obtain information specific to Pittsburgh and the surrounding six counties on the website for the Pittsburgh Bed & Breakfast Association, www.pittsburghbnb.com.

you'll have the ideal opportunity for a memorable experience. You might even make a new friend or two.

North

An Inn Between
$$-$$$ • 161 Deer Creek Rd., Saxonburg
• (724) 352-4899
• www.innbetweenbnb.com

When you arrive at An Inn Between, you'll be treated to homemade pie and ice cream. You'll be staying in your own private, air-conditioned apartment on the 200-acre estate, and you'll enjoy a fireplace, balcony, and your own secluded garden.

You'll be 25 miles from Pittsburgh and only nine miles from the Pennsylvania Turnpike. You're in golfers heaven, and you're also near Moraine State Park, the historic town of Saxonburg, a planetary observatory, a chocolate factory, and a plethora of antique shops. (See our Golf chapter for information on nearby courses.) You might choose to stay right where you are, however. There's certainly enough to do, what with the walking and biking trails; the opportunities for birdwatching; the tennis court; and the two-acre pond where you can row, fish, and swim. Watch for ospreys, egrets, and Canada snow geese seasonally at the pond.

If you're going to be in town on business, note that there's a drafting table where you can set up your computer and plug in your modem. Don't worry about the phone being busy; it's your own private line. The full-sized apartment, which sleeps four people, is also spacious enough to accommodate small meetings. In addition, you'll have access to the fax machine and the copier in the nearby inn office.

Your children are welcome here, and your pets stay in a separate, heated room in the barn designed just for them. You may smoke on the balcony or outside the barn.

Note: Discounts are available for staying here three or more nights, making this splendid accommodation in the same price range as nearby, moderately-priced motels.

Ber-Nita Acres Bed & Breakfast
$, no credit cards • RD 2,
151 Bennett Dr., Ellwood City
• (724) 752-1455, (888) 297-5396
• www.pafarmstay.com\bernita

Ber-Nita Acres, a 92-acre working farm, offers three guest rooms in the owners' large home. Private baths are accessible to, but not adjoining, all of the rooms. A phone is available in the large living room where there's also a television, VCR, and an abundance of family-oriented movies on videotape. You'll be treated to a full country breakfast in the morning.

Your children are welcome to help feed the sheep, cows, and ostriches! From mid-May to October, they'll also be able to watch baby ostriches hatch from eggs in the incubator. For adults and children alike, there are two fishing lakes and a paddle boat, and you won't have to worry about bringing along your fishing poles or life-jackets—it'll all be there waiting for you, just like at grandma's house.

After a long day of play, sink into the Jacuzzi on the covered deck; it's open all year. Smoke under the stars, but not in the house or in any of the outbuildings, and please leave the pets at home.

Heather Hill Bed & Breakfast
$$-$$$, no credit cards
• 268 Rader School Rd., Renfrew
• (724) 789-7911
• isrv.com/bedandb/

Heather Hill offers six air-conditioned guest rooms—five with private baths, one with a wood-burning stove. The bed and breakfast sits on a secluded 180-acre farm about 30 miles from Pittsburgh in Butler County. You can enjoy hiking trails, swimming, paddleboats, a soak in

Bed and breakfast inns provide a more personal lodging experience.

Photo: Courtesy of The John Butler House

the hot tub after a round of bocce, and interaction with the farm animals that share the space.

If you plan to bring children or pets, you'll need to review that with management.

The Inn on Grandview
**$$-$$$ • 310 East Grandview Ave.,
Zelienople • (724) 452-0469
• www.pittsburghbnb.com**

Originally known as the Zimmerman Hotel, the facility has been completely restored and now features four guest rooms furnished with antiques. All offer private baths, air conditioning, televisions, whirlpools, and telephones. Two rooms also offer working fireplaces. Well-behaved children are welcome, but pets are not.

The Inn on Grandview is just a few miles from both the Pennsylvania Turnpike and I-79. That places it in the heart of some splendid outdoor recreation country. Opportunities for golf, tennis, boating, and antiquing will beckon when you stay here. Enjoy a full breakfast at the inn before setting out to enjoy your activities.

The Inn on Vine
**$$-$$$ • 241 Vine St., Kittanning
• (724) 545-7744, (888) VINE INN**

This restored Georgian Colonial home features four guest rooms, all furnished with Vic-

torian antiques. Two rooms offer private baths, while all include phones, television, and air conditioning.

In the heart of downtown Kittanning in Armstrong County, the inn is only one block away from the Allegheny River, and there's a $4 million amphitheater carved into the riverbank, where the Pittsburgh Symphony and other groups perform from time to time. In the summer, the Gateway Clipper docks along the river, and boat and Jet Ski rentals are available a short distance down the street from The Inn on Vine. The inn is also just around the corner from a genealogy library and two blocks from the "Rails to Trails" bike and walking trail. Children 16 and older are welcome, but pets are not permitted.

Maggie West Bed & Breakfast
**$, no credit cards • 605 Pittsburgh St.,
Springdale • (724) 274-8906**

This 1860s mansion, only a few blocks away from the Allegheny River, is within walking distance of small, local shops and restaurants in the heart of Springdale. Of the 20 rooms in the house, four are rented to guests. All rooms feature access to a common television room, parlor, and tea room, while one offers a private bath.

If you need to make a call, use the inn's

portable phone. Children are welcome, but pets are not. Maggie West Bed & Breakfast is about 20 minutes from Pittsburgh when the traffic along Pa. 28 is light.

The Main Stay B&B of Saxonburg
$$ • 214 Main St., Box 547, Saxonburg
• (724) 352-9363
• www.pittsburghbnb.com

The Main Stay is a beautifully restored 150-year-old home in the heart of Saxonburg, about 25 miles north of Pittsburgh. Accommodations include two guest rooms; one suite; and one apartment with a kitchen, living room, and telephone. All accommodations offer air conditioning, private baths, and cable television. If you stay in the rooms or the suite at The Main Stay, you'll share a common phone.

You also can utilize the inn's parlor and library for visiting with old pals or the new friends you'll meet during your stay. The Main Stay is a nonsmoking facility. Children are welcome, but no pets, please. Senior citizens and those staying two or more nights enjoy discounted room rates.

The Outside Inn
$ • 980 Rte. 228, Mars
• (724) 776-0626, (800) 947-2783
• www.sgi.net/outside-inn

The Outside Inn's four rooms, each decorated differently, offer something for everyone, much like the area where the inn is located. Nestled on 50-plus acres of secluded land, the inn, surprisingly, is just one mile from a local fitness center, where you'll enjoy complimentary membership during your stay. You'll be near the Cranberry business district and only 3 miles from the Pennsylvania Turnpike and I-79.

Your room will have a private bath and a television with satellite programming. If you're planning to bring a small child, you might want to ask for the room with the nursery adjacent to it. Please leave your pets at home.

Computer and modem hook-ups and phones are located in each of three sitting rooms, where you're free to host a business meeting, if you like. You'll also have access to a fax machine in the office. When you've had enough work, venture on down to the working wine cellar, sniff the bouquet, and taste a few. You might also take the path back through the woods and visit the hidden garden, where there are ponds, a waterfall, and a gazebo among the trees. Or you could just sit on one of the decks and enjoy the view. You'll enjoy a full, gourmet breakfast in the morning.

Pumpkin Hollow Farm
$, no credit cards • RD1, Box 17,
Cowansville • (724) 545-9117

Pumpkin Hollow is a working, organic farm, affording you the opportunity to get up close and personal with the resident sheep, chickens, and vegetables. You'll also have the chance to enjoy some fishing at the pond, after a hike through a few of the 73 acres that comprise the farm.

At night, you'll retire to guest rooms that include a bath shared by only one other party. One of the two guest rooms offers a television, and a telephone is available in a common area. The owners note that, at the time of this writing, they are planning to add features that will make the guest rooms wheelchair accessible. The sun porch is the designated smoking area.

Children are permitted, but not pets, although arrangements can be made to board your horse while you enjoy your stay. Pumpkin Hollow is about 35 miles from Pittsburgh, about five miles from Kittanning. It's easily accessible from Pennsylvania Route 28.

Step Back in Time
$-$$ • 224 Washington St., Butler
• (724) 283-7509

This charming colonial-style home offers three guest rooms furnished with Victorian period antiques. All of the rooms have private baths, telephones, and televisions, so even as you soak in the claw-foot tub and dream of yesteryear you'll rest assured knowing that all the modern amenities are at your fingertips. Step Back in Time is conveniently located in the heart of downtown Butler, within easy walking distance of offices, shops, restaurants, and area churches.

The facility is an hour from Pittsburgh, thirty minutes from I-79, and quite near Moraine State Park. Just imagine waking up the morning after a hike through the park to a feast of scones, clotted cream, raspberry jam, and warm hospitality.... That's what you'll find at Step Back in Time.

Your children are welcome here. Smoking, pets, and alcohol are not allowed.

Sun and Cricket Bed and Breakfast
$$$ • 1 Tara Ln., Gibsonia
• (724) 444-6300
• www.pittsburghbnb.com

You'll be struck by the appealing blend of old and modern on this 35-acre country estate about 15 miles north of Pittsburgh. Of the two spacious guest cottages, one is a log cabin adjoining the main house, the other a carriage house about 500 feet from the main house. Each is enhanced by antique furnishings and handmade quilts. On the modern side, you'll enjoy private baths, color television, and air conditioning. The cozy log cabin offers a telephone and accommodations for children that offer their parents some privacy. The bright, airy carriage house boasts a microwave and mini-refrigerator. Each cottage has a separate entrance and porch, so you can relax alone while you enjoy the view of the woods surrounding you. (You won't even be able to see the road from where you're sitting!) You'll enjoy a full, gourmet breakfast in the morning.

The owner notes that at least 12 golf courses are within a five-mile radius from here, including the acclaimed Deer Run. (See our Golf chapter for more information.) While other pets are not permitted, Sun and Cricket will board your horse in a pasture you can view from your window.

Victoria House Bed & Breakfast
$$-$$$ • 939 Western Ave., Pittsburgh
• (412) 231-4948, (800) 231-4948
• www.pittsburghbnb.com

It's hard to believe that this exquisite Victorian restoration was once home of the local Knights of Columbus lodge. The owners have preserved one floor tile of the KOC decor, but just about everything else speaks of Victorian splendor—including the $50,000 chandelier in the greeting room.

The facility offers five guest rooms; four suites comprised of bedrooms, sitting rooms, and private baths; and a guest cottage, where smoking is permitted. All accommodations are equipped with phones and computer access, while three have televisions. Complimentary evening cocktails are available in the library.

There's also a 2,000 square-foot ballroom in the house, making it an ideal location for weddings or other special events. Tim, the owner of Victoria House, who happens to be a chef, can cater the dinner for your special event, if you like, and will prepare an elaborate breakfast for you in the morning. In some cases, you can literally enjoy your breakfast in bed.

When you stay here, you'll be in the heart of Pittsburgh's North Side, only a hop, skip, and a jump from the major highways that intersect the Greater Pittsburgh area. You can relax in the enclosed, English-cottage-style garden or take a short walk to such nearby attractions as Three Rivers Stadium, The National Aviary, and the Andy Warhol Museum. You can also walk to the downtown business and shopping district.

Children 13 and older are permitted, but pets are not. If you stay seven nights or more, you'll enjoy a corporate discount.

East

Appletree Bed & Breakfast
$$$-$$$$ • 703 South Negley Ave.,
Pittsburgh • (412) 661-0631
• www.pittsburghbnb.com

Appletree is located about 3 miles east of downtown Pittsburgh, but that's hardly the whole story. It's set in Shadyside, one of Pittsburgh's most diverse and exciting shopping and dining districts, and it's near Chatham College and the university-medical complex in Oakland.

Its location is an attraction, and so, too, are the stately residences that surround it. In this restored 1884 Victorian, eight guest rooms custom-designed by Richard Lauren Interiors of Shadyside feature private baths with robes ready and waiting, telephones, voice mail, VCRs, and air conditioning. Four of the rooms boast Jacuzzis, while six offer fireplaces. Wine and cheese are served on Fridays and Saturdays, and refreshments are always available on request. A trained chef will prepare your gourmet breakfast. Pets are not permitted; children sometimes are welcome—check your circumstances with the innkeeper. Business and AAA discounts are available. Park your car in the lot behind the B&B at no charge.

Campbell House Bed & Breakfast
$$-$$$ • 305 E. Main St., Ligonier
• (724) 238-9812

Amenities abound at Campbell House, where the three guest rooms and two suites are what owner Patti Campbell describes as "eclectic" in decor. Whichever room you choose, you'll find a private bath, air conditioning, cable television, and complimentary snacks and beverages. You also can utilize the common phone and fax machine and receive e-mail messages. Pets are not permitted, but children 12 and older are welcome.

Campbell is the owner of a large collection of Campbell's Soup artifacts—her license plate reads "Soup Kid." At breakfast, make sure you sample one of her "Campbell's Babies," large pancakes with fruit, powdered sugar and optional chocolate. With her "babies" she also passes out "cigars"—sausage links, of course. Mmmmm, mmmmm good.

Enjoy a small discount on your room if you're staying during the week.

Antiques and seasonal decorations make your stay a special one.

Champion Lakes Bed & Breakfast
$-$$ • RD1 Box 285, Bolivar
• (724) 238-5440
• www.pagolf.com

This facility is located on the grounds of Champion Lakes Golf course, right next to Champion Lakes Restaurant. (See our Golf chapter for more information about the course.) Owned by two retired Pittsburgh Pirates, Dick Groat and Jerry Lynch, the bed and breakfast has nine rooms. (Get it? Like nine innings?). Each room has a private bath, phone, television with HBO, and heating and air conditioning system with its own controls.

All of the rooms are named after baseball players, and each room has its namesake's autographed uniform and picture on the wall. You'll choose your breakfast, which is included in the price of your room, from the menu at the restaurant next door.

Ask about special golf getaway packages when you call for reservations. Your children are welcome, but your pets are not.

The Inn at Oakmont Bed and Breakfast
$$$-$$$$ • 300 Rt. 909, P.O. Box 103,
Oakmont • (412) 828-0410
• www.pittsburghbnb.com

The emphasis at this new, federal-style inn is on charming surroundings and gracious ser-

vice. The facility features eight rooms with private baths; two of the rooms also offer a fireplace and whirlpool bath. All of them are furnished with antiques. A special feature in each room is a sleep machine that lulls you off to dreamland with the sounds of tropical rain or the Hawaiian surf.

You'll have a phone in your room and use of the house fax machine. Children over 10 are permitted, but leave the pets at home. Inquire about discounts for extended stays.

One of the chief attractions of the inn is its accessibility to the city. It's a short hop from the Pennsylvania Turnpike and about 20 minutes from downtown Pittsburgh along Pennsylvania Route 28.

When you stay here, make sure you get a good look at the nearby Hulton Bridge spanning the Allegheny River . . . but only if you're not accustomed to seeing lavender bridges.

Shadyside Bed & Breakfast
$$$-$$$$ • 5516 Maple Heights Rd.,
Pittsburgh • (412) 683-6501
• www.pittsburghbnb.com

The first bed and breakfast within city limits, Shadyside Bed & Breakfast may offer the ideal urban setting. It's located just above "Millionaire's Row," the mansions erected by coal and steel magnates along Fifth Avenue. The Shadyside shopping district and Oakland

Who needs a pool when the place you're staying has its own pond?

Photo: Courtesy of An Inn Between of Briar Rose Farm

university-medical complex are nearby. In summer, the facility is surrounded by foliage so lush and beautiful you'll feel splendidly isolated.

Of Shadyside Bed & Breakfast's 10 rooms, all have private baths, and all offer phones, air conditioning, and computer access. You also may use the office fax machine and common kitchen for light food preparation. This elegant bed and breakfast offers a full meal in the morning and, if you feel like a little privacy, not to worry. Several private tables grace the dining room, and you're sure to be able to find a seat at one of them.

For relaxation, try the full-line of spa services, including various hydrotherapy treatments, massages, and other amenities provided on site by Sewickley Spa. The bookcases in the library are stocked with dozens of titles for your enjoyment, and you can enjoy television in the common living room. You might also visit the billiard room—or send the kids there while you unwind. Pets are not permitted.

If you descend the grand staircase of this mansion, you'll notice original stained glass windows. Look closer and you'll see that one window bears the crest of the original owners, the Bergers, an important family in Pittsburgh's turn-of-the-century printing business and for decades thereafter. Adjacent to the Berger crest are those of other Pittsburgh printers, tribute to the worthy competition. It makes you long for the days when families had crests, and competition was indeed worthy.

South

Foggy Mountain Lodge
$$-$$$ • Old Distillery Rd., Stahlstown • (724) 593-1000

Foggy Mountain Lodge is unusually large by local standards. Not only does it offer 12 rooms, but it's also set on 120 lush acres dotted with wooded trails, fields, and a lake. The air-conditioned rooms offer private baths, televisions, and phones, and you'll enjoy the gameroom, which features a pool table and darts. When you're ready to relax, try the outdoor hot tub and the Fireside Dining Room restaurant, where you may smoke in the designated section. (For more on the Fireside, see our Restaurants chapter.) Proprietors Rena and Jeff Stumpf think of Foggy Mountain primarily as a couples retreat, but if you want to bring your children and discuss it with them, they'll probably approve it. Pets are not permitted. Note: the rooms are spread over two buildings, a lodge, and a guest house, and the nightly rate is higher for the lodge. Foggy Mountain Lodge is near Ligonier in Westmoreland County, 1.3 miles from Pa. Route 711.

The John Butler House
$$ • 800 Rock Run Rd., Elizabeth
- **(412) 751-6670**
- **www.butlersgolf.com**

About 40 minutes from downtown Pittsburgh, this facility is located hard by both the Monongahela and Youghiegheny rivers on the grounds of Butler's Golf Course. (See our Golf chapter for more information on the course.) A deck on the house overlooks the course, and you'll be only a mile from the Youghiogheny Trail.

The four guest rooms offer private baths, while a television and phone are available in the common living room. You'll be served a full breakfast at the house, and there's an adjacent restaurant, the Rock Run Inn. (For more on the Rock Run Inn, see our Restaurants chapter.) You'll also enjoy games in the sunroom . . . and the opportunity to learn the correct spelling of Monongahela and Youghiogheny once and for all.

Children are permitted; pets are not. If you have a large party, you may rent all four guest rooms. Check with management for the appropriate fee.

Lady of the Lake Bed & Breakfast
$$$ • 157 U.S. 30 E., Ligonier
- **(724) 238-6955**

There is indeed a lake at Lady of the Lake, a 25-acre lake, to be specific. It's a seasonal home for swans and Canada geese, and it's a picturesque element at this lovely Westmoreland County inn. It offers four rooms in the main house, one cottage, and the opportunity to spend the night on the 60-acre grounds in a tent (you can bring your own or they'll rent you one). The rates for these lodging modes vary quite a bit. Our listing of $$$ applies to the main house. A night in the cottage would be $$$$, while a night under the stars would be $ or less. The rooms offer private baths and television—you're welcome to use the office phone. Lady of the Lake is available for company picnics, and it offers a tennis court, in-ground pool, and paddleboats and canoes for use at the lake. Lady of the Lake welcomes children—a useful feature, since the inn is adjacent to Idlewild Park and Storybook Forest, both popular attractions for kids. You'll find more about them in our Kidstuff chapter. Lady of the Lake welcomes small pets only.

Lesley's Mountain View Country Inn
$$$$ • 10 Mountain View Rd., Donegal
- **(724) 593-6349, (800) 392-7773**
- **www.shol.com\mtviewbb**

Mountain View offers spectacular views of the surrounding Laurel Highlands from each of its eight rooms. These are furnished with period American furniture, including tall-poster beds, and feature televisions, phones, and private baths. The inn permits children 10 and older but does not allow pets. In-room smoking is not permitted, but you can light up at the bar of Lesley's, the restaurant within the inn that also is operated by inn owners Lesley and Gerard O'Leary. For more on Lesley's, see our Restaurants chapter.

Mountain View Bed & Breakfast is about one mile east of the Donegal exit of the Pennsylvania Turnpike, at the extreme eastern edge of Westmoreland County. By the way, don't confuse this inn with Mountain View Inn, a separate Westmoreland County establishment. You can read about Mountain View Inn in our Accommodations and Restaurants chapters.

Ligonier Country Inn
$$-$$$ • U.S. 30 E., Laughlintown
- **(724) 238-3651**
- **www.ligoniercountryinn.com**

This inn may be the region's most capacious and diverse—it offers 23 rooms and two cottages. Each room is furnished differently; here you'll find a brass bed, there a four-poster. All rooms feature private baths, air conditioning, televisions, and telephones with computer ports. The cottages also are different from each other. One is family-oriented and sleeps up to seven people. The other, which offers a working fireplace, is known informally as the "romance cottage." If we have to explain that to you, perhaps you're better off in one of the rooms. Both cottages sport porches that overlook Mill Creek.

Wherever you stay here, you're invited to enjoy the outdoor pool and the adjacent restaurant, also known as Ligonier Country Inn. For more on that, see our Restaurants chapter. You're welcome to use the office fax and copying services, and the good proprietors even will provide massage services for you. Smoking and nonsmoking accommodations are available. Discounts are available for stays of at least two nights. Children are welcome in certain rooms only. If you're staying in the romance cottage, you may bring your dog but no cats, please. Ligonier Country Inn is located about 3 miles from Ligonier in eastern Westmoreland County.

Morning Glory Inn
$$$-$$$$ • 2119 Sarah St., Pittsburgh
- **(412) 431-1707**
- **www.pittsburghbnb.com**

Morning Glory Inn is a restored 1862 brick,

Italianate Victorian home on Pittsburgh's South Side. Not only will you enjoy gracious appointments, but you'll be in the perfect position to experience one of Pittsburgh's most captivating and "hot" neighborhoods. South Side is an unusual blend of professional offices; kicky restaurants and clubs; art galleries; and unusual shops, such as The Bead Mine, where you can string your own necklaces from gem or glass beads. From the Morning Glory, you'll also be able to stroll through the friendly streets to the City Theatre, which offers innovative, New York-quality performances.

The five guest rooms at the Morning Glory Inn offer private baths, televisions, and speaker phones with digital answering machines, as well as Swedish pressure-relieving mattresses for extra comfort. The rooms are all well appointed. For instance, the Margaret Jackson suite offers a queen-size canopy bed, a desk and several chairs, and a sitting-room bathroom complete with chaise lounge. You'll enjoy a walk in the Victorian garden after relaxing on the Spanish porch or in the guest parlors, one of which features a restored 1890 grand piano.

Smoking areas are available on the porch or in the garden. A corporate discount is offered, and you may make use of the office fax machine and copier. You can also hold your business meeting or special event at the Morning Glory Inn. For children's and pet's accommodations, discuss your circumstances with Nancy, the innkeeper. She pledges to be as flexible as she can.

Pine Wood Acres Bed and Breakfast
$$ • Pa. Rt. 1, Scottdale • (724) 887-5404
• www.laurelhighlands.org/pinewoodacres

Pine Wood Acres offers a country getaway. The restored 1880 Westmoreland County farm house overlooks a boulder-strewn creek that attracts wildlife for you to observe, and you also can enjoy birding from the back porch. The three rooms provide private baths and robes, and you'll also find a game room featuring books and puzzles. Television is available in a common area, and management can provide you with the house's portable telephone. If you request it, Proprietor Ruth Horsch will set out afternoon tea. She usually serves a gourmet breakfast seasoned with local, native herbs, but she will gladly cater to your special diet.

If you stay at Pine Woods, you can comfortably travel to Falling Water, Kentuck Nob, and the Youghiogheny "Rails to Trails" Bike Trail. Ruth asks that you discuss with her any plans to bring your children with you. Pets are not permitted.

Rush House
$$-$$$ • 810 E. Maiden St., Washington
• (724) 222-2430

This restored Victorian home features four bedrooms and one suite, all of which have air conditioning and private baths. Rooms are furnished with period pieces highlighted by antique clocks. You'll want to take advantage of the Rush House's cozy Tea Room. You can't bring your pets, but your children are welcome.

Rush House is within walking distance of Washington and Jefferson College as well as the shopping areas of Washington. One historical note: Rush House is built over Catfish Creek, said to derive its name from the fish Native Americans caught there centuries ago. Sorry—the cat' no longer bite.

Sunnyledge Boutique Hotel
$$$$ • 5124 Fifth Ave., Pittsburgh
• (412) 683-5014

With eight rooms, intimate enough to be a bed and breakfast, Sunny Ledge is Pittsburgh's only boutique hotel—and a sumptuous one it is. All of the rooms boast marble baths with Jacuzzi tubs, wets bars and mini-bars, fluffy bathrobes, king-size beds made up with Egyptian cotton linens, two-line speakerphones with modem hook-ups, and cable television. The décor is contemporary with eclectic touches, similar to what you might find in a Ritz Carlton or Four Seasons.

You'll find a restaurant and full bar and room service in this restored mansion; note that, as Sunnyledge is not a true bed and breakfast (we've just included it here because of its size), breakfast is not included in the price of the room. See our Restaurants chapter for more on dining at Sunnyledge; in the meantime, we'll tell you that the hotel offers a delicious Sunday brunch with such tempting entrees as lobster club sandwiches, spinach and feta streudel, and banana rum French toast. Sunnyledge is within walking distance of Shadyside, Carnegie Mellon University, and the Oakland medical complex; it's a 10-minute car or bus ride from downtown.

Weatherbury Farm Bed and Breakfast
$ • 1061 Sugar Run Rd., Avella
• (724) 587-3763
• www.weatherburyfarm.com

If a vision of more than 100 acres of rolling meadows, gardens, fields, and valleys appeals to you, then you're the ideal guest for Weatherbury Farm. Your kids will like it too—they're welcome here. Pets are not permitted.

Because this is a working farm with cows, sheep, ducks, and geese, you can expect a hearty and filling breakfast—bountiful, they call it here. In fact, you are cordially invited to help with the farm's chores before you eat in the morning.

The four guest rooms feature private baths but no phone or television, in keeping with the agrarian theme. Feel free to enjoy the outdoor swimming pool while the kids cavort on the playground.

Woolley Fox Bed and Breakfast
$$$ • 61 Lincoln Hwy. E., Ligonier
• (724) 238-3004
• www.woolleyfox.com

The two guest houses at Woolley Fox impart distinctly different personalities, but both luxurious guest houses offer separate bedroom and kitchen areas, private baths, air conditioning, and working fireplaces. One of the guest houses features a balcony overlooking a pool and waterfall, while the second boasts a cathedral ceiling and an awning-covered back deck. Both are furnished with antiques and original hooked rugs. The rooms have no telephones, but you can use the phone in the common area. The inn, surrounded by stone walls, is perched on a secluded woodland hillside in Westmore-land County, remote enough to promote privacy and romance yet not far from the attractions of downtown Ligonier. Woolley Fox does not permit children or pets.

West

Country Road Bed & Breakfast
$$$, no credit cards • Box 265, Moody Rd., Clinton • (724) 899-2528
• www.pittsburghbnb.com

This country estate near Pittsburgh International Airport offers you an appealing choice of accommodations: in one of two cottages or in a 200-year-old log cabin with a fireplace. All of the accommodations are equipped with small kitchens, private baths, televisions, and VCRs. Children are permitted, but management needs to review your plans for pets.

You'll enjoy a fully stocked fishing pond, an outdoor pool, and a Jacuzzi, and you can take advantage of complimentary airport transportation.

The Inn on College Hill Bed & Breakfast
$, no credit cards
• 3233 6th Ave., Beaver Falls
• (724) 843-6048

The mission oak-style inn draws its name from its location near Geneva College, about three miles south of the Pennsylvania Turnpike. Often, guest lecturers and performers at Geneva College stay here, and you'll love conversing with them.

The facility offers four air-conditioned guest rooms furnished mostly with antiques; two have private baths. A telephone and television are available in a common area. Review your plans for bringing children 12 and older with the management. Neither pets nor smoking are allowed.

When you wake up well rested, you'll be ready to feast on the country continental breakfast. If you tuck one of the fresh muffins or biscuits into your overalls as a tasty reminder of the inn, chances are no one will mind. Note that you'll need to make a reservation to stay here, as the inn can't accommodate drop-ins.

INSIDERS' TIP
For the enjoyment of their guests, a number of Pittsburgh bed and breakfast inns collaborate on Murder Mystery Weekends.

McKinley Place Bed & Breakfast
$$ • 132 McKinley Rd., Beaver Falls
• (724) 891-0300
• www.mckinleyplace.com

McKinley Place offers four rooms with televisions, VCRs, phones, computer/modem ports, and private baths. Rooms are decorated in English country style, with Laura Ashley prints and wicker and antique furniture in each room.

While the address for McKinley Place is Beaver Falls, the 60-year-old Colonial house is actually a mile from the town of Chippewa, near chain stores, a large antique mall, and all the good restaurants. You'll still have that secluded feeling, though, because the bed and breakfast is on 3½ wooded acres.

You and other guests will have a private entrance. Breakfast time is the social time at McKinley Place, and you'll enjoy a full, gourmet breakfast that takes into account your special dietary needs.

The Pittsburgh International Airport is only 15 to 20 minutes away. Your children are welcome, and your pets may stay at the nearby kennel. (Check with the proprietors for kennel reservation information.)

The Whistlestop Bed and Breakfast
$-$$ • 195 Broad St., Leetsdale
• (724) 251-0852
• www.pittsburghbnb.com

This 1888 brick Victorian about 20 miles west of Pittsburgh was constructed by the Harmonists, an order that founded several western Pennsylvania towns. It features two guest suites with private baths, phones, air conditioning, and cable television, as well as a pair of two-bedroom suites that each share a bath. The two-bedroom suites also have phones, air conditioning, and cable television.

The Whistlestop is only two miles from Sewickley, a charming Ohio River town with many galleries and antique shops for you to explore. It's also very near the popular historic site Old Economy village, where the Harmonists once lived. Children are welcome, but the innkeeper asks to review your plans for pets.

Restaurants

If you thumb through this chapter, you'll notice that it's a very large one. Pittsburgh and the surrounding areas boast everything from the traditional meat-and-potatoes, old-style restaurants you'd expect to Cambodian, Indian, and Middle Eastern restaurants. On Pittsburgh's trendy Southside, there's even an all vegetarian/vegan restaurant, art gallery, and antique store combination, Zenith Tearoom.

As in most places, the diversity of Pittsburgh's ethnic restaurants is largely dependent on the diversity of its immigrant population. One of the largest populations of immigrants, historically, is Italian. Thus, you might expect that one of the largest categories of ethnic restaurants is Italian. Another factor in Pittsburgh's restaurant scene is the large college crowd. Some students seek out traditional American youth fare, hot dogs and fries, likely to be found at the Original Hot Dog Shop, or "The O," as it's known by Insiders. Other, more health conscious types seek organic or vegetarian fare, easily found at The Co-op Café at East-End Food Co-op, at Zenith, or at most ethnic restaurants.

As you travel outside the city of Pittsburgh into the six-county surrounding area, you'll find less ethnic diversity and more good home-cooking, as in Butler, where Morgan's Diner has been a local fixture longer than some members of our writing team have been alive. Don't even say "soup starter kit" while you're at Morgan's; it would be like hitting a wrong note with a master pianist in the audience.

In short, if you're in our area, you're likely to have access to almost any kind of food you've got a craving for. Now, what we can't promise is that it will be right next door, unless you're inside the city proper. Suppose you just want to wander around an area and choose a restaurant with the shortest wait list or the most delicious-sounding specials posted on the menu outside its door? Then we suggest you head for Downtown, Shadyside, or Atwood or Craig Street in Oakland.

To find the area where you'd like to dine, take note of where it is in relation to Downtown: north, south, east, or west of it. To check out the restaurants serving the type of food you're looking for, see the descriptive headings in each of those sections. For instance, if you want to eat Chinese or Japanese in Shadyside, find the East section, then the respective headings within it.

Now, get out there and go to dinner, or lunch, or breakfast, or tea... and don't be afraid to venture into a place we just didn't have room to include. If it looks good to you, it probably is. We hope you'll enjoy dining in the Pittsburgh area—we sure do.

Downtown

American

Boulevard Deli
$ • 322 Blvd. of the Allies,
Pittsburgh • (412) 281-4300
Boulevard Deli is a popular spot for take-out lunches, and it also offers a seating area for 26 patrons. Sandwiches here all bear the names of Pittsburgh neighborhoods and features, such as "The Mt. Washington," mountainous roast beef piled high over cheddar cheese and snow-capped with cole slaw; and "The Mon," tuna salad on a bagel with rivers of melted cheddar. You

Price Code

In addition to aiming to include representative, good restaurants of every flavor, we've also aimed to include places for every pocketbook and occasion. You'll find economical lunch spots as well as places where you'd want to propose or close that most important business deal. Here's how we've indicated the price range at each establishment:

$	$1 to $15
$$	$16 to $25
$$$	$26 to $60
$$$$	$60 to $100

In this town of business travelers and independent-minded individuals, we're not assuming you'll be dining with anyone else, so each price range is based upon the range of entrée costs, from lowest to highest, for one person. For instance, when we checked, at the Red Bull Inn in Robinson, the lowest price for an entrée was $9 and the highest, $20; thus, we've characterized the price range of entrees there as $-$$. Get it?

also can order salads and soups, and you can select from a small number of continental breakfast items. Boulevard Deli offers extensive catering services as well. It does not accept reservations or credit cards, and it does not serve alcohol. Smoking is not permitted. Boulevard Deli is open for breakfast and lunch Monday through Friday.

British Bicycle Club
$$ • 923 Penn Ave., Pittsburgh
• (412) 391-9623

Opening day at British Bicycle Club coincided with the wedding of Prince Charles and Lady Diana. Owners John and Robert Cain sent the Royals an invitation to the club's grand opening; alas, no response was forthcoming. Nevertheless, the opening was a smash, and British Bicycle Club continues to be a popular spot with conventioneers, thanks to its location a few blocks from the David L. Lawrence Convention Center. The restaurant serves lunch and dinner Monday through Friday, featuring steaks and chops as well as chicken and seafood selections, sandwiches, and a popular steak salad. It offers a full-service bar but does not designate smoking and nonsmoking sections. By the way, the restaurant offers no real British connection, but it does sport vintage cycling pictures on its walls.

The Carlton
$$-$$$ • 500 Ross St., Pittsburgh
• (412) 391-4099

You're in for an elegant dining experience at The Carlton, which is located in One Mellon Bank Center. It would be hard to cite the restaurant's specialties, because the menu changes each day to keep the dining experience fresh. You can always count on veal and fresh seafood. Lunch and dinner specials might include Seafood Wellington, veal portabella, sesame-seared mahi-mahi, or crab potato cake with citrus ponzu and wasabi aioli.

The wine list is extraordinary. It covers 42 pages and 475 selections, with each selection priced just $10 over cost, per the philosophy of Proprietor Kevin Joyce, named Pittsburgh Restaurateur of the Year four years in a row. The wine list was designated the best in town by *Pittsburgh Magazine* in 1995 and has been the city's *Wine Spectator* award winner six years straight. Reservations are recommended, and The Carlton accepts major credit cards. While the restaurant does not offer banquet facilities as such, it can accommodate private parties of up to 150 people. The Carlton is open Monday

through Saturday but does not serve lunch on Saturday.

The Common Plea
$$$$ • 310 Ross St., Pittsburgh
• (412) 281-5140

You are summoned to an important duty at The Common Plea, to wit: "The Bearer is summoned to savor a selection from the following menu and to adjudicate the value thereof." That's what the menu, in the form of a legal summons, advises patrons. As you can see, the restaurant gets plenty of mileage from its location in the city's legal and political district. As for its food, service and atmosphere, the verdict is in, and it's thumbs up.

The Common Plea serves its food in a seemingly endless succession of courses, so bring a hearty appetite. Entrees include pasta, seafood, veal, beef, and lamb selections, many of them priced daily with the market. The lounge provides an intriguing selection of single-malt Scotch whiskeys as well as such specialty cocktails as Chocolata, a martini concocted with vodka and white creme de cacao. The wine list is extensive. If you're of a mind, you can pamper yourself with a 5-liter bottle of 1993 Robert Mondavi "Reserve" Pinot Noir—for $600.

The restaurant offers banquet facilities for up to 70 people. It serves dinner Monday through Saturday, lunch Monday through Friday. The Common Plea closes from 2:30 to 5 PM, though the lounge remains open during those hours. Smoking and nonsmoking sections are available during lunch and dinner.

Eadies Kitchen
$ • 500 Grant St., Pittsburgh
• (412) 391-3993

This restaurant in One Mellon Bank Center specializes in lighter fare for breakfast and lunch, and is a popular spot among Grant Street workers for a quick and affordable meal. The menu, chalked on a blackboard above the ordering counter, features soups, pastas, burgers, hoagies, and salads, as well as four or five hot entree specials. Eadies also provides catering services for downtown offices, including cakes prepared by the pastry chef at The Carlton; on the Friday before Father's Day in 1997, Eadies shipped 41 cakes to Downtown offices where Dad was being honored. The restaurant is open Monday through Friday for breakfast and lunch.

Eadies operates a companion restaurant at the same address called Eadie's Market, which specializes in take-out lunches Monday through Friday. Actually, you'll have to take your Eadie's

Market lunch out, as there's no seating. Neither restaurant serves alcohol, and neither accepts reservations or credit cards.

The Forbes Room
$ • 400 Fifth Ave., Pittsburgh
• (412) 232-2000

The Forbes Room is one of three restaurants you'll find in Kaufmanns department store. All are popular with Downtown shoppers, with The Forbes Room offering perhaps the most formal dining of the three. Specialties include crab cakes, which The Forbes Room prepares from scratch, and the chicken Waldorf salad. You'll find a tempting dessert selection as well, headlined by chocolate amaretto cake and pineapple pie. The Forbes Room offers a lounge, a bar list, and banquet facilities for up to 40 people. It serves lunch only Monday through Saturday, closing on Sundays. The Forbes Room is located on the 11th floor of Kaufmanns and provides a scenic view of Downtown and the three rivers from its expansive picture windows.

Frenchy's Restaurant & Cocktail Lounge
$$$ • 136 Sixth St., Pittsburgh
• (412) 261-6476

You will find French-inspired entrees at Frenchy's, but they're a small part of a diverse menu that also includes seafood, beef, chicken, pasta, and veal selections. Frenchy's offers lunch and dinner specials, which might include twin filet mignon with seasoned mushrooms or boneless chicken pepperoni with red sauce and cheese. The restaurant offers a full-service bar and a wine list, and it accepts reservations.

A fixture in Downtown's theater district for more than three decades, Frenchy's offers lunch and dinner Monday through Saturday. It's usually closed on Sundays but opens on show nights. When you call for the Sunday schedule, you also can ask about the restaurant's catering services and its banquet facilities, which can accommodate up to 50 people.

Froggy's
$-$$ • 100 Market St., Pittsburgh
• (412) 471-3764

Owner Steve "Froggy" Morris is one of the region's most colorful restaurateurs, a devotee of sports who once hosted a local sports radio show. The decor reflects Froggy's interests, with sports memorabilia covering nearly every inch of wall space without any apparent organizing principle. In one section, for example, you'll find pictures of Don Shula and Joe Louis above

a four-shot sequence of Ben Hogan and his golf swing... all of it framing a photo of Froggy himself in harness racing regalia. Dominating this tableau are 15 LeRoy Nieman prints and an elk head hung over the bar, with sports caps adorning the antlers.

The decor sets the mood for the fun experience here, which includes large portions and strong cocktails. Froggy's specializes in steaks and ribs, but you'll also find such lunch and dinner specials as seafood Devonshire and mussels Parmesan, and many seafood, dinner salad, and sandwich selections. You can enjoy outdoor dining on the third floor deck in season—a rock band performs there Wednesday through Friday evening. On those evenings, Froggy's also features live piano entertainment. Reservations are suggested on weekends. Froggy's accepts major credit cards. It's generally closed on Sundays but is open then when the Steelers play at home.

The Garden Cafe
$$ • Liberty Ave. and Sixth St., Pittsburgh
• (412) 392-4879

You'll enjoy this outdoor cafe at Heinz Hall, the glittering performing arts hall. The cafe is set in the courtyard and features a fountain and a waterfall, creating an inviting, relaxing atmosphere. The Fluted Mushroom, a prominent Pittsburgh caterer and Heinz Hall's concessionaire, provides sandwiches and salads, and the cafe can accommodate up to 250 for outdoor events. The cafe serves alcohol, although it does not offer a bar or wine list. It accepts reservations for parties of six or more. As the dining area is outdoors, smoking is permitted anywhere. The Garden Cafe serves lunch Monday through Friday from May through September—weather permitting, of course.

Jimmy's Post Tavern
$ • 110 Smithfield St., Pittsburgh
• (412) 562-0238

Owner Jimmy Costanzo says this about his operating philosophy: "We've been in business 20 years, and we're still dedicated to the working man. We have no frills, no specials, just good quality food and large portions." Whether you enjoy lunch or early dinner here, you'll find a menu that's true to Jimmy Costanzo's philosophy. (Note that the kitchen at Jimmy's closes at 4 PM, so that's a very early dinner.)

"Jimmy's Famous Fish" is the signature sandwich, and you'll find many other sandwich and burger selections as well as soups, salads, and a few vegetarian options. Jimmy's offers a full bar as well as catering services through a separate company called Jimmy's Corporate Catering. The restaurant is open Monday through Friday.

Jimmy Costanzo operates two other restaurants Downtown, including Up Over Jimmy's, which as you might guess, is upstairs from Jimmy's Post Tavern, and Jimmy's Downtown Pizza & Lounge, which is just across the street from the tavern.

Kason's
$-$$ • 311 Fourth Ave., Pittsburgh
• (412) 391-1122

Kason's is a large—it seats 215 people—lively restaurant that serves lunch and dinner Monday through Friday while entertaining private parties seven days a week. The menu offers primarily lighter fare, such as sandwiches, salads, pastas, burgers, and Mexican dishes, but you'll also find a limited entree list that includes steaks, ribs, chicken dishes, and a few seafood selections. To accommodate its large crowds, Kason's offers two full-service bars. A DJ spins tunes each Friday night. Kason's has been providing good food and entertainment at the same location since 1981.

Mahoney's Restaurant
$$ • 949 Liberty Ave., Pittsburgh
• (412) 471-4243

Mahoney's is a quick walk from the David L. Lawrence Convention Center, thus a popular spot for conventioneers. It serves lunch and dinner Monday through Friday, closing on Saturdays and Sundays. While the menu is diverse, the most popular items are dinner salads, such as the steak salad and the grilled chicken salad. Mahoney's offers daily specials for each meal. You'll find an upstairs billiards room as well as a full service bar with daily happy hour specials and a complimentary buffet on Friday evenings. Reservations are accepted. Mahoney's offers banquet facilities for up to 60 people.

Michael's
$ • 400 Fifth Ave., Pittsburgh
• (412) 232-2887

Michael's is part of the 11th-floor dining complex of Kaufmanns department store. Michael's serves lunch Monday through Saturday, focusing on lighter fare and quick service as a courtesy for busy Downtown shoppers and workers. You'll enjoy the salad buffet as well as Michael's Marketplace Salad, cashew chicken salad served with a frozen fruit mold and homemade nut bread. Michael's offers a lounge and banquet facilities for up to 40 people. Reservations are accepted. Michael's is closed on Sundays.

Mitchell's Restaurant, Bar & Banquet Center
$ • 304 Ross St., Pittsburgh
• (412) 471-3663

Since 1903, the Mitchell family has operated restaurants in Pittsburgh, first in East Liberty, now in Downtown in the heart of the city's legal and political center. Many city and Allegheny County employees dine here; if you want the latest political buzz, you'll likely hear it at Mitchell's. The restaurant specializes in inexpensive, home-cooked meals. The menu features seafood and poultry items, dinner salads, and sandwiches. Mitchell's offers a full-service bar and capacious banquet facilities, which have hosted 400 people.

Mitchell's accepts major credit cards but not reservations. It serves lunch and dinner Monday through Friday. On Saturdays, only the bar is open. While the restaurant is formally closed on Sundays, it will host banquets on those days.

Morton's of Chicago
$$$-$$$$ • 625 Liberty Ave., Pittsburgh
• (412) 261-7141

You'll know pretty early in your experience at Morton's that you're in a classy restaurant. As you enter, you'll spy the private liquor lockers where such celebs as Mario Lemieux keep their supplies for entertaining guests. Even if you don't achieve that status, you'll enjoy the attentions of a staff that won *Pittsburgh Magazine's* 1997 award for excellence in service. That award also cited Morton's steaks, for which the restaurant is known. The menu also offers such entrees as Sicilian veal chops, domestic rib lamb chops, and seafood selections that include shrimp Alexander and broiled Brock Island swordfish steak. When you're ready for libations, Morton's offers a full-ser-

INSIDERS' TIP

The Strip District, just east of Downtown Pittsburgh, is the city's most vital food marketplace, offering fresh produce, meat, and seafood brought in daily. Many of the region's restaurateurs shop there every day. You'll find it a lively, exciting venue for your own fresh food shopping.

Downtown Pittsburgh offers numerous fine dining options.

Photo: Courtesy of Greater Pittsburgh Convention & Visitor's Bureau

vice bar and a wine list that earned the *Wine Spectator* Award of Excellence from 1995 through 1999. You can smoke in the restaurant's private dining rooms and also buy your cigars here. Morton's serves dinner daily, and it can accommodate banquets of up to 80 people—it also entertains private parties for lunch. Reservations are recommended. You'll find Morton's on the ground level of CNG Tower.

The Mozart Room
$$$ • Liberty Ave. & Sixth St., Pittsburgh • (412) 392-4879

Here's a find known primarily to Insiders—a group that now includes you. The Mozart Room is a dining room within Heinz Hall, one of the region's principal halls for the performing arts. The Mozart Room offers pre-performance or pre-concert dinners prior to events in Pittsburgh's Cultural District; your ticket to that evening's event gains you admission to The Mozart Room (you still have to pay for the food). Contemporary American meals are prepared and served by The Fluted Mushroom, a prominent Pittsburgh caterer and Heinz Hall's concessionaire, and are drawn from a seasonal menu that features such entrees as pan-roasted loin of veal.

One of the most appealing aspects of the experience here is the decor, notably the crystal chandeliers and Corinthian columns found throughout Heinz Hall. The Mozart Room, which is entirely nonsmoking, offers a wine list. Reservations are required, and you must wear what management calls proper attire. Banquet facilities can accommodate up to 80 people. The Mozart Room offers occasional Sunday brunches, and it sometimes opens before events staged at venues other than Heinz Hall. Call for details about brunches and those special dinner performances.

The Original Oyster House
$, no credit cards • 20 Market Sq., Pittsburgh • (412) 566-7925

Since 1870, The Original Oyster House has been delighting Downtown patrons with its variety of seafood—crab cakes, fish sandwiches, clams, shrimp, and of course, its signature oysters. This is a lively, informal spot, with many patrons preferring to sit or stand at the bar/counter while they eat. Booths are available, and around them you'll see one of the oddest collections of photographs you're ever likely to find in a restaurant. Staring at you, with toothy smiles each, will be Miss America contestants in group photos representing many years of the pageant. These have been preserved from the collection of the restaurant's original owner, a Miss America buff. Each time he attended the pageant, he returned with a group photo. The Original Oyster House is open from 9 AM to

11 PM Monday through Saturday. It's closed on Sundays. Reservations are not accepted.

Pittsburgh Fish Market
$$$ • 1001 Liberty Ave., Pittsburgh
• (412) 227-3657

Seafood is the principal theme here, with a seemingly endless variety of tasty variations. Chef Alexander Young recreates the lunch and menu daily, so that you'll always have new selections from which to choose. Watch for items such as Chilean sea bass, Florida black grouper, Maine wolfish, and Alaskan halibut under "Today's Catch." One entree that's always on the menu is the PFM Bucket, which features a 11/4-pound Maine lobster, little neck clams, Dungeness crab, Maine mussels, redskin potatoes, and corn on the cob. You'll need a hearty appetite for this one.

PFM also features chicken, steak, chops, and

If you're a meat-and-potatoes eater, you've got options in Pittsburgh.

sushi and sashimi. The extensive wine list offers a taste guide to help you distinguish those that are dry, for example, from those that are sweet. You also can select from 17 varieties of bottled beer, 11 types of beer on tap, and four varieties of sparkling water. You can buy a cigar at the humidor or t-shirts, hats, polo shirts, and aprons emblazoned with the PFM logo. If you'd like a taste of PFM in your own home, the restaurant offers seafood for sale at a special counter. PFM is located in Liberty Center, at the eastern edge of town across from the Greyhound Station. If you're interested in dinner on a Sunday, note that PFM opens at 4 PM.

The Promenade Cafe
$$-$$$ • 600 Commonwealth St., Pittsburgh • (412) 391-4600, ext. 5304

Part of the Hilton Hotel, the Promenade Cafe is open daily for breakfast, lunch, and dinner, and it also serves brunch each Sunday. The dinner menu offers extensive selections of dinner salads and sandwiches, and a more limited selection of entrees. Breakfast and lunch are fun here. The breakfast menu runs to three pages. For lunch, try the Chinese buffet each Monday, featuring a "Wok it to Me" stir fry station, or the Wednesday buffet that highlights foods of a different nationality each week.

Reservations are accepted, and the cafe offers a wine list and banquet facilities (through the hotel). For cocktails, you can repair to the adjacent Scenes lounge, which features jazz on Friday and Saturday evenings. For more on that, bop over to our Nightlife chapter.

Rosenbaum's Deli
$ • 614 Smithfield St., Pittsburgh
• (412) 391-4944

Many delicatessens are so cramped for seating space that they provide their patrons little dining privacy. That's not the case at Rosenbaum's, a spacious deli that offers two floors of seating. It features a large selection of sandwiches, soups and salads, with prices on all large salads reduced each Wednesday. Rosenbaum's does not serve alcohol, and it does not have a smoking section. Reservations are not accepted. Rosenbaum's serves exclusively lunches, but you can enjoy yours as early as 9 AM. The deli is open Monday through Friday.

The Ruddy Duck
$-$$ • 1 Bigelow Sq., Pittsburgh
• (412) 281-3825

Finding a place to dine on a major holiday sometimes can be a problem. That problem is solved by The Ruddy Duck, which serves breakfast, lunch, and dinner 365 days a year. It's part of the Ramada Hotel, so you'll find banquet facilities that can accommodate up to 1,000 people. The menu features veal, pasta divalo, and a stuffed Parmesan chicken dish as highlights. In season, you're welcome to dine on the patio, though there's no view to speak of.

The Ruddy Duck offers a full-service bar and a wine list. During happy hour, 4 to 7 PM Monday through Friday, you'll enjoy free hors d'oeuvres. The restaurant accepts major credit cards, and you can reserve a table at all times except those nights when the nearby Mellon Arena is hosting an event. The Ruddy Dock offers a schedule of ethnic food festivals as well as specially priced cocktails; to keep up with these, ask for a monthly schedule. By the way, if you forget the phone number, it spells 281-DUCK.

Ruth's Chris Steak House
$$$ • 6 PPG Place, Pittsburgh
• (412) 391-4800

If you've visited a Ruth's Chris Steak House in other cities, you'll be familiar with the menu and high quality of service at this restaurant. Steaks, of course, are the specialty, but the restaurant also offers an appealing selection of fresh fish that varies daily with the catch. You usually can find fresh lobster and grilled salmon on the menu, as well as coconut shrimp with a honey mustard sauce that makes an unusual appetizer.

The restaurant offers a full-service bar and a 14-page wine list, with prices up to $500 a bottle. Reservations are suggested for both lunch and dinner. While the restaurant is open seven days a week, lunch is served Monday through Friday only. The dinner menu is available all day.

Seventh Street Grille
$$$ • 130 Seventh St., Pittsburgh
• (412) 338-0303

Set in the heart of the theater district, Seventh Street Grille is a popular spot before and after shows and concerts. It serves lunch and dinner daily, which is somewhat unusual, as many theater district restaurants close on Sundays. Mesquite grilled items are among the specialties here, as you'll enjoy such items as tuna nicoise, salmon fillet, lite chicken, and boneless breast of duck from the grill. Quesadillas, with your choice of six fillings, also are popular. The restaurant offers a bar and a wine list as well as a selection of 77 bottled and 13 draft beers. Reservations are accepted. Seventh Street Grille offers banquet facilities for up to 70 people.

The Smithfield Cafe
$-$$ • 639 Smithfield St., Pittsburgh
• (412) 281-5452

The Petrolias family has operated The Smithfield Cafe at the same location since 1933. If that's not a record, it's still a heckuva lot better than average. The restaurant serves breakfast, lunch, and dinner Monday through Friday, breakfast and lunch only on Saturday; it accepts reservations for lunch and dinner. It opens on Sundays only to accommodate large conventions in Downtown. Breakfasts are quite popular here. Breakfast specials are economically priced, and waffles are a regular feature of the menu.

"The Famous Smithfield Devonshire" is a favorite of lunch patrons, while the diverse dinner menu offers beef, chicken, and seafood selections as well as salads and "mix & match" pasta—you select the pasta and match it with your choice of sauces. The cafe offers a full-service bar and banquet facilities for up to 150 people. On Wednesday and Friday evenings, The Smithfield Cafe hosts karaoke.

Souper Bowl Restaurant & Lounge
$ • 910 Fifth Ave., Pittsburgh
• (412) 471-0416

Here's an unpretentious spot in the Uptown neighborhood, a few blocks from both Downtown and the Mellon Arena. You'll find a variety of soups and sandwiches, several specials each day and a Taco salad special each Wednesday. During happy hour from 4 to 6PM, you'll enjoy special prices on cocktails and the extensive selection of beers. Souper Bowl is open Monday through Friday. It accepts major credit cards and offers banquet facilities for up to 100. Reservations are not accepted.

Southwest Bistro
$-$$ • 129 Sixth St., Pittsburgh
• (412) 261-8866
• www.citysearch.com

Run by native Texan Michael Crawford and his wife Cheryl Lowitzer, Southwest Bistro features menu selections unlike any others we know of in Pittsburgh. While the number of entrees is around only 10, you're certain to find plenty of taste packed in each. The bistro's specialty is smoked duck with ancho-chile demi-glace and shiitake mushrooms. Also with the ancho-chile demi-glace, another dinner entrée often ordered is grilled centercut pork loin topped with roasted red pepper jelly and a pineapple-jicama salsa. On the vegetarian side, you'll find saffron rice topped with black beans, with a medley of side dishes surrounding it: ginger carrot puree; braised red cabbage; brandied portobella mushrooms; green chile grits; grilled garlic tomatoes; and a poblano, leek, and red pepper side dish. Michael orders all the wines himself from special, smaller vineyards (we give them a thumbs-up), and you'll get a great price on a bottle—$10 above cost. To complement your Southwest experience, beer and margaritas are also available. Something else to look forward to at the bistro is the desserts; two of our favorites are the Belgian chocolate mousse and the caramel flan.

Southwest Bistro is open for lunch during the week from 11 AM to 2 PM and for dinner Tuesday through Saturday, beginning at 5 PM. Formal banquet facilities are not available, as this really is a bistro; however, you may be able to book the entire restaurant for your party of up to 55 people. With occasional exceptions during odd hours, Southwest Bistro is a non-smoking zone.

The Terrace
$$-$$$ • 530 William Penn Pl., Pittsburgh
• (412) 553-5235

Sitting in the lobby of the Westin William Penn Hotel is one of our town's most enjoyable experiences; when you dine at the hotel's restaurant, known as The Terrace, you'll enhance that experience. The Terrace offers breakfast, lunch, and dinner Monday through Saturday, brunch only on Sunday. Each meal has a distinct personality, and power breakfasts are popular here.

Dinner is a more leisurely affair. Wheeling and dealing gives way to lingering dinners over such entrees as seared duck breast, roast lamb rack, curry roasted cod, and bronze-skin salmon. On Tuesday and Friday evenings, you'll enjoy a special package that includes hors d'oeuvres, a cigar (Sinatra label), cognac or Scotch whiskey, and a local Jazz entertainer every Friday night. The Terrace offers two full-service bars, a wine list, and banquet facilities for up to 150 people.

The Tic Toc Restaurant
$ • 400 Fifth Ave., Pittsburgh
• (412) 232-2307

The ornate clock outside Kaufmanns department store is one of the city's most recognizable landmarks. As far back as the 1930s, Kaufmanns appreciated the importance of this landmark, and so it named its first floor restaurant to reflect the clock's popularity. Today, it's still convenient to look up and catch the time while dashing about downtown.

While The Tic Toc Restaurant has the look and feel of a coffee shop, it goes beyond that to offer such breakfasts as home-made waffles and a dessert menu that's about 15 items strong. It's open from 9 AM to 6 PM Monday through Saturday, closing on Sundays. The Tic Toc Restaurant serves beer and wine. It does not accept reservations.

Top of the Triangle
$$-$$$ • 600 Grant St., Pittsburgh
• (412) 471-4100

This is the top of the Golden Triangle, 62 stories up in USX Tower. No downtown restaurant offers a broader view of the city, and Top of the Triangle's large picture windows assure that you'll enjoy the view from every seat in the house. The most popular menu selections are the Angus strip steak and the grilled double-cut veal chop with porcini goat cheese risotto and marsala glace de viande. Other interesting entrees include jumbo prawns with black beans, banana chutney, and papaya jam; the cedar plank salmon with grilled fennel-citrus quinoa; and the pappardelle pasta with roasted tomato and yellow peppers, arugula, feta cheese, and grilled leeks.

Top of the Triangle serves lunch and dinner daily. You'll enjoy specially priced drinks during the daily happy hour and complimentary hors d'oeuvres each Monday and Friday evening. Smoking is not allowed in the dining room. The restaurant offers a bar, a wine list, and banquet facilities for up to 400 people. Reservations are suggested. Speaking of banquets, the male member of our writing team exchanged vows with his wife in the first wedding ceremony staged at the Top of the Triangle. That was in 1974. Must be something about that view that contributes to longevity.

Up Over Jimmy's
$ • 110 Smithfield St., Pittsburgh
• (412) 562-0239

Located upstairs from Jimmy's Post Tavern, this restaurant—which serves lunch only—is true to owner Jimmy Costanzo's philosophy of serving working people on a budget. You'll find reasonably priced entrees such as Maryland crabcakes and broiled swordfish, as well as a diverse selection of sandwiches and several specialty salads. And of course, "Jimmy's Famous Fish Sandwich" is always available. Up Over Jimmy's is a popular spot for banquets and meetings, often hosting political functions. Up Over Jimmy's is open Monday through Friday.

Cambodian

The Lemon Grass Cafe
$-$$ • 124 Sixth St., Pittsburgh
• (412) 765-2222

Restaurateurs are a colorful breed with engaging tales to tell. Spend some time, however, with The Lemon Grass Cafe owners Kim Hong and her son, Bophanara "Bo" Meng, and if the mood is just right, you'll hear stories shocking in their cruelty and nearly incredible with their examples of commonplace heroism. It's the story of native Cambodians Kim and Bo, of course, who in 1979 escaped Khmer Rouge "killing fields" and re-education camps that claimed the lives of 21 members of their immediate family. After enduring four years of re-education, they escaped to Thailand as the first part of their journey to Pittsburgh.

Now, they operate both The Lemon Grass Cafe and a sister Downtown restaurant called Phnom Penh (see write-up below). The menu at the cafe offers a variety of Cambodian dishes, including red and green curry; spicy mussels; and fried rice with sausage, eggs, carrots, peas, and scallions. For many of the entrees, you have the option of chicken, beef, or shrimp as the base. You'll also enjoy the green papaya salad; the signature lemon grass soup; and the shark fin soup, which includes crab meat, roast pork, egg, shredded ginger root, bamboo shoots, black mushrooms, and scallions. The cafe does not use butter or cheese in any of its dishes.

The cafe serves lunch and dinner Monday through Saturday, dinner only on Sundays. It does not serve alcohol. Reservations are accepted. The cafe does not designate smoking or nonsmoking sections. It can accommodate banquets of up to 80 people.

When you're here, take a minute to shake hands with Kim and Bo. If the mood is just right, they might have some tales to tell you.

Phnom Penh
$-$$ • 410 First Ave., Pittsburgh
• (412) 261-4166

The second of the downtown restaurants operated by Kim Hong and Bo Meng, Phnom Penh offers a menu similar to that of its sister restaurant, The Lemon Grass Cafe. Phnom Penh, however, supplements its Cambodian cuisine with a generous selection of Chinese entrees such as General Tso's Chicken and cashew chicken or shrimp. You also can enjoy Lemon Grass soup here. Phnom Penh serves lunch and dinner Monday through Friday, dinner only on Saturdays. It's closed on Sundays. Reservations are accepted. Phnom Penh does not serve alcohol—you're invited to bring your own—and it does not designate smoking and nonsmoking sections. It provides banquet facilities for up to 55 people.

Chinese

Chinatown Inn
$$ • 520 Third Ave., Pittsburgh
• (412) 261-1292

The Yee family has operated Chinatown Inn for three generations, serving Cantonese, Szechuan, and Hunan selections. It's located near Grant Street, the center of city and Allegheny County political and legal activity, so you'll be rubbing shoulders with politicos when you dine here. The lunch and dinner menus include beef, seafood, and poultry entrees as well as a limited vegetarian menu. Chinatown Inn offers a full-service bar and a wine list, as well as banquet facilities for up to 100 people. Lunch and dinner reservations are accepted, as are major credit cards.

Mandarin Gourmet
$-$$ • 305 Wood St., Pittsburgh
• (412) 261-6151

Mandarin Gourmet serves lunch and dinner

INSIDERS' TIP
When you're in Downtown Pittsburgh and not sure what you want for lunch, try one of the three food courts that offer a variety of restaurants in a single complex. You'll find them at Warner Center, Fifth Avenue Place, and PPG Place, all within walking distance in downtown Pittsburgh.

Monday through Saturday. You'll find a broad selection of pork, beef, poultry, seafood, and pasta items as well as vegetarian selections. Check out the "Chef's Suggestions" section for a number of interesting combinations, like sizzling two delicacies, featuring beef and scallops, and dragon and phoenix, with lobster and General Tso's chicken. Hot and spicy items are marked with a red star. Mandarin Gourmet offers a full-service bar, and it accepts reservations. It offers banquet facilities for up to 300 people. You'll find a sister Mandarin Gourmet in the North Hills, which offers a buffet as well as a full menu.

Greek

Christos
$-$$, no credit cards • 130 Sixth St., Pittsburgh • (412) 261-6442

For three years, Christos Malacrinos served as a chef for Jackie Onassis aboard the yacht Christina. Now, he's bringing the benefits of that experience to Downtown Pittsburgh diners. Christos serves lunch and dinner daily, offering such entrees as spanakopita, lamb kabob, chicken kabob oreganato, and moussaka—you can complement them all with Greek Easter bread. But the real star of the menu is a dessert called ekmek, which Malacrinos says he developed and prepared especially for Onassis. It's a white cake topped with honey syrup, custard, cinnamon, and whipped cream, and you can order a version with a chocolate cake base as well.

Christos offers an outdoor dining area and banquet facilities for up to 55 people. It does not serve alcohol—you're invited to bring your own—and it does not designate smoking and nonsmoking sections. Christos normally does not accept reservations, but it will take lunch reservations for parties of six or more on days when the nearby theaters are staging performances.

Italian

Asiago
$$-$$$ • One Oxford Centre, Pittsburgh • (412) 392-0225

This elegant restaurant in One Oxford Centre on Grant Street features European cuisine of French and Italian influence. The selections include pasta, beef, veal, poultry, and fresh seafood. Among its most popular items are

crabcake Valencia with a scarlet orange beurre blanc and veal siago, which is topped with roasted peppers, asiago cheese, and pesto, and laced with chianti bordelaise sauce. You'll find a full bar and an outstanding wine list, as well as banquet facilities for up to 70 people. Reservations are suggested for dinner and accepted for lunch parties of five or more. Parking is complimentary with dinner reservations. The restaurant, which accepts all major credit cards, is closed on Sunday.

Bravo Franco Ristorante
$$$ • 613 Penn Ave., Pittsburgh • (412) 642-6677

Located in the heart of the Cultural District, Bravo Franco offers both indoor dining in an intimate room and dining al fresco on its sidewalk patio. The menu features chicken, seafood, pasta, and beef selections, with the steaks cut thick. A popular selection is the bowtie and salmon pasta, served with a light tomato cream sauce. Bravo Franco offers a full-service bar, an extensive wine list and banquet facilities for up to 60 people. Reservations are requested. Bravo Franco does not designate smoking and nonsmoking sections, but it tries to accommodate patrons of each persuasion. The restaurant offers lunch and dinner Monday through Saturday. It's open on Sundays only when the nearby theaters are staging performances. Call ahead to check the Sunday schedule.

Caffe Amante
$$$ • 120 Fifth Ave., Pittsburgh • (412) 391-1226

Caffe Amante is the principal restaurant in Fifth Avenue Place, the retail and office complex that features distinctive needle-type ornamenting. Caffe Amante specializes in continental and Northern Italian fare, with seafood, veal, chicken, and pasta entrees. The restaurant offers a full-service bar and an extensive wine list, and it can accommodate banquets. Reservations are suggested. Caffe Amante serves lunch and dinner Monday through Saturday. It's closed on Sundays. Entrée prices are at the lower end of $$$.

Carmassi's Tuscany Grill
$$$ • 711 Penn Ave., Pittsburgh • (412) 281-6644

Carmassi's specializes in Northern Italian fare. You'll enjoy such entrees as chicken and shrimp saute; penne arrabiatta, which consists of grilled lobster and shrimp with red onions in a spicy tomato sauce over a penne bed; and veal

Asian cuisine has found a home in Pittsburgh.

nights. The menu features steak, veal, chicken, seafood, and pasta selections. Banquets are an important service of Costanzo's, as it can accommodate up to 200 people. It offers a full-service bar. Reservations are recommended for lunch; not usually needed for dinner. Costanzo's is open every day except Sunday.

F. Tambellini Seventh Street
$$$ • 139 Seventh St., Pittsburgh • (412) 391-1091

F. Tambellini offers a wide variety of lunch and dinner selections, including beef, veal (including ossu buco, or veal shank), seafood, and pasta selections. The common denominator among long-time patrons, however, is considerable affection for the restaurant's fried zucchini—a must when you dine here. The restaurant offers a full-service bar and an extensive wine list, and it accepts reservations for parties of eight or more. The Puccini Room hosts banquets for up to 100 people. F. Tambellini is open Monday through Saturday; with its location in Downtown's theater district, it also opens on Sunday show nights. It's best to call to determine F. Tambellini's status on any Sunday. Entrée prices here are at the lower end of $$$.

Jamie's On The Square
$$-$$$ • 435 Market St., Pittsburgh • (412) 471-1722

Jamie's offers a diverse menu that includes beef, seafood, veal, chicken, and pasta selections. Popular entrees include crab cakes, which are deep fried with jumbo lump crab meat and served with Dijon mustard sauce, and Jamie's Surf and Turf, featuring charbroiled beef tenderloins and skewered shrimp and scallops, served with a tomato caper sauce. Jamie's offers a full-service bar and a wine list. It serves

San Remo, which features veal medallions sauteed with artichoke hearts, roasted peppers, and a marsala demi-glace. Carmassi's also serves a pre-theater "Prix Fixe"—a fixed-price feature with a different entree each day. Carmassi's offers a full-service bar, an extensive wine list, and banquet facilities for up to 80 people. Reservations are accepted. Carmassi's serves dinner Monday through Saturday, lunch Monday through Friday. It opens on Sundays only on performance days at the nearby theaters. If you're thinking about Sunday dinner here, it's best to call ahead.

Costanzo's Italian Bar and Grill
$-$$ • 240 Fourth Ave., Pittsburgh • (412) 232-0706

Costanzo's offers two separate personalities, both of them appealing. By day, it's a popular spot for lunches. By night, it swings, offering DJs or bands Wednesday through Saturday lunch and dinner Monday through Saturday, closing on Sundays. Reservations are recommended for dinner, but not accepted for lunch. You'll find Jamie's in the busy Market Square section of Downtown.

La Scala Ristorante
$$-$$$ • 144 Sixth St., Pittsburgh
• (412) 434-6244

This classy restaurant in the heart of the theater district features primarily Northern Italian selections, including seafood, veal, beef, chicken, and pasta entrees. If you're in the mood for light dining after the theater, you'll enjoy La Scala's homemade desserts. The restaurant offers a bar and a wine list, as well as banquet facilities for up to 80 people. The dining room normally is nonsmoking, but La Scala will waive that rule if the restaurant isn't too full. Reservations are recommended. La Scala offers lunch and dinner Monday through Friday, and only dinner on Saturdays. It's usually closed on Sundays but opens on show nights. Call to confirm La Scala's status on any Sunday.

Piccolo Piccolo Ristorante
$$$ • 1 Wood St., Pittsburgh
• (412) 261-7234

Piccolo Piccolo is one of the restaurants people often name when asked about the finest in town. The restaurant specializes in Roman-style food. Among its most popular selections is the antipasto buffet, which comes with your entree or serves as a meal in itself. You'll find veal, chicken, seafood, and pasta selections, as well as steaks and chops. When you're really hungry, try the delizia del mare, a mixture of lobster, crab claw, shrimp, and other shellfish simmered in garlic and white wine and served on a bed of angel hair pasta.

Piccolo Piccolo offers a full-service bar and a 12-page wine list, as well as banquet facilities for up to 65 people. It accepts major credit cards and recommends reservations for lunch and dinner. The restaurant is open on weekends from 4 to 9 PM. General Manager Frank Sacco is the second generation of his family to participate in Piccolo Piccolo's ownership. Shuttle service is available to and from hotels and major events in the area.

Scoglio Uptown
$$ • 429 Fourth Ave., Pittsburgh
• (412) 263-0546

Located only a few paces from Grant Street, Scoglio Uptown specializes in Northern Italian cuisine. Among its most popular menu items are broiled Virginia spots almondine and sauteed crabcakes with herb mustard sauce. You can select from eight sauces to top any pasta dish you order. The restaurant offers a full-service bar and banquet facilities for up to 75 people. Reservations are recommended. Scoglio Uptown serves lunch and dinner Monday through Friday.

Japanese

Hana Japanese Restaurant
$$ • 1 Graeme St., Pittsburgh
• (412) 471-9988

This Market Square restaurant offers an extensive Sushi bar as well as such entrees as sesame chicken, chicken, steak, or salmon teriyaki, and scallops or shrimp flambe. For libations, you'll enjoy the Kamikaze Lounge. Reservations are accepted; they're usually more important for lunch than they are for dinner. Hana serves dinner Monday through Saturday, lunch Monday through Friday. It's closed on Sundays.

Pizza

Jimmy's Downtown Pizza & Lounge
$ • 105-107 Smithfield St., Pittsburgh
• (412) 394-9600, (412) 566-9660

The ubiquitous and hard-working Jimmy Costanzo operates this restaurant, along with two others just across Smithfield Street. One of the strongest attractions here is that you can place your orders for pizza, hoagies and submarines, and soups and salads as late as 1:30 AM, making it one of the latest-closing restaurants in all of Downtown. The menu also includes several pasta entrees and of course, "Jimmy's Famous Fish Sandwich."

Monte Cello's Italian Restaurant & Pizzeria
$ • 7th and Liberty Aves., Pittsburgh
• (412) 261-2080

When you have time for a quick lunch only but still want to get away from the office, hurry on down to Monte Cello's. You can avoid the lines at the counter by helping yourself to pizza by the slice and sandwiches at the express lunch buffet—and enjoy your meal in the dining area. Monte Cello's offers such unusual pizza toppings as steak and onions, and chicken and broccoli. You also can choose from a limited number of entrees, soups, and salads. Monte Cello's does not serve alcohol. It accepts reservations for parties of 10 or more, and it offers catering and delivery services. Monte Cello's serves lunch and dinner Monday through Saturday.

Villa Reale
$ • 628 Smithfield St., Pittsburgh
• (412) 391-3963

Villa Reale calls its pizza "perfect." That may be an exaggeration, but only a slight one, as Downtown shoppers and workers have been enjoying the restaurant's pizza since 1976. You can order yours with such unusual toppings as roasted red peppers or pineapple. Villa Reale also features a limited selection of entrees—pasta with broccoli and pasta with ricotta cheese are among patrons' favorites—and plenty of sandwiches and salads. The restaurant offers a lounge and a limited wine list, as well as banquet facilities for up to 50 people. It serves lunch and dinner Monday through Saturday.

Seafood

The Steelhead Grill
$$$ • 112 Washington Pl., Pittsburgh
• (412) 394-3474

When The Steelhead Grill opened in 1997, it was named by *Esquire* magazine as one of America's top 10 new restaurants. It's operated by Myriad Restaurant Group, the force behind such restaurants as Montrachet, TriBeCa Grill, Layla, and Nobu in New York, and Rubicon in San Francisco. As you would expect, Steelhead boasts all the features—excellent food, classy environment, attentive service—that you would expect in a restaurant that attracts national attention. Specialties include grilled steelhead salmon and tuna seared rare with soba noodles and a mushroom broth. You'll also find beef, chicken, and pasta entrees, as well as a vegetarian "plate of the day."

Steelhead offers a lounge, an extensive wine list, and banquet facilities for up to 50 people. It serves breakfast, lunch, and dinner Monday through Friday and a breakfast buffet on Saturdays and Sundays. While Steelhead closes each Monday through Friday from 2 to 5 PM, the lounge remains open for eating and drinking during those hours. Reservations are recommended for dinner and lunch. When you call for reservations, remember that the phone number above spells FYI-FISH. The principal dining area is nonsmoking, but smoking is permitted in the lounge. The Steelhead Grill is located in the Pittsburgh Marriott City Center near the Mellon Arena. For more on the hotel and its banquet facilities, see our Accommodations chapter.

North

American

The Bending Room
$ • 418 Third Ave., Ford City
• (724) 763-2901

The Bending Room serves dinner only from Tuesday through Sunday. The menu offers diverse American fare, with beef, poultry, and veal selections as well as sandwiches and daily pasta and seafood specials. It offers a full-service bar and a wine list, and it can accommodate up to 120 people for banquets.

Bonello's Family Restaurant
$-$$ • 353 Butler Rd., Kittanning
• (724) 545-2601

For buffet buffs, Bonello's is boffo. On Wednesdays and Thursday, you can sample the chef's buffet, a dinner spread that features such entrees as lasagna, cabbage rolls, and chicken. Fridays bring the super seafood buffet, while the highlight of Saturdays and Sundays is the American buffet, offering ribs and roast beef. Did we mention the breakfast buffet each Saturday and Sunday? The salad bar at Bonello's seems like a buffet itself, offering about 50 items. Banquet facilities for up to 100 people are available. This Armstrong County restaurant accepts reservations. Bonello's is open daily for breakfast, lunch, and dinner. And don't worry about getting lost trying to find this old-time gem; there's a giant plastic cow out in front of the restaurant.

The Clark Bar & Grill
$-$$ • 503 Martindale St., Pittsburgh
• (412) 231-5720

Although this building housed the original Clark Bar production facility, you won't find any of those chocolate bars here, as the candy company now is based in Pittsburgh's northern suburbs. You will find a restaurant that serves lunch and dinner Monday through Saturday, and each Sunday that brings an event to Three Rivers Stadium. The menu is limited but trendy, offering ribs, steak, grilled crab cakes, sandwiches, and dinner salads. The wine list is limited, but the bar is exceptionally well stocked, offering 12 brands of vodka and 10 types of single-malt Scotch whiskey, among other delights. The restaurant accepts reservations. The restaurant designates smoking and nonsmoking sections. It's a long field goal from the stadium on the city's Northside.

Damon's

$$$ • 855 Freeport Rd., Fox Chapel
• (412) 782-3750
7221 McKnight Rd., North Hills
• (412) 367-7427
50 Miracle Mile Shopping Center,
Monroeville • (412) 858-7427
511 Clairton Blvd., Clairton
• (412) 653-7427

You'll find four Damon's restaurants in the area—two in the North Hills, one in Monroeville in the eastern suburbs, and one in the South Hills. Each offers the same combination of fun food, around-the-wall TVs, and unusual games. The Fox Chapel restaurant, set in Waterworks Mall, is the original Damon's in this region, so we'll tip our cap to them and profile that Damon's in this section.

The restaurant may be best known for its prime rib and ribs; prime rib is available after 4 PM Monday through Saturday, but the St. Louis-style ribs are available for lunch and dinner. In fact, the lunch and dinner menus are identical, with the exception of the prime rib noted above. You'll also find chicken, pasta, seafood, and sandwich selections, as well as a special menu for kids' under 10. For an unusual appetizer, try the onion loaf—if you're really in a daring mood, go for the "Mother Loaf." Adults will enjoy a full-service bar, a wide selection of beers, and a more limited wine list, plus happy hours that run from 5 to 7 PM Monday through Friday and 10 PM to midnight Sunday through Thursday. Enjoy half-price appetizers during this extended get-happy times.

If you'd like some upbeat entertainment with your meal, try the Damon's clubhouse, which features computer keyboards that offer trivia games viewed on wide-screen TVs; kids enjoy their own trivia time, 5 to 7 PM each Wednesday. Damon's accepts major credit cards as well as reservations Sunday through Thursday. On Friday and Saturday, you can call ahead for priority seating when you're en route. Damon's offers banquet facilities.

Gunner's Grill & Pub

$$$ •143 N. Main St., Butler
• (724) 283-6061

Owners Greg and Laura Walter traveled throughout the world when Greg served in the Air Force, sampling exotic fare. They've brought a touch of that exotic flavor to Gunner's Grill & Pub in downtown Butler. In addition to the standard steak, seafood, pasta, and chicken dishes served for lunch and dinner, you can sample such unusual dishes as elk, caribou, black bear, rattlesnake, and wild boar—or whatever else chef Don Potter has bagged that day. Alligator is a staple of the appetizer menu, and you'll enjoy the raw bar each Friday.

Gunner's offers more than 100 microbrews and 17 varieties of beer on tap. If you want to enjoy a post-alligator cigar, you'll find a humidor on the premises. Reservations are accepted for lunch and dinner.

Hardwood Cafe

$$-$$$ • 646 Pittsburgh Rd., Butler
• (724) 586-5353

On those cold Southwestern Pennsylvania nights, you'll enjoy dining by the fire at Hardwood Cafe, which features a two-story fireplace. You'll also enjoy a diverse menu that offers pasta and chicken dishes as well as pizza and burgers. You can opt for lunch and dinner specials each day except Sunday when you'll still be able to choose from the wide variety of selections on Hardwood's menu. Reservations are needed on weekends and accepted on weekdays. The Hardwood Cafe offers banquet facilities for up to 50 people. The restaurant is conveniently located on Pa. Rte. 8. Like the entrees available, prices at the café encompass a broad range; however, those that are $$$ are at the lower end.

The Home Plate Cafe

$, no credit cards • 300 Stadium Cir.,
Pittsburgh • (412) 323-5058

The Home Plate Cafe is the formal name for the press lounge in Three Rivers Stadium. For years, baseball writers have regarded it as one of the finest such facilities among National League towns. The private Allegheny Club, which operates the cafe, has opened it to the public for lunches. It's a well-kept secret in town, but as an Insider, you now have the skinny on this restaurant.

From Monday through Friday, it offers economical and tasty lunches. Typically, there are several daily specials and other selections. If you're not partial to the specials, however, the staff will whip up a made-to-order cold cut sandwich for you, and you still can partake of the side dishes, daily soup, dessert specials, and salad bar. The cafe does not serve liquor. While it does not accept credit cards, it will accept personal checks with appropriate identification. All seating is nonsmoking, but in fair weather, you're invited to dine outdoors in the press box, where smoking is permitted. The cafe can accommodate banquets for up to 80 people, and it requires reservations for parties of 12 or more.

When you dine here, you'll feel like a genuine sportswriter . . . and you don't even have to

Elegant dining at The Grand Concourse.

Photo: Courtesy of Greater Pittsburgh Convention & Visitor's Bureau

days only. Reservations are recommended for Saturdays, accepted at other times.

James Street Restaurant
$$-$$$ • 422 Foreland St., Pittsburgh
• (412) 323-2222

For good food and good jazz, try James Street Restaurant on Pittsburgh's North Side. The restaurant features a number of Cajun- and Creole-style dishes, including chicken and shrimp jambalaya and chicken andouille gumbo, and sauteed chicken in a stew of onions and peppers over rice. You'll find lunch and dinner specials, a full-service bar, and a wine list.

James Street also is one of the city's most popular havens for jazz. On Tuesday, Thursday, Friday, and Saturday evenings, the stage typically is turned over to such top local performers as drummer Roger Humphries and saxophonist Kenny Blake. Wednesdays bring a double treat. First, the Pittsburgh Banjo Club holds an open practice session at the restaurant. Then Five Guys Named Moe treat patrons to a show featuring jazz from the '40s and '50s. There's a cover charge only for the occasional national act.

Reservations are recommended. James Street offers banquet facilities for up to 150 people. It's open for lunch and dinner Monday through Saturday, and you can enjoy Sunday brunch here when the Steelers play at home. If you're wondering about the name, you do turn on James Street to get there.

Kaufman House
$$ • 105 South Main St., Zelienople
• (724) 452-8900

You can have a memorable dining experience here, as each month brings wild game specials that include such dishes as elk, ostrich, and wild boar sausage. The less adventuresome will enjoy the prime rib and fried chicken selections from the regular menu. Each Wednesday and Thursday, Kaufman House features specially priced "Dinner for Two" features.

The restaurant offers a bar, a wine list, and banquet facilities for up to 50 people. You'll need reservations on Fridays, Saturdays, and

wear mismatched clothes. The café is open from 11:30 AM to 2 PM on weekdays.

J-Barn Country Inn
$-$$ • 495 Monroe Rd., Sarver
• (724) 353-3300

This Butler county restaurant is a pleasant country inn that offers such appealing country-style fare as ribs, ham, seafood, steak marinated on the premises, marshmallow fruit salad, fried mushrooms, and homemade banana bread and apple butter. Outdoor grilling is one of their specialties. If you like what you're eating, you can stop at the inn's country store and pick up J-Barn baked goods and other branded foods. The store also features crafts fashioned by local artisans. J-Barn is open Wednesday through Sunday for dinner, with lunch served on Sun-

RESTAURANTS

Sundays. Kaufman House serves breakfast, lunch, and dinner daily.

Kenny B's
$ • 411 Butler Rd., Kittanning
• (724) 545-2122

This Armstrong County restaurant offers a diverse menu that features lunch specials and the "catch of the day" each evening. Kenny B's holiday buffets are especially popular, as is its Sunday brunch. It offers a lounge and a wine list, and it accepts reservations. Kenny B's provides banquet facilities for up to 185 people. The restaurant serves lunch and dinner Monday through Friday, dinner only on Saturdays, and brunch and menu offerings on Sundays until 4 PM.

Morgan's Diner
$$ • 127 Oneida Valley Rd., Butler
• (724) 282-2800

Here's a pleasant throwback—a diner that serves breakfast all day and hearty American fare for lunch and dinner. Beyond the signature steakburgers, Morgan's offers daily specials that include creamed chicken and biscuits, sirloin tips and noodles, and scalloped potatoes and ham. Morgan's accepts no reservations.

You'll find real home-cooked food at Morgan's; even the pastries are made from scratch. The diner is especially famous for its fried chicken, homemade soups, the shakes made from real ice cream and milk, and its apple dumplings. There's an extensive menu, and you'll feel like you're at Grandma's house when you see the five kinds of potato dishes available. That reminds us, if you're a vegetarian, you're not likely to find a conventional entrée, but you can load up on veggie side dishes and maybe one of those yummy shakes. It's worth it. If you're in Butler, don't miss this tasty landmark.

Shamrock Inn
$ • 917 Western Ave., Pittsburgh
• (412) 231-2468

Shamrock Inn is an unpretentious restaurant on the North Side, near Three Rivers Stadium. You'll find a solid selection of sandwiches, as well as entrees and a few dinner salads. The salad bar is a particularly popular feature. You can enjoy the lounge and choose from a limited wine list. Reservations are accepted; you

might want to consider them, as Shamrock Inn typically draws large crowds. The restaurant offers banquet facilities for up to 200. Shamrock Inn serves breakfast, lunch, and dinner Monday through Friday. Only the lounge is open on weekends.

Silky's Crow's Nest
$$ • 19th St. and River Rd., Sharpsburg
• (412) 782-3701

When you dine at Silky's, the Allegheny River will be your cheerful companion. The restaurant takes full advantage of its riverfront location by offering a nautical decor, outdoor dining with a view of the river and the dam at Highland Park, and bands performing on a barge in the river each weekend throughout the warm weather months. (Sorry, there's no food available on the barge.)

The lunch and dinner menus offer primarily lighter fare as well as daily specials, but you will find such dinner entrees as Shrimp scampi, filet mignon, and pan-fried Maryland crab cakes. You'll enjoy a full-service bar with a broad selection of beers as well as a limited wine list. The restaurant offers banquet facilities for up to 150 people. It accepts reservations for parties of six or more.

Silky's is a few miles north of Downtown. It's open Tuesday through Friday in the summer, Tuesday through Saturday at other times.

Springdale Restaurant
$, no credit cards
• Pa. Rt. 66,
New Bethlehem
• (814) 275-1914

Springdale Restaurant is in Armstrong County just south of the Clarion County line. It's popular locally for its hot sausage breakfast and homemade soups and pies. Most dinners are priced under $8, so you won't beat the price. Springdale offers banquet facilities for up to 30 people. It does not serve alcohol, and it has no designated smoking and nonsmoking sections. The restaurant doesn't accept reservations.

INSIDERS' TIP

If you spot unsanitary conditions at an Allegheny County restaurant, call the county health department, (412) 687-ACHD. They pledge to investigate.

Tata's Family Restaurant
$$ • 5 Lyn-Mar Plaza, Lyndora
• (724) 287-7359

Since 1971, the Milasincic family has operated Tata's—you pronounce it TUH Tuh's, by the way—and it has the feel of an old-time family restaurant. Located just outside the City of Butler, Tata's offers daily lunch and dinner specials; all entrees include visits to the food bar, a buffet of salads and hot foods. You'll also find specially priced seniors' and children's menus. Reservations aren't required, but Tata's will accept them for larger parties. The restaurant offers banquet facilities for up to 110 people. Entrees are priced at the lower end of $$. Smoking is not permitted in the restaurant.

W. Ricks Taproom & Grill
$-$$ • 269 Meridian Rd., Meridian
• (724) 482-2970

Located just outside the City of Butler, W. Ricks offers a diverse menu that includes steak, seafood, and lamb selections regularly; prime rib is available after 4 PM on Wednesdays, Fridays, and Saturdays. You'll find daily lunch and dinner specials and a children's menu. W. Ricks offers a full-service bar and a wine list. Reservations are accepted but not required.

Asian

Mandarin Gourmet
$$$ • 4812 McKnight Rd., North Hills
• (412) 366-9111

Mandarin Gourmet serves lunch and dinner daily, including a buffet for each. You'll find a broad selection of pork, beef, poultry, seafood, and pasta items as well as vegetarian selections. Check out the "Chef's Suggestions" section for a number of interesting combinations, such as sizzling two delicacies, featuring beef and scallops, and dragon and phoenix, with lobster and General Tso's chicken. Hot and spicy items are marked with a red star. Mandarin Gourmet offers a full-service bar, and it accepts reservations. If you're Downtown, try Mandarin Gourmet's sister restaurant on Wood Street.

Sichuan House
$$ • 1900 Murray Ave., Pittsburgh
• (412) 422-2700
1717 Cochran Rd., Mt. Lebanon
• (412) 563-5252

If you like broad menu variety, you'll love Sichuan House, which features 175 distinct entrees at both of its locations—in the city's Squirrel Hill neighborhood, in the South Hills, only a few miles from Downtown. Beef, seafood, chicken, pork—all are well represented at Sichuan House, which serves both lunch and dinner. Among diners' favorites here are shrimp with snow peas; stuffed bean curd; pan-fried

Cantonese noodles with seafood; and leeks with smoked ham, Taiwanese style.

The menu clearly highlights "hot and spicy" items in red, so you'll always know what's in store for you. Sichuan House offers a small selection of "lean" entrees and free delivery, within a limited service area for take-out selections. The restaurants accept reservations for parties of five or more.

When you want to enjoy the food at Sichuan House at a slightly reduced rate, try their "Family Dinner." It features a flat rate for each member of your party, no matter what entree each selects. It's a great way to work your way through that menu.

Tai Pei Chinese Restaurant
$$-$$$ • 1124 Freeport Rd., Fox Chapel
• (412) 781-4131
5528 Walnut St., Pittsburgh
• (412) 683-2332

When you choose Tai Pei for lunch or dinner, you can select from a limited wine list or enjoy the full-service bar. The extensive menu offers plenty of beef, lamb, chicken, pork, and seafood selections, ranging from such traditional favorites as General Tso's chicken (the General's shrimp is available as well) and Peking duck to more daring entrees, such as crispy prawn, Szechuan style. You'll know if you're ordering a "hot and spicy" selection—these are highlighted in red on the menu.

Tai Pei offers a limited selection of "Dieter Gourmet" entrees as well as specially priced family dinners; entree selection for family dinners is limited. The restaurant accepts major credit cards and reservations for lunch and dinner, and provides free lunch delivery for take-out orders. The Fox Chapel location is about 10 miles north of Pittsburgh and only 1 mile south of Sichuan House, while you'll find its sister restaurant in Pittsburgh's Shadyside neighborhood. Entrees are priced at the lower end of $$$.

German

Max's Allegheny Tavern
$-$$ • 537 Suismon St., Pittsburgh
• (412) 231-1899

If it's sausages, schnitzel, and other German delights you hunger for, you'll find them at Max's Allegheny Tavern on the city's Northside. The restaurant offers daily lunch and dinner specials. If you can't settle on just one German entree, try Max's Sampler Platter—you'll get three entrees with your platter. The restaurant also offers beef and seafood selections prepared with a German touch. You'll find a full-service bar and a wine list, as well as banquet facilities for up to 80 people. Max's accepts reservations for parties of five or more. It's open daily for lunch and dinner and features brunch each Sunday.

Penn Brewery Restaurant
$$ • Troy Hill Rd. and Vinial St., Pittsburgh • (412) 237-9402
• www.pennbrew.com

Gemutlich! That's how you'll describe Penn Brewery after you visit this bright, informal restaurant on Pittsburgh's Northside. Tom and Mary Beth Pastorius operate both the restaurant and the adjoining microbrewery, which produces Penn Pilsner and a variety of other beers. There's more than a touch of authenticity here, as Tom Pastorius traces his lineage to Franz Daniel Pastorius, who is credited with establishing the first German settlement in America in 1683.

The menu features such German fare as schnitzel, sauerbraten, schweinebra-ten, and potato pancakes, as well as dinner salads and beef, chicken, and seafood entrees. You'll find lunch and dinner specials, a full bar, a limited wine list, and banquet facilities for up to 200 on Sunday, up to 100 on other days. If you're planning to hold a birthday party here, you can bring in your own cake, but be sure to ask about the restaurant's "cutting fee," which applies even if the staff doesn't actually cut the cake; this cost can be on the prohibitive side.

You'll be entertained on Wednesday evenings by a strolling accordion player, on Friday and Saturday evenings by a live band. Special events also are fun here. These range from Oktoberfest and Caribbean Night to the annual Pennsylvania Microbrewery Fest, when patrons can sample the wares of more than 30 brewers. But for Oktoberfest, these events are irregularly scheduled, so it's best to call for details about these special events.

The restaurant accepts reservations for parties of eight or more. Penn Brewery serves lunch and dinner Monday through Saturday.

Irish

Blarney Stone Restaurant and Catering Service
$$$ • 30 Grant Ave, Etna
• (412) 781-1666

When Proprietor Tom O'Donoghue came to Pittsburgh from County Kerry in 1974, he brought a piece of the "oulde sod" with him.

It's preserved in a glass-topped square on Blarney Stone's ceramic floor. When you enter Blarney Stone, you have the opportunity to set foot on Irish soil.

Be that as it may, the good folks at Blarney Stone asked us to advise you that they serve American as well as Irish dishes. Consider yourself advised. You'll find such Ireland-inspired selections as County Cork Salad, Shannon Chef Salad, and Irish smoked salmon, as well as American entrees that include Maryland crab cakes, prime rib, duck breast, and lamb chops. The restaurant serves dinner Tuesday through Sunday, lunch Tuesday through Friday, and a Sunday brunch. It's closed on Mondays. Blarney Stone offers a full-service bar, a wine list, and banquet facilities for up to 500 people—it's a popular spot for corporate functions. Reservations are accepted. Smoking and nonsmoking sections are designated for lunch, but the dining room is nonsmoking for dinner.

It's in the area of entertainment that Blarney Stone shows its Irish. It celebrates St. Patrick's Day with a week of lunch and dinner shows as well as an Irish buffet. During November, it hosts Irish singing groups. Several times each month, Blarney Stone presents a musical revue called *The Flavor of Pittsburgh* accompanied by an "ethic buffet" featuring foods of various nationalities. And there's swing dancing on Fridays.

Italian

Bravo! Italian Kitchen
$$ • 4976 McKnight Rd., Ross
• (412) 366-3556

This is a family restaurant that understands families, passing out crayons, coloring books, and pizza dough to each youngster who visits. While your kids are occupied with those pursuits, you get a chance to enjoy the signature Pasta Bravo, rigatoni with wood-grilled chicken and button mushrooms in a roasted red pepper sauce. Chicken scalopini romano also is popular here. Located in the North Hills, Bravo! serves lunch and dinner daily. It offers a full-service bar and a wine list. Reservations are not accepted.

Falsetti's Villa
$$, no credit cards • Pa. Rt. 128, North Buffalo • (724) 763-2266

This Armstrong County restaurant specializes in Italian food and seafood selections. Among the most popular items are the Italian platter, which includes spaghetti, lasagna, rigatoni, ravioli and a meatball, and scrod Villa. The restaurant offers a full-service bar and a wine list. Reservations are accepted Sunday through Thursday. Located near the county seat of Kittanning, Falsetti's Vila serves lunch and dinner daily.

Mama Rosa's Restaurant & Lounge
$-$$ • 263 Old Plank Rd., Butler
• (724) 287-7315

Yes, Virginia, there is a Mama Rosa—Mama Rosa Fusca, who founded this restaurant with her family. Mama Rosa no longer is active in the business, but she still drops in to watch as the staff prepares the hand-made pasta that is the restaurant's signature. In addition to pasta, you can select from steak, seafood, chicken, and veal dishes. The restaurant offers daily lunch and dinner specials as well as a line list. Mama Rosa's offers catering services as well as banquet facilities for up to 50 people.

Michael's Lake Arthur Restaurant & Motel
$-$$ • 970 New Castle Rd., Butler
• (724) 865-9838

Michael's sits on U.S. Route 422, about 7 miles from Moraine State Park. If you've enjoyed an active day at Moraine, you'll also enjoy repairing to Michael's to sample the rock shrimp linguini, chicken parmigiana, and barbecued ribs. Michael's serves lunch and dinner, offers a full-service bar and wine list, and can accommodate up to 65 people in its banquet facilities. Reservations are available. The number of rooms at the motel is limited.

Montemurro's
$$-$$$ 1822 Main St., Sharpsburg
• (412) 781-6800

Montemurro's has been an institution in Pittsburgh since the 1960s, when it operated in the city's Morningside neighborhood. It's now located just across the Allegheny River from Morningside in the northern suburb of Sharpsburg, only a few miles north of Downtown, but the quality food and service remain the same.

You'll find a broad selection of seafood, headed by the Montemurro Spots, which are prepared English style. The menu also features pasta, veal, and beef selections as well as several entrees for vegetarians. If you're looking for something light and tasty, try the French-fried provolone—it's been a fixture of the menu since 1964. The chef also offers daily dinner specials that are strong on seafood, including selections such as a broiled seafood sampler and broiled red salmon with sauteed leeks and tomatoes. The restaurant's sauces, soups, and dressings are available for take-out.

Montemurro's features a full-service bar and an extensive wine list; selections range from a single glass for as little as $4 up to a $119 bottle of Dom Perignon. Banquet facilities can accommodate up to 400. For a special treat, try Montemurro's dinner theater, which has featured such musical and comedy acts as Little Anthony and Pat Cooper. Shows are offered about once a month, except for a summer hiatus, and are priced separately from dinner. Montemurro's serves lunch and dinner and accepts reservations for each.

Natili Restaurant & Lounge
$$ • 104 W. Wayne St., Butler
• (724) 287-5033

Natili Restaurant & Lounge is a familiar sight at the corner of Wayne and Main in downtown Butler; it's been operated continuously by the same family since 1939. It features what owner Vince Tavolario describes as traditional dishes from the Abruzzi region of Italy, including many selections based on Natili's homemade pasta. The restaurant, which is closed on Sundays, offers lunch and dinner specials as well as a full-service bar and wine list. Reservations are accepted. The restau-rant's banquet facilities can accommodate up to 75 people.

Live bands, fronted by such noted Pittsburgh performers as trombonist Harold Betters, are featured each Friday and Saturday evening. Twice each month, a guest pianist sits in. It's none other than Vince Tavolario, who dazzles his dinner guests with an eclectic repertoire that features jazz, rock, and standards. Tavolario and his family also operate the nearby Natili-North Restaurant & Carry Out.

Serventi's

$-$$ • 438 S. Chestnut St., Butler
• (724) 287-4474

Serventi's is an institution in downtown Butler—it's been serving its popular Italian-American fare there since 1973. You'll find a broad selection of steak, seafood, chicken, and veal dishes, as well as daily lunch and dinner specials. Serventi's offers a full-service bar, a wine list, and banquet facilities for up to 30 people. Reservations are accepted but not required.

Mexican

Mad Mex

$-$$ • 7905 McKnight Rd., Ross
• (412) 366-5656
370 Atwood St., Pittsburgh
• (412) 681-5656

You'll find Mad Mex in both the North Hills and near the University of Pittsburgh campus in Oakland. We're not sure what Mex is mad about—it's certainly not the menu, which is varied and entertaining. You'll find a broad selection of dishes that the restaurants consider "California-Mexican." These include such interesting variations as Heavy Duty Judy's Curry Chicken Burrito, with marinated chicken, white rice, pineapple, and raisins topped with a curry sauce, and grilled chicken chick pea chili burrito, packing a lot of tastes into one burrito. The restaurants offer a generous selection of microbrews as well as "Big Ass Margaritas," which probably don't require further explanation, and happy hour specials. Each location serves lunch and dinner daily, and the Atwood Street restaurant is open until 2 AM each day. Reservations are not accepted.

This is a fun place with good food, but take it from an Insider—don't expect a quiet rendezvous here. Mad Mex is for an evening when you feel like good background music and loud conversation.

East

American

Baldonieri's Mill Creek Restaurant

$$ • Springer Rd., Ligonier
• (724) 238-3636

You'll dine in style here in a restored 18th century barn furnished in wormy chestnut and boasting a working fireplace and a 2½-story cathedral ceiling. The diverse menu is particularly strong on seafood selections, such as lobster ravioli and Po River catfish. Choucroute, a traditional Alsacian dish featuring braised pork loin, sausage, and sauerkraut, also is popular. Reservations are accepted. Baldonieri's offers a full-service bar, a wine list, and banquet facilities for up to 350 in the barn's loft. That's also the scene of entertainment—acoustic guitarists on Saturday nights. Baldonieri's serves dinner only Wednesday through Sunday. It's closed on Mondays and Tuesdays.

Baum Vivant

$$-$$$ • 5102 Baum Blvd., Pittsburgh
• (412) 682-2620

At this unobtrusive Shadyside restaurant, owners Toni and Becky Pais have created an unusual and compelling menu that blends elements of French, Northern Italian, and Portuguese cuisine—often in the same entrees. That approach is so innovative that Baum Vivant captured *Pittsburgh Magazine's* Blue Ribbon Award as Pittsburgh's best restaurant for six consecutive years. Don't miss this place if you're making a tour of Pittsburgh's finest dining spots.

The menu changes up to eight times each year, but entrees typically include such items as tiger shrimp Mediterranean; wild boar medallions with braised white cabbage in a riesling sauce; a medley of shrimp, lobster, scallops, clams, and mussels with Isreali couscous; and caribou tenderloin with figs in a porto wine sauce. Appetizers include ostrich as well as tenderloin of kangaroo with kiwi sauce, and you can choose from four types of caviar. Baum Vivant offers a full-service bar and a wine list with roughly 150 selections. Smoking is permitted at the bar only. The restaurant can accommodate banquets for up to 20 people. It serves dinner only Monday through Saturday, and is closed on Sundays. Reservations are highly suggested.

The Bistro

$$$ • 216 W. Loyalhanna St., Ligonier
• (724) 238-9545

You'll find The Bistro at the Ramada Inn Historic Ligonier. Specialties include crabcakes, pasta dishes, grilled steak, salads, and sandwiches. You also can dine more informally at Cappy's Deli, which features the same wine list and much of the same menu as The Bistro.

The Bistro serves breakfast, lunch, and dinner—including a buffet—each day but Sunday. Brunch is offered on Sundays. The Bistro does

Special occasions call for white tablecloths and fine crystal.

wiches, salads, and burgers. The Reuben sandwich, which is topped with cole slaw, is particularly popular, as is The Yinz Burger, lovingly named for that peculiar Pittsburgh term and highlighted with barbecue sauce procured from another Pittsburgh favorite, Iron City Beer. (For a wistful explanation of the term "yinz," see our Area Overview chapter.) Dinner entrees are available as well. C. J. Barney's serves lunch and dinner daily. The restaurant provides a full-service bar and banquet facilities for up to 250 people.

not designate smoking or nonsmoking sections. The hotel offers banquet facilities for up to 80 people. The restaurant offers occasional special events, such as theater nights; these are irregularly scheduled, so you'll need to call for details. The Bistro is closed from 1:30 to 4:30 PM daily.

Buffalo Blues
$$-$$$ • 216 S. Highland Ave., Pittsburgh
• (412) 362-5837

This Shadyside restaurant specializes in wings, barbecued foods, and blues. The wings come topped with your choice of 11 different sauces, ranging from "Who Do Voodoo" to "Hotter' an Hell." The barbecue menu includes ribs, chicken, and seafood, and you can pick from three different sauces. Fresh fish, jambalaya, and fajitas round out the menu. Buffalo Blues offers a full-service bar and a limited wine list. It offers both catering services and banquet facilities for up to 50 people.

On Friday and Saturday evenings, you'll enjoy the restaurant's signature live blues performances. There's often a cover charge for national acts but none for local groups. By the way, the restaurant's phone number is easy to remember—36 BLUES. Again, the most expensive entrees are priced at the lower end of $$$.

C.J. Barney's
$ • 3909 Forbes Ave., Pittsburgh
• (412) 621-2149

C.J. Barney's has been a fixture on the University of Pittsburgh campus for more than three decades, serving primarily lighter fare—sand-

The Candlelight Dining Room
$$$ • 1001 Village Dr., Greensburg
• (724) 834-5300

You'll find The Candlelight Dining Room at Mountain View Inn, a charming hotel described in our Accommodations chapter. You don't have to be a hotel guest, however, to enjoy the dining room. It's open 361 days a year, closing only for major holidays, and serves breakfast, lunch, and dinner. The breakfast menu is especially large and compelling, featuring such unusual selections as Laurel Mountain Toast—oatmeal bread dipped in egg, grilled and topped with honey maple syrup, raisins, pecans, and orange marmalade—and Eggs Chestnut Ridge, two eggs on zucchini cakes topped with a roasted garlic cheese sauce.

The dinner menu is seasonal. Depending on the season, you'll find such entrees as ostrich medallions with mango and raspberry puree, and grilled raspberry chicken. The menu offers a generous selection of seafood and homemade desserts. If you're here on Sunday, you may opt for a family-style dinner. The restaurant offers an extensive wine list and a tavern with an attractive selection of single-malt Scotch whiskeys. Reservations are recommended for lunch and dinner. Smoking is permitted only in the tavern. The dining room closes daily from 2 to 5 PM, but you're welcome to eat in the tavern during those hours. The Candlelight Dining Room offers banquet facilities for up to 500 people. You'll find Mountain View Inn about 1 mile north of U.S. Route 30.

Cappy's
$ • 5431 Walnut St., Pittsburgh
• (412) 621-1188

If you're trying to keep your diet free of fried foods but still love to eat out, try this Shadyside restaurant. Cappy's does not fry any of its foods, preparing them instead on the grill or in a high-heat convection oven. The restaurant offers a diverse selection of burgers, sandwiches, and salads. Cappy's features a full-service bar but does not designate smoking and nonsmoking sections. Reservations are not accepted. Cappy's serves lunch and dinner daily, breakfast on Saturday and Sunday. Late breakfasts are available on weekdays.

The Carnegie Café
$ • 4400 Forbes Ave., Pittsburgh
• (412) 622-3225

For one of the most engaging and civilized dining experiences in town, try The Carnegie Cafe, a feature of The Carnegie in Oakland. The cafe serves lunch only, and you don't have to pay admission to the museum to dine here. The cafe specializes in sandwiches and salads, including roasted vegetable Napoleon salad and portabella mushroom panini. You'll find a bar as well as wine and beer lists. You'll enjoy the view of the museum's fountains, a series of geyser-like water jets. In fair weather, you can dine al fresco in the Fountain Court. (Be warned that the view outclasses the food; however, dining here is still worth doing.)

When The Carnegie Theater is staging performances, the cafe often hosts themed dinners for theater patrons. It can entertain up to 160 patrons at those dinners, and it's also available for wine-tasting parties and sponsored or corporate conferences. Lunch reservations are recommended. The entire cafe, including the Fountain Court, is nonsmoking. The Carnegie Cafe serves lunch Tuesday through Saturday, but it does open on Mondays when the Museum is open. It's best to call to determine the Monday schedule.

Carson St. Deli
$, no credit cards • 17th and E. Carson Sts., Pittsburgh • (412) 381-5335

This is a popular South Side spot for apres-performance eats. Not only does the deli offer a broad selection of sandwiches (including vegetarian selections), soups, salads, and desserts, but it also stays open until 3 AM on summer Fridays and Saturdays. Many musicians repair here after their South Side gigs—you can compare notes with them as you enjoy the sidewalk café tables. On occasion, the musicians perform impromptu concerts here, but you

never can be sure when that might happen. It's all part of the ambiance that helped Carson St. win the 1997 Best Deli in Pittsburgh award from *In Pittsburgh.*

The deli does not designate smoking and nonsmoking sections, and it does not serve alcohol. Reservations aren't accepted, needless to say. Carson St. Provides catering and delivery services. It's open daily but closes at 6 PM on Sundays.

Chelsea Grille
$-$$$ • 519 Allegheny Ave., Oakmont
• (412) 828-0570

Chelsea Grille is part of Oakmont's one-two culinary punch operated by brothers Danny and Tommy Monaco. It serves dinner daily, lunch Monday through Saturday. The menu covers a lot of ground, offering beef, seafood, and chicken entrees, fajitas, barbecued ribs, pasta and Italian selections, and dinner salads. Chelsea Grille offers a full-service bar, a wine list, and facilities that accommodate up to 60 people for banquets. Reservations are accepted. The most expensive entrees are priced at the lower end of $$$.

Dunning's Grill
$ • 1100 S. Braddock Ave., Swissvale
• (412) 243-3900

Here's a pleasant neighborhood restaurant that's popular with those who live and work in Pittsburgh's eastern suburbs. Burgers, pasta, and grilled chicken salad are among the hottest sellers. Don't let the salads fool you. They're served over a bed of mixed greens and French fries; you'll want to bring a hearty appetite when you order one. Dunning's offers a full-service bar and banquet facilities, available only on Sundays, for up to 55 people. The restaurant does not accept reservations. Dunning's serves lunch and dinner Monday through Saturday; it's closed on Sundays except for private parties.

The Elbow Room
$-$$ • 5744½ Ellsworth Ave., Pittsburgh
• (412) 441-5222

The Elbow Room has been a fixture in the city's Shadyside neighborhood for more than 40 years, offering a diverse lunch and dinner menu that's particularly strong on salads. Steak salads may be the most popular selections, but you'll also find portabella, grilled eggplant, grilled chicken, spinach, and many other dinner salads. You also may choose from an extensive sandwich selection and a more limited entree list.

The restaurant offers a Sunday brunch, a full-service bar, and a limited wine list. It accepts reservations and provides banquet facilities for up to

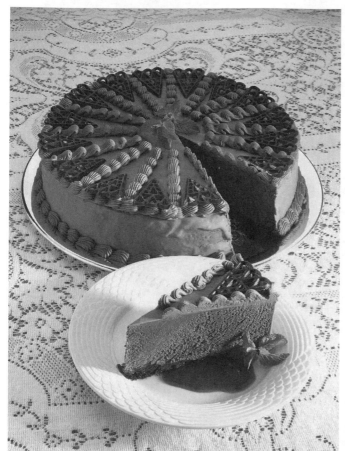

Make sure you save room for dessert!

rack of lamb as well as beef and seafood selections. Chef Gary Klinefelter is an attentive host, preparing salad dressings and other foods from scratch. Reservations are suggested. The dining room serves dinner daily. Alcohol is not served, but you should feel free to BYOB. The dining room is closed on Mondays.

Gullifty's
$ • 1922 Murray Ave., Pittsburgh
• (412) 521-8222

Gullifty's has won *Pittsburgh Magazine's* award for the best desserts in town for the past 17 years! When you're ready to indulge your sweet tooth, you can sample the restaurant's peanut butter truffle pie, its macadamia truffle torte, or its chocolate intemperance. The piece de resistance is the "Killer Cookie," featuring a chocolate chip and walnut cookie topped with vanilla ice cream, bananas, chocolate syrup, and whipped cream. It's so loaded with taste that Gullifty's requires 15 minutes to prepare it.

The restaurant's menu features soups, dinner salads, sandwiches, burgers, Mexican fare, pasta, and a limited entree list. Gullifty's offers a significant number of meatless dishes; these are so noted on the menu. Among the most popular sandwiches is Gullifty's Meshugna, grilled corned beef served open face with cole slaw and Russian dressing on two potato pancakes. Gullifty's offers a full-service bar, a limited wine and beer list, and banquet facilities for up to 40 people. It does not accept reservations. It serves lunch and dinner daily as well as Saturday and Sunday brunches. You'll find Gullifty's in the center of the Squirrel Hill business district.

Hemingway's Cafe
$ • 3911 Forbes Ave., Pittsburgh
• (412) 621-4100

The spirit of Papa Hemingway comes alive each Tuesday evening when this restaurant on the University of Pittsburgh campus hosts po-

100 people. In fair weather, you'll enjoy dining on the patio, which is especially nice as it boasts a large tree in the center and is surrounded by vine-covered garden walls. The Elbow Room is next door to Club Havana, which features Latin dance classes and other evening entertainment, so you can make a night of it at these side-by-side establishments. For more on Club Havana, see our Nightlife chapter.

Fireside Dining Room at Foggy Mountain Lodge
$$$ • Old Distillery Rd., Stahlstown
• (724) 593-5050

In 1998, proprietors Rena and Jeff Stumpf realized their dream of opening a rustic country inn and a companion restaurant in the Laurel Highlands. For more about the inn, turn to our Bed and Breakfast and Country Inns chapter. For dining, you'll enjoy the diverse menu, which features the popular roast New Zealand etry readings. Some readers are scheduled, while other Tuesdays feature open sessions. If the hunger for literature makes you literally hungry, you can select from a varied menu including sandwiches; salads; pasta dishes; and some poultry, seafood, and beef dishes. Hemingway's offers a full-service bar, wine and beer lists, and banquet facilities for up to 60 people. The cafe serves lunch and dinner daily, and it accepts reservations. When classes are in session, Hemingway's often features easy rock bands on Saturday nights. Call to check.

Hoffstot's Cafe Monaco Restaurant & Lounge
$$$ • 533 Allegheny Ave., Oakmont • (412) 828-8555

Hoffstot's is a pleasant restaurant near the Allegheny River and the Hulton Bridge. Along with the neighboring Chelsea Grille—the restaurants are operated by brothers Danny and Tony Monaco—it gives Oakmont an attractive dining tandem. Hoffstot's offers a diverse menu with beef, seafood, veal, and Italian selections, as well as dinner salads. Steaks are popular, as is the shrimp Monaco—shrimp and jumbo lump crab meat baked in butter, garlic, lemon, white wine, and oregano—and sea scallops Palermo. You'll find a lounge and a wine list that includes 11 "reserve" or premier wines. Hoffstot's offers weekday banquet facilities for up to 60 people. It serves lunch and dinner daily; make it a late lunch on Sundays, when the restaurant opens at 1 PM. Reservations are accepted.

Jaden's
$ • 4727 William Penn Hwy., Monroeville • (412) 373-8575

Jaden's is a family restaurant that's open daily for breakfast, lunch, and dinner, with daily specials offered for each meal. If you're hankering for a hearty breakfast, try Jaden's Ultimate, featuring two hot cakes topped with your choice of strawberries, blueberries, or cherries; two eggs; potatoes; and a side of bacon, sausage, or ham. Dinner entrees include beef, chicken, pastas, and seafood selections. Save room for a slice of homemade pie or the waffle sundae. As a family restaurant, Jaden's doesn't serve alcohol.

Jimmie Monzo's Blue Angels Restaurant & Lounge
$$$ • 200 Pleasant Unity Rd., Latrobe • (724) 539-3980

Jimme Monzo's is located on the third floor of the Arnold Palmer Regional Airport main terminal; when you dine here, you'll get up close and personal with arriving and departing planes. The restaurant serves breakfast, lunch, and dinner daily as well as Sunday brunch, offering an eclectic menu that features beef, chicken, veal, seafood, and pasta selections. Nightly specials include spaghetti (Monday), prime rib (Thursday), and an Italian surf and turf buffet (Friday). Jimmie Monzo's offers a small bar and a wine list. Reservations are recommended for parties of six or more. Smoking is permitted at the bar only. Entrees are priced at the lower end of $$$.

John Harvard's Brew House
$-$$ • 3466 William Penn Hwy., Wilkins • (412) 824-9440

John Harvard's serves lunch and dinner daily. Among the most popular entrees are chicken pot pie, meatloaf, and fish and chips, and you'll also find beef, seafood, and pasta entrees as well as daily specials. You'll find a full-service bar and a wine list; as befitting a brew house, John Harvard's also offers an extensive selection of ales and lagers. Other features include a humidor and cigar list and a retail area for merchandise imprinted with John Harvard's logo. The restaurant offers banquet facilities for up to 35 people. Reservations are recommended for weekends for eight people or more, accepted at all times. John Harvard's is located on U.S. Business Route 22.

Kazansky's Restaurant and Delicatessen
$ • 2201 Murray Ave., Pittsburgh • (412) 521-4555

Kazansky's has been pleasing Squirrel Hill patrons for decades. It features Jewish-style specialties, including homemade soups, dinner salads, a limited entree list, and a broad selection of sandwiches. These include the Yoy (pronounced oi-ee), the Double Yoy, and the Triple Yoy, all built around corned beef and based on a characteristic exclamation of Pittsburgh Steelers commentator Myron Cope, as in "Another penalty? Yoy." You'll also find The Marv Albert, comprised of beef tongue and Swiss cheese on pumpernickel. "Sink your teeth into this one," the menu advises. Hey, we don't endorse 'em, we just report 'em.

Kazansky's offers a retail section and a takeout counter, which is one of the region's busiest places on Christmas Eve, when patrons line up to purchase meat and dairy trays for their guests. Kazansky's serves beer but no other alcohol, and it does not accept reservations. You won't find designated smoking and nonsmoking sections. Kazansky's serves breakfast, lunch, and dinner daily.

The Lamplighter Restaurant
$ • 330 U.S. Rt. 22, Delmont
• (724) 468-4545

For more than 40 years, The Lamplighter has been a hub for dining and entertainment in Westmoreland County. In fact, the restaurant offers so many activities and specials—such as a daily early bird menu and dance bands each Saturday—that you're advised to pick up your monthly activities calendar in the lobby. Prime rib and fresh seafood are the menu headliners, and you'll also enjoy the Monday-to-Friday lunch buffet and the Sunday breakfast and dinner buffets. The Lamplighter offers a lounge, a wine list, and banquet facilities for up to 400 people. Reservations are suggested. The Lamplighter serves breakfast, lunch, and dinner daily.

Lesley's Restaurant
$$$ • 10 Mountain View Rd., Donegal
• (724) 593-6349, (800) 392-7773

Lesley's offers intimate dining in a restored chestnut barn nestled in the foothills of the Laurel Highlands at Mountain View Country Inn. Dining is leisurely and memorable here, as you'll enjoy such entrees as scallop pasta with roasted peppers and Beef Wellington. The menu changes weekly, but you can get a preview—as well as some of Lesley's most popular recipes and wine list—by visiting the restaurant's Web site, www.shol.com/mtviewbb. The site also will introduce you to the companion Lesley's Mountain View Country Inn. For more on that, see our Bed and Breakfasts chapter.

Lesley's offers a full-service bar and an extensive wine list. Smoking is permitted at the bar only. The restaurant serves dinner only from Wednesdays through Saturday, and reservations are suggested. You'll find the restaurant about 1 mile east of the Donegal exit of the Pennsylvania Turnpike.

Ligonier Country Inn
$-$$ • U.S. Rt. 30 E., Laughlintown
• (724) 238-3651

Located in eastern Westmoreland County, Ligonier Country Inn serves dinner Tuesday through Sunday, as well as a Sunday breakfast and a Sunday brunch buffet. It's closed on Mondays. The menu features beef, chicken, pasta, and seafood selections, as well as specials and a vegetarian feature of the day. You'll find a full-service bar, a wine list, and banquet facilities for up to 300 people. Reservations are recommended.

You can transform your trip here into a relaxing vacation by staying at the adjacent bed and breakfast inn, which shares the name Ligonier Country Inn. For more on that, see our Bed and Breakfasts chapter. Both the restaurant and the bed and breakfast are owned and operated by P.J. and Maggie Nied, so you can be assured of uniform service whether you're lodging or dining. There's an outdoor pool here, and the Nieds plan a busy summer schedule of pool parties featuring live music. Call them for details.

Ligonier Tavern
$-$$ • 137 W. Main St., Ligonier
• (724) 238-4831

This is a fun spot, where everyone seems to have a good time, whether they're dining indoors or alfresco on the front porch or balcony. Your enjoyment will increase when you discover that the tavern makes all its sauces and desserts from scratch. Popular menu items are the crab cakes and fresh mozzarella and tomato chicken. Make sure you save room for the signature Loyalhanna cheesecake—two layers of New York and chocolate cheesecake over an Oreo cookie crust and topped by fudge icing. Try it and you'll know why everybody's smiling.

The tavern offers a full-service bar and a wine list, as well as catering services and banquet facilities for up to 150 people. It recommends reservations on Fridays, Saturdays, and Sundays. Ligonier Tavern is open daily for lunch and dinner.

Moré Restaurant
$$-$$$ • 214 N. Craig St., Pittsburgh
• (412) 621-2700

Since 1971, this Oakland restaurant has been pleasing its patrons with a varied lunch and dinner menu that includes beef, seafood, chicken, veal, and pasta entrees; Virginia spots and shrimp scampi are among the most popular selections. Nor does the variety stop there, as Moré lists 16 appetizers and 10 desserts, ensuring that your dining experience here can be complete. The restaurant offers a full-service bar, an extensive wine list, and banquet facilities for up to 80 people. It serves lunch and dinner daily. Reservations are recommended. On Wednesday through Saturday evenings, feel free to sing along at the piano bar.

New York New York
$-$$ • 5801 Ellsworth Ave., Pittsburgh
• (412) 661-5600

New York New York is not especially near Pittsburgh's Cultural District, but the Broadway theater posters on the walls of this Shadyside restaurant will make you feel as if you're treading the boards. The menu is eclectic, featuring beef, pork, chicken, seafood, and pasta entrees. The restaurant offers a full-service bar, a wine list, and live piano entertainment Wednesday through Saturday evenings. Reservations are accepted, recommended for parties of eight or more. One of the most memorable features of New York New York is its upstairs patio, a colorful enclosed porch decked with flowers. The patio seats 100 diners—ask for it when the weather is right. New York New York is open daily for dinner only, and it also features Sunday brunch. While people of all walks of life patronize New York New York, it's a particularly great place to meet other gay and lesbian diners.

Original Hot Dog Shop
$, no credit cards • 3901 Forbes Ave., Pittsburgh • (412) 621-7388

When you consider the University of Pittsburgh, you may think of such wonders as the towering Cathedral of Learning or the Nationality Classrooms that celebrate the region's ethnic heritage. Ask alumni what they recall about their undergraduate days, however, and the landmark they're most likely to name is the "O," the affectionate nickletter for Original Hot Dog Shop. Since 1960, the O has been serving up hot dogs, burgers, wings, subs, and pizza. French fries are particularly popular here—the O goes through 40,000 pounds of them every 10 days. (Note: A small order of fries could fill a dinner plate, so don't dare order two unless you're dining with four or five people! Also note that you won't be eating heart healthy here.) You'll find a full-service bar and a broad selection of beers. The O serves lunch and dinner daily, staying open until 3:30 AM during the week and 5 AM on weekends. It does not accept reservations, of course. If you're looking for a leisurely candlelight repast with muted string music in the background, this is not the place for you. But if you want to experience the sights and cacophony of an urban college hang-out in motion, the O is a go.

Pamela's
$, no credit cards • 5527 Walnut St., Pittsburgh • (412) 683-1003
3703 Forbes Ave., Pittsburgh
• (412) 683-4066
5813 Forbes Ave., Pittsburgh
• (412) 422-9457

If you like your hotcakes stacked high and stuffed full, Pamela's is the place for you. Each of Pamela's three locations—Shadyside, Oakland, Squirrel Hill—specializes in breakfasts that are available in the afternoon as well. Pamela's offers banana walnut, strawberry, chocolate chip, and apple walnut hotcakes, a variety so tasty and appealing that *Pittsburgh Magazine* has selected them the best pancakes in town for five years. Breakfast fare also includes waffles, omelets, and French toast. For lunch, Pamela's offers sandwiches and salads. Pamela's does not serve alcohol, and it does not accept reservations. The restaurants are open daily for breakfast and lunch, and the Oakland location at 3703 Forbes Avenue serves dinner daily until 8 PM.

Peppermill Inn
$$$ • 4733 William Penn Hwy., Monroeville • (412) 372-9878

You won't find many restaurants with a separate lobster menu, but that's an attraction of Peppermill Inn. You can enjoy lobster tails, lobster Newberg, or lobster in a surf and turf combination. The eclectic menu also offers homemade pasta selections as well as beef, veal, chicken, and additional seafood entrees. It would be hard not to find something you like at the Peppermill. The restaurant offers a full-service bar, a wine list, catering services, and banquet facilities for up to 70 people. Reservations are recommended for weekends and accepted at all times. Peppermill Inn does not designate smoking and nonsmoking sections. It serves dinner daily, lunch from Monday through Saturday.

Pittsburgh Deli Co.
$ • 728 Copeland St., Pittsburgh
• (412) 682-DELI
• www.pghdeli.com

This bright, airy Shadyside deli serves lunch and dinner daily; you also can enjoy a late night bite, as the deli is open until 2 AM daily. You'll find gourmet sandwiches, Jewish-style foods, and homemade baked goods, and you can enjoy it all in the downstairs dining area or the bar area upstairs. Speaking of the bar, Pittsburgh Deli Co. offers a full array of drinks and roughly 100 varieties of beer. It provides catering services and can accommodate banquets of up to 100 people on site. Smoking is permitted in the second-floor bar area only. The deli features live jazz, rock, and acoustical bands on some Wednesday and Saturday evenings. The entertainment schedule is irregular, so it's best to call for details.

Prima Classe
**$$$$ • 325 McKinley Ave., Latrobe
• (724) 539-0500**

This small, elegant restaurant is set in a turn-of-the century railway dining car. That's fitting, since it's located at the still-active Latrobe Train Station, where Joseph DiSalvo and his father Gaetano have created a dining complex. The DiSalvos will make your dining experience here memorable. Joe himself will wait on you, while Gaetano—the executive chef for the complex—will prepare your food. The menu is aural, so you won't need your glasses here. It features such gourmet Italian entrees as veal stuffed with prosciutto and provolone and sauteed in a wine and mushroom sauce, and shellfish in a red bouillabaisse.

Prima Classe offers an extensive wine list. Reservations and proper attire are required. The restaurant is nonsmoking, but you can puff to your heart's content at the adjoining Joey D's Sala Da Fumo, a cigar salon that hosts several cigar-based special events each year and offers private lockers for members. Prima Classe serves only dinner, and only on Friday and Saturday evenings. For a visit to its sister restaurant, DiSalvo's Station Restaurant and Banquet Facilities, see the profiles of Italian restaurants in the East section.

The R&R Station Family Restaurant and Inn
**$ • 19 W. Main St., Mt. Pleasant
• (724) 547-7545**

While the Pennsylvania Railroad that once served the Mt. Pleasant railroad station is gone, the still-active Highlander steam train shuttles passengers the 7.9 miles between this station and Scottdale. All that railroad history is the inspiration for The R&R Station Family Restaurant and Inn, which includes both a restaurant and a 17-room hotel. For more about the hotel, see our Accommodations chapter.

The restaurant, furnished with rails, flashing lights, and other railway memorabilia, serves breakfast, lunch, and dinner daily, and it's open round the clock on weekends. You'll find daily specials for each meal. Particularly popular are such homemade desserts as Death By Chocolate, chocolate cake topped by chocolate ice cream, chocolate syrup, hot fudge, and chocolate whipped

cream. That can put a little kaboom in your caboose. Speaking of which, libations are served in The Caboose Lounge. Reservations are recommended. The restaurant does not designate smoking and nonsmoking sections. It offers banquet facilities for up to 50 people.

Ritter's Diner
**$, no credit cards • 5221 Baum Blvd.,
Pittsburgh • (412) 682-4852**

Most of the region's night owls know Ritter's—not only has it been a fixture since 1951, but it's also one of the few round-the-clock restaurants in the area, closing only on major holidays. In 1996, this Shadyside restaurant scored a double from *Pittsburgh Magazine,* winning both the "Best Breakfast (nonchain)" and "Best Late Night Bite" awards. The menu is diverse, offering entrees, salads, sandwiches, and daily lunch and dinner specials. Make sure you save room for the rice pudding, a specialty of the house. Ritter's does not serve liquor or accept reservations. It offers banquet facilities for up to 75 people. Don't expect to eat heart healthy here; just enjoy yourself at this quintessential diner.

River's Edge
**$$ • 4616 Allegheny River Blvd.,
Penn Hills • (412) 793-6167**

Since 1958, River's Edge has been serving patrons from its perch on a bluff above the Allegheny River. You'll enjoy a great view of the river when you dine at River's Edge, which serves dinner only Tuesday through Saturday. The menu features veal, seafood, and pasta selections as well as daily specials. The restaurant offers a wine list and a bar—the bar provides the best view of the river. It accepts reservations for parties of four or more, and it offers banquet facilities for up to 110 people. In the fall and winter months, River's Edge features live piano entertainment Thursday through Saturday. The restaurant does not designate smoking or nonsmoking sections.

The Road Toad
**$-$$ • U.S. Rt. 30 E., Ligonier
• (724) 539-7623**

The Road Toad is one of those places that

INSIDERS' TIP
Our region has been honored with a culinary term—"Pittsburgh rare." If you order your meat Pittsburgh rare, it will be charred on the outside, rare on the inside. The term probably dates to the region's days as the hub of steelmaking, but we like to think it refers to our people: crusty on the outside, tender on the inside.

RESTAURANTS

fairly hops with energy—diners indoors, diners outdoors, the Loyalhanna Creek rushing by just below the restaurant. The menu features beef, chicken, seafood, and pasta selections as well as a lengthy list of sandwiches and pitas. Outdoors at the Back Bay Grill, they'll grill just about anything you order. The Road Toad offers a full-service bar and accepts reservations for parties of eight or more. It can accommodate 50 people for indoor banquets, 150 for outdoor affairs. The restaurant offers occasional live music; it's best to call for details. When you call, remember that the phone number spells 539-TOAD. The Road Toad offers lunch and dinner Tuesday through Sunday.

Ruthie's Diner
$ • U.S. Rt. 30 E., Ligonier
• (724) 238-9930

If you're a diner fan, make sure you drop by Ruthie's for the homemade soups, pies, and apple dumplings. The fare is filling and economically priced. Ruthie's serves breakfast, lunch, and dinner daily, and it's open until midnight on Fridays and Saturdays. Ruthie's does not serve alcohol, and it does not accept credit cards. It accepts reservations Monday through Friday only.

Tivoli Restaurant
$$-$$$ • 419 Rodi Rd., Penn Hills
• (412) 243-9630

Rodi Road is a busy commercial thoroughfare that doesn't look like it could easily accommodate fine dining. That's just what you'll find, though, at Tivoli, which features a menu rich in seafood, veal, and homemade pasta selections. Veal roaise, prepared with artichokes, mushrooms, provolone, prosciutto, and sherry, is a popular entree, and you can order it in a combination with scrod. Sole belle meunierie also rates highly with Tivoli patrons. You can select from nine types of pasta—including whole wheat linguini—and top your pasta with your choice of 17 sauces. Tivoli offers a full-service bar and an extensive wine list as well as banquet facilities for up to 220 people. Reservations are suggested.

Tivoli serves dinner Tuesday through Sunday, lunch Tuesday through Friday. It's closed on Mondays. You can reach Rodi Road, in the eastern suburb of Penn Hills, from U.S. Business Route 22.

Union Grill
$-$$$ • 413 S. Craig St., Pittsburgh
• (412) 681-8620

South Craig Street is a happening venue in Oakland, situated between the campuses of the University of Pittsburgh and Carnegie Mellon University and drawing considerable traffic from each. Union Grill is one of the chief contributors to the bustle of activity, offering indoor and outdoor dining and a menu that's sure to please almost everyone. It offers such specialties as Bourbon Street Pasta, fresh vegetables and fettuccine tossed in a spicy Cajun sauce and flavored with a shot of Jim Beam bourbon, and calypso chicken, a chicken breast rubbed with Calypso spices and topped with peppers, mushrooms, onions, tomatoes, and mangoes.

The selections don't stop there. Union Grill offers seafood and salsa specials each evening, a "Build a Burger" feature, dinner salads, sandwiches, and vegetarian selections. For libations, you'll find a full-service bar and a wine list offering what the house calls "rock bottom prices." Union Grill serves lunch and dinner daily, and it also offers a late night menu each day. Reservations are accepted for parties of seven or more.

Vallozzi's
$-$$ • U.S. Rt. 30 E., Greensburg
• (724) 836-7663

Vallozzi's is a veritable oasis amid the arid shopping malls and heavy traffic that mark this section of U.S. Route 30. It's a warm and inviting restaurant—an Italian villa, the proprietors call it—that's been honored by Distinguished Restaurants of North America, The National Restaurant Association, and *Wine Spectator*. The menu has a distinct Italian flavor, with such entrees as cappelletti lobster, with spinach and portabella mushrooms in a buttery tomato sauce, and Salmon Vallozzi, grilled salmon with artichokes, tomatoes, scallions and portabella mushrooms, served in an asiago cream sauce over angel hair pasta.

The wine list offers 325 different selections, and you'll also find a lounge. Parties up to 16 will enjoy seating in the secluded Wine Cellar or the semiprivate Arbor Room. Reservations are recommended. Vallozzi's serves lunch and dinner Monday through Friday, dinner only on Saturdays. It's closed on Sundays. A few entrees are priced slightly higher than $$.

Caribbean

Donsvilles' Jamaica, Jamaica
$ • 6008 Broad St., Pittsburgh
• (412) 361-1631

Donsvilles' specializes in such Jamaican dishes as curry shrimp; curry goat; jerk chicken; and escovitch, a red- or yellow-tailed snapper

Le Mont Restaurant offers a stunning view of the Pittsburgh skyline.

Photo: Courtesy of Le Mont Restaurant

fried and sauteed with spicy peppers, vinegar, tomatoes, and onions. The menu is rich in Jamaican foods—make sure that's what you want, since you won't find any alternative selections. Donsvilles' accepts reservations. It does not serve alcohol or designate smoking and nonsmoking sections. The restaurant serves lunch and dinner Monday through Saturday, and it's closed on Sundays. You'll find Donsvilles' in Pittsburgh's East Liberty neighborhood near North Highland Avenue, one of the neighborhood's principal thoroughfares.

Chinese

China Palace
$$ • 5440 Walnut St., Pittsburgh
• (412) 687-7423
4059 William Penn Hwy., Monroeville
• (412) 373-7423
409 Broad St., Sewickley
• (412) 749-7423

China Palace offers some of the best Chinese food in the area, with the nicest ambiance. China Palace offers a compelling variety of entrees, including salmon sizzler; orange-flavored beef; and Three's Company, which combines lemon chicken, General Tso's Chicken, and chicken with vegetables. You'll find a broad variety of seafood, beef, chicken, and pork selec-

tions, with hot and spicy items noted on the menu. China Palace offers a bar and a wine list, but it does not accept reservations. It serves dinner daily, lunch Monday through Saturday, and is open on Sundays only for holidays. Note that the phone number of each restaurant sports the same last four digits, which spell the word RICE.

Evergreen Chinese Restaurant
$ • 3500 William Penn Hwy., Wilkins
• (412) 825-8088

Evergreen offers a varied menu that features beef, chicken, pork, and seafood selections, but the most popular item here is the daily lunch and dinner buffet. The buffet features nearly 40 items, including about one dozen entrees. Evergreen offers a special buffet price for children, and senior citizens receive a discount on any order. The restaurant accepts reservations, and it offers banquet facilities for up to 70 people. It does not serve alcohol. Evergreen is located about 2 miles from Exit 6 of the Pennsylvania Turnpike on U.S. Business Route 22, a commercial corridor that spans Wilkins Township and Monroeville.

The House of Chiang
$-$$ • 120 McKee Pl., Pittsburgh
• (412) 681-5169

The House of Chiang, located near the western edge of the University of Pittsburgh campus, serves lunch and dinner daily. It specializes in Cantonese and Szechuan fare, including such favorites as moo goo gai pan over rice and cashew chicken. The diverse menu offers an uncommon number of lunch specials, highlighted by 20 combination plates. Although you won't find a bar here, the wait staff will serve alcohol you've brought yourself. Reservations are not accepted.

Jade Garden
$-$$ • 4450 William Penn Hwy., Murrysville • (724) 733-2281

If you like to share plates with your dining companions, try Jade Garden's "Happy Family Dinners." They're specially priced, and you can select from 13 entrees. The menu also offers beef, lamp, pork, chicken, vegetarian, and seafood selections. General Tso's chicken is a popular pick, as is seafood in bird's

Traditional meets modern at Pittsburgh's Italian eateries.

nest, which features sauteed shrimp, scallops and lobster with Chinese vegetables over a crispy base. The restaurant offers a full-service bar and a wine list, and it can accommodate banquets of up to 40 people. Reservations for parties of five or more are accepted. You'll find Jade Garden on U.S. 22 in Westmoreland County, just east of the Allegheny County line.

Jimmy Tsang's Chinese Restaurant
$$-$$$ • 5700 Centre Ave., Pittsburgh • (412) 661-4226

Jimmy Tsang's offers selections representing the four major Chinese styles—Mandarin, Hunan and Szechuan, Shanghai, and Cantonese. Popular features of the lunch and dinner menu include shrimp with lobster sauce; Manchurian noodles; and a whole fish, which might be red snapper or sea bass. If you order that whole fish, the folks in the kitchen will need about 40 minutes to prepare it. The restaurant in Pittsburgh's Shadyside neighborhood

also offers an extensive roster of vegetarian entrees, combination dinners for up to six people, daily lunch specials, and a limited early bird menu with specially priced entrees.

Jimmy Tsang's features a full-service bar and an extensive wine list, as well as banquet facilities for up to 300 people. Reservations are accepted for parties of four or more. Jimmy Tsang's is open daily but serves dinner only on Sundays. Prices for the most expensive entrees are at the lower end of $$$.

Peking Gourmet Kitchen
$$ • 2018 Murray Ave., Pittsburgh • (412) 421-1920

Since 1960, Peking Gourmet Kitchen has been pleasing Squirrel Hill diners with its broad menu representative of all Chinese regions. You'll find such entrees as Szechuan spicy eggplant; ginger chicken with spicy sauce; and happy family, a medley of shrimp, beef, chicken, and roast pork with Chinese vegetables and topped by a brown sauce. Hot and spicy items are so noted on the menu. Peking Gourmet Kitchen, which serves lunch and dinner daily, offers a limited wine list. It accepts reservations, but it does not permit smoking.

Continental

Lucca
$$-$$$ • 317 South Craig St., Pittsburgh
• (412) 682-3310

Lucca styles its food as European, inspired by Italian flair. Read the menu and you'll get an idea of the international flavor. You'll find Crisfield County crab cakes, calamari gaetta, lump crabmeat spring roll, and shrimp taquito. The menu changes daily for lunch and dinner and offers seasonal complements; for instance, it features lamb in the spring, pasta in the summer. Staples of the menu are the mixed grille, which combines samplings of filet mignon, lamp chop, leg of duck, and Italian sausage, and the seafood mixed grille.

You'll find a full-service bar, and a sommelier will guide you through the ample wine list. Reservations are recommended. Lucca offers banquet facilities for up to 30 people. The restaurant serves lunch and dinner Monday through Saturday. Eat out on the patio when the weather is nice—if you can grab a table.

Greek

The Harris Grill Cafe
$-$$ • 5747 Ellsworth Ave., Pittsburgh
• (412) 363-0833

Delightful front and back patios with tables sheltered by umbrellas are the signature of this Shadyside restaurant. You'll enjoy such Greek entrees as chicken or lamb souvlaki and such Greek appetizers as spanakopita and grape leaves. The menu also offers a limited number of beef, chicken, and seafood entrees, as well as sandwiches, salads, and pizza. The cafe serves lunch and dinner daily, and it offers a full-service bar and a wine list. It does not accept reservations in the summer, when the patios are in particular demand, but you can reserve tables in the other seasons. The cafe does not designate smoking and nonsmoking sections.

Suzie's
$$ • 1704 Shady Ave., Pittsburgh
• (412) 422-8066

Hidden around the corner from the busy Forbes Avenue thoroughfare in Squirrel Hill, Suzie's is a pleasant spot that offers a road range of traditional Greek dishes, including moussaka, spanakopita, and pastitsio, as well as Greek salads and homemade desserts. You'll also enjoy the Greek background music. Suzie's serves lunch and dinner Monday through Saturday, dinner only on Sundays. It serves beer and wine, and it accepts reservations for parties of five or more. Suzie's offers catering services. It's a nice place to go for a quiet dinner.

Indian

India Garden
$-$$ • 328 Atwood St., Pittsburgh
• (412) 682-3000
3815 William Penn Hwy., Monroeville
• (412) 372-0400
• www.indiagarden.net

For three consecutive years, from 1996 to 1998, India Garden was awarded *Pittsburgh Magazine's* gold meal in the Indian food category. The dining room is large and inviting, and if you come for lunch, you'll be attracted immediately by the daily buffet, which features more than 25 items. India Garden prepares its food in a clay oven, giving it a distinctive taste. The extensive menu offers such popular entrees as tandoori chicken and tandoori shrimp as well as a generous selection of vegetarian entrees.

India Garden does not serve alcohol, but patrons are invited to bring their own. Reservations are required. The restaurants, which serve lunch and dinner daily, offer banquet facilities for up to 230 people. You'll find the Pittsburgh restaurant on the University of Pittsburgh's Oakland campus, the Monroeville location on U.S. Business Route 22 near the Pennsylvania Turnpike.

Prince of India Restaurant and Tavern
$-$$ • 3614 Fifth Ave., Pittsburgh
• (412) 687-0888

Located near the University of Pittsburgh campus and the Oakland medical complex, Prince of India serves lunch and dinner daily. Its daily lunch buffet is popular, as is its mix grill tandoori, a medley of seekh kabob, boti kabob, chicken tikka, and tandoori chicken and shrimp, served with chutney. The menu includes beef, lamb, seafood, vegetarian, and biryani entrees, and you'll enjoy the selection of 10 breads baked in Prince of India's clay oven. The restaurant offers a bar and a wine list. Smoking is permitted at the bar only. Prince of India doesn't accept reservations.

RESTAURANTS

Sree's Foods
$ • 2107 Murray Ave., Pittsburgh
• (412) 422-0663
$ • 606 Main St., Sharpsburg
• (412) 781-2306

Where else but Sree's can you find an entire Indian meal to go for under $5? Mr. and Mrs. Sree started their business with a take-out cart at Carnegie Mellon. Now, they offer take-out from more prestigious digs as well—restaurants in Squirrel Hill and Sharpsburg. Prices are a couple of dollars higher at the restaurant in Sharpsburg, but you can eat in there on Friday and Saturday evenings when the restaurant is open for dinner. You can't eat in at the Squirrel Hill location, but when you get home you'll enjoy this delicious, medium to very hot, spicy food. Vegetarian entrees are always offered.

Star of India
$-$$ • 412 S. Craig St., Pittsburgh
• (412) 681-5700

Dinner fare includes a variety of chicken, lamp, beef, and shrimp selections as well as biryani, a rice and raisin base topped by shrimp, chicken, lamb, or beef. You'll find a number of vegetarian entrees, and the Monday-through-Thursday lunch buffet includes vegetarian choices. Star of India does not serve alcohol, but you can bring in your own. It accepts reservations. The restaurant does not offer designated smoking or nonsmoking sections. If you become a regular patron here, the personable Star of India waiters will greet you as a friend.

INSIDERS' TIP

Through its "Dining With Heart" program, University of Pittsburgh Medical Center designates selections at local restaurants that meet program standards in cholesterol, fat, and sodium content. Participating restaurants usually mark those entrees with a small red heart. You can get your free list of participating restaurants from UPMC at (412) 647-UPMC or (800) 533-UPMC.

International

Road to Karakash
$15 • 320 Atwood St., Pittsburgh
• (412) 687-0533

We really didn't anticipate an "International" category; technically, there is no international cuisine. But how else do you categorize Road to Karakash, an underappreciated jewel of a restaurant that features foods from a wide variety of Asian and African nations and regions? You'll find such unusual entrees as doro wat, Ethiopian chicken curry in spiced herb butter; Moroccan beef tagine, beef stew with onion, mushrooms, tomato and cauliflower; Parsi

shrimp curry; and Malaysian devil's pork curry. Other selections include Yemeni lentil stew, and aush, an Afghani noodle soup served with split peas, kidney beans, and a spiced mint yogurt cream, all topped with lamb and tomato sauce.

Located near the University of Pittsburgh's Oakland campus, Road to Karakash serves lunch and dinner Monday through Saturday (It's closed from 2:30 to 5 PM on those days.), closing on Sundays. It does not serve liquor or accept reservations. The dining room is nonsmoking. Road to Karakash likes to call itself "a spice odyssey." It's a trip you'll want to take.

Italian

Carbone's
$-$$ • U.S. Rt. 119, Crabtree
• (724) 834-3430

Carbone's accepts reservations for parties of six or more, but you probably don't have to worry about getting seated here. With a seating capacity of 650, Carbone's can pretty much guarantee a table whenever you arrive. It's operated by Natale "Buzzy" Carbone and his sister Natalie Carbone—Carbone's has been in their family since its opening in 1938. An interesting bit of family lore: Natale and Natalie were named to honor their grandfather, who was born on Christmas—"Natal" in Italian.

It will seem like Natal when you dine here. A house specialty is braciole, steak stuffed and rolled in tomato sauce. Save room for Carbone's homemade desserts such as angel pie, made with strawberries, coconut, and whipped cream cavorting on a vanilla wafer crust. Carbone's offers a bar, a wine list, and banquet facilities for up to 300 people. It serves dinner only Monday through Saturday, closing on Sunday. Carbone's is about 6 miles north of Greensburg in Westmoreland County on Route 119.

La Cucina Flegrea
$$-$$$ • 2114 Murray Ave., Pittsburgh
• (412) 521-2082

In the Naples region of Italy, centuries of volcanic activity left a ring of craters. La Cucina Flegrea, which can be translated as "burning plains," takes its name from that geographic feature. This intimate Squirrel Hill restaurant seats only 30 and specializes in Neapolitan dishes such as gamberoni Michelangelo, sautéed tiger shrimp with artichoke hearts and sun-dried tomatoes in a wine sauce, and polpette Flegrea con pasta, homemade meatballs with pasta in a red sauce. La Cucina serves dinner Monday through Saturday, closing on Sundays. Reservations usually are accepted only on weekdays. The restaurant does not serve alcohol—you can bring your own wine for a $3 per bottle corking fee—and it does not permit smoking.

Del's Bar & Ristorante DelPizzo
$-$$ • 4428 Liberty Ave., Pittsburgh • (412) 683-1448

Del's, as this establishment is popularly known, has been a Bloomfield fixture since the Del Pizzo family opened it in 1949. It offers lunch and dinner daily, providing a broad selection of steaks and chops, pasta, chicken, veal, and seafood dishes. You can easily make a meal of Del's Gourmet pizza. The restaurant offers daily luncheon specials, with specially priced drinks if you eat at the bar. Wednesday night is Buffet Night. Del's offers irregularly scheduled entertainment in the form of karaoke—it's best to call for details. The restaurant offers a wine list, and it accepts reservations. Banquet facilities for up to 100 people are available.

DeNunzio's Italian Restaurant
$$-$$$ • 700 Lowry Ave., Jeannette • (724) 527-5552

You'll enjoy the creative menu at DeNunzio's. It features veal, chicken, beef, and seafood entries, as well as two pages of pasta entrees. But the showstoppers may be the tenderloins of beef garnished with shrimp and prepared in a Cajun style, and the veal Florentine, which is layered with shrimp and lump crab meat and prepared in a white wine sauce. Denunzio's offers a bar, an extensive wine list, and banquet facilities for up to 50 people. The restaurant can accommodate two banquets simultaneously. Reservations are recommended. DeNunzio's serves lunch and dinner daily. You'll find it in Westmoreland County about 1 mile north of U.S. Route 30. The most expensive entrees are priced at the lower end of $$$.

DeNunzio's Italian Restaurant
$$-$$$ • 2644 Mosside Blvd., Monroeville • (412) 374-7120

This is a sister restaurant of the Jeannette DeNunzio's but offers a somewhat less extensive menu. It also aims more for families, offering more booths than its Jeannette counterpart and covering the tables with paper on which kids are invited to color. In fact, the restaurant holds occasional coloring contests for its young patrons. Another difference: the Monroeville restaurant cooks in a wood-fired oven, providing a distinctive taste for its food. The restaurant offers a full-service bar and an extensive wine list. It serves lunch and dinner daily. Reservations are accepted for parties of four or more; others may call ahead for priority seating. The Monroeville DeNunzio's is about 1 mile west of the Pennsylvania Turnpike.

D'Imperio's Restaurant
$$-$$$$ • 3412 William Penn Hwy., Wilkins • (412) 823-4800

D'Imperio's is a classy restaurant with an appetite for fun as well. Shrimp Sorrento, enhanced with a taste of lemon and vodka, is a popular selection, and you'll find a wide variety of veal, lamb, chicken, seafood, and pasta entrees. Executive Chef Joseph Schilling offers at least three soups—including his signature seafood bisque—for every meal, and he also offers what D'Imperio's calls its "Culinary Geek" showcase of daily entree specials. The restaurant accepts reservations, and it offers a full-service bar and banquet facilities for up to 250 people. It serves dinner Monday through Saturday, lunch Tuesday through Friday. D'Imperio's is closed on Sundays.

A restaurant that calls its specials a "Culinary Geek" showcase clearly knows how to entertain, and you'll find a number of entertaining touches here. As you walk in, you'll enjoy viewing the ample wine collection in cabinets decorating the lobby areas. You can participate in the restaurant's wine-tasting events, held on most Friday evenings, and you can trip the light fantastic at a summer series of "Al Fresco Friday Feasts," which feature dinner and drinks as well as dancing. Al and the geeks move indoors if it rains on their feast. Call D'Imperio's for a schedule of special events.

DiSalvo's Station Restaurant and Banquet Facilities
$$-$$$ • 325 McKinley Ave., Latrobe • (724) 539-0500

Some enterprising entrepreneurs located their businesses in renovated train station. The DiSalvo family has gone them one better, creating a dining complex in an active train station. You'll find this Westmoreland County restaurant, as well as a sister restaurant called Prima Classe, in the Latrobe Train Station, where two Amtrak trains stop daily. In addition to deploying a railway motif in their decor, the DiSalvo's have created a special Steelers training camp package built around Amtrak's service. The package, offered only when the Steelers are training at nearby St. Vincent College in July and August, includes round-trip train fare from Pittsburgh, lunch at DiSalvo's, and an afternoon at training camp.

The menu offers beef, chicken, seafood, and pasta selections. Favorites include Filet DiSalvo, filet mignon stuffed with prosciutti ham and provolone cheese and laced with bordelaise sauce and mushrooms; and DiSalvo's Station Seafood Platter, a medley of lobster, clams, shrimp, scallops, deviled crab, oysters, and sole. You'll also enjoy the early bird menu featuring a limited selection of specially priced dinner entrees from Tuesday through Saturday. Reservations are suggested for all meals. DiSalvo's offers an extensive wine list and can accommodate up to 350 people for banquets. The restaurant is nonsmoking, but if you want to light up, you can repair to the adjoining Joey D's Sala Da Fumo, a cigar smokers' lair that's part of the complex.

DiSalvo's serves dinner Tuesday through Sunday, lunch Tuesday through Friday, and brunch on Sundays. It's closed on Mondays. For more on Prima Classe, see the Fine Dining profiles in the East section. The most expensive entrees are priced at the lower end of $$$.

Lombardozzi Restaurant & Lounge
$-$$ • 4786 Liberty Ave., Pittsburgh
• (412) 682-5785

Lombardozzi is one of a number of fine Italian restaurants in Pittsburgh's Bloomfield neighborhood, where you can still hear Italian spoken all along Liberty Avenue. The restaurant features pasta, seafood, veal, chicken, and beef entrees. It's particularly proud of its fettucine Lombardozzi, which includes lump crabmeat, shrimp, scallops, and clams in a red or a white sauce, and its veal Lombardozzi, which is crowned with lump crabmeat and shrimp. Lombardozzi offers a popular lunch buffet—the line-up changes daily—as well as a full-service bar and an extensive wine list. It accepts major credit cards and reservations for lunch and dinner. The restaurant provides banquet facilities, with a special menu for up to 150 people. Several entrees are priced slightly higher than $$.

Mariani's at the Pleasure Bar
$-$$ • 4729 Liberty Ave., Pittsburgh
• (412) 682-9603

Mariani's at the Pleasure Bar has been a fixture in Bloomfield since the 1940s; the Mariana family has operated it since 1963. The atmosphere is cozy here, the menu strong on pasta dishes. The Pleasure Bar, as it's popularly known, also offers beef, chicken, veal, and seafood selections, as well as a children's menu. Patrons are especially fond of the Italian tripe, served with mushrooms and sweet or hot peppers in tomato sauce, as well as the eggplant parmigiana and the homemade manicotti. The list of daily specials is extensive. The Pleasure Bar offers a full-service bar, a limited wine list, and banquet facilities for up to 50 people. It accepts reservations for parties of four or more on weekends, for parties of any number at other times. It's open daily Monday through Saturday until 10:30 PM and on Sunday from 4 to 10 PM only.

Minutello's Restaurant & Lounge
$-$$ • 226 Shady Ave., Pittsburgh
• (412) 361-9311

The Minutello family has operated this East Liberty restaurant for more than 40 years, attracting a loyal clientele. The restaurant features a diverse menu, with veal, beef, chicken, seafood, and pasta entrees. You'll also find specialty pizzas and salad and sandwich selections. Minutello's offers a full-service bar, a wine list, and an extensive selection of domestic and imported beers and microbrews. Reservations are accepted. The restaurant is open daily for dinner and serves lunch Monday through Saturday; it's open from 1 to 9 PM on Sundays. Takeout, catering, and delivery are available.

Pasta Piatto
$$-$$$ • 736 Bellefonte St., Pittsburgh
• (412) 621-5547

Pasta is the specialty at this restaurant in the heart of the Shadyside commercial district. The menu features no fewer than nine types of pasta—all of them homemade—with varied selections in each category. You'll also find other Northern Italian fare, including steak, veal, chicken, and seafood selections. Just reading the menu here is a satisfying experience. Pasta Piatto offers a useful children's menu. It has a bar and an extensive wine list. Pasta Piatto serves dinner daily, lunch Monday through Saturday.

Persichetti's
$-$$ • 101-101 S. Third St., Jeannette
• (724) 527-5553

This Westmoreland County restaurant offers a diverse menu that's especially strong on seafood, with such selections as Persichetti's Lobster Crock and the land and sea trio, a medley of chicken breast, jumbo gulf shrimp, and sea scallops. You'll also find beef, veal, chicken, and pasta selections as well as dinner salads, sandwiches, and pizza. Persichetti's offers daily specials; on Wednesdays, the special is barbecued ribs. The restaurant offers a lounge, a wine list, and banquet facilities for up to 30 people. It serves lunch and dinner Tuesday through Sunday, closing on Mondays. Reservations are accepted on weekends for parties of five or more, on weekdays for parties of any size.

Spadaro's Restaurant & Lounge
$-$$ • 4430 William Penn Hwy., Murrysville • (724) 327-5955

Spadaro's serves lunch and dinner daily, and it also hosts banquets for up to 175 people. Seafood and pasta are popular selections here; you can combine them in an entree called seafood pasta, featuring shrimp, scallops and langostinos in a light, creamy wine sauce over angel hair pasta. You'll also find veal, chicken, and beef selections as well as a lounge and a wine list. Reservations are recommended on weekends, accepted at all times. Spadaro's is located on U.S. Route 22 in Westmoreland County, just east of the Allegheny County line.

The Tarentum Station Restaurant
$$-$$$ • 101 Station Dr., Tarentum • (724) 226-3301

The Tarentum Station was constructed in 1892 as a stop for the Pennsylvania Railroad. Such notables as William Howard Taft, William Jennings Bryan, Kit Carson, Carrie Nation, and Chief Ironstone road the Pennsylvania to Tarentum, an Allegheny River town. When train traffic declined, the station was converted to a restaurant in 1983. When you dine here, you'll get a little flavor of the train station—and a lot of flavor in your meal.

The menu features beef, seafood, veal, chicken, and pasta selections, as well as dinner salads, such as an enticing grilled eggplant salad. Among the most popular selections is the Pittsburgh steak, a New York strip steak marinated in seasoned butter, then placed in a white-hot cast iron skillet, resulting in a charred exterior and a rare interior. You'll find a bar and a wine list that includes domestic, Italian, and Australian selections but eschews French brands. Tarentum Station offers banquet facilities for up to 40 people. It serves dinner daily, lunch Monday through Friday. Reservations are recommended. You can get here by taking the Tarentum exit off Pa. Route 28.

Japanese

Sushi Too
$-$$$ • 5432 Walnut St., Pittsburgh • (412) 687-8744

As its sister restaurant on the South Side, this Shadyside establishment features sushi—its phone number spells out 68-SUSHI—and such other Japanese fare as tempura and teriyaki. You'll find an attractive list of chef's specials, including garlic shrimp and lemon chicken. You'll enjoy a visual treat if you order the beef or seafood shabu shabu; both of these meals for two are prepared at your table. Sushi Too offers a bar, a wine list, and a Tatami Room that can accommodate banquets of up to 30 people. Reservations are accepted for parties of six or more. When you enter Sushi Too, take a minute to admire the replica Japanese garden in the lobby; it will help set an appropriate mood for your meal. (By the way, no smart comments about our editors. The Shadyside restaurant is Sushi Too; the South Side restaurant is Sushi Two.) The most expensive entrees are priced at the lower end of $$$.

Korean

Young Bin Kwan
$-$$ • 4305 Main St., Pittsburgh • (412) 687-2227

In ancient times, Young Bin Kwan was the name of a house in Korea that hosted the Chinese ambassador and his retinue on official visits. That blending of cultures is the defining feature of this Bloomfield restaurant, which features Korean, Chinese, and Japanese fare—and a separate chef for the dishes of each nationality. Be advised that because the menu is so eclectic, prices vary widely. Young Bin Kwan serves lunch and dinner. It offers a full-service bar, a limited wine list, and banquet facilities for up to 100. Reservations are accepted.

Kosher

Yacov's Restaurant
$, no credit cards • 2109 Murray Ave., Pittsburgh • (412) 421-7208

Yacov's selections all are meatless, which makes the diversity of the menu that much more interesting. You'll find Israeli and Italian entrees, as well as soups and vegetarian chopped liver. When you eat at this restaurant in the heart of Squirrel Hill, you'll be intrigued by the art on Yacov's walls, including a series of primitive-style paintings that depict Biblical scenes—Moses receiving the commandments, the Tower of Babel, David about to slay Goliath.

The dining room is nonsmoking. Yacov's does not serve alcohol, and it does not accept reservations. It offers catering services. The restaurant serves lunch and dinner Sunday through Thursday, lunch only on Friday until 3 PM, as it closes for the Jewish Sabbath.

Mexican

Casa Chapala
$-$$ • 122 N. Market St., Ligonier
• (724) 238-7399

This is a bright, airy restaurant in downtown Ligonier that features foods primarily from the Mexican interior. Among diners' favorites are chile Colorado, chicken en mole—chicken in a salsa of tomato and spices, served with rice and beans—and mole ranchero, an especially hot and spicy blend with chunks of pork and cactus. The restaurant offers a full-service bar and banquet facilities for up to 120 people. It accepts reservations. Casa Chapala is open for lunch and dinner Tuesday through Sunday. It occasionally offers such entertainment as a guitarist—you'll need to call for coming attractions.

Cozumel
$-$$ • 5507 Walnut St., Pittsburgh
• (412) 621-5100
U.S. Rt. 30 E., Greensburg
• (724) 836-2653

Cozumel offers a diverse menu at both its Shadyside and Greensburg locations, but you're most likely to remember the ostrich fajitas and taco salad. The restaurant features a number of tempting combination platters as well as limited children's and vegetarian menus. Cozumel offers a full-service bar, a wine list and a broad selection of Mexican beers. It features live music each Saturday night—there is a cover charge even if you're dining there. Cozumel serves lunch and dinner daily.

The Fajita Grill
$-$$ • 5865 Ellsworth Ave., Pittsburgh
• (412) 362-3030

This Shadyside restaurant offers dishes from four Mexican regions—Central, Puebla, Gulf Coast, and Caribbean. In addition to a broad selection of fajitas, you'll find such intriguing entrees as marinated jumbo shrimp in chipotte sauce and chicken in a pumpkin seed sauce. The restaurant does accept reservations and does not serve alcohol—you're invited to bring your own. There's no smoking here, even if you're dining on the patio. The Fajita Grill serves dinner Tuesday through Sunday, lunch Tuesday through Friday. It's closed on Mondays.

Middle Eastern

Ali Baba
$-$$ • 404 S. Craig St., Pittsburgh
• (412) 682-2829

Ali Baba has been pleasing Oakland patrons since 1972. Particularly popular are its shish kebab and its hummus, which are part of a broad selection of entrees and a la carte items. The restaurant serves beer but no other alcohol, and it accepts reservations for parties of five or more. It provides take-out service. Ali Baba serves dinner daily, lunch Monday through Friday. It's located between the campuses of the University of Pittsburgh and Carnegie Mellon University and easily accessible from each. Don't miss it.

Khalil's II
$-$$ • 4757 Baum Blvd., Pittsburgh
• (412) 683-4757

Before he opened Khalil's II, Mikhail Khalil worked for 12 years as the chef at a predecessor restaurant at the same Shadyside site, so you know this restaurant is a labor of love. Shishkabob is a popular entree, as is samket el pasha, catch of the day baked in lemon and garlic and topped with pine nuts and sesame sauce. You won't find much in the way of fried foods here, as Khalil, grills, broils, or oven-bakes most of the fare. The restaurant features a full-service bar, a wine list, and banquet facilities for up to 125 people. It's open for dinner only from Tuesday through Sunday, and it's closed on Mondays. If you're wondering about the name, Khalil also operated Khalil's I and Khalil's III some years ago, but these no longer are extant.

Open Flame
$ • 2103 Murray Ave., Pittsburgh
• (412) 422-8170

Until another Insider told us about the homemade Middle Eastern food here, we just walked right by this unassuming, small restaurant. That was years ago; we've enjoyed many tasty bites since then. Open Flame is known mostly for its take-out and delivery; it's a favorite of Carnegie Mellon students too hard at work to leave their dorm rooms, even for a trip to nearby Squirrel Hill. However, there are six tables and a small counter inside the restaurant, and it's a fine place to dine very informally and fairly quickly. It sure beats fast food! Enjoy the variety here; even vegetarians will find plenty to choose from. We especially like the falafel sandwiches, the spinach pies, and the baklava.

Pan Asian

The Spice Island Tea House
$ • 253 Atwood St., Pittsburgh
• (412) 687-8821

When you visit Spice Island, you'll be embarking on a culinary journey of Southeast Asia. The restaurant features the cuisine of Burma, Indonesia, Malaysia, Singapore, Thailand, and lesser known regions of Southeast Asia. Among the intriguing selections are five-spiced chicken of Malaysia; Burmese barbecued chicken; pad Thai; Singapore rice noodle; Java fried rice; Sumatran corn and shrimp fritters; and gado gado, an Indonesian salad. There are plenty of vegetarian choices. Dining here is a fulfilling—and filling—journey; it's a trip you'll want to take. The restaurant is near the University of Pittsburgh campus in Oakland, and is owned by a Carnegie Mellon graduate. It serves lunch and dinner Monday through Saturday, closing on Sundays, although it occasionally hosts banquets on Sundays. It does not serve alcohol, and it does not accept reservations. The Spice Island dining room is nonsmoking.

Peruvian

La Feria
$ • 5527 Walnut St., Pittsburgh
• (412) 682-4501

Unique is an overused word, but we're pretty sure La Feria is unique in this regard: you won't find another combination Peruvian restaurant and imported crafts store in Southwestern Pennsylvania. Owners Luisa Porras and Pamela Cohen founded this Shadyside complex in 1992, not really sure how the market would respond. They needn't have worried. Residents and visitors alike have been charmed by the products of Peruvian artisans as well as the Peruvian cuisine.

The restaurant features rotating specials—there's always a vegetarian dish—that include such entrees as locro de zapallo, a pumpkin and potato stew; tacu tacu, a black bean and rice

casserole baked with hot peppers and served with fried bananas and sweet potato chips; and ajide gallina, shredded chicken cooked in a creamy sauce with crushed peanuts, aji peppers, garlic, and onions. La Feria serves lunch and dinner Monday through Saturday, closing on Sundays. It does not serve alcohol but invites patrons to bring their own. The restaurant seats only 36 people, so the smoking section is rather small. Reservations are accepted for parties of six or more.

Filipino

La Filipiana
$-$$ • 5321 Butler St., Pittsburgh
• (412) 781-8724

This restaurant is located in the city's Lawrenceville neighborhood along the Allegheny River, not known for restaurants, but inside you'll find the only Philippino restaurant in the region. A feature on the menu is the Taste of La Filipiana, a seven-course dinner for two that features entrees representing three geographic regions of the Philippines. Groups of 10 or more can make arrangements to dine any day of the week. La Filiapiana received the designation as Best in Ethnic Cuisine from *Pittsburgh Magazine* from 1994 to 1998. The restaurant is open all week from 5 to 10 PM for dinner, and 11 AM to 4:30 PM for lunch. Bring your own wine or beer, but La Filipiana bans liquor.

Pizza

Mineo's Pizza House
$, no credit cards • 2128 Murray Ave., Pittsburgh • (412) 521-9864
713A Washington Rd., Mt. Lebanon
• (412) 344-9467

Most pizza lovers have their favorites; for many Pittsburgh residents, their favorite pizza comes from Mineo's. In fact, Mineo's was named the town's best pizzeria for the past six years by *City Paper*. The restaurant offers outlets in Pittsburgh's Squirrel Hill neighborhood and in Mt. Lebanon in the South Hills. In addition to its standard pizza, Mieno's offers Sicilian and white varieties as well as options for thick crust and extra sauce. The menu also features subs, calzoni, and largely pasta-based entrees. You can order pasta party trays as well. Mineo's does not serve alcohol, and it doesn't accept reservations. It does not designate smoking and nonsmoking sections, as most orders here are for take-out rather than to be enjoyed in the small dining area. It's open daily for lunch and dinner.

Vento's Pizza & Dairy
$, no credit cards • 420 N. Highland Ave., Pittsburgh • (412) 361-9197

How important is this 50-year-old establishment to its East Liberty neighborhood? In 1998 when the city moved to acquire the buildings in this block to make way for an important new Home Depot store, it worked with Al Vento to find a convenient new location for his restaurant. The result: Vento's and Home Depot are neighbors.

In addition to its signature pizza, Vento's offers such lunch and dinner specials as pepper steak, fish, and chicken parmesan, as well as a variety of hoagies and other sandwiches. Vento's does not serve liquor, and it does not accept reservations. The seating area is small, so there are no smoking and nonsmoking sections. Vento's is closed on Sundays.

Seafood

The Nest
$$$ • 407 Clay Ave., Jeannette • (724) 527-9880

Lobster and shrimp dominate the interesting menu at this Westmoreland County restaurant. No fewer than 11 entrees feature lobster or shrimp, and the lobster and shrimp scampi includes both. The headliner of the lobster group is the 22-ounce lobster tail; this must have been one of those tails that wagged the lobster. You'll also find crab cakes, orange roughy, and scallops on the menu as well as a few beef, veal, and lamb selections. The Nest offers a full-service bar, a wine list, and banquet facilities for up to 125 people. Reservations are suggested for weekends and accepted at all times. The Nest serves dinner only from Tuesday through Saturday, closing on Sundays and Mondays.

Simmie's Restaurant and Lounge
$-$$ • 8500 Frankstown Rd., Penn Hills • (412) 731-4689

Located just over the city line in Penn Hills, Simmie's offers such seafood dishes as Caribbean shrimp scampi and twin Maine lobster tails and a variety of fresh fish specials that change with the catch. Barbecued ribs also are popular here. If you'd like to enjoy both seafood and beef, try the surf and turf combina-

tion. Happy hour each Monday through Friday from 5 to 7 PM brings specially priced cocktails and hors d'oeuvres, and senior citizens enjoy a discount on their meals each Wednesday.

Simmie's serves lunch and dinner Monday through Saturday, opening at 1 PM on Saturdays. It opens on Sundays only for some holidays. It offers a full-service bar and a wine list, and it accepts reservations for parties of seven or more. If you leave Simmie's with an enduring taste for fresh fish to take home, you can satisfy your urge at the adjacent Frankstown Fish Company.

Thai

O'cha Restaurant
$$ • 321 South Ave., Verona • (412) 828-1517

This small restaurant just off Allegheny River Boulevard—the main street through Verona—seats only 30, but its patrons regularly travel for miles for the diverse selection of Thai and Chinese food. Popular menu items include royal fish—deep-fried halibut with mushrooms, peppers, and green onions in hot chili sauce—and pad Thai, a stir fry with chicken or shrimp, eggs, bean sprouts, green onions, and ground peanuts. If you're not exactly sure what entree names mean, the unusual menu will help; it offers colorful photos of each selection as well as pictures of Thailand's attractions. O'cha does not serve alcohol. It accepts reservations and, by closing its dining room, can accommodate banquets for up to 30 people. The restaurant offers lunch and dinner Monday through Friday (though it closes from 2 to 5 PM on those days), and dinner only on Saturdays. It's closed on Sundays.

Thai Place
$$-$$$ • 809 Bellefonte St., Pittsburgh • (412) 687-8586

When you're in Pittsburgh's Shadyside neighborhood and ready for a taste of pad Thai, that signature Thai dish that here is prepared with shrimp and ground peanuts in a flavorful sauce, Thai Place is the place to go. The diverse menu also includes such favorites as tiger prawns, which are spiced with red curry sauce and coconut milk and served with mixed vegetables, as well as a broad selection of beef, chicken, pork, seafood, curry, and vegetarian entrees. Thai place offers a wine list and a retail section, where you can purchase crafts, silk products, and neckties—all fashioned in Thailand. The restaurant offers a wine list, and it recommends reservations. Thai Place serves dinner daily, lunch from Tuesday through Sunday.

Vegetarian

The Co-op Cafe
$ • 7516 Meade St., Pittsburgh
• (412) 242-7726

Many Pittsburgh shoppers appreciate the East End Food Co-op as a great source of organic and natural foods. In the rear of the Co-op is a nice find for vegetarians and vegans, and anyone else wishing to have a healthy, tasty meal—the Co-op Café. The café offers seating for about 20 people, and foods are served cafeteria-style from a hot bar and a salad bar. The cafe features lunch and dinner Monday through Friday, and breakfast until 1 PM on Saturdays and Sundays. The breakfast menu includes hotcakes, omelets, and a variety of tofu dishes. The lunch and dinner menu offers a limited number of soups, salads, and entrees that change daily, including linguine prima vera and spinach quesadilla. The cafe's soups are vegan, and other vegan options are available. Smoothies and fresh juices are also served, and you may want to pick up one of the café's cookies made without white flour and sugar, if you've got sweet tooth. They're really satisfying.

The Co-op Cafe does not serve alcohol, and it does not accept reservations or permit smoking. The café can be a little noisy, what with shoppers checking out the adjacent deli case and the kids that are a constant feature of this environment, so don't plan that crucial business lunch or romantic rendezvous here. Come here if you want to meet other like-minded souls or enjoy a quick bite, though—and pick up your groceries at the same time. If you're interested in joining the Food Co-op, management would be happy to explore that with you. The Co-op Cafe is in the North Point Breeze neighborhood, about 2 miles from the Edgewood-Swissvale exit of Interstate 376 (the Parkway East).

South

American

Armstrong's Restaurant
$ • Baptist and Grove Rds., Castle Shannon
• (412) 885-1033

When you're out shopping at Castle Village Shopping Center, you'll enjoy a respite at Armstrong's, which is located in the mall. You'll find the same menu for lunch and dinner here, an Italian-accented menu with selections such as pasta and manicotti. Daily specials include such items as stuffed chicken breast, beer-battered fish with macaroni and cheese, and meat loaf. It's hearty fare. In fact, Armstrong's has received a "Best Buy for the Buck" award from *Pittsburgh Magazine*. The restaurant features a full-service bar. It offers catering services, and its entire menu is available for take-out. Armstrong's doesn't take reservations.

The Back Porch
$$ • 114 Speers St., Belle Vernon
• (724) 483-4500

The Back Porch is set in a restored, antique-packed 1806 home along the Monongahela River in Washington County. You'll enjoy dining on the veranda or on the sun porch and choosing from a diverse menu. Appealing selections include charcoal-broiled ribs marinated in brown sugar and soy sauce, tuna topped with feta cheese and a lemon herb vinaigrette, and a mixed grill that highlights three different items each day. The Back Porch offers a full-service bar, and extensive wine list and banquet facilities for up to 50 people. (The banquet space is not available on Saturdays.) Smoking is permitted only in The Side Door, a casual dining room located downstairs. The Back Porch serves dinner Tuesday through Sunday, lunch Tuesday through Friday, and reservations are recommended for all meals. It's closed on Mondays.

Barry's on the Avenue
$$ • 939 Jefferson Ave., Washington
• (724) 222-6688

In Washington County, Barry's is a popular spot for seafood and steaks. Seafood selections include blackened tuna, swordfish, and salmon, while if you're hungry for beef, it would be hard to look past Barry's 40-ounce Porterhouse steak. Barry's offers a lounge that's cigar-friendly as well as an extensive list of California wines. Reservations are accepted. The restaurant hosts banquets—primarily on weekdays—for up to 40 people. Barry's on the Avenue serves lunch and dinner daily. You'll find it just off Exit 6 of Interstate 70.

Blue Lou's Bar & Grill/Mario's South Side Saloon
$-$$ • 1514 E. Carson St., Pittsburgh
• (412) 381-5610

Blue Lou's and Mario's once were distinct, although commonly owned, establishments that stood side by side on East Carson Street. In recent years, however, the owner has knocked out the interior dividing walls, so they function as a single entity with a common menu and amenities. It's a lively, vital place with a pool table fun menu headlined by "Blue Lou's Famous BBQ Ribs," which are roasted for eight hours before they hit the grill. You'll also find seafood, chicken, and pasta selections, as well as dinner salads and an extensive sandwich menu. The creative dessert menu features chocolate chip baked potato and chocolate razz-a-matazz pie, cheesecake swirled with fudge and topped with a layer of raspberry and white chocolate.

The restaurant offers a broad selection of specialty coffees and cocktails; order one of the cocktails and you can keep the imprinted glass as a souvenir. (Note: the cocktails carry sexually explicit names that probably aren't appropriate for children.) As another tip of the cap to regular patrons, those who drink 10 yards of beer—not necessarily at the same sitting—have their achievement commemorated on a small plaque that will hang in the restaurant. Drink prices are reduced during happy hours, and ladies enjoy specially priced drinks and free wings each Wednesday evening.

The restaurant accepts reservations and offers banquet facilities for up to 80 people. While the restaurant accommodates nonsmokers, management advises that smoke from the bars tends to affect all dining areas.

Bobby Rubino's Place for Ribs
$$-$$$ • 10 Commerce Ct., Pittsburgh
• (412) 642-7427

Like the man says, this Station Square restaurant is a place for ribs, for both lunch and dinner. Other barbecued selections include chicken and ribs, and you can order prime rib after 4 PM daily. Other entrees include rainbow trout, served for lunch and dinner, and lunch specials like roasted turkey platter and a jumbo chicken sandwich.

Bobby Rubino's offers an appealing variety of specialty cocktails, such as "Top Notch Butterscotch" with butterscotch schnapps, and "Buoys 'n Berry," concocted with tropical schnapps and raspberries. The wine list is more limited. You can reserve a table Monday through Thursday. Bobby Rubino's offers banquet facilities for up to 150 people.

Cafe Allegro
$$ • 51 S. 12th St., Pittsburgh
• (412) 481-7788

The Pittsburgh Steelers may have won four Super Bowls, but Cafe Allegro has an even more impressive championship record. For six consecutive years, 1993 through 1998, *Pittsburgh Magazine* and its readers named Cafe Allegro Pittsburgh's "Best Overall Restaurant." Considering that the region sports about 7,200 restaurants and taverns, that's a remarkable distinction, indeed. When you visit Cafe Allegro, you'll see the blue quartz trophy emblematic of the title.

Chef Nolan changes the menu with the seasons. Depending on the season, you may find such entrees as horseradish-crusted red snapper with garden salsa; veal saltimbocca; or Chef Nolan's Bouillabaisse, prepared with market-selection seafood. One specialty impervious to seasonal changes is the grilled calamari—it's enjoyed an uninterrupted 12-year run on the menu. Cafe Allegro offers a full-service bar and an extensive wine list, as well as banquet facilities for up to 40 people. It's open daily for dinner only.

Cafe Bullwinkle
$ • 1100 Bower Hill Rd., Mt. Lebanon
• (412) 278-7777

You may not get fan mail from flounder at Cafe Bullwinkle, but you'll find plenty of other attractions at this informal South Hills restaurant. It features sandwiches and pasta dishes and is especially prominent for its daily 99-cent beer specials—one specially priced beer is featured each day. Beer is the only alcoholic beverage served here. Cafe Bullwinkle offers live bands Thursday evenings, karaoke on Wednesday evenings. Reservations are accepted for parties of eight or more. Cafe Bullwinkle does offer designated nonsmoking seating, but it remains fairly smoky regardless. All-you-can-eat specials are offered during the week, and Café Bullwinkle also does catering.

Callahan's Sports Grill
$ •18 Great Southern Shopping Center,
Bridgeville • (412) 221-2235

Callahan's is a popular spot for kids' parties—and adult bashes for that matter—and you'll know why as soon as you step inside and get the full impact of the 32 televisions that surround you. Partygoers will enjoy the pool table, electronic darts game, and video/pinball arcade where kids can win prizes for their performance. You'll also enjoy the lunch and dinner menus, which feature primarily lighter fare such as sandwiches, wings, and an all-you-can-eat crableg special from 5 to 10 PM each night. Callahan's offers a full-service bar. The restaurant accepts reservations for parties of eight or more. The grill opens at 4 PM during the week and at noon on weekends.

Cheese Cellar Café
$$ • 25 Station Sq., Pittsburgh
• (412) 471-3355

While the menu is diverse, many diners choose Cheese Cellar to enjoy its specialty fondues. In fact, you can "fondue" your way through each course of lunch or dinner, starting with the Sam Adams cheddar and beer fondue for your appetizer and topping off your meal with chocolate fondue, which is flavored with orange liqueur and served with fresh fruit, pound cake, and marshmallows.

Another attraction of Cheese Cellar is its outdoor seating. The restaurant offers an extensive list of specialty coffees and cocktails, as well as a more limited wine list. Cheese Cellar accepts reservations Sunday through Thursday. It offers banquet facilities with menu facilities for up to 60 people.

Cheese Cellar offers several discount programs. Through one, you'll get your discount card punched each time you dine at Cheese Cellar, with a free lunch when your ticket is completely punched. The other discount program is for birthday celebrants. If you dine at Cheese Cellar on your birthday, you'll enjoy a discount that's equal in percentage to your birthday. If you eat here when you turn the big Four-Oh, for example, your discount is 40 percent. And they throw in a free chocolate mousse besides.

City Grill
$-$$ • 2019 E. Carson St., Pittsburgh
• (412) 481-6868

When you're cruising the South Side and get that hankering for something from the grill, try City Grill. Burgers are the most popular items here, but City Grill also grills steaks, shrimp, and a variety of appetizers. Salads and a delicious grilled chicken sandwich are also available. The desserts are popular here, too. City Grill offers a full-service bar and a wine list, but it does not accept reservations or designate smoking and nonsmoking sections.

The Colony
$$-$$$ • Greentree and Cochran Rds.,
Scott • (412) 561-2060

The Colony offers all the elements of a fine dining experience: an inviting dining room, top food, an award-winning wine list, and romantic piano music on Friday and Saturday nights. The list of entrees is comparatively short, but the entrees are all quality. You'll find New York prime sirloin and prime filet mignon, medal-

lions of pork tenderloin served in a green peppercorn Dijon sauce, and such seafood selections as centercut swordfish and filet of Norwegian salmon. The Colony offers a full-service bar and a wine list that won the *Wine Spectator* 1997 Award of Excellence. The restaurant's banquet facilities can accommodate up to 40 people. The Colony serves dinner daily. Reservations are recommended.

Fat Head's South Shore Saloon
$ • 1805 E. Carson St., Pittsburgh
• (412) 431-7433

When you have an appetite that won't quit, bring it to Fat Head's for one of their oversized sandwiches called "Headwiches." They headline a menu that includes primarily informal selections—burgers, subs, wings, salads, and munchies—as well as a limited selection of full entrees. Fat Head's offers a full-service bar that draws heavy evening crowds. It does not accept reservations, and it does not designate smoking and nonsmoking sections. Fat Head's serves lunch and dinner daily. Note: If you're a feminist, you may be turned off by the mural depicting near-naked women.

Grandview Saloon
$$ • 1212 Grandview Ave., Pittsburgh
• (412) 431-1400

Grandview Saloon combines a great view of the city from the top of Mt. Washington with hearty, informal dining. If you're really into the view, try the saloon's outdoor deck, which will put you right out on the mountain. Reservations aren't accepted for the deck, but you can reserve a table indoors for both lunch and dinner.

Portions are large here, but perhaps none larger than the 1-pound fish sandwich, one of the saloon's most popular items. You'll find a broad selection of burgers, salads and pasta, and you can kick things off with such unusual appetizers as Greek spinach pie and pepperoni roll. Grandview Saloon offers a limited wine list and a full-service bar, which celebrates a daily happy hour from 6 to 8 PM with discounted drinks and hors d'oeuvres. The saloon accepts major credit cards, and its banquet facilities can accommodate up to 30 people.

Houlihan's
$-$$ • 15 Freight House Shops,
Station Square, Pittsburgh
• (412) 232-0302

You'll usually find something inviting happening at Houlihan's. The Station Square restaurant serves lunch and dinner daily, and it also offers a late night menu, serving until 12:30

AM. For dinner, you'll find beef selections that are prepared on a wood-fired grill, as well as chicken and fajita entrees and salads and sandwiches. A specialty of the house is an appetizer called 'Shrooms—jumbo mushroom caps filled with herbs and garlic cheese, then lightly battered and fried and served with a horseradish and Dijon sauce. The restaurant offers a lounge, a wine list, and banquet facilities for up to 75 people. For entertainment, Houlihan's provides either a DJ or a band—sometimes both—each evening as well as nightly happy hours with complimentary hors d'ouevres and specially priced drinks. The restaurant accepts reservations Sunday through Thursday but not on Fridays and Saturdays. The dining room offers a section for smokers after 5 PM; before then, you can smoke in the lounge.

LeMont Restaurant
$$-$$$ • 1114 Grandview Ave., Pittsburgh
• (412) 431-3100

LeMont has been an important Pittsburgh institution since 1960, offering both a splendid Mt. Washington view of Pittsburgh from 20-foot windows and an elegant dining experience. LeMont has been honored by the Distinguished Restaurants of North America and *Wine Spectator,* and it has earned *Holiday Magazine's* award for dining excellence for 37 consecutive years. That recognition suggests the comprehensive excellence you'll enjoy here. Popular entrees include roasted raspberry duck and steak Diane, which is prepared tableside, as well as such game specials as antelope and zebra. Vegetarians will enjoy the vegetable strudel, an herb-laced medley of garden vegetables and rice nestled in streudel dough.

The wine list is extensive, as is the selection of coffees and the array of desserts. Crepes Suzette and strawberries and bananas flambe are two of the more tantalizing desserts. Banquets are an important component of LeMont's services, so important that they've captured their banquet menus in a helpful four-color pamphlet that you can request. The restaurant can accommodate up to 500 people for a special event. LeMont serves dinner daily, and reservations are suggested.

Louis Tambellini Restaurant
$$ • 860 Saw Mill Run Blvd., Pittsburgh
• (412) 481-1118

Just for the heck of it, we counted the entrees Louis Tambellini Restaurant was offering on the night we visited. When we reached 44 regular entrees and 19 dinner specials, we were too hungry to bother with the salads and sandwiches,

though those are plentiful as well. We were more than ready to eat. The extensive menu here will tempt you, and the restaurant will satisfy your temptation. You'll find beef, veal, seafood, and pasta selections. Specials include such entrees as filet of Norwegian salmon, filet of Florida grouper, and steak filet with sweetbreads and bacon strips. The restaurant offers a full-service bar, a wine list, and banquet facilities for up to 120 people. Banquets are not booked for Saturday nights. Louis Tambellini Restaurant serves lunch and dinner Monday through Saturday, closing on Sundays. Reservations for parties of eight or more are accepted. You'll find the restaurant just south of the Liberty Tunnels on Pennsylvania Route 51.

Maxwell's
$-$$ • 340 Race Track Rd., Washington
• (724) 222-6200

Located in the Meadow Lands Holiday Inn, Maxwell's offers a varied selection of food and entertainment. Its menu features such unusual specialties as shrimp Jessica, shrimp stuffed with provolone cheese, wrapped in bacon and broiled; and pecan crusted walleye, which is served with an herb sauce. Maxwell's also offers beef, chicken, veal, and pasta selections, and it features prime rib on Fridays and Saturdays. It offers a lounge, a wine list, and banquet facilities (through the hotel) for up to 550 people.

For entertainment, Maxwell's provides a jazz band on Friday evenings from 9:30 PM to 1:30 AM. In addition the adjoining Nitelite nightclub features live music and dancing Thursday through Saturday evenings. Maxwell's serves breakfast, lunch, and dinner daily as well as a Sunday brunch. The dining room closes from 2 to 5 PM daily, but you're welcome to eat in the lounge during those hours. Reservations are accepted; they're recommended for Sunday brunch and for weekend evenings.

Peppercorns
$-$$ • 3821 Willow Ave., Castle Shannon
• (412) 344-7856

Peppercorns is an intimate South Hills restaurant that lavishes considerable care in the selection and preparation of its food. They prepare their own ravioli, which is featured in such dishes as lobster ravioli and salmon ravioli. You'll also enjoy the roasted sesame salmon, served with spicy peanut noodles. The menu offers beef, veal, chicken, and seafood selections. Peppercorns does not serve alcohol, but you're invited to bring your own for a nominal service fee. The restaurant offers banquet facilities for up to 50 people. It serves dinner Monday through Saturday, closing on Sundays. Reservations are recommended. The dining area is nonsmoking.

Pittsburgh Steak Company
$-$$ • 1924 E. Carson St., Pittsburgh
• (412) 381-5505

This South Side steak restaurant is more than just a steak restaurant. To be sure, you'll find a broad selection of steaks, but you also can choose from seafood, chicken, and pasta entrees as well as salads and sandwiches. Fried zucchini is a popular appetizer here. Pittsburgh Steak Company offers a full-service bar and a wine list, and it accepts reservations for parties of eight or more. It provides banquet facilities for up to 96 people. The restaurant serves dinner daily, with lunch offered Monday through Saturday.

Shootz Cafe
$ • 2305 E. Carson St., Pittsburgh
• (412) 488-3820

Shootz describes itself as "an upscale cafe and billiards club," rather an unusual combination for these parts, where billiards clubs don't necessarily cater to the upscale. Shootz combines dining, drinking, and billiards so well that *City Paper* named this South Side establishment the region's best bar for billiards for five consecutive years from 1993 through 1997. The menu features primarily lighter fare, including sandwiches, salads, and pizza, as well as a limited list of full entrees. You won't go thirsty here, as Shootz offers a number of drink promotions, including nightly beer specials and a highlighted "Brewery of the Month."

When you're ready to take cue in hand, 18 billiards tables await you. Shootz hosts regular leagues and tournaments, but players of any skill level are welcome. In fact, many corporations host staff parties at Shootz, which can accommodate up to 500 people for such events. You'll also find a small retail area, where you can pick up a Shootz golf shirt and other logo-emblazoned material. Shootz serves lunch and dinner Monday through Sunday and remains open until 2 AM on Friday and Saturday. Reservations are required for parties of eight or more. Shootz does not designate smoking and non-smoking sections.

The Tin Angel
$$$$ • 1200 Grandview Ave., Pittsburgh
• (412) 381-1919

When you dine at The Tin Angel, you'll enjoy that splendid Mt. Washington view of the city below, as well as the delights of an innovative menu. You'll get that sense of creativity right away, with the restaurant's signature fresh vegetable boat and home-made clam dip. The boat brings such unusual starters as stuffed grape leaves and baby pickled eggplant. When you're ready for your entree, try the Black Forest Filet, charbroiled filet mignon stuffed with pitted black cherries and topped with a bernaise sauce. You'll also find other beef, chicken, veal, and seafood selections. The Tin Angel offers a full-service bar, a wine list, and banquet facilities for up to 50 people on week nights, up to 30 people on Saturday nights. The restaurant serves dinner Monday through Saturday, closing on Sundays. Reservations are suggested.

Chinese

Golden Palace
$ • 206 Shiloh St., Pittsburgh
• (412) 481-8500

Golden Palace can't boast of the spectacular city view that other Mt. Washington restaurants offer, but it does provide a diverse menu and tasty food. It offers entrees representing all regions of China. Among the more interesting selections are Golden Palace Seafood Combination—shrimp, scallops, lobster, and crab meat with black mushrooms, broccoli, baby corn, and snow peas—and The Four Happiness, chicken, shrimp, beef, and roast pork sautéed with vegetables in a brown sauce. Golden Palace serves lunch and dinner daily. It offers a full-service bar, a wine list, and banquet facilities for up to 75 people. Reservations are accepted for parties of 10 or more.

Sesame Inn
$$-$$$$ • Station Square, Pittsburgh
• (412) 281-8282
715 Washington Rd., Mt. Lebanon
• (412) 341-2555
2975 Washington Rd., McMurray
• (724) 942-2888
711 Browns Ln., Ross
• (412) 366-1838

Sesame Inn operates four restaurants in our primary service area—one at Station Square, two in the South Hills, the fourth in the North Hills. The menu is the same at each, so no matter which one you choose, you can be sure of the quality that persuaded both the *Pittsburgh Post-Gazette* and the *Tribune-Review* to name Sesame Inn the region's Best Chinese Restaurant.

The lunch and dinner menus are quite extensive, featuring poultry, beef, lamb, pork, seafood, and vegetarian selections. Among the most popular dinner choices are General Tso's chicken, salmon with black bean sauce, and the four duck entrees on the menu. Hot and spicy dishes are marked with a star, so you shouldn't be taken by surprise. Sesame Inn offers a full-service bar and a wine list, and it accepts reservations and major credit cards. Each restaurant offers banquet facilities for up to 60 people.

Continental

Cliffside Restaurant
$$$ • 1208 Grandview Ave., Pittsburgh
• (412) 431-6996

Through its large picture windows, Cliffside offers one of Mt. Washington's best views of the city and three rivers below. A piano player performs on Friday and Saturday evenings to enhance the atmosphere. The menu is attractive as well, drawing from a variety of sources and traditions. Cliffside's most popular entree is Veal LaFayette, veal medallions sautéed with artichoke hearts, Butler County mushrooms, black olives, and Marsala wine and laced with scallions. You'll also enjoy the chicken dragina, chicken breast stuffed with cheddar cheese and apple and glazed with a sauce of raisins and honey, and the pepper steak, a New York strip steak lightly marinated and topped with whole green peppercorns, heavy cream, and brandy. Cliffside serves only dinner daily. It offers a full-service bar, an ample wine list, and banquet facilities for up to 60 people. Reservations are recommended. While Cliffside does not designate smoking and nonsmoking sections, it will try to accommodate those who prefer nonsmoking areas.

English

London Grille and Pub
$$ • 1500 Washington Rd., Mt. Lebanon
• (412) 563-3400

Located in The Galleria Mall in the South Hills, London Grille and Pub offers formal and informal English-accented dining. In the dining room, you'll enjoy such traditional English dishes as fish and chips; shepherd's pie, a lamb-based dish with onions and potatoes; and steak and Guinness pie, beef tips braised with Guinness Ale, beef gravy, onions, carrots, and potatoes. If you're in a particularly British mood, try the bangers, grilled British sausage served with English mustard and mashed potatoes. The pub offers lighter fare and features the same menu for lunch and dinner.

In addition to a full-service bar and a wine list, London Grille offers a broad selection of bottled beers and English ales. Reservations for the dining room are recommended on weekends. London Grille offers banquet facilities for up to 40 people in its glass-covered atrium. The dining room and pub are open daily for lunch and dinner, and the restaurant offers a Sunday brunch.

French

Le Pommier
$$ • 2104 E. Carson St., Pittsburgh
• (412) 431-1901

The number of French restaurants in the region is seriously limited; once you've dined here, you'll likely agree that one is more than enough when it's as satisfying as Le Pommier. Among the specialties are Muscovy duck, served on currant red wine sauce, and Elysian Fields farm lamb, served with spicy brown mustard sauce. Also featured are a nightly seafood selection and chef's specials, which include such unusual fare as Thai-style curried seasonal vegetables. French wines dominate the extensive wine list, but you'll also find American wines. Le Pommier offers a full-service bar and banquet facilities for up to 90 people. It serves dinner only Monday through Saturday, closing on Sundays. Reservations are accepted.

Italian

Angelo's Restaurant
$-$$ • 955 W. Chestnut St., Washington
• (724) 222-7120

You won't have to worry about the track record here. The Passalacqua family has operated Angelo's at the same location for more than 60 years, a tribute to the quality of the food and service. It's fitting that one of the signature entrees bears the family name. It's called Pasta Lacqua, and it features sautéed green beans tossed with a light tomato sauce and served with fettuccini and romano cheese. You'll find a full-service bar and an extensive wine and liquor list. Angelo's is a nonsmoking restaurant. Reservations are preferred at Angelo's, which is located in downtown Washington.

Bruschetta's
$$-$$$ • 19th and E. Carson Sts.,
Pittsburgh • (412) 431-3535

Bruschetta's is a cozy South Side spot that

two side dishes, a popular feature with patrons. The diverse menu includes pasts and seafood selections as well as such specials as meat loaf and stuffed chicken breast. Each Monday, Calabria's offers a lunch buffet—it's never the same as it was the previous Monday. The restaurant offers a wine list, a limited-service bar, and banquet facilities for up to 65 people. Calabria's accepts reservations for parties of nine or more.

Influences of many ethnic groups are evident in Pittsburgh cuisine.

The Living Room
$$ • 1778 N. Highland Rd., Bethel Park
• (412) 835-9772

Located along U.S. Route 19 in the South Hills, The Living Room offers an appealing variety of food and entertainment. In addition to a diverse selection of pasta and seafood dishes, the restaurant features ossu buco, which is a veal shank, and chicken Vesuvius, a sauteed chicken breast with hot peppers and sausage. You'll find an extensive wine list and a full-service bar, a special area for cigar smoking, and banquet facilities for up to 75 people. The Living Room opens at 5 PM daily for dinner only accepts reservations and major credit cards. Call to find out about selected weeknight and weekend entertainment.

Paparazzi Ristorante
$$-$$$ • 2100 E. Carson St., Pittsburgh
• (412) 488-0800

Paparazzi specializes in Northern Italian fare . . . and a whole lot more. Regulars at this South Side restaurant particularly enjoy the veal and shrimp cangelosi, which is sautéed with artichokes, mushrooms, and red roasted peppers and served in a wine, lemon, and butter sauce. You'll find other veal and seafood entrees, as well as pasta and chicken selections and an appealing variety of freshly baked breads. The entertainment doesn't end with the food, how-

features both indoor and outdoor dining. The menu offers beef, chicken, seafood, and pasta entrees as well as such interesting veal selections as veal Zurich, which is sautéed with fried onions and Swiss cheese in a marsala wine sauce. If you're in the mood for pasta, try the rotolo, pasta rolled with sausage, mushrooms, and onions and topped with marinara and fontinella cheese. Bruschetta's serves lunch and dinner Monday through Saturday, closing on Sundays, when its dining room is available for banquets up to 50 people. The restaurant offers a full-service bar, and it accepts reservations for parties of six or more. It does not designate smoking and nonsmoking sections.

Calabria's
$-$$ • 3107 Library Rd., Castle Shannon
• (412) 885-1030

Hearty portions are the theme at this South Hills restaurant. Each dinner entree comes with ever, as Paparazzi features live blues and jazz bands Wednesday through Sunday evening, and you can enjoy both your meal and the sounds in an outdoor seating area. Paparazzi offers a full-service bar, a wine list, and banquet facilities for up to 100 people. Paparazzi serves dinner daily, lunch Monday through Saturday. Reservations are accepted Fridays and Saturdays only.

Pasquarelli's Restaurant
$$ • 1204 Grandview Ave., Pittsburgh
• (412) 431-1660
631 Painters Run Rd., Upper St. Clair
• (412) 221-0350

The Pasquarelli brothers—Gino, Joseph, and Mario—emigrated from Italy in 1970 and founded these restaurants only 10 years later. They brought rich Northern Italian flavors and tastes with them, as represented by a variety of veal dishes including ossu buco alla Melanese and Veal Chop Alla Pasquarelli, veal stuffed with prunes and broiled in the brothers' special sauce. You'll also find beef, chicken, seafood, and pasta entrees. The restaurants offer full-service bars; if you ask to see the wine list, they'll bring you a volume so thick and authoritative that it's called "The Bible." The Grandview Avenue restaurant, which offers a great Mt. Washington view of the city, serves dinner each day and accepts reservations for parties of any number. The Upper St. Clair restaurant serves dinner Tuesday through Sunday, and it accepts reservations for parties of five or more. Each restaurant offers banquet facilities for up to 90 people.

Union Grill
$$ • 13½ E. Wheeling St., Washington
• (724) 222-2860

The diverse menu at Union Grill is likely to satisfy most tastes. Italian selections include an appealing assortment of pastas and specialty pizzas as well as fried zucchini. If you're in the mood for American fare, try the popular Rueben sandwich. Union Grill—not to be confused with a different but similarly-named restaurant in Pittsburgh's Oakland neighborhood—offers a full-service bar, a wine list, and banquet facilities for up to 40 people. Reservations are suggested for weekends and accepted at all times. Union Grill serves lunch and dinner Monday through Saturday, closing on Sundays.

Viaggio
$$$ • 2302 E. Carson St., Pittsburgh
• (412) 488-0646

Located on Pittsburgh's South Side, Viaggio specializes in Venetian Italian fare, offering lunch and dinner daily. The dinner menu offers a broad selection of fish, chicken, and pasta dishes, while for lunch you can get really crazy and build your own pasta by mixing and matching from six pastas, seven sauces, and four meats.

One of the most appealing aspects of Viaggio is its libations. The wine list is deep, as is the selection of domestic and imported beers and microbrews. You also may select from a variety of small batch bourbons, single malt Scotch whiskeys, and 13 specialty-brew coffees. Viaggio recommends reservations for lunch and dinner.

In keeping with the swinging Carson Street scene, Viaggio offers outdoor dining. You might call before you drop by Viaggio's; when we last called, they were closed temporarily for the renovation of their HVAC system.

Japanese

Kiku Japanese Restaurant
6 and 7 Commerce Ct., Pittsburgh
• (412) 765-3200

Sushi and tempura for lunch and dinner are Kiku's specialties and its most popular menu items. You'll find plenty of other entrees at this Station Square restaurant, however, including chicken and swordfish teriyaki and shabu shabu, featuring thinly sliced beef with fresh vegetables. You dip the ingredients into a boiling broth, cook them to your liking, and enhance to taste with ponzu and sesame sauce.

Kiku offers an interesting selection of specialty cocktails and Japanese wines and beers, as well as a list of domestic and European wines. Reservations are suggested for dinner. Kiku accepts major credit cards and can accommodate up to 30 people for banquets.

Sushi Two
$ • 2122 E. Carson St., Pittsburgh
• (412) 431-7874

As the name implies, sushi is the star at this South Side restaurant, but you'll find many other options such as tempura, teriyaki, and such "Chef's specials" as chicken cheese roll; eggplant and string beans; and fantasy shrimp, which is sautéed with asparagus in a creamy sauce. Sushi Two offers a full-service bar, and can accommodate banquets of up to 30 people in its Japanese Tatami Room. The restaurant offers lunch and dinner daily, although you'd better make it a late lunch on Sunday, as opening time is 1 PM. Also note that the restaurant closes from 3 to 5 PM Monday through Friday.

Its sister restaurant, Sushi Too, is located in Pittsburgh's Shadyside neighborhood.

Mexican

Hungry Jose's
$ • 227 S. Main St., Washington
• (724) 228-1311

If business takes you to Washington, take your dining business to Hungry Jose's—it's only two blocks from the county courthouse. In addition to a wide variety of Mexican fare, Hungry Jose's also offers Italian and American entrees. The restaurant's The Cantina bar offers a number of specialty margaritas as well as a generous selection of beers on tap. Hungry Jose's offers banquet facilities for up to 50 people. It does not designate smoking and nonsmoking sections. The restaurant serves dinner each day and lunch each day but Sunday.

Jose and Tony's Mexican Restaurant
$ • 1573 McFarland Rd., Mt. Lebanon
• (412) 561-2025

Here's an unpretentious restaurant in the South Hills. You'll order at the counter and transport your food to your table without the intervention of wait staff, but you'll be pleased with the broad selection of tacos, burritos, tostadas, and other Mexican treats. The restaurant offers combination entrees, Mexican-style pizzas, and a limited children's menu. From Monday through Thursday, you'll enjoy "Taco Hour" from 5 to 7 PM, when tacos and pitchers of beer and soda pop are half price. Jose and Tony's offers a full bar—with specially priced margaritas each Monday—and a limited wine list.

Margaritaville
$ • 2200 E. Carson St., Pittsburgh
• (412) 431-2200

Margaritaville specializes in varieties of margaritas, of course. The menu offers both Mexican and American fare, including some hearty Mexican combination platters that will test your appetite. You'll find a bar and a beer list, and you can enjoy your meal or drink in an outdoor seating section. Maragaritaville does not designate smoking and nonsmoking sections. It serves dinner

daily and lunch during the week. Reservations are accepted on weekends only.

Middle Eastern/ Mediterranean

Amel's
$ • 435 NcNeilly Rd., Baldwin Twp.
• (412) 563-3466

Amel's is an institution—it's been serving customers in the South Hills since 1952 and has been operated continuously by the Reiland family since 1968. You'll appreciate that experience and commitment when you dine on fresh seafood on a bed of homemade pasta, or the lamb kabobs that may be the most popular menu item. Amel's offers daily lunch and dinner specials as well as a full-service bar. It accepts reservations, and provides banquet facilities for up to 30 people.

Seafood

Monterey Bay Fish Grotto
$$ • 1411 Grandview Ave., Pittsburgh
• (412) 481-4414

If you have any doubts that this bright, classy Mt. Washington establishment, take a close look at the waiters. They're all sporting bright aqua vests with schools of fish cavorting across them. The menu and its rich selection of seafood will provide another clue. Among the favorite entrees here are Maryland crab cakes, ahi tuna—served sesame style with a lemon butter soy sauce—and an Atlantic salmon dish called Rido Grille House, salmon marinated in a house teriyaki sauce, chargrilled and topped with a honey lime glaze. The restaurant also offers beef, chicken, and pasta selections.

You'll find a bar and an extensive wine list; Monterey Bay pledges to sell its wines at only $10 over cost. It also offers banquet facilities for up to 100 people. It serves dinner daily, lunch Monday through Friday. Reservations are recommended. We probably don't have to remind you, but don't forget to admire the particularly fine view of the city, enhanced by Monterey Bay's 10th-story location and its glass elevator.

INSIDERS' TIP

Only restaurants with Sunday licenses can serve liquor on Sundays and on election days when the polls are open. If you're not sure if your favorite restaurant has this license, don't hesitate to ask.

RESTAURANTS

Solomon Seafood
$$ • 222 Hall Ave., Washington
• (724) 222-0898

Solomon is a popular Washington County spot for salmon, orange roughy, and tuna, and it supplements its seafood offerings with steak and pasta entrees. It's located near Interstate 70 and a few minutes from the campus of Washington and Jefferson College. The Solomon wait staff will serve your liquor orders. The restaurant serves lunch and dinner Monday through Saturday, closing on Sundays. You can't reserve tables on Fridays and Saturdays, but your reservations will be accepted at other times.

Spanish

Mallorca
$$ • 2228 E. Carson St., Pittsburgh
• (412) 488-1818

As the sun streams through the skylight, accenting the colors in the hanging plants, and the tuxedoed wait staff attends your every need, you'd swear you were actually in Spain, enjoying the creative recipes of proprietor Antonio Pereira. It's a touch of Spain on the South Side. Mallorca offers a full-service bar, a robust wine list more than 200 brands deep, and outdoor garden seating seasonally. It accepts weekday reservations for parties of any number and weekend reservations for parties of five or more. Mallorca serves lunch and dinner daily. In fact, it closes only one day—Christmas Eve. "My staff cooks for me 364 days a year," Periera says. "On Christmas Eve, I cook for them."

Vegetarian

Zenith Tea Room
$ • 26th and Sarah Sts., Pittsburgh
• (412) 481-4833

Zenith Tea Room offers soups, salads, sandwiches, and daily specials for lunch and dinner. Representative specials include linguini with onions, walnuts, and Gorgonzola, and wild rice pilaf with celery, onions, cashews, and mushrooms. The menu changes weekly. If you leave your e-mail address with owners Mary Kay Morrow and David Goldstein, they'll send you weekly updates. Also, if you follow the stricter vegan diet, Zenith Team Room can accommodate your needs with various menu items as well on request, in some cases.

Zenith does not serve alcohol, but you're invited to bring your own. It does not accept reservations or allow smoking. The tea room can accommodate up to 40 people for banquets. It's located in the same South Side building as the delightful and quirky Zenith Gallery and antique shop—in fact, you'll be seated among antiques and art in the dining area. For more on Zenith Gallery, see our chapter on The Arts.

The tea room serves lunch and dinner Tuesday through Saturday, brunch only on Sunday. Zenith is closed on Monday. It's located in a residential area and is not particularly well marked. You'll find it just by following the numbered streets. Don't give up; this is one of our favorite restaurants. Vegetarian is gourmet here, and the portions are large, too.

West

American

Alexion's Bar & Grill
$ • 141 Hawthorne Ave., Green Tree
• (412) 276-2018

Here's a nice neighborhood restaurant where you can enjoy lighter fare and sports—both spectator and participant. For your culinary enjoyment, Alexion's offers a large sandwich menu as well as salads, pizza, and wings. You'll enjoy lunch and dinner specials as well as discounted drinks during happy hour each Monday through Friday. If you're a sports buff, you'll enjoy the restaurant's seven televisions and its darts and other games as well as the sports posters that grace the walls. Alexion's offers a full-service bar. It does not accept reservations, and it does not designate smoking and nonsmoking sections for dinner. For lunch, nonsmokers are invited to eat in the upstairs dining room away from the bar. Alexion's is near the Crafton-Green Tree exit of Interstate 279 (the Parkway West), a few miles from Downtown. It serves lunch and dinner Monday through Saturday and offers special entertainment on Christmas, Halloween, and St. Patrick's Day. Call for details.

Boots Open Flame Grill
$-$$ • 1402 Riverside Dr., Bridgewater
• (724) 728-8002
1025 Washington Pike, Bridgeville
• (412) 220-9676

Part of the family of restaurants operated by Lou Pappan, these establishments specialize in wings and barbecued ribs. You'll also find an extensive selection of sandwiches. The

Bridgewater restaurant is in Beaver County, while the Bridgeville restaurant is in southwestern Allegheny County. Each serves liquor but does not accept reservations. They're open daily for dinner, serving lunch on Sundays only.

Casey's Grill
$-$$ • 7195 Eastwood Rd., Beaver Falls
• (724) 846-3700

You'll enjoy breakfast, lunch, and dinner at Casey's Grill, which is located in the Holiday Inn on Pa. Route 18. (For more on this Holiday Inn, see our Accommodations chapter.) The dinner menu includes steal and seafood selections as well as such specialty salads as tuna almond salad, steak salad, and Cajun chicken salad. Each Saturday night there's a surf and turf buffet and a champagne brunch each Sunday.

Casey's Grill provides entertainment—either a disc jockey or a band—on Friday and Saturday nights. The restaurant offers a full-service bar and a wine list. Reservations are suggested for Fridays and Saturdays and holidays. Casey's is open daily but closes from 2 to 4:30 PM each day. It's located just off Exit 2 of the Pennsylvania Turnpike.

Clark's Restaurant
$$ • 333 Rouser Rd., Coraopolis
• (412) 269-9100

Airport Office Park, with its impersonal buildings, is an unlikely setting for a top restaurant. Don't be fooled by Clark's location in the park, for you'll find a restaurant that's warm and classy. The flower-bedecked dining room is an oasis in the desert of gray concrete, getting you in the right mood for the menu, which features beef, seafood, and pasta selections, as well as sandwiches, burgers, and dinner salads. Clark's offers a full-service bar and an extensive wine list. If you're in the mood for a $225 bottle of Chateau Lafite de Rothschild, you'll find it here. Reservations are recommended. Clark's offers banquet facilities for up to 100 people. It serves dinner Monday through Saturday, lunch Monday through Friday. Clark's is closed on Sundays.

DeMartino's Restaurant
$$ • 1100 Washington Ave., Carnegie
• (412) 279-7700

At DeMartino's, you'll find a varied menu highlighted by homemade pasta selections, seafood entrees, sandwiches, and salads. Friday nights bring a seafood buffet, while the feature on Tuesday through Thursday is specially priced dinners for two. DeMartino's offers a full-service bar, a

wine list, and banquet facilities for up to 100. Reservations are accepted. The restaurant serves lunch and dinner Tuesday through Saturday, breakfast on Saturdays, and brunch on Sundays. It's located on Pa. Route 50.

Dockers Restaurant and Tavern
$-$$ • 500 Market St., Bridgewater
• (724) 774-7071

Dockers is a delightful spot along the Beaver River, near Exit 13A of Pa. Route 60. In season, you can dine outdoors on a deck that overlooks the Beaver, and you can feed the ducks—Dockers will provide the bread—that call the river home. If watching those ducks dine sparks your appetite, repair to the restaurant to select from a diverse menu that includes prime rib, burgers, seafood and dinner salads. Dockers offers a full-service bar, and it provides banquet facilities for up to 110 people. It accepts reservations but for Friday and Saturday after 6 PM.

Grand Valley Inn
$$$ • 452 Constitution Blvd., Fallston
• (724) 843-9000

This Beaver County restaurant offers a menu that's interesting and diverse. Entrees range from crab cakes to a filet mignon dinner for two, to dinner salads, including a popular pork loin salad. You'll also find chicken and pasta selections as well as lunch and dinner specials. Grand Valley offers a full-service bar, a wine list, and banquet facilities for up to 100 people. It accepts reservations. Grand Valley is open Tuesday through Sunday. If you enjoy the restaurant's player piano music, you might seek out Grand Valley co-owner Scott Watson and tip your cap. He created the instrument from an unused piano he had around the house.

Greentree Cafe
$$-$$$ • 812 Noblestown Rd., Green Tree
• (412) 276-3557

Greentree Cafe is a fooler. If you're not dissuaded by the unassuming exterior, you'll find an intimate room that seats only 36 and offers a diverse, intriguing menu. Veal and beef dishes are popular, and you'll also be tempted by such interesting selections as filet and shrimp brochette and nutty Norwegian—fresh Norwegian salmon dusted with almonds and topped with brown butter sauce. The restaurant serves lunch and dinner Monday through Saturday. It does not serve liquor—you're invited to bring your own wine and beer—and it does not designate smoking and nonsmoking sections. Reservations are suggested. You'll find Greentree Cafe off the Crafton-Greentree exit of Interstate 279 (the Parkway West), just a few miles from Downtown.

J.W. Hall Steak and Seafood Inn
$-$$ • 2284 Brodhead Rd., Hopewell Township Shopping Center, Aliquippa • (724) 375-6860

As the name suggests, J.W. Hall specializes in steak and seafood for both lunch and dinner. It also features such homemade desserts as Dutch apple pie; peanut butter fudge pie; and turtle cheesecake, which is covered with caramel, hot fudge and pecans. Maybe they need to add desserts to their name. The restaurant offers a full-service bar and a wine list, as well as banquet facilities for up to 40 people. It does not accept reservations.

Kathy's Country Kitchen
$, no credit cards • 3403 Old Darlington Rd., Darlington • (724) 827-2558

Kathy's is one of those old-fashioned restaurants that offers solid American food at reasonable prices. Breakfast, lunch, dinner—you can get them all here seven days a week, and Kathy's stays open round the clock on Fridays and Saturdays. Staples of the menu include sausage over homemade biscuits, breaded vegetables and zucchini, and Kathy's Large Steak and Cheese Sandwich. For dessert, try the bread pudding or rice pudding. Kathy's does not accept reservations, and it does not serve alcohol. Kathy's will close off part of the dining room to accommodate banquets.

Manion's Idlewood Inn
$ • 2749 Noblestown Rd., Greentree • (412) 922-9560

There's never an idle moment at the Idlewood Inn. On Thursday, Friday, and Saturday evenings, you'll enjoy live entertainment, ranging from bands to DJs. Thursday is karaoke night. On Sunday, large crowds gather to watch NASCAR races and Steelers games and to enjoy the accompanying free buffet, live guitar entertainment, and specially priced beer. Did we mention the free happy hour buffet Monday through Friday from 5 to 7 PM? The scene is so lively that Idlewood captures it all in a monthly schedule that you can pick up when you're here.

The food is primarily lighter fare, including burgers, wings, and salads. Each Tuesday through Thursday evening, wings—in 10 different flavors—are priced at 15 cents each. Idlewood offers a full-service bar. It does not accept reservations, and it does not designate smoking and nonsmoking sections. It offers banquet facilities for up to 150 people, and it serves lunch and dinner daily. You can reach it off the Green Tree-Crafton exit of Interstate 279 (the Parkway West).

Manny's Rook Station Cafe
$ • 201 Hawthorne St., Greentree • (412) 429-9353

Manny's is a neighborhood restaurant, set near an abandoned railroad station, and it offers primarily informal fare. Wings, sandwiches, turkey burgers, and Maryland crab cake sandwiches are popular selections. Manny's offers lunch and dinner specials as well as a full-service bar, where you'll enjoy happy hour discounted beers. Reservations are not accepted. Manny's serves lunch and dinner every day.

Mr. C's Restaurant & Lounge
$ • 2820 Duss Ave., Ambridge • (724) 266-4466

When you visit Mr. C's, a family restaurant in Beaver County, try The Pittsburgher—you choose the meats and cheeses—Mr. C's will add Italian bread, marinated cabbage, tomatoes, and French fries, all piled on the sandwich. It's the most popular item on a menu that includes beef, seafood, veal, and pasta selections. The restaurant offers a full-service bar. It does not accept reservations, and it does not designate smoking and nonsmoking sections. Mr. C's serves breakfast, lunch, and dinner daily.

Pappan's Family Restaurant
$ • 2527 Darlington Rd., Chippewa • (724) 843-5813

"And you're gonna like it!" With that famous tag line for his television commercials, "Uncle" Lou Pappan became something of a celebrity in town, attracting attention for his restaurants as well. This one is located in Beaver County, but you'll also find Pappan's Family Restaurants outside our primary coverage area in New Castle and Oil City. As the name suggests, they're family restaurants with economical meals and diverse menus. Fried chicken is a popular selec-

INSIDERS' TIP

In Pennsylvania, restaurants with 50 seats or more must offer nonsmoking sections.

tion, and you'll find daily specials as well. The restaurants serve breakfast, lunch, and dinner daily. They don't serve liquor, and they don't accept reservations. Take it from Uncle Lou— you're gonna like it!

Red Bull Inn
$-$$ • 5205 Campbells Run Rd., Robinson • (412) 787-2855

Located just off the Parkway West about 6 miles from Pittsburgh International Airport, Red Bull Inn serves dinner daily, lunch Monday through Friday. Specialties include an extensive salad bar, prime rib, and the restaurant's trademarked Lobster Pot. You'll enjoy live piano entertainment in the two-story lounge each Friday and Saturday. The lounge is large enough that if you sing off key, no one will be sure the offender is you. Red Bull Inn offers a full-service bar, a wine list, and banquet facilities for up to 80 people. It accepts reservations for parties of six or more.

Red Hots Cafe
$-$$ • 11 W. Mall Plaza, Carnegie • (412) 276-2855

Ribs and wings are the hot items at Red Hots Cafe, which also offers Cajun-style dishes and such unusual selections as buffalo burgers and special salads. The restaurant offers a full-service bar and a limited wine list. For entertainment, try the pool room and the live bands and DJs on Friday nights. Red Hots Cafe can accommodate up to 50 people for banquets. It accepts reservations for parties of six or more. The restaurant serves dinner Monday through Sunday (except from May through August when it's closed on Sundays), and it's open for lunch Monday through Friday.

Temperanceville Tavern
$ • 424 Main St., Pittsburgh • (412) 920-1300

Read the menu at this West End restaurant and you'll discover an operating philosophy: "Remember that you're in Pittsburgh, not at the Ritz. You enter as a customer but you leave as our friend. If you have a suggestion, problem, or question, please let us know at once. (We probably won't do anything about it but we like to keep track of these things.)" Some of that, of course, is tongue in cheek, but the economical prices here are pretty serious. The menu boasts "Five Buck Samiches," including the London Grille fish sandwich (see the "South" section for a profile of London Grille, a sister restaurant to Temperanceville Tavern), and "Nine

Buck Suppers," featuring hobo skillet and "Better Than Your Mom's Liver."

The tavern offers a full-service bar and banquet facilities for up to 50 people. You won't find a designated nonsmoking section. Temperanceville Tavern accepts reservations for parties of six or more. The tavern serves dinner from Monday through Friday, lunch from Monday through Friday. It's closed on weekends. If you're hungry on Sunday, better try the Ritz.

Tramp's Grill & Bar
$ • 412 Greentree Rd., Pittsburgh • (412) 921-7194

The owners of this West End establishment operated a downtown restaurant for years but found they preferred a neighborhood atmosphere. You'll like it, too. Tramp's offers lunch and dinner specials, a lot of sandwiches, and a limited dinner entree list. Its "jumbo cut" wings are a popular selection. You'll find a full-service bar and draft beer specials each Monday and Thursday. Tramp's offers banquet facilities for up to 50 people. Reservations are not accepted, and there is no designated smoking section. It's open Monday through Saturday and on Sundays when the Steelers play at home.

Willows Inn Family Smorgasbord
$ • Pa. Rt. 68, Industry • (724) 643-4500

No need to describe the menu here—there isn't any. This Beaver County restaurant offers exclusively buffet dining, serving lunch and dinner Tuesday through Sunday. That's not to say that the fare is the same every day. The DiMaggio family, which owns both the restaurant and the adjoining Willows Inn hotel, vary the buffet line-up to provide some fun. Wednesday is Italian Night, while the Friday buffets feature seafood. On Thursday and Saturdays, barbecued pork ribs are the featured item. Willows Inn offers a lounge and banquet facilities for up to 200. Reservations are recommended for parties of eight or more. Willows Inn is near Beaver, the county seat of Beaver County. For more on the hotel, see our Accommodations chapter. Note that seniors get a discount on the cost of the buffet.

Wooden Angel Restaurant
$$-$$$ • 308 Leopard Ln., Bridgewater • (724) 774-7880

For more than 30 years, Alex Sebastian has operated this Beaver County restaurant on his personal philosophy of customer satisfaction. For example, Wooden Angel offers an extensive wine

RESTAURANTS

list that features only American brands, which Sebastian believes should be promoted. It's a personal vision to be sure, but Wooden Angel executes it so well that many regard it as one of the region's finest restaurants.

The menu is attractive and diverse, featuring such entrees as rack of lamb; lobster cannelloni; Tuscany sautéed chicken; and angel hair Cantonese, with gulf shrimp and sea scallops atop the pasta bed. Wooden Angel offers a full-service bar, and it hosts jazz bands each Thursday and Friday evening. It can accommodate up to 100 for banquets. Reservations are recommended. For more informal dining, try Casual Cafe, a bistro located within Wooden Angel. Casual Cafe does not accept reservations. The Wooden Angel and the café are closed Sunday and Monday.

Chinese

Asian Gourmet Chinese Restaurant
$ • 507 Fifth St., New Brighton
• (724) 847-2992

Happy Garden specializes in buffet Hunan and Szechuan dishes, including the popular yushaing, which features beef or chicken complemented with green pepper, onions, carrots, bamboo shoots, and water chestnuts—all topped by a hot and spicy brown sauce. The restaurant does not serve alcohol, but you're invited to bring your own beer or wine. Happy Garden does not designate smoking or nonsmoking sections. It recommends reservations.

Greek

Evergreen Family Restaurant
$ • 816 Ohio River Blvd., Rochester
• (724) 775-8885

One of the attractions of this Beaver County restaurant is its availability. It's open seven days a week for breakfast, lunch, and dinner. You'll find steak and seafood selections and many homemade entrees and deserts. Evergreen Family Restaurant does not serve alcohol, and it does not accept reservations.

Italian

Aracri Greentree Inn
$ • 1006 Greentree Rd., Greentree
• (412) 921-4601

Aracri serves lunch and dinner Monday through Saturday, offering a healthy selection of special entrees that changes regularly. You'll find seafood, pasta, beef, chicken, and veal selections, including such entrees as Norwegian salmon prepared "lightly Cajun" with linguini and red clam sauce, and linguini al Scoglio, a linguini base topped with clams, shrimp, scallops, and lump crabmeat in a white or a red sauce. Aracri offers a full-service bar and a limited wine list as well as banquet facilities for up to 60 people. It accepts reservations.

Guiseppe's Italian Restaurant
$-$$ • Pa Rt. 18, Beaver Falls
• (724) 843-5656

In addition to its broad selection of Italian food for lunch and dinner, Guiseppe's offers dining themes Thursday through Sunday evenings. Thursday's specialty is prime rib. Fresh seafood is featured on Friday, while family style dining is Sunday's concept. The restaurant offers a full-service bar and a wine list, and it offers banquet facilities for up to 20 people in one room and 30 in another.

Mario's Family Italian Restaurant
$$-$$$ • 926 Brodhead Rd., Moon
• (412) 262-3020

The breadth of its menu and wine list is a strong appeal of Mario's which is located near Pittsburgh International Airport. The menu offers beef, veal, seafood, and pasta selections, as well as homemade soups. A favorite of diners is Mario's Own Hot Sausage Casserole, featuring ziti and hot Italian sausage baked with provolone cheese and a plum tomato sauce. The wine list runs to 190 selections, and you can enjoy the full-service bar as well.

Mario's can accommodate banquets of up to 20 people. It offers dinner only Monday through Saturday. Reservations are accepted Monday through Thursday only. The restaurant is closed on Sundays.

The Primadonna Restaurant
$-$$ • 801 Broadway Ave., McKees Rocks
• (412) 331-1001

Primadonna has won a clutch of awards for its food and service. The *Post Gazette, Pittsburgh Magazine,* and *City Paper* have all called it the Best Local Italian Restaurant. But the most important tribute to Proprietor Joseph Costanzo, Jr., that hangs on a Primadonna wall is from one Tommy Lasorda, Los Angeles Dodgers executive and sometime gourmand, when he's not hawking weight control products. "You, the Dodgers, and the Italians are all great," Lasorda wrote.

We agree with all that, except maybe the part about the Dodgers. You will find great things on the menu here, highlighted by 33 different made-to-order pastas. Seafood, beef, chicken, and veal entrees complement the pasta selections. Popular selections include portafoglio-delizia—a pocket of veal filled with ham, cheese, artichokes, and mushrooms and simmered in sauce—and chicken zummo, chicken breast filled with a hot stuffed pepper, pepperoni, melted provolone cheese, and prosciutto ham, all breaded, baked, and topped with a tangy tomato sauce.

Primadonna serves dinner from Monday through Saturday. Reservations are not accepted. It offers a full-service bar and a wine list. You'll find it in the western suburb of McKees Rocks, about 5 miles from Downtown Pittsburgh.

Mexican

Chi Chi's Restaurante
$ • 600 Beaver Valley Mall, Monaca
• (724) 774-9206

This chain restaurant is located in Beaver Valley and offers lunch and dinner daily. Among its most popular menu items are fajitas and fried ice cream. Chi Chi's offers a full-service bar, and it accepts reservations for parties of six or more. Each Monday through Thursday, you can take advantage of specially priced mixed drinks. While Chi Chi's does not feature banquet rooms, it sometimes can provide its dining room to host events for up to 50 participants.

Seafood

Wright's Seafood Inn
$$-$$$ • 1837 Washington St., Heidelberg
• (412) 279-7900

Wright's Seafood Inn has been a tradition with local seafood lovers since 1898 when it was opened by the Wright family. It's still operated by their descendants, who have added a few touches here and there, such as outdoor dining in the summer months.

While the menu offers token beef entrees, tasty seafood is the name of the game here. You'll find shrimp, crab, and lobster selections flown in fresh seasonally as well as seafood pasta and some tempting combination platters. Particularly appealing is Bedford broil, a medley of Boston scrod, Atlantic salmon, Maine lobster,

swordfish, and sole broiled with lemon dill or teriyaki. For dessert, you'll enjoy the confections from Wright's made-from-scratch bakery. Wright's offers a lounge, an ample wine list, and banquet facilities for up to 120 people. Reservations are accepted. You'll find Wright's just off Pa. Route 50, less than 10 miles from Downtown Pittsburgh.

Multiple-location Restaurants

Our region boasts a number of locally owned restaurant chains. Each offers family dining, and each is quite popular. Rather than numb you with lengthy lists of addresses and phone numbers, in each case we've described the food and experiences that pretty much apply to all restaurants in the chain. The phone number and address listed are those of corporate headquarters; they'll be happy to help you locate a specific restaurant within the chain.

Eat'n Park
$ • 100 Park Manor Dr., Robinson
Township
• (412) 788-1600

It was in 1949 that Eat'n Park rolled out its first restaurant, a 13-seater in the South Hills section that featured a revolutionary concept: patrons, attended by carhops, could eat in their automobiles. The concept was wildly popular, so popular that Eat'n Park had to close early on opening day due to the crush of curious patrons. Car-hop service has vanished along with the Ramblers, Packards, and Studebakers that queued up that first day, but Eat'n Park's popularity remains. It's the region's largest restaurant chain, boasting more than 70 locations in Pennsylvania, Ohio, and West Virginia. With more than 7,000 employees and annual sales exceeding $150 million, Eat'n Park is a major corporate player in the region . . . and a responsible one. It donates at least 5 percent of its annual pretax profits to community initiatives.

The restaurants are family-oriented, featuring menus with more than 150 choices. Most offer such features as a breakfast buffet; a soup and salad bar; a Sunday brunch; and a bakery, where you can order home-made pies for takeout and pick up some of Eat'n Park's signature Smiley cookies. Many of the restaurants are open 'round the clock and offer a midnight buffet. If you contact Eat'n Park, they'll send you a directory of their restaurants, complete with maps and a checklist of features. The restaurants don't serve liquor, and they don't accept reservations. They serve breakfast, lunch, and dinner daily.

Kings Family Restaurants
$ • 1180 Long Run Rd., McKeesport
• (412) 751-0700

Hartley C. King opened his first restaurant in the eastern community of North Versailles in 1967. His concept of economical family restaurants with signature desserts grew so popular so quickly that today, Kings Family Restaurants includes 31 locations in Allegheny, Butler, Westmoreland, Crawford, Mercer, Venango, Blair, and Lawrence counties. All Kings restaurants serve breakfast, lunch, and dinner daily, and all offer 20 daily dinner specials priced under $5.

When you're ready for dessert, you'll enjoy Hartley's Choice ice cream, which also is available for take-out. The Hartley's Choice private label also features tea and coffee selections. Kings does not serve alcohol. Some, but not all, restaurants offer banquet facilities.

Primanti Bros.
$, no credit cards • 3191 Industrial Blvd., Bethel Park • (412) 854-2700

In the 1930s when Pittsburgh was primarily a factory town, Primanti Bros. had a brainstorm: why not pile everything—meats and side dishes—on a sandwich and create a meal that could be eaten during a rushed lunch hour? Some sixty years later, that idea is still popular, even though the region no longer depends as heavily on manufacturing. Sandwiches here begin with thick slices of Italian bread; wedged

between them are your choice of meats as well as any cole slaw or French fries you order. The result: just about the most robust sandwich you'll find anywhere, imitated by many but equaled by few. If you must break down and cut your sandwich with a knife and fork, it's okay —you won't be the first.

Primanti Bros. offers restaurants in Downtown, Oakland, South Side, the Strip District, Robinson, and Three Rivers Stadium. They serve lunch and dinner— hours at the Three Rivers location depend on the day's activities at the stadium—and the Strip District restaurant is open 'round the clock. Most serve alcohol, but none designates smoking and nonsmoking sections. Reservations are not accepted.

Valley Dairy
$ • 1562 Mission Rd., Latrobe
• (724) 537-7111

Valley Dairy offers old-fashioned, unpretentious dining where meals are filling and economical. It serves breakfast, lunch, and dinner daily and is especially popular for its breakfasts. If you serve two eggs, hash browns or home fries, and toast for $1.89, chances are you will be pretty popular, too. Desserts are plentiful here; you have more than 20 to choose from, including such traditional favorites as All American Banana Split and rainbow parfait. Valley Dairy does not accept reservations, and it does not serve alcohol. In our six-county service area, you'll find Valley Dairy restaurants in Kittanning, Richland, Butler, Greensburg, Latrobe, and Washington. Other Valley Dairy locations are in Fayette, Indiana, and Cambria counties. Valley Dairy, which has been in business for over 60 years, boasts award-winning ice creams and desserts.

Nightlife

When we divvied up this book's chapter assignments, and discussed nightlife in Pittsburgh, each of us laughed. Now, don't get us wrong... there is plenty to do after dark here in "the 'burgh." It's just that when we considered our own nightlife, we quickly surmised we each had none. Zip. Well, not much, anyway. You've got the picture.

Well, lest you think this chapter is a real dud, we collected the thoughts and impressions of seasoned, out-on-the-town friends... and yes, at least one of us even ventured out to discover a few of these hot spots in person!

In this chapter, we give a sampling of entertainment possibilities throughout our coverage area. Admittedly, some Allegheny County neighborhoods, like the Strip District and Station Square, really party the night away in sharp contrast to the more sedate evenings in rural counties. Yet we think you'll find something appealing from our list of jazz clubs, bars and brewpubs, coffeehouses, lounges and nightclubs, sports bars, and movie theaters. Within each of these categories below, we've followed our traditional geographic breakdown.

Rest assured, Pittsburgh nightlife isn't always synonymous with roaring crowds and pulsating music. You'll find those elements, for sure. But you'll also discover neighborhood cafes where patrons play board games, sip cappuccino, and make their own entertainment through lively conversation. If artistic venues or the performing arts appeal to you, turn to our Arts chapter for myriad ideas.

For those who do enjoy a spirited evening in the literal sense, let's discuss a few caveats. First, the drinking age in Pennsylvania is 21. Restaurants with a liquor license are permitted to serve alcohol until 2 AM. Sunday sales are based on a formula involving the establishment's ratio of food to alcohol sales (you won't find sales in the state liquor stores or at beer distributors on Sundays, however).

Second, you may be asked for identification, so be prepared if you have that youthful look about you. Also, be ready to pay a cover charge at some clubs. The amounts vary even from night to night at the same club or night spot, depending upon that night's entertainment.

Third, always designate a driver who won't partake of alcoholic beverages. Be sure to consult this chapter's taxi listing to arrange cab transportation, for your own safety and everyone else's. Unlike some cities, you usually must call for a cab in Pittsburgh unless you're at the airport or a major hotel—you won't necessarily find the cabbies cruising the streets for fares.

Fourth, dress appropriately, or call the phone numbers provided if you're unsure of the dress code. Remember, as a former industrial town, Pittsburgh is a bit more conservative than New York, Los Angeles, or cities in Florida (like Key West, for example).

Finally, there are two factions that deserve mention, and we didn't want you to think we're excluding them. One is the teen scene, and the other is gay nightlife. In our region, neither has a wealth of clubs devoted to them, although they're out there if you look. When we discovered clubs, concert venues, or other entertainment of particular interest to these crowds, we've noted that in the text in order to give you some guidance.

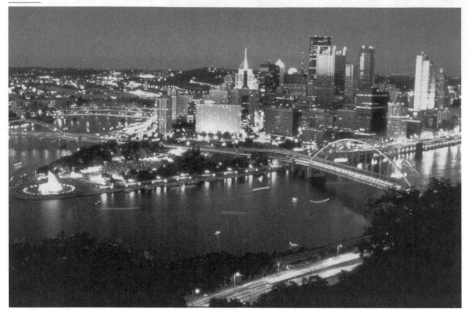

The city skyline at night is best seen from Mt. Washington.

Photo: Jeff Greenberg

Be sure to call for a cab if you're unable to drive home safely:

Yellow Cab Company of Pittsburgh .... (412) 665-8123

Peoples Cab Company .... (412) 681-3131

Limousine Service .... (412) 782-5466

Above all, enjoy your night out on our town. Pittsburgh might lag behind a few other major metropolitan areas, but sure enough, it's a happening kind of place!

All Jazzed Up

Downtown/Uptown

Boardwalk
1501 Smallman St., Pittsburgh
• **(412) 281-3680**

Every Monday evening in the warmer weather months, you'll find live jazz performances on the Pepsi Floating Stage. The Boardwalk, on the shores of the Allegheny River in what's known as the Strip District, attracts boaters who dock and climb aboard these float-ing barges anchored to the shore. Other music is featured on other nights, including disco, oldies, and steel band rhythms.

Crawford Grill
2141 Wylie Ave., Pittsburgh
• **(412) 471-1565**

Though the days of the legendary jazz greats in the 1930s, '40s, and '50s are long gone, the enthusiasm for the music hasn't waned. You'll sway at this club while enjoying soul food and drinks every Friday and Saturday night. The Crawford Grill is in the heart of Pittsburgh's African-American community, close to downtown.

Hill House
1835 Centre Ave., Pittsburgh
• **(412) 392-4400**

Mellow out every Sunday evening at the Hill House in Pittsburgh's Hill District in this uptown area that's the center of the African-American community. Local and visiting jazz artists take the stage. There's free parking at Hill House or in lots nearby.

Scenes Outdoor Cafe
**Pittsburgh Hilton and Towers,
600 Commonwealth Pl., Pittsburgh
• (412) 391-4600**

Don't miss the nightly jazz bands, martinis, and cigar bar here at the Pittsburgh Hilton and Towers outdoor cafe. Of course, this night spot is only open in the warmer weather months, so call ahead if you're unsure. The summer menu specializes in grilled salads, burgers, turkey wraps, and portabello sandwiches. It's open daily until 9 PM.

North

James Street Tavern
**422 Foreland St. at James St., Pittsburgh
• (412) 323-2222**

Jazz bands, quartets, and trios perform here on the North Side many nights each week. Dinner, snacks, drinks, and a fun atmosphere are the highlights beyond the cool tunes you'll hear. Menu specialties from New Orleans like Jambalaya are particular hits. Reservations are suggested for this night spot with two floors of fun and entertainment.

East

Foster's Bar & Grill
**100 Lytton Ave., Pittsburgh
• (412) 682-6200**

Set in the Holiday Inn in Oakland, this local night spot features live jazz each Sunday evening from 7 until 11 PM. Pittsburgh Jazz Society bands perform, and anyone joining the society at the door receives a discount off drinks and food. Sunday brunch includes a jazz performance as well, as do Friday and Saturday evenings.

Valhalla Microbrewery & Restaurant
**1150 Smallman St., Pittsburgh
• (412) 434-1440**

Come to Valhalla in the Strip District for brick oven-baked pizzas, burgers, and wings. Live jazz is performed Wednesday through Saturday evenings. For more information about this night spot, turn to "Bars and Brewpubs" later in this chapter.

South

Paparazzi
**21st St. and Carson St., Pittsburgh
• (412) 488-0800**

Various local artists perform in this South Side establishment. The upstairs dining room serves Italian cuisine for those who want a little dinner before listening to jazz and blues tunes. Tuesday is Euro-Club night with a disc jockey, and ladies receive half off drink prices. No entertainment is typically planned on Mondays.

West

Casual Café
**Wooden Angel, Leopard Lane, Beaver
• (724) 774-7880**

Jazz and piano favorites are provided many evenings in this café at the Wooden Angel Restaurant in Beaver County. Particularly known for its wine selection, this night spot definitely attracts an upscale crowd. There's no cover charge.

Temperanceville Tavern
**424 S. Main St., Pittsburgh
• (412) 920-1300**

If you want jazz and blues on the west side of the rivers, come to the Termperanceville Tavern Wednesday through Saturday. Located in the West End community, this night spot attracts a happy hour crowd that comes out to hear local bands perform.

Bars and Brewpubs

Downtown

Froggy's
**100 Market St., Pittsburgh
• (412) 471-3764**

One of the best hang-outs in the city, Froggy's is the place to be for juicy steaks, an extensive wine list, or just to take in the wonderful art collection. This bar is usually closed on Sundays, except when the Steelers play on home turf. Live bands and disc jockeys perform. There's a piano bar Tuesday through Saturday evenings.

Kason's
**Bank Tower, 311 Fourth Ave., Pittsburgh
• (412) 391-1122**

At this Downtown hot spot, you'll find

plenty of young professionals relaxing after work with good food and drinks at Happy Hour on Fridays from 5 to 7 PM. In this cozy atmosphere that's dimly lit, enjoy the dance floor with tunes from a disc jockey and a $1 buffet each Friday.

Ruddy Duck
Ramada, One Bigelow Sq., Pittsburgh
• **(412) 281-3825**

Cheese and fruit plus hot items are on the hors d'oeuvres menu for the professionals needing to unwind following their Downtown workdays. Check out events on the Ruddie Buddie Calendar, published each month. In fact, if you visit this local lunch and evening spot, be sure to ask them to add your name and address to the mailing list. It's free. Different nights feature microbrew samples, snack attacks, and special promotions for sporting events. Happy Hour runs from 5 until 7 PM.

Top of the Triangle
USX Tower, 600 Grant St., Pittsburgh
• **(412) 471-4100**

Sixty-two floors up with a stunning view of the Golden Triangle below, patrons enjoy the sounds of the piano bar Friday and Saturday evenings. On Friday, there are complimentary hors d'oeuvres during Happy Hour from 5 to 7 PM.

North

Blarney Stone
30 Grant Ave., Etna
• **(412) 781-1666**

You won't want to miss this hot spot, especially around St. Patrick's Day when Irish musicians and dancers put on an extra entertaining performance. Various performers come here, and reservations are suggested for dinner theater packages. For one fixed price, usually on weekends, you get your meal and entertainment. This ranges from approximately $15 to $20 per person. On nights when individuals perform, expect to pay a slight cover charge.

Moondogs
378 Freeport Rd., Blawnox
• **(412) 828-2040**

Just two miles north of the Highland Park Bridge,

Moondogs features some of Pittsburgh's finest local rock 'n' roll talent. On different nights you'll hear from local musicians including native rocker Norm Nardini. Most bands and comedy acts are booked in advance and advertised in the alternative weekly papers (see our Media chapter). Past events have included Pajama Party night, open stage comedy, and contests to win a $1,000 guitar. The tunes range from country and rock to reggae and blues. Moondogs menu is limited to pizzas, tacos, nachos, and a variety of other light snacks.

Penn Brewery
Troy Hill Rd. and Vinial St., Pittsburgh
• **(412) 237-9402**

Enjoy the ambiance of restored 19th-century brewing buildings as you sample at least a dozen varieties of German beers brewed on the premises. This North Side hangout offers an award-winning selection of microbrews, plus its own famous Penn Pilsner beer. There is live entertainment each and Saturday. On the last Thursday of every month, enjoy the sounds of live swing and jazz. German and American cuisine is served in the dining hall with traditional family-style tables (see our Restaurants chapter). The outdoor biergarten is fun in warm weather. Plus, there's free parking in the covered lot next door.

East

Baggy Knee Cafe
9 E. Pittsburgh St., Greensburg
• **(724) 832-5733**

This upscale bar attracts what locals call the courthouse crowd comprised of after-hours professionals. Occasionally a live band will perform, but this is a rarity. It's mostly an eatery for dine-in or take-out service as well as a place to imbibe favorite beers or mixed drinks. It is reported that Harrison Ford enjoyed himself here while in town to make movies.

Bloomfield Bridge Tavern
4412 Liberty Ave., Pittsburgh
• **(412) 682-8611**

Local bands, including alternative rock, rhythm and blues, and new wave artists, perform here in Bloomfield, where ethnic food such as pierogies (a

Polish specialty) always hits the spot as a late night treat. And be sure to wash them down with imported beers.

Church Brew Works
3525 Liberty Ave., Pittsburgh
• **(412) 688-8200**
• **www.churchbrew.com**

Does the name intrigue you? We admit, it might seem strange, but in Lawrenceville you'll find handcrafted ales and lagers served in a turn-of-the-century Catholic church-turned-pub. In fact, you'll find a gleaming steel and copper kettle sitting behind glass on the famous altar. Strange, we know, but it's true.

Brews featured include Pipe Organ Ale, Bell Tower Brown Ale, and Pious Monk Dunkel. You won't go hungry either, with wood-fired pizzas, buffalo strip steak, and other American cuisine. The outdoor Hop Garden is open everyday. If you come because you're curious, you won't be the only ones. The Food Network visited Church Brew Works and Primanti Brothers (see write-up below) for separate shows.

INSIDERS' TIP
Please remember, don't drink and drive. Always have a designated driver in your group.

Foundry Ale Works
28th St. and Smallman St., Pittsburgh
• **(412) 338-9050**

In the city's Strip District, this pub features American ales made from natural ingredients. You'll find a different brew, from Foundry Lite Ale to the Foundry Brown Ale, that is sure to appeal to everyone's differing taste buds. The food is equally tempting with a selection of baby back ribs, seafood, steaks, and chicken done on wood-burning grills. Fresh pizza is prepared in the wood-fired oven. Free parking makes this place even more appealing.

John Harvard's Brew House
4566 William Penn Hwy., Pittsburgh
• **(412) 824-9440**

Nestled into the Shoppes at Penn Center in Wilkins Township, John Harvard's is certainly a restaurant with wonderful appetizers, entrees, and desserts to go with any beverage. There are those, however, who only go for the microbrews and the ambiance of looking in at the stainless steel tanks. Each month, John Harvard's hosts a brewery dinner with samples of their brews, with complementary food dishes at one all-inclusive price (see our Restaurants chapter for details). If you sit in the bar area, you can watch

sporting events or whatever else happens to be on the television as entertainment.

Mullaney's Harp and Fiddle Pub
24th St. at Penn Ave., Pittsburgh
• **(412) 642-6622**

Not just on St. Patrick's Day, but every day it's Irish Old World atmosphere here in the Strip District. Enjoy at least 10 different draft beers, grilled specialties, outdoor seating, and traditional live music. Tuesdays feature Celtic dancing. Be prepared to pay a $3 cover charge after 9 PM on weekends, when you'll find Irish bands playing.

Valhalla Microbrewery & Restaurant
1150 Smallman St., Pittsburgh
• **(412) 434-1440**

Everyone raves about the awesome outdoor deck as much as the array of ales and lagers in this Strip District brewpub. Some brews have unique names such as "Eric the Red," "Big Olaf" or "Thor's Wild Wheat." Valhalla's menu features New American cuisine, including brick oven pizza, burgers, and wings. Live jazz is performed Wednesday through Saturday in the evenings.

Yuppies
241 E. Main St., Mt. Pleasant
• **(724) 547-0430**

Run by the owners of the Casa Nova Lounge in Somerset County, this bar is frequented by gay clientele. It has been in business for nearly 10 years, and has become a popular watering hole.

South

DJ Mike's Cafe
4962 Library Rd., Bethel Park
• **(412) 835-9915**

Here at DJ Mike's, enjoy music (including country western) with a disc jockey, bands, and karaoke too. If the variety of sounds doesn't get you on the dance floor, entertainment like the dart board will ensure a fun time.

Excuses Bar & Grill
2526 E. Carson St., Pittsburgh
• **(412) 431-4090**

If the music menu of live blues, R&B, plus rock 'n' roll doesn't tempt you, then the 24 imported beers surely will. Feast on wings and munchie delights. Friday, enjoy Greek music. Depending upon the entertainment on Saturdays, there may be a cover charge of $2 or $3.

Gandy Dancer Saloon
Landmarks Bldg., One Station Square, Pittsburgh • (412) 261-1717

In what was once the main passenger waiting area of the Pittsburgh & Lake Erie Railroad, the Gandy Dancer makes natives and those from out-of-town feel right at home. Crowds come here for the cozy feel this bar affords, complete with music from the baby grand piano. Listen to every tune imaginable, from Gershwin to ragtime and even the Pittsburgh Steeler fight song. Enjoy free hors d'oeuvres Monday through Friday.

Jellyrolls
Station Square, Pittsburgh • (412) 391-7464

Here on the South Side, Jellyrolls opens at 5 PM Friday evenings, and at 7 PM Wednesday through Saturday. There's karaoke available upon request every Friday from 5 to 8 PM. Crowds come on Wednesdays through Saturdays to hear the dueling piano players perform on stage. Two players hammer out an all-request evening of music from the '70s, '80s, and '90s.

Margaritaville
2200 E. Carson St., Pittsburgh • (412) 431-2200

You won't go hungry here with a plentiful Mexican and Tex Mex menu. Reservations are suggested if you have a large group coming here. Of course, as the name implies, this spot is famous for its substantial margaritas. Band entertainment is limited to Thursday evenings, as most other nights it's too crowded.

Nick's Fat City
1601-1603 E. Carson St., Pittsburgh • (412) 481-6881
• www.nicksfatcity.com

Enjoy live music almost nightly. Don't miss seeing the Hall of Stars, or stars of local entertainment, that is. Doors open at 8 PM in this art-deco club reminiscent of the 1930s nightclubs. There's no cover charge Tuesday through Thursday. Beer specials are offered from 8 PM to 12 AM daily, and happy hour drinks come at $1 per drink from 9 to 11 PM.

The Sandbar
Sandcastle Park, Pittsburgh • (412) 462-6666

If you didn't spot a glimpse of the Gateway Clipper Fleet, you'd think you were on Venice Beach. So says their ad for this beach bar along the banks of the Monongahela River. Having experienced Sandcastle's family fun during the day (see Kidstuff), adults claim this spot at night to enjoy a little alcoholic refreshment.

West

Kangaroos Outback Café
Two Robinson Plaza, Pa. Rt. 60 and Park Manor Dr., Pittsburgh • (412) 788-9003

At this Australian-themed pub in suburban Robinson Township, a typical week might look like this: Tuesday is guest bartender night, Wednesday is all you can eat ribs and wings (die-hard fans love the wings here), and Thursday is college night. All that's before the weekend, which offers more music and fun. A DJ brings you the tunes Tuesdays through Saturdays. On Fridays and Saturdays, get ready to dance to top-40 hits.

Kelly's Down By The Riverside Saloon
1458 Riverside Dr., Bridgewater • (724) 728-0222

Kelly's is one-of-a-kind in this Beaver County community. Set on the banks of the Beaver River, you'll enjoy the tropical island they've set up outdoors with palm trees, equatorial plants, and lots of sand. Inside, there's also action at the bar. Tuesdays are devoted to different Irish balladeers. Thursday, there's karaoke. During the summer months, Fridays and Saturdays have reggae, and Sundays there is steel drum music. During the winter, it's usually blues bands for your listening pleasure. A bar menu feaures sandwiches and burgers.

Quaker Steak & Lube
The Pointe, 110 Andrew Dr., Pittsburgh • (412) 494-3344

Now fans of Quaker Steak & Lube's famous chicken wings don't have to travel all the way to

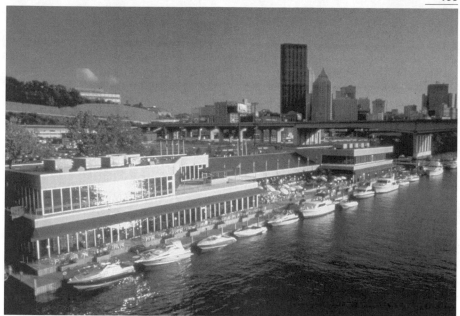

Many establishments are built along the waterfront in Pittsburgh, especially in the popular Strip District along the banks of the Allegheny River.

Photo: Courtesy of Greater Pittsburgh Convention & Visitor's Bureau

Sharon in Mercer County. The eatery's newest location recently opened off the Parkway West at The Pointe. Don't miss the many flavors of wings, but do watch out for the atomic ones. They're potent, and if you want them, you'll have to sign a release form. Of course, there are burgers, steaks and other fare on the menu The ambiance isn't quite what made the Sharon store a favorite, but the car motif is still very prevalent. At the bar, you can even purchase beer to go.

Coffeehouses

Downtown

Barnes & Noble
339 Sixth Ave., Pittsburgh
• **(412) 264-1866**
• **www.barnesandnoble.com**
  This chain of bookstores is famous for its Starbucks coffee bars. Consult the newsletter in the store nearest you to see when poetry readings might occur. Barnes & Noble is also located on Murray Avenue in Squirrel Hill, at The Pointe in North Fayette Township, in Cranberry Town-

ship, at the Waterworks Mall, and in Greensburg near Westmoreland Mall (see Shopping chapter).
  Of course, if you're savoring Starbucks coffee, know the choices include café au lait (a French staple of espresso served piping hot and mixed with steamed cream), caffe latte (a large espresso served with a double shot of steamed milk), cappuccino (espresso coffee served steaming hot, topped with frothed milk) and regular espresso (finely ground dark coffee).

North

Borders Books & Music
1170 Northway Mall, Pittsburgh
• **(412) 635-7661**
• **www.borders.com**
  The Borders chain of book and music stores has three locations in Pittsburgh. Each provides a monthly newsletter with its literary as well as music offerings. If you're looking for a more sedate evening sipping a cappuccino and listening to the sounds of jazz, guitar, acoustic music and many other varieties, then hang out here. Other locations include Monroeville Mall Boulevard in the east suburbs, and at Norwin Center in the South Hills (see Shopping chapter).

East

Dick's Diner
Pa. Rt. 22, Murrysville
• **(724) 327-4566**

Open everyday, Dick's Dinner isn't opulent, but that doesn't matter to its followers. This late night coffee shop and restaurant is known by east suburbanites for its great prices, tasty food, homemade desserts, and casual atmosphere.

Electra Cafe
1814 Penn Ave., Pittsburgh
• **(412) 471-3895**

If you're in the mood for some great coffee, a luscious dessert, and quiet ambiance with friends, head to the Electra Cafe in the Strip District. Order sandwiches and soup off the menu board. Also tempting are the special hot chocolates and cigars. Large tables are conducive to board games or cards, but if you want to play, bring your own as they aren't provided.

Enrico's Tazza D'oro Café & Espresso Bar
N. Highland Ave., Pittsburgh
• **(412) 362-3676**

Owner Amy Enrico grew up in an Italian family and created this café with European flare. She searched the entire country for a coffee broker, and now conducts "cupping" sessions some evenings where coffee drinkers learn to appreciate the qualities and characteristics of particular types of coffee. Poetry readings occur Friday evenings with brunch on Sundays. Dine on the great sandwiches made on the European panini grill.

Hemingway's Cafe
3911 Forbes Ave., Pittsburgh
• **(412) 621-4100**

Enjoy poetry readings every Tuesday at 8:30 PM. While there's no live musical entertainment here, you can savor the delicious menu items including appetizers, wings, seafood dishes, and a full range of pastas in addition to the full bar.

Primanti's
46 18th St., Pittsburgh
• **(412) 263-2142**

If you took a poll of Pittsburgher's favorites for late-night bites to eat and early morning cups of coffee, we bet Primanti's (pronounced Pra-MAN-tees) in Pittsburgh's Strip District would rank at the top. We know of no place else where you'll find the fries and slaw inside (yes, inside!) the sandwich.

Primanti's is open 24 hours. Besides, the prices are very reasonable. People come here for the camaraderie and the reputation. You've just got to say you've been to Primanti's! And while other Primaniti locations have popped up on the Pittsburgh landscape (E. Carson Street on the South Side, Forbes Avenue in Oakland, Market Square and Cherry Way, Downtown, and in Robinson Township), this is the flagship location—the one and only that counts, according to some!

Steamers Espresso Cafe
424 Allegheny River Blvd., Oakmont
• **(412) 828-5506**

Steamers closes around 8:30 PM most evenings, except Friday and Saturday nights when the café remains open until 11 PM. Plans are on tap to add acoustic guitar entertainment in the near future, but for now, patrons clamor to answer the trivia question of the day. In fact, when owners gave the Trivia Board a rest, popular demand brought it back. The menu here is limited to pastries and elaborate desserts, but you'll surely enjoy the hot and cold coffees, plus several loose leaf teas to choose from.

The Café Photo Forum
5884 Ellsworth Ave., Pittsburgh
• **(412) 661-5800**

Based in Shadyside, this small brick building is the city's hang-out for its artistic community. With food, art, photography, and jazz, who could blame the artists for hanging out here? There has been live music on Friday and Saturday nights until midnight in the past, but best to call the phone number (above) for recorded information. Try the outdoor garden café, the full service bar, or book a private party by reservation. Why is it called the Photo Forum? Well, for one thing, you'll see handsomely mounted professional photos, all for sale.

INSIDERS' TIP

While we've pointed this out previously, do remember that the Strip District is perfectly decent. It's a happening kind of place by day, club and coffee spot by night.

South

Beehive Coffee Shop
1327 E. Carson St., Pittsburgh
• **(412) 488-4483**

There is no planned entertainment here at

this South Side coffee shop. Feel free, however, to simply hang out with friends and create your own form of recreation. Board games and chess sets are available to use if you want to join in with this hip, laid-back crowd.

Another Beehive Coffee Shop sits in Oakland at 3807 Forbes Avenue. Call them at (412) 683-4483, but know that on Tuesdays, you'll hear acid jazz, on Wednesdays there is Techno music, and on Thursdays, it's retro '80s music. Fridays and Saturdays feature local and national bands, with top 40s also a part of Saturday's fun. On Sundays, get ready to watch *The Simpsons* and *The X Files* on the big screen, which also airs pro wrestling with punk rock music on Mondays.

Cafe Au Lait
13th St. and E. Carson St., Pittsburgh
• **(412) 431-5910**

With coffees like "Funky Monkey" and "Milky Way Cappuccino" you can tell there's some true brew and specialty teas served here on the South Side. The menu is a bit more extensive, though, with cakes, pastries, bagels, sandwiches, and soups. This night spot stays open until midnight Sunday through Wednesday (they stay open until 1 AM on Thursdays). On Fridays and Saturdays, the doors don't close until 2 AM. Until then, enjoy live entertainment, the Internet, computer and board games, as well as library selections.

Cafe Bean
31 E. Wheeling St., Washington
• **(724) 228-1799**

Close to Washington & Jefferson College, this spot attracts an eclectic crowd. Occasionally, there is music provided by the local radio station, but the ambiance here is created more by the conversation and diversity among the patrons. Some of those customers comment that this place is a throwback to the '60s with its rhythmic sounds as background music.

West

Cappuccino City And Gourmet Coffee
441 Beaver St., Sewickley
• **(412) 749-0766**

If you're in the mood for excellent pastries, gourmet coffees, and herbal teas, stop in. There's no regular entertainment, but look for signs posted in the window (or call to inquire) because the owner books occasional music events. The atmosphere here is a little more casual than in some of the neighboring cafes (like Starbucks).

Common Grounds
234 Bridge St., Beaver
• **(724) 728-5282**

Special coffees, cappuccino, and lattes make this a literal perk-up spot. But if the beverages don't do it, the acoustic music will. Occasionally, you'll find Mario singing Frank Sinatra and Tony Bennett tunes on selected Saturdays. For serious tea drinkers, the fancy tea room can be reserved for parties of 2 through 20 people. Dress in this room is more formal than in the rest of the café.

Starbucks Coffee
425 Beaver St., Sewickley
• **(412) 741-9184**
415 Seventh Ave., Pittsburgh
• **(412) 471-3422**
210 Sixth Ave., Pittsburgh
• **(412) 642-9066**
1719 Penn Ave., Pittsburgh
• **(412) 281-4898**
1717 Cochran Rd., Pittsburgh
• **(412) 563-7813**
6304 Forbes Ave., Pittsburgh
• **(412) 421-6244**
3462 William Penn Hwy., Pittsburgh
• **(412) 823-5328**

Brewing is their business. In recent years, Pittsburgh has seen an increase in stand alone Starbucks coffee shops beyond those in the Barnes & Noble bookstores (which we mentioned above). So stop by not only in the morning, but also well into the evening. Downtown locations include Chamber of Commerce Building and at One Oliver Plaza. Also, enjoy the Strip District shop, the Mt. Lebanon location, the Squirrel Hill's Starbucks, and the Wilkins Township store. Some Starbucks offer periodic entertainment such as acoustic guitar or folk music, usually on the weekends.

Lounges, Dancing, Music & More

Downtown

Cairo
333 Fourth Ave., Pittsburgh
• **(412) 261-0881**

With the sounds of jazz and funk, this club caters to the African-American crowd with its raised dance floor, multiple bars, and lounges. Happy hour runs from 5 to 7 PM. Don't miss the weekly drink specials.

Pegasus
818 Liberty Ave., Pittsburgh
• **(412) 281-2131**

It's got a glittery look and a techno sound for dancing. Happy hour here is from 5 to 7 PM, but watch for drink specials as well. This is perhaps Pittsburgh's most visible gay bar.

North

Ghost Riders
1805 N. Main St., Butler
• **(724) 283-4401**

With top-40 sounds on Fridays, and country tunes the rest of the weekend, Ghost Riders is for a diverse crowd. There's no liquor license here, so it's bring your own bottle.

Horrah's
401 Perry Hwy., Pittsburgh
• **(412) 931-3990**

The sound is definitely from the '90s, and the lighted dance floor, bar games and pool tables give everyone in the crowd a chance to enjoy more than dancing if they wish. Horrah's claim to fame is its drink specials. Wednesdays feature karaoke, and Thursdays you'll find a DJ.

Jetz
2801 Freeport Rd., Harmarville
• **(412) 828-9442**

Jetz attracts the younger, under-21 crowd, on Fridays, Saturdays, and Sundays. Since there aren't that many clubs for this age group, you can see it's a popular place on weekends.

3 B's Lounge
309 S. Main St., Zelienople
• **(724) 452-9959**

There's a lot to entertain you here in Butler County. Thursdays, play pool here. A disc jockey is on hand Friday, and a different band performs every Saturday night. Roughly once a month (usually on Wednesdays or Thursdays) it's open stage. If you feel like playing the hockey game, or joining in at the pool tables, you're in luck. Dart boards and pinball machines are popular fun here also.

3 B's features a full menu with everything from salads to prime rib.

East

Area 51
2106 Penn Ave., Pittsburgh
• **(412) 434-1144**

This club opened in the Strip District in 2000, as part restaurant, part dance club with a uniquely sci-fi theme. Walking through the multilevel club makes you think of films. Downstairs, there's a bar lit up with fiber optic lights reminiscent of Star Wars. The DJ booth acts as the command center for this night spot with four bars, a VIP lounge, a smoke-proof dining room, and 51 micro-brews, not to mention the specialty drinks. And you can't miss the dozen large-screen televisions throughout.

Club Chameleon
2545 Penn Ave., Pittsburgh
• **(412) 338-1988**

New York-style club music is heard here on a spacious dance floor with the ultimate in sound and lighting. Free parking is available nearby this Strip District club.

Club Havana
5744 Ellsworth Ave., Pittsburgh
• **(412) 661-2025**

Martinis, cigars, and Latin sounds are all here at Club Havana. In the warm weather months, the patio is open. Salsa and merengue dance lessons are offered many evenings between 8 and 10 PM.

Club Millennium
112 18th St., Pittsburgh
• **(412) 281-6100**

If you're not used to an unusual indoor and outdoor dance floor, come here to check out this unusual feature. This club describes itself as high energy. Since it's an upscale nightspot, the dress code (dressy casual) is strictly enforced. Valet parking is available. Club Millennium is open Wednesday through Sunday. Fridays feature happy hour.

Donzi's
**Boardwalk,
1501 Smallman St.,
Pittsburgh**
• **(412) 281-1588**

Patrons get to choose here between dancing under the lights inside this popular night spot, or sim-

INSIDERS' TIP

Check the weekend entertainment sections in your local newspapers for listings of movies currently playing, and a whole host of other nightlife possibilities. Most of these sections appear on Friday, although some may be published on Thursdays.

Saints and sinners alike can imbibe at the Church Brew Works.

Photo: Courtesy of Greater Pittsburgh Convention & Visitor's Bureau

ply mingling with the crowds along the Boardwalk outside. Thursday is oldies night. On Sunday, you'll find a disc jockey. Other nights you'll hear mostly top-40 music.

Four Points Hotel – Klub Kokomos
Pa. Rt. 30, 100 Sheraton Dr., Greensburg
• **(724) 836-6060**

You'll find live entertainment here many nights, including a backyard beach party in warm weather months at Klub Kokomos every Thursday night from 5:30 to 10 PM. This wild night features two lighted beach volleyball courts, drink specials, disc jockeys, and much more.

Four Points Hotel – Prospect Lounge
Pa. Rt. 30, 100 Sheraton Dr., Greensburg
• **(724) 836-6060**

Tuesday through Sunday you'll find various bands performing top-40 dance music. A different band rotates on the schedule each week. The dress code here is rather casual, but the

atmosphere's a little dressier than Klub Kokomos (listed above).

Graffiti
4615 Baum Blvd., Pittsburgh
• **(412) 682-4210**
• **www.graffitishowcase.com**

Graffiti showcases national recording artists and local musicians such as Bonny Raitt, Nirvana, Hootie and the Blowfish, and many more talented performers. In fact, Graffiti has been rocking Pittsburgh for nearly 20 years. Call for a listing of upcoming events and ticket prices. Unless otherwise stated, all concerts are geared toward an over-21 crowd. There are frequent exceptions, though, so do call or check the weekly alternative newspapers for the upcoming events.

INSIDERS' TIP
Check out live theater productions by consulting our Arts chapter.

Have A Nice Day Café
1700 Penn Ave.,
Pittsburgh
• **(412) 201-1200**

Featuring a raised and lighted dance floor, this is

certainly a nightclub unlike any other cafe you've discovered (in the true sense of the word café!). Despite the name, you'll enjoy sounds of the '70s and feel you're back in that decade as you look upon the walls plastered with celebrities the likes of television's Farrah Fawcett, former president Richard Nixon, and superstar Elton John.

At Have A Nice Day Café, don't miss the drinks served in your very own fishbowl! Doors open at 5 PM. After 9 PM, you must be 21 years of age or older.

Metropol
1600 Smallman St., Pittsburgh
• **(412) 261-2221**
• **www.sportsrock.com**

There's a semi-private club upstairs, with a multi-level (and large) dance floor downstairs. If you like to dance, you can surely work up a sweat here with the variety of sounds ranging from new wave and modern hits to electronica. There are plenty of disc jockeys to keep the music hot.

Rosebud
1650 Smallman St., Pittsburgh
• **(412) 261-2221**
• **www.sportsrock.com**

Another club in the city's Strip District, Rosebud offers a little taste of every kind of music. The variety includes Tuesdays "Girls Night Out" showcasing local and national female musicians, and other nights that have disco, funk, and dance music. Special events require advanced ticket purchases.

Yesterday's Restaurant & Lounge
233 W. Otterman St., Greensburg
• **(724) 836-6996**

People come from all over for the wings here at Yesterday's, where folks also enjoy oldies music from the '50s through '70s, provided by the disc jockey five nights a week until 1 AM. Sunday, don't miss karaoke. Yesterday's is closed Mondays. There are children's items on the menu, so you might consider bringing the family to Yesterday's.

South

Blues Cafe
1832 East Carson St., Pittsburgh
• **(412) 431-7080**

Stop in for a Monday night jam session here on the South Side. Various artists are featured throughout most weekends with different blues

bands all the time. The Blues Cafe now serves Primanti sandwiches (read more about Primanti's above under coffee houses). Typical cover charge is $2.

CJ Deighan's
2506 W. Liberty Ave., Pittsburgh
• **412-561-4044**

While the clientele at many of the other alternative bars and nightclubs in Pittsburgh is mostly men, CJ Deighan's is a happening place for women, with the majority of patrons being of that gender. During winter months, the nightclub's busiest season, Friday and Saturday nights boast DJs, and there are often bands or other live entertainment scheduled. In the summer, there's a DJ on Saturday night only. If dancing isn't really your thing, belly up to one of the two bars or shoot some pool. Call CJ Deighan's to check the live entertainment schedule year-round. And get yourself over there; it's a nice place.

Chauncy's
Station Square, Pittsburgh
• **(412) 232-0601**

Different nights bring on new sounds. Tuesdays, enjoy music from the '50s through '70s. Wednesday, it's swing. Thursday, dance to rhythm and blues selections as well as hip-hop. On Friday, you'll be all set for the '90s tunes. Saturday is reminiscent of John Travolta with the '70s disco sounds. Finally, on Sundays, it's top-40. Drink specials are always on tap. Proper dress is required (no sneakers). Cover charges apply Tuesday through Sunday.

Funny Bone
Station Square, Pittsburgh
• **(412) 281-3130**
• **www.funnybonelive.com**

If you couldn't guess from the name, this club will keep you laughing with its evenings of comedy, music, and magic. Showtime is 7:30 PM most nights. Tuesdays feature the All U Can Laugh Comedy Buffet. Fridays, be prepared for shows at 8 and 10:30 PM. Saturday, the fun starts at 7:15, 9:30 or 11:30 PM. Reservations are recommended.

Lava Lounge
2204 E. Carson St., Pittsburgh
• **(412) 431-5282**

Most every night disc jockeys keep the pace hopping at the Lava Lounge. On Mondays, there is a variety show. The mood here is set by the different décor—the feeling of a subterranean organic environment with a deep-cushioned pit booth. Wednesdays and Thursdays give you the chance to visit with no cover charge, but expect to pay $2 to $4 on other evenings.

Nitelite
Holiday Inn Meadowlands,
340 Racetrack Rd., Washington
• (724) 222-6200

Join the upscale crowd assembled here for dancing, drinks, and wonderful evening entertainment. Nitelite isn't far from the race track, so once your wagering is finished for the evening, head on over.

Pepsi-Cola Roadhouse
Rt. 18, Burgettstown
• (724) 847-9448
• www.pepsiroadhouse.com

Pepsi-Cola Roadhouse is a unique dining and entertainment experience, with a seating capacity in excess of 800. With tables of four, every seat yields an up close and personal view of the performers, who range from country and western entertainers to pro boxing and night-at-the-races events. Take Route 22 west (off the Parkway West) and continue on until you reach the Burgettstown-Florence exit.

Quail Hill
Pa. Rt. 19 S.,
Washington
• (724) 745-0333

One mile north of Racetrack Road, you'll find Quail Hill, a restaurant lounge with light fare, cocktails, and live music. Performers vary, but previous groups and individual artists have included jazz, blues, rock, and country music.

West

Boots
1420 Riverside Dr., Beaver
• (724) 728-8002

If you're into country and western music come to Boots, where beers are served from plastic boot glasses (that double as take-home souvenirs).

But that's not the only thing that makes this quite a different hang out. The menu (try the ribs) is presented as a newspaper. Peanut shells get thrown on the floor. If you time your visit right, you'll get to witness one of the many line dances the wait staff occasionally performs.

However, that's not all they're known for. Servers here at Boots also write the daily specials on each table cloth—upside down!

Cahoots
101 Marriott Dr., Pittsburgh
• (412) 920-8078

Laugh with the local comedians during an open mike session each Thursday evening, then come back Friday for live blues bands performing. On Saturday, it's oldies night. Expect to pay a $3 to $5 cover charge on weekends.

Sports Bars

North

Clark Bar & Grill
503 Martindale St., Pittsburgh
• (412) 231-5720

Housed in the old Clark Candy Building on the North Side, there's a definite sports atmosphere to this popular hangout across from Gate B at Three Rivers Stadium. Come in for the great grilled entrees, delicious salads and sandwiches, and supreme pastas. Drinks are moderately priced. Even better than the food and libation, however, is the art deco atmosphere, including autographed jerseys, baseballs, hockey sticks, and much more celebrating Pittsburgh sports.

Headwaters Pub
Three Rivers Stadium, Pittsburgh
• (412) 321-2800

Enjoy the upscale atmosphere of this stadium pub before and after the games, and watch all the on-field action on the five-foot screen. Snacks, sandwiches, and wonderful specialties available for your dining delight. Headwaters is only open on game nights.

Legends
Sheraton Inn Pittsburgh North,
910 Sheraton Dr., Mars
• (724) 776-6900

Open seven days a week, Legends offers eight television screens around the bar. This Butler County night spot serves your favorite mixed drink or beer plus light fare such as sandwiches.

INSIDERS' TIP
If you're a recovering alcoholic, head to Club Alternative at 615 McClure Street in Homestead. There's a big dance floor, a house disc jockey and snack bar. Call (412) 462-5777.

East

Champs
5832 Forward Ave., Pittsburgh
• **(412) 422-6414**

This Squirrel Hill haunt is a favorite for Steeler games and other local sports. It's open every day from mid-afternoon until 2 AM. However, for Steeler's Sundays, come on in at noon to start the fun.

Damon's
Miracle Mile Shopping Center, Monroeville
• **(412) 858-7427**
7217 McKnight Rd., Pittsburgh
• **(412) 367-7427**
511 Clairton Blvd., Pittsburgh
• **(412) 653-7427**
855 Freeport Rd., Pittsburgh
• **(412) 782-3750**

This is certainly the place for barbecued ribs, but you'll also find sports fans congregating here. Other house specialties include reasonably priced sandwiches, salads, and entrees for the whole family. In the Pittsburgh area, visit other Damon's locations in the North Hills, South Hills, and at the Waterworks Mall.

Dino's Sports Lounge
Pa. Rt. 30, Latrobe
• **(724) 539-2566**

Winner of the 1997 Pittsburgh Wing Cook Off at Station Square, Dino's is a popular spot for sports fans. If you don't want to watch the 10-foot big-screen television, park yourself near one of the 16 to 18 smaller sets. In addition to the great sandwiches and wings for which the lounge is known, there are also two Indy racecar simulators, pinball and golf machines, and a dart board.

The Loft Lounge
475 Willow Crossing, Greensburg
• **(724) 838-9335**

With entertainment provided throughout the week, you'll find more than sports fans here. There is a disc jockey playing tunes Tuesday through Sunday evenings. Jazz bands perform every Sunday from 3:30 until 7:30 PM. For those who focus primarily on sports, they'll find three televisions and one big-screen TV.

Oakmont Tavern
814 Allegheny River Blvd., Oakmont
• **(412) 828-4155**

With five televisions that let you see your favorite sports action, we'll term this a sports bar, even though you can have lunch or dinner also. After all, the walls are adorned with old photos of Forbes Field, Pirate baseball, and more. The menu features sandwiches, hoagies, and appetizers. Mexican dishes are apparently the hit of the house.

South

Forbes Field Tavern
2901 Sarah St., Pittsburgh
• **(412) 431-9463**

Forbes Field, for those with a primitive Pirates baseball background, was the predecessor of Three Rivers Stadium. Centered in Oakland, the baseball park was demolished to make room for expansion at the University of Pittsburgh. Today, this tavern bears its name with old memorabilia adorning the walls, including scorecards and plenty of photographs. Enjoy Budweiser drafts for only 75 cents all day, every Monday.

Woodson's All-Star Grille
One Station Square, Pittsburgh
• **(412) 454-2600**

Sports fans of all ages will enjoy the sports memorabilia here, so feel free to bring the entire family to this night spot bearing the name of former Pittsburgh Steeler Rod Woodson. With over 30 televisions, this is definitely the place to catch Penguins hockey, Steelers football, or any other popular team on the tube. It's also reported that Rod Woodson appears frequently!

West

Butya's Tavern
5576 Steubenville Pike, Pa. Rt. 60,
Pittsburgh • **(412) 787-1919**

The autographed memorabilia hanging on the walls gives just the right team spirit to watch popular games on television while enjoy good food and drink. Recently completed for the summer season is a sand volleyball court with an adjacent pavillion for outdoor serving. Based in Robinson Township, Butya's is known for its tasty fish sandwiches.

Zooky's Tavern
Pa. Rt. 51, Fallston
• **(724) 843-9464**

Between Beaver and Chippewa, Zooky's offers more than just great wings and beer. There's the trivia game patrons play on television, competing against participants in other bars around the country. Of course, that's when fans aren't watching a major sporting event. So whether it's food, beverages, or just plain fun, Zooky's has all three.

Movie Theaters

This obviously is not a comprehensive list, but here we've given the largest and the most popular theaters and spots for movie lovers.

Andy Warhol Museum
117 Sandusky St., Pittsburgh
• (412) 237-8300
• www.warhol.org

While the art comprises most of the attraction here, there is a theater that screens Andy Warhol films. It's on the first floor of the museum, and sometimes easily missed by those who only browse the exhibits or eat in the café. The Warhol is open Wednesday and Sunday, 11 AM to 6 PM, and Thursday, Friday, and Saturday, 11 AM to 8 PM. It's closed Mondays and Tuesdays. Admission to the theater is included in the cost of a museum ticket. Adults will pay $7, seniors are charged $6, and students and children older than 3 pay $4 for admission. Carnegie members pay nothing to enter.

Carmike Cinemas—Cranberry
Rt. 19 N., Cranberry
• (724) 772-3111
• www.carmike.com

Carmike Cinemas is a chain with several suburban locations throughout the Pittsburgh region. This cinema in Cranberry has eight screens showing popular first-run movies. Try the others closer to you at South Hills Village, (412) 835-7700; the Galleria in Mt. Lebanon, (412) 531-5551; Pleasant Hills, (412) 655-0500; Century Square Plaza, (412) 655-8700; and Delmont, (724) 468-3553.

Carnegie Science Center Omnimax
One Allegheny Ave., Pittsburgh
• (412) 237-3400
• www.carnegiesciencecenter.org

Read more about this attraction in both the Attractions and Kidstuff chapters. However, here we wanted to highlight the Rangos Omnimax Theater which shows one or two different films on any given day. Double-feature presentations are the norm on weekends. Expect to pay approximately $4.50 to 6.50 for tickets, unless you want exhibit passes and other tickets, or unless you attend a double feature. Members are admitted at lesser charges.

Dependable Drive-In
Moon Clinton Rd., Coraopolis
• (412) 264-7011

Drive-in theaters are so rare, we've chosen to list this one. Why not enjoy a throw-back to the 1950s and take the family out to this theater? Enjoy the per car admission as opposed to per person charges too!

Destinta Theatres
Rt. 30 and Rt. 48, N. Versailles
• (412) 824-9200 • www.destinta.com

Opened in June 1999, this 20-screen complex bills itself as "luxury for less" because it boasts VIP luxury boxes, highback recliner seats, large party rooms, a video arcade, a full concession stand, and a gourmet coffee bar. Visit another location in the west suburbs at Rt. 50 West in Bridgeville, (412) 914-0999.

Harris Theater
809 Liberty Ave., Pittsburgh
• (412) 471-9700

The Harris Theater is often the site of films for Pittsburgh Filmmakers. You can read more about both the theater and the organization in our Arts chapter.

Loews Cineplex
Rt. 30 to Warren Dr., N. Versailles
• (412) 823-3992

There's tough competition in this area of North Versailles, with Loews Cineplex opening less than six months after Destinta Theatres. Built on the site of the former Greater Pittsburgh Drive-In, Loews offers 22 screens showing recent Hollywood releases.

Regent Square Theater
1035 S. Braddock Ave., Pittsburgh
• (412) 241-2332

Like the Harris Theater, this facility hosts the Pittsburgh Filmmakers. Find out the showings by calling the phone number, checking the web at pghfilmmakers.org, or reviewing the listings in the alternative weekly papers.

Showcase Cinemas
McKnight Rd., Pittsburgh
• (412) 931-1870
• www.showcasecinemas.com

Built in the 1970s, many of these cinemas have been added onto. The North Hills location on McKnight Road boasts 12 screens. There's Showcase Cinemas West in Robinson Township (412) 787-5788, with 15 screens, and Showcase East in Wilkins Township, with 12 screens.

Shopping

If you've read other chapters so far, you probably know that Pittsburghers are proud of our sports teams. But there's one sport we love that you won't read about in that chapter: shopping.

Indeed, browsing for bargains, finding fresh produce, or uncovering valuable antiques is a true treasure hunt in these parts. Then, there's gearing up for your garden, outfitting the kids, or finding a fun flea market. If all these venues don't complete your search, your local mall surely will. Throughout the region, major malls and strip plazas dot the landscape.

However, there has been controversy surrounding shopping as well, most notably concerning the proposed Market Place at Fifth and Forbes Avenues. This issue has been in the news so much that headline writers merely write "Fifth/Forbes" and we all know what it means.

Essentially, Mayor Tom Murphy has pushed for development of an historic but slightly run-down retail corridor in Downtown Pittsburgh. A plan by Chicago-based Urban Retail Properties would transform this space into an 18-hour mecca of upscale shops, restaurants, and movie theaters. Sounds great, until you realize that the project would raze 68 buildings, and save, if feasible, about 13 building facades of historical or architectural value. Preservationists fear this will destroy the charm and character of Downtown. Well, we can't solve the ongoing debate here, but architecture aficionados can turn to our Architecture chapter to learn about preservation groups, and die-hard shoppers can merely dream that someday we may have an FAO Schwartz, Tiffany's, or Nordstrom to call our own.

For the moment, shoppers will not go through withdrawal or have to do without. Whether it's window shopping or stock piling for the next snow storm, you're set. Peruse the following list, which we hope will help you on your way. Using our normal geographic breakdown to guide us for the most part, we'll also break this chapter into other sections, beginning with places where you can boost the Downtown economy, then focusing on shopping within the city limits before heading out to the suburbs. In addition, we felt particular types of stores deserved their own sections within this chapter, so look for added focus on books and music, specialty merchants, consignment shops, antique dealers and flea markets, and farmers' markets as well. Hardly comprehensive, we've tried to include the highlights such as major malls and outlets, while also steering you toward out-of-the-way shops and independent merchants you won't want to miss. Several of these entrepreneurs have stellar reputations in the region for providing only the finest.

Downtown Shopping

Pittsburgh is fortunate to have a rather compact central business district, defined by the banks of its rivers on each side. From Point State Park to the Mellon Arena, we call this area the Golden Triangle. Within the Golden Triangle, there are three major department stores Pittsburghers rely upon for their shopping needs.

Kaufmann's
**400 Fifth Ave. and Smithfield St.,
Pittsburgh • (412) 232-2000**

This is the home of the famous Kaufmann's clock, which hangs outside the store. If anyone tells you to meet them under this famous landmark, now you'll know exactly what they mean. Inside, you'll find plenty of merchandise as this is Pittsburgh's oldest department store (in our Architecture chapter you'll read about the Kaufmann family and their legendary summer retreat). This is the original Kaufmann's, and the oldest name in Pittsburgh retailing. The store carries moderately priced to expensive merchandise including jewelry and cosmetics, men's, women's, and children's fashions, home furnishings, and housewares. You'll also find that in the downtown store, space is rented out to private vendors selling everything from a quick bite to eat to gourmet chocolate or books.

This Downtown flagship store offers a parking garage across the street with a convenient skyway. On the first floor, you'll find the beloved Tic Toc Shop Restaurant (see our Restaurants chapter for more on this and Kaufmann's other eateries). Watch out for the Day & Night sales, which bring patrons mostly to the suburban locations including Beaver Valley, Ross Park, Monroeville, and Westmoreland Malls, Robinson Town Centre, Century III Mall, South Hills Village, and Shenango Valley Mall in Mercer County.

Lazarus
**301 Fifth Ave., Pittsburgh
• (412) 291-2200**

At a cost of $78 million, Pittsburgh unveiled its new Lazarus store in the fall of 1998. Years before, Lazarus (a regional department store chain that had acquired the Joseph Horne Co.) operated out of a location near Gateway Center on Penn Avenue and Stanwix Street. Today, as you walk along downtown, you'll come upon the store at Fifth Avenue and Wood Street. In fact, you might see first the four terra cotta masks salvaged from the façade of the old building that was torn down to make way for the glimmering department store. The third floor is devoted to all merchandise female, and you'll even find a mammography screening center run by Allegheny University Hospitals. You'll find

suburban locations at Beaver Valley, Ross Park, Century III and Monroeville Malls as well as at South Hills Village and Natrona Heights.

Saks Fifth Avenue
**513 Smithfield St., Pittsburgh
• (412) 642-6700**

While much smaller than the world-famous Saks Fifth Avenue in Manhattan, this location lends a certain appeal to a certain upscale clientele. It's got all the same top names in fashion and fragrance as its New York counterpart. It's within easy walking distance of the other two major department stores, and rounds out Pittsburgh's list of major Downtown retailers. For the moment, that is.

Other Downtown Stores

Respected names in fine clothing—Brooks Brothers (600 Smithfield) and Larrimor's (Grant Street & Fifth Avenue)—have stand-alone stores Downtown.

During the city's second Renaissance, new downtown office towers and retail centers sprouted. The Shops of One Oxford Centre along Grant Street and Fourth Avenue nest inside a five-level atrium and showcase fine fashion labels like Armani and Ralph Lauren. Hardy & Hayes, with its selection of Tiffany and Baccarat merchandise, is another anchor tenant in Oxford Centre. The White House is a store with one dominant color in clothing! Shoppers wishing to continue their boost to the economy don't even need to venture outdoors, for there is a skywalk that connects Oxford Centre to covered parking and Kaufmann's.

Closer to Gateway Center at Third and Stanwix sits PPG Place, an architectural jewel that includes specialty shops, mostly with interesting cards and gifts. Just blocks away, Fifth Avenue Place Arcade Shops (at Fifth & Liberty Avenues) features two floors of boutiques, fashionable shops, and gift merchants.

Other finds within the Golden Triangle include Warner Centre, a retail arcade fashioned out of a former movie palace along Fifth Avenue; Burlington Coat Factory, which opened its doors at Sixth and Smithfield; and several jewelry stores making up what is known as the diamond district right around the Clark Building on Liberty Avenue.

INSIDERS' TIP

It's a taxing subject, but you will want to know that in Pennsylvania, most clothing is not subject to the state's 6 percent sales tax. Within Allegheny County, the sales tax levied is 7 percent.

SHOPPING

Farmers' Markets

Most communities offer farmers' markets beginning in May or June and running through the fall harvest season. Check with your municipality or borough for more details, but here's a list of a few more popular farmers' markets.

Downtown

City-County Building Farmers' Market
400 Grant St., Pittsburgh
    Fridays from 11 AM to 1 PM

Marketplace
Fifth Ave. Place, Stanwix St. and Penn Ave., Pittsburgh
    Monday through Friday from 7 AM to 5 PM

East

East Liberty Farmers' Cooperative Market
344 N. Sheridan Ave., Pittsburgh
    Saturdays from 5 AM to 12 PM, open year-round

Greensburg Market
W. 2nd St., Greensburg
    Tuesdays from 3 to 6 PM

Highland Park Farmers' Market
Pittsburgh Zoo parking lot
    Mondays from 4 to 8 PM

Irwin Borough Farmers' Market
Main St. and Fourth Ave., Irwin
    Saturdays from 9 AM to 12 PM

Ligonier Country Market
Baldonieri's Mill Creek Restaurant parking lot
    Saturdays from 7 AM to 12 PM

Monroeville Lions Club Farmers' Market
Gateway Campus Dr., Monroeville
    Saturdays from 9 AM to 1 PM

Verona Borough Farmers' Market
736 E. Railroad Ave., Verona
    Thursdays from 4 to 8 PM

South

Mt. Lebanon Farmers' Market
Washington Rd. and Shady Dr. East
    Wednesdays from 4 PM until dusk

South Side Farmers' Market
S. 18th St. and Sidney St.
    Tuesdays from 4 to 8 PM

Washington Farmers' Market
Washington, PA
    Monday, Wednesday, Friday from 5:30 PM to dusk
    Saturday and Sunday from 12 to 5:30 PM

West

Ambridge Farmers' Market
Park Rd. and Route 65
    Thursdays from 4 to 7 PM

Beaver Farmers' Market
Beaver County Courthouse Parking Lot
    Saturdays from 10 AM to 1 PM

Moon Township Farmers' Market
Robin Hill Park
    Tuesdays from 3:30 to 6:30 PM

North

Butler County Cooperative Farmers' Market
Chestnut St. and W. Diamon St., Butler
    Mondays and Wednesdays from 3 to 6 PM
    Saturdays from 7:30 AM to 12 PM

North Side Farmers' Market
East Park (across from main entrance to Allegheny General Hospital at Cedar Ave.)
    Fridays from 4 to 8 PM

Shopping Districts On The Outskirts

While not within the Golden Triangle, many other areas boast wonderful shopping. Several are within city limits.

East

South Craig Street Shopping
Oakland section of Pittsburgh

In the heart of Pittsburgh's education and healthcare community, you'll find one-of-a-kind gifts and other worldly surprises. Among the local merchants are Caliban Book Shop, (412) 681-9111, for books of the scholarly variety; the Irish Design Center, (412) 682-6125, filled with Irish imports like sweaters, fashionable woolens, and decorative household items; and Papyrus Designs, (412) 682-3287, featuring unique desk accessories, gift wrapping supplies and fine stationery.

Shadyside Shopping
Along Walnut St. and Aiken St. as well as Ellsworth Ave.

Not far off of Fifth Avenue, heading east is the fashionable Walnut Street of Shadyside. This community is known for cafes, restaurants, retail chain stores, and local specialty shops and galleries. The best finds may be at the independent establishments such as Clay Place, (412) 682-3737, with sculptures and ceramics; Glassworks, (412) 682-5443, boasting names like Baccarat, Lalique, and Swarovski; and Feathers, (412) 621-4700, which as the name implies is filled (literally!) with comforters, quilts, and pillows. You can read about SW Randall Toyes & Gifts in our Kidstuff Chapter and review our Bookstore section below for Journeys of Life information.

Squirrel Hill Shopping District
Forbes and Murray Aves., Pittsburgh

Searching for perhaps the best homemade bagels in Pittsburgh? In the heart of Pittsburgh's Jewish community, you won't want

to miss Bageland, (412) 521-1067. Other favorites include Adele's Ladies Apparel, (412) 421-1991, for fine fashions, and Linton's, (412) 421-9700, for women's designer clothing and bridal selections. Little's Shoe Store, (412) 421-3530, is actually big! That's right, no matter whose feet you intend to fit into the shoes, you should be able to find a pair here. And after a day of heavy duty shopping, why not walk to Barnes & Noble (see Bookstores below) for some coffee in the café and a relaxing book.

Strip District
Several blocks from Downtown at 11th Street to 33rd Street

Named for the strip of flat land that runs from the edge of downtown to the beginning of Lawrenceville, one thing is for sure: People come to the Strip for the hectic atmosphere, novel merchandise, and above all else, great food! As we've told you in other chapters, The Strip is very decent!

Gourmet delights abound, with everything from authentic Mexican ingredients at Reyna Foods, (412) 261-2606, to the wonderful seafood selection at Robert Wholey & Co., (412) 261-3693, and Benkovitz Seafoods, (412) 263-3016.

Looking for Italian bread, buckets of fresh olives, imported cheeses, and a variety of pastas? Head to the Pennsylvania Macaroni Co., (412) 471-8330, Jimmy & Nino Sunseri Co., (412) 255-1100, or Stamoolis Brothers, (412) 471-7676.

While it's true that you'll breathe in a new aroma on virtually every corner of the Strip, there are a few other non-edible finds in this trendy shopping district. Known for its noise-activated toys and wacky gadgets, the Mike Feinberg Co., (412) 471-2922, supplies everything from partyware and gifts to Pittsburgh sports team merchandise. Come Halloween, look your spookiest with the help of Costume World, (412) 281-3277.

Sidewalk vendors in the Strip peddle everything from T-shirts to compact discs and cassette tapes. And you will not go hungry while you shop. Sidewalk grills offer barbeque ribs, chicken, and pork, Chinese specialties, as well as hot dogs and hamburgers. Stop in at a coffee shop or bakery for a cup of fresh brew, and a freshly baked pastry or biscotti. It's all

INSIDERS' TIP

More Amish merchandise is found in Smicksburg-Dayton, Armstrong County. Call for a free brochure with area map and merchant descriptions, available from the Armstrong County Tourist Bureau at (724) 548-3226. Amish shopping is also covered in our Daytrips & Weekend Getaways chapter for those headed to Lawrence and Mercer counties.

SHOPPING

here—dozens of stores to tempt your palate and pocketbook—in Pittsburgh's Strip District.

South

The Shops at Station Square
Across the Smithfield Street Bridge at
Carson Street • (412) 261-9911

Imagine an old railroad station with its freight house and passenger operations. That hurried exchange of merchandise between boxcars and wagons is somewhat replicated today as savvy shoppers dart in and out of the chic stores comprising the Shops At Station Square.

Since the 1970s when the Pittsburgh History & Landmarks Foundation launched a site study and plan for a retail complex, the Shops at Station Square have brought distinction to this section of the South Side.

Today this indoor mall boasts restaurants and maybe one or two chain retailers, but mostly purely Pittsburgh establishments. S.W. Randall Toyes & Giftes carries the obvious. St. Brendan's Crossing features Celtic charm with fisherman's knit sweaters, woolens, and wraps. And The Landmark's Store is the place to go for books about Pittsburgh as well as a few unique souvenir items.

Shoppers who want charming boutiques and off-the-beaten-path stores that focus on Pittsburgh's diverse ethnic heritage come to Station Square. Parking and restaurants are nearby, as is the Monongahela Incline, taking visitors or commuters to the heights of Mt. Washington. The "T" light rail station is also a permanent fixture. Indeed, many downtown shoppers park at Station Square and ride the T across the river.

Suburban Malls

East

Westmoreland Mall
Rt. 30 East, Greensburg
• (724) 836-5025

Anchor tenants here include Kaufmann's, JC Penney, Sears, and the Bon-Ton. In terms of size, Westmoreland ranks second in the region. You'll find the usual stores here, and a few unique ones, including the Disney Store, Victoria's Secret, Limited and Limited II, Champs, Old Navy, and Paul Harris.

The Waldenbooks is a large-format store. Gloria Jean's coffee stand is a fixture in the food court. Built in the late '70s, Westmoreland Mall was refurbished in the mid-'90s, taking on a thoroughly modern look.

Monroeville Mall
Monroeville Mall Blvd. (off Rt. 22),
Monroeville • (412) 243-4800

Built in 1969, this was one of the region's first major malls. In addition to large department stores such as Kaufmann's, Lazarus, and JC Penney, Monroeville Mall boasts the usual regimen of franchises and national chains, including Victoria's Secret, the Disney Store, WQED Store of Knowledge, Payless Shoes, Lechter's, Lerners New York, Warner Brothers Studio Store, Kay's Jewelers, and more. Behind the mall itself sits the Monroeville Mall Annex with Burlington Coat Factory, Office Max, Dick's (sporting goods), and other merchants. The food court and full-service restaurants keep you well fed. There's the Playground Day Care Center for the kids, valet parking, and stroller rentals available.

South

Century III Mall
Rt. 51, Clairton Rd., West Mifflin
• (412) 653-1220

The largest mall in the region (in terms of square footage), Century III boasts anchor department stores Kaufmann's, JC Penney, and Sears, in addition to specialty retailers Old Navy and Wickes Furniture as well as nearly 200 other stores and services. National chains such as American Eagle Outfitters, Gap and Gap Kids, Lerners New York, Motherhood Maternity, Parade of Shoes, and Fredricks of Hollywood are offered here. In past years, shoppers have been rewarded with the Mallperks program as they earn points toward huge discounts on travel, entertainment, and merchandise. A food court and full-service restaurants are available.

Washington Crown Center
(formerly the Franklin Mall)
1500 W. Chestnut St., Washington
• (724) 228-4270

Anchor tenants at this Washington County mall include Kaufmann's, Sears, Ames, and the Bon-Ton (a smaller regional department store). Banks, jewelers, and shoe stores are

Shoppers of all ages enjoy the eclectic atmosphere of Station Square.

Photo: Courtesy of Greater Pittsburgh Convention & Visitor's Bureau

found here in addition to names you'll recognize like the Gap, Old Navy, American Eagle, Victoria's Secret, Bath & Bodyworks, and American Outfitters. There is a small food court on the premises. Customer services include stroller rental and wheelchair loans, shopping bags, and senior citizen discount cards.

The Galleria
Rt. 19 S., Mt. Lebanon
• **(412) 561-4000**

Opened in 1989, this upscale mall property boasts some national chains and other retailers that operate solely at this location in Pittsburgh. Enclosed parking for inclement weather is one perk at the Galleria. Shops include Godiva Chocolatier, Sox Appeal, Restoration Hardware, Williams-Sonoma, Talbots, and Ann Taylor. The London Grille is one of the restaurants within the complex.

South Hills Village
Rt. 19 & Fort Couch Rd., Bethel Park
• **(412) 831-2900**

Built in 1965, and revamped in 1993, South Hills Village is a fixture in the South Hills communities of Bethel Park, Mt. Lebanon, and Upper St. Clair. Kaufmann's, Lazarus, and Sears department stores anchor this mall, with the

usual national chains and franchises such as Banana Republic, Brookstone, Elizabeth, Eddie Bauer, Discovery Channel Store, Museum Company Store, Natural Wonders, the Disney Store, and the WQED Store of Knowledge. In recent years, strip malls and other merchants have taken up camp nearby.

Washington Mall
301 Oak Spring Rd., Washington
• **(724) 222-7390**

Outside of JC Penney, there are no major department stores here. However, the mall has a Toys R Us and Home Depot outside the main building as well as several banks, barbers and hair salons, a general store, and local Victorian gift boutique and ladies apparel store called Lang's.

West

Airmall
Pittsburgh International Airport
• **(800) ITS-FAIR**

If you arrive at the airport early for your flight, you might want to consider carrying more than your suitcase on your next trip. Try a shopping agenda and credit cards! That's right, the Airmall makes it possible to shop for much more than last minute souvenirs. In fact, Pittsburgh International consistently scores as one of the nation's leading airports based upon the stellar shopping alone.

BAA Pittsburgh oversees the airport shopping mall, and one rule for retailers here is that prices are guaranteed to be the same as they are at local malls. And while you will find some familiar names here (like Eckerd Drugs, The Body Shop, and Victoria's Secret), you'll also find niche stores like Waterstone's Booksellers, The Discovery Channel Store, Perfumania, Tie Rack, and the PGA Tour Shop. Most shops require going through security checks to the airside building, although a handful of merchants are located landside. Food court vendors as well as sit-down restaurants are available, and there is Kidsport if the youngsters need to play a spell. (See our Getting Here, Getting Around chapter for more details on the airport.)

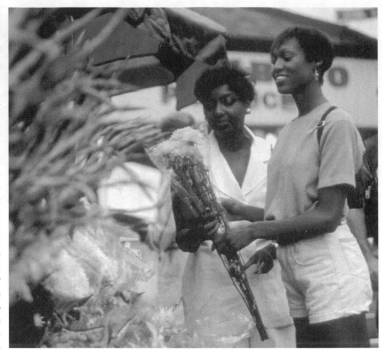

If you're looking for anything fresh, including flowers, then head to Pittsburgh's Strip District.

Photo: M.G. Ellis courtesy of Greater Pittsburgh Convention & Visitor's Bureau

Robinson Town Centre
Park Manor Blvd., Robinson Township
• **(412) 391-7887**

An outdoor strip mall with some freestanding stores and buildings, this complex just keeps on growing. Kaufmann's Department Store is the most significant recent addition. Ikea (see Specialty Stores in this chapter) is an anchor retailer along with Phar-Mor, Dick's, Ames, Marshalls, and T.J. Maxx. Family Bookstores have a location here, along with Pier 1 Imports and many other chains.

The Pointe at North Fayette
**Summit Park Dr. at Quinn Dr.,
North Fayette Township**
• **(412) 394-4355**

Directly across from Robinson Town Cen-

tre on the other side of the Parkway West sits The Pointe, which looks a little like a strip mall but is almost more of a shopping district because its buildings are not connected in many locations. Don't miss Barnes & Noble, Home Place, Sam's Club, Wal-Mart, Home Depot, Half-Priced Books, Petsmart, and many other major retailers. You won't go hungry either. Turn to our Restaurants chapter for more detail on dining options here. To get to The Pointe, take the bridge from Robinson Town Centre, or if you're coming from the airport on I-279, exit at Montour Run. You'll find Summit Park Drive about a half-mile up the road on your left.

Parkway Center Mall
Parkway Center Mall Dr., Greentree
• **(412) 922-1741**

Just off the Parkway West and having its own exit, Parkway Center Mall offers shopping to local residents. Don't expect to find major department stores. There's merely a Kmart, Syms, Phar-Mor, Comp USA, and Giant Eagle. But there are also a few smaller chains. And there is Bugle's Children's Outlet, one of only two locations in Pittsburgh (the other is in the North Hills).

Beaver Valley Mall
380 Beaver Valley Mall, Monaca
• (724) 774-5573

Beaver County's major shopping locale, this mall has all the major department stores in the region—Lazarus, Kaufmann's, Sears, and JC Penney. In addition, you'll find the typical mall stores such as Lerners New York, the Wall, Victoria's Secret, the Disney Store, and Waldenbooks, a convenient food court, and two sit-down restaurants—Chi Chi's and Humphrey's.

North

Ross Park Mall
1000 Ross Park Mall Dr., Ross Township
• (412) 369-4400

Nestled in the North Hills, Ross Park Mall includes a collection of major department stores such as Kaufmann's, Lazarus, JC Penney, Sears, and Service Merchandise. Here's you'll find all the other stores you've grown accustomed to in mall locations such as Ann Taylor, Casual Corner, Baby Gap and Gap Kids, Lane Bryant, Talbot Kids, Victoria's Secret, and the Disney Store. Ross Park Mall was built in 1986.

The Waterworks Mall
Freeport Rd., O'Hara Township
• (412) 366-2250

This outdoor strip mall is located in the Fox Chapel Area with the usual merchants you would find at most indoor locations such as Lechter's, Dress Barn, Toy Kingdom, Old Navy, and Famous Footwear. No major department stores have branches here except for discounters like Marshall's, Hill's, T.J. Maxx, Dunham Sports, and Ames. However, you will find gourmet groceries within the Giant Eagle supermarket, as well as musical selections in the Barnes & Noble.

Cranberry Mall
Rt. 19 & Freedom Rd.,
Mars • (412) 366-2250

Department stores in this Butler County mall include discounters like Big K (Kmart) and Ames along with Phar-Mor, and Giant Eagle and Shop N Save grocery stores. Within the mall are also hair salons and banks as well as chains like American Eagle, Big Lots, Dollar Tree, Famous

Footwear, Petland, JoAnn Fabrics, and Fashion Bug. You'll find other retailers near this outdoor mall in the growing community of Cranberry Township.

Clearview Mall
101 Clearview Cir., Butler
• (724) 285-5722

Anchor tenants include Ames, JC Penney, Sears, the Bon-Ton, and Boscov's. Typical mall outlets and chain stores such as Bugle Boy, Zale's and King's jewelry stores, Casual Corner, Paul Harris, Bath & Bodyworks, American Eagle, and Lerner New York also make their home in the Clearview Mall. There is a food court, as well as plenty of restaurants and eateries within the complex and along the mall periphery.

Books & Music

Downtown

Barnes & Noble Booksellers
339 Sixth Ave., Pittsburgh
• (412) 642-4324

A frequent lunchtime hangout for the working crowd, this Barnes & Noble location also offers a handy selection of computer software. As with all Barnes & Noble stores in the area, there is a Starbucks coffee bar serving up cappucinos, fancy desserts, and other goodies. Author events and children's story times are held regularly. Check the in-store bulletins for dates and times. There are several Barnes & Nobles in Greater Pittsburgh. Additional locations are on Murray Avenue (Squirrel Hill), The Pointe (North Fayette, across from Robinson Town Centre), Cranberry Township, and at the Waterworks and Westmoreland (along Route 30 East). Both the Waterworks and Westmore-land locations offer music departments in addition to cafes.

Bradley's Book Attic
400 Fifth Ave.,
Pittsburgh
• (412) 232-9506

Browse for books here on the ninth floor of Kaufmann's Department Store. Bradley's carries a full selection of fiction, non-fiction, and children's books. The store stocks remainders and some new releases.

INSIDERS' TIP

General Nutrition Center (GNC), located in many malls throughout the country, was founded in Pittsburgh in 1935 as a health food store. Back then, the main product was yogurt. Today, GNC stocks a variety of vitamins, health foods, and natural products.

Pittsburgh Products

Pittsburgh Pride extends to gift giving. No matter if you're a sports fan, beer connoisseur, Christmas collector, or card player, there's a Pittsburgh product for you or your loved one. Here's a sampling of some of the most popular and useful items we've found:

• Couch potatoes will want to curl up with nearly 20 different videos produced by WQED/Pittsburgh. From Frank Lloyd Wright's *House On The Waterfall* or *Kennywood Memories* to *The Strip Show* or *Pittsburgh's Greatest Sport Heroes,* each video costs $19.95 plus tax. These are available at WQED Store of Knowledge locations or by calling (800) 274-1307 or (412) 622-1307.

• Hometown Treasures reproduces local landmarks like the Allegheny County Courthouse in ceramic. Perfect for your Christmas train displays, these reproductions are available at The Landmarks Store in Station Square or can be ordered by phone at (412) 765-1042.

• A made-to-order basket from The Brewery Store pretty much proves that Iron City Beer is indeed "a 'burg thing." Place a gift basket order by calling (412) 692-1114.

• Pittsburgh playing cards and Pittsburghese mugs from ABELexpress will give your next bridge or card club gathering something to talk about. Showroom visits are by appointment only, but you can order by phone at (412) 279-0672.

• Afraid of getting lost? *Finding Yourself In Pittsburgh* ($5.95) is a colorful series of maps to help you navigate across Pittsburgh's bridges and boulevards. Published by Informing Design, this map is carried in many local bookstores.

• And while you're buying books, don't forget to read *Mario Lemieux: Final Period* (Triumph Books), the inspirational story told mostly through pictures of how this shy Canadian teenager overcame battles on and off the ice to become one of hockey's all-time greats.

• Job seekers will appreciate the professional contacts found in *The Pittsburgh*

If visual arts are your passion, check out Alexander Patho Photography, (412) 486-1621, www.pathophoto.com. Alexander who has forty years of experience in color photography, has specialized in taking photographs of Pittsburgh since 1983. His limited and open edition photographs grace many prestigious locations in Pittsburgh, among them the mayor's office and the Chamber of Commerce boardroom.

Photo: Courtesy of Alexander Patho Photography

Job Source, a book published by Benjamin Scott Publishing. This resource retails at $16.95 and is in most major bookstores. Adams Media publishes the *Pittsburgh Job Bank 2000,* which retails for $16.95.

•Learn all about Pittsburgh's history by reading *Pittsburgh: Story of an American City* by Stefan Lorant. It sells for $39.95 at area bookstores.

•Sacred Heart Elementary School has published a cookbook from historic Pittsburgh. It's called *The Heart of Pittsburgh* ($17.95). Call (412) 441-1582.

•Savor the city's skyline with the Pittsburgh PC Screensaver ($29.95) which shows off impressive photos right on your computer. It's available from New Pittsburgh Publications, along with their *Images of Pittsburgh* video ($19.95) by calling (412) 681-8528.

•*Pittsburgh For Kids: A Guidebook and Directory for Grown-ups and Kids* is published by the McEwan School. Copies are sold in local bookstores as well as through mail order. Call (412) 361-7559.

•Kids and their grownups will enjoy buying up prime real estate like Station Square, The Benedum, or Isaly's as they play the "Pittsburgh In A Box" board game ($24.95), produced by Late for the Sky Production Company. Find it in specialty gift shops or Kaufmann's, especially around the holidays.

Kirner's Catholic Bookstore
219 Fourth Ave., Pittsburgh
• (412) 261-2326

Since Kirner's carries much more than books within this family-run store, we classify this as more of a gift shop. It's been in business for over 115 years. Merchandise includes a most extensive selection of Catholic Bibles, books, clerical apparel, first communion merchandise, and gifts for all occasions, including Christmas, Easter, weddings, baby congratulations, and confirmation gifts.

East

Basilica Gift Shop
St. Vincent College, Latrobe
• (724) 532-5060

Gifts for the soul abound here. The shop is a project of the St. Vincent Archabbey, whose 190 Benedictine monks, many of whom teach at the college, operate priories worldwide. The spiritual stock includes religious medals, prayer books and Bibles, small statuary, and artwork, as well as cookbooks and gift items.

Borders Books & Music
200 Mall Blvd., Monroeville
• (412) 374-9772

The most recent location in the Borders chain to open in Pittsburgh, the Monroeville store offers book lovers and music fans a wall-less concept in shopping. Unique spaces are de-signed for the children's area and the café, which includes coffee, soft drinks, pastries, salads, and desserts. The store's music department sits at the center behind the information desk. Author signings and discussions are regularly held, along with a full array of children's story times and events, as well as live entertainment in the café on weekends. Check the current newsletter for details. Additional Borders locations in the area are at Rt. 19's Norman Center (South Hills) and along McKnight Road, Ross Township (North Hills).

Chapters
191 Hillcrest Shopping Center,
Lower Burrell • (724) 337-7303

Nestled in a suburban shopping center, you'll find friendly staff that helps shoppers find books they love—usually a hallmark of this kind of independent bookseller. Chapters offers gift certificates and special orders for hard-to-find titles. Check to see when there might be story times for children. This store used to be a Little Professor Book Center until early in 2000.

Jay's Book Stall
3604 Fifth Ave., Oakland
• (412) 683-2644

It was at this popular independent bookstore that novelist Michael Chabon once worked part-time while he was a student at the University of Pittsburgh. Jay's offers a general selection of fiction and non-fiction, children's, literature and more.

Duty-free shopping for passengers leaving the country is available at Concourse C at Pittsburgh International Airport.

Photo: Debbie Norrell

SHOPPING

Media Play
4100 William Penn Hwy., Monroeville
• (412) 374-1266

With a grand new opening at Monroeville's Miracle Mile Shopping Center in June 2000, this national book and music chain is new to the Pittsburgh area. The media superstore, as it calls itself, offers 60,000 CDs and 20,000 video titles in addition to thousands of children's and adult books, toys, and interactives. In essence, Media Play is comprised of four smaller stores in one—music, video, books, and computer software/video games. Other locations opening in 2000 within Greater Pittsburgh include Ross Park Mall and Robinson Towne Centre.

Mystery Lovers Bookshop
514 Allegheny River Blvd., Oakmont
• (412) 828-4877

The only book store in Pittsburgh devoted exclusively to the passion of mystery novels, Mystery Lovers Bookshop offers a warm atmosphere, knowledgeable staff, authors signings, writers' group meetings, children's events, and an in-store coffee bar. Orders by phone can be placed using their toll-free number, (888) 800-6078.

The Book Center
University of Pittsburgh, Pittsburgh
• (412) 648-1452

The main supplier of textbooks to university students, this store (colloquially called the Pitt Book Store) also offers a full range of con-

sumer and trade books as well as periodicals and children's books. Merchandise such as Pitt sweatshirts, T-shirts, mugs, and other mementos are also available.

North

Bookworks
1139 Freeport Rd., Aspinwall
• (412) 782-6661

Nestled in the Fox Chapel Plaza, this bookstore has a homey feel to it. Stocking a general selection of non-fiction, fiction, and children's books, it's sure to please avid readers who delight in traditional, independent booksellers. Occasionally, the store will host a book signing when an author is local or visiting town.

Cokesbury Books & Church Supplies
19015 Perry Hwy., Mars
• (724) 776-6150

Stocking church supplies and curriculum materials, this store also carries books and gift items merchandised to the general public. Compact discs, cassettes, videos, pictures, and greeting cards are also available.

Family Christian Stores
10517 Perry Hwy., Wexford
•(724) 935-9460

Carrying a full range of Christian Bibles, storybooks, music, gifts, and church supplies, this chain used to be known as Family Bookstores. You'll find additional locations at Robinson Town Centre, Bridgeville, West Mifflin, Monroeville, and Natrona Heights.

Record Rama Sound Archives
4981 McKnight Rd., North Hills
• (412) 367-7330

Boasting over three million sound recordings in stock, this is the place to browse for a day's (or several) worth of music. Compact discs, CD singles, cassettes, and more are carried here. There's a large selection of used CDs, cleaning and storage products, reference material, and phonograph needles for those of you who still spin vinyl. This store is so busy, the ad states that they do not answer the telephone on Saturdays!

Waldenbooks
Highland Mall, Natrona Heights
• (724) 224-5444

There are many Waldenbooks locations throughout Western Pennsylvania. Some are larger than others. At Westmoreland Mall, for instance, there is a large-format store with a more extensive children's book and product selection. Each store offers author signings throughout the year. Additional locations at Century III Mall and South Hills Village (South Hills), Ross Park Mall (North Hills), Monroeville Mall, Waterworks Mall, Clearview and Butler Malls (Butler County), and at the Beaver Valley Mall (Beaver County).

South

Camelot Music
477 South Hills Village, Bethel Park
• (412) 835-6930

This chain of music stores can be found all around Pittsburgh with locations at Ross Park Mall, Beaver Valley Mall, and Century III Mall as well.

Literati
246 Washington Rd., Pittsburgh
• (412) 388-5040

In a Mt. Lebanon location that was "born to be a bookstore," this store opened in January 2000. It's certainly unique. Customers pay $5 just to enter this literary setting, where you'll find reading and games in addition to the light menu of soups, sandwiches, and coffees.

The admission charge isn't the only reason we call it one-of-a-kind, for you cannot purchase books at Literati. Here you can come to read and browse all you want. If you're enthralled with one in particular, you may rent the book to take home for a nominal charge. The shop has limited hours. It's open Monday, Tuesday, Wednesday, Friday and Saturday from 6 to 10 PM, and Sundays from 12 to 4 PM. On Thursdays, Literati is closed. Store owner Patti McGuire plans special events from time to time so do call for more information.

Randy's Alternative Music
1210 E. Carson St., Pittsburgh
• (412) 481-7445

In this South Side store, you'll find new and used CDs, tapes, and records, including many hard-to-find items not typically found in the traditional chain music stores.

Sam Goody
South Hills Village, Bethel Park
• (412) 831-9557

Another chain establishment for music lovers, you'll also find two stores Downtown (at Warner Centre and Fifth Avenue Place). Additional locations are at Forbes Avenue, Oakland, Beaver Valley Mall, and Westmoreland Mall.

West

Coconuts Music
1990 Park Manor Dr., Pittsburgh
• (412) 788-0223

Located at Robinson Town Centre, this is the only Coconuts store locally, and perhaps one of the largest music stores around. Coconuts carries the latest in compact discs, cassettes, and music accessories as well as videos and DVDs.

National Record Mart
Various Locations • (800) 860-8863

Known as National Record Mart or NRM Music, this chain has well over two dozen stores throughout Western Pennsylvania. By calling the toll-free number, you're sure to find a location near you carrying compact discs, cassettes,

INSIDERS' TIP
Used book dealers can often turn up rare finds you've searched a lifetime for. Look in your Yellow Pages Directory under "Book Dealers - Used & Rare" for stores nearest you.

SHOPPING

videos, and more. Other stores within the NRM chain include Oasis, Music X, Vibes, and Waves.

Penguin Book Shop
420 Beaver St., Sewickley • (412) 741-3838

Here's another independent bookstore of general nature. Kids can browse upstairs while adults look over the selection of fiction, non-fiction, current bestsellers, and greeting cards.

Specialty Shops
Downtown

Candy-Rama
212 Fifth Ave., Pittsburgh
• (412) 281-7350

Generations of Pittsburgh kids (and grown children!) have enjoyed discovering the plentiful selection of candy at this downtown store. Indeed, it's a favorite stop during the lunch hour or on virtually any shopping trip to the city. Candy-Rama has an additional location at 264 Fifth Avenue, and you can stop by its warehouse at 3340 Smallman Street in the Strip District.

Curtain Call
Penn Ave. and Sixth St., Pittsburgh
• (412) 392-3313

Stop by this new coffee bar and retail store run by the Pittsburgh Symphony—a perfect complement to the Cultural District according to many arts patrons. In this 2,100-square-foot space, you'll find CDs, books, jewelry, and symphony-related merchandise. Demonstrations and lectures are offered occasionally so call for more information.

Bailey Banks & Biddle Jewelers
One Mellon Bank Center, Pittsburgh
• (412) 391-4440

You'll find this stores in the lower lobby of One Mellon Bank Center along Grant Street, Downtown. This leading jeweler offers the finest in jewelry, better watches, corporate gifts, and giftware, including crystal and porcelain pieces. Clients come here for custom design work and repairs. With 29 windows, it's a great place to window shop as well! Look for additional locations at South Hills Village and Ross Park Mall.

Honus Wagner Co.
320 Forbes Ave., Pittsburgh
• (412) 471-3045

Sports fanatics will flock to this store named for one of the greatest Pirate players ever, since many sporting goods and apparel items are stocked here. This includes athletic shoes, team merchandise, brand-name athletic workout suits, coats, shorts and shirts, footballs, baseballs and gloves, tennis, racquetball and squash racquets, and golf accessories. Really, anything that's sports-related and small is available here. Because of its downtown location, Honus Wagner Co. doesn't stock golf clubs and other large items. But with almost 75 years in business, it's a store to check out.

J.R. Weldin Co.
413 Wood St., Pittsburgh
• (412) 281-0123

A favorite stationer and travel supply store, you'll find the usual office supplies that most businesses and professionals need. But here, you'll also discover wonderful gifts for the career-minded, including fine pens, stationery, desk accessories, and much more. There's a bountiful selection of greeting cards and unusual gifts that you typically don't find elsewhere.

Pennsylvania Culinary School
705 Liberty Ave., Pittsburgh
• (412) 566-2433

Gourmet cooks head for the retail store at Pennsylvania Culinary School in the Clark Building, Downtown. You'll find cookbooks (why of course!), textbooks, small wares, cutlery, chef wear, and other culinary products. And if they don't have what you want in stock, they'll be happy to locate it for you.

East

Basket Styles
903 Elizabeth St., Churchill
• (412) 351-2742

No request is too big or small for a custom-made gift basket for personal celebrations or corporate gift-giving. Baskets created for the usual occasions of holidays, new babies, weddings, birthdays, and Valentine's Day. Non-traditional baskets include new promotion, comfort, and the ever-popular Pittsburgh baskets. Owner Pamela Price will arrange personal delivery to area hospitals or ship worldwide. Corporate accounts can be established, and credit cards orders are also accepted by phone.

Delallo Italian Market Place
Pa. Rt. 30, Jeannette
• (724) 523-5000

Since 1950 this family name has supplied its

own brand of pastas, peppers, tomato sauce, oils, and vinegar to Pittsburgh-area supermarkets. In Jeannette, you can visit the large Italian market where the complete selection of Delallo products is stocked on the shelves. In addition, you'll find an extensive counter of ready-made foods (both hot and cold entrees and salads), fresh breads, candies, and Italian supplies.

Journeys of Life
810 Bellefonte St., Shadyside
• (412) 681-8755

You'll find new age gifts that are hard to come by—things like feng shui cures, hand-crafted meditation fountains, candles, and aromatherapy products—on the store's first floor. Upstairs, discover a selection of books on life issues for kids and adults. Lots of 12-step recovery books and materials are found here as well.

Phantom of the Attic
3766 William Penn Hwy., Rt. 22, Monroeville • (412) 856-4403

There aren't many stores specializing in comic books, magic cards, and collectible cards. But you'll find those items here, as well as at Phantom locations along South Craig Street in Oakland and at Parkway Center Mall.

Pittsburgh Center for the Arts Shops
6300 Fifth Ave., Pittsburgh
• (412) 361-0873

The Pittsburgh Center for the Arts Shops feature original and handcrafted jewelry, ceramics, functional and decorative works, paintings, prints, glassware and more. You'll find this location at Fifth & Shady avenues in Shadyside. Galleries and shops are open Monday through Saturday, from 10 AM to 5:30 PM and on Sunday from 12 to 5 PM. The store is accessible for those with physical challenges. In prior years there were other suburban locations, but all operations and sales have been consolidated into this location.

Rolling Rock Gift Shop & Visitor's Center
behind the brewery on Ligonier St., Latrobe • (724) 539-3394

Operated by the Latrobe Brewing Company, this gift shop offers sweatshirts with different logos as well as glassware, gift items, baseball caps, can coolers, jackets, and golf shirts. No beer is for sale here because of the state liquor laws, but there is a beer distributor about two blocks up the road. It's open Tuesday and Wednesday from 9:30 AM until 5 PM. Thursday and Fridays, the store stays open until 6 PM, and on Saturdays it closes at 3 PM.

The Toy Box
108 S. Market St., Ligonier
• (724) 238-6233

Quality toys, games, and puzzles for children of all ages are found here. Phone orders are welcome as well. Popular brand names include Avanti, Brio, Bburago, Erector, Folkmanis, Playmobile, Steiff, and Tucker Jones.

Willi's Ski Shop
3838 William Penn Hwy., Rt. 22, Monroeville • (412) 856-1230

Complete ski furnishings including clothing and equipment in addition to snowboarding and tennis accessories. Additional locations are at Seven Springs Ski Resort, in the North Hills and South Hills.

West

The Country Mercantile
220 Rt. 30, Imperial
• (412) 695-7251

Country crafts fill the shelves of this quaint little store in rural Imperial, not far from Pittsburgh International Airport and just minutes from Robinson Town Centre. Fresh ground coffees, unique teas, candles, crafts, bears, baby items, and other gift suggestions stock the store. Visitors who sign the guest register are invited to special open houses held throughout the year for refreshments and an advance peek at new holiday-themed merchandise.

INSIDERS' TIP
Thrift stores such as Goodwill, Salvation Army, and St. Vincent De Paul stores are plentiful throughout the region. Turn to your Yellow Pages directory for a complete listing, for there are dozens to choose from.

Ikea
2001 Park Manor Blvd., Robinson Town Centre
• (412) 747-0747

The only store of its kind in the Pittsburgh region, this Swedish furniture and home furnishings retailer offers a thoroughly modern and well-stocked showroom, cafeteria-style restaurant and cafe areas, and a supervised ball room

SHOPPING

for young children, as well as convenient self-service and efficient check out. Known for its inventiveness and thriftiness, the Ikea concept will be kind on your budget. Most components are easy to assemble, but it's best to thoroughly take your measurements for coming to the store. Design specialists are on hand to assist you. Ikea is open every day except Thanksgiving, Christmas, and Easter Sunday.

The Open Mind
439 Beaver St., Sewickley
•(412) 741-1888

New age, spirituality, self-help, and recovery books stock the shelves along with a limited children's selection. Gift items include jewelry, incense, candles, bath salts, greeting cards, music, and videos. Call to find out when you might catch appearances by a massage therapist, palm reader, or psychic.

Volkwein's Music
138 Industry Dr., RIDC Park West
• (412) 788-5900

Anyone who is serious about music in Pittsburgh knows Volkwein's for its fine reputation selling musical instruments, band and orchestra accessories, and sheet music. Private instruction, voice lessons, and instrument rentals are also available. Phone orders are welcome.

North

Carlisle's
409 E. Ohio St., Pittsburgh
• (412) 321-2421

Carlisle's is truly a Pittsburgh wedding tradition, offering only the finest in bridal gowns and fashions for bridesmaids and mothers. You'll find names like Vera Wang and Janell Berté on the racks. Carlisle's has been serving Pittsburgh since 1888. Carlisle's is conveniently located on the North Side, just off of I-279 North. Many shop here for formal wear for other occasions as there is also an adjacent tuxedo shop.

Duncan Comic Books and Accessories
1047 Perry Hwy., Pittsburgh
• (412) 635-0886

Find more than just comic books here, for there are toys, gifts and cards to choose from here as well as a large selection of action figures. You'll also find a plentiful array of used books to browse through.

New Dimension Comics
20550 Rt. 19, Mars
• (724) 776-0433

Located in Cranberry Township, New Dimenion stocks over 60,000 back issues of comic books, and a 40-foot wall of new releases. This is the place to browse for collectible card games, too. Your children will also delight in the action figures.

Wendell August Gift Shoppe & Forge
620 Madison Ave., Grove City
• (724) 458-8360

Allow some time for a tour of the Wendell August Forge in Mercer County, established in 1923 in Brockway and moved to Grove City in 1932. Signs are well-placed along major routes into town. It's one of the few remaining forges in the country that continues to produce forged aluminum, pewter, bronze, sterling, and silver articles entirely by hand, using no production machinery.

The Showroom houses a historical collection of artifacts and a complete line of giftware that has been commissioned by corporate executives, leading companies, and even the U.S. Congress. Visitors witness the artisans hammering and chiseling artforms as part of the free, self-guided tours available Monday through Saturday. Do call before making the trip to make sure the Forge and/or Showroom is open, since it's a bit of a drive from some communities in our coverage area.

South

Gram & Gramps
1720 Washington Rd., Bethel Park
• (412) 831-4726

Not only will you find a great selection of top-quality toys (including Brio, Thomas, and Playmobile), but you'll also be able to outfit the kids in this all-in-one store. Named for doting grandparents, it's probably appropriate. While prices on the toy merchandise are competitive, the clothing lines are a little upscale. But then, grandparents only want the best!

INSIDERS' TIP
Many regional malls offer cinemas either within the mall complex or nearby. Plan to take in a new box office release before or after your shopping excursions!

Retailers like this at Oxford Centre dress up in full display during the holiday season, better known as Sparkle Season in the city.

Photo: Courtesy of Greater Pittsburgh Convention & Visitor's Bureau

McGinnis Sisters Specialty Foods
**3825 Saw Mill Run Blvd., Route 51,
Brentwood • (412) 882-6400**

If you're in the market for supreme cuts of meat, plentiful produce, fresh fish, gourmet cheeses, and ready-made pasta salads, McGinnis Sisters is the place to go. With one other location at 4311 Northern Pike, Monroeville, the McGinnis Sisters stores host occasional Saturday events with samples of seasonal items. Special orders are accepted. Why not join in a cooking class also? Find out more by calling the store near you.

Send Me No Flowers
**606 Weyman Rd, Whitehall
• (412) 885-4888**

Gift baskets that express what flowers can not are the idea here. Choose from many selections including baskets to pamper, celebrate special occasions, comfort with chocolate or coffee, or welcome home a new baby. You can place your orders toll-free at (800) 680-3277.

The Riverside Shoppes
**127 Speers St., Lower Speers
• (724) 483-2290**

Situated midway between Washington and New Stanton and just two minutes off Route 70, this complex sits along a wooden walkway and cozy courtyard. In this colonial setting, you'll find 16 shops awaiting you with everything for the home, for the luxurious bathroom, for a gourmet kitchen and much more.

Consignment Stores

East

Music Go Round
**Holiday Center, Rt. 22, Monroeville
• (412) 856-8742**

If you need musical instruments that don't cost bundles, then head here. This store is great for the parents of aspiring musicians just taking up an instrument in school. You'll find guitars, drums, clarinets, flutes, and all the other popular instruments as well as speakers, amplifiers, and accessories.

Play It Again Sports
**Holiday Center, Rt. 22, Monroeville
• (412) 372-3380**

You'll find all types of used sports equipment here—everything but hunting, fishing, and archery equipment. Weights, benches, and

accessories, inline skates, hockey, baseball, golf, tennis, exercise, croquet, volleyball, skiing, snowboarding, and lacrosse equipment fills the store. Other locations within the region are found at at Edgewood Town Center, Pleasant Hills, North Hills, Cranberry (Butler County), Bridgeville, and McMurray (Washington County).

Repeats
**5871 Forbes Ave., Squirrel Hill
• (412) 422-3340**

This clothing shop for women carries better sportswear, formal wear, suits and dresses, accessories such as shoes, purses, some jewelry, and hats. Name brands like Armani and Liz Claiborne are common. You'll find extended Thursday hours but the store is closed Sundays.

Second Chance Resale Shop
**500 Garden City Dr., Monroeville
• (412) 372-4308**

Established since 1985, this shop offers only the finest in family clothing in all sizes as well as select, small household items. Designer labels in women's fashions are sought after and displayed the most.

South

Yesterday's Best
**141 Main St., New Eagle
• (724) 258-8112**

Here in Washington County, this old house is full of everything on consignment that's related to the home. Dishes, pots and pans, linens, furniture, and antiques are here, but no clothing.

West

Second Hand Rose
**411 Walnut St., Sewickley
• (412) 741-5909**

Men's, women's, and children's gently worn apparel is found here, along with accessories, ties, shoes, and hats. Some designer labels available, as well as selected formal wear, suits, and dresses.

North

Kids' Consignment III
**3463 Babcock Blvd., Pittsburgh
• (412) 364-7282**

This store carries gently used children's items

At the core of Pittsburgh International Airport are over 100 stores and services with prices that mirror any local retailer.

Photo: Debbie Norrell

including baby through childhood clothing, cribs and furniture, sports equipment, toys, accessories, and books.

Once Upon A Child
10648 Perry Hwy., Wexford
• (412) 933-1660

Outfit the kids for less here at Once Upon A Child. Not only will you find play and dressy clothing for the kids, but a selection of quality used toys and children's furnishings. Strollers, portable cribs, and potties prevail too. There's also a Monroeville location in Holiday Center Shopping Plaza (near PharMor).

Outlet Shopping

North

Prime Outlets at Grove City
Interstate 79 at the Grove City/
New Wilmington Exit • (888) 545-7221

In 1994, the Grove City Factory Shops, smack between the towns of New Wilmington and Grove City, put this region in the news as savvy shoppers combed racks and roamed aisles of outlets in search of the ultimate bargain. Now, the complex is called the Prime Outlets. With the fourth phase completed, the shops now include 533,000 square feet—a virtual

shopper's mecca. The more than 130 stores here include Ann Taylor, Liz Claiborne, Calvin Klein, Eddie Bauer, London Fog, and many other popular retailers.

From Downtown Pittsburgh, count on at least an hour's drive (perhaps less from northern suburbs). Shuttle buses run daily to take shoppers around the outlets—it's *that* big. Customer services (located in the food court) include gift certificates, stroller rentals, wheelchair loans, area tourist information, coupon books, and lost and found services.

East

Horizon Outlet Center
Route 601 N., Somerset
• (814) 634-0720

Just off the Pennsylvania Turnpike at Somerset lies another outlet complex that has been serving up finds for outlet shoppers over many years. Open in April 1990, the Horizon Outlet Center is approximately one hour from Pittsburgh (less perhaps from the eastern suburbs). Retailers here include Adolfoll, Bass Shoes, Levi's, Polo Ralph Lauren, and Van Heusen.

During the winter months, these outlets may close a little early (say 6 PM) whereas they are open into the evening in the summer and busy holiday months. You'll find abbreviated hours on some holidays as well.

Lenox Factory Outlet
Rt. 31 East, Mt. Pleasant
•(724) 547-9555
Located in Mt. Pleasant, The Lenox Factory Outlet saves you 15 to 20 percent off suggested retail prices on quality china and crystal gifts, dinnerware, stemware, and barware. At The Lenox Factory Clearance Center, save up to 60 percent off suggested retail prices of seconds, overstocks, discontinued and special products. The outlet is open from 9 AM to 6 PM.

L.E. Smith Glass Company
1900 Liberty St., Mt. Pleasant
•(724) 547-3544
At L.E. Smith Glass Company, they've been crafting handmade glass for nearly a century. Using many techniques of original artisans, today's craftsmen mold, shape, heat, and cool beautiful glassware. Factory tours are available Monday through Friday from 9:30 AM to 3 PM. The Factory Outlet & Giftware Store is open daily until 5 PM, but it's closed on weekends from January through March, and on all national holidays. Don't miss the annual "Christmas in July" sale held during the first two weeks of the month.

INSIDERS' TIP

Drive toward New Wilmington from the Prime Outlets (along Rt. 208) and you can't miss The Volant Mill, a major tourist stop and shop! Built in 1812, it operated as a grist and flour mill until 1963. Today, it sits across the street from the mini-mall of refurbished train shops.

Antiques & Flea Markets

East

Ages Ago Antiques
722 Allegheny River Blvd., Verona
• (412) 828-9800
Moderately priced antiques here include furniture, lamps, lace, glassware, pottery, rugs, collectibles, toys, and paintings. The store is open Monday through Saturday from 9 AM to 4:30 PM, but it's closed Sundays. In the evenings, the hours are by appointment only.

Hanna's Town Antiques &
Collectibles Show
Between Routes 119 & 819 in Historic
Hanna's Town • (724) 836-1800
Three miles north of Greensburg, in a large open field, you'll find this show and sale held several times each year. This one-day market ends up being more like a two-day event, according to those who frequent it. Technically held on Sundays, some bargains can be found throughout Saturday. Antiques and collectibles are offered as well as some yard-sale type articles.

Mullin House Antiques
16 Mullin Ave., Mt. Pleasant
• (724) 547-4690
Specializing in antique furniture, Mullin House also offers lamps, clocks, decorative items for the home, old music boxes and musical instruments, glassware, prints, pictures, and lots more. Browse through the six rooms filled with furniture and accessories, each according to a theme.

South

Antiques Downtown
88 S. Main St.,
Washington
• (724) 222-6800
This store carries a general line of antiques, including Duncan & Miller and other American hand-made glass. They specialize in glass and china. Bring your Civil War (or any war) collector here because the shop offers swords, badges, pins, books, and other military memorabilia.

The Antiques Fair at the Meadows
Race Track Rd., North Strabane Township
• (724) 228-3045
Recently voted the best flea market by *Pittsburgh Magazine* readers, this Washington County flea market offers some 600 different dealers who put out their wares the last Sunday of each month from February through November. Better quality antiques and collectibles are featured. There are indoor as well as outdoor dealers from 8 AM to 3 PM.

Trader Jacks
99 Steen Rd., Kirwan Heights
• (412) 257-8980
This year-round indoor and outdoor flea market usually offers lower end merchandise for true bargain hunters. The feel here is definitely more like a yard sale, but you may find some antiques and collectibles among the merchandise. Come weekends from 7 AM until 3 PM.

A quaint shopping experience at Nemacolin Woodlands.

Photo: Courtesy of Nemacolin Woodlands Resort & Spa

Where The Toys Are
45 West Pike St., Canonsburg
• (724) 745-4599

Indeed an antique store, this place specializes in turn-of-the-century through baby-boomer era toys, old Barbies and other dolls, trains, vehicles, action figures, TV-show and movie tie-in toys, comic characters, GI Joe and Star Wars figures, and memorabilia. This unusual store is open from 10:30 AM until 5 PM, Monday through Saturday. Where The Toys Are is closed on Wednesdays.

Whiskey Run Antiques Southpointe
Rt. 19 S., Canonsburg • (724) 745-5808

Named because of its location in the 1794 Whiskey Rebellion area, this shop sits between Pittsburgh and Washington off of I-79. Over 40 professional dealers offer upscale antiques, including 18th- and 19th-century country and formal furniture along with appropriate accessories such as glassware, pottery, and silver. Appraisals, clock repairs, and lamp repairs are offered as well. It's open daily from 10 AM to 5 PM.

West

Leonard's Antiques & Uniques MegaMall
2586 Constitution Blvd., Rt. 51, Chippewa • (724) 847-2304

Over 300 dealers in this former Kmart building offer antiques, some collectibles (though no fad merchandise like Beanie Babies), and other higher-end items. The rule is "if you can find it selling in typical stores, you won't find it here." You'll find more attractive booths here. It's open daily from 10 AM to 8 PM, except for Sundays, when it closes at 6 PM. Leonard's is closed also on Christmas, Easter, and Thanksgiving.

Linder's
701 Yunker St., McKees Rocks
• (412) 771-6566

Linder's features fine art and antiques from England, Ireland, Europe, and the United States, Linder's also carries new and traditional furniture, oriental carpets, and more. If you're in the mood for upscale merchandise, come here Monday through Friday from 10 AM until 6 PM. Evening hours are by appointment only. Saturdays, you can shop from 10 AM to 4 PM, and on Sundays browse from 12 to 4 PM.

The Antique Emporium
818 Seventh Ave., Beaver Falls
• (724) 847-1919

Here you'll find three floors devoted to antiques and collectibles from over 75 quality antique dealers. There are no crafts and only a few reproductions. But you'll find the usual array of furniture, military wares, glass, and collectibles. Most days the store is open from 10 AM until 5 PM, but there are extended Friday hours until 8 PM. On Sundays, the hours run from 12 to 5 PM.

Twin Highway Flea Market
Steubenville Pike, Rt. 60,
Robinson Township
• (412) 787-1617

Held weather-permitting on the grounds of the old Twin Highway Drive-In movie theater, this flea market features yard-sale merchandise from individuals who set up their tables very early on a Sunday morning. It runs from mid-March to mid-October, on Sundays only, from 6:30 AM until 2 PM. You'll find it next to Butya's Restaurant on Rt. 60, Robinson Township.

North

Country Corner Indoor Flea Market
Rt. 839, Dayton • (814) 257-8491

Local crafts, collectibles, Amish furniture, gift items, new and used merchandise—there's something for everyone at this Armstrong County flea market. It's open Tuesday through Saturday from 9 AM to 5 PM, and on Sunday from 1 to 5 PM only. On Mondays you must make an appointment.

North Hills Antique Gallery
Church Rd. & Rt. 19, Wexford
• (724) 935-9804

Here's a co-op establishment with 15 dealers handling a variety of antiques, Depression-era glass, kitchen collectibles, Hummels, stained glass windows, furniture, pictures, toys, cameras, and more. There's war and sports memorabilia here also. It's open daily from 10 AM until 5 PM.

Wildwood Peddlers Fair
2330 Wildwood Rd., Hampton Township
• (412) 487-2200

This indoor and outdoor flea market is held weekly, featuring an eclectic mixture of brand new items, coins, collectibles, and antiques to typical yard-sale quality merchandise. It's open on Sundays from 6 AM until 4 PM.

Attractions

Sightseeing around this diverse city is more than an afternoon's entertainment or a day away from it all. Pittsburgh is particularly rich with memories of eras past, parks as pleasurable as you'll find, and culture that flourishes here.

Whether you choose to spend your leisure time learning, poking through Pittsburgh's past, exploring nature, or simply seeing the sights, opportunities abound for you throughout the entire region.

Note that we're deviating from our usual geographic headers in this chapter—most of these attractions are worth driving to, even if they're not in your immediate area. You can look forward to learning about educational venues, touring famous homes, venturing out to parks and other fun places, and browsing through some of our notable museums.

While many of the most popular attractions are situated in or near the City of Pittsburgh, and within Allegheny County, a fair number await your discovery in surrounding counties. So enjoy the listing presented here. Your fun-filled opportunities will soon transform into fond memories. And you'll keep coming back for more!

Educational

The Carnegie
4400 Forbes Ave., Pittsburgh
• (412) 622-3288

Culture, history, and art appreciation abound in our area because of renowned turn-of-the-century Pittsburgher Andrew Carnegie, who resolved at an early age to use his phenomenal wealth for benevolent purposes. This led to the creation of Carnegie Institute, Carnegie Library, as well as the Carnegie Music Hall and Lecture Hall, the Museum of Art, and the Museum of Natural History. Today, these entities all fall under the organizational banner of The Carnegie.

Since Mr. Carnegie, who rose from working class ranks, was committed to creating resources he could have used in his formative years, he was deeply concerned about details of architecture in the buildings that are now landmarks in the Oakland neighborhood.

Inside, pick up a visitor orientation map of the Museums of Art and Natural History. This will guide you through three floors of exhibits including the famed Dinosaur Hall (See Kidstuff), the natural history gallery, the Benedum Hall of Geology, Hillman Hall of Minerals & Gems, Walton Hall of Ancient Egypt, and the Heinz Architectural Center (See Architecture). Additional displays feature African and North American wildlife, botany, fossils, insects, amphibians, and reptiles, as well as the Wyckoff Hall of Arctic Life.

Upstairs is the permanent collection of the Scaife Galleries as well as exhibitions of limited runs. Concerts are held in the Music Hall. (See the Arts chapter).

Before leaving the Carnegie, walk through the Hall of Sculpture, made famous as a backdrop in the movie *Flashdance*. Each holiday season, the Hall of Architecture hosts a display of beautifully decorated Christmas trees (see Annual Events).

A coffee cart is available inside the complex, and the Museum Cafe serves meals during certain hours (see Restaurants). A brown bag lunch area is located in the basement with vending machines for sandwiches, snacks, and beverages.

Finally, Andrew Carnegie's legacy is predominantly felt through his contribution to literacy with the entire system of Carnegie Libraries, with branches throughout the city. The main library is part of the Oakland complex, next to the Music Hall and post office. Highlights here include the Pennsylvania Room, the Foundation Center, and the Ready Reference telephone unit, as well as the general holdings of the book, video, and periodical collections.

Hours at the museum are Tuesday through Saturday from 10 AM to 5 PM, and Sunday from 1 to 5 PM. Friday hours might be hard to remember, but in the summer (June through August), the museum is open from 10 AM to 9 PM, giving patrons a little more time (perhaps after work on a summer's eve) to wander around the air-conditioned museum. Mondays, during July and August, you can explore from 10 AM until 5 PM.

Carnegie Library is open Monday through Thursday, 9 AM to 9 PM, Friday and Saturday from 9 AM to 5:30 PM, and Sunday from 1 to

INSIDERS' TIP

A total of 218 covered bridges remain standing throughout Pennsylvania. The common nickname for many of these structures was "the kissin' bridges." Well, you can probably figure out why!

5 PM. Admission to the library is free of charge. Admission to The Carnegie Museum of Natural History and Museum of Art is $6 for adults, $5 for senior citizens, and $4 for children (ages 3 to 18). Children younger than 3 and members are admitted free of charge.

Carnegie Science Center
One Allegheny Ave., Pittsburgh
• (412) 237-3400

Along the north shore of the Ohio River is the Carnegie Science Center, recognizable because the USS Requin Submarine moors along the banks of the river. This facility was borne of the older institution known as Buhl Planetarium. Now, it boasts not only a new planetarium and observatory, but indoor displays of science, technology, and health care as well as the miniature railroad display that's open almost year-round (see Annual Events).

Rangos Omnimax Theater film presentations, hands-on learning, and a guided tour of the submarine, commissioned during World War II, are available (see Kidstuff). The center extends its hours in the summer at times. Regu-

Old Economy Village hosts tours and special events in Beaver County.

Heinz Hall for the Performing Arts is home to the Pittsburgh Symphony Orchestra.

Photo: Courtesy of Pittsburgh Symphony Orchestra

Nationality Classrooms
157 Cathedral of Learning, Univ. of Pittsburgh, Pittsburgh
• (412) 624-6000

Twenty-six classrooms (and the number continues to grow) in this towering cathedral depict the city's diverse ethnic heritage through their individual architecture and decor. In the 1920s, over a quarter of Pittsburgh's population had been born abroad, and another fifth were the offspring of foreign-born parents. At Pitt, one of every three students was foreign-born or the child of immigrants.

Thus, chancellor John Gabbert Bowman and others conceived of these special rooms so as not to disappoint visitors who saw the impressive structure outside. Each was funded by ethnic committees, designed by native architects, and built with materials from the countries they represent. Access to the classrooms is by tour only. Recorded tours are offered if you like. Student guides are also available between 11 AM

lar hours, Sunday through Friday, 10 AM until 5 PM and Saturday 10 AM to 9 PM. An Explorer Pass for adults costs $14; $8.50 for children.

Tickets are also sold separately for Omnimax, submarine and laser shows, and exhibits, if you prefer to see only one part of the center. For instance, to see the exhibits only, admission costs $6.50 for adults, and $4.50 for seniors (65 and above) and children (ages 3 through 18). For the Omnimax theater alone, expect to pay $6.50 or $4.50. The submarine tour alone costs $4 or $2, respectively. Combination ticket packages are available and prices are listed at the desk and given by telephone on the automated information line (call number given above). Senior discounts are extended on Tuesdays. Purchasing a membership to the science center allows complimentary admission. Parking is a flat $3 rate.

and 3 PM on most days. The Nationality Rooms are open Monday through Saturday, 9:30 AM to 3 PM , and Sunday, 11 AM to 3 PM. Admission rates are $2 for adults, $1.50 for seniors (60 and above), and 50 cents for children (ages 8 to 18). Children (8 and younger) are free.

Historical

Air Heritage Museum
Beaver County Airport, 15 Piper St., Beaver Falls • (724) 843-2820

This museum boasts a rich heritage of aviation with vintage aircraft, war planes, and aeronautical artifacts. Volunteers at this museum work hard to make some of these old "war birds" or aircraft fly again. Some of the aircraft date back to the 1920s. Visitors can shop for flying paraphernalia in the gift shop. Proceeds from

ATTRACTIONS

the planes' appearances in air shows, movies, and commercials help to support the restoration process. as do donations from the public and gift shop sales. Here, you'll find that behind every plane is, of course, a war story to go along with it! The Air Heritage Museum is open to the public from 10 AM to 4 PM, most days except holidays. A $2 per person donation is requested.

Senator John Heinz Pittsburgh Regional History Center
1212 Smallman St., Pittsburgh
• **(412) 454-6321**

Named in memory of the late U.S. Senator John Heinz, this center in the Strip District is home to the Historical Society of Western Pennsylvania, and serves as a museum and depository of regional history. Four floors of exhibits tell of building a life in Western Pennsylvania from 1750 to the present. Many of the displays are interactive, informative, and entertaining. A library and archives is housed on the sixth floor.

The center's first floor

The Andy Warhol Museum on the city's North Side was created to house many of this Pittsburgh native's collection.

Photo: Courtesy of Greater Pittsburgh Convention & Visitors Bureau

offers a video inside an actual trolley car, reminiscent of Pittsburgh's past. There are also famous neon signs depicting well-known merchants and companies through the years. Large staircases and elevators take you to the exhibit areas, starting with the second floor and its dramatic contrast of Pittsburgh in the pioneer days with its status today (as seen through a large screen image). A 10-minute orientation video introduces the exhibits you'll see on this floor of the permanent collection.

On the museum's third floor, children enjoy the Discovery Place (see Kidstuff). Changing exhibit galleries grace the fourth floor where past displays have included Toy Bop, Glass: Shattering Notions, and the History of Heinz 57 (a history of the Heinz Company).

The Heinz History Center is open daily from 10 AM to 5 PM. The library is open Tuesday through Saturday, 10 AM until 5 PM. The Center is closed Thanksgiving, Christmas, and New Year's Day. Cost for adults is $6, $4.50 for seniors (65 and above) and students (with ID), and $3 for children (ages 6 to 18). Children younger than 6 are admitted at no cost.

Beaver Area Historical Museum
East End Ave., Beaver
• **(724) 728-5431**

Housed in the renovated Pittsburgh and Lake Erie Railroad freight station, this museum tells the story of Beaver County. Residents and visitors alike will enjoy the collection of artifacts

ATTRACTIONS

and information about life in years past. Some of the exhibits include a Revolutionary War uniform and equipment, Civil War weaponry, archaeological specimens from area digs, and examples of local pottery. Publications and gifts are featured in the museum shop. The historical attraction is open on Wednesdays and Saturdays from 10 AM until 4 PM, and on Sundays from 1 to 4 PM. Admission is free of charge.

Butler County Heritage Center
119 West New Castle St., Butler
• **(724) 283-8116**

After searching for more than 20 years for a place to archive its artifacts and memorabilia, residents of Bulter County found just such a site. In 1994, the Butler County Heritage Society purchased a three-story building that opened the following year, with a 4,500-square-foot exhibit entitled "Made In Butler County," which includes an original Bantam jeep, the Bantam Hollywood prototype convertible sports car, and displays representative of Butler industries both past and present. Metered on-street parking is available. The Heritage Center is open weekends May through October.

Pennsylvania Trolley Museum
Off Race Track Rd., Washington
• **(724) 228-9256**

South of Pittsburgh in Washington County, vintage streetcars depict transportation from another era. Home of "A Streetcar Named Desire," these relics are rebuilt and restored for your enjoyment. Kids especially enjoy the special events such as Santa's visit each year (see our Kidstuff and Annual Events chapters).

Allow at least two hours to completely experience the museum. Please note the museum is closed during the months of January, February, and March, but reopens on weekends in early April through December 31 from 11 AM to 5 PM. It's open seven days a week, Memorial Day through Labor Day, from 11 AM to 5 PM. Admission costs $6 for adults, $5 for seniors (65 and above), and $3.50 for children (12-15). Children younger than 12 receive free admission.

Meadowcroft Museum of Rural Life
401 Meadowcroft Rd., Avella
• **(724) 587-3412**

Experience life in the 19th century, as it was in Western Pennsylvania. This 200-acre living history museum in Washington County offers

ATTRACTIONS

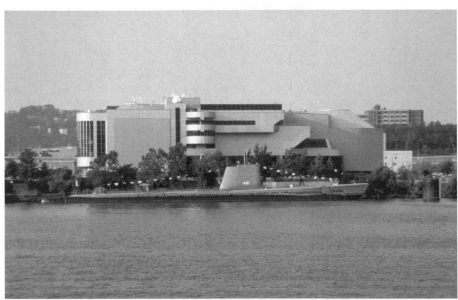

The Carnegie Science Center sits along the banks of the Ohio River, with its World War II submarine as a tourist attraction.

Photo: Kevin Sell

Idlewild Park, in the Laurel Highlands of Westmoreland County, offers a trolley ride through the only life-size Mister Rogers' Neighborhood of Make-Believe.

Photo: Courtesy of Idlewild Park

lessons on rural life for the entire family (see Kidstuff). Meadowcroft introduces you to the Native Americans, frontier settlers, farmers, lumbermen, coal miners, and conservationists who have shaped rural Western Pennsylvania. You'll get to try your hands as spinning wool or attend a class in a one-room school. Included on the grounds are wooden paths, gardens, a picnic area, a gift shop, a cafe, and a modern visitors center. Meadowcroft is open Memorial Day through Labor Day, on Saturdays from Noon to 5 PM and on Sundays from 1 to 5 PM. Groups of 20 or more can call for appointments. To enter, adults pay $6.50; senior citizens, $5.50; children (ages 6 through 16), $3.50; and children younger than 6 are admitted free of charge.

Harmony Museum
218 Mercer St., Harmony
• (724) 452-7341

Surrounding the diamond in the village of Harmony are many of the original buidings erected by the Harmonists, immigrant German separatists in the early 1800s. Johann George Rapp was a German vinetender-turned-prophet. Several of his followers traveled with him to the New World, fleeing religious persecution and finding the freedom they could not have in their European homeland. Rapp purchased acreage in Western Pennsylvania. Their religious fervor prospered, until in 1807, they adopted celibacy, a step toward the ultimate extinction of the group. Subsequently, the Mennonites settled here from 1815 through much of the 19th century.

The Harmony Museum, including the Wagner House and Ziegler log house, as well as the Harmonist cemetery, Father Rapp's hillside seat, and the Mennonite meeting house and cemetery, are under the direction of Historic Harmony. Appointments are recommended for the weekends. Tours are given Tuesday through Sunday, 1 to 4 PM, year-round. General admission is $3.50; seniors (60 and above) pay $3; children (ages 6 through 12) get in for $1.50; children (6 and younger), free of charge.

Old Economy Village
1400 Church St, Ambridge
• (724) 266-4500, (724) 266-1803

Visit the third and final home of the Harmony Society here at Old Economy Village in Beaver County. This National Historic Landmark is administered by the Pennsylvania Historical and Museum Commission. The Harmonists were one of America's most successful Christian communal groups. Wearing Harmonist dress, interpreters take you through the museum building, cabinet shop, community kitchen, baker house, wine cellar, store, and George and Frederick Rapp Houses, all of which were built between 1825 and 1830. Browse through four buildings and the gardens independently. Original objects owned by the Harmonists are displayed. Tours are conducted Tuesday through Saturday, 9:30 AM to 3 PM, and Sunday, 1 to 3 PM. If you're visiting in the fall or winter, the tours end at 2:30 PM. Old Economy Village is closed Mondays and winter holidays. Special holiday decorations and activities are seen at particular times throughout the year (see Annual Events). Admission costs $5 for adults (age 13 and older), $4.50 for seniors (60 and older), $3 for children (ages 6 through 12), and $13 for a family (with members all living in the same household).

Fort Necessity National Battlefield & Braddock's Grave
U.S. Route 40, Fayette County
• **(724) 329-5512**

Along what's called The National Road (otherwise known as Route 40), there's a little bit of history from the French & Indian War. Here, on July 3, 1754, a French and Indian force surrounded George Washington's "fort of necessity" and forced his only military surrender. Fort Necessity park grounds and visitor center are run by the National Park Service and open to the public, daily from 8:30 AM to 5 PM throughout the year (except for Christmas Day). Besides the battlefield, don't miss other related sites, including the grave of British General Edward Braddock, a commanding officer who was mortally wounded in the war and buried just up the road. Jumonville Glen was the site of Washington's first skirmish with the French. And the park also operates the Mount Washington Tavern, built in 1828 to serve travelers along the National Road.

Picnic facilities are available during summer months. Start at the visitor center with the audio-visual program and exhibits before moving through the grounds, where on a warm day you'll see Indians demonstrating crafts and telling the story of survival at Fort Necessity.

Fort Ligonier
Rtes. 30 and 711, Ligonier
• **(724) 238-9701**

Another battle site of the French & Indian War, Fort Ligonier is located on U.S. Route 30 and Pa. Route 711 in Westmoreland County. On October 12, 1758, the British overcame few French and only a few hundred Indians forces. The fort is open daily April 1 through October from 10 AM to 4:30 PM. Fort Ligonier Days occur each October (see our Annual Events chapter). Admission rates are $5 for adults and $2.25 for children ages 6 to 14. Children younger than 6 are admitted free of charge.

Heralded Homes

Armstrong County Historical Museum
300 N. McKean St. and Vine St., Kittaning
• **(724) 548-5707**

This Federal-style house was built in 1842 and added on to with a spacious wing in 1990. It was known as the McCain House before the change to its present name. Today, it's a museum offering the public seasonal exhibits, a historical and genealogical library, and an educational classroom center. It's open Wednesdays and Saturdays from 2 to 5 PM, but during the winter months, this attraction is closed. Special tours can be arranged by appointment.

Clayton
Penn Ave. and Homewood Ave., Pittsburgh
• **(412) 371-0600**

Henry Clay Frick and his wife Adelaide purchased this as their home in Pointe Breeze in 1882. Clayton, as the house was called, was an example of the Italianate homes built following the Civil War. But the Fricks, wanting a new look, had the house remodeled, giving it steep roofs and gables. (See our Architecture chapter.)

The Frick's daughter Helen Clay Frick inherited the home, and after she died in 1984, it was willed to the family's foundation. In 1990, Clayton opened to the public, and is now part of the Frick Art & Historical Center (see the Arts chapter). There is free parking. The center is open Tuesday through Saturday, from 10 AM until 5 PM, and on Sundays from Noon until

INSIDERS' TIP
If you're new to Pennsylvania, or would just like a switch, purchase a zoo license plate to save the wild animals. Created by the Pennsylvania Zoological Council, these green plates are easy to spot. Inquire at the Pittsburgh Zoo or National Aviary.

ATTRACTIONS

6 PM. Clayton is closed on Mondays. Tours of Clayton cost $8 for adults, $7 for seniors, and $6 for students. Members are admitted free of charge.

Hartwood
215 Saxonburg Blvd., Pittsburgh
• (412) 767-9200

In the northeastern suburbs of Pittsburgh lies the Hartwood estate, 629 equestrian acres with stables, gardens, and summer music and theater performances. The Tudor mansion is fully furnished with English and American antiques, and there is a gate lodge designed by Alfred Hopkins. This is the site of the special holiday lights tour (see Annual Events). Mansion tours are conducted by reservation only. Hartwood is closed January through March and major holidays, but is open April 1 through December 31. Hartwood opens its doors Wednesday through Saturday, 10 AM to 3 PM and Sunday, 12 to 4 PM. It's closed Mondays and Tuesday. Admission costs $5 per adult, $3 for seniors (60 and older), $3 for children ages 13 to 17, $2 for children ages 6 to 12, and $1 for children 5 and younger.

Passavant House & Buhl House
243 S. Main St. & 221 S. Main St., Zelienople • (724) 452-9457

Local history abounds in this Butler County community where these two homes have been converted to museums. Baron Dettmar Friederich Basse, an aristocrat, invited daughter Zelie and her husband Philipp Louis Passavant to join him at the land he'd purchased in the early 1800s. The couple's five children were born in Passavant House, which dates back to 1808. Their progeny continued their hardworking tradition, establishing churches, hospitals, orphanages, and schools in the area.

Son Charles married the granddaughter of Christian and Fredericka Buhl, another famous name to Western Pennsylvania, associated with the Buhl Planetarium and the former Boggs and Buhl Department Store on the city's North Side. Buhl House, built in 1805, houses a museum of the Buhl family in its 10 rooms. Contact the Zelienople Historical Society (telephone listed above) for tours. Admission includes a guided tour of both homes, with the general ad-

mission price set at $3.50 per person. Children (younger than 18) and students cost $2.50. Children (younger than 6) are admitted free of charge.

Rachel Carson Homestead
613 Marion Ave., Springdale
• (724) 274-5459

At the birthplace and childhood home of ecologist Rachel Carson (1907-64), there are guided tours available to homestead visitors. Carson's 1962 best-seller Silent Spring helped launch the environmental movement. This legendary home is open weekends only, from 10 AM to 4 PM Saturday and from 1 to 5 PM Sunday, or by appointment at other times. The homestead is closed in January and February. Admission costs $5 for adults, $3 for seniors, and $2.50 for kids 4 to 18.

Fallingwater
Mill Run (Off Rt. 40), Fayette County
• (724) 329-8501

Frank Lloyd Wright's spectacular house set atop a waterfall is an architectural masterpiece of the 20th century. Back in the 1930s, Pittsburgh department store owner Edgar J. Kaufmann and his wife Liliane commissioned Wright to design their weekend retreat at Bear Run, 90 minutes south of Pittsburgh. Tucked among the rhododendrons, the house uses cantilevers enabling the terraces of the living and bedroom levels to extend over the rushing falls without visible support.

Now under the care of the Western Pennsylvania Conservancy, the house can be toured by visitors, but reservations are suggested. Children younger than 9 are not permitted, but there is group baby-sitting at $2 per hour per child at the Visitors Pavilion. With the many stairs, considerable walking is required, so make arrangements for special assistance in advance if you feel you'll need it. (See also our Daytrips and Architecture chapters).

Fallingwater is closed from early January through late February. In-depth tours are available at 8:30 AM for $40 (weekdays) or $50 (weekends). Regular tours are conducted on weekends until the middle of March. This famous architectural masterpiece is open March through December, Tuesday through Sunday from 10 AM to 4 PM.

INSIDERS' TIP

Powdermill Nature Reserve, in the Laurel Highlands, offers woodlands, streams, fields, and ponds for its educational programs run through The Carnegie Museum of Natural History. It's open during the warm-weather months.

Rollercoasters are among the main attractions at Kennywood Park.

Photo: Courtesy of Kennywood Park

Kentuck Knob
Chalk Hill, Ohiopyle
• **(724) 329-1901**

High above a mountain overlooking the Youghiogheny River Gorge near Fallingwater is another of Frank Lloyd Wright's creations. Built of native stone and tidewater cypress, this house was commissioned by the I.N. Hagan family of Uniontown. Contemporary sculpture and historic artifacts enhance the secluded setting. Children under 9 are not permitted (no childcare provided). Though not as renowned as Fallingwater, Kentuck Knob is available for touring. Kentuck Knob is open daily, except Mondays, 10 AM to 4 PM. In-depth tours are available at 8:30 AM for $30 (weekdays) or $35 (weekends). Or, take a regular tour, available on weekdays during the summer at $10 per person and $15 per person on weekends. Winter tours cost $15 per person.

LeMoyne House
49 E. Maiden St., Washington
• **(724) 225-6740**

Discover why LeMoyne House is a trail to the Civil War. This historic 1812 structure once was an abolitionist home and shelter to escaping slaves. The house is named for Dr. Francis Julius LeMoyne, who converted words into action, at great personal risk, as he sheltered escaping slaves on the Underground Railroad, established a college for African-Americans, and rescued Washington College from bankruptcy. LeMoyne House is administered by the Washington County Historical Society, which makes tours available. The property is open from February through mid-December, Tuesday through Friday, 11 AM to 4 PM, and Saturday and Sunday, 12 to 4 PM. Admission is $4 for adults and $2 for students.

Linden Hall
RD 1, Dawson
• **(724) 529-7543, (800) 944-3238**

Listed on the National Register of Historical Sites, Linden Hall Mansion and Recreation Center was built in Fayette County in 1913, with its grand view of the Laurel Highlands. Enjoy 35 rooms of the exquisite English Tudor mansion featuring signed Tiffany windows, an Aeolian pipe organ, wonderfully restored Victorian furnishings, and original paintings. In addition, there are gardens and trails for warm-weather walks. The estate offers lodging, dining, and recreation. Tours are conducted daily March through October, 11 AM to 3 PM

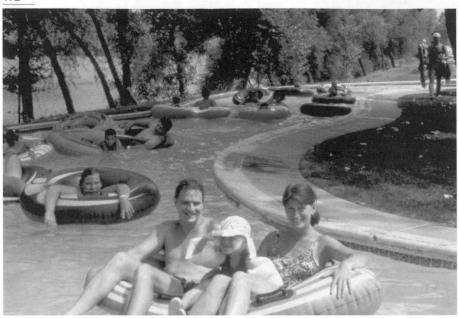

A float down the lazy river raft ride is cool refreshment at Sandcastle water park.

Photo: Courtesy of Sandcastle

(weekends, by reservation). If you want to visit in November and December, you may, but by appointment only. To enter, adults can expect to pay approximately $8. Seniors are charged $7, children (12 and older), $4, and children under 12 are admitted free of charge.

On the Wild Side

Idlewild Park
Route 30, Ligonier
• **(724) 238-3666**

Set in the Laurel Highlands of Westmoreland County, Idlewild is an amusement park where you'll want to pack for a picnic. Theme areas include Story Book Forest, Mister Rogers' Neighborhood of Make-Believe, H2OHHH Zone, Jumpin' Jungle, Hootin' Holler, and Raccoon Lagoon. Enjoy major amusement rides in the Olde Idlewild area, and live entertainment occurring on stage. (See our Kidstuff chapter for more). This family fun land is open from May 31 to Labor Day, but is closed on Mondays, except holidays. Adults and children pay $16.95 everyday, and seniors (55 and older) are charged $12. Children 2 and younger are admitted free of charge. For those who discover there is sim-

ply too much fun to explore in one day, ask about the "Next Day Pass" at guest services. There's no cost to park at Idlewild.

Kennywood Park
4800 Kennywood Blvd., West Mifflin
• **(412) 461-0500**

A historic park and roller coaster capital, Kennywood has long had a commitment to upgrading its rides and keeping its Allegheny County grounds family-friendly. (See our Kidstuff chapter). Kennywood has brought generations of Pittsburghers lots of thrills and old-fashioned fun. Enjoy live performances, community and school picnics, ethnic pride days, and fall fantasy parades. Ride-all-day passes cost $18.95 on weekdays and $22.95 on Saturdays and Sundays. General admission tickets (rides not included) are available to adults for $7.50 and to seniors (65 and older) for $6.50. During the last week of August, there is a Fun Finale each evening. A ride-all-evening pass costs $12.

Sandcastle
1000 Sandcastle Dr., West Homestead
• **(412) 462-6666**

Set along the Monongahela River banks in Allegheny County, this is where Pittsburgh beats the heat during the summer. That's because there are 15 twisting and turning waterslides, a gentle Lazy River to float down, several pools, and the self-proclaimed World's Largest Hot Tub for adults. The park has undergone recent renovations that added the 20,000-square-foot Mon-Tsunami wave pool.

Landlubbers play volleyball, snack on food, or visit the gift shops along the old fashioned boardwalk. Oasis Miniature Golf and the exciting Formula 1 Speedway give your trip to Sandcastle added activities. The adjacent Riverplex entertainment complex boasts an amphitheater, big top circus tent, grassy areas, and tree-lined walkways.

Sandcastle is open daily from early June through early September. Hours are 11 AM to 6 PM in June and September and 11 AM to 7 PM in July and August. A Whitewater Pass entitles you to all water attractions and costs $16.95 for adults and $12.95 for seniors. The Super Pass, good for five separate visits, costs $39.95. To ride the Formula 1 Speedway, you must be at least 58 inches tall and pay $4. Children 3 and younger are admitted free of charge, and parking plus boat docking is also free of charge.

Whitewater Rafting
Ohiopyle • (800) 272-4141

Ohiopyle Falls in Fayette County had its name derived from the native words "Ohio pehelle" which mean white frothy water. Indeed, thousands enjoy white water rafting in this most famous site in the Appalachians. Ohiopyle State Park has hiking and bicycle trails, picnic areas, camping, as well as cold and warm water fishing. During the winter months, many enjoy sledding, cross country skiing, and snowmobile trails. Whitewater rafting trips are available through Wilderness Voyagers (telephone listed above), April 1 through November 1. The reservation office is open year-round. Anyone can use the bike trail, free of charge, but it's best to call when reserving pavilions or organizing a rafting trip.

Nature's Best

Pittsburgh Zoo & Aquarium
One Wild Place, Pittsburgh
• (412) 665-3640, (800) 474-4966

If you feel like monkeying around, head to Highland Park, where the primates show off just for you. The elephants, zebras, and giraffes roam the African Savanna, and the Siberian tigers and snow leopards explore the Asian Forest. Youngsters can enjoy Kids Kingdom (see Kidstuff) and the young elephant, born in 1999. (If you're counting on seeing the baby elephant,

Dinosaur Hall is one of the popular exhibits for families and school children at the Carnegie Museum of Natural History.

ATTRACTIONS

call ahead for the exact times.) In addition, a recent capital campaign allowed for a renovated aquarium, making the Pittsburgh Zoo one of only six zoos in the country with a major aquarium.

Did you know that the zoo is open year-round? Well, it is, and it closes only on Christmas Day. Don't miss the special evening hours during the holiday season (see Annual Events chapter). At all other times, the zoo is open Memorial Day through Labor Day 10 from AM to 6 PM. Labor Day through Memorial Day, the zoo opens at 9 AM until 5 PM. Entrance gates close an hour before the park closes. Admission is as follows: Adults, $6.50; seniors, $4.75; children (ages 2 to 13) $4.75; children younger than 2 pay nothing. Members of the zoo are also admitted free of charge. Strollers are available for rent at a nominal charge.

National Aviary
Allegheny Commons West, Pittsburgh
• **(412) 323-7235**

This bird zoo is indeed called the National Aviary. Though it receives no federal funding, Congress granted the North Side aviary the national designation in 1993. Over 400 of the world's most colorful and exotic birds live here in this, the nation's largest indoor bird display, independent of a larger zoo. The Aviary is open daily, except Christmas Day, 9 AM to 5 PM. Adults will pay $5 and seniors (60 and older), $4. Admission for children (ages 2 to 12) costs $3.50 and those younger than 2 are admitted free of charge.

Phipps Conservatory and Botanical Gardens
Schenley Park, Pittsburgh
• **(412) 622-6915**

Donated by Henry Phipps, one of the city's turn-of-the-century millionaire industrialists and philanthropists, this conservatory is a 13-room Victorian glasshouse full of beautiful gardens. Visit one of the country's finest bonsai collections or take the kids to the Discovery Garden (see Kidstuff). You don't need to fly to Arizona to view desert plants, or head to the Caribbean to see tropical palms, ferns, and other flora that are right here for you to enjoy. A $30 million expansion project that will quadruple the size of this facility will be unveiled in 2002.

Phipps is open Tuesday through Sunday, 9 AM to 5 PM. Phipps admission is $6 for adults, $5 for seniors 60 and above, $4 for students with ID, and $3 for children (ages 2 through 12). Children younger than 2 and Phipps members enter without charge. Metered parking is right in front of the conservatory.

Pivotal Points of Interest

Andy Warhol Museum
117 Sandusky St., Pittsburgh
• **(412) 237-8300**

Pop artist Andy Warhol, born into a Pittsburgh family that emigrated from Eastern Europe, began his career right in this city. After attending Saturday art classes and college at Carnegie Institute and what now is Carnegie Mellon University, Warhol moved to New York, working as a commercial artist and becoming famous for his experimentation with silkscreens (from which he made photographically derived paintings). Upon his sudden death in 1987, The Andy Warhol Museum was constructed on the city's North Side. Seven floors house celebrity portraits, pop paintings (including Heinz boxes, Marilyns and Campbell's soup cans), Warhol's sketchbooks, and a film gallery. The Warhol is open Wednesday and Sunday, 11 AM to 6 PM, Thursday, Friday, and Saturday, 11 AM to 8 PM. It's closed Mondays and Tuesdays. Adults will pay $7, seniors are charged $6, and students and children older than 3 pay $4 for admission. Carnegie members pay nothing to enter.

Jimmy Stewart Museum
845 Philadelphia St., Third Floor, Indiana
• **(800) 83-JIMMY**

Though an attraction of Indiana County, this museum is a definite Western Pennsylvania highlight for those who follow Hollywood and its legends. Located in Jimmy's hometown of Indiana, where his father once owned a hardware store, the museum gives you a chance to see many of Stewart's accomplishments in film, radio, and television. Tributes to Jimmy Stewart's military service, family life, and public service are also housed here. The museum is closed Monday and Tuesday, January 1 through April 1, Christmas Eve and Day, New Year's

---

INSIDERS' TIP

If you're interested in specific historic homes or small history centers, check the operating hours. Some are closed for weeks or months during the year.

Eve and Day, Good Friday, Easter Sunday, and Thanksgiving. However, it's open 10 AM to 5 PM other days of the week, and on Sunday, 12 to 5 PM. Adults pay $5; seniors (60 and above), students and military, $4; and children (ages 7 to 17), $3. Children younger than 7 get in for free.

Pittsburgh's Inclines
Carson St., Pittsburgh
• **(412) 381-1665 (Duquesne Incline) and (412) 442-2000 (Monongahela Incline)**

Pittsburgh once had over a dozen working inclines at the turn of the century. Now, the Monongahela and Duquesne Inclines remain, transporting commuters and tourists to and from Grandview Avenue atop Mt. Washington to the City of Pittsburgh below. The Monongahela Incline was the city's first in 1870. Declared a historic structure by the Pittsburgh History and Landmarks Foundation, it's been registered a National Historic Landmark as well.

Today, it's operated by the Port Authority Transit (PAT). For a panoramic view, a ride on one of these is a must, night or day. (See our Getting Here, Getting Around chapter). The inclines operate daily starting at 5:30 AM until 12:45 AM On Sundays, service begins at 7 AM.

Washington County Covered Bridges
Various locations, Washington County
• **(800) 531-4114**

Travel back in time to some of the century-old covered bridges (of which there are 25 in this county alone). All are listed on the National Register of Historic Places. Romantics call these "kissing bridges" for their seclusion, and animal lovers herald their barn-like appearance for helping the animals cross streams. A helpful map is offered through the Washington County Tourism office (telephone number listed above). A covered bridge festival is held each fall (see Annual Events).

ATTRACTIONS

Kidstuff

To see the world through a child's eyes indeed lends a new perspective, particularly on Pittsburgh. Kids, this chapter is for you mostly, but also for mom and dad, family and friends, and anyone else who simply wants to have fun.

Since play is the child's work, it's impossible to list every spot across so many counties where kids can enjoy themselves as they learn and grow. In these pages, you'll find the highlights and the things you most definitely won't want to miss.

Savvy parents might also peruse the Attractions and even the Arts chapters, particularly for older children or those who have interests in more sophisticated subjects like history, art appreciation, and landmarks. As another entire chapter, Recreation offers a range of equally fun activities that can burn off some of that boundless energy.

Separate chapters cover Shopping and Restaurants as well, so if you're looking for family-friendly places to eat, shops in which to outfit the kids, or if you need to stock your home with a few new toys, it's best to turn to these listings. However, you'll find that most of the museums and attractions listed in these pages do offer gift shops with appropriate memorabilia and merchandise. That may come as a double-edged sword, bringing on the chorus of "Mom, can I have that?" but these stores are often very educational in nature.

Because children teach us to throw structure to the wind sometimes, we've abandoned our usual geographic breakdown for this chapter. Instead, get ready to stretch your mind, discover and explore, go a little crazy in between, and savor the delights of Pittsburgh's seasons.

We've tried to present current prices, but there are instances where class or exhibit fees do fluctuate. Thus, it's best to call before heading out (and perhaps disappointing a child).

So lace up your sneakers and get ready to enjoy a day (or several) of being inquisitive, overjoyed, and yes, probably tired at the end of it all. Oh, but the fun you'll have!

Stretching the Mind

Kids' Classes
Community College of Allegheny County Main Campus, 800 Allegheny Ave., Pittsburgh • (412) 237-3100

Think of this as kids' college of sorts, as youngsters attend a variety of classes at one of the community college campuses near you. There are offerings at the Boyce, North, South, and Allegheny campuses. Most sessions meet on Saturdays, with some classes held on particular evenings. Kids can acquire new skills or sharpen existing ones as they take art, acting, basketball, babysitting, cheerleading, dance, computer, language, writing, fencing, swimming, or other classes. Sessions are also offered for SAT preparation and verbal self-defense, just to name a few of the courses available for your child's educational advancement.

In outlying counties, many community colleges offer similar fare for the younger set. It's best to contact the schools in your area for their continuing education brochures. Use these numbers to help you:

Take a ride through Mister Rogers' Neighborhood of Make-Believe at Idlewild Park.

Photo: Courtesy of Idlewild Park

Butler County Community College
(724) 287-8711
Community College of Beaver County
(724) 775-8561
Westmoreland County Community College
(724) 925-4000

Classes at The Carnegie
4400 Forbes Ave., Pittsburgh
• (412) 622-3288

Culture, history, and art appreciation abound here at the home of the Carnegie Museum of Natural History and the Carnegie Museum of Art. The schedule changes each semester, so it's best to call for a catalog, or perhaps pick one up at your local library. Previous offerings have included painting, puppet-making, sculpting, and architectural classes on the art side. Explore everything from bugs and bears to dinosaurs, Disney animals, reptiles, and archaeological findings. Also, there are classes specifically designed for homeschoolers. The prices for these always fluctuate, so it's best to call for further details.

Dinosaur Hall
Carnegie Museum of Natural History,
4400 Forbes Ave., Pittsburgh
• (412) 622-3131

This world-famous collection of dinosaur bones and fossils is perhaps the most popular attraction at the museum with children of all ages. Eleven different species are on display in

addition to the other fossils of animals that lived around the same Mesozoic Era. For children, these non-threatening monsters are simply amazing, especially in size. The Tyrannosaurus rex stands 20 feet tall here, and dominates the far end of Dinosaur Hall. While at the Museum of Natural History, don't miss Bonehunters Quarry, an interactive exhibit that re-creates an area of Dinosaur National Monument in Colorado and Utah.

Hours at the Carnegie museums are Tuesday through Saturday, 10 AM to 5 PM, and Sunday, 1 to 5 PM. The museum stays open until 9 PM on Fridays from June through August, 10 AM to 9 PM, and opens on Mondays in July and August from 10 AM to 5 PM. Admission to The Carnegie Museum of Natural History and Museum of Art is $6 for adults, $5 for senior citizens, and $4 for children (3-18). Children younger than 3 and members are admitted free of charge.

Children's Discovery Room
Carnegie Museum of Natural History,
4400 Forbes Ave., Pittsburgh
• (412) 622-1950

Tucked away downstairs in this museum is a room where kids can touch, explore, ask questions, and find answers to many intriguing facts. Individual boxes of artifacts can be checked out to explore while in the room (grown-up supervision with these sets is requested). The room's handful of aquariums contain fish, hermit crabs, and turtles.

KIDSTUFF

Kids can sniff spices and learn where they come from, and in general, explore to their heart's (and hands'!) content. All children younger than 12 must be accompanied by an adult.

Discovery Room hours are Tuesday through Friday 1 to 3 PM, Saturday 10 AM to 4 PM, and Sunday 1 to 4 PM during the school year. In the summer, the room is open weekdays and Saturdays 10 AM to 4 PM as well as on Sunday from 1 to 4 PM. Admission to The Carnegie Museum of Natural History and Museum of Art is $6 for adults, $5 for senior citizens, and $4 for children (3 to 18). Children younger than 3 and members are admitted free of charge.

Pittsburgh Children's Museum
10 Children's Way, Pittsburgh
• (412) 322-5058

In the historic landmark Old Post Office Building on the city's North Side, this museum offers outstanding exhibits throughout its three floors. Luckey's Climber is an amazing two-story indoor jungle gym. Riverscape recreates Pittsburgh in the 1920s where children can role-play, while The Studio is a section where kids create their own silkscreens. The little ones won't want to miss the puppet exhibit featuring some of Fred Rogers' famous puppets as well as some Jim Henson (of Muppets fame) creations. Stuffee, the museum's health-teaching exhibit, doesn't mind at all if he's poked and prodded.

Previous exhibits have included the Welcome to Mister Rogers' Neighborhood exhibit, made possible by the Grable Foundation. In honor of Mister Rogers' 30th anniversary on public television, this exhibit will travel to other children's museums but come back for a permanent stay in Pittsburgh.

The Children's Museum is closed on Mondays and major holidays, but open Tuesday through Thursday from 10 AM to 5 PM. On Fridays, visit from 10 AM to 8 PM. Saturdays, hours are 10 AM to 5 PM, and on Sundays, the museum opens from noon to 5 PM. Adults pay $5 per person for admission, with $4.50 charged for seniors and children (2 to 18). Children younger than 2 are admitted free of charge, and museum members receive complimentary admission as well. Each Thursday, everyone's admission is discounted to $3.50.

Carnegie Science Center
One Allegheny Ave., Pittsburgh
• (412) 237-3400

With it's focus on science and technology, it's no wonder the Carnegie Science Center on the North Side makes kids feel like inventors, young astronauts, and even magicians. The center isn't limited to children's activities, but certainly kids can learn so much from the interactive exhibits and Omnimax large-format films. They can momentarily pretend they are meteorologists on the evening news, and they can watch a demonstration of science in the kitchen.

Ports of Discovery is a three-part water-related area featuring a living Pacific coral reef aquarium. Kids can explore the planets and stars at the Henry Buhl, Jr. Planetarium & Observatory. Young history buffs shouldn't miss a tour of the USS Requin, a World War II diesel-electric submarine moored on the banks of the river (this one's not recommended for very young children). And do note that the miniature train display, while closed each February for refurbishing, is open most other months of the year. You'll avoid the crowds if you time your visit outside the holiday season (see our Annual Events chapter).

The center features an educational division with programs for school groups, students, families and educators. Scouts can earn badges at the science center's scout workshops. Using NASA resources, there's even a young astronauts program exploring space travel. Periodically, school students compete in science fairs, and the Carnegie Science Academy for teens fosters a fun, interactive environment for students in grade 9 through 12 with a love of science and exploration.

The center extends its hours in the summer at times. Regular hours, Sunday to Friday, 10 AM to 5 PM and Saturday 10 AM to 9 PM. An Explorer Pass costs $14 for adults, $8.50 for children.

Tickets are sold separately for Omnimax, the submarine, and laser shows and exhibits, if you prefer to see only one part of the center. For instance, to see the exhibits only, admission costs $6.50 for adults, and $4.50 for seniors (65 and above) and children (3 to 18). For the Omnimax theater alone, expect to pay $6.50 or $4.50. The submarine tour alone costs $4 or $2, respectively. Combina-

---

INSIDERS' TIP

Did you know that the *Mister Rogers' Neighborhood* fan in your house could help you shop through the mail? That's right, you can request a catalog from Family Communications featuring the puppets, books, videos, and other merchandise, including a trolley of your very own. Call (412) 687-2990.

tion ticket packages are available and prices are listed at the desk and given by telephone on the automated information line (call the number given above). Senior discounts are extended on Tuesdays. Purchasing a membership to the science center allows complimentary admission. Parking is an additional $3.

Kindermusik
Various locations • (800) 628-5687

This flexible curriculum that brings out the magic in music appeals to children between the ages of 18 months to 5 years. The goal isn't necessarily to make a musician out of your child, but to make your little one eager to learn and more alive through musical activities. These include 30-minute classes of singing, moving, listening, and playing simple instruments for those younger than 3, and 45-minute classes for kids ages 3 to 5. Those who enroll can take advantage of the parent orientation, family newsletters, and bring-a-friend days. Early registrants receive a 10 percent discount. The eastern suburbs location at Beulah Church may provide information for this site. Contact them at (412) 798-SONG. To find a Kindermusik location closer to you, try the toll-free number above or do a class locator search on the kindermusik.com website.

Discovering History

Senator John Heinz Pittsburgh Regional History Center
1212 Smallman St., Pittsburgh
• (412) 454-6321

Home of the Historical Society of Western Pennsylvania, this museum and depository of regional history isn't limited to children alone (see our Attractions chapter). However, there are several displays and features that will interest your youngsters. Start on the first floor of the Strip District museum, where kids can board an old street car, the way it used to be in Pittsburgh before the days of light rail transit and PAT buses. Kids will also delight at the robots giving them directions.

Children are certainly welcome to browse the exhibits throughout the building, but they will especially enjoy the Discovery Place (no relation to the Discovery Room we mentioned above) on the third floor, which is just for them. This room offers hands-on exploration with interactive exhibits and games. Kids can interview an object, travel through time, interview a shoe, and climb in a steel mill. Past exhibits at the History Center have included Top Bop, a collection of the best toys ever created.

The Heinz History Center is open daily from 10 AM to 5 PM. The library is open Tuesday through Saturday, 10 AM until 5 PM. The Center is closed Thanksgiving, Christmas, and New Year's Day. Cost for adults is $6, $4.50 for seniors (65 and above) and students (with ID), and $3 for children (6 to 18). Children younger than 6 are admitted at no cost.

INSIDERS' TIP
Bookstores throughout the region often feature story times, Saturday craft and story sessions, and other events for children during school breaks and throughout the summer months. Check with your local book seller, particularly the large superstores, for their individual offerings.

Pennsylvania Trolley Museum
Off Race Track Rd., Washington
• (724) 228-9256

Just 30 minutes south of Pittsburgh, kids can climb aboard a streetcar, hear the clang of the bell, and feel the powerful electric motors and the heavy clatter of steel wheels over the rails. These vintage streetcars are fun to ride and learn about. Volunteer craftsmen rebuild and restore these relics. Allow at least two hours to completely experience the museum. Please note the museum is closed during the months of January, February, and March, but reopens on weekends in early April through December 31, from 11 AM to 5 PM. It's open seven days a week, Memorial Day through Labor Day from 11 AM to 5 PM. Admission costs $6 for adults, $5 for seniors (65 and above), and $3.50 for children (12 to 15). Those children younger than 12 receive free admission.

Meadowcroft Museum of Rural Life
401 Meadowcroft Rd., Avella
• (724) 587-3412

This 200-acre living history museum in Washington County offers lessons on rural life for the youngsters as well. Each summer, there's a hands-on history day camp where children experience life in 19th century Western Pennsylvania. Kids shop at the general store, visit the blacksmith, and join Ma in preparing a meal on a woodstove. Then, after lunch, there's class

Everyone's Favorite Neighbor

He's been the subject of parody, yet his sweater hangs in the Smithsonian. Children play with merchandise bearing his legacy, and families travelling through Pittsburgh International Airport stop to admire the display, commemorating his important anniversary on public television. Yes, 30 years have gone by since Fred Rogers began bringing his gentle voice and nurturing demeanor into our living rooms, but his style and grace are as needed today as they were back in the turbulent '60s.

Fred McFeely Rogers was born in Latrobe, Westmoreland County. After graduating from Rollins College, Fred surprised everyone with his decision to work in television. He rejected the pies-in-the-face humor aimed at young audiences in the '50s, and was determined to find a better approach for this powerful medium.

Pittsburgh's Fred Rogers celebrated his 30th year on public television in 1998.

Photo: Courtesy of Family Communications

In New York, he worked briefly as an NBC floor manager, but later, he wanted to return to Pittsburgh and a start-up station, the first community-supported station in the country. "My friends thought I was crazy. I was in line to be a network director," he says of those days. And though it took eight years to complete additional studies at Pittsburgh Theological Seminary, Rogers was ordained with the special mission of working through the media. (See our Media and Worship chapters).

While gaining that seminary degree, Rogers was influenced by what he calls the "giants" in the field of child development—people like the late Margaret McFarland, Benjamin Spock, and Eric Erikson. Much of the *Mister Rogers Neighborhood* material, all written by Fred himself, emerged from the insights he gained from his mentors.

Today, Fred Rogers is as focused on his objective as he was when he first began producing the *Neighborhood* through his non-profit company, Family Communications. He lives in Pittsburgh with his wife Joanne, a concert pianist. His own two sons are now grown and married, there are grandchildren added to the Rogers' family.

While some parents poke fun at him and his slow, quiet approach, most have grown to admire the way he reaches out to their youngsters, becoming an important teacher in their lives. "Any adult who is honest with children and cares to spend time with them and cares to appreciate them can make a difference," he says. "Parents need to know how important they are in the life of their children. They really are their pre-school child's world. They are the axis."

The world has shown its thanks with numerous awards and recognition. In 1997, both the Daytime Emmys and the Television Critics Association saluted Fred with lifetime and career achievement awards. That same year, he was named Pittsburgher of the Year. The accolades just keep pouring in for this man. In 1998, Rogers got a star on the Hollywood Walk of Fame, and in 1999 he was given the TV Hall of Fame Award by the Academy of Television Arts & Sciences as well as another Emmy, this time for outstanding performer in a children's series.

The honors will surely continue, as Rogers remains steadfast in his work. A favorite quote that guides him perhaps gives us the most personal insight into this man. Translated from Saint-Exupery's *The Little Prince*: "What is essential is invisible to the eye." Indeed, Mister Rogers appreciates every day, every person, just the way they are. We Pittsburghers cherish him in return, just the way he is.

in a one-room school, learning a craft skill, and playing historical games. This one-day camp is for ages 6 through 12, and runs from 10 AM to 4 PM. Registration costs $25 per child. (See the Attractions chapter for more information on Meadowcroft).

Fort Necessity National Battlefield & Braddock's Grave
U.S. Route 40, Fayette County
• (724) 329-5512

Most kids have had to study about the French & Indian War in school, so why not show them a little history to supplement the studies! Right off Route 40 in Fayette County, or what is commonly called the National Road, visit George Washington's "fort of necessity," so named because a large force of French and Indians attacked Washington's army of 400 here. While this battle wasn't a success for Washington, the war's outcome had great impact on global affairs. The French lost much influence in North America, while the English colonies began to pay taxes levied upon them to help pay for this expensive war. Independence became a dream of some settlers.

Quietly up the road

from Fort Necessity, a single marker memorializes the final resting place of British Major General Edward Braddock. Braddock was the leader of an ill-fated expedition along the Ohio River trying to capture the French-held Fort Duquesne. Don't drive too fast along this road, for you just might miss it!

Fort Necessity park grounds and visitor center open daily from 8:30 AM to 5 PM. Picnic facilities are available during summer months. It's best to start your visit at the visitor center with its audio-visual program and exhibits before moving through the grounds. On a warm day, you'll find costumed Indians demonstrating crafts and telling the survival story at the fort.

In addition to the battlefield and the aforementioned grave of General Braddock, Fort Necessity features other historical sites of interest to kids. Jumonville Glen was the site of Washington's first skirmish with the French. And the park also operates the Mount Washington Tavern, built in 1828 to serve travelers along the National Road. Admission to Fort Necessity, which includes the fort, the museum exhibits, and the Mount Washington Tavern, costs $2 per person.

INSIDERS' TIP
Tired of driving your kids here and there? Port Authority of Allegheny County offers Summer Ride Passes for kids 18 years and younger. Call (412) 442-2000.

KIDSTUFF

Children 16 and younger are admitted free of charge.

Fort Ligonier
Rts. 30 and 711, Ligonier
• (724) 238-9701

If your children studied the French and Indian War, visit Fort Ligonier in Westmoreland County, which served as a staging area for the 1758 Forbes campaign that resulted in the capture of Fort Duquesne (Pittsburgh). The enemy arrived here October 12, 1758, with about 1,200 French and only a few hundred Indians, who were retreating to begin preparations for the long winter ahead. With their strength in numbers and mortar fire, the British were victorious. The new battery, constructed in a $2.3 million restoration project, is built on the site of the original defense fortification of 1758. This historic site is open daily, May 1 through October 31. Fort Ligonier Days occur each October (see the Annual Events chapter). It's open from 10 AM to 4:30 PM Monday through Saturday and Noon to 4:30 PM on Sundays. Admission rates are $6 for adults, $5 for seniors, and $3 for children 6 to 14. Children younger than 5 are admitted free of charge.

Going Crazy

Idlewild Park
Rt. 30, Ligonier
• (724) 238-3666

This family theme park in Westmoreland County includes Story Book Forest, Mister Rogers' Neighborhood of Make-Believe (the only one in the country), H2OHHH Zone (water slides and pool), Jumpin' Jungle, Hootin' Holler, and Raccoon Lagoon (kiddie rides). Kids will enjoy major amusement rides like a Ferris wheel and other traditional amusement park attractions in the Olde Idlewild area, and live entertainment on stage. Idlewild offers shaded picnic tables and grills, so be sure to pack a basket in this beautiful area of the Laurel Highlands. Pavilions can be reserved for large groups. Refreshment stands are numerous, and there's a large restaurant.

Previous highlights at Idlewild have included the Royal Hanneford Circus, and annual appearances of everyone's favorite charac-

ters from Mister Rogers' Neighborhood. Height requirements apply on the park's faster rides. There are changing facilities for the water attractions, and lockers for rent to store your belongings. But they aren't large, so pack light.

This family fun land is open from May 31 to Labor Day, but is closed on Mondays, except holidays. Adults and children pay $16.95 everyday, and seniors (55 and older) are charged $12. Children 2 and younger get in free. For those who discover there is simply too much fun to explore in one day, ask about the "Next Day Pass" at guest services, which gives you a discount on your second day's visit. There's no cost to park at Idlewild.

Kennywood Park
4800 Kennywood Blvd., West Mifflin
• (412) 461-0500

Named as a Pennsylvania Historic Landmark and having celebrated its 100th year anniversary in 1998, Kennywood in Allegheny County is a roller coaster capital. The park has been named the favorite traditional amusement park of the National Amusement Park Historical Association for more than a decade running.

One of the most popular rides is the Pitt Fall, which hoists riders to the top of a black and gold tower, then plummets them at a free fall of nearly 65 miles per hour. Technology and innovation have set Kennywood apart for years. Noah's Ark, a walk-through "haunted" ark built in the 1930s, was totally refurbished in 1996-97 so that it might sail into the 21st century. Guests are now thrilled by high-tech scenes such as the Elevator of Doom, which provides the illusion that you're in a falling, crumbling elevator.

Coasters at Kennywood are the main attraction. Don't miss the Thunderbolt and the Jack Rabbit rollercoasters, if your children are old enough (and brave enough!). There's also the Racer and the Exterminator to thrill you. Be prepared to get drenched on the Log Jammer flume ride. And, here at Kennywood, you don't need a learner's permit to drive the Turnpike.

Throughout the year, but especially in the summer, Kennywood features live performances, community and school picnics, ethnic pride days, and fall fantasy parades. A cafeteria style restaurant is available as well as numerous re-

INSIDERS' TIP
Contact the Special Kids Network at (800) 986-4550 for information on services for children with special health needs. Directories of summer day camps, residential camps, and leisure and recreational activities are available.

Children enjoy the indoor Luckey's Climber, just one activity at the Children's Museum on Pittsburgh's North Side.

Photo: Courtesy of Children's Museum

15 twisting and turning waterslides, a gentle Lazy River to float down, several pools, and the self-proclaimed World's Largest Hot Tub (for adults), you understand why people flock to Sandcastle when the mercury soars. Little tikes love Wet Willie's Waterworks.

There's plenty of fun on land as well, with volleyball, food and gift shops, and an arcade on the old fashioned boardwalk. Oasis Miniature Golf and the exciting Formula 1 Speedway add landlubber fun to your trip to Sandcastle.

Sandcastle is open daily from early June through early September. Hours of operation are 11 AM to 6 PM, June and September, and 11 AM to 7 PM in July and August. A Whitewater Pass entitles you to all water attractions and costs $16.95 for kids and adults and $12.95 for seniors. The Super Pass, good for five separate visits, costs $39.95. To ride the Formula One Speedway, you must be at least 58 inches tall and pay an additional $4. Children 3 and younger are admitted free of charge, and parking (or boat docking, if you get here via the river) is also free of charge.

freshment stands. Height requirements do apply on some rides.

Ride-all-day passes cost $18.95 on weekdays, and $22.95 on Saturdays and Sundays. General admission tickets (rides not included) are available to adults for $7.50 and to seniors (65 and older) for $6.50. During the last week of August, there's a Fun Finale each night. Ride-all-evening passes cost $12 per person.

Sandcastle
1000 Sandcastle Dr., West Homestead
• (412) 462-6666

This is Pittsburgh's wettest playground, just minutes outside the Golden Triangle along the Monongahela River in Allegheny County. With

Just Ducky Tours
Station Square, Pittsburgh
• (412) 402-DUCK

It's a boat, it's a truck... no, it's a duck! That's right, Just Ducky Tours offers an amphibious tour vehicle to shuttle passengers throughout the city as they learn a little about Pittsburgh and its waterways. This fully narrated tour begins at Station Square, a building formerly housing the Pennsylvania and Lake Erie Railroad and now a shopping/restaurant mecca on the city's South Side. Quacking your way along, you'll see Pittsburgh's past and present along Grant Street and the historic Penn Station before moving into the Strip District (yes, it's G-rated—the Strip is the infamous produce/food shopping area) and then the Cultural District.

Kids squeal with delight at the tour's highlight, when the Duck boat makes its way effortlessly off the dry land, splashing down into the Allegheny River to continue the tour! Adults ride for $12, with students (with ID) and seniors costing $11, and children 12 and younger $8. The duck tour is wheelchair accessible, and the boats are equipped with heat and canopies for inclement weather. Tours operate from April through November at various times throughout the day beginning at 10:30 AM and ending at 6 PM (except in October and November, when it gets dark earlier). Call to book your reservation and get ready to quack away!

INSIDERS' TIP

Have you ever camped along with the mummies and the dinosaurs? Overnight Adventures is a program for scout troops, school clubs, and youth and church groups at the Carnegie Museum of Natural History, for grades 1 through 12. Call (412) 622-3289 for information.

Chuck E. Cheese
1025 Washington Pike, Bridgeville
• (412) 257-2570
3800 William Penn Hwy., Monroeville
• (412) 856-5044

Chuck E. Cheese and his band are on stage for you in the Chartiers Valley Shopping Center, and in Monroeville. So take the kids to this popular restaurant for pizza, music, and lots of fast-paced, indoor fun. Watch them climb their way to the skycrawls or shimmy down a slide. Older kids and tiny tots are bound for the ball pit, and there are plenty of arcade games for your pre-teens too.

Chuck E. Cheese has a hand-check, child identification system to keep children from leaving without their parents. Party packages available, but do make weekend party reservations at least one month in advance. Enjoy the non-stop fun (and noise!) Sunday through Thursday, from 11 AM to 9 PM. On Friday, hours are 11 AM to 11 PM, and on Saturday, you can eat and play from 10 AM to 11 PM. For summer hours (Memorial Day to Labor Day), the weekday closing is extended until 10 PM. Prices vary on the menu, so call if you're curious.

Wildwood Highlands
2330 Wildwood Rd., Pittsburgh
• (412) 487-5517

Wildwood Highlands is North Park's family

fun center, with miniature golf, go carts, bumper boats, a driving range, an arcade, and a complete menu for meals and snacks. Woody's Den is an area of the park especially suited for kids ten and younger. This site can accommodate small groups of children as well as large corporate gatherings. Teen parties are also available. Wildwood Peddlers Flea Market is adjacent to this family fun center (see our Shopping Chapter).

The center sells tickets for go karts, bumper boats, and Woody's Den. Tokens are required for the driving range, miniature golf, and game room. Call the automated information line (number above) for complete price information. However, miniature golf costs $4.95 for adults and $3.50 for children ages 4 to 10, and it's free for kids 3 and younger with a paying customer. Indoor play costs $4.75 for children 4 and older, $3 for 2- and 3-year-olds, and it's free for babies 1 and younger. At the driving range, a half-bucket costs $3 and a full bucket costs $5. Tickets are available in different price amounts, but for $20 you can receive 17 tickets.

Wildwood Highlands is open year-round, but the hours vary seasonally. Generally, it's open Sunday through Thursday from 11 AM to 9 PM, and on Fridays and Saturdays from 11 AM to 10 PM.

Caddie Shak
Rt. 31 E., Donegal
• (724) 593-7400

From sports to animals—there's something sure to please young and older kids alike. Try the challenge of two miniature golf courses, bumper boats with water cannons, three go-kart tracks, batting cages, an arcade, driving range, beach volleyball, a kiddie area, horseback riding, paintball, and a picnic grove that's perfect for birthday parties. Height requirements apply on all tracks and bumper boats.

Caddie Shak, in Westmoreland County, is open Memorial Day through Labor Day, Monday through Thursday, 10 AM to 10 PM; and Friday through Sunday, 10 AM to 11 PM. Spring and fall hours are more limited, generally from 4 to 9 PM on weekdays and 10 AM to 10 PM on weekends. Admission is free, but each activity costs a certain number of tickets. Tickets cost

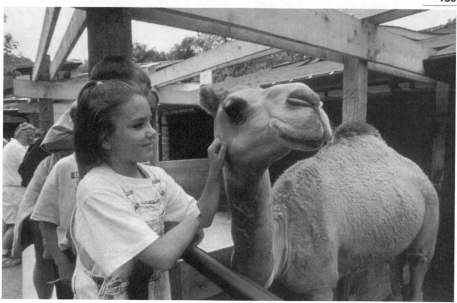

Kids can meet the animals at the Pittsburgh Zoo & Aquarium.

Photo: Terry L. Way courtesy of Commonwealth Media Services ©

$1 apiece, but you can purchase 24 tickets for $20, 125 tickets for $100, and 255 tickets for $200. Paintball costs $21 and more.

Dino Kingdom
Parkway Center Mall, 1165 McKinney Ln., Greentree • (412) 922-3466

This is where prehistoric fun rules! Dino Kingdom is an indoor recreation site for kids age 2 through 12, featuring games like skee ball that spit out tickets to exchange for trinkets. As you might guess from the name, there's a dinosaur theme throughout. There's a soft-play jungle gym, kiddie rides, and a toddler area for little ones 3 and younger. A full-service menu will keep the kids and their grownups from getting hungry. Dino Kingdom's open Monday through Saturday from 10 AM to 10 PM, and on Sunday from 11 AM until 8 PM. Admission costs $3.50 per person on weekdays and $4.50 on weekends, which start Fridays at 6 PM.

Fun Fest Entertainment Center
2525 Freeport Rd., Harmarville • (412) 828-1100

Kids will enjoy the range of activities at this indoor entertainment complex. Pick from cosmic bowling with laser lights and fog rising above the lanes, laser tag games with computerized scorekeeping, and much more. Fun Fest is open from 9 AM until midnight Sunday through Thursday. On Friday and Saturday, the center stays open until 3:30 AM.

Bowling costs $2.50 per game for adults and $2 per game for each child Monday through Friday. On Saturdays and Sundays, it costs a little more at $3 per game, per person. Every day after 6 PM, the bowling price is $3.25 for everyone. Laser Storm costs $4.75 per game per person during the week, but after 6 PM and on weekends, the price goes up to $5.25. Reservations are strongly suggested.

Safari Sam's
8001 Rowan Rd., Cranberry Township • (724) 779-1991
925 Broadhead Rd., Moon Township • (412) 604-0500

For a ball-jumping, tunnel-crawling, game-playing good time, head to Safari Sam's in Cranberry in Butler County or in Moon in Allegheny County. This is an indoor playground like others designed

INSIDERS' TIP

Even Mister Rogers came to meet the baby elephant at the Pittsburgh Zoo & Aquarium. His production crew taped an episode of *Mister Rogers' Neighborhood* featuring the African elephant calf and her family herd.

KIDSTUFF

for kids 2 to early teen where tokens operate the interactive games. A full-service restaurant menu features pastas, salads, sandwiches, and pizza. Birthday party packages are available.

Safari Sam's is open Sunday through Thursday, 10 AM to 9 PM, and Friday and Saturday, 10 AM to 10 PM. Adults are admitted free (with children); but older children (5 and older) cost $5.99; children 2 to 4 get in for $4.99; and children younger than 2 are admitted free.

Gymboree Play Programs
Mt. Lebanon Christian Church,
Cedar & Hollycrest blvds., Pittsburgh
• (724) 933-0033
Fox Chapel, Boyd Community Center,
1220 Powers Run Rd., Pittsburgh
• (724) 335-1410
Bethel United Presbyterian Church,
418 Beatty Rd., Monroeville
• (724) 335-1410
Cross Roads Presbyterian Church,
3281 Wexford Rd., Gibsonia
• (724) 933-0033

Gymboree specializes in developmental play programs for newborns through 5-year-olds, with over 40 pieces of colorful play equipment, upbeat music, movement, creative games, and activities to improve self-esteem. It's a great opportunity for youngsters to socialize with children their own age. To enroll a child, the fee is generally $140 for a period of 14 weeks. There is also a first-time enrollment fee of $20. Additional siblings can attend at a slightly lesser rate, so ask at the location near you.

Talkin' Toys

The Center for Creative Play
5 Station Square East, Pittsburgh
• (412) 281-8886, ext. 46

Your children can play with over 1,000 toys and computer programs, climb the three-story playhouse, create their own puppet shows, experience the sensory room with its unusal lighting and relaxation (designed for special needs children, but enjoyed by all), and romp in the ball pit.

Family membership entitles you to borrow any of the toys or software for an entire month. The center's computer lab has software for both PCs and Macs, with packages for all ages, plus access to the World Wide Web for parents. Developmentally appropriate toys are plentiful for all ages. Perhaps the most appealing part of this center is that you can bring the whole family. Young children and their teen siblings will not be bored.

Fully accessible for children with disabilities and special needs, this fun zone is right across from the subway stop at Station Square. Party packages are available in a special, brand-new room. Adults are admitted free (with children) and all children enter for $4 apiece. Babies under a year old pay nothing. Family memberships begin at $30 per year and entitle you to unlimited visits for your immediate family and the ability to borrow three toys at a time for one month. Higher membership levels, including some that include grandparents, are available with additional benefits and discounts.

The Center is open Monday, Wednesday and Friday from 10 AM to 5 PM, and on Tuesdays and Thursdays from 10 AM to 7 PM. Saturday, visit the Center from 9 AM to 2 PM. The Center is open selected Sundays (usually once a month), but call to find out prior to your planned visit.

Pittsburgh Toy Lending Library
S. Aiken and Baum Blvd., Pittsburgh
• (412) 682-4430

Created as a safe, clean, inexpensive place for children, parents, and caregivers, the Toy Lending Library operates from the First United Methodist Church at the corner of S. Aiken and Baum Boulevard. Children from birth through kindergarten are welcome to come and explore or attend free classes. Developmentally appropriate toys enhance motor, social, sensory, cognitive, imaginative, and language skills.

A resource reference library helps parents and caregivers, and informal meetings provide friendly information exchange on such topics as nursing and potty training to selecting a school. The Parent Enrichment Program features speakers from Children's Hospital leading various sessions. Family membership costs $35 per year for those who can volunteer to help. For non-volunteers, it's $60 annually. Visitors are also welcome to stop by on a pay-per-visit basis. Cost is $4 per child over one year of age. Members enjoy toy

Fiddlesticks, the mascot of the Pittsburgh Symphony, helps educate and entertain children with music.

Photo: Courtesy of Pittsburgh Symphony

Fort Necessity helps fill kids' active imaginations.

Photo: Courtesy of Laurel Highlands Visitors Bureau

borrowing and party privileges as well as newsletter subscription. This toy library is open Monday through Saturday, generally 9:30 AM until 2 or 3 PM, but it varies depending upon the day. Please call before heading out with your little ones! On Tuesday evenings, the toy library is open from 5 to 7 PM.

Disney Store
South Hills Village, Bethel Park
• (412) 831-5010

Save the trip to Orlando by coming to one of six Disney Stores in the Pittsburgh area. Cast members will assist you in finding Disney collectibles, clothing, toys, videos and stuffed animals. And if you think the Disney Store is strictly for children, you'd be mistaken. There are plenty of adult items, including desk accessories, books, and apparel including ties for men and sleepwear for all ages. Don't miss the sale rack, and enjoy Disney's trademark customer service. In fact, if you purchase an item at one of the Disney theme parks and need to return it, the cast members at the Disney Stores can often assist you. In addition to this South Hills Village location, you'll find the Disney Store at Monroeville Mall, Ross

Park Mall, Century III Mall, Beaver Valley Mall, and Westmoreland Mall.

Gram & Gramps
1720 Washington Rd., Pittsburgh
• (412) 831-4726

Not only will you find a great selection of top-quality toys (including Brio, Thomas, and Playmobile) but you'll also be able to outfit the kids in this all-in-one store in the South Hills. Named for doting grandparents, it's probably an appropriate moniker. While prices on the toy merchandise are competitive, the clothing lines are a little upscale. But then, grandparents want only the best!

Once Upon A Child
10648 Perry Hwy., Wexford
• (412) 933-1660

Holiday Center, Rt. 22, Monroeville
• (412) 374-9932

Outfit the kids for less here at Once Upon A Child, featuring gently used merchandise. Not only will you find play and dressy clothing for the kids, but also a selection of quality used toys and children's furnishings. Strollers, portable cribs, and potties prevail

INSIDERS' TIP

While you'll read about Eat 'N Park Restaurants in the Restaurant chapter, do know that children receive a free Smiley Face cookie with meals here. The menu items, crayons, and coloring placemats also make this a must-stop!

too. If you'd like to sell children's items you no longer need, please note that the stores accept only top-quality merchandise, which clerks check for missing pieces and stains. Appointments aren't necessary, but you can visit with your sale items from 10 AM until 6 PM, Monday through Saturday. You should plan to return that same day to collect what they will not buy from you, and of course, to receive payment.

S.W. Randall Toyes and Giftes
806 Ivy St., Pittsburgh
• (412) 687-2666
630 Smithfield St., Pittsburgh
• (412) 562-9252
5856 Forbes Ave., Pittsburgh
• (412) 422-7009
Station Square, Pittsburgh
• (412) 471-8800

Generations of Pittsburgh families have shopped at S.W. Randall for classic toys such as Brio and Lego sets, quality stuffed animals, dolls, board games and other children's favorites.

The Toy Box
108 South Market Street, Ligonier
• (724) 238-6233

Quality toys, games, and puzzles for children of all ages are found here. Phone orders welcome as well. Brand names include Avanti, Brio, Erector, Folkmanis, Playmobile, Steiff, and Tucker Jones. The Toy Box is open Monday through Friday, 10 AM to 6 PM; Saturday, 10 AM to 8 PM; and Sunday, from noon to 5 PM.

Toys R Us
3735 William Penn Hwy., Monroeville
• (412) 373-8043
Rt. 18 & Valley View Dr., Monaca
• (724) 728-0525
4000 Oxford Dr., Bethel Park
• (412) 831-3410
2003 Cherry Dr., Pittsburgh
• (412) 364-4062
275 Clairton Blvd., West Mifflin
• (412) 655-0677
2001 Park Manor Blvd., Pittsburgh
• (412) 787-1770
Donahue Rd., Greensburg
• (724) 836-8813

The Pittsburgh region is well covered when it comes to popular toy stores. Toys R Us is the national chain of toy superstores featuring everything from infant clothing, cribs, layettes, and diapers to children's toys, bicycles, outdoor play equipment, electronic games, even Halloween costumes. There are extended hours during the months preceding the holidays so do call prior to heading out. Most of these stores are found near our major suburban shopping malls.

WQED Store of Knowledge
Monroeville Mall, Monroeville
• (412) 374-1255

These stores bear the name of Pittsburgh public television station, which all children in Pittsburgh know as the origination of *Mister Rogers Neighborhood* along with broadcasts of *Sesame Street* and other programs. Thus, kids can find merchandise from their favorite PBS shows, as well as puzzles, science, weather, magic, and other educational toys and games. Adults will enjoy the selection of videos from programs aired on WQED, as well as some unusual gift items for their age. You'll find additional locations at Ross Park Mall the North Hills, and at South Hills Village in Bethel Park.

Exploring Nature

Round Hill Farm
651 Round Hill Rd., Elizabeth
• (412) 384-8555

Take the kids to see a real working farm, while there's one still left! Open year-round with tours conducted from April through November, Round Hill in southern Allegheny County has picnic areas in the summer, so be sure to pack a lunch. Kids will enjoy the self-guided tour, especially if there's a cow that needs some milking. Though retired, the county police department's riding horses remain on the farm along with their friends, the sheep and chickens. In fact, exotic chickens that they are, some even lay beautifully colored eggs. Ask about the "Day on the Farm" program for fifth and sixth graders whereby the students go on hayrides, have snacks, and fix their own lunches on the farm. Normal hours are from 9 AM to 2:30 PM.

INSIDERS' TIP

Giant Eagle supermarkets make shopping just a bit easier with the Eagle's Nest play centers in many of the larger stores. It's free for children ages 3 to 9. Check with your store for requirements.

KIDSTUFF

Pittsburgh Zoo & Aquarium
One Hill Rd., Pittsburgh
• **(412) 665-3640,**
(800) 474-4966
• **www.zoo.pgh.pa.us**

If your idea of fun is seeing others act out, head to the Pittsburgh Zoo. At this 77-acre natural habitat facility, primates show off their antics in the fog-shrouded indoor rain forest; elephants, zebras, and giraffes roam the African Savanna; and Siberian tigers and snow leopards explore the Asian Forest. Your own children can act as animalistic as they like (under your supervision, of course!) at Kids Kingdom, where they'll have a roaring good time on play equipment that replicates animal motions and behaviors. They'll pass through a petting area to touch a friendly goat or see the Australian grey kangaroos up close. Another recent fun addition: a baby elephant, who checked in at just over 200 pounds at birth. Youngsters won't want to miss the baby elephant, but be sure to call the hotline to check the times when the baby is shown to the public.

In 1994, the zoo became a non-profit organization owned and operated by the Zoological Society of Pittsburgh. Privatization has been a tremendous success with zoo attendance soaring. In 1998, the Zoo celebrated its 100th birthday, amidst celebrations including national broadcasts on *Good Morning America*. The centennial year's work included a few surprises, among them an exotic dragon, and a pair of koalas.

The Pittsburgh Zoo is open year-round. Special evening hours are held during the holiday season (see Annual Events). Otherwise, the zoo is open from Memorial Day through Labor Day 10 AM to 6 PM. Labor Day through Memorial Day, the zoo opens from 9 AM until 5 PM. Entrance gates close an hour before the park closes. Admission is $6.50 for adults, $6.50; $4.75 for seniors; $4.75 for children 2 to 13; and children younger than 2 pay nothing. Members of the zoo are also admitted free of charge. Strollers are also available for rent at a nominal charge.

National Aviary
Allegheny Commons West, Ridge Ave.,
Pittsburgh • (412) 323-7235

While it receives no federal funding, the National Aviary on Pittsburgh's North Side was granted the national designation by Congress in 1993. This sanctuary proves that the Pittsburgh Penguins hockey players aren't the only birds in town! Over 400 of the world's most colorful and exotic birds live here in this, the nation's largest indoor bird display, independent of a larger zoo. Kids will love the cacophony and the mysterious-looking books flying overhead. The Aviary is open daily, except Christmas Day, 9 AM to 5 PM. Adults will pay $5 and seniors (60 and older), $4. Admission for children (ages 2 to 12) costs $3.50, and those younger than 2 are admitted free of charge.

Savoring the Seasons

Discovery Garden
Phipps Conservatory and Botanical
Gardens, Schenley Park, Pittsburgh
• **(412) 622-6915**

Located in Schenley Park in Pittsburgh's Oakland section, among the blossoms and bonsai, the indoor and outdoor Discovery Garden is designed especially for children. Kids can pot their own plants, learn about botany with the garden ambassadors, and partake of other special activities. Phipp's Discovery Garden is open May 2 through October 31, and the hours vary depending upon the weather. A $30 million expansion project that will quadruple the size of this entire facility will be unveiled in 2002.

Phipps is open Tuesday through Sunday, 9 AM to 5 PM, weather permitting. Admission is $6 for adults, $5 for seniors 60 and above, $4 for students with ID, and $3 for children (ages 2 to 12. Children younger than 2 and Phipps members enter without charge. Metered parking is in front of the conservatory.

Pumpkin Farms
Various locations

Picking your way through a pumpkin patch each October is a fun way for the kids to enjoy autumn's colorful changes. The only thing more exciting than picking your own great pumpkin is carving it once you get it home.

Many pumpkin farms exist in the Greater Pittsburgh area, offering selections as tiny as two pounds to giant-sized ones needing a small truck to haul it home. Besides picking a pumpkin, however, children can often find their way through cornstalk mazes, take a hay ride, play on outdoor equipment, enjoy a petting zoo, have a pony ride, and help the family shop for other produce, including fall specialties and baked goods. Here are a few of the better-known pumpkin patches around Pittsburgh:

Janoski's Farm, Rt. 30, Clinton (3 miles from the airport), (412) 899-3438

Kaelin Farm Market, 2547 Brandt School Rd., Franklin Park, (724) 935-6780

Reilly's Summer Seat Farm, Ohio Township, (412) 364-8662

Schramm's Farm Market & Greenhouse, 291 Crisswell Rd., Butler, (724) 282-3714

Schramm's Farms & Orchard, Harrison City Rd., Westmoreland County, (724) 744-7320

Soergel's Farm, Brandt School Road, Wexford, (724) 935-1743

Trax Farms, Rt. 88, Finleyville, (412) 835-3246

Simmons Farms, 170 Simmons Rd., McMurray, (724) 941-1490

Bridgewater Pumpkinfest
214 Bridge St., Bridgewater
• (724) 775-8919

Held the second weekend in October, this giant pumpkin contest and Little Miss Pumpkinfest contest are things the kids will love. Children will enjoy the games, food, crafters, and a fireworks display. (See our Annual Events chapter). Visit the Pumpkinfest in Beaver County on Saturdays from 10 AM to 8 PM, and on Sundays from noon to 6 PM.

Houston Pumpkin Festival
American Legion Picnic Grounds, Houston
• (800) 531-4114

Sponsored by the Houston Volunteer Fire Department, there's more pumpkin fun at this Washington County fall festival. Kids will enjoy the petting zoo, pony rides, pumpkin decorating, and an orange pumpkin bouncer. (See our Annual Events chapter for more). This festival takes place on October Saturdays from 10 AM to 7 PM, as well as Sundays from 10 AM to 5 PM.

Great Miniature Railroad & Village
Carnegie Science Center,
One Allegheny Ave., Pittsburgh
• (412) 237-3400

A true Pittsburgh holiday tradition, this display is a great way for families to teach children what the region looked like decades ago. Strollers are welcome. (See the Annual Events chapter for additional information). Thanksgiving through end of January, and then throughout year, after temporary refurbishing. Regular hours are, Sunday through Friday, 10 AM to 5 PM and Saturday 10 AM to 9 PM. To see the exhibits only, admission costs $6.50 for adults, and $4.50 for seniors (65 and above) and children (3-18). Combination ticket packages are available and prices are listed at the desk and given by telephone on the automated information line (call number given above). Senior discounts are extended on Tuesdays. Purchasing a membership to the science center allows complimentary admission. Parking is a flat $3 rate.

Penn Hills Train Display
Penn Hills Municipal Building,
12245 Frankstown Rd., Penn Hills
• (412) 798-2147

During December, this month-long train display is brought to the community by the Penn Hills Police Department, which converts its shooting range into a holiday exhibition each year. Kids will enjoy unusual scenes such as the Batcave and the military airport. Browse the display on weekdays from 5 to 9 PM and on weekends from 1 to 9 PM. A $1 per person donation toward local charities is asked at the door.

Santa's Trolley
Pennsylvania Trolley Museum,
Off Race Track Rd., Washington
• (724) 228-9256

Kids can make special crafts at the trolley museum and ride with Santa aboard one of the vintage trolley cars this museum is known for. A Lionel train display is also a part of the holiday season. Visitors can even operate the Lionel trains on the museum's large "you run it" display. (See our Annual Events and Attractions chapters.) Hop aboard the trolley from 11 AM to 5 PM. Admission rates are $6 for adults, $5 for seniors (65 and older), and $4 for children (2 to 15). Those younger than 2 are admitted for free.

INSIDERS' TIP

Carnegie Museum's Discovery Room does fill up on weekends, during holidays, and at other busy times. Free passes are distributed on a first-come, first-served basis. So check in at the room early to avoid disappointing your youngster.

KIDSTUFF

Festivals and Annual Events

No matter what your favorite interest, hobby, sport, or recreation, chances are good you'll find events throughout the Greater Pittsburgh area that will make you smile, and keep you plenty busy. Perusing this list will give you an overall picture of the broad range of activities and events our area has to offer at special times of the year—everything from county fairs and farm shows, marathons and parades, to ethnic celebrations and holiday festivities.

Unless indicated otherwise, events can be enjoyed free of charge, though specific portions of a festival or event—like food or a special performance—might require some cash outlay. For those festivals or special events which require an admission or entry fee, we've given the most current price level, but please know these are subject to change each year so it's best to check before heading out.

We also give approximate dates and times for anything particularly special occurring within the activities and celebrations listed, but again, it's always best to call the sponsoring organization or group before making plans to attend. Where expositions are listed spanning many days, even entire weekends, we've left out the times because they vary. Again, our advice is to call in advance. Many of the shows at the David L. Lawrence Convention Center run well into the evenings. And of course, bring along enough money to any festival to cover the food, beverages and crafts you might want to purchase. This is often the case even if there is no formal admission charged.

Rather than format this chapter geographically, we've followed the calendar, starting in January and ending up at the holidays. So grab your camera, put on your walking shoes, and get ready to have some fun.

January

Beaver County Annual Snow Shovel Contest
Economy Park,
Legionville Hollow Rd.,
Ambridge • (724) 846-5600

Contestants in this event ride on their favorite snow shovels, trying for the fastest time, as they slide down a 160-foot hill. You must be at least 5 years old to participate. Four different divisions are offered—for boys 13 and younger, girls 13 and younger, and adults, with a modified race for all ages.

This modified class simply means those with "improved shovels." Registration starts at 11 AM, and the contest begins at 1 PM. The winner is the person with the fastest time to the bottom, where a trophy awaits. There is no charge to participate so bundle up, grab your shovel, and enjoy!

Recreational Vehicle Show
David L. Lawrence
Convention Center,
1001 Penn Ave., Pittsburgh
• (412) 565-6000

The latest in recreational vehicles, including travel trailers, mo-

*Thousands flock each year to see the Great Miniature Railroad & Village
on display at the Carnegie Science Center*

Photo: Courtesy of Carnegie Science Center

tor homes, fifth wheels, custom and conversion vans, campers, park models, pop-up camping trailers, truck caps, and utility trailers are on display on the convention center floor. Representatives are handy to answer questions you might have or help put you behind the wheel of your own Winnebago. If nothing else, just seeing the limitless camping possibilities primes you for summer and all its allure in the months ahead. Adult admission costs $6, $5 for seniors, and $4 for children (6 to 16). Those younger than 6 are admitted free of charge.

Pittsburgh Boat Show
**David L. Lawrence Convention Center,
1001 Penn Ave., Pittsburgh
• (412) 565-6000**

This annual display of boats, big and small, along with the latest in other assorted watercraft, makes people in this boat-crazy region pray for an early spring on the three rivers. Included on the showroom floor are personal watercraft (like Jet Skis), fishing boats, ski boats, plus house boats. You can even take boating exams and classes for various safety certifications, though advance registration may be necessary. Beginning January 2000, anyone operating a personal watercraft in Pennsylvania must possess a valid boating safety certificate. Be sure to enter the contests (sometimes there's a cash giveaway contest) and peruse

the accompanying flea market to find a bargain treasure to add to your watercraft. Admission costs $7, with children 12 and younger admitted free of charge if accompanied by an adult. Each person who completes a boating safety class for certification receives free admission to the Boat Show as well.

February

Winterlude Festival
**Various locations throughout Greensburg
• (724) 838-4362**

This month-long major arts extravaganza celebrates the performing and visual arts all across Westmoreland County. The Grand Finale will conclude the event at the restored Palace Theatre, Greensburg. Hours do vary, with locations throughout the county. As the event is diverse with many different activities, please check your local paper for particular listings and the prices charged at any particular show, display, concert, or screening.

Custom Car Show
**David L. Lawrence Convention Center,
1001 Penn Ave., Pittsburgh
•(412) 565-6000**

This unusual show features automobiles, hot

rods, motorcycles, and monster trucks for the car fanatics, or simply the mildly curious. If you've ever fathomed sitting on a Harley, imagining the wind flowing through your hair, this is the place to come live out that fantasy! Celebrity appearances are also a part of the weekend. Adults can expect to pay $9, children (4 to 11) $4, and those younger than 4 years of age are admitted free.

Pittsburgh Automobile Show
David L. Lawrence Convention Center, 1001 Penn Ave., Pittsburgh
• **(412) 565-6000**

A Pittsburgh tradition, this show brings out the best in local automobile dealerships. Local dealers newest models, plus manufacturers' prototypes of cars of the future, are on display. So picture yourself driving the car of your dreams. Here, you can hop right in behind the wheel (at least for a brief moment of glory!). The admission charge for adults is $7 with children (6 to 16) paying $5, and those younger than 6 admitted free of charge.

Greenberg's Train & Dollhouse Show
ExpoMart, 105 Mall Blvd., Monroeville
• **(412) 856-8100**

This is America's premier toy train and miniature railroad event, complete with a dramatic train layout, displays, and a huge dollhouse marketplace. In addition, there are ongoing how-to clinics, door prizes, and the latest in hobby books. This show will definitely give you plenty of project ideas to fill the remaining winter days! Adults will pay approximately $6, and children (6 to 12) $2. Those younger than 6 receive complimentary admission.

March

Charter Day
Old Economy Village, 14th & Church Sts., Ambridge • (724) 266-4500

This free one-day event at Old Economy Village features exhibits of many old handcrafts, including spinning and blacksmithing, with the intent to introduce you to how the Harmonists lived (see our Attractions chapter for details about the Harmonists). There are crafts available for purchase and musical enter-

tainment every year. You'll feel you're stepping back in time with craft demonstrators dressed in clothing of centuries past. Plus, German food is typically on each year's menu. Do note that the hearty meals are served inside, which might be a welcome reprieve from the still-chilly temperatures. Though depending upon what the winter has allowed, you might see an early preview of the flowering spring bulbs and perennial herbs sprouting. Tours of Old Economy Village are conducted Tuesday through Saturday, 9 AM to 3 PM, and Sunday, 12 to 3 PM. Old Economy Village is closed Mondays and winter holidays.

Pittsburgh Home & Garden Show
David L. Lawrence Convention Center, 1001 Penn Ave., Pittsburgh
•**(412) 565-6000**
• **www.pghhome.com**

A very large and popular event among Pittsburghers, the Home & Garden Show usually features well over 1,400 exhibits highlighting the latest in products for your house, yard, and garden. Information on interior design, landscaping, lawn care, furnishings, cooking, and other related topics is plentiful, and of course, you won't want to miss your chance at winning any number of prizes in various contests and give-aways. This past year, WTAE-TV had a broadcast center where children could pretend they were anchors on a newscast. For a small donation, they went home with a video of their audition! Adult admission costs $8.50, and children (6 to 12) pay $3.50. Those younger than 6 are free of charge.

St. Patrick's Day Parade
Downtown Pittsburgh • (412) 621-0600

Usually held the Saturday morning before St. Patrick's Day, this annual parade brings out the best Irish eyes in the city. The parade runs from Mellon Arena down Grant Street to the Boulevard of Allies, and there's a reviewing stand at Stanwix Street. Sponsored by the Irish Society for Education and Charities, the parade includes everything you'd expect on St. Patty's Day: floats, celebrities, and lots of green on display. Usually you can count on seeing approximately 200 different parade entries, and it seems to be a tradition to watch the parade from parking garages (for a better view, and to stay dry in the unpredictable March weather). Of course, there's no charge to view the parade, so come out, wear your green shirts and hats, and be a little Irish for the day! Plenty of parties follow throughout the day in the Downtown area.

Spring Flower Show
Phipps Conservatory and Botanical Gardens, Schenley Park, Pittsburgh
• (412) 622-6915

The arrival of spring brings new blossoms and a bouquet of color at this Schenley Park conservatory in the Oakland neighborhood. Call for notice of special activities, including the annual Mother's Day Flower Sale, held each spring. The Flower Show lasts for about a month, while the Mother's Day sale runs the weekend of that special holiday. Phipps is open Tuesday through Sunday, 9 AM to 5 PM. Phipps admission is $6 for adults, $5 for seniors 60 and above, $4 for students with ID, and $3 for children (ages 2 to 12). Children younger than 2 years old and Phipps members enter without charge. Metered parking is right in front of the conservatory.

April

Shrine Circus
Mellon Arena, 66 Mario Lemieux Pl., Pittsburgh •(412) 642-1800

The Shriners have all that it takes for a festive circus adventure, with traditional clowns, wild animals and their trainers, magic tricks, illusions, and other zany surprises. Kids eyes may light up at the fire rings lit for animals to jump through in the darkened arena. Ticket prices average approximately $10. There are usually eight shows (including three on Saturday) over the course of a long weekend.

Easter Egg Hunts
Trax Farms, 528 Trax Rd., Finleyville
• (412) 835-3246

Held on numerous weekends leading up to Easter in this South Hills town, kids hunt for Easter eggs, enjoy pony rides, learn button making, have their faces painted, and walk away with a bag of goodies, treats, and other surprises. Of course, no egg hunt would be complete without a visit from the celebrated rabbit himself—the Easter Bunny. There's no admission charge for kids to hunt, though some of the other activities require money.

Antiques Show at the Carnegie
The Carnegie, 4400 Forbes Ave., Oakland
•(412) 622-3131

This show runs concurrently with other regular museum attractions and exhibits and features fine quality glass, furniture, jewelry, porcelain, silver, and various other works of art. The antiques are brought in and displayed by more than 50 different dealers, representing many states across the country. This isn't garage-sale stuff—they can be quite pricey, but certainly worth the look and price of extra charge. Tickets for the Antique Show cost $8 for members of the Carnegie and $10 for non-members, though for $15 you can buy a ticket spanning all three days of the Antique Show. To browse the exhibits and/or make a purchase, you'll spend your time in the Music Hall Foyer and Hall of Architecture for the most part which are consumed by this annual show.

Maple Syrup Festival
Brady's Run Park, off of Rt. 51, Beaver County •(724) 774-7090

Held at the Brady's Run Park Lodge, this festival celebrates the annual spring bounty of the areas millions of maple trees. Come for the all-you-can-eat pancake breakfast and stay for demonstrations and old-time crafts, including lace making. The lines for breakfast can be long, but the wait is worth it, locals report. The concept is to tap the trees and explain the boiling down process through which maple syrup is made. Admission rates (including breakfast) are $4 for adults. Children 10 and younger are admitted free of charge. The event runs from 8 AM until 4:30 PM.

Spring Festival
Trax Farms, 528 Trax Rd., Finleyville
•(412) 835-3246

Step into spring with three days of celebrating flowers, sunshine, and getting back into the fresh air at this South Hills farm. Garden lectures, display gardens, kids' activities, farm

INSIDERS' TIP

The "engineers" of the Carnegie Science Center's Miniature Railroad hosted behind-the-scenes tours to commemorate the 45th Anniversary of the Railroad in 1999. Call to investigate any such offerings in future years.

animals, demonstrations, giveaways, and other prizes are all part of this long weekend of celebrating the outdoors. There's no admission charge for the spring festival, so come, learn, and just have fun.

May

University of Pittsburgh Medical Center/ City of Pittsburgh Marathon and 5K
Downtown through the North Side, South Side, and Oakland neighborhoods, Pittsburgh
• (412) 647-7866

Crowds line the streets of the city on this Sunday morning race that takes over 3,000 runners over bridges, up hills, and through 12 of the city's neighborhoods. Perhaps the most intriguing part for spectators is the fervent neighborhood block parties cheering the runners as they pass through, and many times providing musical entertainment. What an uplift for the runners!

The race starts at the City-County Building and concludes at the finish line in Point State Park. Registration fees for marathon runners are $50 prior to April 7 and $65 after April 7. The 5K race costs $15 for runners and walkers before April 7 and $20 after that date. Several classes and distances take off before the main event, the marathon, gets under way shortly before 9 AM.

More than $100,000 in prize money is awarded for the top men, women, masters and wheelchair participants. The Center for Sports Medicine routinely offers a series of seminars pertaining to the races.

The Society for Creative Anachronism holds its annual international event in Northern Butler County.

Photo: Courtesy of Butler County Chamber of Commerce & Tourism

Cinco De Mayo
Station Square, Smithfield and Carson Sts., Pittsburgh • (412) 562-9900

This Mexican festival marks the anniversary of the day the Mexicans defeated the French at the Battle of Puebla in 1862 (Cinco de Mayo means May 5th). Music, drinks, and food all have a Mexican flare here. There is no cover charge to attend, but individual vendors may charge for food and beverages.

Greek Food Festival
419 S. Dithridge St., Pittsburgh • (412) 682-3866

In years past, more than 20,000 people have stopped in for an appetizing dose of Greek food and culture at this week-long festival in the Oakland neighborhood. Greek lunches and dinners, plus dancing and live entertainment each evening are found at St. Nicholas Greek Orthodox Cathedral's community center. Imagine smelling the aroma of dishes you typically do not cook at home such as moussaka, pastita, and baklava. Normal hours run Sunday, Noon to 8 PM; Monday through Friday, 10 AM until 2 PM (lunch); and Monday through Thursday 5 to 9 PM (dinner). On Friday, dinner is served from 4 until 10 PM. Prices for various parts the festival vary each year so do call closer to the actual event.

Ambridge Nationality Days
Merchants Street from 4th to 8th Sts., Ambridge • (412) 266-3040

Held as an open air street fair, this is a three- or four-day celebration of ethnic pride that offers tasty foods from all over the world along with live entertainment, crafts, and special children's activities and attractions. Traditional dancing has always been a part of the event, and you can count on three blocks of fabulous food stands with the aromas of Greek, American, Italian and other cuisines wafting through the air. Italian, German, Croatian, Greek, Russian, Vietnamese, Scottish and even African American dishes are represented. The festival begins at 10 AM and lasts until 9:30 PM. As this is a street fair, there is no admission charge, just the cost of your food and beverages purchased.

National Pike Festival
Route 40, Washington, Fayette, and Somerset Counties • (800) 840-0274

Numerous towns in several counties participate in this festival along the historic National Pike, which we know today as Route 40. Washington (Washington County) and Uniontown (Fayette County) are two of the larger cities the road passes through as it cuts diagonally across the southwest corner of the state. Arts and crafts, antique cars, displays, food, and entertainment are all a part of the event. In years past, two wagon trains started at opposite ends of the route, traveling along and making encampments along the way. The best advice we can give you is to check the local newspapers

closer to the actual festival (or call the number above) for particular offerings you're interested in, as this event covers three large counties. So get ready for a full range of fun, traveling back in history.

Pittsburgh Children's Festival
134 Allegheny Center, Pittsburgh • (412) 321-5520

Youngsters will enjoy all the festivities, many of which are educational, at this North Side festival for the performing arts. Past performers have come from as far as South America, Europe, Asia, Australia, and certainly from other North American cities to perform. The event typically spans five days filled with puppetry, acrobatics, storytelling, participatory art projects, facepainting, and sometimes paddle boat rides. Look forward to the parade that's been a part of previous children's festivals. Local schools may even have booths of their own with children's activities. There is a $3 per person admission charge, but do know that shows are additional.

Pittsburgh Folk Festival
David L. Lawrence Convention Center, 1001 Penn Ave., Pittsburgh • (412) 565-6000

Usually held around Memorial Day weekend, this is a festive three-day ethnic event. More than 20 nationalities prevalent in the Pittsburgh area celebrate their heritages with colorful costumes, authentic folk dancing, native dishes, delicious desserts, and an international marketplace. In years past, tickets cost $5. Children 12 and younger enjoy free admission.

June

Three Rivers Arts Festival
Gateway Plaza and Point State Park, Pittsburgh • (412) 481-7040

A Downtown tradition for decades, new exhibitors and performers are introduced daily as a part of this 17-day festival. All types of art, crafts, dance, music, and food make this a memorable start to anyone's summer. Lunchtime for Downtown office workers will never be the same after meandering the line of food booths at the entrance of Point State Park.

FESTIVALS AND ANNUAL EVENTS

Just imagine watching the sizzling steak sandwiches and fried vegetables, let alone the aroma of hot sausage, Chinese foods, and dozens of other tasty treats.

Most artists offer their work for sale, including handcrafted jewelry, pottery, photography, paintings, fiber art, and finished calligraphy. As years go by, the expanse of the arts festival has covered more of the Downtown urban setting including the Art Institute of Pittsburgh and Wood Street Gallery (on second floor of the Wood Street T station at Liberty Ave.).

The Three Rivers Arts Festival runs from the beginning of June through mid-month, and is free to the public. See the Getting Around chapter for tips on parking downtown or taking public transportation.

Historic Harmony House Tour
Harmony Museum, 218 Mercer St., Harmony, Butler County
• **(724) 452-7341**

Normally held the first Saturday in June, this event gives visitors the chance to tour the historically and architecturally significant Harmony House that lies in the historic district (Exit 27 off I-79, east of Zelienople). The site actually consists of five houses in addition to the museum buildings. Since the tour is self-guided, you can use the map to go at your own pace, and it costs $10 per person. Tours are given Tuesday through Sunday, 1 to 4 PM, year-round. General admission is $3.50 for adults, $3 for seniors (age 60 and above), and $1.50 for children ages 6 through 12. Children younger than 6 years of age are admitted free of charge.

Mountain Top Bluegrass and Craft Festival
Mountain Top Park, Tarentum, Armstrong County • **(888) 224-1511**

Some of the top national bluegrass pickers and strummers come to Pittsburgh for the region's premiere bluegrass festival. It brings a touch of Appalachia to Pittsburgh no doubt! This event, typically the first weekend in June, features the family fun of live music, crafts, workshops, horse-drawn wagon rides, camping, a petting zoo, and much more. There's also been a pig roast in previous years. You'll find there's no admission charge,

but donations are accepted to support the local and national talent.

Mellon Jazz Festival
Various locations, Pittsburgh
• **(412) 234-3275**

Each June, the hottest performers bring the coolest jazz to the city at one of many outdoor concerts held throughout city parks and plazas. Many concerts are free while others ask a ticket price. If there is a major headliner, the event may even be moved to one of Pittsburgh's performing arts concert halls. Most Mellon Bank locations have more up-to-date information at their counters, listing the individual performers, performance times, and public locations each year.

Greater Pittsburgh Renaissance Festival
Route 31, west of New Stanton
• **(724) 872-1670**

During late June through late July each year (yes, a time span of five fun-filled weekends), this recreation of a 16th-century village brings together crafters, acting troupes, combat jousting, musicians, and food purveyors in a village setting to celebrate the arrival of the king and queen. The Westmoreland County festival is an appealing history experience for all ages. Children will particularly enjoy the Children's Dell and petting zoo. Held over five weekends, the event was moved to a new site in recent years on Route 31 East, seven miles west of New Stanton in southwestern Westmoreland County. Take exit 24A on I-70 (for those of you traveling that route). Admission is $9.75 in advance or $10.95 at the gate for adults, and children (ages 5 to 12) pay $4.50 in advance or $5.95 at the gate.

Big Butler Fair
Butler Fairgrounds, Rt. 422, Prospect
• **(724) 283-2222**

Usually run from the end of June through July 4, this event takes place along Rt. 422, 61/2 miles east of I-79. Livestock, horse and farm product demonstrations, exhibitions, and rides are all a part of this traditional county fair. In addition, browse the food stands, and enjoy country entertainment, harness racing, and

INSIDERS' TIP

If you plan to attend the Great Miniature Railroad & Village at the Carnegie Science Center, know in advance that holidays are the peak period. Over 6,000 visitors each day pass through in the week between Christmas and New Year's. So plan to stand in line.

The Gateway Clipper Fleet shines amid the fireworks along Pittsburgh's rivers.

Photo: © 1994 AngelArt

annual Beaver County event held in Ewing Park, Ellwood City. The fun begins at 11 AM and keeps going strong until 10 PM. Enjoy the free admission. On-site parking is available for $2 though you might park at no charge in outlying areas if you're willing to walk a few blocks.

Fourth of July Fireworks at the Point
Point State Park, Pittsburgh
• (412) 255-2352

Fireworks displays are ignited in numerous Western Pennsylvania communities, but this one is perhaps the most spectacular. The Pittsburgh Symphony Orchestra performs a rousing patriotic concert under the stars and fireworks at The Point. Fireworks are courtesy Zambelli International of New Castle, Lawrence County (also known as the fireworks capital of the world). The music and fireworks extravaganza comes at no cost, but do bring a blanket to spread out in Point State Park, and be prepared for the massive crowds and traffic jam exiting the city. The festivities get underway at dusk.

other grandstand events. In years past, there's been a petting zoo and a confederate railroad, too. Gates open at 9 AM, and the carnival begins at 1 PM. Cost is $7 per person, but if you come before 5 PM, pay only $5 per person. Children younger than two years old are admitted free of charge, and parking comes at no cost as well.

July

Ellwood City Arts, Crafts & Food Festival
Ewing Park, Ellwood City
•(724) 758-5630

More than 200 craft booths, art shows, entertainers, and food booths are offered at this

Westmoreland Arts & Heritage Festival
Twin Lakes Park, off Rt. 30, Westmoreland County •(724) 834-7474

Art comes alive at this kaleidoscope of creative expression usually held around the July 4th holiday in Unity Township. What makes the booths appealing are their juxtaposition around the lake. Get ready for arts, crafts and music—everything from woodworking, painting and photography. Past festival goers have enjoyed poetry readings and performances by the Westmoreland Symphony, polka bands,

FESTIVALS AND ANNUAL EVENTS

fiddlers, oldies music, country, and rock 'n' roll groups. International food booths offer a culinary complement as well. This festival begins at 11 AM and runs until 8 PM. Shuttles and wheelchair accessible vans run from the Westmoreland and Greengate Malls. Roundtrip shuttle tickets cost $2 per person.

South Side Summer Street Spectacular
E. Carson St., Pittsburgh
• (412) 481-0651

A carnival-like atmosphere with a parade, fireworks, riverfront races, and live entertainment makes this Pittsburgh's largest neighborhood festival, held amid the South Side's coffee shops and novelty stores. As the event is an open-air celebration of fun and food, there is no admission charge, but be prepared to pay for food and drinks.

Apollo Moonlanding Celebration
Owens Field, Rt. 56, Apollo
• (724) 478-1114

Normally held during the third week in July, you'll find rides, games, and fireworks at this one-day Armstrong County celebration of the anniversary of landing on the lunar surface each July. What else would you expect from a town that bears the name of the famous space program! The fun begins at 6:30 PM and continues until 11 PM.

August

Three Rivers Regatta
Point State Park, Pittsburgh
• (412) 261-7055

This free, family-oriented weekend is full of thrilling air shows, on-land events, Formula 1 powerboat races, hot air balloon races, fireworks, and waterskiing demonstrations. In prior years, the live music made coming out to the Regatta special even if you never saw the water attractions. Local musician Donnie Iris has performed as well as the group Blood, Sweat and Tears. The "Anything That Floats Race" has also been a regular event, with teams creating some type of seaworthy (in theory, anyway) transportation out of materials not usually used for boatmaking. And one year, beer lovers not only sipped their favorite brew, they learned how it was made in a trailer-classroom created for the event.

Beaver County Riverfest
Ohio River at Riverfront Park, Rochester
• (724) 775-1200

This celebration of the region's rivers brings out residents of Beaver County for outdoor activities, fireworks, food, and great music. Bands typically perform on a stage constructed on the riverfront, and boaters enter a contest to determine the best decorated among them. Look up and you'll see skydivers, too. As this is open air, there's no admission charge, but you'll pay for food and other purchases.

Two Shadyside Arts Festivals
Walnut St. and Ellsworth Ave., Pittsburgh
• (412) 681-2809

Note there is a little rivalry of sorts between these two Shadyside festivals, but we couldn't alert you to one without the other. One festival encompasses the area between Walnut Street from S. Negley to S. Aiken Avenues. The Ellsworth Avenue celebration takes place between Maryland Avenue to Spahr Street.

Nightly outdoor jazz performances, workshops, and over 200 designers of American collectibles exhibiting their wares are a part of these large community events. Recycled art and neon art plus multi-dimensional pieces have been on display for serious art aficianados in years past. Both festivals showcase local talent, and there is running shuttle service from various points in Shadyside to avoid any parking nightmares. A few of these shuttle points include Shadyside Hospital, the Pittsburgh Center for the Arts, and Sacred Heart Academy.

Washington County Agricultural Fair
Washington Fairgrounds, 2151 N. Main St., Washington • (724) 225-7718

Agricultural and commercial exhibits, rides, games, entertainment, tractors, animals, the 4-H and FFA exhibits, a market livestock sale, and refreshments are all a part of this week-long county-wide fair, now over 200 years old. Trolley service to fairgrounds is provided by the Pennsylvania Trolley Museum. Admission costs $6 for the event that runs from 8 AM until 11 PM.

INSIDERS' TIP

Many smaller train displays are presented locally each December, such as the one the Penn Hills Police display at their municipal building. Call your own borough or municipality for local exhibits.

Hookstown Fair
**One mile from Rt. 168 and Rt. 30,
Hookstown, Beaver County
• (724) 728-0212**

This week-long fair, over 50 years old, has entertainment, tractor pulls, rides, a demolition derby, fireworks, food, and plenty of other fun, including live country music. There is no official Beaver County fair, but this one takes on that type of ambiance. Admission costs $6 for adults and children. However, seniors can enter free before 5 PM. Parking is plentiful in this open area that resembles a big old farm.

Caribbean & Reggae Festival
**Station Square, Smithfield & Carson Sts.,
Pittsburgh • (412) 562-9900**

There aren't many other places inland where you can find Caribbean steel drums, calypso music, and the pulsating sounds of reggae, but this South Side festival is one of them. The Island Market Place features Carribbean clothing, jewelry, and crafts, while the food court serves up a zesty menu of Caribbean food and drinks. As this festival is open air in nature, there is no admission charge.

Westmoreland County Fair
**Westmoreland Fairgrounds, RD 2,
Greensburg •(724) 423-5005**

Generally held over a week in the middle of August, this county fair has the usual rundown of rides, entertainment, food, and fun that residents look forward to each summer. Look to the local papers or call the number listed above for the current admission charges and any special attractions taking place.

September

Ligonier Highland Games
**Idlewild Park, Rt. 30, Ligonier
• (724) 851-9900**

The first weekend after Labor Day brings a Scottish fair to Ligonier, featuring bagpipe bands, Highland dancing, Scottish fiddling, children's games, exhibits, and more. Friday and Saturday evening activities include dinner and entertainment at Mountain View Inn, by reservation only. Event hours for Saturday and Sunday are 9 AM until 6 PM. Admission charges are $10 for adults and $5 for children 6-12. Those younger than six enter at no cost. Parking is free as well. Group discounts are available.

Annual Pennsylvania Arts & Crafts Colonial Festival
**Westmoreland Fairgrounds, R.D. 2,
Greensburg • (724) 863-4577**

Experience the pride and skill of colonial men and women in over 170 booths as they create hand-thrown pottery, hand-crafted furniture, dried floral arrangements, stained glass, tole and decorative painting and much more. In years past, there have been military encampments, a fife and drum group, a Civil War string band, carriage rides, children's activities and refreshments at this multi-day event. Rates for adults are $4.50, $4 for seniors, and $1 for children 6 to 12. There are indoor as well as outdoor exhibits so come rain or shine!

Pittsburgh Irish Festival
**I.C. Light Amphitheatre,
Station Square,
Pittsburgh
• (412) 661-1221**

Irish and Celtic folk music is the focus of this festival, usually held around the second weekend in September, running from Friday night through most of Sunday. Get ready for a long list of performers and bands. Previous years the talent has included the Great Big Sea band, Tommy Maken and the Makem Brothers, David Kincaid, and Mike Gallagher. There's plenty of traditional Irish dancing too. Admission in past years has been $7 for adults, $3 for children (3 to12), and complimentary tickets for children two and younger. A three-day pass costs around $14.

Penn's Colony Festival
**North Park, Allegheny County
• (412) 487-6922**

This is the closest thing you'll find to Colonial Williamsburg, and we've got it here in western Pennsylvania! This is an 18th-century colonial marketplace featuring 230 American folk artists and cottage craftsmen with authentic entertainment and food. Demonstrations here have included sheep clipping and wool preparation, soapmaking as done in colonial times, and hand stenciling for the kids. Come Friday

---

INSIDERS' TIP

During the month of December, many churches offer dramatic presentations of the journey to Bethlehem, free of charge, as a gift to their communities. Keep an eye out for mentions of these in community newspapers, and through word of mouth.

FESTIVALS AND ANNUAL EVENTS

starting at 1 to 6 PM, or Saturday and Sunday from 10 AM until 6 PM. Admission in prior years has been $5.50 for adults, $4.50 for seniors (65 and above), and $3.50 for children (8 to 15). Children 7 and younger receive complimentary admission. Parking is free of charge.

Covered Bridge Festival
Various locations throughout
Washington County • (724) 228-5520

Traditionally held the third weekend in September, there's old-fashioned hospitality in store at this festival among the rolling hills of southwestern Pennsylvania. Old-time fiddlers perform in addition to the arts and crafts, antique cars and engines, guns, and other artifacts that are displayed. Country-style food is also available at different covered bridges throughout Washington County. In prior years just under a dozen of the covered bridges in the county were featured, and each one has its own natural flavor. There are approximately 218 covered bridges that remain standing in the Commonwealth of Pennsylvania. The exploring begins at 10 AM and continues until 5 PM. Admission and parking for this covered bridge festival are free of charge.

Richard S. Caliguiri/City of Pittsburgh Great Race & Walk
Frick Park to Point State Park, Pittsburgh
• (412) 255-2493

This race is always held the last Sunday in September. Nearly 11,000 runners from around the world, many donning hilarious costumes, compete in this annual 10K great race, 5K run, and 5K walk, held in honor of the late Richard S. Caliguiri, former mayor of Pittsburgh. Caliguiri died in 1988 after a lingering illness in the prime of his political career. The race begins at Frick Park and moves to Point State Park Downtown, where it concludes. Early bird registrations save you money. If you submit them before July 14, the fee is $14. Then, those registering before September 8, pay $16. Thereafter, it costs $22 to register.

Oktoberfest
Penn Brewery, Troy Hill Rd. & Vinial St.,
Pittsburgh • (412) 237-9402

This traditional event is held on the last two weekends in September to coincide with the actual Oktoberfest in Germany. The North Side's German heritage is in full swing as the Pennsylvania Brewing Company marks this event. Dine in the brewery restaurant on such traditional German fare as Schnitzel,

sauerbraten, and potato pancakes. In the outdoor tent, there's often grilled wurst and chicken, pork, and strudel. Ongoing entertainment provided by German bands and a strolling accordionist complete the ambiance. And of course, there are plenty of beers to sample. Celebrate your German heritage (or pretend to!) on Fridays and Saturdays from 5 PM to midnight, or on Sundays from 4 to 10 PM. The hearty aromas will tempt you, so bring along money for your food and beverage purchases.

October

Bridgewater Pumpkinfest
214 Bridge St., Bridgewater
• (724) 775-8919

The second weekend in October, the Beaver County community of Bridgewater blocks off several streets to celebrate autumn in this charming area filled with antique and specialty stores. Previous favorites of this festival include the pumpkin pie bake-off, the giant pumpkin weigh-off, and Little Miss Pumpkinfest. There have also been adult and children's games, food vendors, crafters, and a spectacular fireworks display. Of course, the prime attraction is the weigh-off, which often requires flatbed trucks and farm equipment just to maneuver the pumpkins, some of which weigh hundreds of pounds. If nothing more, bring the kids out to watch! This pumpkinfest is held Saturday, 10 AM until 8 PM , and on Sunday from noon until 6 PM. As it's open air in nature, there is no admission charge except for your purchases.

Meadowcroft Maize Days
Meadowcroft Museum,
401 Meadowcroft Rd., Avella
• (724) 587-3412

This festival is usually around the third weekend in October. Experience autumn in its glory with this celebration of corn and Western Pennsylvania's farming heritage, featuring corn shelling and grinding, cornhusk doll making, children's games, and old-time music. Learn to make apple butter and enjoy horse-drawn wagon rides too. Meadowcroft is only open on Saturdays and Sundays this time of year. To enter, adults pay $6.50 and children pay $3.50.

Houston Pumpkin Festival
American Legion Picnic Grounds, Houston
• (800) 531-4114

Sponsored by the Houston Volunteer Fire Department in Washington County, this fall festi-

The National Pike Festival recalls one of the country's great migrations.

Photo: Courtesy of Laurel Highlands Visitors Bureau

val features baked goods, crafts, entertainment, a children's petting zoo, pony rides, pumpkin decorating, and an orange pumpkin bouncer. Bring the kids on Saturday from 10 AM until 7 PM, or on Sundays from 10 AM until 5 PM.

American Indian Gathering
Community College of Beaver County, One Campus Dr., Monaca
• (724) 775-8561

Usually held around the second weekend in October, this weekend-long event is held at the college's Golden Dome. There's Native American dancing, crafts on display and for purchase, food, as well as seminars about American Indians. In past years the organizers charged $2 for admission for adults, seniors, and older children. Those ages 5 to 12 enter at $1, and children younger than 5 are admitted free of charge.

Fort Ligonier Days
Rt. 30 and Route 711, Ligonier
• (724) 238-4200

This three-day Westmoreland County festival commemorates the battle at Fort Ligonier in 1758 during the French and Indian War. It's the largest celebration in town with 150 juried craftspeople, merchant sidewalk sales, entertainment, antique window displays, and a huge parade on Saturday at 11 AM. There are over 30 food booths around the diamond, or bandstand area. Look for an official program to guide you through the festival. It's a supplement to *The Ligonier Echo* newspaper. Admission rates are $5 for adults, and $2.25 for children (6 to 14). Children younger than six are admitted free of charge.

Fall Foliage Cruises
Along the Allegheny River, Armstrong County • (724) 548-3226

All month long, you're invited to board boats of the Gateway Clipper Fleet to experience the beautiful autumn foliage along the Allegheny River in Armstrong County northeast of Pittsburgh. The atmosphere is relaxing as you see the region from a totally different (waterfront) perspective. Cruises, which have in the past cost around $20 per person, are offered throughout the month of October and sail from 1:30 until 4:30 PM.

Fall Flower Show
Phipps Conservatory and Botanical Gardens, Schenley Park, Pittsburgh
• (412) 622-6915

Fall foliage is on display indoors with the splendor of autumn accented in the various rooms of the Schenley Park conservatory in Oakland.

Phipps is open Tuesday through Sunday, 9 AM to 5 PM. Phipps admission is $6 for adults, $5 for seniors 60 and above, $4 for students with ID, and $3 for children (ages 2 to 12). Children younger than 2 years old and Phipps members enter without charge. Metered parking is right in front of the conservatory.

The Pennsylvania Arts & Crafts Christmas Festival
Washington Fairgrounds, 2151 N. Main St., Washington • (724) 863-4577

This festival, held also in late October and early November, boasts over 165 exhibit booths with artists and craftspeople displaying hand-thrown pottery, handcrafted furniture, dried floral arrangements, stained glass, clothing, quilts, children's toys, wrought iron, and lots more. Santa Claus and Emmett the Elf are here for children. Trolley rides are also available. Exhibits are displayed in five heated buildings, Friday and Saturday, 10 AM until 8 PM, and on Sunday from 10 AM until 6 PM. Admission is $4.50 for adults, $4 for seniors (65 and above), $1 for kids (age 6 to 12), and complimentary for children younger than 6.

November and December

Sparkle Season & Light Up Night
Various locations throughout Downtown, Pittsburgh • (412) 566-4190

Light Up Night traditionally kicks off the holiday shopping season within the Golden Triangle, known as Sparkle Season. Light Up Night begins at 5 PM on a Friday evening and lasts until midnight. Downtown office buildings remain lit, and retailers have their holiday displays illuminated.

PPG Plaza is aglow in luminaria and its own towering tree. Several trees, including the Unity Tree (formerly the Joseph Horne Co. tree) at Penn Avenue Place, are unveiled, and there is the creche at the USX Plaza (read more about it in the Worship chapter).

Looking down at the city from Mt. Washington is a great vantage point, especially for the fireworks.

Throughout the rest of Sparkle Season, activities, events, and displays appear throughout the city to celebrate Christmas, Chanukah, Kwanzaa, and New Year's. One such display is the Santa Exhibit at the PPG Wintergarden. The "Celebrate the Season" parade is the Saturday after Thanksgiving. And if you feel worn out, take the Holly Trolley shuttling downtown

shoppers throughout the Golden Triangle. It's free of charge, and stops at the major plazas, department stores, in the Cultural District, and at the Heinz History Center in the Strip District.

Sparkle Season brochures are available at the major Downtown buildings with a complete list of events and special shopping hours during the holiday season.

Beaver County Festival of Trees
Brady's Run Park, off of Rt. 51, Beaver County • (724) 775-4510, (724) 843-0594

This winter wonderland—indoors, mind you—lasts a long weekend and has approximately 50 decorated trees, continuous entertainment, a Santa snack bar, visits by Santa, and a talking Frosty the Snowman. Community groups and businesses decorate these trees which are sold at the end of the festival. There's a Santa's gift shop and a model railroad on display in the park's large recreation center. Thursday hours are from 5 to 9 PM. All other days, come around noon and stay until 9 PM. Admission costs $2 for everyone except those 12 and under, who are admitted free of charge.

Eckerd Drug Celebration of Lights at Hartwood
Hartwood Acres, 215 Saxonburg Blvd., Indiana Township • (412) 767-4043, (412) 594-4729

This annual outdoor drive-through light show features animated scenes using 1.5 million lights and over 300 miles of electrical wiring. Illuminted reindeer, snowmen, candy canes, and other holiday figures are synchronized to holiday music. Previous displays have used in excess of 5.5 million lights!

Hours for this colorful show are Sunday through Thursday, 5:30 to 10 PM, and Friday and Saturday from 5:30 to 11 PM. A donation of $7 per carload is suggested, and the money benefits the Salvation Army's Project Bundle-Up, providing winter coats, hats, and gloves to those who need them. Other charities may participate also. Hartwood Acres is a county park in Indiana Township. Enter from Saxonburg Boulevard and exit onto Middle Road in Hampton Township.

Overly's Country Christmas
Westmoreland Fairgrounds, RD 2, Greensburg • (800) 9OVERLY

One of America's largest light displays (according to *Good Housekeeping* magazine), this extravaganza began at the home of the late Harry E. Overly years ago. But it grew too massive and was moved to the fairgrounds.

Another drive-through event, Overly's Country Christmas boasts animated displays, more than 800,000 lights, a gift shop, outdoor barbecue, cookie barn, bonfires, and a manger scene with live animals. Rides on a horse-drawn sleigh or wagon are also a part of the fun. Overly's Country Christmas is open daily for a couple of weeks before Christmas, usually from 5 to 10 PM. Cost on Monday through Thursday is $6 per car, and on the weekends, it's $8 per car.

Clayton Holiday Tours
**The Frick Art & Historical Center,
7227 Reynolds St., Pittsburgh
• (412) 371-0600**

From mid-November through the New Year's holiday, visitors to the Frick Art & Historical Center can enjoy extended hours and special holiday tours of Henry Clay Frick's Clayton. This 23-room, turn-of-the-century residence is the only surviving estate in Pittsburgh's East End (Pointe Breeze), the once-fabled millionaire's row. Watchful holiday guests at Clayton might even catch a glimpse of Father Christmas, dressed in Victorian costume. They certainly gather a sense of the closeness associated with Frick holidays at Clayton. Of course, the mansion is decorated with pine, poinsettias, and other winter blooms, and the scent of evergreens prevails. For families with children ages 6 to 12, the Frick presents Family Holidays at Clayton, special tours for kids, on several Saturdays in December from 9:30 until 11:30 AM. Cost is $10 for one adult/one child for non-members, and $7 for members. Additional children cost $5 ($3 for members).

Hours during the holiday season are Tuesday through Saturday from 10 AM until 5 PM, and Sunday from noon until 6 PM. Evening tours (which run until 8 PM) are offered on selected days so it's best to call for the exact dates each year. The Frick Art Museum and Car and Carriage Museum are open until 9 PM on selected evenings also. Tours of Clayton cost $8 for adults, $7 for seniors, and $6 for students. Members are admitted free of charge.

For more information about Clayton and the Frick museums, turn to our Architecture and Arts chapters.

INSIDERS' TIP
Don't miss the display of life-size Santas from around the world at the PPG Place Wintergarden in Downtown Pittsburgh each holiday season.

ZooLights
**Pittsburgh Zoo & Aquarium, One Hill Rd.,
Pittsburgh •(412) 665-3640**

Brought to the zoo by AT&T, ZooLights transforms the zoo into a display of more than 500,000 lights from 5:30 PM until 8:30 PM closing time each night for approximately six weeks. Visitors can stop at various indoor locations for hot cocoa, to see the indoor zoo exhibits, or merely to warm up from the brisk night air. The Pittsburgh Zoo is closed on Christmas Eve and Christmas Day. Admission to ZooLights costs approximately $4 for non-members and $3 for Zoo members. Parking for ZooLights is free.

Santa's Trolley
**Pennsylvania Trolley Museum,
off of Race Track Rd., Washington County
• (724) 228-9256**

The trolley begins operation the day after Thanksgiving and runs for three weekends. All aboard the Santa Express! Kris Kringle arrives in true trolley fashion to kick off the holiday season's popular Santa's Trolley. Children and their families can ride with Santa aboard one of the vintage trolley cars while listening to the sounds of Christmas carols. Kids can make special crafts, and visitors can operate the Lionel trains on the museum's large "you run it" display. Santa's Trolley pulls out regularly from 11 AM until 5 PM. Admission rates are $6 for adults, $5 for seniors (65 and above), and $4 for children (2 to 15). Those younger than 2 are admitted for free.

Great Miniature Railroad & Village
**Carnegie Science Center,
next to Three Rivers Stadium,
One Allegheny Ave., Pittsburgh
• (412) 237-3400**

Whereas many other train displays close up shop after the holiday season, this North Side one stays open Thanksgiving through the end of January, and throughout many months of the year.

This is a true Pittsburgh tradition. The railroad display began in the 1950s, but because of the limited space, had to be dismantled each spring. Now, the 2,300-square-foot exhibit, featuring new models each year, is left in place, closed only periodically for refurbishment (during the month of February and immediately before Thanksgiving for several weeks). The miles of train display features O-gauge railroad and beautiful animated scenery showing the region's history.

Regular hours run Sunday through Friday from 10 AM until 5 PM, and on Saturday from10 AM to 9 PM.

Admission costs vary. Adults can see the exhibits for $6.50, children (3 to18) and seniors (65 and above) pay $4.50, and science center members are free. For more detailed prices for the rest of the science center facility and attractions, turn to the Attractions chapter.

LeMoyne House Candlelight Tours
E. Maiden St., Washington
• (724) 225-6740

Typically this event is held the first weekend in December. Sponsored by the Washington County Historical Society, these evening candlelight tours show the LeMoyne House decorated for Christmas with costumed actors portraying members of the LeMoyne Family. Admission rates are $4 for adults and $2 for students. Candlelight hours run from 5 to 9 PM.

Candlelight Christmas at Old Economy Village
Old Economy Village, 14th & Church Sts., Ambridge • (724) 266-1803, (724) 266-4500

Traditional German Christmas decorations and legends are displayed in the historic village of the 19th-century Harmony Society, here in Beaver County. Food, crafts, and entertainment are always a part of the annual festivities. More than 25 rooms are decorated for the season, nightly from 5 until 9 PM. Please know that this event is held for only two days, usually at the start of December, so do call in advance or you might miss out. The village, lit only by the glow of candlelight and with the scent of pine prevailing, is sure to put you in the holiday spirit! The tour takes you out of the hustle and bustle of the season, allowing you to focus on simplicity. Cost is $6 per person. For those interested in the special Christmas Dinner Tour, cost is $40 per person, and reservations are necessary. The dinner typically takes place after the two-day tours, but again, call for the exact day and times.

Holidays at The Carnegie
The Carnegie, 4400 Forbes Ave., Pittsburgh
• (412) 622-3131

Stop in to see this annual Christmas tree exhibit that illuminates the Hall of Architec-

ture. Each year, there's a different theme. Past trees have celebrated the Russian czars, French impressionists, and Victorian England. Traditional carols echo throughout the great halls of the museum and art galleries. Previous exhibits have included rare nativity scenes and spiritual paintings. Concerts are performed most days.

Admission to The Carnegie Museum of Natural History and Museum of Art is $6 for adults, $5 for senior citizens, and $4 for children (3 to 18). Children younger than 3 and members are admitted free of charge. Call for the Carnegie's Holiday Program Guide.

Festival of Lights
Ligonier Valley Library, W. Main St., Ligonier • (724) 238-6818

This is a month-long display of decorated trees and wreaths designed by local families within Westmoreland County along with those contributed by area businesses and the Ligonier Valley Historical Society. There's also a holiday boutique with handcrafted items. Cost for adults is $2. Children are admitted for 50 cents.

Holiday Open House at the Nationality Rooms
Cathedral of Learning, Fifth Ave. & Bigelow Blvd., University of Pittsburgh, Pittsburgh
• (412) 624-6000

For the month, 24 nationality rooms representing European, Middle Eastern, Asian, and African cultures are on display with holiday decorations representing their individual traditions and heritages. Guides appear in national dress, and there are continuous performances, and sometimes also delicious ethnic foods. Rooms are open from noon until 4 PM daily.

Candlelight Evenings at Phipps Conservatory and Botanical Gardens
Phipps Conservatory and Botanical Gardens, Schenley Park, Pittsburgh
• (412) 622-6958

Throughout December, the Conservatory remains open later than usual during the holiday season each year. The rooms are dressed for the holidays with lights and festive decorations. Special tours can be arranged.

Phipps admission is $6 for adults, $5 for seniors 60 and older, $4 for students with ID, and $3 for children (ages 2 to 12). Children younger than 2 and Phipps members enter without charge. Metered parking is right in front of the conservatory.

First Night
Various locations throughout Downtown, Pittsburgh • (888) PGH-FEST

Go out with a big bang, as the expression says! Pittsburgh's First Night Celebration occurs each year for families. It's the city's way of planning a safe alternative for New Year's Eve. Events and locations vary, but package deals are available so that families can book a room at a downtown hotel. Public transportation into the downtown area is also offered. Performances in year's past have included Joe Negri from *Mister Rogers' Neighborhood* and Margo Lovelace

Puppets, among others. Fireworks are courtesy Zambelli International of New Castle, Lawrence County (also known as the fireworks capital of the world).

In past years, those who wanted to attend all events had to purchase a First Night button costing $15 for adults and $5 for children (6 to 12). Children younger than free did not have to pay. But if you just want to see what's happening in the open-air spaces, there is no cost for First Night. Check the daily newspaper for particulars each year, including special parking and public transportation hours.

Architecture

As the sun sets on Pittsburgh's Golden Triangle, it lights the pinnacles of PPG Place and reflects off several other shimmering skyscrapers that are our city's architectural gems. These dominant corporate headquarters, including the mighty USX Tower, add aesthetically as well as economically to our city. Often, the modern buildings reflect the transitions our companies have undergone—companies such as PPG Industries (Pittsburgh Plate Glass decades ago) and USX Corporation (formerly United States Steel).

Today, nothing is half-veiled in smoke the way many buildings erected in 19th-century Pittsburgh were back when heavy industry polluted the skies. And plenty of these structures merit close attention, especially for aficionados of great architecture. In this chapter, discover the highlights, including the works of famous architects and a brief tour of architectural masterpieces you won't want to miss.

Of course, with any remarkable achievement and improvement comes controversy, and Pittsburgh has had it share. For instance, Downtown Pittsburgh was a picture of urban vitality back in the late 1940s. Well before shopping malls, many Downtown merchants thrived in Italianate, Victorian Gothic, or art deco buildings.

In an effort to restore such commercial vitality to the Downtown area, Mayor Tom Murphy and the city's Urban Redevelopment Authority have struggled with a plan that will forge ahead into the future while saving at least some semblance of the past. As you might guess, it's hard to merge the wishes of the preservationists with the needs of modern merchants. At this writing, it's hoped that many important architectural facades can be maintained while making way for new construction of shopping and entertainment complexes.

You will notice in this chapter that we depart from the geographic breakdown we've used in other chapters throughout this book. Instead, we start with information on history and preservation efforts, and we close the chapter with a short list of important buildings and bridges, some of which are broken down by region. The highlight of the chapter is our Downtown walking tour, which features many of Pittsburgh's most important buildings. If you've never taken a walking tour, now's your chance.

In keeping with the architectural theme, this chapter focuses more on the structural aspects of design than the historical appeal. So you won't find descriptions of buildings simply because they are old. Of course, architecture and history overlap, and where appropriate, you might want to refer to our History chapter.

Now, get ready to read about the fascinating creations and works of building art brought about by names such as Hornbostel, Janssen, Klauder, Osterling, Richardson, and Wright. Their contributions quite literally made our city what it is today.

Architectural Periods

From the formation of Fort Pitt after the British took hold of the Pittsburgh Point in 1758, this city has enjoyed a rich discussion of its structural heritage. This settlement phase was followed by the Georgian simplicity of 1785 to 1830. The latter-day form of Georgian style is what we now call the Federal style.

The Greek Revival period came next, followed by the mid-Victorian era. The Manchester and Mexican War Streets neighborhoods on the city's North Side remain primarily Victorian examples of architecture. Unfortunately, this mid-Victorian style was thought by some to have a harsh appearance.

New ideas characterized the years following the Civil War. Helping to propel these insights was the American Institute of Architects, which became a national organization in 1857. Architectural schools, exhibitions, and journals became recognized forces. All of this focus culminated in a time of experimentation, most notably in East Coast cities such as Boston and Philadelphia. Henry Hobson Richardson was one of these experimental architects.

Richardson, his firm based in Brookline, Massachusetts, submitted his plans to rebuild the Allegheny County Courthouse and Jail in 1883. (In May 1882, fire had gutted the rotunda of the second county courthouse, reducing the building to a sandstone shell.) The first and original jail structure had been built in the Downtown Market Square area (known as the Diamond in years prior).

The simplicity of Richardson's Romanesque design was alluring with its rounded arches, rugged stone walls, and Byzantine leaf carving. He was formally chosen for the job from among competitors in 1884.

Of course, the original jail and courthouse site was ten feet higher due to a hump, commonly referred to as Grant's Hill, that was eventually lowered in 1912. Subsequent widening of Grant Street required that the entrances be lengthened in the 1920s. But to look upon the finished structure is to see the beauty of the intricate carvings, the rise of the tower, the way in which the sun grazes the exterior stone, and most certainly the handsome grand staircase Richardson created.

The Allegheny County Courthouse and Jail are regarded as the finest works of architecture in the city. Richardson is quoted as saying, "If they honor me for the pygmy things I have already done, what will they say when they see Pittsburgh finished?" Sadly, the architect passed away before his vision was realized. Work did not conclude on these structures until 1888, two years after he died. (See walking tour below.)

Additional Architectural Strides

As the application of architecture became more professional around the country, Pittsburgh felt the effects as well. The Carnegie Technical Schools, founded in 1900 and the predecessor of today's Carnegie Mellon University, incorporated architecture into its curriculum in 1905. Architects sought more modern ways of designing. American architects practicing their trade between 1890 and 1930 are loosely categorized as Eclectics.

Henry Hornbostel, a partner in the New York firm of Palmer & Hornbostel, won the 1904 competition for the master plan of the Carnegie Technical Schools. During the next two decades, Hornbostel carved out his architectural domain, quite literally, in the Oakland-Shadyside area. Among the buildings he designed were the Rodef Shalom Temple, Soldiers' and Sailors' Memorial, the U.S. Bureau of Mines building (now a part of CMU), the Schenley Apartments, and the University Club in Oakland. Two Downtown buildings, the City-County Building and the Grant Building, are also among Hornbostel's creations.

Major Eclectic buildings erected during the Great Depression include the Gulf Building and Mellon Institute (both Downtown), East Liberty Presbyterian Church (in East Liberty), Buhl Planetarium (on the North Side), and the Cathedral of Learning and Heinz Chapel (both in Oakland at the University of Pittsburgh). Engineers, contractors and suppliers were accustomed to the whims, even fantasies, of architects during this time. However, as material became more expensive and money in short supply during the war years, Eclecticism steadily declined. (Read more detail of these noteworthy buildings later in this chapter).

INSIDERS' TIP

The booklet "Pittsburgh In Your Pocket: A Guide To Pittsburgh-Area Architecture," is reasonably priced at approximately $5, and is available at the Landmarks Store in Station Square.

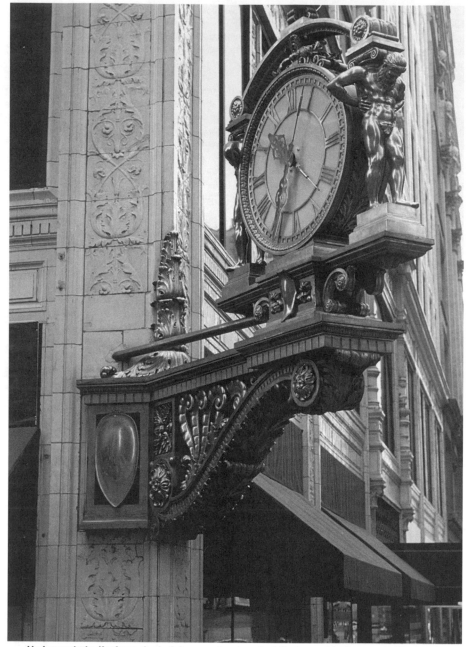

Underneath the Kaufmann's clock is a popular place for folks to meet in Downtown Pittsburgh.

Photo: Courtesy of Kaufmann's Department Store

Pittsburgh's Renaissance

It wasn't until the 1950s that the architectural effects of Pittsburgh's first Renaissance could actually be seen, although plans for revitalization had begun years before. Soon after World War

II ended, smoke abatement became one of the city's priorities. Business and government leaders—Republican Richard King Mellon and Democrat David L. Lawrence, chief among them—joined forces for the future. Mellon and Lawrence were indeed a powerful pair, convincing the city's populace to listen to their ideas for Pittsburgh's Renaissance.

The Fort Pitt Blockhouse was saved, but freight terminals at what is now Point State Park gave way to create the Gateway Center office complex. It's interesting to note that many ideas had surfaced to create the Point as we know it today. Among the visions tabled were those Edgar J. Kaufmann, the department store owner, commissioned from his own architect, Frank Lloyd Wright. Grandiose schemes were quietly put aside for they lacked any concern over cost and were considered to be extravagant for the times.

The building boom continued all over the region. In the 1950s, the lower Hill District was cleared to make room for the Civic Arena, now known as the Mellon Arena. Structures on the North Side in the former city of Allegheny made way for Allegheny Center. Other buildings, particularly those of historical significance, were saved in part by the Pittsburgh History & Landmarks Foundation, founded in 1964.

Also during this time, buildings began to display their corporate products. The firm of Harrison & Abramovitz showed off the functional and decorative uses of aluminum in the Alcoa Building, erected in the early 1950s. The firm did the same years later in 1970, designing the U.S. Steel Building (now the USX Tower).

In the mid-1970s, Landmarks turned its attention to another large-scale property, the Pittsburgh & Lake Erie Railroad complex. With an eye toward commercial revitalization, Landmarks saw potential in this site along the south shore of the Monongahela River. Why not try the notion of historic preservation coupled with urban development? The result is what we know today as Station Square on the South Side. Five historic railroad buildings were saved and adapted beside several new buildings.

Renaissance II

Pittsburgh's second Renaissance altered the skyline yet again. Although the 680-foot main tower of PPG Place still doesn't match the height of the USX Tower (at 841 feet), the complex architecturally changed the city forever. Perhaps no other structure since Klauder's Cathedral of Learning or Richardson's County Courthouse has had the impact of PPG Place.

Here we see Gothic translated into plate glass by architect John Burgee with Philip Johnson. The six buildings that comprise PPG Place were completed in 1984 and are leased to various retailers and businesses.

Also in the 1980s, the old Jenkins Arcade was razed to make way for Fifth Avenue Place. This and the CNG Tower are smaller, yet substantial additions to the city as well, since the former houses an upscale shopping complex (see our Shopping chapter) and the latter the corporate headquarters of Consolidated Natural Gas.

The work and architectural achievements continue. Architect Michael Graves has designed a new center in the Cultural District in the Public Theater and Office Building that opened in 1999. And at this writing, a regional banking center is proposed by Mellon Bank, and plans for new stadiums and shopping establishments are underway.

Since the city is home to two internationally known programs in architectural education, at Carnegie Mellon University and the University of Pittsburgh, this region will surely see more forward movement in the architectural scheme of things. Whether it's a new engineering marvel spanning one of Pittsburgh's famous rivers, or a new skyscraper designed for aesthetic as well as economic purposes, rest assured the future of Pittsburgh will be beautiful to behold.

INSIDERS' TIP

Architecture lovers will appreciate the limited edition, handmade ceramic model of Henry Hobson Richardson's Allegheny County Court House. It even lights up and comes with a historic narrative. While it's the most expensive in the series of Pittsburgh ceramic models (approximately $145 plus tax), it's made locally and numbered for each collector. Look for it at the Landmarks Store in Station Square. Part of the proceeds from the sales benefits the work of the Pittsburgh History & Landmarks Foundation.

Architectural Exhibits

Hall of Architecture
The Carnegie, 4400 Forbes Ave., Pittsburgh
• **(412) 622-5550** • **www.clpgh.org**

In this grand space, architecture has been an important part of The Carnegie since it opened in 1895. Carnegie Institute, designed by Longfellow, Alden & Harlow, was an outstanding example of academic Classicism. The Hall of Architecture, which opened in 1907, became a major feature of the Carnegie, with 144 full-scale plaster casts of building fragments—pulpits, columns, portals and pediments, even an entire facade capturing the history of Western architecture.

Here you can see the east and west fronts of the Parthenon as well as a portal of the north transept of the Cathedral of Sainte-Andre at Bordeaux. Browsing through this skylit space, designed especially for the display of these casts, you will see samples of columns, pillars, and doorways from Romanesque, Italian Byzantine, French Gothic, and many other periods of historic architecture.

The Hall of Architecture is one of three surviving cast courts today, and it is the only one in North America. It's not uncommon to see groups of students gathered within the room studying the displays. Indeed, the purpose of the hall's creation was so that everyone, not just those who could afford to travel abroad, could study the form and detail of architecture in full scale.

The Hall of Architecture is open during regular museum hours, Tuesday through Saturday, 10 AM to 5 PM, and Sunday, 1 to 5 PM. On Fridays from June through August, it's open from 10 AM to 9 PM, and on Mondays in July and August, 10 AM to 5 PM. Admission is $6 for adults, $5 for senior citizens, and $4 for children (ages 3 to 18). Children younger than 3 and members are admitted free of charge.

The Heinz Architectural Center
Carnegie Museum of Art,
4400 Forbes Ave., Pittsburgh
• **(412) 622-5550** • **clpgh.org**

Founded in 1990, The Heinz Architectural Center honors the memory of Henry J. Heinz II, who during his lifetime combined a deep interest in architecture with a commitment to Pittsburgh. Here you'll find architectural drawings, photographs, models, artifacts, and related items. While the center's scope is international,

Remodeled by architect Frederick J. Osterling, the Clayton estate is now part of the Frick Art & Historical Center in Pointe Breeze.

Special Distinctions

As you tour the region, take special note of buildings bearing the National Historic Landmark designation, which acknowledges the highest possible recognition conferred upon a building or site by the Secretary of the United States Department of the Interior.

Additionally, the *National Register of Historic Places* is the official listing of the country's historic sites worthy of preservation. Here, the Pittsburgh History & Landmarks Foundation awards the Historic Landmark plaque to architecturally significant buildings in Allegheny County. Though such a plaque identifies the property for its heritage, it does not guarantee protection. In Pittsburgh, however, there are City Historic Districts and City Historic Structures, and these cannot be legally altered or demolished without approval of a review commission.

it still places significance on the architecture of Western Pennsylvania.

Cicognani Kalla Architects designed the Heinz Architectural Center with galleries specifically suited for the exhibition of drawings, a study room, and support spaces. Every few months these exhibits change.

On permanent display, however, is the office designed and used by esteemed architect Frank Lloyd Wright in San Francisco from 1951 until his death in 1959. In this unique space, Wright divided a nondescript 20- by 40-foot room into three interlocking spaces—a reception area, a drafting room, and a personal office. Wright's fondness for Asian art is very much apparent. Those interested in further details can tour this office the first Saturday of every month from 1 to 1:30 PM. Meet at the Museum of Art Store. Although reservations aren't necessary, space is limited.

Throughout the rest of the center, much of the collection of drawings, models, prints, and photographs represents the 19th and 20th centuries. Designs for residential, institutional, commercial, and industrial buildings as well as examples of engineering, landscape, furniture, and interior design are included.

A special affiliation between The Heinz Architectural Center at The Carnegie Museum of Art and the Royal Academy of Arts in London allows these two institutions to collaborate on exhibitions, publications, and programs of mutual interest.

The Architectural Center is open during regular museum hours: Tuesday through Saturday, 10 AM to 5 PM, and Sunday, 1 to 5 PM. On Fridays from June through August, the center is open from 10 AM to 9 PM; on Mondays in July and August, hours are 10 AM to 5 PM. Admission is $6 for adults, $5 for senior citizens, and $4 for children (ages 3 to 18). Children younger than 3 and members are admitted free of charge.

Architectural Preservation

Pittsburgh History & Landmarks Foundation
One Station Square, Ste. 450, Pittsburgh
• **(412) 471-5808** • **www.phlf.org**

This nonprofit historic preservation organization was founded in 1964 to explore and assess regional architecture and preserve Pittsburgh's history.

Landmarks, as the foundation is known, compiled the first countywide architectural site survey in the nation and has published many studies of regional architects, buildings, and landscape design, including the hefty book, *Pittsburgh's Landmark Architecture,* written by Walter C. Kidney and published in 1997. Many books and publications produced by Landmarks can be found at the Carnegie Library or in local bookstores.

Since 1965 the Pittsburgh History & Landmarks Foundation has offered a variety of walking tours throughout the Golden Triangle where visitors and even lifetime Pittsburghers can learn from trained docents. These range from one-hour walking tours of the Downtown area to customized, in-depth excursions filling one or two days. Walking tour field trips for school groups can also be arranged.

By becoming a member of the Pittsburgh History & Landmarks Foundation, you'll save on tours, publications, and educational programs, get special invitations and a newsletter, and have access to the foundation's James D. Van Trump Library of architecture and historical materials.

Downtown Walking Tour

Though there are guided tours available, there's nothing to keep you from discovering Pittsburgh's streets, structural facades, and architectural highlights on your own. Lace up your comfortable walking shoes, and come along on our own Insiders' tour of Downtown. Our tour will be as brief or as long as you prefer. There may be some buildings you'll want to browse for a while, and other facades you may want to skip. The choice is yours. But if you took a few minutes to stop, read, and look at each mention, we're guessing you'll complete the tour in about two hours. As we said, it all depends upon your gait and your curiosity.

Our starting point will be Station Square, where you can easily park your car in the parking garage or outdoor lot. Our best advice is to bring along this book, and plan your walking adventure in good weather. That way, you can stop along the sidewalk, follow the directions of where to turn next, and read about the structure you're passing.

Station Square
South Side, Pittsburgh

On a 40-acre site on the south bank of the Monongahela River that was once the center of a bustling railroad and a complex of operational buildings sits a major tourist attraction, office complex, and shopping mall called Station Square.

In the late 1870s, the Pittsburgh & Lake Erie Railroad consisted of coal freight, boxcar leasing, and passenger service at the northwest corner of Carson and Smithfield streets.

Architect William George Burns was chosen to create a new train station, which was extolled in an 1896 issue of *The American Architect*. Building began in 1899. Upon completion, the structure and its interior were extensively praised. The Chicago firm of Crossman and Sturdy was responsible for the interior, and the watercolor for the waiting room was written about in the *Pittsburgh Architectural Club Exhibition Catalog of 1900*.

The vestibule and waiting room were filled with decorative details—marble, mosaic, and

INSIDERS' TIP

To learn more about Pittsburgh architecture, enroll in one of several classes offered through Pitt's Informal Program at the University of Pittsburgh. These cover the 18th and 19th centuries, the period from 1890 through 1950, and the years from 1950 to 1990. Call (412) 648-2560.

stained-glass elements. Pittsburgh historian James Van Trump called it "the finest Edwardian interior in the city," second only to the Carnegie Music Hall foyer.

By 1970, when other forms of transportation had made the railroad somewhat obsolete, the ornate spaces were empty, and the terminal complex, with a great barrel-vaulted ceiling in the waiting room, was a prime focus of restoration. The Allegheny Foundation, a Scaife family trust, provided the necessary funding to the Pittsburgh History & Landmarks Foundation to sponsor this restored site, which would be dubbed Station Square.

Today, the old waiting room is now the Grand Concourse restaurant (see our Restaurants chapter), and natural light shines through the clean stained glass. The Gandy Dancer Bar was fashioned out of part of the former baggage area.

The dingy, tarnished and faded facades have been polished in other buildings as well. The former shovel warehouse was transformed into an office complex. The freight house underwent a metamorphosis into a modern-day arcade of shops, restaurants, and entertainment possibilities. Smaller structures like the gate house and express house were also remodeled.

Plenty of commuters find the parking at Station Square convenient for workdays or stadium games as they board the Gateway Clipper Fleet of sightseeing and dinner cruise vessels. Special events are sometimes held on the grounds as well (see Annual Events).

Standing just outside the Landmark's Building at Station Square, we'll step on to the bridge deck to continue our tour. One of the oldest and most remarkable bridges in Allegheny County, the Smithfield Street Bridge used to be called the Monongahela Bridge.

Smithfield Street Bridge
Downtown and South Side, Pittsburgh

Visitors to Station Square can't miss this bridge spanning the Monongahela River, for it's one of Pittsburgh's oldest and most remarkable. When engineer Gustav Lindenthal designed it in 1981-83 (with Stanley L. Roush, the architect for the bridge's portals), it replaced the Monongahela Bridge, a covered wood truss. The forces of the two 360-foot main lenticulartruss type spans seem to cancel each other out. An arch thrusts outward on the upper cord. The lower chord pulls inward. Several restorations have taken place since the original design. In 1995, the Roush portals and main spans were repainted in their original colors—deep blue for the trusses, brown for the flooring, and a creamy yellow for the portals. Designated a national historic civil engineering landmark, notice as you walk across the bridge that the upper chord visually cancels out the lower chord.

Victorian Fronts
Various locations along Fort Pitt Blvd., Pittsburgh

Standing at the traffic light across the bridge, you'll see to your left the Victorian fronts of the buildings along the 200 block of Fort Pitt Boulevard that comprise a commercial row of dwellings.

Cross Fort Pitt Boulevard at the light and walk one block north on Smithfield Street to First Avenue.

Keep walking three more blocks, crossing the Boulevard of the Allies and Third Avenue and stopping at Fourth Avenue. Here at the corner of Smithfield Street and Fourth Avenue, you could take a rest if you like on one of the outdoor benches right outside Dollar Savings Bank.

Dollar Savings Bank
348 Fourth Ave., Pittsburgh
• (412) 261-7539

Philadelphia architects Issac Hobbs & Sons created this bank in an era when the word Victorian was usually the equivalent of "monstrosity." This structure was begun in 1868 and completed in 1871. The strong columns at the Fourth Avenue entrance suggest solidity. The lions on each side are masculine in detail. Fourth Avenue used to be the investment district, and many buildings here have a rather masculine look to them.

When you get up from your brief bench reprieve, turn left down Fourth Avenue, quickly passing the Times Building (336 Fourth Avenue). This is one of architect Frederick J. Osterling's most successful designs, in Richardson Romanesque fashion, with its rounded arches.

Shortly across the street you'll see the awnings and brass sign that designate The Bank Tower (307

Fourth Avenue), built in the 1890s. Architects Alden and Harlow are responsible for the semicircular, grand staircase. Cross the street and stroll into The Bank Tower's lobby (if the building is open). Glancing up the stairwell, you'll see the marble intarsia of the balustrade.

Once you're finished admiring the building, exit on Fourth Avenue and turn right, continuing toward the shimmering glass tower we know as PPG Place. You'll cross Wood Street, passing both the Investment Building (239 Fourth Avenue) and the Benedum-Trees Building (221, 223, 225 Fourth Avenue) on your right.

Burke's Building
209 Fourth Ave., Pittsburgh

Immediately before PPG Place on the right is a tiny building of great architectural significance. This is the Burke's Building, Pittsburgh's oldest commercial structure.

As the oldest commercial building in the Golden Triangle, the Burke's Building is what remains of the Greek Revival period. When the great Downtown Fire of 1845 destroyed many buildings, this one was fortunately spared. This small building was designed by architect John Chislett in 1836, and is now the home of the Western Pennsylvania Conservancy. It's small, but with the plaque outside, you shouldn't have any trouble finding it. It's literally right next door to PPG Place.

PPG Place
One PPG Place, Pittsburgh

Witness the spectacle of PPG Place, the shimmering tower we've been saying you'd find. You can't miss this plate glass complex with the tower rising 680 feet into the Downtown sky. In fact, young movie fans affectionately refer to the structure as "the Inspector Gadget building," since that Disney film used Pittsburgh and PPG Place as its backdrops. But this is only its more recent claim to fame.

In 1979, PPG Industries, wanting to make a one-time gift of significant proportions to the city, commissioned architects to show off the company's product of plate glass. The site chosen was a stretch of land from the Boulevard of the Allies, through Third and Fourth Avenues to Market Square. But you don't just decide to construct a towering complex without much scrutiny.

PPG heard the many fears that their design

INSIDERS' TIP
Ask for the brochure on Heinz Memorial Chapel Weddings if you're thinking of getting married at this historic landmark.

might block the midday light and forever harm the appeal of nearby Market Square. The company involved city planners in selecting architects Philip Johnson and John Burgee. While the original intent might have been to build a single tower, the final plan included six buildings, with the tower (One PPG Place) serving as corporate headquarters for PPG Industries. The complex was completed in 1984.

To meet the city's 20 percent open space requirement, the architects and planners created a formal plaza on the east side of the tower between Third Avenue and Fourth Avenue. This area not only allows the sun to shine down upon the concrete, but it provides the lunchtime crowds a pleasant site for brown bagging it. Festivals sometimes use the space for outdoor events, and the plaza has also been the venue for special receptions. During December, you can't miss the brightly decorated Christmas tree—the focal point of the plaza.

Philip Johnson saw Pittsburgh as Gothic. The tower, with its silver-gray glass that you can't see through, has eight wonderful pinnacles reaching up to the sky. In fact, the building is glazed with nearly 20,000 pieces of reflective glass—the company's flagship product—that catch the sunset over the Point nightly. Inside the lobby of this headquarters building sits the PPG Wintergarden, where the annual Christmas Santa display is a popular attraction (see our Annual Events chapter).

From the Burke's Building, keep walking along Fourth Avenue, literally a few steps, and open the glass doors to Two PPG Place, one of the complex's six buildings, on your right. Go through the second set of doors entering the retail arcade (the food court escalators greet you, should you need a beverage by now). Out the glass doors directly ahead of you is Market Square, once known as the Diamond. From the mid-1790s until 1852, it accommodated not only market stalls but also the first Allegheny County Courthouse.

Market Square is currently used as a small, open-air space for rallies, political announcements, and even concerts in warm weather. Workers often eat lunch on the benches, appreciating the ambience and sunshine. But now, Market Square has the

added distinction of controversy. Mayor Tom Murphy is proposing a retail development plan that, if approved, would mean the razing of several buildings of historical or architectural significance. Preservation groups have their own propositions for saving the buildings, and it seems every day the newspaper includes a new development in this back-and-forth saga.

Continue straight from your glass door departure point with one warning. Duck the pigeons! They do flock in Market Square, much to the chagrin of most every resident and visitor. As you walk, you will pass several small shops, and the 1902 Landmark Tavern. This building, along with the Oyster House restaurant, are Market Square's oldest structures.

The street you are walking on is not marked with a street sign. When you get to the intersection at Fifth Avenue, however, you will find an inscription on the curb stating this is Graeme Street.

From Fifth Avenue On

Turn right on Fifth Avenue and begin walking east toward Kaufmann's Department Store. A two-block walk will put you at the intersection of Fifth Avenue and Smithfield Street, with Kaufmann's on the far right corner. Notice the popular Kaufmann's Clock, under which many a rendezvous for Pittsburghers has taken place. But wait! Don't cross the street (unless you're meeting someone, of course).

We want you to turn left at this juncture, crossing Fifth Avenue as you proceed north on Smithfield Street. Walk two blocks (passing Saks Fifth Avenue on your left) until you come to Sixth Avenue, where you will take another left to explore two of Pittsburgh's architecturally significant churches, and a club for the powers that be.

Trinity Cathedral
322 Sixth Ave.,
Pittsburgh
• (412) 232-6404

You'll know you're in the right place when you see Trinity Cathedral. Detroit architect Gordon Lloyd designed this house of worship in 1871, using the decorated Gothic of early 14th-century England as his style for this Episcopal cathedral. While a fire

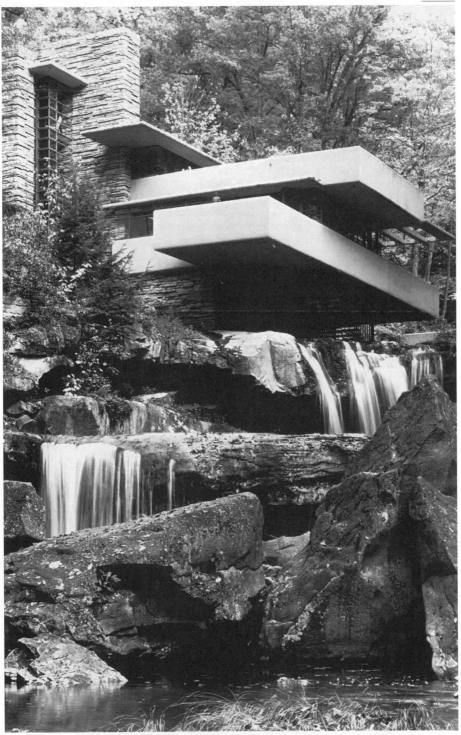

*Fallingwater's dramatic design and unique natural setting are a dream to visitors,
professional photographers, and artists.*

Photo: Robert P. Ruschak courtesy of the Western Pennsylvania Conservancy in 1969 damaged portions of the structure, the interior still reflects its original mid-Victorian appeal. Outside, there's a historic courtyard, and some of Pittsburgh's oldest graves inhabit the cemetery.

First Presbyterian Church
320 Sixth Ave., Pittsburgh
• (412) 471-3436

First Presbyterian Church is next door to Trinity, just a step away. On property donated by the Penn Family (William Penn was the founder of Pennsylvania), Philadelphia architect Theophilus Parsons Chandler began constructing the church in 1903, completing it two years later. The cathedral-like front is reminiscent of 13th- and 14th-century English Gothic. Inside, the nave windows (all but one) are by the Tiffany Studios, and the sanctuary itself boasts a rectangular preaching space. Notice also the raised side galleries.

Duquesne Club
325 Sixth Ave., Pittsburgh
• (412) 391-1500

Exiting First Presbyterian on Sixth Avenue, directly across the street sits the bastion of what some would say was the "old boy network" in Pittsburgh. At the Duquesne Club, women were once excluded as leading industrialists conducted countless business transactions. The architectural firm of Longfellow, Alden & Harlow designed the club between 1887 and 1889. Alden & Harlow added to the main front in 1902, and further remodeling was completed by Janssen & Cocken, as they added a tower in 1930 to 1931.

Return up Sixth Avenue to Smithfield Street and proceed past Mellon Square on your right, an outdoor park atop an underground parking garage. This puts you at a street called William Penn Place (the same street is named Cherry Way a few blocks south of here). Walk one more block to Grant Street, and cross it. You can't miss the skyscrapers such as the USX Tower, the tallest building in Downtown Pittsburgh.

Turn left and walk past the USX Tower, which we'll describe in detail soon. En route, notice how Grant Street offers a handsome view of old architecture juxtaposed next to modern-day skyscrapers.

There's the First English Evangelical Lutheran Church (615 Grant Street), the Gulf Tower, and the Koppers Building (both at Seventh Avenue and Grant Street). Continue your walk to the end of Grant Street.

At the traffic light, you will see where Port Authority buses turn onto the East Busway. Cross this stretch of pavement at the light to The Pennsylvanian.

The Pennsylvanian
Grant St. and Liberty Ave., Pittsburgh

You'll know you are in the right place as you peer up at the former train station's beaux-arts rotunda—a 1900 architectural student's dream, and the first sight rail passengers used to see of our city upon arrival.

Inside the rotunda, on pendentives beneath the skylit dome, four women's heads once smiled down upon tablets naming four destinations of the Pennsylvania Railroad. Passenger service diminished in the 1940s, and soon buses used the rotunda, so large was its scale. Eventually the bus traffic ceased as well. In 1988, a restored Union Station became the Pennsylvanian apartment complex. Many of the architectural highlights from the heyday of the trains remain in place today.

We'll soon end our walking tour taking you past the gem of Pittsburgh architecture—Richardson's Allegheny County Courthouse. But there are a few more substantial structures for you to recognize. For instance, there's the USX Tower as you make your way south back along Grant Street (in the opposite direction you came from).

USX Tower
600 Grant St., Pittsburgh

At 841 feet high, the USX Tower is the tallest building in Downtown Pittsburgh, and one of the tallest buildings between New York City and Chicago. Once known as the U.S. Steel Building (before the company merged with Marathon Oil), it towers 64 stories into the sky. Harrison & Abramovitz started construction in 1968 and completed the project in 1971. The skyscraper is made of an exposed frame of Cor-Ten weathering steel, a rust-resistant steel originally developed for the insides of grain hopper rail cars that could not be painted. However, the Cor-Ten finish did need to be painted, as the rust that formed washed off onto other nearby buildings. Interestingly, the columns and girders are filled with water to resist fire (and anti-freeze to prevent the expansion of frozen water).

If you keep walking on the left sidewalk next to the USX Tower, you will pass One Mellon Bank Center, corporate headquarters of Mellon Bank. If you're on the other side of Grant Street (across the street from the USX Tower), you'll pass both the Westin William Penn Hotel and Two Mellon Bank Center on your right.

Westin William Penn Hotel
530 William Penn Place, Pittsburgh
• (412) 281-7100

The Westin William Penn Hotel is an American Renaissance masterpiece erected by industrialist Henry Clay Frick betwen 1914 and 1916. Designed by Janssen & Abbott, the hotel was enlarged in the late '20s by their successor firm, Janssen & Cocken.

Inside, the Palm Court Lobby has been restored to its original splendor. This is where guests today enjoy afternoon tea and piano music. For a lovely dining experience, the setting is the Terrace Room, framed in carved walnut with original Rococo ceiling and murals depicting Fort Duquesne during the Revolutionary War.

The centerpiece of this hotel, however, is the art deco classic of black marble and Carrara glass, gold detailing, and exotic murals in the Urban Room, named for designer Joseph Urban. This famed room resides on the 17th floor. For years, this hotel was known simply as the William Penn Hotel—named after Pennsylvania's founder—until its purchase by the Westin hotel chain in 1984.

Two Mellon Bank Center
501 Grant St., Pittsburgh

First called the Union Arcade, this was one of Henry Clay Frick's buildings all in a row. He chose architect Frederick J. Osterling to build the Union Arcade, with its prominent rotunda roof. The project was begun in 1915 and finished two years later. Osterling designed this 237-foot Gothic building using carved gray sandstone, terra cotta, and green granite exterior trim, and plenty of bronze, marble, and terra cotta inside. You'll also notice the specially designed light fixtures and leaded glass.

In 1922, The Union Trust Company purchased the building from the Frick estate and quickly remodeled the building the next year, naming it the Union Trust Building. The main vault held more than a billion dollars in silver, cash, and securities. The most significant architectural change was Grecian, but it blended well with the original Gothic design.

As then Mellon National Bank merged with the Union Trust Company in 1946, the character of the building changed a bit as the new owner allowed closing in and flooring over the excess corridor space from the second through fourth floors. When Mellon completed its new corporate headquarters in the 1980s, this site later became Two Mellon Bank Center. Though offices occupy the upper floors, the first floor still has several shops. If nothing more, cut through the building on a rainy day to escape the elements and admire the rotunda.

From where you stand on either side of the street, you can't miss the beautiful detailing of the Richardson's Romanesque design in the Allegheny County Courthouse and Jail.

Allegheny County Courthouse and Jail
Between Grant St. and Ross St., Pittsburgh
• (412) 350-5300 (for courthouse tours)

New technical approaches to design may have originated elsewhere, but they soon found their way into Downtown Pittsburgh. When Henry Hobson Richardson's Romanesque design was selected, its simplicity was the alluring element, with its rounded arches, rugged stone walls, and Byzantine leaf carving. Richardson was formally chosen from competitors in 1883 to move ahead with this project to replace the second county courthouse, which had been gutted by fire.

Since Richardson hailed from Boston (where his famous Trinity Church stands), the stone brought in for the courthouse was quarried in Massachusetts, and many Boston stone carvers and contractors came to Pittsburgh to work for the architect.

Richardson designed each court facility to be self-contained and lighted both from the courtyard and the street. Judges' chambers, jury, and consultation rooms were planned for the building's turrets. The tower, at 325 feet high, dominated the skyline until the Frick Building forever altered the view in 1901.

One courtroom—Judge Raymond Novak's courtroom—has been restored to its original splendor. The lighting and paint were replicated, and a beam in Richardson's work exposed (rather than have drop or artificial ceilings). Much of the furniture used in the restored courtroom today is vintage. Shepley, Rutan & Coolidge, an architectural firm led by Richardson's son-in-law George Shepley, designed and purchased much of the courthouse furniture.

County offices frequented by the public were situated below the courtrooms. Prisoners were transported securely across a built-in bridge, known as the "bridge of sighs" over Ross Street. One theory regarding this peculiar name was that prisoners walking the raised bridge would sigh upon finishing their route to the courthouse. Others say the name comes from the 16th-century bridge between the Doge's palace and the city prison in Venice, Italy.

A plaque affixed to the courthouse details what used to be called Grant's Hill. This section of street you are standing on used to be significantly higher, so much so that the original entrance was on what's now the second floor. In 1912, the hump was leveled to ease traffic.

The Allegheny County Courthouse and Jail are regarded as the finest works of architecture in the city. Because Richardson passed away in 1886, the buildings were completed after his death. The inscription near the grand staircase at the entrance of the old law library reads "In memory of Henry Hobson Richardson, architect (1838-1886). Genius and training made him master in his profession. Although he died in the prime of life, he left to his country many monuments of art, foremost among them this temple of justice."

Classical and gothic architecture were used when Richardson employed the rounded arch, his best-known element, adapted from Romanesque architecture of the early 11th century. Indeed, his style has been called Richardson Romanesque, and this particular distinction means that the architect built the structure. A building said to be Richardsonian Romanesque was inspired by the famous architect but not built by Richardson himself. Two R's, one written backwards and sharing the straight line with the next R, is the signature logo carved into one of the architect's great works.

Richardson used granite in such a way that the stone carver's skill revealed rather than concealed the natural stone. Frank Ellis Alden, a senior member of Richardson's design staff, supervised the construction of both the courthouse and jail. Eight months after the jail's completion in June 1886, and by now after his boss's passing, Alden formed his own architectural firm in Pittsburgh—Longfellow, Alden & Harlow, later Alden & Harlow. The courthouse was completed in April 1888 by Shepley, Rutan & Coolidge, a firm that completed several Richardson designs and went on to construct others in the Pittsburgh area.

In 1904 Frederick J. Osterling was commissioned to expand the county jail. A new round tower at Fifth Avenue and Ross Street was added in keeping with Richardson's original ideas. In 1976 trees and shrubbery were planted and benches added, making the Courthouse courtyard into a public park that's now a popular summer lunchtime spot for Downtown workers.

Having outgrown the space, the Jail was vacated in 1995, and prisoners are now housed in a new facility along Second Avenue, with its exceptional view of the river. Thus, the accommodations have been jokingly dubbed "the Hilton on the Mon." The old jail that Richardson built is being renovated for additional courtroom space.

You can tour the Allegheny County Courthouse, and you have many options, including an organized tour sponsored by the Pittsburgh History & Landmarks Foundation. If you want to do a self-guided tour, obtain the booklet "H.H. Richardson's Allegheny County Courthouse and Jail." (See Architectural Tourism in this chapter.) One caveat of guiding yourself through this masterpiece—stop to admire the design of the three-story staircase, made of Indiana limestone with original lighting fixtures. It's a celebration of the Richardson Romanesque arch—the new architectural style this famous architect created with his artistry and talent!

City-County Building
Grant St., Pittsburgh

Next door to the Courthouse, the City-County Building, along Grant Street between Forbes and Fourth avenues, is one of Henry Hornbostel's contributions to the skyline. Civil proceedings within Allegheny County take place here. It represents work toward the end of this architect's career in the art deco mode.

Beginning his work in 1915, and finishing two years later, the architect had one distinct advantage in that by the time he began working, the hump on Grant Street had been lowered. The open corridor inside the structure allows light to shine through. At the bottom of the outside steps, a statue of Pittsburgh's beloved mayor, the late Richard S. Caliguiri, stands as a tribute to his legacy.

This ends our walking tour of Downtown Pittsburgh. From reading other entries in this chapter, there might be additional buildings or bridges you'd like to explore. However, this tour has given you the highlights (and a little healthy exercise!).

From the City-County Building, return to your origins at Station Square by following Fourth Avenue one block west to Smithfield Street, turn left, and walk again back to the Smithfield Street Bridge, crossing it to Station Square. Or, if we've tired you out, take the T (light rail transit) from Gateway Center, Wood Street or Steel Plaza stations, and get off at Station Square. The fare is minimal.

Clayton, former residence of the Frick family, is popular among art and architecture aficionados.

Other Architecture In Detail

Downtown

Frick Building
437 Grant St., Pittsburgh
• **(412) 281-1260**

Directly across the street from the courthouse, Henry Clay Frick made a number of real estate investments in a closely aligned group of buildings. His Frick Building robbed the county buildings of their dominance. Finished in 1902, the building included the new and unusual for that time, things like hydraulic elevator machinery, a basement generating plant, and washrooms for the whole building (on the tenth floor). Bronze telephone booths remain in the lobby. D.H. Burnbaum & Co. were the Chicago architects that created this building between 1901 and 1902.

Heinz Hall
Sixth St. and Penn Ave, Pittsburgh
• **(412) 392-4900**

In the late 1960s, the Heinz Endowment bought the old Penn Theatre, one of many silent-movie theaters that also had a stage. Originally built between 1925 and 1926 by the Chicago firm of Rapp & Rapp, Heinz Hall was remodeled in the early 1970s by the local firm of Stotz, Hess, MacLachlan & Fosner. The firm turned the old entrance into a large foyer window, and it used architectural terra cotta to match the off-white exterior. Viennese baroque is the style for this center of performing arts that is home to the Pittsburgh Symphony (see our Arts chapter).

Benedum Center
719 Liberty Ave., Pittsburgh
• **(412) 456-6666**

With Heinz Hall establishing the fact that a former theater could be successfully converted into a performing arts complex, the former Stanley Theatre was looked upon as another conversion prospect. Built in the late 1920s by Philadelphia architects Hoffman-Henon, it was remodeled and enlarged between 1985 and 1987 by the firm of MacLachlan, Cornelius & Filoni. To learn more about the performances at the Benedum, turn to our Arts chapter.

Bouquet's Redoubt
Point State Park, Pittsburgh

This 1764 structure is better known as the Fort Pitt Blockhouse. Of the original Fort Pitt, we have only one structure remaining, known as Bouquet's Redoubt (better known as the blockhouse). Built too late to see any action in the French & Indian War, it has suffered its drama during peacetime through floods and a variety of uses. In 1894, the wealthy Mary Croghan Schenley gave the Blockhouse to the Daughters of the American Revolution. The Fort Pitt Society restored the structure and maintained it as a museum that is open to the public, to this day.

Koppers Building
436 Seventh Ave., Pittsburgh
• **(412) 227-2001**

The Koppers Building, completed in 1929, was the headquarters of Heinrich Koppers company. Koppers was the 1908 inventor of a by-product coke oven, one that captured wastes, recycling and utilizing a product that would have otherwise been dispersed into the air and rendered useless. He had moved his business to Pittsburgh in 1915. This building's chateau roof was made of copper, of course, and the lobby spaces are among the best art deco works in the city.

Gulf Tower
707 Grant St., Pittsburgh
• **(412) 263-6000**

In the 1920s, Grant Street was extended northward. More real estate became available in the city. Directly opposite the new Koppers Building, the Gulf Oil Company built a 44-story, 582-foot tower that would be the city's tallest building until the USX Tower was constructed in 1970. Trowbridge & Livingston, an architectural firm from New York, were commissioned. E. P. Mellon served as an associate architect for the project. At the top of the building, neon tubes forecasted the weather. When Gulf and Chevron merged companies in 1984, New York developers acquired the property, and today it has become office space rented out to companies.

Regional Enterprise Tower
Sixth Ave. and William Penn Way, Pittsburgh

Built by Alcoa in 1953, this building served as the company's headquarters until 1998, when everyone moved to a new facility on Pittsburgh's North Side. The firm of Harrison & Abramovitz designed the building that sits between Smithfield and Grant Streets, and of course, the idea was to showcase aluminum in every possible way—from the electrical work to cladding. It's a wonder of industrial design, with a system in place that allows all windows to be washed from the inside. In fact, the windows

swing completely around, and are sealed with inflatable gaskets that have rounded corners. And the rounded corners, necessitated by the window-cleaning system, change this structure's entire appeal. When completed, the building was hailed as a daring experiment in modern office buildings. Today, the 30-story Regional Enterprise Tower has become a regional resource center, housing economic development groups, among others.

North

Allegheny Post Office (now the Pittsburgh Children's Museum)
10 Children's Way, Pittsburgh
• **(412) 322-5059**

Though now converted into a museum for children (see our Kidstuff chapter), the former Allegheny Post Office on the North Side is architecturally significant for its Early Italian Renaissance style. The central domed space inside is tall and much like a mosque. In a sense, Pittsburghers get to see more of the building as a children's museum, since they were restricted to the counter and outer corridors as a post office.

Armstrong County Courthouse
Market St. and Jefferson St., Kittanning
• **(724) 548-3226**

This courthouse is a late Greek Revival structure that boasts a Corinthian porticoed central pavillion. It was erected in 1858, and a left wing was added in 1871. While the courthouse was constructed first, the jail was built in 1873. Clarion County sandstone was used in each.

Butler County Courthouse
Main Street, Butler
• **(724) 285-4731**

Built in 1886, the Butler County Courthouse is Richardsonian in its style, of mixed Gothic and French architecture. James P. Bailey of Pittsburgh was its architect. Later enlarged and modernized between 1907 and 1908, this building contains a clock at least 100 years old, which dutifully ran without motorized assistance until 1940.

Carnegie Library of Pittsburgh (Allegheny Regional Branch)
Allegheny Square, Pittsburgh
• **(412) 237-1890**

Completed in 1890, this was the first Carnegie Library commissioned. Designed by architects Smithmeyer & Pelz of Washington,

D.C., the library interior has been updated over the years. The adjacent Carnegie Hall is now a theater rather than an auditorium where speakers like evangelist Kathryn Kuhlman held services. Still, there are some excellent finials to look at as well as the urn on the Library tower, and a lyre on the Carnegie Hall gable.

Hartwood Acres
215 Saxonburg Blvd., Pittsburgh
• **(412) 767-9200**

New York architect Alfred W. Hopkins constructed this large country estate in 1929 in Indiana Township. It was the property of Mary Flinn Lawrence, daughter of the well-known contractor William Flinn. Its main house, which can be toured by the public, is typical of 1920s rural Tudor styling. Allegheny County maintains the property today for recreational and cultural use. (See our Attractions chapter).

Mother House of the Sisters of Divine Providence
La Roche College, 9000 Babcock Blvd., Pittsburgh
• **(412) 367-9300**

Religious and academic buildings are clustered around the towering Mother House with its chapel, here on the North Hills campus of La Roche College. John E. Kauzor was its architect in 1927. While many of the other buildings are non-descript, the Mother House maintains a North Italian Romanesque style that's splendid.

East

Allegheny Cemetery (Butler Street Entrance)
4734 Butler St., Pittsburgh

John Chislett was the architect for this gateway to the Allegheny Cemetery in 1847. You can see his work on the Butler Street entrance. It's a Tudor Gothic gateway in warm gray sandstone. The cemetery was enlarged 20 years later with a chapel and office. In addition, the Penn Avenue gates were added in 1887.

Board of Education Building
341 S. Bellefield Ave., Pittsburgh
• **(412) 622-3500**

Built between 1926 and 1927, this structure resembles an Italian Renaissance town palace with a few Baroque touches. Architects Ingham and Boyd deserve the honors. Inside, you'll find a landscaped courtyard.

The Carnegie
4400 Forbes Ave., Pittsburgh
• **(412) 622-3131** • **www.clpgh.org**

On land donated by Mary Croghan Schenley, another renowned philanthropist, Andrew Carnegie, offered Pittsburgh a cultural entity that reigns today. Architects Longfellow, Alden & Harlow created Carnegie Institute and the Carnegie Library of Pittsburgh in 1892.

The Italian Renaissance library building was first on the scene, followed by the Music Hall and museums. Outside the Institute, you can't miss the four statues—Galileo, Michelangelo, Bach, and Shakespeare, representing the four branches of science, art, music and literature.

The wealthy Sarah Mellon Scaife donated a massive collection of art. To house it, Edward Larabee Barnes built the Scaife Gallery at the Carnegie Museum of Art in 1974 (see the Arts chapter).

Year-round hours at the museums are Tuesday through Saturday, 10 AM to 5 PM, and Sunday, 1 to 5 PM. On Fridays from June through August, they're open from 10 AM to 9 PM, and on Mondays in July and August, 10 AM to 5 PM. The library is open year-round Monday through Thursday, 9 AM to 9 PM; Friday and Saturday from 9 AM to 5:30 PM; and Sunday, 1 to 5 PM. Admission to the library is free. Admission to The Carnegie Museum of Natural History and Museum of Art is $6 for adults, $5 for senior citizens, and $4 for children (ages 3 to 18). Children younger than 3 and members are admitted free of charge.

Cathedral of Learning at the University of Pittsburgh
Bigelow Blvd. and Fifth Ave., Pittsburgh
• **(412) 624-4141**

John Gabbert Bowman, who was named chancellor of the University of Pittsburgh in 1921, inherited a less than spectacular campus. Although a university skyscraper was virtually unheard of, Bowman had a vision for one here, and he hired Charles Zeller Klauder to ignite and carry it through.

INSIDERS' TIP
Joining the Friends of Fallingwater brings you two annual free admissions to Wright's famous house and other Wright sites around the country, along with a 10 percent discount at the Fallingwater Shop, and a semi-annual newsletter.

Klauder, an eclectic architect from Philadelphia and a specialist in college design, tried to create the perfect plan. Bowman insisted that the building must inspire his students. The chancellor's concept was best articulated when, upon hearing the Magic Fire Music from *Die Walkure,* Bowman suggested that he wanted a climax building, towering higher and higher.

Indeed, Bowman had quite a selling job on his hands. However, with the help of benevolent donors, ordinary laborers, and even young children who took up collections to create the cathedral, the campaign was successful.

Most considered the results beautiful, though some thought it absurd. It's said that Frank Lloyd Wright called the creation "the world's largest keep-off-the-grass sign." Today the Gothic Cathedral of Learning, at 535 feet with 42 stories, towers over much more modest Oakland rooftops.

The Commons Room inside is cavernous, immense, and inspiring. On any given day, you'll find students at quiet study, or occasionally, a special event like Oktoberfest, with the wafting aroma of ethnic foods, only without the beer.

Chancellor Bowman wanted to use the Cathedral of Learning to showcase world cultures. Thus, dozens of classrooms within the cathedral depict the city's ethnic diversity through their individual architecture. Since so many immigrants settled here in the 1920s, these Nationality Rooms seemed a fitting tribute to that heritage (see our Attractions chapter).

But an important caveat in creating these nationality displays was that each room had to be used as a classroom. In addition, no person who was alive could be portrayed in the room. Each is different. The English is patterned after the House of Commons in 16th-century Tudor. The Yugoslav room features pocketknife wood carvings. And the French were the only group that selected the room's location, in this case to be closer to Heinz Chapel. Each room was funded by ethnic committees, designed by native architects, and built with materials from the countries they represent.

Taped recorded tours are offered if you like. Student guides are also available between 11 AM and 3 PM on most days. The Nationality Rooms are open Monday through Saturday,

9:30 AM to 3 PM, and Sunday, 11 AM to 3 PM. Admission rates are $2 for adults, $1.50 for seniors (60 and above), and 50 cents for children 8 to 18. Children 8 and younger are free.

Clayton
Penn Ave. and Homewood Ave., Pittsburgh
• (412) 371-0606

In 1882, Henry Clay Frick and his wife, the former Adelaide Howard Childs, purchased this modest example of an Italianate house built after the Civil War in Pittsburgh's Point Breeze neighborhood. Several years later, in 1890, the Fricks decided to expand and remodel the home, hiring Pittsburgh architect Frederick J. Osterling to carry out the task. Although Osterling proposed a much more elaborate vision than what he finally built, today's Clayton boasts a chateauesque appearance, with steep roofs and gables that bespeak Osterling's style. This architect patterned his remodeling efforts after houses in the Loire River Valley.

Other buildings, including the conservatory, sprouted up along the property. Upon Mr. Frick's death in 1919, his daughter Helen Clay Frick inherited the property. It's reported she was very fond of the home. Though she lived in New York, she visited often and maintained the property. Helen Clay Frick died in 1984, willing the home to the family's foundation. Following her wishes, Clayton was opened as a museum in 1990.

Today, Clayton is part of the Frick Art & Historical Center (see the Arts chapter). You can reserve a spot for a tour of Clayton where you'll notice the renowned art collection the Fricks amassed during their many trips abroad. The stained glass window illuminating the main stairs is by Cottier and Company in New York, and depicts heroines from literature. Many of Mr. Frick's acquisitions remain as they were in the oak-paneled sitting room. The family used to gather for meals in the formal dining room, where they received Theodore Roosevelt in 1902 as the U.S. Marine Corps Band entertained luncheon guests with marches from the lawn.

When you visit Clayton, free parking is available, and there is access for visitors with disabilities. The center is open Tuesday through Saturday, from 10 AM until 5 PM, and on Sundays from noon until 6 PM. Clayton is closed on Mondays. Tours of Clayton cost $8 for adults,

$7 for seniors, and $6 for students. Members are admitted free of charge.

Pittsburgh Athletic Association
4215 Fifth Ave., Pittsburgh
• **(412) 621-2400**

Architect Benno Janssen was responsible for the Pittsburgh Athletic Association, a clubhouse in the manner of a Venetian renaissance palace. It was constructed between 1909 and 1911 of limestone and matching terra cotta. Don't miss the carved ceilings and murals inside.

Soldiers' and Sailors' Memorial
4141 Fifth Ave., Pittsburgh
• **(412) 621-4253**

Built between 1907 and 1911 as a memorial to Civil War veterans, this building was also designed to add to Oakland's cultural scene. Architect Henry Hornbostel modeled the memorial after the Mausoleum at Halicarnassus, one of the seven wonders of the ancient world. Today, it contains a museum remembering all American wars, as well as a dining room and large public auditorium.

Stephen Foster Memorial at the University of Pittsburgh
Forbes Ave., Pittsburgh
• **(412) 624-4141**

Built tight against the Cathedral in 1937 is the Stephen Foster Memorial, a museum to the Pittsburgh composer. It's a combination theater, research library, social center, and shrine to honor another of the city's native sons. The auditorium seats nearly 700. The west wing houses the Foster Hall collection of over 20,000 items pertaining to the late musician. Regular hours for the Stephen Foster Memorial are Monday through Friday from 9 AM until 4 PM (except during University holidays). Weekend and library hours are made by appointment only. Guided tours cost $1.50 for adults and $1 for seniors and school children.

Westmoreland County Courthouse
N. Main St., Greensburg • (724) 830-3000

Built between 1906 and 1908, this public building's style is French renaissance. The bell from a previous brick courthouse in 1798 has been placed in the old jail tower and preserved by the county's historical society.

South

LeMoyne House
49 E. Maiden St., Washington
• **(724) 225-6740**

LeMoyne House is a fine example of early Greek Revival architecture built in 1812 by a French family that had come to America during the French Revolution. The home was passed down through the generations. Today, tours are available (see our Attractions chapter).

Thomas Jefferson Garden Mausoleum
Jefferson Memorial Park,
401 Curry Hollow Rd., Pittsburgh
• **(412) 655-4500**

At this South Hills cemetery, you'll find portions of the former Bank of Pittsburgh building, which came down in 1944. An admirer of this building asked the property's owner to save the temple front. Thus, it's permanent home is this memorial park which is the final resting place for so many generations of Pittsburghers.

Washington County Courthouse
South Main St. and West Beau St.,
Washington • (724) 348-7801

This is the county's fourth courthouse erected between 1898 and the fall of 1900. It's modeled in the beaux-arts classical style from the Italian renaissance. Rising 25 feet above the Courthouse roof are four highly ornamental cupolas whose terra cotta domes rest on sandstone ionic columns.

Within these cupolas rises a large dome. From this summit rises a cupola on top of which rests an 18-foot bronze statue of George Washington. An original statue of Washington stood atop the building from 1900 until 1917, when lightning strikes damaged it beyond repair. The present day statue was erected in 1927, and is protected by lightning rods.

INSIDERS' TIP

If you're a high school senior interested in Pittsburgh's history or architecture, apply for the scholarship awarded by the Pittsburgh History & Landmarks Foundation. Call (412) 471-5808.

West

Beaver County Courthouse
Market St. and Third St., Beaver
• **(724) 728-5700**

Built between 1876 and 1877, the Beaver County Courthouse is made of stone. Additions to the building were completed in 1907, remodeling took place in 1933 following a fire the year before, and another later addition was added between 1973 and 1974. Philadelphia architect David S. Geredel was responsible for the present courthouse.

Best of the Bridges

When you learn about Pittsburgh's path to progress, you learn of some struggle to bring about improvements. Well, for those who thought Plan B—the plan by which voters registered their thoughts on new stadium construction—was controversial, you should have been around for the debate about bridges back in the 1920s.

In 1924, the county's Ultimate Highway System was designed to carry the road system into the 21st century. New boulevards and radial roads connected the city to outlying areas. But what would span the deep ravines, so prevalent in this region?

The Ultimate Highway System was never quite completed, though portions of the plan were built as late as the 1950s. But the plan's legacy is left behind in the form of magnificent bridges—at Sixth, Seventh and Ninth Streets, plus the West End and McKees Rocks bridges, the Liberty, South 10th Street and Westinghouse Memorial bridges—all erected between 1924 and 1940. This achievement cemented Pittsburgh's reputation as the "City of Bridges." Here's a peek at the best of these engineering marvels.

Sixth, Seventh, and Ninth Street Bridges
Allegheny River

Affectionately called the "Three Sisters," these three suspension bridges span the Allegheny River between Downtown and the North Side. Their lyrical design was created in the 1920s as they replaced three adjoining Victorian bridges considered to be too ugly for the times. In 1928, the American Institute of Steel Construction bestowed an award on the Sixth Street Bridge. While several engineers from the Allegheny County Department of Public Works participated in the construction of these impressive spans, Stanley L. Roush served as the architect. In particular, at the site of the Sixth Street Bridge, engineer and designer John Roebling built one of his earlier structures. Roebling, who would go on to construct the Brooklyn Bridge, came from Germany to Pittsburgh in 1832, for he thought Pittsburgh would become the world's industrial center. Roebling invented wire rope and used that technology to build a number of Pittsburgh's early suspension bridges.

Sixteenth Street Bridge
Allegheny River

Spanning the water between Sixteenth Street in the Strip District and Chestnut Street on the North Side, the Sixteenth Street Bridge was designed in 1923 by Warren and Wetmore, the same architects responsible for New York's Grand Central Station. Three truss-arch spans and four masonry piers highlight this bridge. New York's Leo Lentelli created the seahorses that make crossing this bridge even more appealing.

10th Street Bridge
Monongahela River

This bridge runs between South 10th Street on the South Side and the Armstrong Tunnel on the Bluff (near Duquesne University). Sydney A. Shubin was the engineer in 1931 for this Modernistic bridge. Apart from the "Three Sisters" (see description for Sixth Street Bridge), this is Pittsburgh's only extant suspension bridge.

George Westinghouse Memorial Bridge
US Rt. 30

Connecting East Pittsburgh and North Versailles Township, the George Westinghouse Memorial Bridge served as an entrance for railroad passengers for over 50 years. Built in 1930, it's got five concrete arches and a total length of 1,596 feet. Each side's entrance has tall concrete pylons honoring George Westinghouse's development of the Turtle Creek Valley below. The George Westinghouse Memorial Bridge was once compared with other engineering marvels of its era, including the Hoover Dam, the George Washington Bridge, and the Holland Tunnel.

Houses of Worship

Downtown

First English Evangelical Lutheran Church
615 Grant St., Pittsburgh
• (412) 471-8125

Steep-roofed with a 170-foot spired tower

and Gothic elements, this church was built by Andrew Peebles in 1887 and 1888. Inside, worshippers enjoy the Tiffany glass window of the Good Shepherd in the church's sanctuary. Established in 1837, this congregation was the first English-speaking Lutheran congregation west of the Allegheny Mountains.

First Presbyterian Church
320 Sixth Ave., Pittsburgh
• (412) 471-3436

This Downtown church, with its 13th- and 14th-century English Gothic cathedral front, was covered in our Downtown walking tour. Turn to that listing for more detail.

Trinity Cathedral
322 Sixth Ave., Pittsburgh
• (412) 232-6404

Trinity is right next door to First Presbyterian Church, and this too was covered extensively in our Downtown walking tour.

St. Mary of Mercy Roman Catholic Church
202 Stanwix St., Pittsburgh
• (412) 261-0110

Somewhat dwarfed by towering PPG Place, this church holds its own simplicity and strength. Built in 1936 by architect William P. Hutchins, there are two red brick walls gracing the sidewalks on the church's Stanwix Street and Third Avenue sides.

East

East Liberty Presbyterian Church
116 S. Highland Ave., Pittsburgh
• (412) 441-3800

East Liberty Presbyterian Church in its namesake neighborhood of East Liberty was built according to cathedral dimensions, as a gift from Richard Beatty and Jennie King Mellon. Boston architects Cram and Ferguson created this Gothic house of worship that consumes an entire city block.

Heinz Memorial Chapel
East Lawn of the Cathedral of Learning at the University of Pittsburgh
• (412) 624-4157

Next door to the Cathedral of Learning at the University of Pittsburgh is an interdenominational chapel. Chancellor Bowman had insisted upon such a chapel to inspire his students. Thus, in 1938, Charles Zeller Klauder

created the 15th-century French flamboyant Heinz Chapel, with donations from Henry John Heinz and his children. Klauder used several models as inspiration, including Mont-St.Michel, King Louis IX's Sainte-Chapelle, and St.-Maclou at Rouen.

Charles J. Connick, a noted glassmaker from Boston, had responsibility for the spectacular stained-glass windows in this structure that is set off by its tall spire atop the center. Four transept windows represent courage, tolerance, temperance, and truth, and each is 73 feet high.

The present pipe organ in the chapel was made possible through a generous gift of The Howard Heinz Endowment. The third organ to serve this chapel, it has 4,272 pipes (73 ranks) and three electronic pedal stops. The organ, recreated in 1994-95, represents a trend in American organ building to re-use existing materials in an environmentally friendly and musically sound manner. When you hear the organ in this setting, you can literally feel the vibrations around you.

Heinz Chapel is the site of approximately 1,500 events each year, including lectures, memorial services, weddings, and guided tours. The first funeral to be held in this chapel was that of the late Senator H.J. (John) Heinz III, who died tragically in an airplane accident in April, 1991.

Rodef Shalom
4905 Fifth Ave., Pittsburgh
• (412) 621-6566

One of the two synagogues designed by Henry Hornbostel is Rodef Shalom Congregation in Shadyside. Here, the architect used his favorite materials, cream-colored brick and terra cotta. Inside, Hornbostel made use of the light from the skylight, which beams down upon his rich mahogany and gilt interior. The temple also contains stained-glass windows, and beautiful blue and gold chandeliers.

Sri Venkateswara Temple
1230 S. McCully Dr., Pittsburgh
• (412) 373-3380

This Penn Hills temple was the second Hindu temple to be built in the United States, and was constructed in 1979. The Indian scientific and professional community contributed greatly to its establishment. The Tirupathi Shrine from seventh century southern India served as the model here. Two temple domes are constructed of inch-thick stucco over brick and concrete. The sikhara (spire towers) are similarly made.

ARCHITECTURE

Altering Your Home?

If you are a resident of the City of Pittsburgh, you will need permission to make any exterior changes to the front of your home. The Historic Review Commission must review and approve all visible exterior alterations, including demolition, new construction, and additions. For more information, call (412) 255-2243.

St. Paul's Cathedral
Fifth Ave. and N. Craig St., Pittsburgh
• **(412) 621-4951**

Chicago architects Egan & Prindeville designed the twin spires at St. Paul's Cathedral, prominent on the Oakland skyline in this Victorian design. The main structure was built between 1903 and 1906. Two previous Roman Catholic Cathedrals had been Downtown on the site of the Union Arcade (see listing for Two Mellon Center), but Mr. Frick's desire to construct the arcade prompted the cathedral's move to Oakland.

This new cathedral turned away from Victorian colors, yet the actual design was reminiscent of Victorian style. There are no flying buttresses as many large cathedrals might have. Two prominent Catholic architects from our city contributed to the entire complex. Edward J. Weber created the Synod Hall and Chancery of 1914, with its fifteenth-century English look. Carlton Strong built the Rectory in 1926 in a Tudor style.

West

St. Nicholas Chapel
5400 Tuscarawas Rd., Brighton
• **(724) 495-3400**

Constructed in 1992 by architect Tom Terpack, St. Nicholas Chapel, with its three onion domes, is quite a sight in suburban Beaver County. Because it is crafted of cedar logs and shingles, it resembles traditional chapels in eastern Slovakia and the western Ukraine. Windows are located in the upper areas of the church so as not to weaken the main log structure. The wooden entrance doors are carved and framed with logs.

The Wright Stuff

Since Western Pennsylvania is so fortunate to have two great works of the legendary architect Frank Lloyd Wright, we've chosen to give you the highlights in their own special category. Please note that both of these homes you'll read about are outside of our coverage area, but we feel they're significant in the architectural scheme of things, so we're covering them nonetheless. Turn to our Daytrips chapter for more on these architectural gems.

Fallingwater
Mill Run (Off Pa. Rte. 40), Fayette County
• **(724) 329-8501**

Back in the 1930s, Pittsburgh department store owner Edgar J. Kaufmann and his wife, Liliane, commissioned architect Frank Lloyd Wright to design their weekend retreat at Bear Run in the Laurel Highlands, 90 minutes south of Pittsburgh. Tucked among the rhododendrons and sitting atop a waterfall, this masterpiece is more reminiscent of the '60s than the Great Depression.

A devotee of organic architecture, Wright decided to locate the house on top of the waterfall rather than to the side. Who would have thought? But in the spring of 1936, construction began with local contractors quickly trained to implement Wright's techniques.

Built of sandstone quarried on the property, Wright used natural stone to reinforce the concrete and create the image of land meeting nature and vice versa. The elements cause the eye to focus outside. Glass and steel were among the other materials used in this massive project, which back in the 1930s cost approximately $155,000 to construct—modest by today's standards, but consider the times.

The architect believed the Kaufmann family should live with the water, not merely look upon it. Cantilevers enable the terraces of the living and bedroom levels to extend over the rushing falls without visible support. A guest and service wing was added in 1939, and Albert Einstein was among the celebrated guests reported to have stayed with the Kaufmanns.

Inside the house, Wright designed the furniture to echo his themes. Southwestern colors were used throughout the property. While touring the home, you'll notice the stairway opens to the sound of the rushing falls. Nature indeed takes over when the windows on the cantilevers are opened, for there is no physical window structure as we normally experience.

When Edgar Kaufmann, Jr., the son, turned the home over to the Western Pennsylvania Conservancy in 1963, the family requested that the home remain as original as possible. Thus, you'll also see Tiffany lamps, Japanese prints,

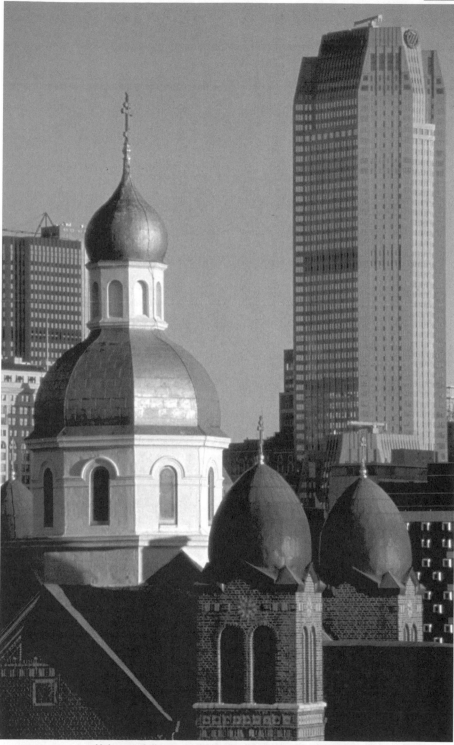

Unique and divergent architecture characterizes Pittsburgh.

Photo: M.G. Ellis

and artwork along with Wright's furniture. Much detail was put into the home—from the novel way the windows open to caning in the closet shelves allowing air to flow in such a damp climate. Even ship-quality wood was used to prevent warping. In 1976, the National Park Service bestowed the National Historic Landmark designation to the property.

Ironically, when Edgar Kaufmann had Wright build this home, he was concerned about structural soundness of his project. Thus, he sought the reassurance of a Pittsburgh firm of registered engineers and steel suppliers for concrete. They had advised that Kaufmann use twice the amount of steel his architect had recommended. Kaufmann took the firm's advice, and reportedly, it infuriated Mr. Wright to the point of a near break in the two men's working relationship. Wright felt the steel would weigh too much, causing the terrace to deflect more than it would naturally.

This disagreement was prescient, for in 1997, temporary shoring was installed under the main floor cantilever because of the gradual but continuing deflection of the first and second levels. In fact, at this writing if you stand at just the right part of the surrounding woods, you can see the famous home's slope whereby the master terrace is seven inches lower than the living room. Computerized analysis along with historical research revealed that the main house had not stopped deflecting since its construction in 1936-38. This was due to inadequate steel reinforcement in the concrete beams of the first and second levels. Robert Silman Associates, a structural engineering firm in New York, designed the final repair plan. Strengthening the main floor concrete beams will eliminate the need for further vertical support from beneath. At that juncture, the temporary shoring will be removed. To fund this massive restoration, the Western Pennsylvania Conservancy has conducted a fund-raising campaign.

Despite the restoration, in-depth tours are available at 8:30 AM for $40 (weekdays) or $50 (weekends). Regular tours are conducted only on weekends until the middle of March, and this famous 20th-century architectural master-

piece remains open through December, Tuesday through Sunday from 10 AM to 4 PM. Reservations are suggested for the hour-long tour. Children younger than 9 are not permitted, but group babysitting at $2 per hour per child is available at the visitors pavilion. For a schedule, call (724) 329-8501. With many stairs, considerable walking is required so call ahead to make arrangements if you need special assistance (see also our Attractions and Daytrips chapters). Note that staircases are narrow, and the stone can be a bit slippery if you aren't agile. No photos or large bags are allowed.

The best route to Fallingwater is to take the Pennsylvania Turnpike to Exit #9 (Donegal). Turn left onto Route 31 East, travel two miles, turn right onto Route 381 South for approximately 19 miles to Fallingwater.

Kentuck Knob
Chalk Hill, Ohiopyle
• **(724) 329-1901**

Not far from Fallingwater is another of Frank Lloyd Wright's famous homes, Kentuck Knob, overlooking the Youghiogheny River Gorge. Kentuck (yes, without the "y") Knob was commissioned by the I.N. Hagan family of Uniontown, a family that owned the Hagan Ice Cream Company. They had come to know the Kaufmann's and fell in love with the idea of a Wright creation of their own (only of a little more modest dimension).

This lesser-known Wright home was built of fieldstone boulders found on the site and tidewater red cypress from South Carolina. Wright based the design on a hexagonal modular grid on one main level because it allows for openness. That hexagonal motif is repeated inside and out, even allowing light to shine through in that geometric pattern. It reflects Usonion design, a precursor to the ranch home that most could afford.

Famous for incorporating nature into each site, Wright made sure light permeated in every room at Kentuck Knob. The outdoors is always present, from the morning sun until dusk. A steep, narrow causeway winds its way up from the road and opens to a gravel courtyard, as you ride in the small tour van leading you to

In Downtown Pittsburgh, old and new architecture coexist beautifully side by side as seen here with the Allegheny County Courthouse and One Mellon Bank Center.

Photo: Jack Wolf

the home site. The double glass entry doors welcome guests just as the copper roof offers shelter to curious tourists. The architect also designed the house's furniture, much of which is built-in, such as the cypress table that conforms to the angles of the dining room. Today, however, Wright's furniture sits beside some contemporary pieces reflecting the tastes of its current owners.

The home is now the property of Great Britain's Lord and Lady Palumbo, dedicated patrons of the arts both in the United States and across the Atlantic. Contemporary sculpture and historic artifacts also enhance the secluded setting. In fact, the Palumbo family's photographs give the house a warm, lived-in feel. Do notice the rather striking and now famous photo of the late Princess Diana, shaking hands in her chic black dress.

But don't expect to meet the owners on your tour. While the Palumbo's occasionally entertain in the house when visiting the United States, they live in the nearby valley.

Please note that improved visitor facilities are in the works, so it's best to make a lunch or restroom stop before coming to Kentuck Knob. And do enjoy the many outdoor sculptures that the Palumbo's have added throughout the 79-acre property.

Children younger than 9 are not permitted, and no organized childcare is provided for touring parents. Though not as renowned as Fallingwater, tours are available. Kentuck Knob is open daily, except Mondays, 10 AM to 4 PM. In-depth tours are available at 8:30 AM for $30 (weekdays) or $35 (weekends). Or take a regular tour available on weekdays during the summer at $10 per person, $15 per person on weekends. Winter tours cost $15 per person.

Architectural Tourism

It used to be that misbehavior unintentionally rewarded you with a tourist's treat. Yes, career criminals got a sneak peak at one of the greatest works of 19th century architecture—the Allegheny County Courthouse and Jail.

Well, now you don't have to misbehave at all to see the same site. "Living Architecture...Alive in Pittsburgh" debuted in 1998 to highlight the region's architectural charm. Aficionados of design, engineering, and architecture can book a package tour, and then partake of two of America's most revered architects—H.H. Richardson and Frank Lloyd Wright.

The Greater Pittsburgh Convention & Visitors Bureau (C&VB) gauged the interest in architectural tourism, found it was there, and has marketed a packaged tour ever since. Pittsburgh History & Landmarks Foundation created pamphlets for tours of the courthouse, and cassette tapes also help visitors take self-guided tours of the North Side and Downtown.

The "Living Architecture...Alive in Pittsburgh" package sells for $199 which includes one night's accommodations at the Westin William Penn Hotel (see entry in this chapter as well as in Accommodations). If you'd like to stay a second night, the price increases to $299. With your package comes the "Pittsburgh in Your Pocket" brochure, a self-guided audio tape set, two unrestricted admissions to The Carnegie and the Andy Warhol Museum, and two admissions to Fallingwater and Kentuck Knob. If you'd like more information, contact the C&VB at (800) 359-0758, or visit their web site at www.pittsburgh-cvb.org.

Another tourism option called The "Wright" Touch Getaway Package is marketed by the Laurel Highlands Visitors Bureau. It focuses on Frank Lloyd Wright's Fallingwater and Kentuck Knob exclusively, and is available from July 15 through November. Prices vary considerably depending upon where you choose to stay in the Laurel Highlands. Generally they range from approximately $80 to almost $200 for a two-day, one-night package. If you're interested, contact the visitors bureau at (888) 234-7268 or visit its website at www.laurelhighlands.org.

For residents or those nearby who don't require accommodations, but do wish to obtain the cassette tape tours, call Pittsburgh History & Landmarks Foundation at (412) 471-5808. The tapes cost $18 plus postage.

The Arts

You don't have to be a connoisseur of fine art or a season subscriber to the symphony to appreciate cultural life in Western Pennsylvania. For sure, there are dozens of opportunities for aficionados of all forms of the arts. In fact, it surprises some visitors and newcomers to learn that Pittsburghers are followers of the opera, in addition to being fans of their football team. But such is the scene here.

For a city our size, Pittsburgh has hidden wealth in its passion for excellent performances, dramatic theater, roving exhibitions, unique films, and the latest in literature and poetry. Combine that passion with plenty of raw talent, and the dedication of organizations that support artistic growth, and you have that rare combination that any arts lover needs to feel challenged, yet overwhelmingly satisfied with the offerings.

In this chapter, we'll abandon our usual geographic breakdown, as the cultural opportunities available here cross regional boundaries. We'll first explore some of the key places where Pittsburgh takes to the stage, for theater, dance, and film. We've got a rundown on local galleries and museums, and a listing of outlets for you creative types, including writers, actors, and musicians. We've also noted some of our area's best artistic support groups.

The Pittsburgh Cultural Trust oversees the development and operation of three of these major theaters—the Benedum Center for the Performing Arts, the Byham Theater, and the Harris Theatre—all located in the 14-block downtown area known as the Cultural District.

The Pittsburgh Cultural Trust was formed in 1984 as the result of the effort of Henry John "Jack" Heinz II. His vision for a downtown cultural district was turned into reality with strikingly restored building facades, murals, and other public art. Handsome brick sidewalks and granite curbs line the district. There's new energy brought about by the economic revitalization of business and the arts community partner together. In December 1999, The O'Reilly Theater opened for public theater patrons to enjoy. Again, Pittsburgh's Cultural Trust was instrumental in this achievement.

Don't forget, we'll close the chapter with a few of the organizations you might turn to for enhancement of your own artistic flare. One thing is certain. In Pittsburgh, you will be pleased with the sounds of symphonies and orchestras, with the sights at major galleries, and with the appeal of theater companies performing a range of works, from Broadway musicals and opera to comedies and dramatic plays.

Get ready to relax and let your spirits soar, as the stage is set and the light shines on all we present. And be sure to turn to our extensive Architecture chapter for details on famous buildings, homes, and bridges, considered works of art in their own right by many.

LOOK FOR:
- In the Limelight
- Dance
- Film
- Galleries & Museums
- Literary Arts
- Music
- Theater
- Artistic & Literary Groups

In The Limelight

Benedum Center for the Performing Arts
719 Liberty Ave., Pittsburgh
• **(412) 456-6666**
Formerly the Stanley Theater, this building is the cornerstone of Pittsburgh's Cultural District. Reopened in 1987 after a $42 million renovation, the Benedum seats 2,800 and is home to the Civic Light Opera, Pittsburgh Ballet Theater, Pittsburgh Dance Council, and the Pittsburgh Opera. The Benedum

Pete Kope and Michele De La Reza in Swan Lake.

Photo: Cylla van Tiedemann courtesy of Dance Alloy

Center also hosts first-run Broadway touring productions. Approximately every five years Andrew Lloyd Weber's *The Phantom of the Opera* visits, and performs here. Registered with the National Trust for Historic Places, the Benedum (as its known for short) is one of the few theaters in the country large enough to stage full-cast, first-run Broadway shows.

You'd never guess from the outside the ornate details and ambiance you'll find within. Feast your eyes on he sweeping staircases, then let your eyes travel up to the domed ceiling, where the crystal chandelier glitters. This center for the performing arts used to be known as the Stanley Theater, a movie palace dating back to 1927.

Byham Theater
101 Sixth St., Pittsburgh
• **(412) 456-6666**
Opened in 1903 as a vaudeville house, and later serving as a 1930s talking motion picture house, the Byham today is Pittsburgh's oldest performing arts facility. With 1,342 seats, the Byham functions as stage to small to mid-sized performing arts productions as well as touring companies in music, dance, and the performing arts for children.

Harris Theater
809 Liberty Ave., Pittsburgh
• **(412) 471-9700**
The Harris Theater is one of Pittsburgh's newest performing spaces within the Cultural District. Home to the Pittsburgh Filmmakers' presentations of independent and foreign films, the Harris Theater also has smaller, live performances, lectures series, recitals, and experimental theater.

Heinz Hall for the Performing Arts
600 Penn Ave., Pittsburgh
• **(412) 392-4900**
No other landmark in this city enjoys the cultural reputation of Heinz Hall, for this great concert hall boasts an international reputation. Back in the 1920s, it was called the Penn Theater. But the Howard Heinz Endowment saved this theater, with its Breche opal and Lavanto marble interior, from the wrecking ball after it closed in 1968. Reopened in 1970 after a 16-month, $11 million renovation, it's now known

as Heinz Hall. With 2,847 seats, it's home to the Pittsburgh Symphony Orchestra, the Pittsburgh Pops, and the Pittsburgh Youth Symphony Orchestra.

O'Reilly Theater
621 Penn Ave., Pittsburgh
• (412) 316-8200

The most recent addition to Pittsburgh's Cultural District is The O'Reilly Theater, home to the Pittsburgh Public Theater. Designed by architect Michael Graves and opened in 1999, the theater's balcony overlooks the lobby's floor laid with a checkerboard of green and black slate. This theater replaced the former Hazlett Theater of Pittsburgh's North Side. With only 650 seats, even if you are in the seat farthest from the stage, you're still not more than 18 rows from the actors. There are many elegant elements to Graves' design, including the two-story, semi-circular wall of seven windows facing the street entrance. Looking at the theater as you enter, you can't miss the grand overhanging effect created by the windows and the copper-covered roof above you. In honor of his leadership of the H. J. Heinz Co. and undisclosed contributions toward the theater's construction, the building is named for former chairman Anthony J.F. O'Reilly.

Greensburg Garden and Civic Center and the Palace Theatre
951 Old Salem Rd., Greensburg
• (724) 836-1123

This non-profit organization owns two facilities—the Center and the Palace Theatre. Each promotes cultural, educational, and civic activities benefiting the residents of Westmoreland County. The Garden & Civic Center is located on Old Salem Road off Route 66, north of Greensburg. The Palace Theatre, home to the Westmoreland Symphony Orchestra, sits in downtown Greensburg at 21 West Otterman Street. Occasionally, the River City Brass Band performs at the Palace Theatre as well.

Post-Gazette Pavillion
Rt. 18 at Rt. 22,
Washington County
• (724) 947-STAR

Located in the sprawling countryside of Southwestern Pennsylvania, this amphitheatre attracts approximately 500,000 concert-goers each year,

mostly in the warm summer months. Live entertainment, from classical composers to the latest in pop-rock music, plus a variety of festivals occur here. The amphitheatre holds 23,000 people (7,200 seated within the open-air pavilion). The spacious hillside allows for 15,800 guests who can watch the large video monitors for close-up views of the stage.

Dance

Pittsburgh Ballet Theatre
2900 Liberty Ave., Pittsburgh
• (412) 281-0360 • www.pbt.org

The Pittsburgh Ballet Theatre celebrated its 30th anniversary in 1999 with Terrence S. Orr as its artistic director. Past performances have included *Dracula, American Salute, The Nutcracker, Coppella, The World Tour, Don Quixote,* and *The Sleeping Beauty.* This dance company takes the stage at the prestigious Benedum Center (see write-up above) for its season each October through May. Tickets range from approximately $20 to $260, depending upon seating in the various tiers and subscriptions. If you become a subscriber, you'll receive the "Spotlight" newsletter, pre-performance lectures, and a liberal ticket exchange policy. To purchase ballet tickets, call the Benedum Box Office at (412) 456-6666.

In addition to fostering its own program, the ballet offers more than 12 levels of dance instruction, with graduates performing with the Pittsburgh Ballet or other national ballet companies. To contact the Pittsburgh Ballet Theatre School, call (412) 281-6727. Classes are offered for children age 4 and older.

Dance Alloy
5530 Penn Ave., Pittsburgh
• (412) 363-4321

Commited to exploring dance as a creative performance medium as well as an educational process, this company exhibits a diverse and dynamic art form. Recent seasons have seen the Dance Alloy embark on a series of cross-cultural collaborations, including work with a Hawaiian hula company. In 1998, the group joined the Reichhold Center for the Arts in St. Thomas, U.S. Virgin Islands, and a recognized Calypso artist from Trinidad to produce a new dance. The

INSIDERS' TIP

In Pittsburgh, distributed free in newspaper honor boxes, is a great way of keeping tabs on the Pittsburgh culture scene, with in-depth interviews and plenty of event listings.

Dance Alloy School of The Carnegie schedules regular workshops throughout the year, consistent with the group's educational mission and its stature as the region's sole professional contemporary dance school. Tickets for a single performance range from $10 to around $24.

Pittsburgh Dance Council
Benedum Center, 719 Liberty Ave., Pittsburgh • (412) 355-0330

The Pittsburgh Dance Council is a hub site of the National Dance Project, a designated consortia of a dozen producers and presenters, each committed to the development of new American work. Performances held at the Benedum Center for the Performing Arts, the Byham Theatre, and sometimes the Eddy Theatre at Chatham College. Previous shows have included *The Harlem Nutcracker, American Indian Dance Theater,* and *Choreographers' Continuum.* Each performance is priced differently, but tickets range from $18 to $55.

Laurel Ballet
300 Hamilton Ave., Greensburg • (724) 837-7230, (724) 832-7391

Founded in the mid-'80s by Artistic Director Eleanor Tornblom, the Laurel Youth Ballet is a semi-professional performing company in Westmoreland County introducing hundreds to the world of dance. Former students have gone on to perform with larger companies, including the Pittsburgh Ballet Theatre and the Pennsylvania Ballet. Each year's schedule includes *The Nutcracker.*

Film

Academy Travel Adventure Films
The University Club, 123 University Pl., Pittsburgh • (412) 321-7668

Celebrating well over 100 seasons, this film series has taken locals to such geographic spots as Mexico, Burma and Vietnam, the Santa Fe Trail, Switzerland, France, Peru, Portugal, Australia, and the Great Lakes. Tickets cost $5, and one child gets in free with each adult ticket. Single memberships will run $14 for a season and double memberships $24. If you're really a fan, you can purchase a lifetime membership for two for $300. Call for information on upcoming film series with dates and times.

Carnegie Travel & Adventure Films
Carnegie Music Hall, 4400 Forbes Ave., Pittsburgh • (412) 622-3379

Join in these fascinating voyages to far off

Duquesne University Tamburitzans entertain around the world, representing Pittsburgh's ethnic traditions.

Photo: Courtesy of Duquesne University

THE ARTS

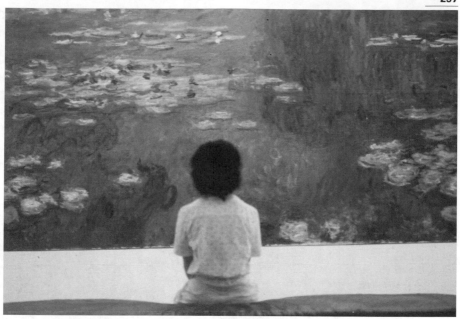

A patron views the permanent collection at The Carnegie Museum of Art.

Photo: C. Exler courtesy of The Carnegie

lands and cultures, including the *Rivers of France, A British Summer, Yellowstone to Sun Valley, The People of Poland, Easter Island, Montana: Beneath the Big Sky,* and even *The Samoan Islands.* There's a fall and spring schedule of travel adventure films offered at the Carnegie Music Hall, and at various locations throughout the suburbs. Sites include Mt. Lebanon High School and Baldwin High School (South Hills neighborhood), and North Hills High School. Sunday afternoon showings are at the Carnegie Music Hall, with evening screenings at suburban locations. Admission costs $6 for adults, $3 for students. Carnegie members are admitted free. Gift certificates are available.

Sweetwater Foreign Film Series
200 Broad St., Sewickley
• (412) 741-4405

Unique films in this series give a glimpse into another world and culture. Past series focused on the Chinese New Year Celebration of the Year of the Tiger and international musicals. The film series is held on Saturday evenings at 8 PM at the Sewickley Center. Admission costs $5 per person.

INSIDERS' TIP

A limited number of scholarships for the Museum of Art adult programs are available through the Scaife Family Foundation. Apply early by calling (412) 622-3288.

Galleries & Museums

Carnegie Museum of Art
4400 Forbes Ave., Pittsburgh
• (412) 622-3288 • www.clpgh.org

One of Andrew Carnegie's benevolent gifts to this city was the Museum of Art, which is operated under the umbrella of The Carnegie. The Carnegie Institute's original Renaissance-style building was designed by the firm of Longfellow, Alden & Harlow, between 1891 and 1895. Alden & Harlow completed new galleries in 1907. And in 1974, the Sarah Scaife Gallery, designed by Edward Larrabee Barnes, tripled the exhibition space in the Museum of Art.

While many turn-of-the-century art museums focused on amassing work of old masters, Mr. Carnegie envisioned a museum collection consisting of "the old masters of tomorrow." Thus, in 1896, he initiated a series of exhibitions of contemporary art, proposing that the museum's collection be formed through purchases from this series.

Early acquisitions included work by Winslow

Homer, James Abbott, McNeill Whistler, and Camille Pissarro. Today's collection includes a continuum of strength in American art from the late 19th century to the present, along with French impressionists, post-impressionist paintings, and other highly significant works of the 20th century.

The permanent collection is housed in the Scaife Galleries, and special exhibitions are reserved for the Heinz Galleries (or the Ailsa Mellon Bruce Galleries for decorative arts). Previous special exhibitions have included *Made in America: Ten Centuries of American Art* (1996) and *Pittsburgh Revealed* (1997). Art classes are available for adults and children (see our Kidstuff chapter). Lunch and Learn programs allow you to learn about the collections with a buffet lunch in the Museum Cafe.

Hours at the museums are 10 AM to 5 PM Tuesday through Saturday, and 1 to 5 PM on Sunday. Fridays, June through August, the museums are open from 10 AM to 9 PM; Mondays in July and August, hours are 10 AM to 5 PM. Admission to The Carnegie Museum of Natural History and Museum of Art is $6 for adults, $5 for senior citizens, and $4 for children (ages 3 to 18). Children younger than 3 and members are admitted free of charge.

Marvin Hamlisch serves as conductor of the Pittsburgh Pops.

Photo: Courtesy of Pittsburgh Symphony

Andy Warhol Museum
117 Sandusky St., Pittsburgh
• **(412) 237-8300**
• **www.warhol.org**

Andy Warhola was the son of Eastern European immigrants (he would shorten his name later in life). Beginning in the fourth grade, Warhol attended free Saturday art classes, and later graduated from Carnegie Tech's College of Fine Arts.

Warhol moved to New York, working as a commercial artist, taking with him from Pittsburgh an appreciation of working-class life. Thus, he created art that played on everyone's fantasies of inaccessible glamour and celebrity, embodied in his famous works of Marilyn Monroe, and Elvis, Jackie Onassis, and Mick Jagger.

Regardless of whether he was correct that everyone would have 15 minutes of fame, Warhol has received that many times over. Who else could create art out of a soup can or ketchup box? Today, the Warhol museum is one of the Carnegie Museums of Pittsburgh and is a collaborative project of Carnegie Institute, the Dia Center for the Arts, and the Andy Warhol Foundation for the Visual Arts.

The collection includes approximately 900 paintings, 77 sculptures and collaborative works, 1500 drawings, over 500 published and unique prints, and more than 400 black-and-white photographs. Also included are wallpaper and books by Warhol, as well as films and videos. Various traveling exhibits come to the museum, including a recent showing of Disney theme park drawings and artwork.

The Warhol is open Wednesday and Sunday, 11 AM to 6 PM and Thursday, Friday, and Saturday, 11 AM to 8 PM. It's closed Mondays and Tuesdays. Adults pay $7, seniors are charged $6, and students and children pay $4 for admission. Carnegie members pay nothing to enter.

The Frick Art & Historical Center
7227 Reynolds St., Pittsburgh
• (412) 371-0600

This six-acre complex in Pointe Breeze is elegantly landscaped with museums and turn-of-the-century buildings, the legacy left by Helen Clay Frick to the people of Western Pennsylvania. Step into the Victorian past to appreciate the architecture and artifacts, in addition to the collection of pre-20th century European art. Helen, the daughter of industrialist Henry Clay Frick and his wife, the former Adelaide Childs, grew up on the estate in Pittsburgh's fashionable East End. After her parents took to New York, Miss Frick maintained her heartfelt feelings toward the home and property.

Today, the Frick Art & Historical Center comprises The Frick Art Museum, Clayton (the restored home of Henry Clay Frick), the Carriage Museum, the Greenhouse, the Museum Shop, the Playhouse, and six acres of sprawling lawns and gardens. Free parking is available in the museum lot. The center is open Tuesday through Saturday, from 10 AM until 5 PM, and on Sundays from Noon until 6 PM. Clayton is closed on Mondays. Tours of Clayton cost $8 for adults, $7 for seniors, and $6 for students. Members are admitted free of charge. Architecture aficionados can turn to that chapter for more information about touring Clayton.

Merrick Free Art Gallery
11th St. and Fifth Ave., Pittsburgh
• (724) 846-1130

Edward Dempster Merrick wanted to be an artist when he was coming of age in New Brighton, Beaver County, back in the mid-1860s. But like others with similar goals, he was told to find a real job rather than live the life of a starving artist. So he did that, working as a telegraph operator, a soldier, and a cowboy before retiring at age 53 to pursue collecting things, including artwork. Merrick's international travels and studies abroad helped him

garner over 200 19th-century European and American paintings in addition to zoological, entomological, and geological collections.

Perhaps not as wealthy as Frick and Carnegie, who also donated their names and money to museums, Merrick's gallery nonetheless brings art appreciation to the area, and hosts special events such as the Victorian Christmas Toy Show. Ask about Saturday art classes and summer art camp for kids. Gallery hours vary depending upon the season (Labor Day through Memorial Day and the summer months), so do call ahead. Admission is free and group tours can be arranged.

Wood Street Galleries
601 Wood St., Pittsburgh
• (412) 471-5605

The Wood Street Galleries showcase various artists' work with different exhibitions, sponsored by businesses and local foundations. Illustrations, paintings, and other forms of art are presented. Gallery hours are as follows: Tuesdays and Wednesdays, 11 AM to 6 PM, Thursday to Friday, 11 AM to 7 PM Saturday, 12 to 7 PM. The gallery is closed Sundays, Mondays, and holidays.

The Mattress Factory
500 Sampsonia Way, Pittsburgh
• (412) 231-3169
• www.mattress.org

No, it's not a place to outfit your boudoir! Rather, we're talking about a former mattress factory warehouse turned art gallery. This collection of contemporary art is located in the historic Mexican War Streets of Pittsburgh's North Side. Since 1977, the Mattress Factory has had both permanent and temporary collections of site specific installations. More than 100 artists from around the world have been hosted here.

Manchester Craftsmen's Guild
1815 Metropolitan St., Pittsburgh
• (412) 322-0800

Located in an inner-city neighborhood, this minority-directed arts education and presenting organization features both art and jazz musicians. Bill Strickland founded the Manchester Craftsmen's Guild over 30 years ago to help inner-city youths. Indeed, the Guild's profile

INSIDERS' TIP

Both the *Pittsburgh Post-Gazette* and the *Tribune-Review* newspapers have sections devoted to the arts and entertainment before each weekend. Check out "Weekend Mag" in the Friday *Post-Gazette* and "The Ticket" in Friday's *Tribune-Review*.

has risen since then. When the *CBS Evening News* broadcast from Pittsburgh in 1999, the program aired a feature about Strickland and the Guild. Chick Corea, Maynard Ferguson, and many other jazz greats have performed here. Tickets typically cost anywhere from $22 to $30, and children 18 and younger are admitted for $10 on Thursday evenings. There are discounts for subscribers and Jazz Society members.

Westmoreland Museum of American Art
221 N. Main St., Greensburg
• (724) 837-1500

Built at the crest of a hill in downtown Greensburg, the Westmoreland Museum of American Art was established in 1949 with the support of the Woods-Marchand Foundation. Ten years later, the museum opened to the public with its mission of acquiring and exhibiting American art. Back in the 1950s, American art was affordable, yet not very prestigious. That's changed today, as exhibitions dedicated to Winslow Homer, Robert Henri, Georgia O'Keeffe, and other great American artists have strong supporters.

Here, contemporary artists counterbalance the more historical nature of some collections, and keep the past and present inextricably woven together for all to appreciate. Educational programs offered include art classes, school outreach, docent-guided tours, lectures, demonstrations, and other special events.

One holiday tradition that families look forward to is the Holiday Toy and Train Exhibition. First begun out of whimsy, it's become a serious collection within the museum. Museum hours are Wednesday to Sunday, 11 AM to 5 PM, and Thursday from 11 AM to 9 PM. It's closed Mondays and Tuesdays, as well as most holidays. Admission is free of charge, but there is a $3 suggested donation box.

Hoyt Institute of Fine Arts
124 Leasure Ave., New Castle
• (724) 652-2882

Tucked away from the commercial district of New Castle (Lawrence County) sits the former home of Miss May Emma Hoyt. Today, the mansion is part of Hoyt Institute of Fine Arts, which serves as a local art gallery offering monthly exhibitions upstairs and downstairs. A range of classes from watercolors, stained glass, ceramics, photography, dance, and even writing are offered at the Institute. The Institute is open Tuesday through Saturday, 9 AM to 4 PM but it's closed Sunday and Monday. You'll find free admission, but a self-guided tour of the West Gallery costs $2 per person.

Literary Arts

Three Rivers Lecture Series
Carnegie Music Hall, 4400 Forbes Ave., Pittsburgh • (412) 622-8866

This lecture series is a non-profit project of Pittsburgh Arts and Lectures. Each year, approximately 12 provocative, entertaining, and informative guests speak in Pittsburgh on a variety of topics. Lectures are normally held at Carnegie Music Hall. Names like Senator John Kerry; authors Tom Wolfe, Andrew Tobias, and Jamaica Kincaid; and humorist Garrison Keillor have presented as part of the series. Individual lectures cost at least $13, with partial series or complete series prices available. The entire schedule of speakers for fall and spring costs approximately $150.

International Poetry Forum
4415 Fifth Ave., Webster Hall, Pittsburgh • (412) 621-9893

Founded in 1966 by Samuel Hazo, Pennsylvania's Poet Laureate, this poetry forum continues as a cultural outreach in Pittsburgh and proves that there is a resurgence of poetry here and around the nation. Poets and performers have included Nobel Prize awardees and many Pulitzer Prize winners. Poets-in-Public is a series at the core of the forum's mission. Poets-at-High Noon presents free poetry events for the public. And Poets-in-Person offers educational outreach and poetry workshops as Pennsylvania poets visit juniors and seniors in high schools. Single ticket prices for readings at the Forum are $12 general admission and $8 for students and seniors. Subscription and group rates also available.

INSIDERS' TIP

Various literary prizes are offered to area writers. One of these, the Drue Heinz Literature Prize, is administered by the University of Pittsburgh Press and carries a $10,000 check and promise to publish. Manuscripts are accepted in May and June for short stories or novellas. For a copy of rules, write to the University of Pittsburgh Press, 3347 Forbes Ave., Pittsburgh, PA 15261.

The Pittsburgh Symphony Orchestra performs around the world.

Photo: Courtesy of Pittsburgh Symphony Orchestra

Music

Pittsburgh Symphony Orchestra
Heinz Hall, 600 Penn Ave., Pittsburgh
- **(412) 392-4900**
- **www.pittsburghsymphony.com**

Under the leadership of Music Director Mariss Jansons, the Pittsburgh Symphony Orchestra continues its heritage of presenting the most talented conductors and musicians. The symphony has completed over 20 international tours, making the PSO truly a world-class orchestra. Previous conductors have included Maestro Lorin Maazel and André Previn. At home, the orchestra offers 24 weeks of subscription concerts annually between September and May, and a year-round Pops series under the direction of Marvin Hamlisch. Concerts are staged in the elegant Heinz Hall for the Performing Arts. Free summer concerts are also offered at various parks. Fiddlesticks, the tuxedoed mascot, teaches children lessons in classical music at selected performances (see our Kidstuff chapter for details).

Pittsburgh Opera
801 Penn Ave., Pittsburgh
- **(412) 281-0912**

Under the direction of Tito Capobianco, the Pittsburgh Opera is world renowned. One of the first to offer English translations, it breathes new life into the classics, and takes to the stage at the beautiful Benedum Center in the heart of Pittsburgh's Cultural District. Past performances have included *Tosca, La Traviata*, and *When A Man Loves A Woman*. Tickets range in price from around $20 to $70. Subscribers get a free opera highlights recording, a subscription to *Renaissance* magazine, ticket insurance, and easy exchange privileges.

Civic Light Opera
Benedum Center, 719 Liberty Ave., Pittsburgh • (412) 281-2822
- **www.pittsburghCLO.org**

Subscribers to the Light Opera enjoy a delightful series of summer Broadway musicals each year performed in the Benedum Center. The 2000 summer series included Barry Manilow's *Copacabana, Evita, The Pajama Game, Buddy, Anything Goes,* and *Parade.* In prior years, *Peter Pan, Joseph and the Amazing Technicolor Dreamcoat, GiGi,* and *Camelot* were on the marquee. Many outreach and education programs are available, including the Academy of Musical Theater. Here, students from 5 through 85 can attend evening or Saturday classes with the finest training in dance, music, and drama.

Three-show package prices range from $33 to $108 and a six-show package costs between $66 and $216. Thursday matinees are available, and subscribers can secure guaranteed seats, a newsletter, free exchange privileges, and discounts to selected restaurants.

River City Brass Band
Various locations
- **(412) 322-7222, (800) 292-7222**

While the word "band" conjures up images of John Philip Sousa marches, this one is very different. The River City Brass Band is one of just two professional brass bands in the country and by far the most active. Season subscribers enjoy concerts at various locations throughout Allegheny County and in Greensburg, Westmore-land County. Concerts are held at the Carnegie Music Hall in the Oakland neighborhood of Pittsburgh at high schools in the South Hills, North Hills, and Monroeville, and at the Palace Theatre in Greensburg. Take 5 flex plans and single concert ticket sales are available. Senior Citizens, students, and groups of 10 or more receive discounted rates. Depending upon the location of the concert, tickets cost between $10 and $31.

> ## INSIDERS' TIP
> **You might be surprised to know that several noted musicians hold ordinary day jobs in and around Pittsburgh. Two examples: Jazz guitarist Joe Negri works as a handyman on the famed Mister Rogers' Neighborhood, while rocker Billy Price writes technical material.**

Butler County Symphony Orchestra
259 South Main St., Butler
- **(724) 283-1402**

Having recently celebrated its 50th season, the Butler County Symphony Orchestra is a regional treasure. Under the tutelage of Elizabeth "Betsy" Heath Charles, musical director and conductor, the symphony features talented musicians and invited guests. Concerts take place at the Butler Intermediate High School. Single season tickets cost approximately $40 for adults and $20 for students. Other pricing plans are available for contributors.

*The Andy Warhol Museum on the City's North Side was created
to house much of this Pittsburgh native's collection.*

Photo: Courtesy of Greater Pittsburgh Convention & Visitor's Bureau

Westmoreland Symphony Orchestra
Palace Theatre, Greensburg
• (724) 837-1850

Performing in the beautiful Palace Theatre in Greensburg, the Westmoreland Symphony Orchestra has provided a musical experience for decades. The orchestra is under the direction of Kypros Markou. Choose from an eight-week Saturday night series, five classical Saturday night concerts, four Sunday afternoons, or three pops concerts. Chamber concerts and holiday programs are also presented. Two Young People's Concerts are held during the school day to introduce youth to classical music. The Orchestra also sponsors a 55-member youth symphony. Single tickets range from approximately $7 to $30. Subscription prices vary according to seating.

American Wind Symphony Orchestra
3600 Penn Ave., Pittsburgh (office address)
• (412) 934-8334

Having recently celebrated its 40th anniversary, the American Wind Symphony Orchestra performs on the banks of Pittsburgh's rivers most every year. The first riverside concerts were performed on a makeshift stage on a derelict coal barge. Robert Austin Boudreau came to Pittsburgh in the 1950s with his dream of comprising an orchestra of woodwind, brass, and percussion players (a symphony without strings) that could give young music professionals performing experience each summer. The ensemble soon developed into the American Wind Symphony Orchestra.

Over the years, it's become a familiar site on the waterways, touring many states and even countries aboard Point Counterpoint II, the orchestra's $4 million floating home. Designed as part of the 1976 U.S. Bicentennial celebration, the boat is an amazing creation of the late architect Louis I. Kahn and architect George Djurkovic, who completed the project. The 195-foot vessel's main feature is its 75-foot wide stage with an acoustical shell that rises on hydraulic lifts for performances. Contemporary art is also strategically placed throughout the decks.

Calliope House
279 Fisk St., Pittsburgh
• (412) 687-8800

Founded in 1976, Calliope is a non-profit educational and presenting organization that promotes traditional and contemporary folk music and its allied arts. All Calliope programs are unique to Western Pennsylvania. The Folk Masters Concert Hall Series, featuring the legends of folk music, holds monthly concerts in the acoustically-acclaimed Carnegie Lecture Hall

THE ARTS

Hello Dolly *took the stage with Jo Ann Worley performing with the Civic Light Opera.*

Photo: Courtesy of Civic Light Opera

in the city's Oakland area. Classes taught at the Calliope Folk Music School include guitar, banjo, fiddle, harmonica, bagpipe, songwriting, country line dancing, square dancing, and even belly dancing!

Pittsburgh Chamber Music Society
315 S. Bellefield Ave., Pittsburgh
• (412) 624-4129

This society brings various chamber music groups to Pittsburgh. Performances are held each season in Carnegie Music Hall, with most Monday concerts commencing at 8 PM. One previous season included the Juilliard String Quartet, St. Luke's Chamber Ensemble, Beaux Arts Trio, and several more string quartets. The season runs from late October through late April. Ticket prices vary.

Pittsburgh Youth Symphony Orchestra
Heinz Hall,
600 Penn Ave.,
Pittsburgh
• (412) 392-4872

Comprised of 90 young musicians, ages 11 to 22, the Pittsburgh Youth Symphony Orchestra was selected as one of five youth

orchestras to participate in the National Youth Orchestra Festival. The musicians take direction from Edward Cumming, resident conductor. Since 1962, the youth symphony has enjoyed affiliation with the Pittsburgh Symphony Orchestra. Free concerts available in the fall and in the spring. However, tickets are required for admission.

Theater

Pittsburgh Public Theater
O'Reilly Theater, 621 Penn Ave.,
Pittsburgh • (412) 321-9800
• www.ppt.org

When this theater burst onto the Pittsburgh scene in September 1975, theater had nearly vanished, except for community and college theater companies. But patrons of the arts and benefactors from many Pittsburgh foundations helped to found the public theater in the early 1970s. Formerly housed on the city's North Side in a building more than 100 years old (the original Carnegie Music Hall, in fact), the theater moved into the state-of-the-art O'Reilly Theater in 1999. Recent productions have included *Pirates of Penzance* and *The Cherry Orchard.* In the past, August Wilson and Shakespearean plays have been performed.

More than 100,000 theatergoers attend presentations at the Public every year, and many more are served through educational outreach programs, including student matinees, post-performance discussions, internships, and classes.

Subscriptions range from approximately $105 to $235, with single performance tickets ranging from $15 to $40. Subscribers enjoy a 35 percent discount off single tickets and $5 off additional tickets. They receive guaranteed and discounted parking, and discounts at selected restaurants.

City Theater
57 South 13th St., Pittsburgh
• **(412) 431-4400**

On the city's South Side, the City Theater makes its home in the restored building that was once the Bingham Street United Methodist Church. This is contemporary theater at its best, staging a vast array of productions, from satire to rhythm and blues musicals, even romantic comedies. Call for information about workshops and special events, including a workshop series for seniors featuring improvisational theater performed by other seniors.

The Playhouse of Point Park College
222 Craft Ave., Pittsburgh
• **(412) 621-4445**

Formerly known at the Pittsburgh Playhouse, this stage is home to the Point Park College Theatre Company, Playhouse Theatre Company, Playhouse Dance Theatre, and Playhouse Jr. The four companies feature students from the Department of Fine, Applied, and Performing Arts at Point Park College. The curtain goes up at the Main Stage of Rockwell & Hamlet Street Theatres, and at the Downstairs Theatre. Cost is approximately $40 for a five-show season. Other package prices are also available.

Theater Factory
Third and Cavitt Aves., Trafford
• **(412) 374-9200**

This small theater company delights audiences with a variety of performances for adults and families. Previous series have included the comedy *Greater Tuna.* Dinner theater is available for all performances. Kidsworks performances are aimed at younger theatergoers.

Artistic & Literary Support Groups

Society for Contemporary Craft
2100 Smallman St., Pittsburgh
• **(412) 261-7003**

Founded by Betty Raphael in 1971 as The Store for Arts and Crafts and People-Made Things, this organization—now called The Society for Contemporary Craft—is a nationally recognized non-profit contemporary arts organization. Exhibits, family workshops, and a children's studio are open for hands-on activities during all public hours. Previous workshops have included puppet making, creating jewelry from beads, and glass studio tours. Exhibitions are held throughout the city, including at The Carnegie. About 30,000 people annually visit Contemporary Craft (its shortened name). Purchases from The Store benefit the society as well as the individual artist. Guided tours and activities available for schools. The society is open Tuesday through Friday, 10 AM to 5 PM Saturday, 9 AM to 4:30 PM.

Pittsburgh Center for the Arts School
6300 Fifth Ave., Pittsburgh
• **(412) 361-0455**

With classes in everything from ceramics, drawing, and music, to yoga stretch and meditation, the Pittsburgh Center for the Arts offers instruction in two locations—Shadyside and in the South Hills. Annually, there are 600 different classes, workshops, and camps provided for adults and children in 20 artistic disciplines. Some say this is the largest community-based art school in the country.

The Center for the Arts Galleries showcase exhibitions of emerging and recognized artists. And the Center for the Arts Shops feature original and handcrafted jewelry, ceramics, functional and decorative works, paintings, prints, glassware, and more. Galleries and shops are open Monday to Saturday, 10 AM to 5:30 PM,

INSIDERS' TIP
Writers requiring library assistance and research by phone can use two regional services. Carnegie Library has a Ready Reference Department at (412) 622-3114, and a similar service is also offered by the Greensburg/Hempfield Area Library at (724) 837-8441.

and Sunday, 12 to 5 PM. For gallery and shop information, call (412) 361-0873. (See our Shopping chapter).

Sweetwater Center for the Arts
200 Broad St., Sewickley
• (412) 741-4405

Founded in 1975, this regional center seeks to stimulate broad-based interest in the arts. Artist-instructors have outstanding qualifications for lectures and demonstrations as well as classes for beginners and experienced artists. The center is wheelchair-accessible. The schedule of classes and workshops includes ceramics and sculpture, cuisine, drawing, house and home, mind and body, painting, photo and filmmaking (see the Film section in this chapter), and traditional crafts.

Associated Artists of Butler County
The Art Center, S. Main St., Butler
• (724) 283-6922

Dedicated to promoting the arts, this group encourages participation in the creative process and assists the community in finding ways to incorporate the arts into daily life. As the oldest cultural organization in Butler County, the AABC relies upon volunteers and now resides in it own facility on South Main Street. The more than 350 members host exhibits throughout the year and offer classes, each lasting approximately eight weeks. Lectures, poetry readings, musical performances and children's art classes are also a part of this group's mission.

Pennwriters
Statewide gatherings at various locations

Pennwriters is a rapidly growing, independent network of writers covering many genres. Established in 1988, the group includes members from all over the Commonwealth who share their knowledge and support fellow writers penning mystery, science fiction, fantasy, romance, women's fiction, children's books, poetry, non-fiction books and articles, greeting cards, and other work. The group now boasts more than 400 members.

Held in either Pittsburgh or in the Harrisburg area, a major writer's conference draws attention (and new members) each May. Throughout the year, area groups meet to learn from guest speakers or fellow members, or simply to network over lunch. Pittsburgh is considered to be in Area 3 of the group's six areas. Officers are elected by the more than 400 members. Author advocacy and other services, including a subscription to *The Penn Writer* newsletter, are the perks of becoming a Pennwriter. For membership information, email: potboils@velocity.net. Dues cost approximately $30 upon renewal but sometimes slightly more for first-time members.

Ligonier Valley Writers
Ligonier, Westmoreland County

A non-profit organization dedicated to encouraging and promoting the craft and business of writing, this group meets informally six times a year to hear from speakers and instructors. Topics tackled by the writers group include travel writing, horror fiction, food criticism, plot development, and the complexities of the publishing industry. An annual conference is held mid-way through each summer featuring outstanding faculty members.

The *Loyalhanna Review* provides talented writers with an outlet for their work. Social events, library resource materials, periodic newsletters and other seminars are the perks of membership. Annual dues are approximately $20 for members ($30 for two members at the same address). For information, write in care of Box B, Ligonier, PA 15658.

Pittsburgh Filmmakers
218 Oakland Ave., Pittsburgh
• (412) 681-5449

Pittsburgh Filmmakers is a media arts center devoted to the artistic expression through film, video and photography. It has provided artists with access to necessary equipment since 1971. The organization provides exhibitions of alternative work ranging from off-beat foreign films to radical showings. Classes are available for credit or non-credit learning.

THE ARTS

Parks

The hills, mountains, streams, and woodlands of Western Pennsylvania provide spacious and splendid settings for parks. In the region, you'll find a happy balance between development and greenways. To its credit, local government has long recognized the value of parks for its citizens. In an era when both the public and private sectors actively seek new revenue sources from growth, they've tended to view the region's park lands as natural resources already producing riches aplenty.

Many of the region's parks were founded through private sector and government cooperation. If you trace the history of parks development here, you'll find that quite a few sit on land once privately owned, then bequeathed to the public by industrialists and philanthropists. Knowing the gems that they inherited, governments tended to buy up adjacent tracts to expand their new parks.

The result is a rich variety of parks ranging from the playground apparatus and tennis courts on the corner to the sweep and majesty of the Allegheny National Forest, Western Pennsylvania's largest scenic and recreation area.

In our descriptions, we've sketched the attractions of 24 municipal parks, 16 state parks, and six federal recreation areas. You'll find many more municipal parks that you'll want to get to know. We've tried to capture both the most popular and heavily used parks as well as those with particularly compelling features. For more information on activities offered in the parks, see our Recreation chapter, where you'll find descriptions and opportunities for many sports and activities.

LOOK FOR:
• Municipal Parks
• State Parks
• Federal Recreation Areas

Municipal Parks

Municipalities in Western Pennsylvania know the value of parks. Virtually every municipality in the region maintains green areas for the relaxation and enjoyment of its citizens. The City of Pittsburgh, for example, operates 29 parks offering picnic shelters, to say nothing of smaller parks and parklets. Our descriptions include only the "crown jewels" of the Pittsburgh parks system—Frick, Highland, Riverview, and Schenley. Clearly, you'll find a great deal more to explore than we could capture here.

If you want to reserve a shelter or ballfield in the City of Pittsburgh or Allegheny County, you'll need to be familiar with the permitting process in each case. For shelters, the City of Pittsburgh launches its permitting period with a "Shelter Day," held each spring in the lobby of the City-County Building. That opening day is reserved for City of Pittsburgh residents, who participate in a lottery for permits. Thereafter, you can reserve your shelter by calling (412) 255-2370. Fees, which include a mandatory alcohol permit, range from $43 to $262. The city will hold your reservation for seven days, and your payment must be by money order or business check only.

For City of Pittsburgh ballfields, organizations currently using fields are entitled to automatic renewals. For the fields that remain, the city permits time slots of 1 hour and 45 minutes. Fees range from $150 to $300. Call (412) 255-2370 for your ballfield permits.

Allegheny County's procedures are significantly different than the City of Pittsburgh's. You can reserve shelters, groves and buildings up to one year in advance—a good idea if you're eyeing one of the large facilities at North Park or South Park. You can make your reservations at the parks (except for Hartwood Acres) or by calling the county at (412) 350-2474. Fees range from $20 to $275. Checks, cash, and money oredrs generally are accepted at all the parks, while North and South Parks accept credit cards. For ballfields at North Park, South Park, and Boyce Park, again, call the county at (412) 350-2474; you can reserve fields at other parks at the parks themselves. You must pay your fee in person—$20 for a three-hour slot—within 48 hours.

North

Belmont Complex
415 Butler Rd., Kittanning
• (724) 548-1067

It would be hard to find a municipal park that offers more comprehensive ice skating facilities than you'll find at Belmont Complex. Operated by the Armstrong County Recreation Authority, the complex feautures ice skating and hockey programs August through April. The budding hockey stars in your family will enjoy skating instruction and youth leagues, while adult teams can compete in the league operated by the complex. If you don't belong to a league, complex officials will find one for you.

The complex also hosts skating shows and high school hockey matches. Perhaps best of all, you can rent the ice complex for your personal or group use. With ice time as precious as it is in the region, that's a rare attraction, indeed.

Skating and hockey are far from the only activities at Belmont Complex. The swimming pool is available on a daily admission basis and to members who pay an annual fee; members are welcome to host their guests. You'll also enjoy various special events. This is a fun place.

Deer Lakes Park
RD#3, Tarentum
• (724) 265-3520

Fishing is the primary theme at Deer Lakes Park, a facility administered by Allegheny County. Over the years, the county augmented the park's existing lake with two additional lakes; all are interconnected and use the same watershed. The state stocks the lake with bluegill, crappie, perch, sunfish, and trout, and bass and catfish also bite. The park's picnic areas all bear the names of fish. Nine picnic shelters and nine groves may be reserved through Allegheny County.

Harrison Hills Park
RD#1, Natrona Heights
• (724) 295-3570

This 500-acre park in the extreme northeastern corner of Allegheny County offers some of the most enticing vistas of any municipal park in the region. From the Watts Memorial Overlook, you'll view a vast expense of the Allegheny River, and your view will take in parts of three neighboring counties—Armstrong, Butler, and Westmoreland. You'll find groves and shelters for relaxation as you enjoy the view, and walking trails and soccer fields if you're in the mood for something less sedentary.

Hartwood Acres
200 Hartwood Acres, Pittsburgh
• (412) 767-9200

The centerpieces of Hartwood Acres are the mansion and riding stables that once were the property of the estate's former owner, Mary Flinn Lawrence, who sold the estate to Allegheny County in 1969. The county has maintained the stables and riding trails and offers tours of the mansion.

Among municipal parks in the region, Hartwood Acres may be unequaled for its beauty, whether lush and green in the summer or a snow-covered picture postcard in the winter. For all that, the principal current attractions are cultural, as Hartwood Acres hosts theater, dance, symphony, and other musical programs in warm weather months. Local restaurants sometimes provide box dinners to patrons of Hartwood performances. Dinner on the lush lawn followed by an evening of theater in the park: Now that's entertainment!

INSIDERS' TIP

Not all municipalities print and distribute brochures about their parks. For the most useful printed information, try: Westmoreland County Bureau of Parks and Recreation, (724) 830-3950 or (724) 830-3951; Washington County Department of Parks and Recreation, (724) 228-6867; and Armstrong County Recreation Authority, (724) 548-1067.

PARKS

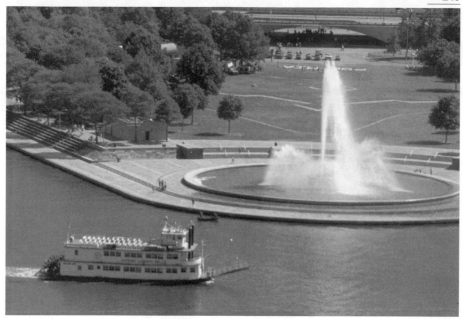

Ships of the Gateway Clipper Fleet set sail at Station Square and sail past the fountain at Point State Park.

Photo: Courtesy of Gateway Clipper Fleet

North Park
Pearce Mill Rd., Allison Park
• **(724) 935-1971**

North Park and South Park are the reigning monarchs of the Allegheny County park system. Visit this sprawling 3,010-acre park and you'll agree that it deserves its crown. Its 75-acre lake is considered the largest man-made body of water in the county; it's bordered by 4½ miles of natural woodlands. If you're a jogger, you won't earn your spurs until you jog around the lake, a popular pastime for many. Anglers utilize the well-stocked lake; even if you don't fish, you can enjoy the lake by renting a boat from the park's concessionaire.

Bicyclists also circumnavigate the lake—the park provides bicycles for rent. The swimming pool may be the largest you'll ever see. Don't count on lap swimming here, though. There are too many swimmers enjoying the pool to allow for that. North Park's 18-hole golf course is exceptionally popular—you'll find a more detailed description in our Golf chapter.

Other amenities include tennis courts, ballfields, a skating rink, and numerous groves and shelters of varying sizes and amenities. The ballfields and groves attract heavy use. If you're planning an outing, it's mandatory that you reserve your grove or picnic area, and we sug-gest that you do so well in advance. You can expect to pay anywhere from $20 to $60 to reserve the space.

Riverview Park
Riverview Ave., Pittsburgh
• **(412) 323-7209**

When the North Side of Pittsburgh was a separate municipality known as Allegheny, local residents raised money to purchase land for a park, which they donated to the community. That land became Riverview Park, a 251-acre facility now operated by the City of Pittsburgh. The park offers many attractive features, including 12 hiking trails that will carry you so deeply into thick woods that you'll swear you've left the city for virgin forest.

You'll enjoy bridle trails—rare enough within the city—as well as a swimming pool, three tennis courts, horseshoe pits, a ballfield, and five playgrounds. Picnickers can utilize six shelters—you'll need permits and reservations for three of those.

The Allegheny Observatory stands near the park's main entrance. Used primarily as a research facility by the University of Pittsburgh, the observatory also hosts credit and informal courses and meetings of the region's amateur astronomers.

East

Boyce Park
675 Frankstown Rd., Plum
• (412) 271-2717

If you're looking for downhill skiing in Allegheny County, Boyce Park is the place. In fact, it's the only place. This park at the extreme eastern edge of Allegheny County offers both lifts and a large ski lodge called Four Seasons. For more on Boyce Park's skiing, see our Recreation Chapter.

Skiing is one of many attractions here, as the county-run park also features a popular wave pool and a large recreational complex. The 1,096-acre park offers tennis courts and picnic groves and shelters all named with a Boy Scouts motif. That's to honor William D. Boyce, the founder of the Boy Scouts, who was born nearby.

Cedar Creek Park
RD#4, Belle Vernon
• (724) 929-4352

The scenic Youghiogheny River provides the northern border for Cedar Creek . . . as well as a host of recreational activities. The Yough offers fishing and canoeing, with river access through a boat launch. You'll also enjoy hiking and bicycling along the Yough River Trail, a work in progress that features about 20 completed miles. The 10-foot-wide trail is finished with crushed limestone, making it wheelchair accessible.

The park also features 19 pavilions available for rental, bicycle and cross-country ski rentals, ballfields, basketball and volleyball courts, horseshoe pits, and sledding and tobogganing areas. You may hunt in certain areas of the park.

You'll take particular pleasure in several special features of the park. Cedar Creek has cut a deep gorge in the northern section of the park—water cascades down shale steps amid steep forested slopes. The park's amphitheater accommodates up to 2,500 visitors for its free summer concert series. Finally, the Mon-Yough Model Airplane Club operates from Cedar Creek Park, so you can expect to see some low-flying craft.

Frick Park
2005 Beechwood Blvd., Pittsburgh
• (412) 422-6538

If there were no Frick Park, someone would have to invent one. Operated by the City of Pittsburgh, this huge urban park touches five city neighborhoods—Squirrel Hill, Point Breeze, Park Place, Regent Square, and Swisshelm Park—and reaches into the adjacent municipality of Swissvale. At 476 acres, it's large enough to host many simultaneous activities without seeming overly crowded, even when dog lovers and their pooches congregate each weekend morning for socializing and play. Frick's walking and jogging trails wind along the park's hills, giving you a workout that few other municipal parks can.

For recreation, Frick Park offers six clay tennis courts, a basketball court, two playgrounds, three ballfields, and a lawn bowling green. For more on lawn bowling in Frick Park, see our Recreation chapter.

The park was bequeathed to the city by industrialist and philanthropist Henry Clay Frick. In accordance with the bequest, 150 acres of the park have been designated Frick Woods Nature Reserve. The Frick Environmental Center manages the reserve and houses Citipark's Environmental Education Program.

Within the reserve, you'll find a meadow, woodlands, and gardens that host a treasure trove of native plant life and are one of the region's most popular birding areas, as home and migratory "stopover" to more than 150 different species. For more on birding at Frick Park, see our Recreation chapter.

> ## INSIDERS' TIP
>
> Each May, the City of Pittsburgh Department of Parks (Citiparks) publishes a "summer magazine," a comprehensive guide to its recreational facilities, including 31 outdoor pools, 29 picnic shelters, 25 recreation centers, and a variety of special programs. To get your free copy, contact Citiparks at (412) 255-2539.

Highland Park
Highland Ave. & Bunkerhill St., Pittsburgh
• (412) 665-3632

For a true Pittsburgh scene, drop by the reservoir at Highland Park any morning at dawn or shortly thereafter. You'll see a parade of walkers and joggers getting in their laps around the reservoir, part of the daily regime for many residents of Pittsburgh's East End. Don't be surprised if you're inspired to join them. Operated by the City of Pittsburgh, the 403-acre park offers eight shelters—all of which you must get a permit to use—woodland trails, a large swim-

PARKS

ming pool, and a companion wading pool. You'll find nine tennis courts, a softball field, and 10 areas with play apparatus. Lake Carnegie is popular with anglers; it's a good place for an afternoon of laid-back fishing, but don't expect to walk away with that trout you've been wanting to mount on your wall. The reservoir notwithstanding, the most popular attraction of the park is the Pittsburgh Zoo & Aquarium, which we'll detail for you in our Kidstuff chapter.

Mammoth Park
RD#1, Mt. Pleasant
• (724) 830-3950

As you drive through eastern Westmoreland County, you'll come across a lake that's mammoth, ergo the name, Mammoth Park. Mammoth Lake spans 27 acres, and it's stocked with trout by the Pennsylvania Fish Commission. When frozen, the lake provides both ice fishing and ice skating. The park offers handicapped-accessible fishing decks.

Another popular water-based activity is the giant water slide, which descends 96 feet from a hillside into the lake. Sounds like a "must-do" for the kids.

When you're dried off and ready for land-based activities, you'll find numerous pavilions available for rental as well as ballfields, play apparatus, sledding and tobogganing areas, and courts for volleyball, boccie ball, shuffleboard, basketball, street hockey, and tennis. You can take it all in from the Mammoth Park observation deck, which provides a panoramic view ranging for almost 10 miles.

Both the Laurel Highlands Radio-Controlled Airplane Club and a BMX club base their operations at the park.

Mt. Odin Park
Tollgate Hill Rd., Greensburg
• (724) 834-2640

Operated by the City of Greensburg, Mt. Odin Park features several picnic pavilions, tennis courts, and a golf course—for more about that amenity, see our Golf chapter. The most compelling attraction of the park, however, is its play area, where you'll find replicas of downtown Greensburg buildings, including city hall, the Westmoreland County Courthouse, and West-

moreland Hospital. The replicas have an open design, so kids can walk through and play inside them. Sounds like an intriguing way to familiarize your youngsters with life in the city.

Northmoreland Park
Rt. 356, Allegheny Township
• (724) 727-7616

Once you get used to the idea of traveling east to Northmoreland in Westmoreland County (We're dizzy just writing it), you'll find a lovely facility developed around the 17-acre Northmoreland Lake. The lake features a winter and spring trout fishery, as well as quality bass and pan fishing. Since the lake is designated a Conservation Lake, special Fish Commission rules apply. Northmoreland provides a wheelchair-accessible fishing deck.

The Boathouse Building offers boat rental and and picnic facilities. You'll find 11 pavilions available for rental, as well as ballfields, play apparatus, cross-country ski trails, and courts for boccie ball and volleyball. Also available for rental is the Activities Building, which features a small kitchen and an air-conditioned reception/meeting room. You may hunt in some areas of the park. The park sports a model radio-controlled airfield and a BMX track, as well as opportunities for horseback riding and equestrian lessons, using either your own horse or one of the park's.

Renziehausen Park
Eden Park Blvd., McKeesport
• (412) 675-5068

This urban park operated by the City of McKeesport offers both recreational and cultural delights. For recreation you can enjoy the park's ballfield, splash pool for kids, seven shelters and a pavilion available for rental, and fishing in Lake Emily, which hosts an annual fishing derby.

For culture and entertainment, visit the International Village, which since 1960 has been hosting a three-day celebration of the region's ethnic heritage, complete with music, dancing, and food. You'll also enjoy The Little Red Schoolhouse, a replication of the city's first schoolhouse, erected in 1832, and entertainment at the park's band shell. Make sure you save time to tour the Rose

PARKS

INSIDERS' TIP

The Commonwealth of Pennsylvania invites you to hunt in many areas of its public parks . . . except for woodchucks, also known as groundhogs, which are protected on most park lands. Sounds like Punxsutawney Phil (of Groundhog Day fame) has been an effective lobbyist.

Garden maintained by the Garden Club of McKeesport. It features 1,500 rose bushes as well as perennials and beds of grasses and herbs. In addition, the club uses the garden as a test bed to introduce new roses to the region. You'll find it difficult to tear yourself away from this beautiful spot.

Schenley Park
Schenley Dr., Pittsburgh
• (412) 622-6904 255-2370

Schenley Park, in the Oakland neighborhood bordering the campuses of both the University of Pittsburgh and Carnegie Mellon University, is one of the crown jewels of the City of Pittsburgh park system. You'll enjoy activities that are marvelously diverse. You'll find a swimming pool, six playground areas, walking and jogging trails, 13 tennis courts and three ballfields. With permits and reservations, picnickers can utilize all five shelters—and you can rent the park's meeting room, a popular site for receptions.

The park's ice rink is one of the region's most popular venues for ice skating—for more information on this activity, see our Recreation chapter. Schenley hosts a number of popular annual events, including the Vintage Grand Prix, the Smoky City Folk Festival, and the Great Ride bicycle race. For more on the Great Ride, see our Recreation chapter. You can lounge on the lawn at Flagstaff Hill—a popular pastime of CMU students—where the city stages its Cinema in the Parks program each summer, or take in the flower shows at Phipps Conservatory and Botanical Gardens.

Schenley Park is rich in history as well as amenities. Much of the park was donated by philanthropist Mary Schenley, and the park's "Oval" for decades was home to harness racing and horse stables. A horrific fire in the early 1970s destroyed the stables and ended the park's equine involvement.

The park also offers a popular 9-hole golf course—the only golf course within City of Pittsburgh limits—and a flying disc golf course that hosts organized competition. For more on these activities, see our Golf and Recreation chapters.

Twin Lakes Park
Twin Lakes Rd., Luxor
• (724) 837-8611

The park takes its name from its twin lakes that provide boating, fishing, ice fishing, and ice skating opportunities. At the Lower Lake's Boating & Concession Building, you can load up on fishing and picnic supplies and rent pedal boats, rowboats, and canoes. The park features three wheelchair-accessible fishing decks.

A broad network of recreational trails is a major attraction at this Westmoreland County-operated facility. You'll find trails for walking, cross-country skiing, and jogging—joggers also can test the exercise stations staged along the trails. If you enjoy the Wilderness Trail, you'll also enjoy the park's environmental and nature center, which provides interpretive programs for schools, groups, and any interested visitors.

For outings, you can rent any of the seven pavilions or the Activities Building, which features a kitchen and a reception hall/meeting room. Twin Lakes also offers play apparatus as well as hunting in designated areas.

South

Cross Creek Park
Rt. 50, Rea
• (724) 228-6867

Operated by Washington County, Cross Creek Park offers hunting and fishing and boating on the 260-acre lake. Bring your own boat and boating permit. (Annual permits are available from the county.) Picnic sites are available free of charge, but shelters must be rented. All shelters feature grills and electrical outlets. You'll enjoy the park's hiking trails.

Mingo Creek Park
Rt. 136, Nottingham
• (724) 228-6867

Mingo Creek Park features a number of activities with an equine theme. You'll find bridle trails for horseback riding—you're responsible for bringing the horse and purchasing an annual permit—and hourly hayrides from 10 AM through 2 PM on weekdays and on weekends in October. Cost for a hayride is $50 per hour for a maximum 25 people.

The park offers 10 shelters of varying sizes, which must be reserved in season, as well as picnic sites available free of charge. Organized groups may camp in the park, and nature walks are available for all. Mingo Creek Park is operated by Washington County.

Round Hill Park and Farm
651 Round Hill Rd., Elizabeth
• (412) 384-8555

This is a park with an agrarian theme. In fact, the 1,101-acre park is built around a modern working farm that's a popular destination

Flowers blossom all year long at Phipps Conservatory in Schenley Park.

Photo: Courtesy of Greater Pittsburgh Convention & Visitor's Bureau

for student groups. The park offers interpretive sessions to thousands of students and other visitors each year. Other attractions of Round Hill, which is located in the southeastern corner of Allegheny County and administered by the county, include a soccer field and picnic groves and shelters.

South Park
Buffalo Dr., Library
• **(412) 835-5710**

At about 2,000 acres, South Park is one of the most capacious and diverse of the region's municipal parks, and if offers just about every recreational activity you would hope to find in a municipal facility. Its wave pool attracts about 100,000 people per season, and its two golf courses totaling 27 holes are exceptionally popular. For more on golf at South Park, see our Golf chapter.

You'll find picnic tables and shelters as well as walking, jogging, and hiking trails. The trails wind through areas that feature both woodlands and open glades. For all that, many joggers eschew the trails for a run along Corrigan Drive, the park's main thoroughfare that was named after the famous "Wrong Way Corrigan." Other amenities include tennis courts, ballfields, horseshoe pits, a deck hockey facility, and a skating rink.

You'll get an eyeful of history at the park as well. Allegheny County, which operates the park, has preserved the homestead of Oliver Miller; it was near that estate that the first shots of the 1794 Whiskey Rebellion were fired. The bathhouse near the wave pool was patterned after the Miller house. You'll also find on Corrigan Drive a memorial to poet Joyce Kilmer, who penned the famous poem "Trees" . . . an appropriate tribute in this lush park.

Ten Mile Creek County Park
Clarksville Rd., Fredericktown
• **(724) 228-6867**

As you might guess, the main attraction in 25-acre, Ten Mile Creek County Park is the creek, where boating is a popular activity. Bring your own boat and annual permit issued by Washington County, which operates this park. You may also fish from the shore of the creek. Shelters with grills and electrical outlets are available for rental. Picnic sites are offered on a first-come, first-served basis.

White Oak Park
3 Muse Lane, White Oak
• **(412) 678-3774**

Operated by Allegheny County, White Oak Park is a botanist's delight, featuring a broad variety of plants and trees, some of them found nowhere else in Pennsylvania. You'll get plenty of exercise if you explore the fauna, as some of White Oak's terrain is quite steep. You can unwind in the park's rental picnic groves and shelters when you've finished exploring the 810 acres.

West

Brady's Run Park
469 Constitution Blvd., Falston
• (724) 847-1312

Brady's Run Park is named for Capt. Samuel Brady, an early pioneer and merciless killer of Native Americans, whose ferocity was fueled by the death of his father and brother in Indian wars of the 1770s. In one of the most interesting examples of early American jurisprudence, Brady was charged with killing Native Americans—and acquitted largely on the strength of testimony of Chief Guyasuta, whose tribe had been relentlessly hunted by Brady.

While the park pays homage to Brady, it is a gentle and peaceful facility operated by Beaver County. It features the Beaver County Ice Arena and the Calland Arboretum, a natural area with walking trails. You'll also enjoy Brady's Run Lodge, a popular site for weddings and other special events; a indoor facility for tennis and walking, with an observation deck; an arena for horse shows; and horseshoe courts that have hosted state championship events.

Settler's Cabin Park
1225 Greer Rd., Oakdale
• (412) 787-2750

Settler's Cabin spans 1,589 acres, unusually large for a municipal park, and it has more of a rugged feel than most municipal parks. Named for an 18th century log cabin that was found on the site, the park's attractive meadows in many cases have been left largely untouched. Allegheny County, which operates the park, has preserved the log cabin for visitors. If you're looking for a getaway only a few minutes from downtown Pittsburgh and Pittsburgh International Airport, you can feel like a settler at Settler's Cabin. It will be easy to feel as if you're exploring a brave new frontier: The park extends to Collier and Robinson Townships, and even into northern Fayette county.

You'll find plenty of amenities, including reasonably priced rental shelters and groves named for Native American tribes. The wave pool and diving platform are extremely popular, as are the park's tennis courts.

State Parks

When the Commonwealth of Pennsylvania established its Department of Environmental Resources in 1971 under Secretary Maurice K. Goddard, it was with the avowed purpose of situating at least one public park within a 25-mile drive of each resident of the state. It might take a surveyor to determine if the state achieved exactly the goal, but one thing the Commonwealth did accomplish was development of a public park system rich in recreational opportunities and environmental wonders.

The state operates 116 parks with a varied and compelling recreational menu. At most, natural or man-made waterways offer fishing, boating, and swimming. Hunting is permitted in most areas of the parks, and you'll find miles of scenic hiking trails, campsites, and picnic areas. Winter brings ice skating, ice fishing, ice boating, sled riding, cross-country skiing, and snowmobiling. Not all activities are offered everywhere, but most parks are diverse enough to satisfy your outdoors needs.

State parks are open year-round, typically from 8 AM until sunset, although some activities are seasonal. Some activities require fees, reservations, or rentals. You may bring your pets to day-use areas, provided you keep them on leashes. The state imposes a number of restrictions on certain activities and uses, including limitations on the horsepower of motorized boats and the length of your stay at certain cabins and campsites. For instance, to boat, in most cases, you'll also need at least one of the following: 1) a State Park launching permit, available at most State Park offices; 2) a State Park mooring permit; 3) a current certificate and number of watercraft registration; 4) current registration for your motorized (electric) boats; or, for your boat registered in another state, 5) a Pennsylvania State Park launch permit and the boat's current registration.

If you call the Bureau of State Parks at (888) PA-PARKS, they'll be happy to provide you with a useful brochure and map of all 116 parks, indicating the activities that each park offers as well as introducing you to park rules and regulations. They'll also send you more detailed brochures on individual parks—they will charge a nominal fee if you ask for more than a few brochures.

We've profiled 16 state parks. To do so, we've had to step out of our six-county coverage area on occasion. We think you'll find the trip worth taking.

Downtown

Point State Park
Commonwealth Pl., Pittsburgh
• **(412) 471-0235**

A state park in downtown Pittsburgh? It's not a misprint, as the Commonwealth maintains this 36-acre downtown oasis right at The Point, where the Allegheny and Monongahela rivers meet to form the Ohio River. The park is steeped in historical significance. It was the sight of the original Fort Pitt, where the British routed the French and founded the city. You can see a portion of the old fort at the park's Fort Pitt Blockhouse museum. The park was created just after World War II as part of the city's Renaissance, yet another historical note.

The park hosts the Three Rivers Arts Festival and a variety of concerts and serves as the finishing point for the Pittsburgh Marathon. The emphasis here, however, is not on doing but on relaxing and, dare we say it, contemplating. With benches that provide views of river traffic and the giant fountain, you can slip away from the day's challenges for a few moments of peace and quiet. This is a rare and welcome city amenity.

North

Clear Creek State Park
RR1, Sigel
• **(814) 752-2368**

Set in Jefferson County just north of our six-county coverage area, 1,676-acre Clear Creek State Park is popular for its own attractions as well as its proximity to Clear Creek State Forest, Cook Forest State Park, and the Allegheny National Forest. If you want to stay long enough to hit all those highlights, you can use this park's family campground, with 53 tent and trailer sites, or opt for cozier accommodations in one of the parks two yurts or 22 rustic family cabins.

Anglers will find stocked and native brook trout in Clear Creek, and northern pike, smallmouth bass, walleye, trout, and pan fish in the nearby Clarion River. Hunters can stalk whitetail deer, bear, squirrel, and wild turkey on 677 acres. The park offers 15 miles of hiking trails, a 390-foot guarded swimming beach, more than 300 picnic tables, and five pavilions available for rental.

For a special treat while you're here, try canoeing on the Clarion River, one of the region's most scenic and pristine waterways. Canoe rental is available from private concessionaires just outside the park.

Cook Forest State Park
P.O. Box 120, Cooksburg 16217
• **(814) 744-8407**

Cook Forest State Park spans 6,668 acres in three counties—Clarion, Forest, and Jefferson. It's north of our coverage area but such a recreational and historical gem that you'll want to visit this park. It's named for John Cook, an early settler whose descendants are buried in a private cemetery adjoining the park. In the 1930s, the park was the site of a Civilian Conservation Corps (CCC) camp; CCC workers helped construct the park's cabins, roads, and trails.

The trails remain an attraction. These include 27 miles of hiking trails, featuring a portion of the 140-mile Baker Trail, which stretches from Freeport in Armstrong County to the Allegheny National Forest. The trails wind through magnificent stands of virgin white pine and hemlock timber stands, which have earned the park the nickname "the Black Forest of Pennsylvania." The trail network includes 4.5 miles of bridle trails and 20 miles of snowmobile trails.

Anglers enjoy the scenic Clarion River, which flows along the park's border and yields trout, warm water game fish, and pan fish, while hunters utilize more than 4,000 acres in search of deer, squirrel, and turkey. You're welcome to canoe on the Clarion, but you'll have to go outside the park for canoe rentals. Cook Forest offers a swimming pool and such winter activities as ice skating, sledding, and cross-country skiing, with ski rentals available.

Picnickers will find tables and two pavilions available for rental. The park offers two organized group tenting areas as well as 24 rustic cabins for rental. Don't miss the Sawmill Craft Center and Theater for plays, musical performances, and displays of crafts by local artisans.

Jennings Environmental Education Center
RR1, Slippery Rock
• **(724) 794-6011**

You can't swim, snowmobile, hunt, or fish here, as Jennings isn't that kind of park. You can, however, learn about ecological and environmental issues . . . then traverse the 300-acre facility and get a hands-on feel for those issues. Jennings just happens to encompass one of the only prairies left in the Pennsylvania area.

The center strives to protect natural ecosystems and provide public education in ecological

PARKS

responsibility. It does so through displays, exhibits, and the natural wonders of the park. These include the blazing star, a prairie plant that sports a cluster of rose-purple flowers at their most colorful in August, and 220 acres of woodland trails that display nearly 400 species of plants and 134 species of birds. Stay on those trails, please, or you may encounter the massasauga rattlesnake. This guy is endangered and not keen on being disturbed.

Kids, this is one place you'll want to take your parents.

Maurice K. Goddard State Park
684 Lake Wilhelm Rd., Sandy Lake
• (724) 253-4833

The park is named for Dr. Maurice K. Goddard, father of Pennsylvania's environmental movement, who served as the founding secretary of the state's Department of Environmental Resources in 1971. Lake Wilhelm dominates the park, spanning more than 60 percent of the facility's 2,856 acres. As you might expect, water-based activities are popular here.

The park features a 200-slip marina and a 48-space dry land seasonal mooring area; the marina provides parking space for 371 cars and trailers. Other amenities include boat rentals and seven launching areas. Nonpowered boats and those up to 10 horsepower are permitted. Anglers enjoy the lake as well, pursuing largemouth and smallmouth bass, walleyes, northern pike, muskellunge, bluegill, crappie, catfish, perch, and sunfish.

More than 1,155 acres are available for hunting—deer and waterfowl are abundant. You'll find 14 miles of hiking trails, 6 miles of mountain bike trails, and 150 picnic tables in the park. Winter activities include ice skating, ice fishing, ice boating, cross-country skiing, and snowmobiling. The park is just north of our principal coverage area.

McConnell's Mill State Park
RR2, Portersville
• (724) 368-8091

The centerpieces of McConnell's Mill are the deep gorge of Slippery Rock Creek formed by glacial activity more than 100,000 years ago and a man-made attraction, the restored rolling grist mill from which the park derives its name. The gorge creates some of the region's best—and

most challenging—opportunities for modern-day hikers, climbers, and whitewater boaters.

Hikers will enjoy 11 miles of rugged trails that provide unparalleled views of the creek. Whitewater boaters can take to the creek in rubber rafts, whitewater canoes, and kayaks, none of which can be rented at the park. Climbing and rappelling are available at the Rim Road Climbing Area and Breakneck Bridge. Warning: They don't call it Breakneck for nothing. You may hunt in designated areas—you'll likely encounter grouse, deer, turkey, rabbit, and squirrel.

Anglers will find trout and bass in the creek as well as a "Delayed Harvest—Fly Fishing Only" area. You won't have camping or swimming opportunities at McConnell's Mill, but you can enjoy more than 150 picnic tables and a ballfield.

Moraine State Park
225 Pleasant Valley Rd., Portersville
• (724) 368-8811

When you take in the majesty of Moraine, you may not believe that this treasured public resource was pocked by the scars of coal mining and oil well drilling as late as the 1950s. The Commonwealth of Pennsylvania undertook the reclamation of strip mined land, plugged 422 gas and oil wells, and created the 3,225-acre Lake Arthur, a restoration of the glacial lake that covered most of Northwestern Pennsylvania more than 10,000 years ago. The result: one of the state's most beautiful and useful parks.

Much of the activity at Moraine centers on Lake Arthur. The lake features 10 boat launching areas—motorized boats up to 10 horsepower are permitted—and you can rent canoes, rowboats, paddleboats, motorized fishing boats, and pontoon boats. Sailing is especially popular on the lake, with sailboats available for rental. The colorful sails form an appealing vista that you can view from picnic areas high above the lake. The Barber Point area of the lake is even suitable for wind surfing. Anglers pursue muskellunge, northern pike, tiger muskellunge, striper, largemouth bass, walleyes, channel catfish, black crappie, and bluegill. For swimmers, the park offers two, large guarded beaches.

You'll find plenty to do away from the lake. A 14-mile portion of the North Country National Scenic Trail courses through the park. A 7-mile paved bicycle trail parallels the north shore of the lake, and you'll also find a 6-mile mountain bike trail that is targeted to experienced off-road bikers. Numerous other trails also offer opportunities for adventure. Approximately 13,600 of Moraine's acres are open season for hunters. Picnickers will discover more than 1,200 picnic tables as well as seven pavilions available for rental.

In the winter, Lake Arthur offers ice skating, ice boating and ice fishing, and you also may enjoy sledding, tobogganing, cross-country skiing, and snowmobiling. For overnight stays, the park provides 11 modern cabins and two organized youth group camping areas. You won't find family campsites, but the area surrounding the park offers plenty of privately operated campsites.

Oh, and just in case you're wondering, "moraine" refers to the soil, rocks, and debris that accumulate at the edges of and underneath a glacier. Now aren't you glad half of Pennsylvania was once covered in ice?

Oil Creek State Park
RR1, Oil City
• (814) 676-5915

It was along Oil Creek that Col. Edwin Drake struck oil in 1859, helping to launch the petroleum industry. Part of the mission of Oil Creek State Park is to preserve and perpetuate the heritage of the oil boomtowns that grew up around Drake Well. The park features displays and historical programs at the Petroleum Centre, once a focal point of the petroleum boom and now the park's visitor center.

Hiking is an important activity in the 7,075-acre park. It provides more than 52 miles of hiking trails that double as biking and cross-country ski trails, and there's also one trail exclusively for bikes—and the occasional park maintenance vehicle. You can rent bikes at the Petroleum Centre. One of the neatest aspects of the park's trail system is its two overnight hike-in shelter areas. Each area offers six Adirondack-type shelters with fireplaces, restrooms, and water. You must reserve these shelters in advance. Warning: if you're along the trails and see railroad tracks, stay off the tracks. The railroad is active.

Anglers flock to Oil Creek, which is known for its bass and trout. If you prefer to be on the water, bring your canoe. Oil Creek is classified as a beginner's stream. You'll find a paved portage path around the creek's ice control dam. Approximately 6,250 acres of the park is open to hunting, with rabbit, deer, squirrel, turkey, and ruffed grouse the most common prey. You'll find picnic areas and shelters, although not nearly as many as other state parks offer. Oil Creek State Park is north of our six-county coverage area.

Pymatuning State Park
P.O. Box 425, Jamestown, PA 16134-0425
• (724) 932-3141

Pymatuning is somewhat north of our principal coverage area, but if you're an outdoors type, you won't mind the extra drive. An act of the Pennsylvania Legislature decrees that the principal purposes of Pymatuning Lake and dam are for controlling floods and the flow of water in the Beaver and Shenango Rivers. The recreational opportunities that follow in the wake of those objectives are awesome.

The lake, spanning Pennsylvania and Ohio, is one of the region's most productive for anglers, yielding walleye, muskellunge, carp, crappie, and largemouth and smallmouth bass, among many species. In one of those jurisdictional quirks that will drive you crazy, if you're a licensed angler in Pennsylvania, you can't fish from the Ohio shore. Similarly, Pennsylvania bans Ohio licensees on its side of the water. On the water itself, however, licensees from both states are welcome. The lake is a popular site for ice fishing in the winter.

Hunting is available in much of the park, including a Goose Management Area where controlled shooting is permitted during the annual waterfowl season. The park features a large protected area for migratory waterfowl. Swimmers will find four guarded beaches. Nonpowered boats and those up to 10 horsepower are permitted on the lake, and you can rent floatboats, rowboats, canoes, and motors, or try ice boating in the winter.

Pymatuning offers a variety of overnight facilities, including 657 family camping sites; an organized group camping area that can accommodate up to 400 people; 194 modern tent and trailer campsites; and modern family cabins. You'll enjoy many picnic tables and 11 pavilions available for rental. Make sure you check out the Linesville spillway, where you may feed the fish and ducks.

Unofficially, this park boasts the most mispronounced name in the region. Try it this way: pie-muh-TOO-ning.

East

Keystone State Park
RD#2, Derry
• (724) 668-2566

If your family has a diversity of outdoor

interests, you'll find that Keystone State Park has facilities to match those interests, all within easy driving distance of Pittsburgh. The recreational theme of this 1,182-acre park is variety. Keystone Lake offers up trout and variety of other fish for anglers and a venue for non-powered and electric-powered boats. You can rent rowboats, sailboats, and canoes. In winter, the lake provides ice fishing and ice skating, while you can sled and snowmobile elsewhere in the park. Swimmers will enjoy a 1,000-foot turf and sand beach.

Hunters can pursue whitetail deer, pheasant, and grouse. Campers will find 100 tent and trailer sites for family camping as well as 11 modern cabins available for rental. Keystone State Park offers 443 picnic tables, several shelters, a ballfield, and hiking and biking trails.

Laurel Hill State Park
1454 Laurel Hill Park Rd., Somerset
• (814) 445-7725

In 1794 during the Whiskey Rebellion, George Washington's troops camped on the site of what is now Laurel Hill State Park. You won't feel the need to rebel here, except perhaps against drudgery. There is much to do and enjoy at Laurel Hill.

The 3,935-acre park offers 12 splendid miles for hiking, including the Hemlock Trail, which features a stand of virgin timber. You'll find four picnic areas with a total of 564 tables, playground equipment, and horseshoe pits. Hunting is permitted in 2,100 acres, and you'll enjoy 70 miles of snowmobile trails in Laurel Hill and the adjacent Forbes State Forest.

Laurel Hill Lake provides many water-based activities, including swimming along a 1,200-foot sandy beach and renting paddleboats, canoes, and rowboats. Both non-powered boats and electric-powered boats are permitted on the lake. Anglers can test the lake 24 hours a day for bass, trout, catfish, suckers, bluegill, perch, crappie, and sunfish. You'll enjoy ice fishing and ice boating when the lake is frozen. If you want to spend some time to enjoy all the amenities, try the family camping areas. Organized groups may camp in tents or in large cabins.

Though technically a bit outside our six-county coverage area, Laurel Hill is part of a trio of adjacent state facilities—along with Linn Run State Park and Forbes State Forest—well worthy of coverage.

Linn Run State Park
P.O. Box 50, Rector, PA 15677-0030
• (724) 238-6623

Set on 571 acres within the Forbes State Forest, in the heart of the Laurel Mountains, Linn Run is a scenic park used primarily for picnicking, hiking, hunting, and fishing, although it offers other opportunities as well. The Adams Falls and Grove Run areas provide a total of 137 picnic tables; Adams Falls also offers a pavilion and play apparatus. If you find you really like the place, you can rent one of the park's 10 rustic cabins for up to a week in season—slightly longer out of season.

More than 400 acres are open for hunting, typically providing squirrel, turkey, deer, and black bear. Anglers will like the availability of trout in Linn Run Stream, while hikers will enjoy a variety of delights. The park itself offers five miles of trails, and it's near three other trails in Forbes State Forest as well as the Laurel Highlands Hiking Trail, which spans 70 miles from Ohiopyle to the Conemaugh River.

Linn Run offers limited horseback riding and snowmobiling, and it is near such other outdoor attractions as Laurel Mountain Ski Area.

Ohiopyle State Park
P.O. Box 105, Ohiopyle, PA 15470-0105
• (724) 329-8591

Ohiopyle State Park is primarily in Fayette County, just outside our coverage area, but its more than 19,000 acres are so spectacular and rich with recreational opportunities that it would be a significant omission.

The focal point of the park is the more than 14 miles of the Youghiogheny River Gorge that passes through the heart of the park, providing some of the best whitewater boating in the Mid-Atlantic region. Just watching the churning water is excitement enough for some; if you're in that category, you'll enjoy a number of scenic overlooks.

Bicycling, too, is a popular Ohiopyle activity, as the park features a 28-mile biking trail, converted from abandoned railroad rights-of-way, that parallels the Yough; bikers will share 9.4 miles of the trail with equestrians. The trail also is suitable for hiking, jogging, and cross-country skiing. Both the Yough and the tamer Meadow Run offer trout to anglers; a disabled-access area is available. Nearly the entire park low Creek is a wonderland of outdoor activities. These begin with ice skating, ice fishing, and ice boating on Yellow Creek Lake—which comprises about one-quarter of the park's 2,981 acres—and include cross-country skiing, snowshoeing, sledding, tobogganing, and snowmobiling in 350 designated acres.

When the weather warms, you can enjoy your non-powered boats and boats up to 10 horsepower, swim along an 800-foot guarded beach, and cast your fishing lines for smallmouth and largemouth bass, walleye, muskellunge, tiger muskellunge, northern pike, yellow perch, bluegill, and catfish. The park's picnic and parking areas can accommodate more than 4,000 people.

Most areas of the park are open for hunting. While the facility is not known for hiking, you will find a number of pleasant, short trails, one of which is dotted with wildflowers in season. Yellow Creek is in Indiana County, just outside our six-county coverage area. State parks are so popular, however, that we want to detail all those within a comfortable drive of Pittsburgh.

Many abandoned railroad lines have been converted to bike trails.

Photo: Courtesy of Laurel Highlands Visitors Bureau

PARKS

is open for hunting and trapping, with typical quarry including deer, turkey, grouse, rabbit, and squirrel. Winter activities include sledding, tobogganing, and snowmobiling, with numerous snowmobiling trails carved from Sugarloaf Knob at an elevation of 2,640 feet.

Picnic areas feature play apparatus, a pavilion available for rental, a softball field, and a volleyball court. If it's all too much to enjoy in one day, extend your stay by reserving a campsite. Ohiopyle offers 237 campsites that you can reserve from April through December. In addition, you can stay at nearby Hosteling International, (724) 329-4476.

Yellow Creek State Park
RR1, Penn Run
• (724) 357-7913

When winter brings a thick snow cover, Yel-

West

Raccoon Creek State Park
3000 Rt. 18, Hookstown
• (724) 899-2200

Raccoon Creek is one of the larger state parks, spanning 7,323 acres, including the beautiful Raccoon Creek Lake. Camping is a particularly popular attraction here. The park offers 172 tent and trailer sites for family camping from mid-April through mid-December, as well as group campsites, group tent camping, and 10 modern family cabins with a furnished living area, kitchen space, and two or three bedrooms. For a special treat, try Lakeside Lodge, a three-bedroom cottage that sleeps nine and is open all year.

The lake yields a wide variety of fish: bluegill, sunfish, bullhead, catfish, yellow perch, walleye, muskellunge, crappie, sauger, large-mouth and smallmouth bass, and brook and rainbow trout. You'll find a turf beach for swimming, a boat launch area, and 42 mooring spaces. Nonpowered boats and electric-powered boats are permitted, and you can rent several types of nonpowered boats at the park. You can also ice fish and ice skate on the lake in season and enjoy sledding, snowmobiling, and cross-country skiing in other areas of the park.

More than 5,000 acres are available for hunting the park's deer, wild turkey, grouse, squirrel, and rabbit. Raccoon Creek offers 16 miles of bridle trails and 5 miles of hiking trails, along which you'll find some of the most singular stands of native wildflowers in the western Pennsylvania region. You may want to call the Wildflower Reserve and Interpretive Center before you head out to check when your favorite flowers will be in bloom; the number is (724) 899-3611. You'll also find 600 picnic tables in the park—some shelters must be reserved. For a historical touch to your outing, visit King's Creek Cemetery on the park's western boundary, where many of the area's pioneers are buried.

Ryerson Station State Park
RR1, Wind Ridge • (724) 428-4254

Technically outside our six-county coverage area, Ryerson Station deserves mention as one of the finest facilities in sparsely populated Greene County. Named for the 18th-century Fort Ryerson which stood nearby, the 1,164-acre park features a variety of winter sports, including ice skating, ice fishing, snowmobiling on 6 miles of trails, and cross-country skiing. You'll find a guarded swimming pool, 10 miles of hiking trails, more than 300 picnic tables, and five pavilions—three of the pavilions are available by reservation only.

Anglers will find trout, warm water game fish, and pan fish in Duke Lake. You can use nonpowered boats and electric-powered boats on the lake. The park provides a launching ramp and a limited number of mooring spaces. For camping, you'll find a 50-site family campground for tents or trailers, as well as organized group tenting areas. Hunting, trapping, and dog training are allowed from the beginning of the fall archery deer season to March 31 of the following year.

Federal Recreation Areas

The U.S. Army Corps of Engineers operates 16 flood control projects in the tri-state area. The principal purpose, of course, is to prevent, or reduce, the damages from flooding. Because the dams hold a pool of water that forms a lake, they also serve a variety of recreational purposes. So popular are these areas that they draw more than 15 million visitors annually.

Generally, you'll find fishing, boating, camping, picnicking, hunting, and cross-country skiing opportunities, as well as hiking, snowmobile, and interpretive trails, although the line-up varies from dam to dam. You may bring your pets to all federal recreation areas. Five of these outdoor playgrounds fall within our six-county coverage area, or close enough to it to merit description below. For unusually well-written and easy-to-follow brochures about all 16 areas, contact the Corps at (412) 395-7500.

Along with descriptions of these recreation areas, we've included information about the Allegheny National Forest. Pennsylvania's only national forest is outside our principal coverage area, but it's such an unusually rich resource that it attracts many visitors from Southwestern Pennsylvania.

North

Allegheny National Forest
222 Liberty St., Warren • (814) 723-5150

For outdoor enthusiasts, the Allegheny National Forest is as much paradise as it is park. It spans 513,000 acres in Elk, McKean, Forest, and Warren counties, about a three-hour drive from Pittsburgh. The only national forest in the state, Allegheny National Forest sits in the rugged plateau country of Northwestern Pennsylvania, with elevation ranging from 1,046 feet to 2,263 feet above sea level. Many creeks and streams cut deeply into the plateau, creating some of the most majestic vistas in the region.

The 12,000-acre Allegheny Reservoir, created by the impoundment of the Kinzua (KIN zoo) Dam, provides a diversity of water-based activities. The reservoir is the centerpiece of 700 miles of waterways that offer anglers muskellunge, smallmouth bass, walleye, northern perch, channel catfish, and some types of trout. To give you an idea of the scale of fish available, the park is annually the site for Cabela's North American Walleye Anglers Team Event. You can boat in the Allegheny and Tionesta reservoirs—many launching areas are available—or try canoeing on such venues as the scenic Clarion and Alleghney Rivers or the Brokenstraw and Tionesta creeks. If swimming or water skiing is your thing, you'll find the Allegheny Reservoir most accommodating.

Hunters can stalk white-tailed deer, black bear, and wild turkey, while campers will find 16 campgrounds including primitive camping areas that you can reach only by boat or hiking trail. Speaking of hiking, you'll find plenty of opportunities here, as 96.6 miles of the North Country National Scenic Trail traverse the forest. Cross-country skiers, snowmobilers, and dirt bikers will enjoy the loop trails that wind through the hills, while bikers will discover several special treats: both the Iowa to Maine Trail and a cross-Pennsylvania bike route pass through the forest.

Many Western Pennsylvanians plan fall foliage excursions to the forest. If you go, check out the Tionesta Scenic Area, part of a 4,000-acre tract of old growth that features venerable beech, hemlock, and sugar maple trees—some of them up to 400 years old. Fall's colors will blaze brightly for you in the Allegheny National Forest. If you're looking for a pretty drive, try the 29-mile Longhouse National Scenic Byway.

You're welcome to bring your pets to the forest, provided you keep them leashed. Saddle and pack animals are permitted in all areas, except for on the forest's hiking and cross-country ski trails.

Crooked Creek Lake
RD#3, Ford City • (724) 763-2764

Crooked Creek is a delight for water enthusiasts, no matter the season. In warm weather, swimmers and sunbathers utilize the sandy peninsula beach, water skiers dot the lake, while anglers reel in bass and sunfish. In cold weather, the park offers two ice skating ponds, a sled riding area, and cross-country skiing. You'll also find a boat launching ramp and no horsepower limit.

Crooked Creek offers hunting, hiking and horse trails, and tent, trailer and group camping. A special feature is the Environmental Learning Center, an interpretive center for groups. Crooked Creek Horse Park, detailed in our Recreation chapter, adjoins the recreation area.

Mahoning Creek Lake
RD#1, New Bethlehem • (814) 257-8017

Anglers especially will enjoy Mahoning Creek Lake—its waters yield northern pike, walleye, muskie, and bass. (The lake is stocked by the Pennsylvania Fish and Boat Commission.) You can score when you hunt here as well, as the Pennsylvania Game Commission leases nearly 1,300 acres for wildlife management and public hunting.

The lake features two boat launching ramps, with boats up to 10 horsepower permitted.

Swimming is not permitted, but you will enjoy 28 acres of campgrounds, with all sites featuring restrooms, showers, and electricity.

East

Conemaugh River Lake
RD#1, Saltsburg • (724) 459-8982

The Pennsylvania Game Commission leases 7,000 acres around the lake for public hunting and wildlife management. The park provides a canoe launch but no other pubic boating due to limited accessibility to the lake. You'll enjoy a picnic area with two pavilions, play apparatus, and nature and hiking trails.

You'll enjoy several sites of historical interest, including traces of the Pennsylvania Mainland Canal and sections of early Pennsylvania railroads.

Loyalhanna Lake
RD#2, Saltsburg • (724) 639-3785

The Loyalhanna Watershed is one of the most scenic areas in Western Pennsylvania, and Loyalhanna Lake captures that majesty. One of the most popular activities here is picnicking at the Damsite Picnic Area—the view of the dam and surrounding woodlands will soothe your jangled nerves.

If you're looking for more active entertainment, try the Black Willow Water Trail, the lake's self-guided boating trail with stations marking natural and manmade features. Anglers will find inlets and coves that yield bass, walleye, crappie, bullheads, and bluegills. The lake offers two boat launching areas and no horsepower limit. You can camp and hunt at Loyalhanna; the Pennsylvania Game Commission leases 2,115 acres for hunting and wildlife management.

South

Youghiogheny River Lake
RD#1, Confluence • (814) 395-3166

Principal activities at Youghiogheny are boating, water skiing, and fishing. Just below the dam, the Youghiogheny River offers some of the most popular rafting and canoeing waters in the Mid-Atlantic region. One boulder-strewn stretch is so popular and challenging it frequently hosts national kayak championships. The lake features five boat-launching ramps.

Anglers find the backwaters and coves rich with walleye and smallmouth bass. You can choose from three campgrounds with facilities ranging from primitive to modern.

PARKS

Recreation

LOOK FOR:
• Participatory
  Sports throughout
  Greater Pittsburgh

The recreation scene in Western Pennsylvania is diverse, creative, and inviting. You'll find an arena and an association for just about every sport and activity that might interest you. If you're not sure just what interests you, don't be afraid to jump feet first into something new. Most of the groups we've profiled below welcome newcomers and offer an instructional component.

Several factors have contributed to the breadth of recreational opportunities. One is the success of the city's professional teams. As the Steelers, Pirates, and Penguins have captured championships that brought them increasing support and media exposure, thousands have been inspired to take to the fields, courts, and rinks to achieve their own levels of athletic enjoyment and rewards. The region's college campuses have played a key role in the growth of certain sports such as rugby; former college players, lacking vehicles to extend their playing days, founded clubs of their own.

Natural geographic resources contribute to the popularity of outdoor activities. The region is blessed with an excellent inland waterway system that provides varied opportunities for fishing, boating, and swimming. The woods of Western Pennsylvania are a hunter's delight, while the region's slopes provide a natural—sometimes stunning—setting for hiking, climbing, and skiing. Add the welcome cycle of the four seasons and you have a region where virtually every sport has its moment in the sun—or snow, as it were.

In our profiles of Western Pennsylvania's recreational activities, we've tried to avoid describing commercial establishments in the belief that you have plenty of other resources to find these. Instead, we've offered information on coordinating associations and interest groups that could be hard to track down otherwise. You won't find descriptions of the region's bowling alleys, for example, but you will learn about the organizations that sanction bowling leagues and tournaments. The exception to this is in the "Yoga" section, in which we've listed several yoga centers. They're hard to find if you don't know where to look.

One caution about phone numbers and addresses. In the case of clubs, these may be accurate only as long as the president or captain keeps the job. As a hedge against shifting organizational responsibilities, we've tried to list the venues where clubs practice and perform, so that you always can make contact by dropping by.

Archery

**Allegheny County
Sportsmen's League**
Rt. 56, New Kensington
• (412) 882-9115
• www.nauticom.net\www\acsl

Archery is a popular activity in Western Pennsylvania, but it's sometimes difficult to identify appropriate sites and organizations. That's because much of the activity occurs inside private shooting clubs; you'd be hard pressed to know that archery takes place at the club. Allegheny County Sportsmen's League can provide you with a directory of shooting clubs. You can use that to find archery facilities.

Chieftain Archery Club is one of the few in the area dedicated exclusively to archery. You'll need to join the club and provide your own equipment to participate. When you do so, you're welcome to bring a guest for a fee of $2. The club sponsors a youth program, with those 18 and under invited to shoot each Friday evening for the nominal fee of $2. Watch for the club's annual Everett Leseuer Invitational, named for the 11-time Pennsylvania champion archer.

Auto Racing

Don Martin's Lernerville Speedway
278 North Pike Rd., Sarver
• (724) 353-1511

Sprints, late models, modifieds, pure stocks . . . Don Martin's Lernerville Speedway has all the variety you could desire in dirt track racing. Moreover, the track often features its divisions in competition on the same evening, creating an unusually diverse program that's sometimes spiced with such special events as demolition derbies. You'll find the track in action from April through September as weather permits. If you plan to enjoy the action from the stands, admission is $10, with discounts for kids and senior citizens. If you'd prefer to get down and dirty on the track, the speedway will welcome your entry as long as your car meets safety specs.

Baseball

Most communities feature an organized youth baseball program. The City of Pittsburgh goes that one better through its B.I.G. ("Baseball Is Great") League Baseball program, (412) 323-7226 or (412) 323-7939. B.I.G. coordinates rookie, pony, and colt leagues that involve about 4,000 youths in organized baseball. The colt and pony leagues play their championship games at Three Rivers Stadium, a special treat for young players.

B.I.G. conducts clinics in association with the Pittsburgh Pirates and also enables community programs to acquire their equipment through B.I.G. and realize the discounts the City of Pittsburgh often enjoys on bulk purchases. B.I.G. administrators will refer you to an organized program in your neighborhood. Perhaps best

of all, if youngsters don't have opportunities to play in their neighborhood, B.I.G. will find spots for them in its program.

Kids in the region's inner city neighborhoods—encompassing both Pittsburgh and its suburbs—will find additional opportunities through Reviving Baseball in the Inner-city (RBI), (412) 231-2300. Major League Baseball sponsors RBI in 70 cities in six countries. In Western Pennsylvania, it's run by the Boys and Girls Club of Western PA in cooperation with Pittsburgh's B.I.G. League Program. Funding for the program is provided by the Roberto Clemente Foundation, an affiliate of the Pittsburgh Pirates.

Locally, about 300 boys and girls from 13 to 18 participate—boys in baseball, girls in fastpitch softball. An All-Star team selected from local participants is eligible for national postseason competition that culminates in a World Series typically held in a Major League Baseball stadium, a thrill for the young players. The program goes beyond baseball to offer career development counseling and advice on conflict resolution. A nice added touch: all teams in the local program sport names and uniforms that honor Negro League teams, such as the Pittsburgh Crawfords and the Homestead Grays. Youths who would like to participate should contact Richard Earl Harris at (412) 363-8469.

Basketball

The city game is healthy in Western Pennsylvania, as men and women of all ages compete regularly in gyms provided by schools, churches, and other institutions. Many such competitions aren't really leagues, as the players "pick up" teams each evening. The best way to find out about these games is through word of mouth or by checking with those schools and churches to determine when games are played.

For youths, many City of Pittsburgh recreation centers sponsor regular competition—3-on-3 for the youngest kids, 5-on-5 for teenagers. Check with your local rec center for its schedule.

If you're in or approaching your second childhood, there's a venue for you as well. The Southside

INSIDERS' TIP

In this chapter, you'll find several different phone numbers for Allegheny Group, Sierra Club, and Hosteling International/ American Youth Hostels, Pittsburgh Council. That's because we've listed the numbers of activity coordinators rather than a central office or hotline number that won't be as immediately useful.

RECREATION

Market House, 1200 Bingham Street, Pittsburgh, (412) 488-8404, a City of Pittsburgh recreation center, runs a gym exclusively for players at least 60 years old. Senior basketball games take place on Fridays from 8 AM to 2 PM, with new teams chosen each week. There are also shuffleboard leagues, a walking club, and opportunities for line dancing. If you don't live in the city, you're still eligible. Call Ray Fisher at (412) 422-6402 for more information. Let the games begin!

Biking

Bikers in Western Pennsylvania have their own signature event—The Great Ride. It occurs each summer and features competition at three distances—15 miles, 25 miles, 35 miles—all within the same race. Sponsored by the City of Pittsburgh, the event will take you up Pittsburgh's hills and along the rivers. It is a great ride, and one you can take every day, since much of the course is considered a bike route. Be advised that, except for the day of The Great Ride, you'll share much of the course with vehicular traffic.

WPW Bicycle Club
P.O. Box 6952, Pittsburgh, 15212
• **(412) 795-4403**
The premier touring organization in the region, the WPW Bicycle Club boasts more than 2,000 members who typically ride from March through November, weather permitting. The club meets monthly and publishes a monthly newspaper and maps depicting nearly 7,000 miles of bicycle routes. Join them and you'll be able to participate in a highlight ride each month as well as the annual Fall Rally in September.

You can keep up with club activities by calling the hotline—the number listed above—or by visiting its web site at trfn.clpgh.org. You'll enjoy riding with the club, as well as the members' offbeat humor. When we sampled the hotline, we were advised that the upcoming highlight event was "an oddball ride for unusual people—the destination depends on your whim." Incidentally, the "WPW" in the group's name stands for "Western Pennsylvania Wheelmen," the club's original moniker ditched for political correctness.

Billiards

Oh so quietly, billiards

has become one of the faster growing sports in the region. You'll find more than three dozen establishments that sport multiple tables, to say nothing of the countless taverns that have installed a table to satisfy the clientele. Among the year's highlights is the Greater Pittsburgh Amateur 9-ball Championships, held each year to benefit the Autism Society of Pittsburgh. Perhaps the best way to keep up with leagues and tournaments is by consulting the publication described below.

Amateur Billiard News
38 Cherry St., Etna
• **(412) 781-6250**
In this free magazine published six times per year, you'll find tournament information as well as current happenings for leagues that feature more than 400 teams. The newsletter highlights men's and women's competitions, as well as mixed events. You'll learn about scratch and handicap leagues as well as those that group players by geography or skill level.

Birding

Audubon Society of Western Pennsylvania at Beechwood Farms Nature Reserve
614 Dorseyville Rd., Fox Chapel
• **(412) 963-6100**
Experience the sights and sounds of a night hike along a moonlit trail. Search for turtles and other creatures in a pond teeming with aqautic life. Follow the colorful tracings of butterflies in a meadow awash with wildflowers. Explore the fascinating lives of birds on a walk through a singing woodland. These and many other experiences await you at Beechwood Farms Nature Reserve, home of the Audubon Society of Western Pennsylvania.

Known as "Pittsburgh's Outdoor Classroom," Audubon at Beechwood offers most extensive, year-round environmental programs for the entire family, from young children to adults. Offerings range from Outdoor Discovery Programs, which provide thousands of school-age children each year with hands-on guided experiences of nature, to programs designed for family participation. Programs range in duration from week-long summer nature camps for children in grades K-5 to two in-

INSIDERS' TIP

Each year at Christmas time, Jim Valimont of the Audubon Society of Western Pennsylvania leads a group that undertakes a regional bird count. You're welcome to join them.

Even youngsters can saddle up for a bike ride in our parks.

novative programs for preschool children as young as 2 months. Audubon at Beechwood also offers a monthly series of bird outings to regional sites; guided bird walks on Wednesday mornings; the annual Christmas Bird Count; and other popular events such as the Secret Gardens Tour of spectacular Fox Chapel gardens and Applejamm, one of the oldest fall festivals in the area. A total of 13,717 people attended the 515 educational programs and activities offering during the 1999 calendar year.

Many thousands more people visit Beechwood Farms all year to enjoy informal outdoor activities on its five miles of nature trails and 134 acres of woodlands, meadows, ponds, and wetlands. Others visit Beechwood to shop at the Audubon Nature Store, with its wide selection of bird feeders, birdseed, and nature-related items. Beechwood also features a modern education center with facilities for children's birthday parties, the new Audubon Center for the Native Plants, and a natural history reference and reading library. Beechwood's trails are open 365 days a year, dawn to dusk.

Boating

Western Pennsylvania's waterways beckon to boaters. Whether you're sailing, canoeing, kayaking, paddling, rafting, or motoring under electrical power, you'll find waters in the region that will accommodate you. Perhaps the best place to start is with a comprehensive state map available free from the Pennsylvania Fish and Boat Commission, (717) 657-4518. The map is free if you pick it up; it's $1 if you ask the Commission to mail it to you. The map depicts nearly 1,000 boating and fishing opportunities in the state and provides a guide to parking, launch ramps, and horsepower limits.

You'll also want a copy of the commission's Boating Handbook, 45 pages of rules and advice. Several of those regulations are particularly noteworthy. You will need to register your boat; the fee, good for two years, ranges from $10 for unpowered boats to $40 for craft over 20 feet. You'll need to display your boat registration number on your boat; kayaks, sculls, and sailboards are exempt from this requirement. The state also provides boat titling, at a cost of $15, to help deter theft. The handbook will familiarize you with state requirements for personal flotation devices and regulations regarding alcohol consumption while you're boating. The commission can provide you with brochures on each topic.

If you're a boater and an angler, you'll get a particular kick from *Pennsylvania Angler & Boater,* the commission's official magazine. It's published six times each year and offers lush color photography, how-to pieces, and commission updates. Cost is $9 annually.

Our Parks chapter will introduce you to boating opportunities at state parks and federal recreation areas. For more specific information about any state or federal facility, contact the Pennsylvania Bureau of Parks, (717) 772-0239; the Pennsylvania Parks Information and Reservation line, (888) PA-PARKS; or the U.S. Army Corps of Engineers, (412) 395-7500.

Hosteling International/American Youth Hostels, Pittsburgh Council
Corner of Fifth and Shady Ave., Pittsburgh
• (412) 362-8181

The council organizes many exciting and challenging outdoors activities, including a broad variety of boating outings. These include frequent canoeing and kayaking adventures, some designated for experienced paddlers only. Since these outings tend to be weather dependent, the group encourages you to call (724) 443-8972 to check the day's plans with event organizers.

You can sail with the council as well. On grand summer days, you'll find the council sailing and racing on Moraine State Park's Lake Arthur. If you'd like to join them but don't know the ropes, take the club's introductory sailing classes and help them maintain their sailboat. You'll learn in a hurry. For more information about sailing, contact the council at (412) 241-0659, or contact the Moraine Sailing Club at (412) 367-3697. The web site for the Moraine Sailing Club is www.moraineclub.org.

Finally, if whitewater paddling is more your thing, the Pittsburgh Council offers a refresher course. Call (724) 933-7261 for membership questions.

Three Rivers Rowing Association
300 Waterfront Dr., Pittsburgh
• (412) 231-8772
• www.threeriversrowing.org

One of the city's most compelling sights is that of crews plying the Allegheny River, intermittently visible through the early morning mist. That vista is brought to you by Three Rivers Rowing Association, a group founded in 1984 with the mission of providing broad-based rowing opportunities in the Pittsburgh area. The group is headquartered on Wash-

ington's Landing, an Allegheny River island about 2 miles north of downtown Pittsburgh. The island houses the group's 15,000-square-foot boathouse, which features large boat storage bays, exercise equipment, lockers and showers, and meeting space.

The association offers orientations, clinics, and other instructional activities to get you started. Of particular interest are the club's programs for special populations. These include programs for youths, seniors, and rowers with certain disabilities. There is also a special summer corporate rowing program. TRRA also offers a variety of sprint racing and tours for kayaks. An adult membership in the association costs $275 annually, with discounts available for students. Much more information is available at www.threeriversrowing.org

Among the highlights of the rowing year is the Head of the Ohio Regatta, typically held in early fall along the Allegheny just before it merges with the Monongahela to form the Ohio. It's a prestigious event, generally drawing several thousand entries. You may not be ready to enter, but you'll love the spectacle of this one.

Bowling

Greater Pittsburgh Ten-Pin Bowling Association
Pittsburgh Women's Bowling
Penn Plaza, Suite 206, Turtle Creek
• (412) 824-4850

Bowling is such a popular pastime in Pittsburgh that you really don't need the help of an organization to get started; just visit your local lanes and ask about leagues. In fact, if you're not in a league, you may find open alleys hard to come by during peak times. That said, the Greater Pittsburgh Ten-Pin Bowling Association and Pittsburgh Women's Bowling perform important functions for local keglers.

The companion organizations, which are run from the same office, sanction leagues and tournaments with the American Bowling Congress. Since more than 15,000 men and women compete locally in sanctioned events, this is a key service. The organizations also sponsor tournaments, present awards for high scores, sponsor a junior bowling program, and publish yearbooks that feature most area lanes and leagues.

INSIDERS' TIP

Each year the city of Washington in Washington County hosts The Pony League World Series at—where else?—Pony League Field.

You can purchase a men's or a women's yearbook for $10 each.

Boxing

As it is at the national level, administration of boxing activities in Western Pennsylvania is somewhat fragmented. However, this is all sorted out on the amateur level with the Golden Gloves tournament held each March. Call Gloria Sztukowski, co-director and chief of officials for the local amateur league, at (412) 298-7373. She'll give you a listing of the gyms where boxing is held in your neighborhood.

Below is a listing of some of the major gyms.

Boyce Police Athletic League Gym
Monroeville • (412) 793-2111

This is a "Black Iron" gym that also offers a weight lifting facility, martial arts, and personal training. Both men and women are welcome. On a professional level, Al McCulley, king of local boxing trainers and promoters, has cultivated the International Boxing Federation (IBF) Lightweight A champion as well as "The Pittsburgh Kid," Paul Spadafora. Greg Beal trains young men from ages 6 and up.

Third Avenue Gym
225 Ross St., Pittsburgh
• (412) 232-3221, (412) 481-3388

This new gym specializes in the art of boxing. You won't find any age limitations here, and children ages 6 through 18 are trained at no fee. The gym is open to the public for martial arts, health and fitness activities, and seminars and education. This gym is associated with the Police Athletic League. Founder and Director Jim Svetic's slogan is "Always for the children!"

Bridge

A true story about bridge in Pittsburgh: A newcomer to town some years ago was invited to a veteran bridge player's house for a private game featuring some of the area's elite players. As the evening progressed, the newcomer smelled something burning. Sure enough, when she looked up, she saw orange flames shooting

ever higher from a wastebasket. "There's a fire in the garbage can," she said. No one moved. No one looked up. Finally, overcoming her shyness as the newest player, she arose and stamped out the fire. No one thanked her or even noticed that she had been gone.

That incident tells you something about bridge in our area. It's not that players are unfriendly, but they are intense. A little thing like a wastebasket fire won't bother them. If you aspire to that level, you can learn bridge at the Jewish Community Center, (412) 521-8011, ext. 225, in Pittsburgh's Squirrel Hill neighborhood, which sponsors instruction at various levels. Older Adult Service and Information System (OASIS), (412) 232-9583, offers bridge classes for senior citizens; the classes usually are fully subscribed. OASIS is located on the 10th floor of Kaufmann's department store in downtown Pittsburgh.

INSIDERS' TIP
The state maintains a convenient "one-call" system to handle both requests for information and reservations of campsites, cabins, and pavilions. Make your one call to (888) PA-PARKS.

Pittsburgh Bridge Association
417 Lloyd St., Pittsburgh
• (412) 241-1981, (412) 683-GAME

If duplicate bridge is your game, you'll want to be in touch with the Pittsburgh Bridge Association, an affiliate of the American Contract Bridge League. Association members will make you aware of as many as 40 games throughout the region each week. The association also stages its own games and publishes a directory including games and the names and phone numbers of 1,400 area players. Cost for the directory is $2.

Camping

If you're an avid camper, you're likely to become mighty familiar with Pennsylvania's state park system. The Commonwealth maintains more than 7,000 campsites in 57 state parks, many of them within an easy ride of Pittsburgh. Check out our Parks chapter for an introduction to camping at Western Pennsylvania state parks, or call the Pennsylvania Parks Information and Reservations line, (888) PA-PARKS, for more comprehensive information and a fee schedule.

State parks offer a variety of overnight options. These include family campsites; group cabins and tent areas; and cabins, both modern and rustic. Whichever option you select, you'll

RECREATION

find most campsites and cabins open from early April until late October. Some sites welcome campers through December, and a handful are open year-round. From Memorial Day through Labor Day, your stay will be limited to 14 consecutive days. At other times, your maximum stay is 21 consecutive days. Most sites are available on a first-come, first-served basis, although you can reserve other sites. The state prohibits alcohol and pets at its sites.

The U.S. Army Corps of Engineers maintains campsites at its recreation areas, although the number can't compare with the total offered by the state. If you lack appropriate camping gear, ask about the "Rent-A-Tent" program, which will provide you with enough equipment to host up to five friends. For information, call the Corps at (412) 395-7500.

You'll find many private campground operators who have opened businesses near state and federal facilities to capitalize on any overflow. You can get a useful list of 180 privately operated campgrounds from the Pennsylvania Campground Owners Association, (888) 660-7262. The list is not comprehensive, since some operators don't belong to the association, but it's a great place to start.

Caving

Several local outdoors groups, while not devoted exclusively to the activity, feature caving on their roster of events. The Explorers Club of Pittsburgh, (412) 963-7534, occasionally explores caves in West Virginia. Allegheny Group, Sierra Club, (412) 351-4068, ventures to caves on Chestnut Ridge. If you contact Allegheny Group, they'll advise you on the degree of difficulty of each outing.

Chess

Pittsburgh Chess Club
5604 Solway St., Pittsburgh
• **(412) 421-1881**
The Pittsburgh Chess Club has been staging tournaments for more than 50 years, making it one of the older chess organizations in the country. Located in a former elementary school in the city's Squirrel Hill neigh-

borhood, the organization stages both club tournaments and those rated by the United States Chess Federation. In addition, the club sponsors instruction and competition at local schools and has reached about 6,000 students through these efforts.

The club's nearly 200 members engage in open play on Wednesdays and Saturdays and in tournament play on Tuesdays. Visitors always are welcome. When you drop by, make sure to check out the extensive chess library, an asset utilized by many researchers.

One of the largest neighborhood chess organizations is the Hill Carnegie Chess and Checker Club, which hosts open play at the Hill District Branch of the Carnegie Library, 419 Dinwiddie Street, Pittsburgh, (412) 281-3753. The club sponsors teams in competitive play, and its nearly 100 members enjoy the club's services free of charge. The group's name is something of a misnomer, though—there's nary a checkers player remaining in the organization.

Climbing

Explorers Club of Pittsburgh
P.O. Box 2815, Pittsburgh
• **(412) 708-1608**
Founded in 1948, the Explorers Club of Pittsburgh is dedicated to two purposes: exploration at home and abroad, and the promotion and instruction of exploratory sciences. The club's 250 members meet monthly and offer instruction in mountaineering and basic and advanced rock climbing. If you enjoy travel, you'll find this group cheerfully peripatetic. Their outings have included rock climbing at West Virginia's Seneca Rocks and ice climbing in Colorado, Canada, and the Adirondack Mountains. They've climbed the Andes and the Himalayas, and enjoyed scuba diving in the Bahamas. Other club expeditions include caving and mountain biking. For your $15 annual membership fee, you'll receive the club's monthly newsletter.

Dog Shows

Western Pennsylvania Kennel Association
208 Old McBride Rd., Canonsburg
• **(724) 746-4794**
The largest kennel club

INSIDERS' TIP

Allegheny Group, Sierra Club, and Hosteling International/ American Youth Hostels, Pittsburgh Council welcome volunteers to help maintain hiking trails throughout the region. So does Friends of the Riverfront, which is developing an 11.5-mile trail around Pittsburgh's three rivers.

Numerous area stables meet the needs of Pittsburgh's horse lovers.

Photo: Courtesy of Nemacolin Woodlands Resort & Spa

RECREATION

in Western Pennsylvania, the Western Pennsylvania Kennel Association stages two all-breed shows each spring, most commonly at the David L. Lawrence Convention Center in downtown Pittsburgh. A portion of proceeds benefit the American Kennel Club's Canine Health Foundation and the local humane societies, so there's a great reason for patronizing the shows.

Annual association dues range from $15 to $20; membership entitles you to free admission to the association's shows as well as its newsletter. There are other kennel clubs in the region. A comprehensive listing is available from the *AKC Gazette,* 5580 Centerview Drive, Raleigh, NC, 27606-3390, (919) 233-9767.

Fencing

Fencers in Western Pennsylvania are relatively small in number, but they are dedicated. With a little help from us, you'll be sure to find a salle, a studio where fencing takes place.

Three Rivers Fencing Center
5533 Ellsworth Ave., #201, Pittsburgh
• **(412) 621-4282**

Three Rivers Fencing Center offers both group and private instruction in foil and saber as well as open fencing on Tuesdays and Thurs-

days. The center offers full-time professional coaches, and its members compete in tournaments locally and throughout the country.

Dress in regular workout clothes when you visit, and don't worry about equipment if you're new to the sport. The center will provide your weapons, jackets, masks, and gloves. You will be responsible for fees for any lessons, and a $8 per night charge for open fencing. If you join the center and pay annual dues, open fencing is included.

Western Pennsylvania Fencing Institute
• **(412) 802-0650**

Fencing is a movable feast at the institute, as this nonprofit organization provides fencing opportunities in a number of neighborhoods, including Squirrel Hill, Monroeville, Mt. Lebanon, the North Hills, Ligonier, and Washington. In some cases, the municipalities engage the institute to provide fencing opportunities for the public. You will be charged for group and private lessons, but open fencing is available for a fee. The institute does solicit donations to help defray costs.

The institute boasts several strengths. First, its three coaches and two apprentices are accredited by the U.S. Fencing Association. In addition, it offers instructions in all three of the sport's weapons: foil, epee, and saber. They'll provide you with all the equipment you need to get started.

Fishing

Fishing in Pennsylvania is a joy that can be utterly different each time you take to the waters. How extensive are the state's fishing opportunities? Consider that a map of state fishing and boating opportunities provided by the Pennsylvania Fish and Boat Commission depicts nearly 1,000 locations for those activities. You'll find state and federal lakes, streams, and impoundments (waters behind a dam) marked on the map, as well as a guide to parking and other facilities. Once you've studied your map, you'll be ready for more specific brochures that detail where you can find trout and warmwater species. All these publications are available from the commission, 3532 Walnut St., Harrisburg, PA, (717) 657-4518.

When you contact the commission, you'll also want to acquire the state's Summary of Fishing Regulations and Laws, a must for all anglers. Some of the regulations won't surprise you. You'll learn that all anglers 16 and older must have a license, with fees ranging from $4 for resident senior citizens to $35 for nonresidents. If you're fishing in Lake Erie or for trout or salmon, you'll need a special permit at an additional cost. You'll also learn about "special regulation" waters, including catch-and-release areas and those reserved for children and anglers with certain disabilities. Did you know that, each year, the state sponsors two "Fish-for-Free" days, when licenses are not required? You'll find this information—and much more —in the summary.

Among the commission's many publications, you'll find two others especially useful. One is the commission's official magazine, *Pennsylvania Angler & Boater*. This is a slick, four-color journal with great photography; first-person articles; tips on where they're biting; and commission updates on seasons, sizes, and regulation modifications. Cost is $9 annually.

The second piece is the commission's pocket guide to seasons, sizes, and creel limits. With this guide tucked into your pocket,

you'll never be out of season or over the limit. For an introduction to fishing opportunities at state parks and federal recreation areas, see our Parks chapter.

Flying Disc

Pittsburgh Flying Disc Society
1818 Morrell St., Pittsburgh
• (412) 734-0321

The Pittsburgh Flying Disc Society administers two types of activities. The first is a golf league, which plays at Schenley Park and Phillips Park in the City of Pittsburgh and Knob Hill Community Park in the North Hills. In golf, players throw discs into a basket posted on a pole about two feet off the ground. The courses wind through wooded areas, so it's a scenic activity as well. The society, which was formed in 1978, awards prizes at each competition. Don't worry if you're new to the sport—you'll receive a handicap that will make you the equal of veteran players.

The second activity is more demanding. It's called ultimate, a blend of football, basketball, and soccer with continuous action. The sport is coed, and you can keep up with it by phoning the ultimate hotline, (412) 521-2441. Ultimate is not a sedentary activity.

The society coordinates clinics, the Professional Disc Golf Association Tour's annual stop at Knob Hill, and Pittsburgh's participation in the World's Biggest Disc Golf Weekend, an international event that attracts 17,000 players. "Why not?" says society President Gary Dropcho. "You don't have to be Arnold Schwarzenegger, run really fast or jump really high." Sounds like our kind of sport.

Football

In the hometown of "The Stillers," you would expect football to be a popular activity. You would be correct, but at the participant level, the game you're most likely to see differs in key areas from the one they play at Three Rivers Stadium. This variation is called "flag football," and it's played on sandlots throughout Western Pennsylvania. In this variation,

RECREATION

players where belts to which two "flags"—strips of cloth or plastic—are attached. A ball carrier is "tackled" when a flag is pulled off his belt.

It can be a hard-hitting game complete with certain oddities. If you've never seen the game before, this will be your first opportunity to witness unsportsmanlike conduct penalties for "shielding the flag." The trouble here is that leagues and personnel are ever shifting. Some leagues are organized by team captains, others by officials' groups. It's hard to find a central organization that stays put. One idea: check with municipal and county field permitting offices. They'll always be able to tell you which groups have fields reserved.

If your youngster wants to play, the path to participation is much easier. Just contact the Boys & Girls Clubs of Western Pennsylvania, 4412 Butler St., Pittsburgh, (412) 682-3031. The organization runs the Dapper Dan Charities/Pittsburgh Steelers Flag Football League, which each year involves about 600 youths as players . . . and another 75 as officials, scorekeepers, timers, and statisticians. The league plays at eight city fields and includes both boys and girls— some playing together on coed teams.

Gymnastics

The sight of elfin young girls twirling gracefully and perilously over imposing apparatus has contributed to an explosive growth of gymnastics facilities in Western Pennsylvania. The region boasts about three dozen gymnastics schools and facilities—more if you include dance schools that also offer gymnastics instruction. No coordinating or trade organization has emerged, so your best bet for information may be USA Gymnastics, (800) 345-4719, which can tell you about its affiliates in our region.

Hiking

With its far-reaching inland waterway network, vast expanses of forest, and many miles of abandoned railroad rights-of-way, Western Pennsylvania is a hiker's paradise. In fact, there are so many outstanding hiking opportunities here that you may want to familiarize yourself with local trails before you set out. You'll find a number of useful resources.

For trails in City of Pittsburgh Parks, the City of Pittsburgh Department of City Planning has produced a colorful brochure called Pittsburgh Outdoors. You can get your free copy by contacting the department at (412) 255-2216. For information on a group of longer and more challenging trails called Heritage Trails of Southwestern Pennsylvania, contact the Southwestern Pennsylvania Heritage Preservation Commission, 105 Zee Plaza, P.O. Box 565, Hollidaysburg, PA, 16648-0565, (814) 696-9380. The commission also can provide you with a useful guide to the rails-to-trails program in the state called *Pennsylvania's Rail-Trails* that details more than 700 miles of such trails. Cost is $12.95, including postage and handling.

We'd also recommend the book *Hiking Pennsylvania,* by Rhonda and George Ostertag, which features 75 hikes of varying difficulty across the Keystone State.

Allegheny Group, Sierra Club
P.O. Box 8241, Pittsburgh, 15217
• **(412) 561-0203**

You'll enjoy the varied outings of the Allegheny Group. The group's hikes average 8 to 9 miles along the region's most scenic trails on Laurel Ridge, Chestnut Ridge, and in such state parks as Moraine, McConnell's Mill, and Raccoon Creek. Allegheny Group rates its hikes as "easy," "intermediate," "strenuous," and "strenuous and exploratory," so you'll always know what awaits you. For the most leisurely outings, try the club's Wednesday rambles. These seldom exceed 4 miles.

The group also organizes backpacking events throughout the region and offers a Basic Backpacking Course each April. The best way to keep up with events is through the club's newsletter at an annual cost of $2.50. You can subscribe by writing to the group at 210 College Park Dr., Monroeville, PA, 15146-1532.

Hosteling International/American Youth Hostels, Pittsburgh Council
830 E. Warrington Ave., Pittsburgh
• **(412) 362-8181**

The group organizes frequent hikes and hiking/backpacking events along such venues as

> **INSIDERS' TIP**
>
> When you're discussing the sports of flying disc golf or ultimate, it's incorrect to use the word "Frisbee" indiscriminately. Frisbee is a brand name; flying disc is a generic term that encompasses several manufacturers.

RECREATION

the Rachel Carson Trail and the Baker Trail, which is about 50 miles north of Pittsburgh. If you don't quite have the time to allot for that, try the group's "Mid-Week Rambles," which are shorter hikes that take place in the Pittsburgh vicinity. A good way to keep up with group activities is through its newsletter. You can get your copy by calling (412) 431-4910 or by going to the open Thursday night meetings held on at the facility on the corner of Fifth and Shady Avenues.

Horse Shows

Fort Armstrong Horsemen's Association
RD#6, Friendship Plaza, Kittanning
• (724) 295-3294
Crooked Creek Horse Park, operated by the Fort Armstrong Horsemen's Association, is one of the mid-Atlantic's most comprehensive equine facilities. Encompassing 113 acres, the park features stable facilities for nearly 150 horses during events only, barns, outdoor arenas, electrical hook-ups for trailers and recreational vehicles, an equine museum, and 300 miles of riding trails. You'll also find pavilions sprinkled through the park. The association sponsors quarter horse, walking horse, and Arabian shows as well as an annual 100-mile sanctioned race. You can lease the park and also utilize the adjoining Crooked Creek Lake and the federal recreation area encompassing it. For more on Crooked Creek Lake, see our Parks chapter.

The Paper Horse
HCR 67 Box OH95, Mifflin
• (717) 436-8893
Fort Armstrong is one of the region's most prominent horse organizations, but dozens of others are active. To keep up with all their events, try *The Paper Horse,* a monthly magazine that will keep you current with many shows in Western Pennsylvania and throughout the Commonwealth. You can subscribe for $12 annually.

Pennsylvania Equine Council
P.O. Box 21, Dallas, PA 16827-0570
• (814) 364-9826
The council is a good place to find a horsemen's group to suit your needs and tastes. It publishes a directory of 30 to 40 such groups as well as a newsletter that will update you on events as well as legislative and other activities. Annual membership costs $10, with discounts for families and those under 19. If you belong to an equine group, you might want to take advantage of the council's fire prevention and rescue program—they'll travel to your barn to offer instruction.

Hunting

Hunting in the Commonwealth is the preserve of the Pennsylvania Game Commission. The commission provides many opportunities for hunters in Southwestern Pennsylvania—check out our Parks chapter for an introduction to which state parks permit hunting—but it's best to know some of the rules before you begin.

It's easy to remember that you must be licensed and wear fluorescent orange safety clothing. But do you know the seasons for each species? The limit on kills for each species? The regulations on goose blinds, dog training, and hunting from tree stands? If you're new to hunting in the state, chances are you'll need some help in becoming familiar with Pennsylvania regulations. If you contact the commission, 2001 Elmerton Ave., Harrisburg, PA 17110-9797, (717) 787-4250, they'll send you "A Digest of Pennsylvania Hunting & Trapping Regulations." You'll want to spend some time with it—it runs 55 pages.

Once you know the rules, you're ready to enjoy the approximately 1.4 million acres in Southwestern Pennsylvania that are open to public hunting. Most common quarry are grouse, squirrel, deer, raccoon, rabbit, turkey, and pheasant. Trappers will find both beaver and red fox within sight of Pittsburgh's suburbs. If you venture east to the Chestnut, Laurel, and Allegheny ridges, you may encounter black bear. One of the better guides to area game is the Pennsylvania Game Commission's "Hunting in Southwestern Pennsylvania." You'll find detailed acreage and game lists for each hunting tract.

A good way to keep up with hunting news in the state is through the official monthly magazine of the Pennsylvania Game Commission. It's called "Game News," and you can subscribe for $12 per year.

Ice Hockey

B.M. (Before Mario), ice hockey was an informal kids' game played whenever the pond froze over. Today, thanks to the influence of Mario Lemieux and the success of the National Hockey League's Pittsburgh Penguins, youth ice hockey in Western Pennsylvania is a sophisticated, complex businesses that has given rise to hundreds of organizations as well as occasional

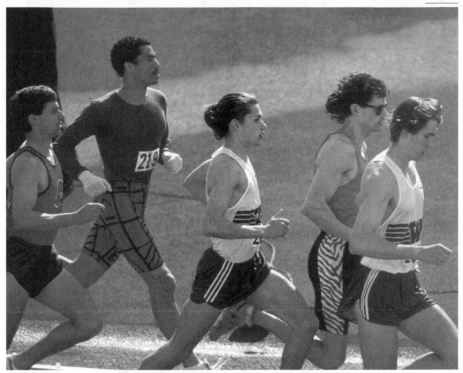

Hit the road in one of the area's many sanctioned races.

jurisdictional squabbling. We'll try to sort out the organizational structure for you.

The Mid-American District of USA Hockey is the coordinating body for amateur youth hockey in Western Pennsylvania, Ohio, West Virginia, Indiana, and Kentucky. Within its region, the district keeps track of 280 organizations, 2,400 teams, and more than 30,000 players and coaches. If you're looking for a hockey organization based in your community, the district will point you in the right direction. You can call their hotline at (412) 884-2922.

For scholastic and collegiate hockey, the coordinating entity is Tri-State Area Hockey Association, (724) 864-8148. TAHA sponsors a scholarship competition and each year awards certificates to Academic All-Stars.

The South Hills Amateur Hockey League, (412) 854-1848, unlike TAHA or the Mid-American District, is not an administrative body. Rather, it stages playoffs for local organizations that include 7,000 kids. The league's web site, pahockey.com, is a great source for information on local organizations and tournaments.

That's a quick guide to the structure of youth ice hockey. Here's a look at some of the most prominent organizations.

Pittsburgh Amateur Penguins Hockey Association
2310 Penn Ave., Pittsburgh
• (412) 767-0421

This program is affiliated with the Pittsburgh Penguins, a relationship that dates to 1983. The Amateur Penguins compete at the highest level of amateur hockey, in the Buffalo-based Empire West League. The program is for youths from 8 to 20 with a serious commitment to hockey. They practice two or three times a week at BladeRunners Ice Complex in Warrendale and Harmarville, pay about $1,500 to the association, and adhere to the group's dress code.

Steel City Stars
706 Heathergate Dr., Fox Chapel
• (412) 767-5049

The Stars are a junior 'C' team. That means a relaxed atmosphere and very little travel. The club, which features three teams with players up to 20 years of age, practices at BladeRunners Ice Complex in Harmarville and plays college hockey squads and other junior 'C' teams. The teams hold tryouts annually before the season starts, but endeavor to find a place for all who want to play. Players are responsible for fees—make sure to inquire about them.

Ice Skating

Ice skating in the region is inextricably linked with ice hockey. Not every ice skater is a hockey player, of course, but hockey teams snap up so much ice time at commercial facilities that it's sometimes difficult for others to find ice time at convenient hours. Public facilities may be your best bet, and two of these merit special attention.

The Schenley Park Skating Rink, operated by the City of Pittsburgh in the Oakland neighborhood, is open year-round for ice skating and in-line skating. In addition to public sessions, the city operates leagues and pick-up hockey programs for ice hockey and roller hockey and rents rink and meeting room time. Call the rink at (412) 422-6523 for schedules and fees.

You also will find ice time for rent at the Belmont Complex, (724) 548-1067, operated by the Armstrong County Recreation Authority, where skating and hockey are two of the principal activities. For more on Schenley Park and Belmont Complex, see our Parks chapter.

Ice skating is a special treat at state parks and federal recreation areas—no hockey teams to contend with here—though you will need cooperation from the weather. Our Parks chapter will introduce you to ice skating opportunities at these facilities. For more comprehensive brochures, contact the Pennsylvania Parks Information and Reservations line, (888) PA-PARKS.

Lacrosse

Pittsburgh Lacrosse Club
217 Seventh St., Apt. 4, Aspinwall
• **(724) 327-8775**
• **www.threeriverslacrosse.org**

Founded in the mid-1960s, the Pittsburgh Lacrosse Club provides just about year-round opportunities. During its outdoor and indoor seasons, from March through June and November through January, respectively, the club competes in the Midwest League and its clubs from Cleveland, Columbus, Chicago, Detroit, and St. Louis. The club plays at two fields in the City of Pittsburgh—Dean Field in Bloomfield and Arsenal Field in Lawrenceville—as well as the Harmarville Sports Complex.

In the summer, the action is less formal but just as enjoyable, when club members welcome local high school and college players for free-spirited competition at Shadyside Academy in Fox Chapel. With only about 35 active players, the club always welcomes new members.

Lawn Bowling

Frick Park Lawn Bowling Association
427 Dorseyville Rd., O'Hara
• **(412) 782-0848**

Lawn bowling in the region is the domain of the Pittsburgh Lawn Bowling Association . . . literally. As far as we know, you won't find lawn bowling anywhere else in the state. The City of Pittsburgh provides lawn bowling rinks at Frick Park, but the association, founded in 1938, raises funds to maintain the facility through private donations and several plant-selling fundraisers each year.

The genteel game is played on rinks that are 120 feet long and 15 feet wide and is distinct from boccie ball, where the course is a gravel pit with sidewalls. The season generally begins in May and lasts until Labor Day, or as long as weather permits. The association engages in league play on Tuesdays and Wednesdays, while pick-up action occurs Thursday and Friday evenings. The action is pretty much continuous on weekends. Newcomers are always welcome—in fact, veteran bowlers will provide complimentary lessons. So give it a try! You won't find lawn bowling anywhere else in Pennsylvania.

Annual membership in the club costs $100 for adults and $25 for youths, with equipment provided. There's also a new youth league offering free supplies and lessons for four weeks. If you're an adult new to the sport, you can play for free in May to determine if you like it. When you join, beyond helping with plant sales, you will be required to wear traditional white dress in tournaments; "No whites, no play," is a venerable club rule. Don't knock it. The sight of the bowlers in their tourney whites on the perfectly smooth green is one of the city's most appealing and relaxing tableaux.

Polo

Darlington Polo Club
Address, Darlington
• **(724) 827-2800**

In 1937, Glenn Watterson founded the Darlington Polo Club. Today, Glenn Watterson

II operates the club, maintaining this unusual asset for the region. The club competes—at the Beaver County field it owns—in the Mid-States Circuit, which also includes clubs from Grand Rapids, Toronto, Lexington, Cincinnati, Virginia, Cleveland, and Columbus. You can catch the club each Friday at 8 PM from May through August. With admission at only $3, you can't beat the price for an evening's entertainment. It's best call ahead if skies are threatening, because rain will force cancellation of the match.

The club welcomes new members, but you must provide your own equine partner. Oh yes. One of the current club members is a young man named Glenn Watterson III. Looks like the Darlington Polo Club has a secure future.

Rugby

Western Pennsylvania is a hotbed of rugby, though the participants themselves aren't sure why. Some attribute it to the popularity of collegiate rugby in the region; as college players graduate, this theory goes, they've created clubs to extend their opportunities to play. In any case, the region boasts at least six major clubs, which always welcome new players. All the clubs profiled below feature spring and fall seasons; most practice during the week and play their matches on Saturday afternoons.

Before you begin play, talk to club members to gauge their intensity. Each of the clubs has developed a "culture," so to speak. You'll want to select the club that best fits you; you're sure to fit in somewhere. Also, if rugby is a little rugged for your tastes, but you'd like to get involved anyway, think about officiating. There's a chronic shortage of officials. Tom Barr, who runs the Allegheny Rugby Referees Society, says you'll be revered. "It's a guy thing not to read the rulebook," Barr says, "so the referees are like shamans." You can reach the society at (412) 488-2212.

Beadling Hooligans Rugby Football Club
1604 McFarland Rd., Pittsburgh
• **(412) 531-7251**

Formed in 1978, the Hooligans perform in both the Allegheny Rugby Union and the Midwest Rugby Union. Edgebrook Field in South Park serves as home field. By their own admission, the Hooligans are perhaps the most social of the area's rugby clubs. It's not that they don't take their rugby seriously. It's just that they take the postgame party just as seriously.

Pittsburgh Women's Rugby Club
1647 Morningside Ave., Pittsburgh
• **(412) 362-8207**

They're nicknamed the "Angels," but there's nothing angelic about the game these women play. They practice twice a week and play their home matches at Frick Park in the City of Pittsburgh's Regent Square neighborhood. Because there are comparatively few women's rugby clubs, the Angels schedule matches against squads from Ohio, Washington, D.C., and other distant cities, so you can expect some travel if you join. New members are most welcome.

Greensburg Area Rugby Football Club
104 North Sixth St., Youngwood
• **(724) 925-1320**

Their nickname is "Gorillas" and they play at Mammoth Park. Does that tell you what you need to know about this club? The club plays in the Allegheny Rugby Union and practices at Lynch Field in Greensburg. The organization welcomes new Gorillas.

Highlanders Rugby Football Club
12 Lennox Ave., Forest Hills
• **(412) 886-1134**

The Highlanders' home games in the Allegheny Rugby Union, part of which is a national organization, take place in Pittsburgh. The Highlanders are a Division 3 team and a good venue for developing your game. The 160-member club is always looking for new members.

Running

You can run to your heart's content in Western Pennsylvania. Many parks offer walking and jogging trails—see our Parks chapter for which parks have the most appropriate facilities. More commonly, runners in the region practice their sport informally, tackling the region's hilly terrain with gusto. A warning is in order: if you're not used to hill running, introduce yourself to Pittsburgh's terrain gradually. You might not realize how taxing hill running can be.

Two of the premier events in the region are staged by the City of Pittsburgh. The Pittsburgh Marathon occurs annually on the first Sunday of May each year, and it's preceded by a festive week that features clinics, receptions, and the occasional merchandise sale. The course falls entirely within city limits, winding across the rivers and offering its share of slopes. In each neighborhood, residents turn out to cheer the

RECREATION

Youth sports fill our parks and fields most of the year.

RECREATION

runners, transforming the marathon into a 26-mile celebration. It is a serious event, however, and has been used as an Olympics qualifier. The marathon features men's, women's, and wheelchair divisions—prize money is awarded in each division—as well as shorter races incorporated within the marathon.

If you're not quite ready for the challenge of marathoning, try the Richard S. Caliguiri Great Race, a 10-kilometer event staged each September. The course begins at Frick Park in Squirrel Hill and ends at Point State Park downtown. The Great Race is extremely popular, typically drawing more than 10,000 runners, so it's a great place to socialize as well.

The Pittsburgh Marathon and the Great Race are the region's signature running events, but there are hundreds of others. The *Pittsburgh Post-Gazette* publishes a schedule of running events each Sunday and produces an annual calendar of races each March. In addition, two organizations can keep you posted on coming events.

Runner's High, 83 Cranberry Rd., Grove City, PA 16127, (724) 458-4435, provides timing services for many of the region's races and publishes a road race directory about once every three months providing details for approxi-

mately 500 races per year in Western Pennsylvania, as well as all such race results. (S. Mark Courtney, founder and principal of Runner's High, meticulously records the names of all finishers in important races.) An annual subscription to the directory costs $10, or you can visit the organization's web site, runhigh.com, for similar information.

A second race timing service, operated by Dave Mapes, provides a free race calendar that catalogues about 80 races per year. You can reach this service at 1202 Grandview Ave., Somerset, PA, 15501, (814) 445-6213. If you enclose a self-addressed, stamped envelope with your request, Dave will send you his calendar free of charge.

Shooting

Allegheny County Sportsmen's League
1028 Hulton Rd., Verona
• (412) 882-9115

Shooting is a popular Western Pennsylvania activity, as witnessed by the more than 40 organized sportsmen's clubs. The Allegheny County Sportsmen's League serves as their umbrella organization, publishing an annual directory of clubs and their facilities. You can contact the organization for a current directory. You'll find facilities for a broad variety of shooting, including skeet- and trap-, high-powered rifle-, and handgun-shooting, as well as a civilian marksmanship program that utilizes older military rifles. Many of the clubs host competitions and leagues, and some feature archery ranges and private lakes for fishing.

Greater Pittsburgh Trap & Skeet
920 King Rd., Bulger
• (724) 796-9111

Most area sportsmen's clubs are private. Greater Pittsburgh Trap & Skeet is one of the few exceptions, offering public facilities as well as hosting a private club. Skeet trap and sporting clays are the organization's most popular offerings. You'll also enjoy rifle-, pistol-, and combat-shooting, as well as an archery range, with all facilities available daily. NSCA shoots are held once a month.

For relaxation, the clubhouse is open all weekend, plus Wednesday and Thursday evenings. Pay by the day or hour, and if you need equipment, ammunition, or ear protection, just knock on the door of proprietor Tex Freund, who lives on the premises. He'll be happy to rent you whatever you need. The guess here is that Tex goes through a lot of ear protection equipment himself.

Skiing

The hills elsewhere may be alive with the sound of music, but in Western Pennsylvania, they're alive with the sights of skiers. With its climate and topography, the region provides excellent skiing venues. You'll find plenty of opportunities for cross-country and downhill skiing, as well as a skiing community that loves its apres ski (the after-ski party). We've highlighted Western Pennsylvania slopes and cross-county trails, but keep in mind that you'll find additional opportunities nearby in West Virginia, Maryland, and New York. Our region boasts a run for just about every skier, whatever your level of experience. Here's the dope on slopes.

Cross-Country Skiing

Cross-country skiing is a staple of many state parks and federal recreation areas. Our Parks chapter will introduce you to local facilities that

offer this activity. Keep in mind that some parks offer well-delineated trails, while at others, the skiers just go with the flow. For more detailed information on particular parks or creation areas, contact the Pennsylvania Bureau of State Parks, (888) PA-PARKS, or the U.S. Army Corps of Engineers, (412) 644-6924.

Several local organizations organize cross-country ski outings. Allegheny Group, Sierra Club, (724) 327-8737, hosts ski-touring treks at such locations as the Laurel Mountains and West Virginia's Canaan Valley. Often, the group doesn't determine its destination until several days before the outing, in the hope of encountering the best weather conditions. It's always best to call ahead. They'll rent you all the gear you need. Participants car-pool for most outings, so you'll be expected to pony up your fair share.

Downhill Skiing

Boyce Park
675 Frankstown Rd., Plum
• (724) 327-8798

You can't beat the convenience of Boyce Park, which is operated by Allegheny County. You'll find it in the easternmost portion of the county, no more than a 30-minute drive from anywhere in the county. Boyce features beginners' and intermediate slopes with a total of nine runs, including moguls, Nastar timing runs with gates, jumps, and night skiing. The vertical drop is 180 feet, and lifts include two double chairlifts, one poma, and one T-bar. You can pay by the day or purchase a season pass. The park provides equipment rentals as well as special group rates on lift tickets.

Kids will have a grand time here with several special events, including an annual Mini-Junior Olympics for boys and girls from 5 to 12 years of age. You can learn the sport at the ski school and try cross-country skiing along the park's trails and hills using your own equipment. Snowboarders will fancy the Alpine Terrain Park and its 200-foot halfpipe. Whichever activity you choose, you'll enjoy apres ski at the Four Seasons Ski Lodge. For more on Boyce Park, see our Parks chapter.

Hidden Valley Resort
Four Craighead Dr., Hidden Valley
• (814) 443-8000, (800) 458-0175

Hidden Valley bills itself as the "Total Winter Fun" place, a handle that seems most appropriate. Spanning 88 acres, the facility boasts an

RECREATION

uphill, per-hour capacity of more than 12,000 skiers who utilize eight lifts, including one quad chairlift, two triples, three doubles, and two handle tows, as well as 17 runs and trails. The vertical drop ranges from 340 feet to 430 feet, so you know you're in for a fun ride. You'll also enjoy more than 50 kilometers of cross-country trails.

Part of Hidden Valley Resort, the ski facility offers a 400-foot halfpipe for snowboarding, as well as snow tubing, sleigh rides, and snowshoeing. You can rent downhill and cross-country ski equipment as well as snowboarding gear. For your pleasure at Hidden Valley, you can pay by the day or purchase a season pass entitling you to unlimited skiing. There's no charge for skiers under 5 or over 70.

You can take advantage of a variety of instructional packages. If you're worried about the kids while you're studying or skiing, drop them at the resort's Mountain Kids Ski Center, which offers babysitting services and organized activities, including a variety of youth ski and snowboard programs.

When you're ready to relax, you'll have the entire resort at your fingertips. You'll find more about the amenities of Hidden Valley in our Accommodations and Golf chapters.

For a report on current ski conditions, call the Hidden Valley hotline, (800) 443-SKII.

Nemacolin Woodlands Mystic Mountain
1001 La Fayette, Farmington
• (724) 329-8555, (800) 422-2736

Mystic Mountain ski area is part of Nemacolin Woodlands Resort & Spa, which tells you right out of the chute that you're in for top-quality activities and amenities. When you leave that chute, the vertical drop is 300 feet. Mystic Mountain is equipped with one regular quad chairlift and one handle bar. You'll find a full line of rental equipment, including cross-country skis and snowboards. Groups of 20 or more receive special discounts on ski tickets and rentals. Hours are 9 AM to 9 PM seven days a week.

If you need some help before you tackle the mountain, the resort offers three group instruction sessions each day. You can supplement that with private lessons including an intense session that lasts three hours. You also may take advantage of a youth program for kids from 7 to 12 years of age. Lunch is included, but ski equipment is not. For other Nemacolin features, see our Accommodations and Golf chapters.

Seven Springs Mountain Resort
RD#1, Champion
• (814) 352-7777, (800) 452-2223

You've reached a certain pinnacle when you ski at Seven Springs—the vertical drop ranges from 360 feet to 750 feet, while the skiable terrain measures 500 acres. Just as breathtaking are the facilities, which include 31 slopes and trails, three quad chairlifts, seven triples, and eight tows. The lift capacity is 24,600 per hour, and the longest run stretches for 1¼ miles. If you're ready to tackle all this, you can rent all the equipment you need and enjoy such related activities as snow tubing. If ever you need help on the slopes, the resort maintains a 150-member ski patrol to assist you.

The resort's Kids' Corner offers child care services as well as a Tiny Tots instructional program. Seven Springs provides a variety of lodging packages, instructional programs, and skiing packages. Of course, you're always welcome to pay by the day. The resort is an accommodating place for apres ski—make sure you try the outdoor hot tubs! Check the hotline, (800) 523-7777, for a report on current ski conditions. See our Accommodations and Golf chapters for more about Seven Springs.

Snowmobiling

You'll find some of the best snowmobiling trails in the region at state parks, forests and game lands and federal recreation areas. The season generally runs until about April 1, or until the weather no longer is conducive. Remember that on state terrain, you'll need a valid snowmobile registration as well as proof of liability insurance coverage. Our Parks chapter will tell you which local facilities offer snowmobiling. For more comprehensive brochures, contact the Pennsylvania Parks Information and Reservations line, (888) PA-PARKS; the Pennsylvania Game Commission, (717) 783-7507; or the U.S. Army Corps of Engineers, (412) 395-7500. For a nominal fee, the Game Commission also will provide you with detailed maps of its lands.

> ## INSIDERS' TIP
> To check the condition of snowmobile trails at state parks, call the state's Snowmobile Hotline, (717) 787-5651. It is a toll call.

McKean Snowriders Club
P.O. Box 27, McKean, PA 16426
• (814) 476-7221

If you're willing to travel a bit for your snowmobiling thrills, you'll find some like-minded riders in Northwestern Pennsylvania. The McKean Snowriders Club belongs to the Erie County Snowmobile Affiliation, an alliance of five groups that plans exciting and challenging outings while undertaking useful projects, such as mapping snowmobile trails. One of the club's favorite rides is along a 175-mile loop in the Allegheny National Forest. The Snowriders welcome participants from Southwestern Pennsylvania.

Soccer

Though it may seem like sacrilege in what was traditionally football country, soccer has become the sport of choice for many area youths. In fact, it's estimated that there are more than 55,000 registered players in the region. It would be difficult, if not impossible, to detail all the region's soccer organizations. Instead, we offer you information on the coordinating agency as well as several of the most important clubs that operate in different geographic regions.

PA West State Soccer Association
855 MacBeth Dr., Monroeville
• (412) 856-8011

Through the United States Soccer Federation, PA West Soccer serves as the overall coordinator for all non-scholastic soccer in this half of the state. Its numbers are impressive, as it encompasses 124 youth clubs with 55,000 members as well as eight adult leagues and 2,000 members. For its members, the association handles registration; scheduling; and referees, who number 2,300 strong.

Of special interest are the association's programs targeted to disadvantaged youths and those with physical and mental challenges. If you're looking for the best soccer opportunity for your particular situation, this is the best place to start. You can visit the group's web site at www.pawest-soccer.org.

Beadling Soccer Club
P.O. Box 435, Bridgeville, PA, 15017
• (412) 221-3880

If you visit Beadling in Pittsburgh's South Hills, they'll be pleased to show you a photograph of the 1898 Beadling club. Needless to

say, Beadling is one of the oldest soccer organizations anywhere. Today, the club administers 20 boys' and girls' teams that play in the Classic League. Beadling also boasts membership in the Continental Alliance, a group of 22 elite clubs. Players range in age from 12 to 20 and must try out for the teams. Some of the teams enter tournaments that take them as far away as France. Youths accepted for the program must provide $500 to cover the club's costs. Club members also participate in less formal adult men's leagues.

Penns Forest Football Club
P.O. Box 17337, Pittsburgh, 15235
• (412) 798-9830

Based in Pittsburgh's eastern suburbs, the club sports 15 teams of youths ages 12 to 19. They play in a number of leagues, including the Classic League, the Premier League, and the National League, with home fields located in Harmarville and the Westmoreland County community of North Huntingdon. Players must try out for teams and are responsible for a $50 registration fee plus all expenses.

Pittsburgh Strikers
P.O. Box 309, Sewickley, PA 15143
• (412) 486-6915

Boys and girls between the ages of 12 to 18 are eligible to try out for the Strikers, who play at a number of fields in the North Hills. The club participates in the Classic League. Be sure to ask about costs, as the Strikers don't publish a fee schedule.

Softball

Softball—the slow-pitch variety—is a popular warm-weather activity in Western Pennsylvania, so much so that it's hard to find an open field at the height of the season. While leagues abound, the sport lacks an overall coordinating body, so that a league appropriate for your skill level may be hard to locate at once. Many teams are company based, meaning you can play only if you work there. Word of mouth may be the best way to find a league, but here are a few suggestions, whether you're searching for a team or your team is looking for a league or tournament play.

One of the neatest opportunities is with the 50 And Older Softball League, (412) 343-5438. Nearly 100 players ages 50 to 83 play twice weekly games at fields in the South Hills. Your $25 fee includes a jersey and cap. The league

RECREATION

uses standard American Softball Association rules, with some modifications. For example, players may not slide into home plate.

If your team is looking for a highly competitive league, try the Pittsburgh Amateur Softball League. Each year the league brings together about 85 men's and women's teams that play at fields throughout Allegheny County. The best teams travel to national tournaments, and the league also sponsors touring youth teams. You can reach the men's division at (412) 488-0844, the women's division at (412) 771-6473.

The Penn Hills Sports Shop Softball League, (412) 795-3636, typically fields a league of about 30 men's teams, most based in the City of Pittsburgh's eastern suburbs. The teams are grouped by ability to assure the most enjoyable competition. One variation here: since the league is not run by a municipality, teams are expected to provide their own permitted fields.

For tournament play, you can get your season off to a running start with the Bud Lite Sports Page Softball Tournament, (724) 325-4964, held each April in Pittsburgh's eastern suburbs. The event usually pits about 30 teams and offers prize money to the winners. All proceeds benefit the Mario Lemieux Foundation.

Swimming

The City of Pittsburgh operates an extensive network of pools, with the outdoor season generally from early June through Labor Day. The network includes 31 outdoor pools as well as the Oliver Bath House on the Southside, which is open year round. The pools are open to city residents and nonresidents alike, although city dwellers receive discounts on admissions fees. The city also offers a discount for recipients of public assistance. For schedules and fee information, contact Citiparks' pool hotline at (412) 594-4645.

You'll also find swimming opportunities at other municipal pools and at state parks and federal recreation areas. Our Parks chapter will suggest some swimming venues for you. Keep in mind that some state and federal facilities offer sand beaches, others turf beaches. Some without lakes have large swimming pools. Food concessions and changing and showering facilities also vary. For comprehensive brochures, contact the Pennsylvania Parks Information and

Reservations line, (888) PA-PARKS, and the U.S. Army Corps of Engineers, (412) 395-7500.

Tennis

The tennis boom may be long over, but the sport continues to flourish here. Most of the courts constructed during the boom of the 1970s remain, and they're more available than ever before. You'll find indoor and outdoor courts aplenty at municipal parks, as well as courts at commercial facilities and private clubs.

The City of Pittsburgh's Citiparks, (412) 244-4188, offers a broad variety of tennis opportunities. If you're a beginner, you'll benefit from free group lessons provided through USA Tennis, a tennis industry program that also barnstorms Pittsburgh's neighborhoods with youth clinics. Citiparks also offers private lessons at $30 per hour and group clinics with varying fees.

You'll soon be ready for the Citiparks Adult Grand Prix Tennis League, which matches singles and doubles players of comparable skills. Some fees are involved. Finally, the Citiparks program includes clinics specially tailored to senior citizens and "munchkins" from 4 to 7 years of age. Munchkins is their word, not ours. When we're charging the net, we have great respect for anyone with a racquet—munchkin or not—on the other side.

Triathlon

Triathlons can be demanding, so demanding that it's sometimes hard to assemble a healthy field year after year. For that reason, you won't find many triathlons in the area; those you do discover won't be steeped in tradition and history.

One of the more established events is the Carnegie Mellon Triathlon, (412) 268-8140, launched in 1987 as a fitness project for Carnegie Mellon University faculty and staff. It's open to all now. The September event includes a 500-yard swim, 12 miles of biking, and a 5K run—all of it contained on CMU's campus and the adjacent Schenley Park.

Perhaps the newest of the area's triathlons is the Friends of the Riverfront Triathlon, founded in 1998 by Friends of the Riverfront to promote the development of riverfront trails

INSIDERS' TIP

The Pittsburgh Marathon served as the men's Olympics qualifying race in 2000. In years past it has also been the qualifier for the women's Olympics trial.

One of the best ski venues is Seven Springs Mountain Resort & Conference Center in Somerset County.

Photo: Neal Palumbo courtesy of Greater Pittsburgh Convention & Visitor's Bureau

local colleges and universities, holistic health centers, and meditation rooms in private homes. There are almost as many forms of yoga and meditation being practiced as there are venues: various schools of Hatha yoga, such as Iyengar yoga, Kripalu yoga, and Ashtanga yoga; Zen meditation; and Kundalini yoga. Because Zen meditation is associated with Zen Buddhism, we've included some information in the Worship chapter. Note also that all the forms of yoga represented here teach some type of meditation as well.

Several of the forms, including Kundalini yoga and gentle forms of Hatha yoga, offer special benefits and/or exercises for pregnant women. Kundalini is especially good for people trying to build strength and balance the internal systems of the body, particularly the immune and glandular systems. That includes people recovering from or coping with severe illness.

Below we've listed contacts for some of the main groups or centers that offer yoga and meditation. We've left out health clubs due to their commercial nature. We encourage you, however, to check out clubs through the Yellow Pages. When you're looking for a yoga teacher, you'll want to find out what form she or he teaches; how the form will help you achieve the results you want; where the teacher was trained and how extensive the training was; and how many years the teacher has been practicing yoga.

and expose Pittsburgh's waterfronts to a greater audience. The event features 20 kilometers of biking and 5 kilometers of running, and, in a departure from the usual event agenda, a 5-K canoeing or kayaking test along the Allegheny River in place of swimming. For information, contact Friends of the Riverfront at P.O. Box 42434, Pittsburgh, PA, 15203, (412) 488-0212.

Yoga and Meditation

You'll find yoga and meditation being practiced in all kinds of venues in the Pittsburgh area: hospitals, health clubs, yoga centers, churches and synagogues, community centers,

The Kundalini Yoga and Yogic Healing Society of Pennsylvania
• (412) 886-1211

Call the number listed above to find a Kundalini yoga teacher in your area or to investigate dates for yogic healing courses. As noted above, Kundalini yoga is appropriate for you no matter what your fitness level is, and yoga classes can range from the very vigorous to the very gentle—many exercises can even be done lying down or sitting in a chair. Kundalini yoga employs sound therapy in nearly every class and meditation. As noted above, the practice is excellent for those of all levels of fitness, including people recovering from or coping with severe illness.

The main form of yogic healing taught in our coverage area is Sat Nam Rasayan, which, loosely translated, means "divine relaxation." Sat Nam Rasayan uses the basic tools of meditation, in a particular way, to sustain a neutral space of healing. If you practice Sat Nam Rasayan, you will learn both how to heal others (and yourself) and how to meditate more deeply and effectively.

Sampurna Yoga Center
411 Mill St., Coraopolis
• (412) 262-5445

Established in 1993, the Sampurna Yoga Center offers ongoing Hatha yoga classes and sponsors special workshops and occasional classes on diet, meditation, Sanskrit and chanting, and other related subjects. The majority of classes are taught by Robert Barton, the director and founder of the center. Other teachers include Robert's wife, Yamuna Devi, who also organizes the special workshops, and two advanced students trained as instructors at the center.

Classes are available for students of all levels. The Hatha yoga traditions that influence the classes at the center include Astanga Vinyasa, Bikrams, Iyengar, Sampoorna, Sivananda, and Vini yoga. The center also offers teacher training in its eclectic method of Hatha yoga. Two main price plans are available at Sampurna: $60 per month for unlimited classes and, for students new to the center, $60 for 60 days of unlimited classes. Other packages are available for people visiting from out of town.

Located in the heart of downtown Coraopolis, the center is 20 minutes west of downtown Pittsburgh, 20 minutes from the North Hills, and 10 miles from the Greater Pittsburgh International Airport. You'll also want to note that Sampurna Yoga Center is a "Fragrance Free Zone."

Yoga Sadhana Studio
East Carson St., Pittsburgh
• (412) 481-YOGA

Located on Pittsburgh's Southside, this studio is on the third floor of an old office building. The space is beautiful with hardwood floors, high ceilings, and windows that offer a view of the sky as well as the gargoyles on the building next door. It's great to stretch up during Cobra pose and catch a glimpse of those gargoyles!

Courses in a variety of forms of yoga, dance, and related disciplines are offered at the center daily. When we called, classes scheduled were beginning, intermediate, and advanced Hatha yoga and Ashtanga yoga; Pilates; intermediate and advanced Modern Dance; Ballet for Modern Bodies; and Flamenco. The studio is continually adding new classes, and workshops on various topics are held there regularly. Integrative Yoga therapy and massage are also available. Drop in for a class for $12. Check out the variety of discount class cards available when you pay a lump sum from $40 to $80 and make a regular commitment to your health and well being.

The studio shares its home with Labco Dance, a modern dance company with up-and-coming choreographers. An art gallery is on the second floor of the building the studio shares. Come, relax, get cultured! Yoga Sadhana Studio is a fun and peaceful place.

Yoga Training Association of Pittsburgh (YTAP)
• (412) 421-1506

Founded by a small group of yoga teachers twenty-five years ago, YTAP's purpose "is to foster education about and practice of the ancient science and art of yoga." Currently, YTAP membership is a mixture of yoga teachers and yoga students of varying levels. Except during summer months, YTAP holds monthly meetings during which a teacher of yoga or a related discipline presents a class. The group also brings in several nationally or regionally known yoga teachers each year and hosts an annual "Yoga Day Out" devoted to showcasing a variety of the forms of yoga and related disciplines available in the Pittsburgh area. YTAP also offers the opportuntiy for those practicing yoga to stay in touch with other like-minded individuals, to make new friends, and to network.

The group publishes five newsletters per year advertising the dates of some of the major yoga events in the area and offering various philosophical meanderings related to yoga and meditation. Periodically, the newsletter includes a simple directory of members; the names of teachers are marked with a "T." If you're a yoga teacher looking for a substitute for one of your classes, this list is one of the best places to start. Yearly membership in the organization was $25 in 2000. We've not listed an address for YTAP, because the organization meets at a different location each month in an effort to make meetings convenient for members living in the various Pittsburgh area neighborhoods.

RECREATION

Golf

Golf in Western Pennsylvania is more than a sport or hobby—it's something approaching a regional passion. The relatively short season may be a handicap, but there are several compelling reasons why golf is so popular here.

Pittsburgh was for many years a leading corporate headquarters town—at one time outranked only by New York and Chicago—as well as a center for manufacturing. Golf always has been a popular getaway for corporate executives, a fondness that tended to trickle down throughout such organizations. Today, even though the region boasts a more diversified economy, that heritage of golf as the ideal vehicle for relaxation and competition remains.

A second pillar of golf's foundation in Western Pennsylvania can be summarized in two words—Arnold Palmer. One of golf's legends, Palmer was reared in Westmoreland County, created several golf courses here, and remains highly visible, staging tournaments for charity, maintaining his offices near his hometown of Latrobe, and popping up on countless television commercials. The rage for golf in Western Pennsylvania is part of Arnold Palmer's gift to the community.

The statistics are impressive. Of Pennsylvania's 705 public and private golf courses, the National Golf Foundation reports that Allegheny County and Westmoreland County rank second and third in the state, respectively, in the number of courses, with a combined total of 81 18-hole equivalents. Butler County is not far behind, ranking sixth.

Of 309 metropolitan areas in the country for which the foundation keeps records, the average golf hole per population rate is 76 holes per 100,000 people. In Pittsburgh, the rate is 101 holes per 100,000 people.

The region boasts courses to suit all tastes and talents, ranging from quick-play executive courses to storied Oakmont Country Club, site of a number of major Professional Golf Association tournaments over the years. You'll find courses carved from mountainsides, a course built atop a slag heap, even a municipal course operated by a university.

In our descriptions below, we've tried to feature most public courses in our service area, though the rate of construction and course openings makes development of a comprehensive list nearly impossible. Unless otherwise noted, costs cited include the price of electric cart rental. Keep in mind that prices change from season to season—you might find slight variations from those we've provided. We've noted where starting times are available, suggested, or required, and we've tried to describe unusual or compelling features of the courses.

Your tour through Pittsburgh's golf courses will be enjoyable, but take care. When you put "the sticks" in your car trunk permanently, because you never know when you'll get a chance to "hit a few," you'll know that the Pittsburgh golf bug has bitten you.

LOOK FOR:
- Public Golf Courses throughout Greater Pittsburgh

INSIDERS' TIP

Arnold Palmer, Latrobe native and patriarch of golf in Western Pennsylvania, won seven professional majors in his career: four Masters, one U.S. Open, and two British Opens. He also won a U.S. Amateur championship.

Public Golf Courses

North

Aubrey's Dubbs Dred Golf Course
P.O. Box 2053, Mercer Rd., Butler
• **(724) 287-4832**

At Dubbs Dred, you'll be playing target golf, hitting over ravines and gullies to tight landing areas. It's a challenging course from stem to stern. Distance for the par 71 course ranges from 6500 yards to 6850 yards. Starting times are required on weekends and holidays, but are optional during the week. Cost is $30. Dubbs Dred offers a limited-service pro shop and a small lounge.

Bostonia Country Club
Box 184, Distant
• **(814) 275-2553**

Bostonia Country Club is located at the northernmost reaches of Armstrong County. Its relatively remote location means you can get on and off the course quickly, and without a starting time. The 9-hole, par 35 course covers 2800 yards. The cost for nine holes during the week is $8, on weekends $10; for 18 holes during the week it's $12, on weekends $14. Annual memberships priced from $120 for students to $500 for families allow unlimited golf. You'll find a newly remodeled pro shop and a snack bar.

Buffalo Golf Course
201 Monroe Rd., Sarver
• **(724) 353-2440**

Perhaps the most challenging hole on Buffalo Golf Course is No. 15, a 438-yard par 4. There's a pond along the right side of a rising fairway, and trees reach out and hang over the green. Distance of this flat, par 71 course ranges from 6138 yards to 6324 yards. Weekend and holiday starting times are available. Cost is $20 weekdays and $30 on weekends, with senior citizen discounts offered during the week. You'll find a pro shop and a snack bar.

Cabin Greens Golf Course
Ford City Rd., Freeport
• **(724) 295-3744**

Cabin Greens is a pleasant, unpretentious 9-hole course that's a great place to get in a quick round after work. The par 36 course ranges from 2462 yards to 2907 yards. Cost is $21 for 18 holes, $18 for nine holes, with senior citizen

discounts available. Starting times are available on weekends and holidays only. Cabin Greens offers a pro shop and a snack bar.

Cherry Wood Golf Course
204 Truxall Rd., Apollo
• **(724) 727-2546**

When Carol and John Chernega designed Cherry Wood, they had golf in mind, of course, and much more. The Chernegas participate in the national Audubon Cooperative Sanctuary Program to promote native habitats and more natural environments. The course design so complements wildlife habitats that the Chernagas have recorded sightings of 50 species—including foxes, mink, wild turkeys and vultures—on Cherry Wood. Perhaps the most important residents are such birds as woodpeckers, which feed on insects and reduce the need for pesticide application.

If you interrupt your commune with nature to golf, you'll find a 9-hole, par 35 course. Distance ranges from 1895 yards to 3115 yards. Starting times are not offered. Cost for a round of 9 holes is $14 during the week and only a dollar more on weekends, with a $2 discount if you play a second round. Senior citizens enjoy a special discount during the week. Amenities include a pro shop, a snack bar, and a driving range with grass tees.

Clover Hill Golf Course
2200 Reis Run Rd., Franklin Park
• **(412) 364-2447**

While this 2300-yard, par 32 course won't test your long-driving ability over its 9 holes, it does place a premium on shot-making. That's especially true at No. 7, a 173-yard par 3 where you'll hit over a lake to a two-tiered green.

Cost for a round of 9 holes is $14, and you can play a second 9 for $6.50. Seniors receive a daily $2 discount. Clover Hill offers neither starting times nor dining facilities, but you will find vending machines in the small clubhouse.

Conley Resort Inn
740 Pittsburgh Rd., Rt. 8, Butler
• **(724) 586-7711, (800) 344-7303**

Could it be that Coleridge was describing Conley's course when he wrote "Water, water everywhere?" Probably not, but you may feel like the Ancient Mariner when you play Conley. Both irrigation and scenic water hazards come into play on five holes. These include No. 7, a 520-yard par 5, where you must hit over water to reach the green.

Distance ranges from 6200 to 6515 yards, with

6345 yards to 7018 yards. Pay special attention to No. 11, a scenic 382-yard par 4. Your second shot must carry over water to a green sheltered behind by a steep hill dotted with flowers. Cost for a round is around $50. If you're looking for accommodations nearby, check out the Sun and Cricket Bed and Breakfast in our Bed and Breakfasts chapter; it's right next to the golf course, just through the woods.

Green Valley Golf Course
647 Lowries Run Rd.,
Ohio Twp. • (412) 364-9980

The fairways at Green Valley are narrow, but there are few hills and and water hazards. If you can position your drive well, you'll find inviting approaches to the greens in most cases. An exception is No. 8, a lovely par 4 where the green sits atop a plateau.

The par 35, 9 hole course covers 2661 yards. Starting times are not available. If you do hit the green on No. 8 in regulation, you can crow about it later at the snack bar. To play the 9-hole course, it costs $8 on weekdays and $9 on weekends. If you'd like to play a second round, it's $5 at all times. Seniors receive a discount during the week.

Hartmann's Deep Valley Golf Course
169 Hartmann Rd., Harmony
• (724) 452-8021

This is an easy walking 18-hole course, popular with senior citizens, with a back 9 dotted by picturesque water hazards. The par 72 course covers 6310 yards, with no starting times necessary. For 18 holes, the cost is $13 during the week and $18 on the weekends and holidays; for 9, it's $7 on weekdays and $10 on weekends. (These prices don't include electric carts, since the course isn't difficult to walk, but carts are available for an extra charge.) Senior citizens receive discounts during the week. Take advantage of the picnic and banquet facilities, as well as the pro shop, snack bar, and the Watering Hole restaurant/lounge.

Lake Arthur Country Club
255 Isle Rd., Butler
• (724) 865-2765

Lake Arthur offers a great finishing hole,

Western Pennsylvania legend Arnold Palmer (left) once welcomed superstar Tiger Woods to a local charity event.

par varying from 70 to 72. The fee is $37 on weekdays and $47 on weekends, with starting times available from Good Friday until December. You'll find a pro shop as well as a full-service restaurant called The Tavern. For more on Conley Resort Inn, see our Accommodations chapter.

Deer Run Golf Club
287 Monier Rd., Gibsonia
• (724) 265-4800

This semiprivate club is open to nonmembers, although members get first crack at tee times. If you don't belong, you may call two days in advance to arrange a starting time. You will enjoy the facilities, which include a pro shop, locker rooms, restaurant, bar, and banquet areas.

Distance of the par 72 course ranges from

GOLF

and the entire course was upgraded recently. The fairway on No. 18 is flanked by lakes with a small landing area between them. Even if you find the fairway, getting your par 4 on this 451-yard challenge is hardly a sure bet.

Distance for the par 69 course is 6629 yards. Cost is $24 on weekdays and $33 on weekends, with senior citizen discount cards available in the pro shop. Lake Arthur offers starting times every day. In addition to the pro shop, you'll find a chipping green, a bar and lounge, and banquet facilities. If you play Lake Arthur and have time for even more fun, stop at nearby Moraine State Park.

Lake Vue North Golf Course
691 Pittsburgh Rd., Butler
• (724) 586-7097

Lake Vue North offers many picturesque holes that feature water hazards and elevated or hidden greens. Distance for the par 72 course ranges from 5690 yards to 6355 yards. Weekend starting times are available. An 18-hole round will cost $40 for two people; a 9-hole round is $18 for two people. Weekday discounts are available for senior citizens. You'll also find a limited-service pro shop, a snack bar, a lounge, and banquet facilities. If your youngster is a budding golfer, ask about Lake Vue North's junior league.

Lenape Heights Golf Course
Rt. 66, Ford City
• (724) 763-2201

Lenape Heights is a 6145-yard, par 71 course that features a pro shop and a sandwich shop. The cost to play this 18-hole course is $29 on weekdays and $33 on weekends, with weekend starting times available.

The signature hole is No. 13, an unusual 531-yard par 5. What makes it so striking is an island, encircled by a moat, in front of the green. Most who try to reach the green in two end up in the moat. There is a pedestrian bridge to the island, which measures about 20 yards across. If your ball somehow stays on the island, it's in play.

North Park Golf Course
Pearce Mill Rd., Allison Park
• (724) 935-1967

One of two golf courses administered by Allegheny County—South Park is the other—North Park is exceptionally popular and does not offer starting times. To avoid the crowds, try to play the course during the late morning, the early afternoon, and on Fridays, when things are a bit slower. The 6805-yard, par 72 course is an open, gently rolling affair with large greens

and no water, a fun outing no matter what your level of play.

Cost for a round is $22.50 on weekdays and $25.50 on weekends. If you're 60 or older, your age entitles you to a $5, 18-hole round of golf and a $3, 9-hole round; these prices don't include carts. North Park offers a pro shop, a putting green, a driving range, and a full-service restaurant. The course is open year-round. For more on the amenities of North Park, see our Parks chapter.

Pittsburgh North Golf Club
3800 Bakerstown Rd., Gibsonia
• (724) 443-3800

Pittsburgh North offers both an 18-hole course and a 9-hole course known to habitues as "The Fox." The 18-hole course, with a 134 slope rating from the back tees, can be challenging. Distance ranges from 5075 yards to 7000 yards, with par at 72 or 73 depending on which tees you play. The course features several tough par 3 holes, including No. 14, a 232-yard challenge where you must hit over water and avoid a sand trap guarding the right of the green. If you miss to the left, you're likely in the water or the accompanying dam.

The Fox, a par 35 course, ranges from 2051 yards to 2796 yards. Weekend and holiday starting times are available. Cost for 18 holes is $26 on weekdays and $33 on weekends, while you can play The Fox for $14. The club features a pro shop, a bar, and a seasonal driving range. Pittsburgh North regularly hosts group functions of up to 150 people, including outdoor barbecues. Three PGA pros are on staff; they offer a golf school.

Rose Ridge Golf Course
4769 Rt. 910, Allison Park
• (724) 443-5020

To give you some idea of the crowds that Rose Ridge attracts, starting times begin at dawn, and the course maintains a fleet of 90 electric carts. The par 72 course measures 6520 yards. You'll enjoy No. 11, a 165-yard par 3 with an elevated tee and a lake guarding the green. You'll also like the sight of Deer Creek, which winds its way for nearly a mile through the course.

Cost is $25, with weekend and holiday starting times available. Rose Ridge features a driving range, a lounge, and a sandwich shop.

Saxon Golf Course
839 Ekastown Rd., Saxonburg
• (724) 353-2130

Saxon Golf Course is a duffer's dream. It

offers 27 holes, with nary a water hazard or sand bunker to be found, and both the 18-hole course and the 9-hole layout are flat. Distance for the par 72 18-hole course ranges from 5131 to 6177 yards, while the tight little 9-hole course, a par 34, covers 2255 yards.

Starting times are available on weekends and holidays. Cost for the 18-hole course on weekdays is $16, on weekends $18 to $20, depending on the time you choose to play; for the 9-hole course, it's $9 all week. You'll find a snack bar, a driving range, chipping areas, and a picnic shelter you can reserve for a group outing. When you get to know course operators Frank Ekas, Sr., and Frank Ekas, Jr., you'll be encountering a bit of local history—Ekastown Road was named for their family, early blacksmiths who helped settle the Saxonburg area.

Shamrock Public Golf Course
481 Grove City Rd., Slippery Rock
• (724) 794-3030

This par 35, 9-hole course is deceptive. While its layout of 2686 yards seems inviting, there are three par 4s longer than 400 yards. You'll also encounter a challenge at No. 2, a 155-yard par 3 with a green surrounded by steep hills. Miss in any direction and you're in double-bogey territory.

Cost for a round of 9 holes is $6.50, and you can play 18 for $12. Carts are available at an additional cost. Starting times are not offered. You'll enjoy the chipping area, snack bar, and banquet facilities.

Stoughton Acres Golf Course
904 Sunset Dr., Butler
• (724) 285-3633

No. 13 at Stoughton Acres will challenge you. It's a 524-yard par 5 that forces you to cross both water and a highway to reach the green. The par 71 course covers 6054 yards. Reserved tee times are available on weekends. You'll find a pro shop and a snack bar. Stoughton Acres does not publish its very reasonable green fees and cart charges. We recommend that you check Stoughton Acres out, especially if you want to play a nice round without emptying out your wallet.

Suncrest Golf Course
137 Brownsdale Rd., Butler
• (724) 586-5508

The front 9 at Suncrest is flat—that will get you in shape for the hillier back 9. Distance for the par 72 layout ranges from 5415 yards to 6243 yards. Cost for a round is $31, with week-

end starting times available. Suncrest offers senior citizen discounts during the week. Facilities include a pro shop and a snack bar.

Venango Trail Golf Club
1305 Freeport Rd., Mars
• (724) 776-4400

If you've cranked up your long game, you can let it out on Venango Trial's No. 8, a 590-yard par 5 with a lake, a creek, and a ravine all threatening you about 400 yards from the tee. A prudent player will lay up before the trouble, but if you're feeling feisty, go for the green on your second shot.

The par 72 course measures 6200 yards. Starting times are available each day. Cost is $32. Venango Trail offers memberships for individual players, senior citizens, corporations, and families. Member benefits include unlimited golf, priority tee times, and discounts in the pro shop and restaurant.

John Sandherr, Venango's director of golf, says you'll be "treated like a king or a queen." In return for such treatment, be prepared to dress a little more royally. Venango does not permit blue jeans or revealing clothing, and all shirts must have collars. You may wear shorts.

Woodlawn Golf Course
917 Bull Creek Rd., Tarentum
• (724) 224-4730

Woodlawn is an enticing par 32, 9-hole course that's not as easy as it looks, despite measuring only 2376 yards. That's because Bull Creek, a natural phenomenon that still supports fish and other aquatic life, runs through the course, coming into play on five holes.

During the week, the cost for a round is $8 for 9 holes and $13 for 18; on weekends, you can play 9 holes for $9 and 18 holes for $14. Senior citizens enjoy a $1.50 discount on weekdays. Woodlawn offers a pavilion for group outings.

East

Carradam Golf Course
2151 Hahntown Rd., North Huntington
• (724) 863-6860

This Jim Harrison-designed course features great finishing holes, as No. 9 and No. 18 sport tree-lined fairways and mounding around the greens. The par 71 course measures 5904 yards. When you're planning your golf outing, note that reserved starting times are available on weekends and holidays only, and that Carradam entertains leagues most evenings. The cost for

GOLF

18 holes is $21 on weekdays and $23 on weekends; the cost for 9 is $11 on weekdays and $14 on weekends. You'll enjoy country-club-quality greens, a fully stocked pro shop, a snack bar, and a picnic pavilion.

Champion Lakes Golf Course
RD #1, Box 285, Bolivar
• (724) 238-5440

Champion Lakes is located in the Laurel Mountains, and the 13th hole offers a particularly beautiful view of the mountains. The fairway on the 380-yard par 4 hole is part of a valley that splits two soaring peaks, while a picturesque lake guards the green.

The fee for the 6608-yard, par 71 course is $35 on weekdays and $40 on weekends. Reserving a tee time is imperative because of the regular schedule of tournaments. Facilities include a restaurant, a bar, a pro shop, and banquet capabilities.

Champion Lakes is the creation of former Pittsburgh Pirates Jerry Lynch and Dick Groat. Groat still resides there during the summer, and so, too, can you—for a little while, anyway. That's because Champion Lakes Bed & Breakfast adjoins the course, with all sleeping rooms named for former Pirates. For more on this B&B, see our Bed and Breakfasts chapter.

Cherry Creek Golf Course
1000 Spyglass Hill, Greensburg
• (724) 925-8665

This par 70, 18-hole course is styled as an "executive course" because of its appealing 4500-yard length. During the week, the cost is $9.50 for 9 holes and $16 for 18; on weekends, the cost is $13 for 9 holes and $21 for 18. (We haven't included the cost of carts, since you'll probably enjoy walking this course.) Senior citizen discounts available. You'll enjoy the pro shop and snack bar, known as Duffers Deli. Cherry Creek takes pride in its smooth, well-manicured greens.

Cloverleaf Golf Club
P.O. Box 55, Delmont
• (724) 468-4173

Cloverleaf offers three 9-hole courses; for your round of 18, you can select any two of the courses. Depending on the combination, the yardage for 18 holes ranges from 6016 yards to 6215 yards, while par ranges from 70 to 72. Your round of 18 will cost you $28, and starting times are not available. You'll find a limited-service pro shop, a snack bar, and a tree-shaded pavilion that is popular with Cloverleaf's 30 leagues.

Donegal Highlands Golf Course
P.O. Box 130, Donegal
• (724) 423-7888

The Laurel Highlands provide a scenic locale for Donegal Highlands, which is located at an elevation of 1,850 feet in southeastern Westmoreland County. Pro Jeff Mowrer doesn't believe the elevation will help your length, but he does commend the view on No. 15, a 487-yard par 5 that, in addition to featuring a hard dogleg right and water on both sides of the green, is flanked by Chestnut Ridge and Laurel Ridge.

The 6153-yard, par 72 course is demanding; its slope rating is 124. Starting times are required daily. Cost for a round is $39.50, while senior citizens can play on Tuesdays and Thursdays for $23.50. You'll enjoy the pro shop, a two-tier driving range with grass tees, and a tavern called The Black Dog Pub.

Four Points Golf
100 Sheraton Dr., Greensburg
• (724) 850-2700

Near the Sheraton Four Points Hotel, Four Points Golf offers a quick-playing 9 holes for hotel guests and any others who care to play. The course does not offer starting times or priority tee times for hotel guests. Cost for a round is $12.50, with a $3.50 discount for a second round. Senior citizens may purchase a $165 annual membership that covers all green fees but not cart costs.

The par 33 course spans 2503 yards. Club pro Bill Sarsfield notes that the course features a continuous cart path for maximum convenience. Four Points offers a pro shop, snack bar, and all the amenities of the hotel. For more on the hotel, see our Accommodations chapter.

The Golf Club at Hidden Valley
One Craighead Dr., Hidden Valley
• (814) 443-8444, (800) 458-0175

Golfing at Hidden Valley Resort will get you high...literally. The course is situated atop a 3000-foot summit in the Laurel Highlands, offering spectacular views of the countryside for up to 30 miles. Your ball will travel well in the rare air, and you'll find the entire experience invigorating.

The par-72 course ranges from 5,027 yards to 6,589 yards and features narrow, tree-lined fairways, You'll hit long here, but the course demands precision. The cost for 18 holes during the week is $40, during weekends $50. The resort also offers weekend golf packages.

Amenities include a pro shop, a driving range, a putting green, and Mulligans Bar and Grill. You may also take advantage of an instructional program that includes camp and private lessons. For more on Hidden Valley Resort, see our Accommodations and Recreation chapters.

Grand View Golf Club
1000 Clubhouse Dr., North Braddock
• (412) 351-5390

If there's a golf course that says "Pittsburgh," it's Grand View. The course sits atop a converted heap of slag, a useless byproduct of industrial operations. The club's owners have done a commendable job reclaiming the land, although if you're interested, you still can make out evidence of the slag at several points along the course.

A round over the 6111-yard, par 71 course will cost you $34 on weekdays and $42 on weekends; senior citizen discounts are offered during the week. Starting times are available, and you'll enjoy a pro shop, a driving range, and a full-service restaurant. Club pro Thomas Beeler points out that from the lofty perch of Grand View, you can see as far away as downtown Pittsburgh to the west and the Laurel Mountains to the east.

Irwin Country Club
594 Simpson Rd., Irwin
• (724) 863-6016

You'll especially like the back nine at Irwin Country Club—that portion of the course was carved from surrounding woods and offers many scenic vistas. The par 70 course covers 5600 yards. Cost for a round is $27 on weekdays and $29 on weekends, with starting times available on weekends and holidays. The club features a pro shop, a lunch counter, and a bar.

Linden Hall
RD#1, Dawson
• (724) 529-7543

Golf is one of many attractive features at this resort about 37 miles from Pittsburgh. The course is scenic, offering compelling views of the Youghiogheny River, but as Linden Hall pro Ron Fronczak points out, it's also a stern test. Most holes have sand traps, and seven holes present water hazards. Yardage on the par 72 course ranges from 5900 to 6675.

Cost for a round is $30 on weekdays and $39 on weekends, with senior citizen discounts available. You also can purchase golf packages from the resort. Starting times begin at 6 AM. In addition to the amenities of the resort; the course features a pro shop; a bar; a restaurant; and a "halfway house," a snack shack after the 9th hole. Linden Hall hosts about 50 group outings each year as well as leagues virtually every weeknight.

Our Accommodations chapter provides a fuller description of Linden Hall's recreation and hotel facilities.

The Madison Club
P.O. Box 519, Madison
• (724) 446-4000

Bill Kossack, pro and general manager at The Madison Club, an upscale facility, challenges you to test your shotmaking skills on No. 8, a 181-yard par 3. You'll hit downhill along a fairway guarded by a massive stone wall. The green is protected by a lake in the rear, a steep hill on the right and a venerable red oak tree on the left.

Distance for the par 72 course ranges from 4905 yards to 6847 yards. Starting times are available daily. Cost is $39 on weekdays and $48 on weekends. Amenities include a driving range, a snack bar, and a picnic pavilion that your group can reserve.

Mannito Golf Club
RD #1, P.O. Box 258, New Alexandria
• (724) 668-8150

To master Mannito, you'll need a sharp game throughout, as the course features two tough closing holes. No. 9 is a 245-yard par 3, while No. 18 is an even longer par 3 at 254 yards. If you get home on regulation on those two tough nuts, you can consider your round a success.

Par for the 6900-yard course is 71. Cost is $25 on weekdays and $30 on weekends, with senior citizen discounts available before noon on weekdays. You can reserve a starting time on weekends. Facilities include a pro shop, a restaurant, a driving range, a chipping area, and a picnic shelter that your group of up to 150 may book.

Manor Valley Golf Course
2095 Denmark Manor Rd., Export
• (724) 744-4242

If you've ever had that

INSIDERS' TIP
The Western Pennsylvania Golf Association, (412) 963-9806, performs several useful services for local golfers. It publishes an annual schedule of amateur tournaments, provides a list of course ratings and slope ratings, and can help you establish your handicap.

GOLF

sinking feeling as darkness closed in and shortened your round, you'll appreciate Manor Valley. The course is one of the few in the region with lights for evening play. A number of Manor Valley leagues don't get underway until 7 or 8 P.M.

The par 72 course measures 6327 yards. Weekend starting times are available. Cost is $27 on weekdays and $28 on weekends, with senior citizen discounts available during the week. Manor Valley offers a pro shop, a snack bar, a bar, several chipping greens, and banquet facilities.

Maplecrest-Monroeville Golf Course
3892 Logan Ferry Rd., Monroeville
• (412) 372-7770

Tucked away in a wooded area far from the frenzy of Monroeville's shopping district, Maplecrest is a scenic 9-hole course where relaxation and quick play are the norm. The par 33 course covers only 2100 yards and presents no bunkers or water hazards.

Cost is $12.50 on weekdays and $14 on weekends. Senior citizens enjoy daily discounts, and starting times are available. Pro Jim Daum offers private lessons as well as instruction through the municipality. Maplecrest sports a pro shop, a snack bar, and many junior leagues—this is one course that courts kids.

Meadowink Golf Course
4076 Bulltown Rd., Murrysville
• (724) 327-8243

To play this 6139-yard, par 72 course, the cost is $20 on weekdays and $25 on weekends, with senior citizen discounts available during the week. (Carts aren't included in these prices, since many people prefer to walk this course.) You can reserve a starting time every day. Meadowink offers a pro shop and a snack bar, as well as one of the toughest par 3s around. From the elevated tee at No. 11, you'll see the green 149 yards away guarded by sand and water in front and left, a steep hillside to the right, and woods in the rear.

"You really need to hit the green," says Meadowink Operations Manager Joyce Miller. "If you can do it, it's a routine hole. If you don't, it's trouble. This is not a place to miss."

Mt. Odin Golf Course
RD#6, Tollgate Hill, Greensburg
• (724) 834-2640

Operated by the City of Greensburg as part of a municipal park, Mt. Odin is an 18-hole course that features a pro shop, a snack bar, a driving range, and considerable league play. Dis-

tance ranges from 4743 yards to 5445 yards, with a par of 70. Cost for 9 holes during the week is $15.50, on weekends $19; for 18 holes, during the week, you'll pay $18, on weekends $25. Senior citizens can purchase a restricted pass ($300) or an unrestricted pass ($350) that covers green fees for the entire season. For more on Mt. Odin, see our Parks chapter.

Murrysville Golf Club
3804 Sardis Rd., Murrysville
• (724) 327-0726

Murrysville Golf Club opened in 1930 with a classic Scottish design—plenty of grass bunkers but no sand. It maintains that philosophy today. The par 70 course spans 5320 yards but features tricky winds to compensate for the moderate distance. Cost is $30, with senior citizen discounts daily. You'll find a pro shop, a snack bar, and a putting green, but no starting times.

Norvelt Golf Club
RD #5, Mt. Pleasant
• (724) 423-5400

This par 72 course covers 6387 yards. You can reserve starting times on weekends and holidays and enjoy the club's pro shop and snack bar. Cost for a round is $24 on weekdays and $31.66 on weekends, with senior citizen discounts offered on Wednesdays.

Oak Lake Golf Course
1208 Oak Lake Rd., New Kensington
• (724) 727-2400

The Conley family owns and operates this 5706-yard, par 72 course, and they've created several signature holes. You'll be tempted by No. 17, a 496-yard par 5 that invites you to go for the green in two shots. First, you must contend with a double dogleg as well as a large sand trap guarding the green. The more conservative approach is to lay up, but if your round needs a pick-me-up, go for it!

Starting times are offered on weekends. Cost for a round is $30, with weekday senior citizen discounts available. Oak Lake features a pro shop, a bar/restaurant, and pavilions for group outings.

Oakmont East Course
909 Hulton Rd., Oakmont
• (412) 828-5335

Oakmont East is the next best thing to storied Oakmont County Club. In fact, the country club owns this public course, a par 72 that measures 5720 yards. Starting times are offered on weekends. Cost for a round is $26 on week-

Nemacolin Woodlands Resort & Spa features a fine resort course.

Photo: Courtesy of Nemacolin Woodlands Resort & Spa

days and $29 on weekends, but seniors may purchase $450 memberships that cover their green fees for a year. Oakmont East features a snack bar and a limited-service pro shop.

Note: During its major tournaments, Oakmont Country Club closes the public course and uses it as a parking lot. It may happen only once every several years, but it is a good thing to know in advance.

RidgeView Golf Course
RR5, Box 172, Ligonier
• **(724) 238-7655**

This 9-hole course provides a sweeping view of Chestnut Ridge in the Laurel Highlands; you'll enjoy that view for much of the 2650 yards of this par 36 course. Cost is $7.75 for a round of 9 on weekdays and $9.50 on weekends, $12.75 on weekdays and $14.50 on weekends for a round of 18. RidgeView offers starting times, a snack bar, a lounge, an outdoor deck, and a limited-service pro shop.

Rolling Fields Golf Course
Hankey Church Rd., Murrysville
• **(724) 335-7522**

You'll be rolling along at Rolling Fields when you reach the challenging No. 13, a 375-yard par 4, with a dogleg left and a severely undulating green. Did we mention that you must hit

over water to reach the green? Get home in four here and you'll have earned your par.

Cost for the 6095-yard, par 70 course is $25, with senior citizen discounts available on weekdays. After your round, you can relax in the snack bar.

Schenley Park Golf Course
Forbes Ave. & Schenley Dr., Pittsburgh
• **(412) 622-6959**

Club pro Bruce Stephen likes to say that Schenley offers the best golfing in the City of Pittsburgh. That's indisputable, since this is the only course within city limits. Part of Schenley Park, the course is owned by the City of Pittsburgh and operated through a lease agreement by a nonprofit corporation affiliated with Carnegie Mellon University.

The par 67 course measures 4620 yards, which is considered executive length. You won't find bunkers or water hazards, but you will have a unique opportunity to hit across roads protected from stray balls by fences, and you'll enjoy a beautiful view of the city skyline as you play. You'll encounter highway hazards no fewer than six times. For your troubles, you'll be rewarded at No. 5, a 122-yard par 3 that probably produces more aces than any other hole in the area. A number of nonprofit organizations stage hole-in-one contests on No. 5.

GOLF

Cost for a round with a pull cart—electric carts aren't available—is $16. If you buy a special "Frequent Golfers" card, you'll get 10 rounds for $100. Schenley offers weekend and holiday starting times, a pro shop, a restaurant, putting greens, and lessons from Stephen. The course is open year-round. For more on Schenley Park, see our Parks chapter.

Seven Springs Mountain Resort
RD #1, Champion
• (814) 352-7777, (800) 452-2223

The golf course at Seven Springs is very much in keeping with the resort. It's beautiful and well appointed. You'll enjoy the facilities, which include a pro shop, locker rooms, and the Tee Top Lounge. The 11th hole is particularly appealing. It's a 195-yard par 3 where the undulating green is guarded by a lake, a bunker, and a large mound. Distance for the par 71 course ranges from 4913 yards to 6360 yards.

Cost during the week is $65.90; on weekends, it's four dollars more. Resort guests may reserve starting times two weeks in advance, while others can get their tee times two days in advance. You can get a good feel for the course by asking pro Fred Haddick for the brochure that will provide a detailed hole-by-hole description . . . including tips on how to approach each hole.

For more information on Seven Springs, see both our Accommodations chapter and our Recreation chapter.

Timber Ridge Golf Course
RR6, P.O. Box 2057, Mt. Pleasant
• (724) 547-1909

You'll enjoy your round at Timber Ridge, if you hit straight. Otherwise, you may get up close and personal with the bunkers featured on just about every hole as well as the water hazards on three holes. Distance for the par 72 course ranges from 5277 yards to 6340 yards. Reserved starting times are available on weekends. Cost is $28 during the week and $31 on weekends, with weekday discounts for seniors. You'll find a pro shop, a bar/restaurant, and banquet facilities for up to 200 people.

Timberlink Golf Course
Rt. 30 W., Ligonier
• (724) 238-7310

This "executive" length course—a par 55 that covers 2375 yards—is attractive of itself, and it's also one of the many features that draw visitors to Ligonier. During the week, the cost to play 9 holes is $6, on weekends $7. An 18-hole round during the week is $10, and on weekends, it's $12. Timberlink does not offer starting times, but you will enjoy the small pro shop and snack bar.

Valley Green Golf & Country Club
RD #2, Box 449F, Greensburg
• (724) 837-6366

Club pro Larry Liprando calls Valley Green one of the region's best walking courses—it's uncharacteristically flat for a Western Pennsylvania layout. The par 72 course measures 6450 yards. Cost for a round is $27 on weekdays and $29.50 on weekends, with weekend and holiday starting times available. You'll find a pro shop, a bar, and a snack bar.

Vandergrift Golf Club
P.O. Box 61, Community Park Rd.,
Vandergrift • (724) 567-7413

Vandergrift Golf Club is semiprivate—nonmembers are welcome to play, but call ahead for weekend starting times. During the week it's first-come, first served.

The 9-hole, par 36 course spans 3136 yards. Cost for 9 holes is $12.50, and you can play 18, using the second set of tees, for $17. (Prices do not include carts, although they are available.) The pro shop is limited, but you'll enjoy a snack bar/grill, a driving range, and a chipping area.

Windyhill Golf Course
603 Windyhill Dr., Plum
• (412) 793-7771

If you're a veteran golfer, this 9-hole course might not be your cup of tea. At 1700 yards, however, it's a great par 30 for juniors and beginners. Cost for 9 holes with a pull-cart (electric carts are not offered) is $6, while you can play 18 holes for $8. You won't need a starting time.

South

Butler's Golf Course
800 Rock Run Road, Elizabeth
• (412) 751-9121

The unusual design of Butler's Golf Course includes four 9-hole courses that you can combine according to your preference, unless heavy crowds prevent that. Whichever two nines you play, the distance is 6606 yards and the par 72. Cost is $33.50 on weekdays and $43 on weekends, with starting times required every day.

The course also entertains many leagues—59 during one recent season. If you're interested in joining a league, club pro Carmen Costa will match you with a group looking for players. One of the great attractions for leagues is the Rock Run Inn, the course's spacious, full-service restaurant that offers a huge and varied menu. In fact, it's a destination dining spot in the Elizabeth area, whether you golf or not, and it offers full banquet and outing facilities.

Costa calls No. 9, a 185-yard par 3, the signature hole, with its peculiar L-shaped green. "If you miss left," Costa says, "you're in the water. If you miss short, you're in the bunker or water, If you miss right, you're in a bunker or on a hill. If it's long, it's in a flower bed." Best advice: Don't miss the green.

Enjoy the driving range, putting green, par 3 practice course, and the popular shotgun outings offered at this course. Call for more information about the latter. Note: Shot-gun outings are events in which everyone playing starts at the same time on different holes—no firearms involved.

Carmichaels Golf Club
RD #1, Box 314, Carmichaels
• (724) 966-7500
Located in Greene County, Carmichaels Golf Club technically is beyond our coverage area, but we thought it worth noting because of the scarcity of courses in the sparsely populated county in the state's southwestern corner. Distance for the par 70 course ranges from 4584 yards to 5393 yards. On the back 9, be prepared to contend with several ponds and many hills. Cost for a round is $27, with starting times available on weekends and holidays. The club offers a pro shop and a snack bar.

Cedarbrook Golf Course
215 Rt. 981, Belle Vernon
• (724) 929-8300
You can select from two 18-hole courses at Cedarbrook. The par 72 Gold Course ranges in distance from 5138 yards to 6710 yards, while the par 71 Red Course ranges from 4577 yards to 6154 yards. Cost to play either is $32 on weekdays and $41 on weekends. Senior citizen discounts are available, and starting times are required. You can visit the pro shop and relax in the full-service The Main Course Restaurant.

Golf course architect Dr. Michael Hurdzan designed Cedarbrook's courses, which feature large flat greens. Don't be

deceived, as the courses offer some stiff challenges. No. 6 on the Gold Course is a monstrous 578-yard par 5 with ever-narrowing fairways. "I don't know if it's ever been reached in two from the back tees," says club pro Bryon Palonder.

On the Red Course, the 531-yard, par 5 No. 10 offers a split fairway divided by an uninviting thicket. The right fairway is longer, the left more dangerous. Which one does Palonder choose? "Whichever one the ball lands in," he says diplomatically.

Chippewa Golf Club
128 Chippewa Rd., Bentleyville
• (724) 239-4841
Architect Jim Harrison designed plenty of water hazards into Chippewa, but he spared you the heartbreak of sand. There's not a single sand bunker on the course. Distance for the par 70 layout ranges from 5104 yards to 6051 yards. Starting times are available each day. Cost is $27.50 on weekdays and $29.50 on weekends, with weekday discounts for senior citizens. Chippewa offers a limited-service pro shop, a snack bar, and a picnic pavilion. Soft spikes are required.

Eighty Four Golf Course
1344 Rt. 519, Eighty Four
• (724) 746-1510
This course features one of the longest holes around. No. 4, a par 5, measures 600 yards with a dogleg right. Get out your driving clothes for this one. The par 70 course measures 5450 yards. Starting times are not available. Cost is $25, with weekday discounts for senior citizens. You'll find a pro shop, a lounge, and a full-service restaurant.

Fort Cherry Golf Club
80 Fort Cherry Rd., McDonald
• (724) 926-4182
Fort Cherry has a number of scenic and challenging holes, perhaps none tougher than No. 4. The par 3, 201-yard hole features water left and right as well as bunkers guarding the green's right side. Distance for the par 70 course ranges from 5888 yards to 6205 yards. Starting times are available in season. Cost is $29 on weekdays and $33 on weekends, with weekday discounts for senior citizens.

In addition to the Fort Cheery Golf Club's pro

GOLF

shop and full-service restaurant, Fort Cherry offers impressive banquet facilities, including a large hall that can accommodate up to 600 guests; a patio bar spacious enough for 100 people; and the Green Room, a glass-enclosed hall overlooking the golf course where you can entertain up to 120 people. These facilities are quite popular for wedding receptions and other functions—you'll want to book them well in advance.

Frosty Valley Golf Course
2652 Hidden Valley Dr., Upper St. Clair
• (724) 941-5003

Frosty Valley once was the course of Hidden Valley Country Club, which relocated some years ago, and this 9-hole course still resembles a country club layout in some ways. The flat course is easy to walk, but water hazards affect six of the nine holes. The par 36 course plays from 2371 yards to 3250 yards. The cost is $13 during the week and $15 on weekends; cart rentals start at $7. Reserved starting times are available on weekends and holidays.

Residents of the adjacent Friendship Village retirement community enjoy complimentary privileges at Frosty Valley. (For more on Friendship Village, see our Senior Scene chapter). Amenities include a pro shop, Mickeys on the Green restaurant, and banquet facilities.

Holly Hill Inn & Golf Center
1110 Towervue Dr., Baldwin Borough
• (412) 882-4222

Holly Hill is situated about 15 minutes from downtown Pittsburgh; if you keep your "sticks" in the trunk, this is a great place to grab a quick round after work, and you won't need a starting time. Distance for the par 33, 9-hole course ranges from 2148 yards to 2480 yards. A round of 9 holes will cost you $14.50, while you can play 18 for $22.50. You'll enjoy the pro shop, restaurant, and banquet facilities.

Lindenwood Golf Club
360 Galley Rd., Canonsburg
• (724) 745-9889

Lindenwood sports 27 new championship holes as well as a new 9-hole executive course. The golf club also features three 9-hole courses that the club configures on a daily basis to give you a different-looking 18 each time you play. Depending on the day's configuration, the distance ranges from 5017 yards to 6699 yards, with par at 71 or 72. This is a scenic course; you won't spy any homes or highways as you play, as Lindenwood is carved from bucolic woodlands.

Amenities include a pro shop, a driving range, a grill room, and banquet facilities. Non-members can reserve a tee time four days in advance. Cost for a round Monday through Thursday is $38; during the rest of the week and on holidays, the cost is $44.

Mt. Lebanon Golf Course
1000 Pine Ave., Mt. Lebanon
• (412) 561-9761

This 9-hole course is operated by the municipality of Mt. Lebanon. While only residents and their guests can play on weekends and holidays, nonresidents are welcome at other times. Cost is $13.50 per weekday for nonresidents and $14 per weekend day; for residents, the cost is $8 per weekday and $9 per weekend day. Discounts are available for juniors and senior citizens. You'll find a pro shop and vending machines.

Distance for the par 34 course is 3034 yards. You'll like No. 2, a 400-yard, tree-lined par 4 with its two-tier green protected by a bunker. The hole typically plays longer due to a stiff wind. If you'd like a tip or two, look up pro Matthew Kluck.

Nemacolin Woodlands Resort & Spa
1001 Lafayette Dr., Farmington
• (724) 329-6111, (800) 422-2736
• www.nemacolin.com

When noted golf course architect Pete Dye designed Mystic Rock at Nemacolin Woodlands, he had a lavish $19 million budget to work with. The course shows it. The par 72, 6832-yard course utilizes Nemacolin's natural assets to create a course as beautiful as it is challenging, with a 146 slope rating. You'll find undulating greens and plenty of water and rock that connect fairways with foliage. Nemacolin hosts the Mystic Rock Charity Pro-Am, which in 1997 attracted no less a player than Tiger Woods. If you think you'd like a tip or two, in order to play your best game, look up pro Delo Mees.

Nemacolin also features a second handsome course called The Woodlands Links, a par 71, 6643-yard adventure with thick woods, high rough, and lakes aplenty surrounding the fairways. The Links is no slouch—the slope rating is 131—but it may seem like a vacation after Mystic Rock.

Resort guests can reserve starting times two weeks in advance; others can reserve their starting times a week ahead of time. Guests can play Mystic Rock for $125, while others pay $150. For The Links, the cost is $79 for all. Whichever course you play, you'll enjoy the extensive facilities, which include a pro shop, a driving range, practice greens and sand traps, and locker rooms. If hunger strikes as you approach the 9th tee at Mystic Rock, pick up the courtesy phone and order from the restaurant just off the 9th green. After you sink that birdie putt, your lunch will be ready for you.

For more on Nemacolin, see our Accommodations chapter.

Riverview Golf Course
Bunola Rd., Elizabeth
• (412) 384-7596

Riverview is an 18-hole layout with dual personalities. The front 9 is tight, demanding precision shot-making, while the back 9 is more open. You'll need most of the clubs in your bag for Riverview.

Distance for the par 71 course ranges from 4871 yards to 6382 yards. You can arrange a starting time in season and take advantage of the pro shop and snack bar. Cost is $32 on weekdays and $41 on weekends, with senior citizen discounts available on weekday mornings.

Rolling Green Golf Course
Rt. 136, Eighty Four
• (724) 222-9671

Distance for this par 71 course ranges from 5621 yards to 6011 yards. Weekend and holiday tee times are available. Cost is $27 on weekdays and $29 on weekends, with senior discounts available every day. Facilities at Rolling Green include a limited-service pro shop, a snack bar, and a picnic pavilion your group can reserve for $35.

Seven Springs of Elizabeth Golf Course
357 Pineview Dr., Elizabeth
• (412) 384-7730

If you're ball has an unerring nose for the water, you'll enjoy Seven Springs of Elizabeth (not to be confused with the similarly named resort). There are no significant water hazards on the 18-hole, par 71 course, or the 9-hole, par 35 course, although both courses feature liberally bunkered greens. The length of the 18-hole course ranges from 5582 yards to 6503 yards. You can reserve a starting time every day, and manage-

ment suggests that you do. Cost for a round is $32.50 during the week and $38 on weekends, with senior discounts available. The course features a pro shop, a lunch counter, and bar and banquet facilities.

South Park Golf Course
East Park Dr. Library
• (412) 835-3545

South Park offers both an 18-hole course and a 9-hole course. As with North Park, the other course operated by Allegheny County, crowds can be huge. Chuck Cullison, pro at all three courses, advises that playing in the late morning or early afternoon is one way to beat the crowds. Starting times are not offered, so you may have to wait to play.

The par 72, 18-hole course covers 6584 yards. It offers a number of tree-lined fairways with tight landing areas. Bring all your clubs, Cullison advises. The 9-hole course is a par 34 that spans 2652 yards. South Park offers a putting green, a chipping area, a pro shop, and a full-service restaurant.

Costs for 18 holes are $14 during the week and $17 on weekends; for 9, you'll pay $9 during the week and $11 on the weekends. Carts are available for an additional fee. If you're 60 or older, you can purchase a $60 season pass. Our Parks chapter provides a more detailed look at the features of South Park.

Village Green Golf Course
4050 Henderson Ave., Hickory
• (724) 356-2282

Enjoy the first half of your outing at Village Green—the back 9 is a lot hillier than the front. Distance for the par 72 course ranges from 5625 yards to 6480 yards. A round will cost you $17.50 during the week and $35 on weekends, with senior discounts offered during the week. If those hills leave you huffing and puffing, you can relax in the pro shop, the bar, or the full-service restaurant.

Willowbrook Golf Course
RD #2, Rt. 201, Belle Vernon
• (724) 872-7272

At 3186 yards, this 9-hole, par 36 course can be

GOLF

Golf in Western Pennsylvania can be a rich and rewarding experience . . . if you can find the dozens of public courses the region offers. You'll find several useful guides. Each spring the *Pittsburgh Post-Gazette* publishes a map that will help you locate courses, as well as a calendar of the season's charity events and competitions. The map and calendar appear as part of the newspaper, so all you have to do is buy that day's edition to get the golf extras.

The Pennsylvania Golf Course Owners (PGO) publishes an annual map of public courses in Pennsylvania as well as a discount book that, for $30, will get you coupons for two rounds for the price of one at more than 50 participating courses. Not all Pennsylvania courses are shown on the map, since some are not PGO members. But the approximately 140 that are listed will get you off to a swinging start. The organization prefers mailed requests, with a self-addressed, stamped envelope enclosed, to 121 Narragansett Drive, McKeesport, PA, 15135. You can reach the PGO by phone at (412) 751-3379 or (800) 872-1483.

deceptive. Just when you think you can take it by storm, you'll find the creek that runs through five holes. Cost for 9 holes is $17.50, and you'll enjoy a reduced rate for a second round of 9. If you're older than 62, snap up the discounted rate of $5 (without cart) for 9 holes. Willowbrook does not offer starting times, but it does feature a small pro shop and a snack bar.

Wyndon Links Golf Club
3001 Race St., Scottdale
• **(724) 887-8858**

Welcome to the fun world of the Yelinek family, proprietors of Wyndon Links . . . and a lot more. The 9-hole course sports a number of unconventional touches, including a heart-shaped green on the 227-yard, par 3 No. 3—a little touch of whimsy after you've crossed a pond and avoided woods to reach the green. You'll also encounter a practice area with a cactus-shaped bunker, to complement the motif of the club's Cactus Star Restaurant.

Distance for the par 36 course ranges from 2457 yards to 3282 yards. A round of 9 holes will cost you $14 during the week and $16 on weekends, with starting times required. In addition the restaurant, you'll enjoy a pro shop, banquet facilities for up to 220 people and a "target driving range" that includes greens sprinkled through the landing area. Wyndon Links hosts accuracy competitions on its driving range. You can see why the course is popular with leagues—they play five nights a week in season.

Another special touch: the Yelineks are real estate developers and have constructed a number of homes that border the 9th hole. They not only will sell you a lot, but their construction company can build your house. Each ho-

meowner gets a golf cart specially equipped with a headlight to tool around the grounds.

West

Black Hawk Golf Course
644 Blackhawk Rd., Beaver Falls
• **(724) 843-5512**

Black Hawk features two 18-hole, par 72 courses, ranging in distance from 6114 yards (No. 1 and No. 2 courses) to 6300 yards (No. 3 and No. 4 courses). Watch out for the fifth hole on No. 3 course. This 420-yard par 4 was voted by local golfers the "Toughest Hole in Beaver County."

"The fairway slopes left to right, so you never have a level lie," says Garen Steele, club pro. "You're hitting into a blind green. You can't miss on any side because of the big hills. Most people take a shorter club and look for bogies and double bogies."

Cost is $27 during the week and $32 on weekends, with senior citizen discounts offered on weekdays before 3 PM. You can relax in the full-service restaurant or book the course and its pavilion for a group outing.

Bon Air Golf Course
505 McCormick Rd., Coraopolis
• **(412) 262-2992**

Bon Air is a popular course with visitors staying at hotels near Pittsburgh International Airport, which is only minutes away. The 5800-yard, par-71 course generally plays quickly, so there's plenty of time to enjoy a round and still make your meeting or flight. Cost is $32.50, with weekend and holiday starting times available. You'll find a snack bar and limited-service pro shop.

GOLF

Hit it straight—trees and woodlands line many of our fairways.

Photo: Courtesy of Butler's Golf Course

Crafton Golf Club
Thornburg Rd., Crafton
• **(412) 921-6203**

Here's a flat 9-hole layout that you'll enjoy walking, since electric carts are not available. The par-35 course measures 3000 yards. Cost for a round, including a pull cart, is $11 on weekends and $10 on weekdays, with senior citizen discounts available. You can't reserve a tee time. The club features a pro shop and snack bar.

Fox Run Public Golf Course
River Rd., Beaver Falls
• **(724) 847-3568**

If you like water, you'll love Fox Run. All of the course's par 3 holes feature water hazards. Twice each year, course personnel fish hundreds of balls from the water and place them on sale at the pro shop for a buck apiece.

The par 72 course covers 6508 yards. Tee times beginning as early as 6 AM are offered on weekends and holidays. Cost for a round is $26 on weekdays and $31 on weekends, with senior citizen discounts available on weekdays. In addition to the pro shop, you'll enjoy the driving range and snack bar.

Grassy Lane Golf Club
470 McCaughtry Run Rd., Darlington
• **(724) 336-5006**

Watch out for the hole they call "The Chute." It's No. 4, a 363-yard par 4 with a narrow, tree-lined fairway that broadens as it approaches the green. This 9-hole, par 36 course covers 3035 yards. Cost is $13.75 with a $1 discount for your second round of 9. Senior citizen discounts are offered during the week.

Only large groups may reserve starting times. Amenities include a limited-service pro shop, a snack bar, a chipping area, and a picnic shelter your group can book.

Hawthorne Valley Golf Club
122 Daniels Dr., Midland
• **(724) 643-9091**

This 18-hole course is popular with evening leagues. If that's when you're planning to play, you might want to call ahead to check whether it's a league night. Starting times are available on weekends.

The par 72 course measures 6237 yards. A round of 18 will cost you $14 during the week and $16 on weekends, with carts available for an additional fee. Senior citizens receive discounts during the week. Hawthorne Valley offers a pro shop and a snack bar.

Marada Golf Course
1434 Rt. 30, Clinton
• **(724) 899-2600**

Only 2 miles from Pittsburgh International Airport, Marada draws quite a few players lay-

GOLF

ing over at the airport. Distance for the 9-hole, par 35 course ranges from 2485 yards to 3090 yards. Arrival and departure times are important here, but you won't need a reserved tee time. For 9 holes, the cost is $9.75 on weekdays and $17 on weekends. For 18, you'll pay $27.50 during the week and $30 on weekends. Senior citizens receive discounts during the week. Marada offers a small clubhouse and a snack bar.

Quicksilver Golf Club
2000 Quicksilver Rd., Midway
• (724) 796-1594

Quicksilver has hosted five events on the Senior PGA tour and three events on the Buy.com tour (formerly the Nike Tour), as well as many tri-state PGA and USGA events. That will give you some idea of the quality of the course. The amenities will reinforce that idea. You'll find a pro shop, a driving range with grass tees, Murphy's Restaurant, and Murphy's Pub. The club's owner, if you hadn't guessed, is Bob Murphy.

Distance for the par 72 course ranges from 5067 yards to 7083 yards. One of the favorite holes of general manager Sean Parees is No. 8, a 199-yard par 3 with a green guarded on three sides by water and sand. The course is a "fair challenge for all golfers with ability," according to Parees. Cost is $55 during peak season, with reduced rates for out-of-season and twilight play. For a $2,000 annual membership, you'll receive a locker, handicap service, a charge account, and the opportunity to reserve starting times 14 days in advance. Nonmembers can reserve tee times six days ahead of time.

Oglebay Resort and Conference Center
Route 88 North, Wheeling, W.Va.
• (304) 243-4000, (800) 752-9436

If you long to play a course that tempts and challenges the pros, try the Speidel Championship Golf Course at Oglebay, longtime host of the West Virginia LPGA Classic. Designed by the legendary Robert Trent Jones, Sr., Speidel is a gorgeous course with compelling views of the hillsides that surround the resort. It's those same hills, however, that create the course's challenge.

One of the toughest holes is No. 17, a 456-yard par 4 with narrow landing areas protected by a line of trees and a steep hill. The green is enormous—about 32 yards deep. The par 71 course plays from 5515 yards to 7000 yards, with a fee of $55—modest, considering the course's heritage.

Just recently, Arnold Palmer designed a new par 71 course at Oglebay. You'll pay $65 to play this one.

You'll enjoy the pro shop, locker room facilities, and the Hamm Clubhouse for dining.

If you're not quite comfortable with the challenge of Speidel or the Arnold Palmer course, you can enjoy the same great Oglebay vistas at the resort's Crispin Golf Course, a 5670-yard, par 71 course. Cost for a round at Crispin is $30.

Oglebay offers a variety of golf packages that include such features as overnight accommodations, breakfast buffets, and a second round at a 50 percent discount. Call Oglebay for details, and see our Accommodations and Daytrips chapters for more information about the resort.

Ponderosa Golf Lands
2728 Rt. 168, Hookstown
• (724) 947-4745

Just as Ben Cartwright was concerned about irrigating his Ponderosa, the owners of Ponderosa Golf Lands have lavished attention on their watering system. It's all computerized, keeping the course green throughout the season.

Distance for the par 71 course ranges from 5525 yards to 6283 yards. Starting times are available in season. Cost for a round is $28.25 on weekdays and $33.25 on weekends. Facilities include a pro shop, showers and locker rooms, and a full-service restaurant.

Rolling Acres Golf Course
350 Achortown Rd., Beaver Falls
• (724) 843-6736

You'll love the unusual timber-frame clubhouse at Rolling Acres. It's a popular spot for banquets, accommodating up to 300 people. In addition, you'll find a snack bar and lounge.

Rolling Acres offers three 9-hole courses, with staff determining your configuration based on the day's volume. The distance for 18 ranges from 5878 yards to 6518 yards, with par varying from 71 to 73. While the courses are mostly free of sand and water, you will find many mounds and grass bunkers. Starting times are offered each day. Cost for 18 holes is $27.50 during the week and $32 on weekends, with senior citizen discounts available during the week.

GOLF

Spectator Sports

In Western Pennsylvania, the term "spectator sports" is almost an oxymoron. The identification of residents with local sports teams is active, emotional, and deep. Spectators in Pittsburgh may be outside the white lines, but we participate nonetheless with our sports teams.

Some have suggested that the local love for sports is rooted in the economic and social history of Pittsburgh. Because many Pittsburgh residents labored long and hard in coal mines and steel mills to feed their families, this theory goes, they turned to sports for recreation, relaxation, and the rewards that were few and far between on the job. They found physical and psychic satisfaction both in their own play and in the success of the teams that represented them.

If that's true, it must be added that the region's emphasis on family helps broaden the affection for sports. In Pittsburgh, sports tends to be a family pursuit. If you check out youth basketball or football games in the area, in addition to the young athletes on the field, you'll most often find Mom and Dad out there, too, volunteering as yardline markers, concession booth operators, and team chauffeurs.

For whatever reasons, we love our sports teams. The metropolitan area supports professional teams in baseball, football, and ice hockey, top-level collegiate football and basketball programs, a harness racing track, and a radio station that features sports programming almost exclusively. In few other communities will you find baseball's home opener regarded as a civic holiday. Here, otherwise dutiful parents cheerfully falsify school excuses to allow their children to attend the game, perpetuating a generations-old tradition.

When our teams win, we dress up in the colors of the local heroes, hang signs of support from office buildings, and party hearty. When the local teams lose, we phone the talk shows to offer heartfelt advice on how the lads can improve—"Get ridda de bums!" would be one example.

The new century is an especially exciting time to be a sports fan in Pittsburgh, as both our baseball and football teams are preparing to move into new stadiums. For the last 30 years, both the Pirates and Steelers have played at Three Rivers Stadium, but starting in 2001, the franchises will go their separate ways. Look for details on the new stadiums in our write-ups of these venerable teams.

Broadcast coverage of local teams deserves special mention. Some who may not appreciate Pittsburgh look at our sometimes half-empty arenas and label us a "bad sports town." What they may not fully understand is that, for reasons that sociologists someday will probe, many local residents—particularly those of a certain age—are notorious stay-at-homers who follow their teams religiously on radio and television but who seldom make it out to the game. For them and for you, we've provided details of the broadcast schedules and personnel for each team.

We've also gathered information on transportation options, points of

LOOK FOR:
- Baseball
- Basketball
- Football
- Horse Racing
- Ice Hockey

interest about the various sporting venues, and specifics about ticket prices. A word of caution about prices: these can vary from season to season, and many of the teams offer more packages than could be detailed here. This is especially true for the teams preparing to move to greener pastures. We've noted the most popular packages and provided the most current pricing information available, but you may encounter some variations.

Baseball

Pittsburgh Pirates

In 1889, the Pittsburgh professional baseball franchise was accused of stealing a second baseman from the Brooklyn organization. Pirates, these rascals from Pittsburgh were called. The name stuck, and today, the Pittsburgh Pirates continue as one of the bedrock franchises of Major League Baseball.

The Bucs (short for Buccaneers), as local fans affectionately call them, have a storied past, with World Series victories in 1909, 1925, 1960, 1971, and 1979. The club has produced 13 Hall of Famers over the years, including Honus Wagner, Pie Traynor, brothers Paul and Lloyd Waner (known as "Big Poison" and "Little Poison"), Ralph Kiner, and such contemporary greats as Roberto Clemente and Willie Stargell, who remains a club official. The Pirates were involved in what may be the most dramatic moment in baseball history—Bill Mazeroski's home run to defeat the heavily favored Yankees in the 1960 World Series.

The Bucs compete in the National League's Central Division, where their rivals are the Chicago Cubs, Milwaukee Brewers, St. Louis Cardinals, Cincinnati Reds, and Houston Astros.

The 2000 season will be the Pirates' last in Three Rivers Stadium. In April 2001, the team will christen PNC Park, a new "old-style" park a few blocks up the Allegheny River from their current home. PNC Park is the latest in a nationwide trend toward retro ballparks. It will feature natural grass (as opposed to the artificial turf at Three Rivers), an asymetrical outfield, and a spectacular view of the Downtown skyline. The park is designed by HOK Inc. of Kansas City, the firm that designed a number of retro parks around the country, including Oriole Park at Camden Yards in Baltimore.

The new park will seat 38,127 people, and will include 69 suites and two restaurants. A 21-foot wall in right field will honor Pirate great Roberto Clemente. The park will be bordered by General Robinson St., Federal St., Stadium Dr. East, and the Allegheny River, and there will be a pedestrian walk along the water.

Three Rivers Stadium has been a serviceable if comparably antiseptic home for the team. For starters, you'll enjoy the huge JumboTron scoreboard in center field, offering not only up-to-date statistics but frequent fan participation games as well. You'll also have fun with the club's mascot, the Pirate Parrot, who tours the stands throughout each game and performs outlandish antics between innings—including shooting hot dogs and tee-shirts into the stands.

If you're not in the parking lots tailgating, you'll find a picnic area for up to 500 people and The Bullpen Lounge restaurant inside the stadium. If you're one who favors no smoking areas, you're in for a treat—smoking is not permitted anywhere in seating areas. The Pirates also maintain a Family Section of 1,300 seats, each priced at $10, where beer consumption is not permitted. Kids will enjoy The Boardwalk, an arcade of games and other amusements.

For those games when you can't make it to the stadium, the Pirates maintain a heavy broadcast schedule to bring the action to you. You can catch all 162 games on radio. Flagship of the 48-station radio network is KDKA-AM in Pittsburgh, 1020 on the dial. For television, cable's Fox Sports Network typically carries a healthy schedule of games each season and is available on most local cable television systems. In addition, Pirates games sometimes are featured on national broadcasts. The popular Lanny Frattare, voice of the Pirates since 1976, is ably assisted by Greg Brown and two former Bucs pitchers, Bob Walk and Steve Blass, he of the button-down humor.

Make sure you pay particular attention to game starting times, as the Pirates vary them to accommodate school schedules and fans concerned about the possibility of chilly weather. Monday through Friday evening games begin at 7:05 p.m. in April, May, September, and October but at 7:35 p.m. June through August. Saturday evening dates begin at 7:05 p.m., no matter the month, while first pitch for all afternoon contests is 1:35 p.m.

The Pirates offer a variety of ticket plans. Prices for individual game tickets range from $5 to $17, with $1 General Admission tickets available for youths 14 and under. The club also features season tickets, multiple-game plans, and discounted packages for groups. If you really want to treat your group to a memorable night at the ballyard, reserve the Grand Slam Box, which doubles as the football press box. Your group of 50 or more will dine in style and enjoy discounted tickets.

INSIDERS' TIP

A number of cable companies serve the Pittsburgh region, meaning that broadcast stations and cable networks that carry sports events are assigned different channel numbers by different cable companies. Always check your local listings to be sure you have the correct channel number.

You can purchase your tickets at the Advance Ticket Window beneath the stadium's Gate A or at a number of off-site locations. These include TicketMaster outlets located in Giant Eagle, Kaufmann's, National Record Mart and Oasis Music and Video, and Pirate Clubhouse Stores in three local shopping plazas—Monroeville Mall, Ross Park Mall, Westmoreland Mall—and Galleria Mall in Johnstown. You also can make credit card purchases over the phone by calling (412) 321-BUCS or (800) BUY-BUCS.

For most games, you'll find $4 parking in the lots that circle the stadium. Other options include public transportation or parking downtown and walking across the Fort Duquesne Bridge to the stadium.

One of the neatest aspects of the Pirates' operation is the club's extensive involvement in the community. The Bucs have a special unit called Pirates Partners to coordinate a far-reaching program of school appearances, youth clinics, neighborhood athletic field restorations, donations of memorabilia, ticket giveaways to disadvantaged youths and autograph appearances—including an annual event at the Pittsburgh Zoo & Aquarium.

In the off season, Pirates Partners each week showcases a player who returns to Pittsburgh for a week of community-based activities. If you're involved in a community group and would like to work with Pirates Partners, call them at (412) 323-5025. You'll find the club is Major League . . . on and off the field.

Basketball

Who says you need a professional basketball team to generate fan excitement and loyalty? While Pittsburgh lacks an NBA team, it doesn't lack for basketball thrills. The city sports three institutions that compete in NCAA Division 1, the best college basketball in the land. Rare is the evening during the season when you can't enjoy a major college game, either in person or in the comfort of your living room.

Actually, Pittsburgh has featured several professional franchises, none of them in the NBA. The Pittsburgh Rens—short for Renaissance—performed in the old American Basketball Association. Later, in the American Basketball League of the late 1960s—the league of the red-white-and-blue balls—the Pittsburgh Condors won the league's inaugural championship behind the swooping grace of Connie Hawkins, who used that experience as a springboard to NBA fame. In the 1990s, Pittsburgh was the brief home of the Piranhas entry in the Continental Basketball Association.

All three franchises were short lived; that entrepreneurs launched them here, however, gives you some sense of basketball's popularity in western Pennsylvania. If you're new to town and wondering if quality basketball is available, have no fear. The city game is alive and well in Pittsburgh.

Duquesne University

The men's basketball program at Duquesne University has long been both an artistic and a popular success. The Dukes have been to the NCAA tournament five times and to the National Invitation Tournament 16 times, capturing the NIT in 1955. Its legendary alumni include Chuck

Three Rivers Stadium is the soon-to-be-demolished home to the Pittsburgh Pirates and Pittsburgh Steelers, as well as many concerts and large gatherings.

Photo: Andrew A. Wagner

Cooper, Sihugo Green, Willie Somserset, and Norm Nixon—perhaps the most recognizable name for current fans, as Nixon was one of the key players in the Magic Johnson-led Los Angeles Lakers dynasty.

The Dukes, coached by Darelle Porter, compete in the Western Division of the Atlantic 10, a conference that features such traditional basketball powerhouses as Temple, Massachusetts, George Washington, Xavier, and Dayton.

Duquesne's home court is the A.J. Palumbo Center, an attractive building that opened in 1988, seats 6,200, and retains the feeling of newness. The center is located on Duquesne's campus along Forbes Avenue, making it quite accessible, as it is only a few blocks from downtown. Parking lots are available near campus as well as around the Civic Arena a few blocks away. You also can shoot for limited on-street parking. Forbes Avenue and the parallel Fifth Avenue are part of many Port Authority of Allegheny County bus routes, so using public transportation to see the Dukes is easy.

The Palumbo Center rarely is sold out, so you can get tickets on game days, through the mail or by calling the ticket office at (412) 232-3853. Individual tickets are priced at around $9 and $14 in advance; you can purchase $5 tickets at the gate. You also may purchase season tickets as a convenience, but there's no discount involved.

Duquesne's TV appearances are limited and difficult to predict from season to season. Typically, regional cable network Fox Sports Pittsburgh offers several games; check local TV listings for those. While we don't recommend staying home to catch the Dukes, if you do find yourself listening to them on WDUQ-FM (90.5 on the dial), you're in for a treat. The broadcast team of Ray Goss and Nellie King is worth not paying the price of admission. Goss, who has been broadcasting Dukes' games since 1968, can squeeze more words into a broadcast—intelligibly— than can any other announcer we've heard.

One other Duquesne note: When you're at the Palumbo Center, several times each game you'll see the crowd rise and chant as one, "Shoo Shoo, Rah Rah." It may sound like a weird new mantra, but it's really a cheer developed by Duquesne's No. 1 all-time fan, the late Maurice "Mossie" Murphy.

Robert Morris College

For much of its basketball history, Robert Morris College played at the junior college level. In 1976, however, the Colonials jumped all the way to NCAA Division 1—and they did it with flair.

The Colonials have reached the NCAA tournament five times since then and have been a mainstay of Division 1 basketball ever since.

Coached by Jim Boone, the Colonials play in the Northeast Conference, which also features such schools as Long Island, Monmouth, St. Francis (New York) and St. Francis (Pennsylvania). Home arena for Robert Morris is the Charles L. Sewall Center for Leadership, a facility that also serves as a business training and meeting hub. Located on the college's Moon Township campus, Sewall Center is only a few miles from Greater Pittsburgh Airport.

While seating capacity at Sewall Center is 3,056, you'll find that tickets on most occasions are readily available. With the top ticket price at about $6—kids get in for $2—and with free parking in several lots around Sewall Center, you'd be hard pressed to enjoy major college basketball more economically. Season tickets also are available, with costs ranging from $50 to $70. For ticket information, call (412) 262-8449.

When you watch Robert Morris play, you'll find that most fans are students . . . some in outlandish garb. During one recent season, some students were so involved with the game that the officials assessed the Colonials a technical foul for student misbehavior. That's the kind of excitement that will capture you when you watch the Colonials.

Catching the Colonials on the air is a bit more difficult. Their games are broadcast on WPIT-AM (730 on the dial), a station not received uniformly well throughout the region during the evening. Likable veteran Chris Shovlin handles play-by-play. WBGN-TV, a low power television station, occasionally airs videotaped replays of Colonials games on. Check your local cable television listings to see if your system carries WBGN. If you live in Beaver County, you may be able to pick up the station directly over the air.

University of Pittsburgh

The University of Pittsburgh has fielded a men's basketball team in every season since 1910, a remarkable achievement that has carried through several world wars and a variety of other dislocations. It is a proud history that includes 7 All-Americans, 13 appearances in the NCAA tournament, 7 appearances in the National Invitation Tournament. Among the highlights: the magical season of 1973-1974, when the upstart Panthers, largely a home-grown squad led by future NBA star Billy Knight, compiled a 25-4 record, losing in the NCAA tournament's Eastern Regional final to eventual champion North Carolina State.

Coach Ben Howland and his Panthers compete in the Big East, one of the premier basketball conferences in the nation. If you follow the Panthers, you'll enjoy such top teams as Georgetown, Villanova, Connecticut, Syracuse, St. John's and West Virginia—all conference members—as well as an attractive non-conference schedule. Big East teams typically contend for top national honors, and Pitt is more than competitive in the conference, with a 1987-88 Big East title to its credit. The brand of basketball you'll see is both fast-paced and physical.

If you're a fan of college basketball, you'll want to catch the Panthers in person on their home floor, Fitzgerald Field House, located on the school's upper campus. The Field House is a cozy arena that seats 6,798, not exactly a sweaty pit striking fear into the hearts of opponents, but a smallish, old-fashioned facility where fans are close to the action. Many fans have reserved the same seats year after year, striking up lasting friendships with nearby ticket-holders.

The Panthers typically schedule a few of their most important games each season at the Mellon Arena, which can accommodate 17,159 fans. When you can't make it to the Field House or the Arena, you can follow the Panthers on radio on WTAE-AM, 1250 on the dial, which carries the complete Panthers schedule. Bill Hillgrove and Dick Groat are the capable, veteran broadcast team—they've been at the mike together since 1978. There is no set television schedule, but local stations and cable and broadcast networks find Pittsburgh and the Big East so attractive that they combine to show about a dozen games each season. You'll see games on local broadcast station WTAE-TV, Fox Sports Network and ESPN.

The ticket policy requires a bit of explanation. When Pittsburgh joined the Big East in 1982, interest in the team skyrocketed, and a seat at a conference game became one of the tougher tickets in town. Day-of-game tickets typically are

INSIDERS' TIP

If you experience car trouble in the Three Rivers Stadium parking lots after a Pirates game, watch for the "Buc Truck," which provides assistance to motorists. You can call the Buc Truck at (412) 362-1900.

When 55,000 people descend on Three Rivers Stadium for a Steelers game, you may be looking for a way to avoid traffic and parking hassles. Port Authority of Allegheny County may have that alternative for you.

PAT operates two special shuttle buses between downtown and the stadium for each Steelers game. The 96C services downtown stops only, while the 96X stops at downtown points and the Civic Arena. Cost for the shuttles is 75 cents each way for adults, 35 cents each way for children 6 through 11. Kids 5 and under ride free.

To reach town, try PAT's special game day express buses which depart from these suburban points: Heidelberg/Green Tree, Whitehall, McKeesport, North Hills, South Hills and Monroeville. Cost ranges from $1.25 to $3.50, depending on the number of zones traversed.

If you really get into bus travel, try PAT's Jerome Bettis Bus Pass, named for the popular Steelers running back nicknamed "The Bus." Buy the pass for $10 and you'll receive free fare on each ride taken on any PAT route all day during Steelers home dates, playoff games included. For information on any of these special plans, call PAT at (412) 442-2000.

For baseball and hockey games, PAT bulks up its fleet but has no special routes.

available for non-conference opponents but may be scarce for Big East foes. Tickets for Fieldhouse games are typically less expensive than games at the Mellon Arena, and games against West Virginia and Syracuse usually carry a premium. Single game tickets can usually be had for $20 or less. You can make credit card purchases over the phone at (800) 643-PITT, and you can access the ticket hotline at (412) 648-8300.

Season tickets are another matter. These are available at prices ranging from $202 to $270, but you must make a contribution of at least $1,000 to the school to be eligible for season tickets.

The university maintains several parking lots on its upper campus to accommodate fans, but if the truth be told, parking on the upper campus can be a crunch. A good way to beat that crunch: park on the lower campus, which offers more on-street parking, and ride the campus shuttle bus to the Field House.

Football

Pittsburgh Steelers

The romance between the Pittsburgh Steelers and their adoring fans is one of the enduring love affairs of sports. The team was founded in 1933 by the late Arthur J. Rooney, one of the grand old men of the National Football League and one of the game's great sportsmen. He launched the Steelers with money won at the race track, and he remained a sharp and successful handicapper until his death. Success couldn't spoil Rooney. He never moved from his house near Three Rivers Stadium, walked to work each day, gave generously to anyone in need, and "loafed," to use the expression he favored, with the friends he had grown up with.

Rooney was beloved, but the Steelers had a hard time winning until the 1970s, when the team under Coach Chuck Noll won four Super Bowls and became a dynasty. Nine Steelers from that era—including Rooney, Noll, Joe Greene, Jack Ham, Mel Blount, Terry Bradshaw, Franco Harris, Jack Ham, and Mike Webster—have been enshrined in the Pro Football Hall of Fame.

Rooney and Noll are gone, but the Steelers success continues under club President Daniel M. Rooney, Arthur Rooney's son, and Coach Bill Cowher, who led the Steelers

INSIDERS' TIP

During World War II, a player shortage forced the Pittsburgh Steelers to combine with the Philadelphia Eagles in 1943, with the Chicago Cardinals in 1944. The 1943 hybrid was called the Phil-Pitt Steagles.

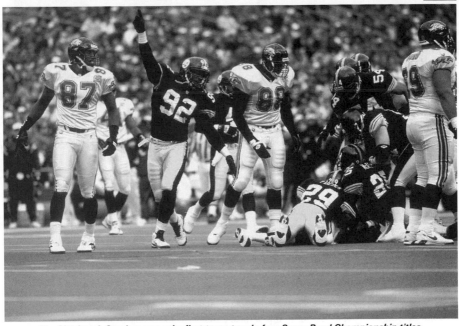

The Pittsburgh Steelers were the first team to win four Super Bowl Championship titles.

Photo: Michael F. Fabus

to post-season appearances in each of his first six years at the helm, an unprecedented coaching performance. Nor has the fans' ardor flagged a bit. Every Steelers home game since mid-1972 has sold out the 58,729-seat Three Rivers Stadium. The waiting list for season tickets is 6,000 names long.

Like the Pirates, the Steelers are packing to leave Three Rivers Stadium. The new football-only stadium, being built right next door to Three Rivers (which will be razed when the new building is complete), will be ready for the 2001 season. The as-yet-unnamed stadium will be horseshoe-shaped, with the open end facing across the River to Point State Park and Downtown. Following the nationwide stadium trend, the new park will have natural grass, every conceivable fan amenity, enormous locker rooms, and a jumbo video screen/scoreboard. It will also have 65,000 seats, several thousand more than Three Rivers. Tickets in this football-mad city will still be tough to come by, though. Even with the expanded seating, the club figures the wait for season tickets is about 10 years long.

That's not great news if you're interested in seeing the Steelers in person. For each home game at Three Rivers, the club puts 2,500 tickets on sale for $35 each. You can purchase up to three tickets for as many as two games; orders are by mail only. Demand is such that the chances of getting a ticket are slim.

There's good news here as well. Because the games are sold out well in advance, the Steelers are able to televise every contest, home or away, preseason, regular season or post season. During the regular season, you'll find Steelers games on KDKA-TV (the local CBS affiliate), WPGH (Fox 53), WTAE-TV (the local ABC affiliate), and ESPN, depending on the day and opponent. Since area cable television systems assign these networks different channel numbers, make sure you check local listings to determine where to catch the Steelers.

Steelers radio broadcasts on WTAE-AM (1250 on the dial), flagship of a 46-channel radio network, are a popular local institution themselves. Bill Hillgrove capably handles the play-by-play, but it is long-time color analyst Myron Cope who excites the crowd. Cope invented the "Terrible Towel"—wave it and good things happen for the Steelers—and you'll see them by the thousands at every game. It's not uncommon for fans watching a Steelers telecast to turn down the volume on their television sets so they can listen to Hillgrove and Cope on the radio. If you listen to a few of their broadcasts, you'll find yourself saying things like "Yoi!" and "Okel dokel," and wondering where on earth you could have picked up those expressions.

Since home games are always sold out, traffic and parking can be troublesome. Most Steelers fans are veterans and know the parking ropes. If you do manage to come by tickets for a game, make sure you leave home early enough for the obligatory tailgate party. Before Steelers games, the parking lots around Three River Stadium resemble a sprawling picnic grounds, with parties ranging from elaborate catered affairs to simple munchfests with center-cut jumbo. What's center-cut jumbo? It's a 'Burgh thing. You'll catch on.

University of Pittsburgh

What do Mike Ditka, Tony Dorsett and Dan Marino have in common? They all are National Football League greats, and they all played collegiate football at the University of Pittsburgh. The Panthers long have been a major college football power, producing such standouts as Joe Schmidt, Hugh Green, Matt Cavanaugh, Bill Fralic, Bill Maas, and Craig "Ironhead" Hayward, in addition to Ditka, Dorsett, and Marino. In all, 46 Panthers have won All-America honors, ranking Pittsburgh No. 6 among all NCAA Division 1-A schools.

> **INSIDERS' TIP**
>
> Three Rivers Stadium could be called "statuesque." Around its perimeter, you'll find statues of former Pirate greats Honus Wagner and Roberto Clemente, and Arthur J. Rooney, founder and patriarch of the Steelers.

Pittsburgh plays in the Big East conference, which means that when Coach Walt Harris and company take the field, they line up against such name opponents as Syracuse, Miami and West Virginia, as well as tough nonconference opponents. Pittsburgh won a national championship behind Dorsett in 1976—its third unanimous national title—and has appeared in 19 bowl games.

The Panthers are awaiting the completion of the new football stadium, which will become their new home. For three-quarters of a century, the team played at venerable Pitt Stadium on Campus, an antiquated facility that was razed to make room for a new convocation center. Until the new stadium is ready in 2001, the Panthers call Three Rivers Stadium home.

Saturday at the stadium on a glorious fall day is a memorable event, and typically an accessible one. While games with such traditional rivals as Penn State, Notre Dame and West Virginia can sell out, tickets tend to be available for most games. Ticket prices are $15 and $20, with youth discounts offered. For "backyard brawls" against West Virginia and Penn State, ticket prices are higher. You also can purchase season tickets and multigame packages. You can get your tickets by calling (800) 643-PITT and using your credit card. For the status of seats for any game, call the ticket hotline at (412) 648-8300.

Horse Racing

Ladbroke at the Meadows

If you've ever thrilled to the beauty of equine athletes as they thunder toward the finish line, then Ladbroke at the Meadows is the place where you'll find that thrill. Located in the Washington county town of Meadow Lands, about 25 miles from downtown Pittsburgh, Ladbroke features live harness racing—the type where the horses pull a sulky with a driver in it—five nights a week during warm weather months, four nights a week during the winter. The races begin at 7:30 PM on Tuesday, Thursday, and Friday, at 6:30 PM on Saturday and Sunday. If you're not currently a fan, the excitement of track announcer Roger Huston calling the action will convert you in a hurry.

When you come to enjoy the races, you'll find much to do. Ladbroke features a full-service restaurant, a sports bar, and a cafe for lighter fare. The kids will enjoy Ladbroke's pinball arcade.

But for the dedicated horseplayer, the real attraction of Ladbroke is the amazing menu of simulcast races that the track offers. The concept is simple. To enhance its own card, Ladbroke imports races from up to 25 harness and thoroughbred tracks across North America—there's even thoroughbred racing from Australia—and shows them to patrons at monitors placed throughout the facility. You can wager on any or all races at any of the tracks featured. The action typically begins just after noon and usually lasts until about midnight, seven days a week.

That's not all. Ladbroke offers that full racing menu at six wagering and dining facilities in the area. Thus, if you can't make it to the Washington County track, you can visit a Ladbroke facility in Greensburg, New Castle, Harmar, Moon, West Mifflin, or Johnstown and take advantage of the same viewing, wagering, and dining options that patrons at the track are enjoying.

Ladbroke heightens convenience even more by broadcasting its live races—as well as about 100 simulcast races from other tracks—into viewers' homes over satellite and via affiliation with local cable television companies. If your cable company features the Ladbroke Racing Network, or if you acquire the appropriate satellite signal decoder, you'll receive 12 hours of racing each day in the comfort of your home. Plus you can wager by phone by opening a Call-A-Bet account with a cash, check, or credit card deposit. To do so, call (800) LADBROK. Ladbroke won't let you bet more than you have in your account, although you can replenish your account at will. If you plan to participate from your home, you can pick up race programs at dozens of neighborhood newsstands and convenience stores.

Finally, the track offers aficionados a high-tech enhancement. If you visit the web site brisnet.com, you can view real-time betting odds at racetracks across the country.

Your experience at Ladbroke can be as simple or as complicated as you like. Some will find a wagering interest—however modest—heightens the enjoyment of the races. For others, the beauty of equine and human athletes in action will be enjoyment enough. Ladbroke also offers group outings that include such features as a race named for your group and a photo of you and your guests in the winner's circle, posed with the winning horse and driver.

Ice Hockey

Pittsburgh Penguins

For many years, the Pittsburgh Penguins were synonymous with their superstar, Mario Lemieux, arguably the greatest National Hockey League performer of all time. When chronic back problems forced Lemieux's retirement at the end of the 1996-1997 season, he went out with a flourish, leading the league in scoring for the sixth time and winning First All-Star Team honors for the fifth time. Most important to Penguins fans, he led the club to two Stanley Cups in 1991 and 1992. After retirement, Mario bought the team, ensuring the future of hockey in Pittsburgh.

Yet even during the apex of Lemieux's career, the Penguins were much more than a one-man team; in their Stanley Cup seasons, they played championship-caliber hockey during Lemieux's prolonged injury-related absences. In the P.M. (Post-Mario) era, led by such stars as Jaromir Jagr, they continue to excel as one of the NHL's top clubs.

The Penguins under Coach Herb Brooks perform in the Northeast Division of the Eastern Conference. That means they skate against Buffalo, Montreal, Ottawa, and Boston on a regular basis. If the regular season isn't enough hockey for you, you also can catch the Penguins in training; their preseason drills are public and take place at the Iceoplex at Southpointe in Washington County.

Home ice for the Pens is the Mellon Arena, but you won't want to call it that. To local fans, it's "The Igloo." The Arena in downtown Pittsburgh seats 16,958 for hockey and features the world's largest retractable stainless steel roof. Chances are you won't get to see the roof in action during hockey season.

One of the best features about The Igloo is its accessibility. Many Port Authority of Allegheny County bus routes end in, or depart from, downtown, making it easy to reach or leave the Arena by public transportation. If you drive, you'll find parking in both the Arena lots and in several nearby indoor garages, but parking can get sticky when crowds are large.

Another good idea—get your tickets in advance. Tickets are accessible for many games, but fans turn out in big

INSIDERS' TIP

A section of Forbes Field, where the Pirates played from 1909 until 1972, still stands in Pittsburgh's Oakland neighborhood.

INSIDERS' TIP

For the sports fan who can't get enough, WTAE-AM, 1250 on the dial, features almost all sports, almost all the time, including live broadcasts, sports news, and local and syndicated talk shows.

SPECTATOR SPORTS

INSIDERS' TIP

A good place to see the Steelers in person is at their summer-training site—St. Vincent College in Latrobe, about 40 miles east of downtown Pittsburgh.

numbers for the best teams and for contests they consider important. The Pens offer season and partial-season plans as well as discounted group packages. For ticket information, call (412) 642-PENS.

If you can't make it to The Igloo, it's still easy to follow the Pens. WDVE-FM, 102.5 on the dial, carries the complete Penguins schedule. On the television side, regional cable network Fox Sports Pittsburgh is the main provider, while local broadcast stations WB22 and WPGH/Fox 53 also air a number of games. Among them, they'll provide you with nearly every regular-season match.

You'll get quite a kick out of the broadcast teams of Mike Lange and Paul Steigerwald on television, Matt McConnell and Peter Taglianetti on radio. The veteran Lange, the lead broadcaster since 1976, is not only sharp and swift in his call, but he also has coined such trademark phrases as "Look Out, Loretta," "Scratch My Back With a Hacksaw," "Buy Sam A Drink (And Get His Dog One, Too)," and the immortal "Elvis Has Left the Building," to signal that a game is out of reach. Most of this Lange-Slang has entered the local lexicon. No less a figure than Sophie Masloff, when she was mayor of Pittsburgh and speaking at a Three Rivers Stadium rally, exhorted the crowd to "scratch her back with a hacksaw" in tribute to Lange.

The Penguins maintain a close relationship with their fans through an active community involvement program. Their initiatives include school visits, scholarships, development of youth hockey and financial support for nonprofit organizations. Perhaps the most innovative aspect of the program is the Penguins Information Booth at the Arena, which nonprofit organizations can use on game days to distribute information to fans. For information about the booth, call (412) 642-1800.

Writing on the Wall

This is a story about an artist, her Pittsburgh sports mural, and the publicist they hired to promote the mural. The artist and the mural both died before their time. The publicist lives, but cautiously.

Judy Penzer was a native New Yorker who had made her mark with sharply

observed, sensitive portraiture. She was especially known for her portraits of female impersonators; many of her works graced the lobbies of off-Broadway theaters. Ever in the vanguard, she was among a group of politically active artists who in 1983 founded New York City's Castillo Cultural Center, which staged multimedia presentations in painting and performance. Her outlook became much grander when she and her brother, real estate developer Richard Penzer, came to Pittsburgh. Judy Penzer made the whole city her canvas, in quite a literal way.

Her brother had acquired a number of downtown Pittsburgh buildings. To achieve a higher profile, he commissioned her to paint a larger-than-life sports mural on one of those structures, the 500 Wood Street Building. I first met the Penzers when the mural project was bogged down in the red tape of zoning permit applications. The Penzers wanted to tackle the problem in dramatic style, by mounting a demonstration against the municipal government. Instead, they hired me to work with the Pittsburgh Zoning Commission to acquire the necessary permits. The commission was quite cooperative, even excited about the prospect of such a signature piece. They were more than pleased to approve the request. With that achieved, I became the publicist for the project.

The mural was ambitious in its design. It would feature five Pittsburgh sports legends—Roberto Clemente, Bill Mazeroski, Mario Lemieux, Jack Lambert and

Joe Greene—in black, gold and white against a bold orange background. The mural would be 135 feet high, 46 feet across, and stretch for 15 stories. It would be visible from many downtown office buildings as well as Mellon Square, a popular gathering area. Judy Penzer developed the pattern for the mural and engaged a professional sign company to apply it to the building. We christened it the "Wall of Fame."

In the summer of 1992, it was finished. The Wall of Fame attracted national attention. It was featured in *Sports Illustrated* and *USA Today*. CBS repeatedly dissolved to it when it appeared the Pirates would reach the 1992 World Series. They didn't, thanks to a late seventh-game rally by the Atlanta Braves.

While the mural was an unqualified success, my relationship with Judy Penzer was more complex. It included friendship and respect but also tension created by the clash of her boldness, even brashness, and my more conservative Pittsburgh attitude. We worked together on other projects, including an even larger mural that she painted on the renovated former Gimbels building downtown. We fought about the Penzers' plans to stage a man-on-the-street poll to build support for the new mural. They loved the poll idea. I found it tacky. I lost. That was our last project together.

Before we parted, she gave me a working model of her portrait of the late Art Rooney, founder and patriarch of the Pittsburgh Steelers. It was much more in the style of the early Judy Penzer: a sober, almost brooding Rooney views his team at work, his eyes shielded by impenetrable glasses that keep his expression a mystery. I intended to hang it, but when my local art dealer suggested he would charge me $300 to frame it, I tossed it in a closet for future action.

On July 17, 1996, Judy Penzer died in the crash of Flight 800 off Long Island. She was 49. The Wall of Fame didn't survive her by much. The 500 Wood

(Continued on next page)

Street Building was targeted for demolition to make way for downtown's new Lazarus department store, a much-needed project for the city and region. My client, the Urban Redevelopment Authority of Pittsburgh, which was planning site development, studied ways of preserving the mural. Salvation would have required brick-by-brick removal of the work, a seven-figure undertaking that nobody's budget would support. When no angel emerged to save it, we all agreed the mural would come down.

On a gray spring Sunday in 1997, the 500 Wood Street Building was imploded. In that last second, Pittsburgh got its final glimpse of Judy Penzer's contribution to the city's sports history. The funny thing is, I don't believe Judy Penzer would have been upset. She knew the mural's impermanence when she created it. It didn't bother her. She always was in the vanguard, looking forward. She would have found a way to convert the implosion into a kicky, gutsy artistic event.

I had mixed feelings about it myself. After watching news coverage of the implosion, I went to the basement and pulled Art Rooney out of the closet. I admire it from time to time but still haven't framed it. Can't be too careful, you know.

—Evan Pattak

Daytrips & Weekend Getaways

We frankly believe that there's so much to see and do in and around Pittsburgh that you'd never need to leave! But for those of you stricken with a case of wanderlust, or just itching to get out in the country, we present a number of destinations for your consideration within a half-day's drive (at most) of the city

Whether you venture just 30 minutes from your home base, take to the highways for a leisurely drive, or even opt for the express airline service offered locally, there are plenty of fascinating escapes just hours from Pittsburgh.

Some of these lend themselves to the affordable family getaway. Others might have the word "golf" written all over them (and for more focus on that subject, turn to the Golf chapter in this book). Educational exploration is certainly prevalent in the area. So is boosting the economy of several sites in Western Pennsylvania. Finally, a few of the destinations you might consider remind us of romance—dare we say, even reminiscent of the second honeymoon you've put off. Well, now is the time to take it!

The day excursions and weekend trips presented in this chapter fall within approximately three hours of Pittsburgh. From the western communities, count on some extra time when traveling east, and vice versa. The only other caveat is to let go, relax, and enjoy yourself exploring new sights, loading your car with new wares, and sampling fine food, entertainment, and hospitality.

Bon voyage!

LOOK FOR:
• Erie County
• Lawrence & Mercer Counties
• Laurel Highlands
• Altoona/State College/Johnstown
• Cleveland
• Oglebay, W. Va.
• Deep Creek Lake, Md.
• Hershey

Erie County

Find out why areas north are Erie-sistible. Roughly three hours from Pittsburgh, Erie County offers something for every member of the family, from amusement parks and water recreation to arts, museums, and fun shopping.

Getting There

Reach the Erie area by taking I-79 north from Pittsburgh. It's a straight shot up one single highway! Once in the area, the Presque Isle Express is a 36-passenger vessel designed to taxi you across the water from Dobbins

Landing to Presque Isle (which isn't really an island, but a nice park with a beach). Weather permitting, the water taxi operates seven days a week from 10 AM until 6 PM. It's wheelchair and bicycle accessible, and maintains a 60-minute schedule.

For more general information about Erie County and environs, contact the Erie Convention & Visitors Bureau at 1006 State Street, Erie, PA 16501, or call (814) 454-7191.

Erie County Attractions

As you might have guessed from the name, Erie County borders Lake Erie, one of the five Great Lakes, and the lake is an integral piece of life here. You'll want to explore the waters of Lake Erie, and what better way to do it than at the Erie Maritime Museum, 150 E. Front Street, (814) 452-2744, on the bayfront.

At the Erie Zoo & Botanical Gardens, W. 38th Street, (814) 864-4091, kids can visit 300 animals exhibited indoors and out. Especially enticing are the dual-level otter exhibit, the white Bengal tiger, and the African wild bird exhibit. Sightseeing train rides are also popular.

Summer is always fun at Waldameer Park and Water World, found at the entrance to Presque Isle State Park, (814) 838-3591, where you'll experience over 75 rides, slides, and attractions. There are fun games, great gift houses, snacks, and food to help pass the time. Conneaut Lake Park, 12832 Center Street, Conneaut Lake (25 miles southwest of Erie), (814) 382-5115, also boasts rides, festivals, and family fun.

Presque Isle State Park, (814) 833-7424, has been rated by *Birder's World* magazine as one of the top birding spots in the country. In addition, you'll find approximately 13 miles of hiking trails in the park (bicycles are not permitted on the hiking trails). A good place to begin your visit is at the Stull Interpretive Center, located near Barracks Beach. Here you'll learn about the park's many resources, including its access for people with disabilities. There's no charge to enter the park.

The Presque Isle Lighthouse, in the park, was built in 1872 and first lit on July 12, 1873. The U.S. Coast Guard still maintains it with its flashing white light. Visitors aren't allowed inside the lighthouse. At Misery Bay and the Perry Monument, you'll find the temporary home of the fleet of ships commanded by Commodore Oliver Hazard Perry in the Battle of Lake Erie. Six of his nine vessels, including two brigs—the *Niagara* and the *Lawrence*—were constructed from local trees along Erie Bay. It was his victory and the War of 1812 that assured we didn't become Canadians!

The Lake Shore Railway Museum, 31 Wall Street at Robinson Street, (814) 825-2724, welcomes visitors Wednesday through Sunday from Memorial Day weekend through Labor Day weekend, in addition to Saturdays and Sundays in September and October. Admission is free of charge to relive the days of the steam locomotive powered trains that ran along Pennsylvania's picturesque Northeast countryside. Walk through a 1926 "Nightstar" sleeping car built by Pullman and see the Centralized Traffic Control board, built in 1943, showing how a single dispatcher controlled large stretches of track at one time.

A day trip for the grown-ups wouldn't be complete without a sampling of Pennsylvania wine. Stop at the Penn Shore Winery & Vineyards, 10225 E. Lake Road, Pa. Route 5, (814) 725-8688, for it's one of the largest and longest established wineries in the state. Mazza Vineyards, 11815 E. Lake Road, (814) 725-8695, offers wine tasting tours daily, seven days a week, year-round.

Erie County Shopping

Are you in the mood for souvenirs? The Nature Shop, at Presque Isle State Park (see write-up above), has books, field guides, and other nature-related items for you to purchase and enjoy from your day trip. Proceeds benefit the state park.

Also, Penn Shore Wines (see above) can ship its vintage, table, and sparkling wines in Pennsylvania via United Parcel Service, if you don't want to take the bottles home with you.

Each season the Mason Farms Country Market, 839 Peninsula Drive, (814) 833-9933, brings exciting treats and

Daytrippers in search of luxury head to the Nemacolin Woodlands Resort & Spa.

Photo: Courtesy of Nemacolin Woodlands Resort & Spa

experiences to store customers. Choose from a large selection of perennials, annuals, and shrubs in the spring, fresh fruit and vegetables over the summer months, pumpkins around Halloween, and country crafts for Christmas.

The Bayfront Gallery, part of the waterfront revitalization, is Erie's artist's co-op located on E. Dobbins Landing, (814) 455-6632. It's open seasonally for its unique blend of antique wares and local artistry.

Customary shopping at chain establishments and some local merchants is found at the Mill Creek Mall, Upper Peach Street, (814) 868-9000. Boasting a Kaufmann's, Elder-Beerman, JC Penney, Sears, HomePlace, and over 200 specialty shops, it's no wonder you could spend the entire day shopping. In fact, the entire Upper Peach Street area has been peppered with more stores and restaurants (see below).

Erie County Accommodations

Featuring in-room movies, coffee makers, an outdoor pool, laundry facilities, and airport transportation, the Holiday Inn Downtown Erie, 18 W. 18th Street, (814) 456-2961 assures you'll be at the center of activity. Enjoy a free breakfast buffet with your room.

The Bel-Aire Hotel, 2800 W. 8th Street, (814) 833-1116, has an indoor, heated pool, Jacuzzi, and fitness center for its guests, as well as restaurants and room service. At Hampton Inn North, 3041 W. 12th Street, (814) 835-4200, the swimming is outdoors, but you can enjoy a complimentary continental breakfast, free HBO, and airport limousines. The Hampton Inn South, 8050 Oliver Road, (814) 866-6800, is accessible to I-90 and nearby I-79. Avalon Hotel, 16 W. 10th Street, (800) 822-5011, is in the heart of downtown Erie, near the Erie Art Museum and the Erie Playhouse. And, for business travel, the Courtyard by Marriott, I-90, Exit 6, (Scott Drive) boasts a full-service hotel with 110 guest rooms, an indoor pool, and several suites. Right next door is the Ambassador Banquet & Conference Center, which will accommodate up to 500 people for business and social functions. Call (814) 866-2773 for both hotels.

Families might prefer renting a cottage near Presque Isle State Park. Presque Isle Cottage Court, 320 Peninsula Drive, (814) 833-4956, offers one-, two-, or three-bedroom individual and deluxe cottages, all with kitchenettes, carpeting, private baths and porches, and some with living rooms as well as decks. There's even a central playground for the kids.

Erie County Restaurants

Oh, the waters—and what better way to experience the wonder of Lake Erie than on a dinner cruise aboard *The Victorian Princess*. Leisurely dinner sailings are offered in Victorian style from April 1 through November 1. Cost is $22 per person for dinner cruises. Group and children's rates are also available. For reservations, call ahead at (814) 459-9696. Dinner (as well as sightseeing only) cruises board at Dobbins Landing.

You can sample various cuisines at area restaurants. Hibachi Japanese Steak House, 3000 W. 12th Street, (814) 838-2495, features food as the name implies. As we mentioned in the shopping description, restaurants have been part of the Upper Peach Street expansion, adding chains such as Don Pablos, Max & Erma's, and the newest site for Quaker Steak & Lube (read a description in Lawrence and Mercer Counties, below). Pufferbelly Restaurant, 414 French Street, (814) 454-1557, operates out of an old Erie firehouse. Spinner McGee's Steakhouse, 4940 Peach Street, (814) 866-7746, is in an old railroad car, and features Western ambiance.

Dock your boats near Dobbins Landing for dinner at Rum Runners, (814) 455-4292, or sit on the verandah at Smugglers' Wharf, (814) 459-4273. There's also the Waterfront Seafood & Steakhouse (814) 459-0606, with seating on three decks. In addition, there are plenty of casual, family-oriented eateries, among them Applebee's, Damon's, Eat'N Park, Perkins, and TGI Friday's at numerous locations throughout Erie County.

Lawrence and Mercer counties

What you know of Lawrence and Mercer counties may be through your children, as each fall, another mass exodus begins for families with college students attending Westminster, Grove City, and Thiel Colleges, the Penn State Shenango campus, and nearby Slippery Rock University. Perhaps you've noticed the beauty of the farm fields on your trips here, but never stopped to truly enjoy the countryside. Maybe you've visited a shop or two, but you haven't taken the time to explore the hidden treasures off the beaten path.

For more information on traipsing through Lawrence and Mercer counties, call the Lawrence County Tourist Promotion Agency at (724) 654-5593, or the Mercer County Tourist Agency at (800) 637-2370.

Getting There

From Pittsburgh, you can reach these counties by driving north on I-79, Pa. 19, or Pa. 60, if you're starting out from Pittsburgh's west suburbs. Pa. 208 runs between the towns of New Wilmington and Grove City, crossing over I-79.

Mercer and Lawrence County Attractions

If you thought Tara was found only in the South, guess again. Tours of Tara—A Country Inn, nestled in the little village of Clark, outside Sharon—are popular for daytrippers. Visitors peruse the antique furniture, books, and an original jacket worn by Vivian Leigh's Scarlet O'Hara in *Gone with the Wind*. There's an antique slave cradle and many other rare finds. The custom-made glass doors in the entry hall were handcrafted and beveled by Bob Lutz & Sons of New Castle, and most definitely add to the elegance of the mansion. (See more about Tara below in Accommodations).

If you're like most visitors, you'll want to allow time to explore the Wendell August Forge, 620 Madison Avenue, Grove City, established in 1923 in Brockway before moving in 1932 to its current location. You can't miss the signs, well placed along the major routes into town. Free tours are available, but to make sure the forge is open when you want to visit, it's best to call (724) 458-8360 or (800) 923-4438.

The forge is one of the few remaining in the country that continues to produce forged aluminum, pewter, bronze, sterling, and silver articles entirely by hand, using no production machinery. The showroom/museum houses a historical col-

INSIDERS' TIP

Be sure to familiarize yourself with safety procedures and the rules of the waterways at Deep Creek Lake, Maryland. Police patrol by boat and will pull you over to run safety checks and inspect for fishing licenses. You will be fined if you're caught boating recklessly or under the influence of alcohol.

lection of artifacts and a complete line of giftware that has been commissioned by corporate executives, leading companies, even the U.S. Congress. Visitors get to see the artisans hammering and chiseling these art forms when they take the free, self-guided tour.

Mercer and Lawrence County Shopping

Byler's Furniture sits off Pa. 18 on Cowden Road, not far from The Cheese House in New Wilmington. Customers keep coming back, and they're quick to praise the Amish man's work on furniture sets and wooden toys. Byler's is open every day from 8 AM to 5 PM, except Sundays and major holidays.

Adventurous shoppers seeking the best prices will track down the authentic Amish shops that make a trip north fun in itself. Visitors can ponder a selection of quilt supplies and fabrics, baby and children's shoes, and have also been known to drive to the Amish harness shops for their custom-made saddles and leather goods. If you get lost, ask the locals to head you on your way to your next stop, since many of these are tucked off on back roads in private homes, without noticeable signage to guide you. (See the Amish Close-up in this chapter.)

Market Street in New Wilmington is the center of retail activity with crafts, antiques, and gift merchandise. Don't miss the New Wilmington Collection of Artisans, 205 S. Market Street, (724) 946-2310, for its vast array of handcrafted gifts and Amish furniture. The Quilting Bee, 126 S. Market Street, offers quilting supplies, colorful fabrics, and classes too. For those in search of antiques, head to Nest Egg Antiques, 139 S. Market Street, where you'll also find J.G. McGill's local artwork.

If you take I-79 and Pa. 208 to New Wilmington, you'll drive through Volant, where you can't miss The Volant Mill, a major tourist stop featuring crafts and gifts. Built in 1812, it operated as a grist and flour mill until 1963. Today, it sits across the street from the mini-mall of refurbished train shops. (See our Shopping chapter for more).

Downtown Sharon, sometimes referred to as the world's largest small town, is full of shopping. It's known for The Winner, 32 W. State Street, which owners Jim and Donna Winner proclaim to be the world's largest off-price fashion store; Reyer's, City Centre, which locals say is the world's largest shoe store, claiming to stock every size; Daffin's Chocolate Kingdom, 496 E. State Street, where candy making is an art; and Kraynak's, 2525 E. State Street, with special Christmas and Easter displays. For more traditional types of chain stores, head to the Shenango Valley Mall located on Pa. 18 and 62 in Hermitage. Anchor stores include Kaufmann's, JC Penney, and Sears.

Of course, if you want to shop until you are absolutely exhausted or spent (literally!), then head to the Prime Outlets along I-79 and Pa. 208. Here you'll find every type of store you could possibly imagine, and prices that sometimes can't be beat. (See our Shopping chapter for more details).

Mercer and Lawrence County Accommodations

With so much to see, you're most likely looking for a place to rest your weary feet. Sprawling development has brought along with it a choice of popular chain motels and hotels, usually clustered off Interstates 79 and 80. But don't overlook the small and elegant, the rural and charming. Several bed and breakfast establishments have thrived, offering a delightful alternative for guests.

At the most elegant end of the spectrum is Tara—A Country Inn at 3665 Valley View Road, Clark, (724) 962-3535 or (800) 782-2803.

A home whose refurbishing was inspired by the movie *Gone with the Wind*, Tara is a graceful 1854 antebellum home—the embodiment of the Old South. Purchased in 1984 by Innkeepers Jim and Donna Winner, it's a frequent stop for travelers who want to tour the grounds and mansion, or dine in one of two restaurants.

Visiting Tara isn't just a culinary experience, or tourist stop to tour. There's a little history lesson as well as your guide tells you about the property, including the formal gardens overlooking the beautiful 450-acre Shenango Lake. No tour is complete without walking through the mansion, a virtual museum of rare and priceless antiques, works of art, and collectibles, many of which the owners purchased on trips abroad.

Each room is decorated differently—many with canopy beds, crystal lamps, marble fireplaces, and sunken whirlpools. Guests enjoy swimming in the indoor spa, sipping afternoon tea on the sun porch, or curling up with a favorite book or videotape checked out of the library.

The Winners own not only Tara, but the Buhl Mansion in Sharon, Mercer County. An art gallery, guesthouse, and spa, this home was built in 1890, and it's listed on the National Register of Historical Homes. The grand oak staircase ascends to the second and third floors. Each suite has a gas fireplace and luxurious bath. For reservations, call (724) 962-3535 or (800) 782-2803.

In recent years, several chain hotels have established themselves, due in large part to the tourist attractions and the outlet shopping. Spend the night in West Middlesex at the Radisson Hotel Sharon, off I-80 on Pa. 18, (724) 528-2501, and relax in the heated indoor pool. Right across the street is the Holiday Inn of Sharon/Hermitage, (724) 981-1530, with its golf packages and outdoor pool facility as well as the Comfort Inn Shenango Valley, Pa. 18 and Wilson Road, (724) 458-6425, which has an indoor heated pool, whirlpool suites, and complimentary breakfasts available.

The Howard Johnson Lodge & Restaurant, 835 Perry Highway (Pa. 19) in Mercer, (800) 542-7674, is just ten minutes from the outlet shops. In Grove City itself, choose from bed and breakfasts like Lynnrose, (724) 458-6425, at 114 W. Main Street, or the Snow Goose Inn, (724) 458-4644, at 112 E. Main Street. The Snow Goose is across the street from Grove City College, while Lynnrose is within a short walking distance. The AmeriHost Inn, a two-story hotel at 1924 Leesburg Road, Grove City, (724) 748-5836, boasts a pool, whirlpool, and saunas.

Within New Wilmington, charming bed and breakfasts abound as well. Consider the Beechwood Inn, an old Civil War home with Victorian decor, found on the road by the same name (175 Beechwood Road to be exact). When your day is complete, sit on one of three covered porches at this inn. Call Beechwood at (724) 946-2342.

Gabriel's Bed & Breakfast at 174 Waugh Avenue, (724) 946-3136, is another Victorian romantic getaway featuring featherbeds, and Behm's Bed & Breakfast nearby at 166 Waugh Avenue, (724) 946-8641, is a gem just blocks from Westminster College. Here you're treated to Nancy Behm's watercolor studio in this 1895 home.

Mercer and Lawrence County Restaurants

At Tara, guests can enjoy Ashley's for gourmet dining and Stonewall's Tavern for lighter fare, including great steaks and salads. Ashley's menu features wine selections honored by the coveted *Wine Spectator* Award of Excellence. Call for reservations at (724) 962-3535.

Quaker Steak & Lube, a popular watering hole famous for its atomic wings and unusual display of race cars and auto memorabilia, is found in the heart of downtown Sharon, 101 Chestnut Street, (724) 981-7221, as well as in Hermitage, on E. State Street, (724) 983-8646. Locals call it "the Lube."

Likewise, the Iron Bridge Inn, (724) 748-3626, is popular for its good food and rustic charm. Despite the name, there's no lodging here, just a restaurant that bills itself as "foodmerchants and brewmasters." Conveniently located on Pa. 19 between Westminster and Grove City, it attracts tourists by day, college crowds by night. Also along Pa. 19 is Rachel's Roadhouse, (724) 748-3193, a sister restaurant literally just down the road, between the Iron Bridge and Route 208.

Longtime area visitors still enjoy pleasant meals at The Tavern in New Wilmington, (724) 946-2020, where the menu is read aloud, or the Penn Grove Hotel, 129 E. Pine Street, Grove City, (724) 458-7400, established long before any golden arches or popular family chains dotted the landscape. At the Penn Grove Hotel, enjoy a Friday evening seafood buffet or a Sunday buffet from 12 to 3 PM.

Laurel Highlands

This scenic expanse in Southwestern Pennsylvania encompasses a broad stretch of more than 100 miles throughout several counties to the south and east of Pittsburgh. With the region named

Swallow Falls, in the beautiful mountains of Western Maryland, is worth seeing during a daytrip to Deep Creek Lake and Garrett County.

Photo: Loriann Hoff Oberlin

in deference to the mountain laurel, you could be in the Laurel Highlands if you're in Greene, Fayette, Somerset, even Westmoreland counties. Since this last county is a part of this book's general coverage area, we'll cover only the highlights here. Indeed exploring the Laurel Highlands for a day, or perhaps several, is a pleasant option.

The Laurel Highlands is a vast area for daytrippers, but if you need assistance, contact the Laurel Highlands Visitors Bureau at 120 E. Main Street, Ligonier, PA 15658, or call (724) 238-5661.

Getting There

There are several routes to take to the Laurel Highlands, depending upon where you depart and which area you'd like to visit. The Pennsylvania Turnpike is popular, with exits at Donegal, Somerset, and New Stanton. Traveling along Pa. 30 or U.S. 40 (the former National Road) in Fayette County will also take you to many of the sites we'll describe here.

Laurel Highlands Attractions

Fallingwater, in Mill Run, (724) 329-8501, was once the weekend retreat of department store owner Edgar J. Kaufmann and his wife Liliane. Tucked away in the Laurel Highlands, architect Frank Lloyd Wright designed this outstanding example of organic architecture. Though there is much walking and many stairs to climb, the curious love to tour Fallingwater. Similarly, Kentuck Knob, located at Chalk Hill, Ohiopyle, (724) 329-1901, is another of Frank Lloyd Wright's creations, though less popular than Fallingwater. Regular tours of Fallingwater are available (see our Architecture and Attractions chapters for details).

Travel back to the French and Indian War at Fort Necessity National Battlefield, along U.S. 40, (724) 329-5512, in Fayette County just southeast of Uniontown. This became George Washington's "fort of necessity" because a large force of French and Indians attacked his army of 400.

Ligonier, in the far reaches of Westmoreland County, is a charming town, known for "the Diamond" town square with its old-fashioned gazebo, ice cream parlor, and antique and craft shops. But most historic is Fort Ligonier, named in honor of Sir John Ligonier, a British commander-in-chief. In 1946, the Fort Ligonier Association was charged with recreating the 1758-1766 garrison, and with building a museum. Though never occupied by the enemy, this fort, and its three-day festival every October, commemorates the battle at Fort Ligonier in 1758 during the French and Indian War. Fort Ligonier Days (see Annual Events) features craftspeople, merchant sidewalk sales, entertainment, antique window displays, and a huge Saturday parade. Of course, there is plenty of great food to sample.

Families will love the beautiful setting of Idlewild Park, (724) 238-3666, with its theme areas, especially suited for kids who want to have fun (see Kidstuff). Another area of noted interest in the Laurel Highlands is Seven Springs (see "Skiing" in Recreation). For thrills of another kind, you won't want to miss whitewater rafting on the Youghiogheny River at Ohiopyle (see Attractions). In addition, there are miles of excellent bike and walking trails throughout the highlands.

The Laurel Highlands also boasts the largest natural cave north of the Mason-Dixon Line. Laurel Caverns, 5 miles west of U.S. 40 on Caverns Road near Uniontown, offers guided and self-guided tours through this limestone catacomb cave with more than 2 miles of passages. Visitors should dress warmly, as the average temperature hovers around 52 degrees Fahrenheit year-round. For information, call (724) 438-3003.

Laurel Highlands Shopping

Outlet shopping in Somerset and Mt. Pleasant is plentiful, but you'll also find many small shops scattered around the Laurel Highlands. Major malls, specialty merchants, and factory outlets are covered in the Shopping chapter; it's best to include this reading in your research.

In Fayette County, you'll find the Uniontown Mall at 1368 W. Main Street, (724) 437-9411. In Connellsville, shop at Youghiogheny Station: Glass & Gallery at 900 W. Crawford Avenue, (724) 628-0332. It's the beautifully refurbished P&LE passenger station just minutes from Fallingwater, Ohiopyle, Nemacolin Woodlands, and Greensburg. The shop offers everything glass, from paperweights to perfume bottles and lamps. Of course, the tourist attractions maintain their own gift shops which you'll want to browse for souvenirs or unique gifts, including Frank Lloyd Wright references and works at Fallingwater.

Finally, it's Christmas year-round at the Christmas Shop & Countree Cupboard along U.S. 40 E., Chalk Hill. Call the store at (724) 439-6500.

Laurel Highlands Restaurants

In Somerset, the Oakhurst Tea Room on Pa. 31, (814) 443-2897, established in 1933, is famous for its smorgasbord and desserts. There's a Friday seafood buffet, and Sunday brunch among other items on the menu. Seven Springs Mountain Resort boasts five restaurants, ranging from snacks at the coffee shop to elegant dining at Helen's, (800) 452-2223.

Look for the innkeeper's menu selections at the Mountain View Inn, (724) 834-5300. Favorites include salmon Oscar, lobster Delmonico, and scallops of lamb with apple butter. Family-style meals are served on Sundays. There are also health conscious menu items and early bird specials.

Vallozzi's, approximately 4 miles east of the U.S. 199 junction, on Pa. 30 E. near Greensburg, features northern Italian specialties for lunch or dinner. However, it's closed on major holidays and Sundays. Call for reservations at (724) 836-7663.

Nemacolin Woodlands offers three full-service restaurants, as well as casual corners to catch a bite. At Lautrec, the menu is French and on the expensive side, with appetizers like escargots and entrees such as chateaubriand or roast rack of lamb. The Golden Trout lunch menu is very reason-

able in price, yet dinner is moderately expensive. Caddyshack is also a good place for lunch in the moderate price range. Take the kids to the Hungry Moose Café or P.J.'s Pizza and Ice Cream Parlor for soup, salads, sandwiches, and a children's menu at relatively inexpensive prices. (For a much more detailed listing of Nemacolin, see our Accommodations chapter).

For more casual dining in a relaxed setting, head to the Sunporch Restaurant along U.S. 40 in the Hopwood Business District, east of Uniontown, (724) 439-5734. River's Edge Cafe in

Confluence features both indoor and outside dining for lunch and dinner. Call for seasonal operating hours, (814) 395-5059.

Laurel Highlands Accommodations

Indeed because much of the Laurel Highlands exists in and around the Pennsylvania Turnpike and other major highways, accommodations are plentiful. Among the highlights, however, is Mountain View Inn, conveniently located between Greensburg and Latrobe in central Westmoreland County. Guest rooms are all unique, some with king-size beds, whirlpool tubs, and fireplaces. Some have the elegant formality of the 18th century, while others are Early American in charm. It's the perfect venue for a romantic weekend. To book a room, call (724) 834-5300.

Seven Springs Mountain Resort (see our Accommodations chapter) is certainly an option as well as the Holiday Inn, 202 Shaffer Street, Somerset, (814) 445-961, or the Hampton Inn, at 324 Laurel Crest Road, (814) 445-9161. In addition to the resort and spa setting of Fayette County's Nemacolin Woodlands, you might also be interested in the Summit Inn Mountain Resort at the Summit in Farmington, (724) 438-8594.

Altoona/State College/Johnstown Area

This area an hour or two east of Pittsburgh is popular for day trips, especially for Penn State fans venturing in the fall to Nittany Lion football games. While the area is accessible for a day, why not stay the night and make it a weekend?

To obtain a visitor's map or area information, call the Allegheny Mountains Convention and Visitors Bureau at (800) 84-ALTOONA. In State College, the staff of the Centre County Convention and Visitors Bureau is available at (800) 358-5466. For specific Johnstown information, contact the Greater Johnstown/Cambria County Convention and Visitors Bureau at (800) 237-8590.

Getting There

There are several routes to take to these destinations. If you're headed to Altoona and State College from Pittsburgh, follow Pa. 22 east and Pa. 220/I-99 north to Altoona and Blair County. Continue on Pa. 220/I-99 and make a right onto Pa. 322 for your destination of State College.

En route to Johnstown, follow Pa. 22 East and you'll find the signs for Johnstown long before Altoona and State College. You could also reach Johnstown going north on U.S. 219 from the Pennsylvania Turnpike.

Altoona/State College/Johnstown Attractions

The Frost Entomological Museum, Headhouse III, (814) 865-1895, in State College has more than 500,000 insects and arthropods, all well preserved and labeled for public display. Each September, highlights at the Great Insect Fair include cockroach races, an insect zoo, and honey extracting and tasting. Also in State College, the Matson Museum of Anthropology, in the Carpenter Building, (814) 865-3853, tracks human evolution with a genetics exhibit, artifacts, needlework, and ceramics of far-ranging cultures. Pennsylvania's prehistoric treasures are found here as well.

Just minutes from I-80 in Nittany Lion Country is Penn's Cave, Centre Hall, (814) 364-1664, filled with glittering stalactites and stalagmites reminiscent of national tourist attractions. You tour this all-water cavern by boat, learning the legend of Indian Princess Nitanee, from whom the Penn State Nittany Lion was named.

Speaking of the Nittany Lion, Penn State's mascot since 1904, stop at the Nittany Lion Shrine near the Recreation Building, on campus. This landmark was created by Heinz Warneke in 1940 from a 13-ton block of Indiana limestone. During the second week of July each year, plan to browse the Central Pennsylvania Festival of the Arts.

New Wilmington's Old Order Amish

Beyond the bonnets and wide-brimmed hats, the plain white farm houses, and the strict code of conduct, the Old Order Amish thrive in the New Wilmington area, approximately one hour north of Pittsburgh. Visitors come to browse in the craft shops, ponder a carpenter's handiwork, or merely enjoy the drive through farm pastures and life at its simplest.

While there are many retailers displaying Amish-made goods, adventurous shoppers seek out their own best buys directly from these creators of country quilts, custom-made leather saddles, and solid wood rockers, cradles, toys or complete dining and bedroom sets. In warmer weather, you'll spot Amish women selling homemade baked goods at roadside stands.

For the Amish, their cottage industries are just that. Many make their living from the bounty of the land or the skill of their hands, using diesel power (with car batteries to start their equipment) instead of electricity and horse-drawn buggies and farm equipment rather than cars and tractors. The average family boasts eight to 10 children, and hard work is a way of life.

Amish education takes place in a one-room schoolhouse where children learn reading, writing, and arithmetic. Religion is taught in the home, not in churches, as small groups gather in homes one Sunday and visit other Amish the next.

Baptism is saved for adulthood, not undertaken at birth. So vital is this passage that teenagers yearn to experience the English world, as they call it, before the commitment is made. Finding young people to hang around with is hardly a problem here, as New Wilmington is also home to Westminster College, a four-year liberal arts college related to the Presbyterian Church (U.S.A).

As you drive along Pa. 18 (north from New Castle or south from Sharon), you'll spot Amish homes and farms by the tell-tale white sheets tied back as curtains in the windows. New Wilmington's Amish are entrepreneurial in spirit, but far less so than their neighbors across the state. There are signs, but they won't knock you over.

Most establishments are open year-round except on Sundays and major holidays. Do stop in and chat, but please don't take pictures at close distances. The Amish prefer to live in the world; they just don't like to be of the world. They're a friendly, honest, and hard-working group of people!

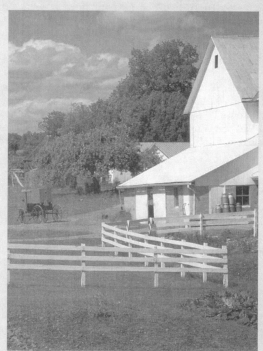

Amish farms dot the rural landscape in surrounding counties, especially in Lawrence County to the north.

Photo: Loriann Hoff Oberlin

Altoona's Horseshoe Curve, 1300 Ninth Avenue, (814) 946-0834, is a historic landmark that tells the story of how railroads were the key in coast-to-coast commerce. The challenge of carrying the Pennsylvania Railroad Mainline over the mountainous terrain was met with the construction of the Horseshoe Curve. You can board a train, say in Pittsburgh, and ride along to see this engineering marvel that was carved out of a mountainside to help trains cross the steep mountain pass. Young rail fans will enjoy the journey, and adults will appreciate the view, as well as the amenities of the visitor center, including shops and the Railroaders Memorial Museum, 1300 Ninth Avenue, (888) 425-8666. Every member of the family will enjoy and learn something about railroad history from the interactive displays here.

Lakemont Park & The Island Waterpark, I-99, Frankstown Road Exit, Altoona, (800) 434-8006, offers over 30 rides and attractions, go karts, miniature golf, and picnic facilities.

To learn the devastation of natural disaster, set out for the Johnstown Flood Museum, 304 Washington Street, Johnstown, (814) 539-1889, where state-of-the-art exhibits and an Academy Award winning-documentary recreate the powerful force that swept through town in May, 1889. The Johnstown Flood National Memorial overlooks the ruins of the South Fork Dam, which burst that May 31. It was indeed one of the worst, if not the worst, flood in American history. At Grandview Cemetery there is the plot where 777 unidentified victims of the flood are buried in the Plot of the Unknown. No admission is charged, and it's open daily from 8 AM until dusk.

The Johnstown Inclined Plane, found at Pa. 56 and Johns Street, (814) 535-5526, was built in 1891, and is one of the steepest vehicular inclines in the world. It is 996 feet long with a 71 percent grade. Witness the spectacular Johnstown view from the observation deck.

Altoona/State College/Johnstown Shopping

In State College, head to the shops along College Avenue. In addition, if you purchase items at the Penn State Bookstore, (814) 863-0205, your purchases directly benefit Penn State scholarships. At the Creamery, 12 Borland Laboratory, University Park, (814) 865-7535, sample and take home some of Penn State's famous ice cream, mushrooms, and cheeses. At Mount Nittany Vineyards & Winery, 300 Houser Road, Centre Hall, (814) 466-6373, you can sip and purchase local wines.

There are specialty shops in Historic Hollidaysburg, (814) 696-0544. Also in the area is the Slinky Toy Outlet at James Industries, found on the Beaver Street Extension, Hollidaysburg, (814) 695-5681, home to the original Slinky toy and many other souvenirs. Take the self-guided tour of Benzel's Pretzel Bakery, 5200 Sixth Avenue, Altoona, (814) 942-5062, ending up with samples and a chance to shop in the outlet store. Boyer Candy Factory Outlet & Emporium, 821 17th Street, (814) 944-9401, contains gift baskets, tins, baking ingredients, and of course, lots of candy for those family members with a sweet tooth!

Johnstown offers shoppers the Richland Mall at 3200 Elton Road as well as the Johnstown Galleria, along U.S. 219, with more than 100 specialty shops. In addition, there is lots of shopping along Johnstown's Scalp Avenue. Twenty minutes south, you'll find outlet shopping in Somerset (see our Shopping chapter).

Altoona/State College/Johnstown Accommodations

In State College, many opt for The Nittany Lion Inn, 200 W. Park Avenue, (814) 865-8500, located near the Nittany Lion Shrine sculpture. Others head to Toftrees Resort and Conference Center, One Country Club Lane, (814) 234-8000, featuring designer guest rooms, golf villa suites, four-star golf, tennis, and swimming. The Atherton Hotel, 125 S. Atherton Street, (814) 231-2100, is just a block from campus. Located downtown, and also a block away from PSU is the Days Inn Penn State, 240 S. Pugh Street, (814) 238-8454, with its heated, indoor pool, sauna, tanning beds, free weights, and nautilus equipment for guests.

If you're looking for a bed and breakfast establishment, The Fairmount, 234 W. Fairmount Avenue, (814) 237-1101, is within walking distance of the PSU campus and downtown. Ten miles away, Reynolds Mansion, 101 W. Linn Street, Bellefonte, (814) 353-8407, is Victorian with fireplaces, whirlpool tubs, private baths, and a billiards room.

The Holiday Inn, 250 Market Street, Johnstown, (814) 535-7777, is conveniently located at the intersection of Pa. 56 and U.S. 219. It's within walking distance of the flood museum and inclined plane, and boasts an indoor pool, hot tub, and exercise room. Just east of U.S. 219, stay at the Comfort Inn, 455 Theatre Drive, (814) 266-3678. While the indoor heated pool is small, some rooms have microwaves, radios, and refrigerators. Special amenities include the free breakfast and newspaper.

Bed and breakfast establishments are also available for a quiet stay in Johnstown. One mile off of U.S. 219, you'll find the Iron Bridge Bed & Breakfast, (814) 845-2106, with five rooms in a secluded, wooded setting. The Iron Bridge is wheelchair accessible. The Windmill Bed & Breakfast, 145 Hostetler Road, Johnstown, (814) 269-4625, boasts a full bath with skylight, equipped kitchen, large great room, and scenic gardens.

Altoona/State College/Johnstown Restaurants

At Toftrees Resort, there are three restaurants—the Down Under Steak House, (814) 234-3053; the 19th Hole Bar and Grill, (814) 234-8000, ext. 561; and Le Papillon, (814) 237-4877, for special functions and occasions.

At the Allen Street Grill, 100 W. College Avenue, (814) 237-4350, entrees are served in the ambiance of the restaurant's historic porch overlooking downtown. Mario & Luigi's, 112 S. Garner Street, (814) 237-0374, has woodburning ovens and rotisserie in view, health-conscious menu items, and carry-out service available. There's another Mario & Luigi's located at 1272 N. Atherton Street, (814) 234-4273. Whisker's Lounge and Courtyard at the Nittany Lion Inn features a pub menu (see listing above).

The Tavern Restaurant, 220 E. College Avenue, (814) 238-6116, is another popular pick for American cuisine. Here, you'll find photos of Penn State and Pennsylvania on the walls.

Native to Penn State's Happy Valley is Zimm's Family Restaurant, 2541 E. College Avenue, (814) 234-2447, with a children's menu, carry-out service, salad bar, and all-you-can-eat daily specials.

At the Incline Station Pub & Restaurant, 709 Edgehill Drive, Johnstown, (814) 536-7550, you can dine at the top of the world's steepest incline. Sunday brunch is a special delight for seniors, who enjoy a discount that day. Surf 'n' Turf Inn, 100 Valley Pike, Johnstown, (814) 536-9250, specializes in steaks and fresh seafood.

Within these areas of Altoona, State College, and Johnstown, there are plenty of casual, family-oriented, and inexpensive chain restaurants as well.

Cleveland

Approximately two hours from Pittsburgh, a drive northwest into Ohio brings you to Cleveland. Yes, the rivalry among football fans is fierce, with the Cleveland Browns pro football team back in the league after a three-year hiatus. But putting those feelings aside, there's plenty to do for families, business travelers, and anyone who wants to see a different set of scenery.

To obtain a visitor's guide to the area, or any additional information, contact the Convention and Visitor's Bureau of Greater Cleveland at (216) 621-5555 or (800) 321-1004.

Getting There

Cleveland is easily accessible from several major interstate highways. From Pittsburgh, take the Pennsylvania Turnpike west to the Ohio Turnpike and continue on Ohio 76 until you join I-77 north. I-80 will also lead you to I-77.

Cleveland Attractions

The Rock and Roll Hall of Fame and Museum, 1 Key Plaza, opened in 1995, with improvements in 1998, to provide information on each of the Hall of Fame inductees. Multimedia

History plays a role in many of our daytrips.

Photo: Courtesy of Nemacolin Woodlands Resort & Spa

productions combine film footage, music, interviews, animation, and still photography to tell the stories of these famous musicians. During the holidays and peak tourist periods, advance reservations are available by calling (800) 493-ROLL.

Amusement parks are popular in Cleveland, especially Cedar Point in nearby Sandusky. Power Point, the newest attraction at this park, opened in 1998. It's the tallest of its kind in the world, an amusement thriller consisting of four towers rising 240 feet, topped with connecting arches. Two of the towers blast riders up, and two will plunge them back down at 50 mph! Get wet at Soak City, and take the little ones to Berenstain Bear Country, Kiddy Kingdom Oceana, and the petting zoo. For details and hotel packages, call (419) 627-2350.

Six Flags/Geauga Lake in Aurora is located on Ohio 43, nine miles north of the Ohio Turnpike, at Exit 13, (216) 562-7131. Take in over 100 rides, shows, and attractions, including the terrifying Mr. Hyde's Nasty Fall and the Serial Thriller, a suspended looping roller coaster. Sea World Adventure Park of Ohio is nearby at 1100 Sea World Drive. Don't miss the 4-D Pirates movie adventure, and of course, Shamu the Whale. Contact the park at (800) 63-SHAMU.

There are more than 300 golf courses in the area, abundant waterways, and many museums located in Cleveland, including The Cleveland Museum of Art, University Circle, (216) 421-7340, where admission is free. Football fans won't want to miss the Pro Football Hall of Fame, 2121 George Halas Drive NW, Canton, (330) 456-8207, about 45 minutes south of Cleveland. Visit the five-building complex, movie theatre, displays, museum, enshrinement halls, and the store.

True Pittsburghers would have a hard time admitting they "might" root for the Cleveland Browns, but if you're going there to cheer on the Steelers, check out the $283 million Cleveland Browns Stadium, seating 73,200 people and standing 12 stories tall.

Leisurely excursions can be had aboard the Goodtime III, a 1,000 passenger, triple-decker sightseeing ship on the Cuyahoga River and Lake Erie. For reservations, call (800) 446-3140. The Observation Deck, located on the 42nd floor of the Terminal Tower, offers breathtaking view of downtown Cleveland, and is open to the public Saturdays and Sundays. Hours vary.

The Convention & Visitors Bureau also has a "Walk Cleveland" booklet featuring a pedestrian's guide to Cleveland architecture and public art. Call (800) 321-1004 for the self-guided booklet.

Cleveland also has lakefront parks and beaches, fishing expeditions, trolley tours, wineries, and breweries to visit. In the winter months, there's even ski resorts to try. Read on for the visitor's guide later in this section which will help you find a weekend (or several) of fun possibilities.

Cleveland Shopping

Downtown Cleveland boasts shopping that includes The Avenue at Tower City Center, Terminal Tower, Public Square, (216) 623-4750, with upscale shopping in a historic landmark. Also, browse the Galleria at Erieview, E. 9th and St. Clair, (216) 861-4343, with its glass enclosed stores such as Williams Sonoma, Eddie Bauer, and the Cleveland Indians Team Shop. In addition, there are unique retail arcades—the Colonial Arcade and the Euclid Arcade. Call (216) 621-0057. With the opening of the new Hyatt Regency hotel complex, there will also be shopping. (See our Accommodations chapter).

Beachwood Place, 26300 Cedar Road, Beachwood, (216) 464-9460, is Cleveland's premiere fashion destination with such department stores as Dillard's, Saks Fifth Avenue, and Nordstroms. Factory outlets include the Aurora Premium Outlets, 549 S. Chillcothe Road, Aurora, (216) 562-2000, just minutes from Sea World and Geauga Lake, as well as the Prime Outlets at Lodi, 9911 Avon Lake Road, Brunswick, (330) 948-9929, 40 minutes south of Cleveland.

Also within Cleveland is a 10-block shopping district on Larchmere Boulevard, where you'll find more than 15 antique shops and art galleries. European pastry shops and fine restaurants line this boulevard as well.

Cleveland Accommodations

In the Cleveland area, you'll choose from more than 15,000 hotel rooms. Some of these are of the elegant nature that befits the Ritz-Carlton Cleveland, 1515 W. Third Street, (216) 623-1300, Renaissance Cleveland Hotel, 24 Public Square, (216) 696-5600, and Marriott Downtown at Key Center, 127 Public Square, (216) 696-9200.

A new 294-room hotel is scheduled to open in downtown Cleveland by the spring of 2001. The Hyatt Regency Cleveland at the Arcade, 401 Euclid Avenue, will be an architectural gem featuring the refurbishment of the Arcade's 62,000 square feet of shops and restaurants. To make advance reservations, call (216) 696-1408.

There are several Holiday Inn locations, including Lakeside City Center, (216) 241-5100, and Beachwood, (216) 831-3300, as well as some Hampton Inn locations, such as Hampton Inn Cleveland/Wickliffe, 28611 Euclid Avenue, Wickliffe, (440) 944-4030, and Hampton Inn & Suites, 16020 Jefferson Drive, Independence, (216) 520-2020.

In addition, try the Fairfield Inn Willoughby, 35110 Maplegrove Road, (216) 975-9922. There are budget and economy-minded motels that dot the landscape, including several Travelodge, Days Inn, and Red Roof Inn franchises. You'll find an extensive listing in the *Greater Cleveland Official Visitors Guide* by calling 1-800-321-1001.

Cleveland Restaurants

Dining in Cleveland is just as abundant as places to stay. The *Nautica Queen* is a luxury cruise and dining ship featuring lake and river cruises. Docked in the Flats Nautica Entertainment Complex, the ship serves up to 400 passengers and runs from April until October. For reservations, call (216) 696-8888.

Seafood reigns supreme on the shores of this city. Hornblower's, 1151 N. Marginal Road, (216) 363-1151, is a seafood house to head to, on the shores of Lake Erie. Barnacle Bill's Crab House, 14810 Detroit, Lakewood, (216) 521-2722, also serves seafood and steaks with its raw bar and beer varieties in a nautical setting. Try some more ales and lagers brewed on the premises of the award-winning local brewery, the Great Lakes Brewing Company, 2516 Market Street, (216) 771-4404, where you'll also dine on fine food.

Sans Souci Restaurant in the Renaissance Cleveland Hotel (see above) specializes in French country fare. It's among Cleveland's better and more expensive restaurants. Morton's of Chicago, Cleveland, 230 Huron Road, (216) 621-6200, is another upscale restaurant serving great steaks, fresh seafood, and shellfish.

Those preferring Chinese can head to Lu Cuisine, 1228 Euclid Avenue, (216) 241-8488, for cuisine from the Shandong province of Northeast China. And for a family-style buffet in a non-smoking atmosphere with Norman Rockwell décor, there are at least a half dozen Hometown Buffet locations around Cleveland. Check the long list in the visitors guide mentioned in accommodations.

Oglebay, West Virginia

Less than two hours west of Pittsburgh sits a playground, golf spot, and shopping destination, complete with lodging and food, all for your pleasure in Wheeling, West Virginia. Oglebay started as a farm, then became the elegant summer estate of Cleveland industrialist Col. Earl W. Oglebay. Later, the property was given to the city of Wheeling for use as a park and recreational site.

Seasonally, there are attractions that may become favorite traditions, such as the Winter Festival of Lights, a spectacular outdoor light show that you drive through during the holidays. Regardless of the time of year, the people of Wheeling have long known of the wonderful offerings of Oglebay. Now, you can also! For reservations or more information on any of the facilities at Oglebay, West Virginia, call (304) 243-4000.

Getting There

Follow I-79 south out of Pittsburgh until you pick up I-70 west in Washington, Pa. Then, follow the signs to Wheeling and Oglebay. It's that simple!

Oglebay Attractions

The Winter Festival of Lights we mentioned above is sometimes called America's largest light display, complete with model trains and a laser light show (every hour, on the hour). Admission is priced by age, per person, not by car as some winter light shows are structured.

During the warmer months, walk through Waddington Gardens, with a different floral display each season. These elegant gardens existed at the turn of the century and have been carefully recreated to cover the hilltop region of Oglebay. From April through October, you can stroll along winding brick pathways among hanging baskets, fragrant flowers, ever-flowing water displays, and the finest of trees.

The Speidel Championship Golf Course, designed by noted golf architect Robert Trent Jones, is a perfect challenge for the serious golfer who needs a change in scenery. There's also a par 3 golf course and driving range. See our Golf chapter for further details.

At the Good Children's Zoo, bears, otters, bison, and rare red wolves are at home in this spacious natural setting. Kids will especially enjoy the 3,000-gallon fish tank and the barnful of friendly domestic animals. Take the 1½-mile train ride, enjoy the playground, and do allow time for the Benedum Science Theater and Planetarium.

In addition, at Oglebay, there is a huge outdoor swimming pool as well as tennis at the Crispin Center. Get your exercise paddling a boat upon Schenk Lake, right on the grounds.

In the winter, if there's enough snow, the par 3 golf course becomes some mild ski slopes. Both cross-country and downhill skiers are accommodated.

Less physical fun can be had touring the beautiful white Mansion Museum's period rooms. Finally, to learn how glass is made, visit Oglebay's Glass Museum with its audio tour.

Oglebay Shopping

Eight distinctive shops complement Oglebay's full range of activities and recreation. But then, shopping is indeed recreation for some!

Start at Carriage House Glass, the most recent addition to the shopping scene, boasting the area's largest selection of West Virginia decorative glass, with items produced right before your eyes.

Christmas in the Gardens is a store located in Waddington Gardens with hard-to-find holiday items, available to you year-round. Next, there's the Mansion Museum Gift Shop, featuring collectibles and a line of specialty gifts. Garden Center Gift Shop has flowers, accessories, and gifts made of natural materials, whereas the Palm Room boasts seasonal plants, herbs, and hanging baskets. These last few shops are also located within the gardens.

Wilson Lodge's Resort Shop features logo merchandise and resort clothing. Golfers are certainly in their element in the Speidel Pro Shop, located in the Hamm Club House on the golf course. Here, they will find golf apparel and equipment. During the off-season when the Festival of Lights operates, this store is decked out for the holidays, and offers shoppers fine gourmet foods and West Virginia wines.

Finally, you and the children will enjoy the Nature Express store at the Good Children's Zoo.

Oglebay Accommodations

Wilson Lodge provides excellent overnight accommodations with modern luxuries such as an indoor pool, Jacuzzi, and fitness center. See our Accommodations chapter for further details.

For those who require additional space, Oglebay offers a choice of cottages, deluxe or standard, rented by the day, the weekend, or the week. Each has a large living area, a fully equipped kitchen, and either two, four, or six bedrooms for sleeping.

Oglebay Restaurants

Ihlenfeld Dining Room in Wilson Lodge serves American cuisine at its finest in a family-friendly setting. The menu features gourmet selections as well as entrees the kids will surely enjoy. Overlooking Schenk Lake and the surrounding countryside, the view is an added attraction each season. Winter guests will enjoy the Festival of Lights, and summer patrons can look out over the lake's 150-foot fountain with its music and colored lights.

Deep Creek Lake, Maryland

Once called "Maryland's Best Kept Secret," Deep Creek Lake in Garrett County, Western Maryland is now well known in many seasons.

Each October, the annual Autumn Glory Festival is reason for a drive not only to witness the spectacular foliage, but to partake of banjo and fiddle contests, square dancing, bag pipes, bands, baseball card shows, and of course, wonderful food.

When it snows (and boy, does it snow in Garrett County!), the slopes at the Wisp Ski Resort are bustling with downhill activity. There are 23 trails, a halfpipe for snowboarders, snowmaking capability, an indoor lodge, and restaurants to warm the hearty. For more information on such winter recreation, turn to our Recreation chapter.

INSIDERS' TIP

The holiday season at Hershey begins in mid-November with a winter wonderland of horse-drawn carriage rides, carolers, Santa Claus, and of course, chocolate! Call (800) HERSHEY for details.

However fun a downhill run is in December, summer is Deep Creek's most popular season. As the largest freshwater lake in Maryland, Deep Creek boasts 65 miles of shoreline. Built in 1925 by the Youghiogheny Electric Company, the lake was purchased by the Pennsylvania Electric Company in 1942. Currently, it's owned by the state of Maryland, and plenty make this their summer playground and weekend retreat.

If you're thinking of spending any time at Deep Creek Lake, pick up a copy of the *Garrett County & Deep Creek Lake Vacation Guide,* updated annually. Contact the Deep Creek Lake–Garrett County Promotion Council at 200 S.

Third Street, Oakland, MD 21550, or call (301) 334-1948 or (301) 387-6171. Pick up a guidebook at the visitors center, located along U.S. 219, or contact the promotion council.

Getting There

From Pittsburgh, you can reach Garrett County from different routes. If you originate south or west of Pittsburgh, take I-79 through Washington (there's a stretch that becomes I-79 and I-70) and continue on I-79 through West Virginia until you pick up Interstate 68 (older maps show this as Highway 48, but the designation was changed some years ago to 68). Follow 68 to the Maryland border, until you reach the Friendsville Exit (approximately four miles after the border). Take Pa. 42 to McHenry, Maryland, the first sighting of Deep Creek Lake.

From points south and east of Pittsburgh, take Pa. 51 South to Uniontown, until you pick up U.S. 40 East. Continue to U.S. 219 at Keyser's Ridge. Follow U.S. 219 south to McHenry, Md.

Deep Creek Lake Attractions

Watersports abound here at Deep Creek. Just be sure to learn the rules of the waterways before taking off in your rental boat, towing a waterskier, or cruising around on your jet ski. For motor boat rentals, consult the vacation guide listed at the conclusion of this section.

Since the lake is home to the *Flying Scot* 19-foot daysailer, sailboat races are a popular activity on weekends. The nautical crowd takes to the water at the yacht club. Kids and adults can learn to sail with weeklong classes conducted by the Deep Creek Sailing School, 365 Back Bay Road, Swanton, (301) 387-4497.

Swallow Falls State Park, where tall hemlocks and four waterfalls cascade along a beautiful backdrop, is a perfect place for camping, picnicking, and hiking the scenic trails.

Funland Family Fun Center, across from McHenry Plaza, U.S. 219, (301) 387-6168, is perhaps the best local amusement besides the annual county fair each August. There's a carousel for all ages, a go-kart track for kids ages 4 and older, bumper cars, miniature golf, and an indoor arcade with video games.

Courses at the Wisp Resort and in Oakland keep the family golfers happy while area trails are prime for mountain bikers. If you prefer to ride horses, there are several stables for pony and horseback rides. Consult the vacation guide listed above.

Deep Creek Lake Shopping

Schoolhouse Earth, two miles north of Deep Creek on Pa. 42, (301) 746-8603, is a country shop with gifts for year-round Christmas shoppers, as well as those searching for cards, handcrafted jewelry, lamps, country accessories, framed calligraphy, music, books, rugs, and more. Antique reproduction furniture and custom framing are also available. For the kids, visit the petting zoo, open daily in the summer season and on spring and fall weekends, weather permitting.

There's nothing like a good book to read in the warm sunlight. Head to the Book Mark'et & Antique Mezzanine, 111 S. Second Street, Oakland, (301) 334-8778, for books, cassettes, CDs, and a complete children's area. Newly added antiques make this a must stop. At Mountain Village Shops, U.S. 219 across from Arrowhead Market, there's Expanding Horizons, (301) 387-5700, for more books and music.

Within Mountain Village Shops, check out The Tourist Trap, (301) 387-7900, for souvenirs, gifts, swimsuits, music, cards, and miscellaneous gifts. The Christmas Chalet, (301) 387-SHOP, is exactly what the name implies, with Christmas-themed gifts and collectibles.

Need your fishing tackle, a current fishing license, camping supplies, or live bait? No doubt about it, you need Johnny's Bait House, U.S. 219, (301) 387-FISH. And when you reel in the big one, be sure to bring your prize catch by for weighing and measuring. You just might win a patch and have your name published in the paper, and that's no fish tale! Johnny's is accessible by car—or by boat if you're on the water.

Arrowhead Market, along U.S. 219 next to Alpine Village, has expanded over the years to be a

Fallingwater makes a lovely daytrip to the Laurel Highlands.

Photo: Courtesy of Western Pennsylvania Conservancy

one-stop shopping establishment for almost any provision you need. Open 24 hours, the store stocks baked and canned goods, fresh meats and produce, roasted chickens, ready-made sandwiches and beverages, as well as newspapers and beer. Arrowhead even has a business service center, photo developing center, gas station, and it's accessible by boat with its own dock. Call (301) 387-4020 for more information on the store's provisions and services.

Yoder's Country Market, Md. 669, Grantsville, (800) 321-5148, is not necessarily at the lake itself, but if you are traveling U.S. 40, or if you plan to eat at Penn Alps, we'd be remiss if we didn't tell you about it. Do stop for country fare, including jams, jellies, baked goods, and other Amish specialties.

Deep Creek Lake Accommodations

Depending upon your personal preferences, you'll find many types of accommodations at Deep Creek Lake. For those families opting to rent a cottage, contact Railey Rentals, (800) 447-3034, or A&A Realty Rental, (800) 336-7303. If having direct access to the waterfront is important to you, be sure to ask for it. Cabins advertised as having "lake access" could still mean the lake is a considerable hike from your accommodations.

Campers will find several state parks nearby, with Deep Creek Lake State Park, (301) 387-5563, providing a beach, boat launch, and camping facilities. Camping trailers up to 29 feet in length are permitted in Maryland state parks, and there are electric hookups. Improved campgrounds provide centrally located washhouses, toilets, lavatories, and hot-water showers. Cabins are available, some with wheelchair access. Make your site reservations up to one year in advance, especially for the busy summer months. Some parks do permit pets.

Vacationers may also prefer motels, hotels, or a bed and breakfast inn, and there are plenty of these in the area. For a complete listing, consult the vacation guide. Alpine Village, (800) 343-5253, sits right off U.S. 219 next to Arrowhead Market. With a private beach and outdoor pool, the village includes some cottages and some motel rooms. Point View Inn, (301) 387-5555, also sits along U.S. 219 offering lakefront access, boat docking, a private beach, and a restaurant on the premises.

The Wisp Hotel & Conference Center is a center of summer and winter activity. In addition to taking to the ski slopes, golf course, and hiking trails, you can swim a few laps in the indoor pool. However, the Wisp does not have a beach, and it's a walk to the waterfront. For reservations, call (800) 462-9477. Affiliated with the Wisp are the Will O' The Wisp Prestige Condominiums, U.S. 219, (301) 387-5503, with an indoor pool, whirlpools, a sauna, fireplaces, exercise and game rooms, a sandy beach, boat docking, and a restaurant.

The bed and breakfast crowd will want to check out the Carmel Cove Inn, Glendale Road, (301) 387-0067. This former monastery boasts beautifully appointed rooms with fireplaces, whirlpool baths, and private decks. Guests can swim from the dock, fish from shore, or enjoy other amenities like the great room with billiards and cable television. Lake Pointe Inn, off Marsh Hill Road, (800) 523-LAKE, is 13 feet from the water's edge and a five-minute walk from the Wisp Resort. All rooms have lake and/or ski slope views. There's a private dock, too.

Deep Creek Lake Restaurants

Penn Alps Restaurant and Crafts Shop, half a mile east of Grantsville, (301) 895-5985, isn't exactly at Deep Creek, but it's en route from Pittsburgh. So plan to stop for Amish-style food, along with their soup and salad bar. Visit the artisan village next door.

Not far from McHenry is McClive's Restaurant & Lounge, (301) 387-6172, where you can dine with a spectacular view of the lake. Early bird specials begin at 5 PM, and boat docking is available. In the mood for a light bite or happy hour? The Courtyard Patio Lounge is downstairs.

Next to Arrowhead Market, Pizzeria Uno Restaurant & Bar, (301) 387-4866, features a great view of the lake if you choose deck seating in the summer. Just a few steps away is their Honi-Honi Bar, a Deep Creek watering hole for decades. Live music takes the stage on summer weekends, where families or couples often sit out on the open lawn. Both establishments are accessible by boat dock.

Across the street, Dr. Willy's Seafood Company, (301) 387-7380, is a carry-out fish market that's great for a quick bite to eat. If you prefer a more formal sit-down dinner, drive just a bit further on U.S. 219, turning onto Glendale Bridge Road. Here you'll find the Silver Tree Ristorante, (301) 387-4040, featuring nightly specials, including Italian entrees. Right next door is the Silver Tree Harbor, a much more casual lakeside seafood bar, accessible by boat as well.

Sip a cappuccino with a croissant or enjoy the country French or American cuisine at the Cornish Manor Restaurant & French Bakery, Memorial Drive, Oakland, (301) 334-6499, only 10 miles south of Deep Creek Lake. Reservations are required for lunch and dinner, and the restaurant is closed on Sundays.

Hershey

Otherwise known as Chocolate Town, U.S.A., Hershey is the sweetest place on earth. To be floating high up in the air at Hersheypark, the popular amusement park, you only need to breathe in the scent of cocoa to know where you are! The sweet smell drifts from the factory into the park.

A three- to four-hour drive east from Pittsburgh, Hershey is definitely a weekend getaway as opposed to a day trip. But if you can spare a few days, head on out to see the town Milton Hershey pretty much created for his employees. The Hershey Entertainment & Resort Co. will assist you in supplying information and/or booking your stay. Call them at (800) HERSHEY.

Getting There

Take the Pennsylvania Turnpike east about 200 miles to Exit 19 (Harrisburg), then follow Route 283 North. Join Route 322 East into the town of Hershey. Amtrak runs trains daily to Harrisburg, the state capital. If you book reservations at the Hotel Hershey or Lodge (see below), you may be able to take advantage of free shuttle service (which is also available for those flying into Harrisburg International Airport, 15 minutes away).

INSIDERS' TIP

If you plan to shop in a traditional Amish establishment, do arrive well before dusk, since there are no electric lights to help you size up the merchandise.

Attractions

Turn-of-the-century confectioner Milton Snavely Hershey didn't actually start out in chocolate. Caramels were his focus, and he did very well in business. But he made an interesting discovery along the way: it was the chocolate adhering to the caramels that children licked off and seemed to enjoy the most. Thus, Hershey sold his Lancaster Caramel Company for $1 million but shrewdly resevered the rights to sell chocolate. And sell he did, building a company town rich in benevolence, and just plain fun to visit. Hershey opened his chocolate factory in 1905.

Hersheypark, (717) 534-3900, began as a place for his employees and their families to relax. It was largely picnic grounds, built in 1907. Today, it's one of the cleanest and most exciting amusement parks in the country. Ride the Great Bear, an inverted steel looping roller coaster; the Sidewinder; the Comet; one of several water rides; or some kiddie rides. Children love to determine their ride status by measuring their height against popular candy bars, posted throughout the park.

Adjacent to Hersheypark is ZooAmerica, (717) 534-3860, opened as the Hershey Zoo in 1910 as a place for Mr. Hershey to showcase his wild animal collection. Now, there are more than 200 animals for everyone to see. Hours for both Hersheypark vary according to the month, but the park generally opens at 10 AM. ZooAmerica is open daily, year round, from 10 AM until 5 PM, with the exception of Thanksgiving, Christmas and New Year's Day. Call the toll-free info line, (800) HERSHEY, for more information. Admission for these two attractions falls under the one-priced admission plan, which changes most seasons. Ride height restrictions apply.

Many years ago, tours of the Hershey factory used to attract a million people each year. When the tours became too popular to manage, they were stopped and the education shifted elsewhere. Visit Chocolate World, (717) 534-4900, for a Disney-like tour of chocolate production and facts. You'll ride through the displays in automated cars, and as you exit, reach out your hand for that complimentary candy bar! Admission to Chocolate World is free. Hours vary depending upon the season so be sure to call the toll-free Hershey information line listed above.

What better way to learn about the town Mr. Hershey built (complete with chocolate kiss-shaped street lamps on Chocolate Avenue) than by riding the Hershey Trolley? Visit Trolley Works, (717) 533-3000, right inside Chocolate World, to purchase your ticket for this fun-filled and educational ride through town. You'll learn how Milton Hershey gave so much back to the community that during the depression he kept many townspeople employed by building a community center, a sports arena, a stadium, and the palatial Hotel Hershey (see description below). In addition, you'll learn that Milton and his wife Catharine, unable to have children of their own, founded a school for needy children, today known as the Milton Hershey School.

What began as a rose garden in 1937 became the Hershey Gardens, (717) 534-3492, a 23-acre botanical display garden that includes Butterfly House, representing over 25 different North American plant species. It's located on Hotel Road across from the Hotel Hershey, and is open from 9 AM until 6 PM, mid-April until October 31. During the summer months, the Gardens stay open on Fridays and Saturdays until 8 PM before Labor Day. Admission is charged according to age.

A short walk from Hersheypark and Chocolate World is the Hershey Museum, (717) 534-3439. It's a self-guided tour that explains how Milton Hershey overcame business failures to create his chocolate empire, and how he became the philanthropist he's remembered as today. There's a Discovery Room for young children. The museum is open from 10 AM until 5 PM. Memorial Day through Labor Day, the museum stays open until 6 PM, and it's closed Thanksgiving, Christmas, and New Year's Day. Admission is charged according to age.

Shopping

Most of the Hershey attractions have gift shops on the premises. One you won't want to miss is the giant candy feast-land inside Chocolate World. In fact, the ride lets you off at the entrance of the gift area. Here, you'll find some types of candies packaged differently than you're used to in stores back home, in addition to shirts, hats, mugs, ornaments, and more. The Hershey Museum and Hershey Gardens also offer gift shops, and in Hersheypark and ZooAmerica there are multiple chances to purchase souvenirs.

The Factory Stores at Hershey, (717) 520-1236, give you plenty of stores. You'll find the usual array of outlet establishments for men's and women's apparel, children's clothing, footwear, books, stationery and gifts, home furnishings and housewares, intimate apparel, leather goods and luggage, and much more. They're located at 46 Outlet Square in Hershey, just one block east of Hersheypark, on Hersheypark Drive. Visit Monday through Saturday, 9:30 AM until 9 PM, and on Sundays from 11 AM until 5 PM, but hours may be shorter during the winter months so do call in advance.

Accommodations

Built with European charm, the Hotel Hershey is elegant with its Mediterranean design, luxury amenities, and guest services. You'll enjoy valet parking, concierge service, 24-hour room service, baby sitting, laundry services, indoor and outdoor pools, bike rentals and carriage rides, therapeutic massages, saunas, tennis, golf, lawn bowling, and much more. The Fountain Lobby, with hand-carved wooden balustrades, custom-painted tile, and the famous painted cloud ceiling, is a wonderful display of craftsmanship. The Hotel Hershey certainly rivals some of the finest hotels in the world.

At the Hershey Lodge and Convention Center, you'll enjoy fitness facilities, indoor and outdoor pools, miniature golf, concierge service, and valet parking as well, in addition to the many meeting and business facilities. Kids will love the free chocolate bars upon check-in too!

For reservations at either the Hershey Hotel or the Hershey Lodge and Convention Center, call the reservations and information line at (800) HERSHEY.

The Milton Motel, located at 1733 E. Chocolate Avenue, (717) 533-4533, offers comfortable, more budget-conscious accommodations. Amenities include free coffee, free HBO/ESPN, a heated swimming pool, a game room, and senior discounts.

Campers will appreciate the Hershey Highmeadow Campground featuring over 290 camp sites on 55 beautiful acres of countryside. Choose from cabins, with electricity and small kitchen equipment, or sites for camping and recreational vehicle hookups. There are two outdoor swimming pools, plus a kiddie pool, playgrounds, a country store, self-service laundry, a game room, recreational facilities, and more. Contact the information line at (800) HERSHEY for further information on camping in Hershey.

Restaurants

The most exclusive restaurant at Hershey is the Circular Dining Room, built in the Hotel Hershey so that no guest would have to settle for a corner table. The cuisine is contemporary American with an extensive wine list. The dining room overlooks formal gardens and a tranquil reflecting pool. For more casual fare, try The Fountain Café.

At the Hershey Lodge and Convention Center, choose from several restaurants on the property including the Hershey Grill for steaks, seafood and pasta. Lebbie Lebkicher's Eatery & Pub features an all-American menu. The Hearth restaurant is a little more formal, but is known for its warm ambiance and Sunday brunch.

Reservations are recommended at any of the Hershey restaurants, with the exception of The Cocoa Beanery coffee shops and the lounges. Call (717) 534-880 for the Hotel Hershey and (717) 520-5401 for the Lodge and Convention Center.

At Chocolate World, visit the Chocolate Town Café for overstuffed sandwiches, salads, home-style meals, and great, chocolate-y (what else!) desserts. For more information, call (717) 533-2917.

Neighborhoods and Real Estate

LOOK FOR:
• Neighborhoods
• Real Estate

At various times in its history, Pittsburgh has been defined by its rivers and bridges, by its steel mills and coal mines, by its sports teams. More than anything else, however, Pittsburgh is a city of neighborhoods, of residential communities that are both distinct and distinctive. In its relatively small space of less than 59 square miles, the city proper officially includes 90 neighborhoods. Beyond the city itself, Allegheny County spans 130 municipalities. Add the neighborhoods in the other five counties in our coverage area and you have a region blessed with hundreds of attractive places to live.

Pittsburgh's emphasis on neighborhoods has firm roots in both topography and history. The region's riverfronts and mountains serve as natural boundaries to neighborhoods. Traveling across town in Pittsburgh can mean traversing hills and major waterways, providing some incentive to remain close to home. This was especially true during Pittsburgh's industrial heyday, when workers did not want to live too far from their mills and factories.

Perhaps even more importantly, Pittsburgh was settled by immigrants who tended to cluster together, taking comfort in the familiarity of people and customs from their native lands. The principal waves of immigration ended many decades ago, yet even today, the center of activity in many neighborhoods remains the local church constructed by early immigrants.

All of which provides Pittsburgh's neighborhoods with unusual solidity. Most neighborhoods in the region feature business districts—ranging from several stores to several blocks or more—to assure that residents can meet their shopping needs without leaving the neighborhood. The region also has witnessed the growth of neighborhood-based development organizations, known locally as community development corporations, which inspire neighborhood development and involve residents in their own well-being.

Most Pittsburghers live in single-family residences, although this is hardly the exclusive style. Many of the city's elegant older homes have been subdivided into apartments, and larger multi-unit buildings dot the region as well. Region-wide statistics on apartment life are not completely reliable, but a good guess is that about 30 percent of City of Pittsburgh residents live in rental properties, condominiums, or cooperative housing.

Many residents spend their entire lives within their neighborhoods. Call it parochial if you will, but it's an enduring strength of Pittsburgh that contributes to the richness of residential life here. If you doubt it, consider this: in 1994, the crime rate in Southwestern Pennsylvania was the lowest of all metropolitan areas with at least 1 million residents. Can there be any doubt that Pittsburghers' commitment to community contributes to the low crime rate?

Outside the city proper, you'll find a broad diversity of styles in residential communities. Pittsburgh has many close-in suburbs of both the affluent and working class variety. A number of nearby cities, such as Greensburg and Beaver, blend both sophistication and charm. If rural life is more your style, you can be in lush farm country by driving about 20 minutes—in just about every direction—from downtown Pittsburgh.

From riverfront to mountaintop living, from homes with spacious grounds to those with party walls, you're pretty likely to find the style of living you prefer in Pittsburgh's attractive neighborhoods.

In describing some of Pittsburgh's neighborhoods below, we could present only a fraction of the communities where you might choose to live. We've tried to pick neighborhoods that are interesting of themselves and others—such as an Allegheny River town or an affluent suburb— that may be representative of a larger number of communities.

One final word about Pittsburgh's neighborhoods. Maps may formally delineate neighborhood boundaries, but cartographers don't necessarily have the last word. Pittsburghers will heatedly defend their perceptions of their neighborhoods in utter defiance of what the maps may say. On certain corners in the city, you can talk to residents and discover that you are simultaneously in Bloomfield, Garfield, Lawrenceville, Shadyside, and East Liberty. Don't fight it. Ultimately, neighborhood in Pittsburgh is more than a place. It's a state of mind, a creed, a way of life. Don't be surprised if it becomes your way of life very soon.

Neighborhoods

Downtown

Why not downtown? Downtown life offers proximity to the city's vital center, with its primary business facilities—and many of its cultural amenities—within easy walking distance. Remember that you can traverse the entire length or breadth of downtown in less than 30 minutes. If you're living downtown, you're close to everywhere.

Downtown living is almost exclusively high-rise living, in such buildings as Gateway Towers near Point State Park; The Pennsylvanian, a refurbished former railroad station at downtown's edge approaching the adjacent Strip District; and Washington Plaza, an apartment complex near the Mellon Arena. You'll find additional luxury apartments just across the Seventh Street Bridge in a complex called Lincoln at North Shore.

A newer downtown residential style is lofts, which were late to come to Pittsburgh but are available from a small number of developers.

Most downtown residences bring you both convenience and views of the rivers. Downtown boasts about 3,000 residents, many of whom belong to a residents' association.

North

Aspinwall

A scenic community just north of Pittsburgh, Aspinwall is an appealing blend of the old and new. About half its homes are sturdy brick affairs predating World War II that sell for $46,000 or less. The town also features recently constructed dwellings that can bring as much as $150,000. Rental properties are popular in Aspinwall, as fewer than half its homes are owner-occupied.

The business district is particularly appealing. With the Allegheny River as its backdrop, the commercial section features a variety of small specialty shops with a handsome, old-fashioned decor. If you're of a mind to promenade, parasol upon your shoulder, this is the perfect setting for it.

If shopping plazas are more your metier, you'll find the Waterworks Mall conveniently placed along Route 28, which also connects Aspinwall to Pittsburgh's North Side, about 6 miles away. Other amenities include the Pittsburgh Zoo & Aquarium, which is just across the Allegheny River, and St. Margaret Memorial Hospital, which, through the mysteries of politics, is located in the City of Pittsburgh without being contiguous to any part of the city.

With a population of just under 3,000, Aspinwall has been able to preserve its considerable charm.

Butler

Between 1992 and 1996, Butler County saw the creation of more manufacturing jobs than any other county in Pennsylvania. That augurs well for employment in Butler County and the city of Butler, the county seat. Among the leading employers are steelmaker ARMCO Inc., with a major complex just outside Butler, and the Veterans Affairs Medical Center and its sprawling hospital/residential complex.

Residential style in Butler is a mix of affordable single-family homes and rental properties. Though no official figures exist, some longtime Butler residents believe that four of every 10 Butler residents live in rental units. Renovating older homes is a popular pursuit here.

The city of just more than 15,000 residents was named for a Revolutionary War general. It's accessible from Pittsburgh, about 25 miles away, by Route 8, which also serves as a gateway to communities further to the north.

Cranberry

Cranberry has been perhaps the hottest growth area in Western Pennsylvania. This Butler County township was for many years a largely rural community when folks discovered that its location—at the juncture of the Pennsylvania Turnpike, Interstate 79, and Route 19—meant easy access from and to just about everywhere. That signaled the start of a growth spurt that hasn't stalled yet. In 1996, the township added 277 new single-family units, the largest number of any municipality in the Pittsburgh region.

The average home price is about $175,000, and many lots include spacious grounds. About 17 percent of Cranberry residents live in rental units. Shopping is a breeze at the many malls along Route 19.

Cranberry is full of seeming contradictions. Turn away from the busy shopping plazas and you'll quickly find yourself in unspoiled terrain without sidewalks. The shape of the township's development remains a topic of considerable debate among residents. One owner of a large unimproved site, upset with Cranberry's development rules, threatened to cut down every tree on his property if the process wasn't liberalized. He reached a compromise with elected officials, and the amazing development of Cranberry continued.

Fox Chapel

One statistic tells you much of what you need to know about Fox Chapel: The average home price here is more than $350,000, an extraordinary figure for the Pittsburgh area where affordable housing is the norm. Housing prices beyond $1 million are not uncommon in Fox Chapel.

As you might guess, homes here are large, frequently set back from streets atop winding drives and lush grounds. Mansions may be a word out of favor, but whether they're politically correct or not, you'll find plenty of them here. The community is so woodsy that town fathers on occasion must develop ways to cope with a deer overpopulation that threatens residents' shrubbery.

There's more to Fox Chapel than gorgeous homes. The borough maintains six parks totaling 280 acres, and it's home to the Beechwood Farms Nature Reserve and Hartwood Acres, an Allegheny County park that is a popular summertime site for theatrical and musical performances. For more on Hartwood Acres, see our Parks and Recreation chapters.

You won't find much of a commercial district, but residents can purchase just about everything they need at the Waterworks Mall and other Route 28 shopping plazas. If you're driving from downtown, you'll reach Fox Chapel in about 25 minutes. If Fox Chapel is your home, you won't mind the drive.

INSIDERS' TIP

The Pennsylvania sales tax is 6 percent in all local counties but Allegheny. There, you'll pay 7 percent. Funds raised by the extra 1 percent are earmarked for support of such regional assets as libraries and parks. A number of items, such as food and clothing, are exempt.

Harmony

In 1804, Johann George Rapp and his religious separatist followers abandoned the German duchy of Wurttenberg and began constructing a communal town in what today is Butler County. They gave the name Harmony to the town they built along the banks of the Connoquennessing, in the hope that it would reflect their communal style. The Harmonists developed other communities in Western Pennsylvania as well.

Ultimately, the Harmonists' experiments died out, but the town they constructed retains much of its original charm. Its shopping district features an appealing variety of antique and artisans' shops. Approximately 1,200 people live here, most in single-family dwellings but some in rental units. You'll find no highrises here.

Among Harmony's leading employees are Sippel Company, a steel fabricator, and Paragon Trade Brands, which produces diapers.

Kittanning

The county seat of Armstrong County, Kittanning shares many qualities with its fellow Allegheny River communities, including attractive riverfront homes and vistas. Single-family homes dominate the town, although recent developments include three highrise buildings featuring housing for the elderly.

Large employers in this community of about 5,100 include Alltel Pennsylvania, a telecommunications provider, and Standard Products, a rubber company. As a county seat, Kittanning boasts its own daily newspaper and proximity to several hospitals and a branch of Indiana University of Pennsylvania.

Kittanning is about a 40-minute drive from Pittsburgh along Route 28, which becomes a high-speed highway once it leaves Pittsburgh.

McCandless

The Town of McCandless is representative of Pittsburgh's burgeoning North Hills in many regards. Most residents live in single-family homes, with more than half the town's dwellings built after 1970. The average home price is just less than $138,000. Residents have access to the many malls and shops along Route 19 and McKnight Road.

What makes McCandless noteworthy, even among Pittsburgh's splendid northern suburbs, is that it sits squarely in the middle of North Park, one of the jewels of the Allegheny County park system. The park offers such activities as fishing, boating, biking, tennis, jogging trails, swimming, golf and ice skating—read more about it in our Parks chapter. If you live in McCandless, North Park is your back yard.

Mexican War Streets

Near as we can tell, Pittsburgh did not play a prominent role in the Mexican-American War. Nevertheless, this City of Pittsburgh Northside neighborhood features streets like Palo Alto and Monterrey named for battles and heroes of that conflict. The community was developed in the 1860s and 1870s—perhaps the freshness of the war in the minds of the developers helps account for the homage to the soldiers who fought it.

The neighborhood is one of the city's architectural showcases. Carefully restored row houses reflect a broad variety of styles, with Greek revival doorways, Gothic turrets, stained glass, and Richardsonian stonework. Many residents are longtime homeowners, while some homes here are purchased as investments. Because owners have such different purposes, prices of Mexican War Streets homes vary a good deal—from $30,000 for "fixer-uppers" to $100,000 and more for fully restored Victorians.

If you live in the Mexican War Streets, downtown is less than 2 miles away, and you'll be within walking distance of such amenities as Allegheny General Hospital, Three Rivers Stadium, the Carnegie Science Center, and the shopping district of East Ohio Street. Plus, when someone asks what in the heck Buena Vista Street is doing in Pittsburgh, you'll have an answer of sorts.

Observatory Hill

Not often can you find stately older homes with such features as window seats, carved wooden doors, front porches, and third-floor rental units. It's rarer still when such homes sell for an average price of $39,000. That's what you'll find, though, in Observatory Hill, a neighborhood at Pittsburgh's northern boundary.

The neighborhood draws its name from Allegheny Observatory; perhaps a more important feature for you is Riverview Park, one of the city's grandest, which features acres of open greenery and such activities as picnic shelters and hiking, biking, and riding trails. See our Parks chapter for more on Riverview Park.

Observatory Hill is home to both a public elementary school and a public high school. It's several miles from downtown Pittsburgh, although the steepness of the neighborhood's hills encourages driving to town rather than walking. No matter. If you live here, you won't want to leave too often.

Troy Hill

Whoever coined the term "neighborhood" probably was inspired by a vision of Troy Hill—or a community very like it. Troy Hill was settled by European immigrants, and today, this City of Pittsburgh neighborhood retains the look and feel of an Old World village.

From its base near the Allegheny River, Troy Hill winds up a series of steep hills to a plateau that overlooks the city and the river. Here you'll find brick and frame row homes and solid single-family houses, with not much in the way of rental units. Prices for homes—between $20,000 and $35,000—are yet another attractive old-fashioned feature.

With few entrances and exits from the neighborhood, Troy Hill has been able to retain much of its close-knit character, contributing to a low crime rate and a genuine sense of community.

East

Bloomfield

While many City of Pittsburgh neighborhoods boast a strong European heritage, in Bloomfield, that heritage is alive and well in daily activities. Just east of downtown, Bloomfield was settled by Italian immigrants, many of whom passed on their homes, language, and traditions to their descendants. As a result, the bustling business district along Liberty Avenue is dotted with ristorantes and grocerias. When you walk along Liberty Avenue, don't be surprised when you hear residents conversing in Italian.

Homes here typically are small but well maintained, providing a quaint quality to the narrow streets. The average Bloomfield home sells for about $50,000.

Amenities include West Penn Hospital and Dean Field, a football field beneath the Bloomfield Bridge where the legendary Johnny Unitas got his start. Dean Field was one of the first gridirons in the city to boast an artificial surface. Never mind that the playing area is only 70 yards long. Johnny U. graduated to the big time from Dean Field, and that's an inspiration for all the kids in Bloomfield.

Edgewood

This community just east of the City of Pittsburgh spans less than one square mile, yet it is something approaching a living book of the region's history. A farming community until the mid-19th century, Edgewood took on an industrial character with the growth of Union Switch & Signal Company. Today, as industry has declined, Edgewood is a lovely community of just under 4,000 residents, with large, inviting homes throughout the borough but especially prominent along tree-lined Maple Street.

Edgewood boasts two shopping hubs—a string of small shops along South Braddock Avenue, and Edgewood Towne Center, a popular mall that draws shoppers from throughout the eastern suburbs and Pittsburgh's eastern neighborhoods. With its location along I-376 (the Parkway East), Edgewood is about a 15-minute drive from both downtown Pittsburgh and the Pennsylvania Turnpike.

An oddity: if you walk a certain six-block route here, you can pass through four municipalities: Edgewood, Wilkinsburg, Swissvale, and the City of Pittsburgh. You don't win anything. It's just an interesting quirk.

Greenfield

Greenfield borders Squirrel Hill to the east. Homes here generally top out at $80,000 or less, so if you'd like to be within walking distance of the conveniences in Squirrel Hill at a lower price, this may be the neighborhood for you. Greenfield, too, offers many conveniences, including a senior citizens center, baseball field, and public pool, as well as shops, doctors' offices, and service businesses. A considerable percentage of Greenfield's residents are former steel mill workers. If you're interested in relocating to Greenfield, you may want to pick up a copy of the *Greenfield Grapevine*, a small monthly newspaper published by a Greenfield neighborhood organization. You can usually find a copy at the Giant Eagle on the corner of Murray Avenue and Loretta Street.

Greensburg

Once you spy the gleaming dome of the Westmoreland County Courthouse, you know you're in a city with character. That's Greensburg, a rather small city with an outsized appetite for culture. While Greensburg's population is just over 16,000 and the city spans only about 5 square miles, it is home to three institutions of higher learning—Seton Hill College, the University of Pittsburgh's Greensburg campus, and Westmoreland County Community College—as well as the popular Westmoreland Museum of American Art; the Westmoreland Symphony Orchestra; and the Palace Theatre, a downtown hall for performing arts.

The city offers many large, gracious homes as well as a growing number of planned developments that feature single-family homes, townhouses, condominiums, and rental units. Shopping here is fun. You'll have the option of browsing downtown establishments or heading to the large malls that just about surround the city.

Greensburg is about 30 miles east of Pittsburgh along Route 30. Perhaps more importantly, it sits at the foothills of the Laurel Highlands and so serves as the gateway to the popular recreation areas located there. You'll be delighted by Greensburg, a city of sophistication and charm.

Hill District

Live in the Hill District and you'll be part of a community steeped in history. Because of its adjacency to downtown Pittsburgh, the Hill District has been home to immigrant groups of many nationalities. Today, it boasts a primarily African-American population and is the center of African-American culture. Among the most important institutions in the neighborhood is Hill House, a multifaceted facility that sponsors social and educational programs as well as cultural events.

For many decades, the neighborhood has been the hub of the city's jazz activities, attracting multi-racial fans to such historic centers as the Granada Theater and the Crawford Grill and nurturing such international jazz stars as Pittsburgh natives Earl Hines, Erroll Garner, George Benson, Billy Eckstine, Stanley Turrentine, and Mary Lou Williams. Much of the neighborhood's joie de vivre was burned out in rioting in the late 1960s; today, organizations such as the Hill Community Development Corporation are working to restore that inviting quality, through programs including restoration of the Granada.

The neighborhood is a blend of older housing and inviting new developments such as Crawford Square, a mixture of about 500 rental and for-sale units that looks for all the world, with its grand trees and cul-de-sac drives, like a suburb plunked down in the heart of the city.

The Hill District also is a center of religion—you'll find no fewer than 40 churches in the neighborhood.

Live in the Hill District and you'll be a comfortable walk from downtown . . . and a resident of one of the city's historically important neighborhoods.

Latrobe

Welcome to Mr. Rogers' neighborhood. And Arnold Palmer's. And Rolling Rock Beer's. And the banana split's. All had their start in this community of about 9,300 in Westmoreland County, about 35 miles east of Pittsburgh.

> **INSIDERS' TIP**
>
> When you're in the Pittsburgh neighborhood of Lawrenceville, check out the *Doughboy*, the statue that commemorates those who served in World War I. The commercial/residential streets around the statue are known as Doughboy Square.

Latrobe is rich in history. It was mentioned, although not by its current name, in a 1750 entry in the diary of Christopher Gist, the surveyor credited with being the first explorer to cross the Allegheny Mountains heading west. Today, Latrobe is an appealing blend of urban and rural life. You'll find residential styles of all varieties. About 70 percent of Latrobe residents live in single-family homes, while the market value of residences is between $30,000 and $200,000. Venture just a few minutes outside downtown Latrobe and you'll be surrounded by fertile farmland.

With its central location along Route 30, the town is important to the commerce of Westmoreland County. Among the largest employers are Latrobe Area Hospital, with a staff of more than 1,500 at its main facility, and Kennametal, a Fortune 500 company that produces cutting tools. The area's industrial directory lists about 200 manufacturers, a reliable source of employment for local residents.

One of Latrobe's cultural centers is St. Vincent College, which is operated by the Benedictine Monks. In addition to hosting a number of important lecture series, the college each summer serves as the training site for the Pittsburgh Steelers.

Can you say, "Go, Stillers?"

Ligonier

When Westmoreland County residents refer to "the Diamond," they're not talking about precious stone deposits or a baseball field. Rather, they're referring to downtown Ligonier, where the shopping area—in the shape of a diamond—is one of the region's most charming. You'll find a variety of quaint shops as well as a bandstand that is the center of the town's civic activities.

Ligonier is one of the most prestigious addresses in the region; some who live elsewhere have second homes in Ligonier. Residences can be breathtaking, with woodlands stretching to the backyards and pristine streams coursing through the properties. Not all homes here are quite that

With Pittsburgh's rugged terrain, many of its neighborhoods are carved out of hilltops.

Photo: Jeff Greenberg

spectacular—the Ligonier Valley offers a broad mix of income levels—but it is those picture-postcard dwellings that provide Ligonier with its reputation.

Located in the Laurel Highlands, Ligonier is close to some of the region's most popular resorts as well as Idlewild Park, an amusement park with an unusual rustic flavor. See our Kidstuff chapter for a more complete description of Idlewild Park. Also an enduring attraction is Fort Ligonier, an important British redoubt in the 18th-century struggles for supremacy with the French.

"We offer a tranquil respite from the fast-paced tempo of living today," the town fathers are wont to say. Come to think of it, maybe there is a diamond in Westmoreland County after all.

Oakland

Oakland may be the city's most cosmopolitan neighborhood, drawing on its university-medical complex for a rich variety of residents, visitors, and amenities. The neighborhood is home to the University of Pittsburgh, Carnegie Mellon University, and Carlow College, attracting students, faculty, and visitors who contribute to the neighborhood's vitality.

The medical complex, including the University of Pittsburgh Medical Center, Children's Hospital, and Magee Women's Hospital, is among the most highly regarded in the world. Dr. Jonas Salk developed the polio vaccine here, and it serves as the base for Dr. Thomas Starzl, one of the world's transplant pioneers. See our Healthcare chapter for more details on Oakland's hospitals.

The style of life in Oakland covers a wide range. Beyond the transient community of students, the neighborhood boasts a solid residential base. South Oakland features streets of closely built homes that stretch all the way to I-376 (the Parkway East), where they overlook the Monongahela River. Schenley Heights features large older homes, while at Oakland's eastern end, you'll find many attractive high rises, where residents live in close proximity to hospitals, doctors' offices, and such cultural amenities as The Carnegie. Our chapter about The Arts contains a complete description of The Carnegie. The average Oakland home price is about $73,000.

Though Oakland is only about four miles from downtown, it contains two shopping districts—student-oriented businesses along Forbes Avenue, and more upscale galleries, shops, and restaurants near The Carnegie along South Craig Street.

In a word, Oakland will energize you.

Oakmont

If you follow the professional golf tour, you've heard of Oakmont. It's the home of Oakmont Country Club, which has hosted a number of PGA and U.S. Open tournaments through the years and is considered one of America's premier country clubs. As you travel from the Allegheny River up steep Hulton Road toward the country club, you'll see many well appointed homes with spacious grounds.

The commercial district is a charming slice of small town Americana, featuring professional offices and artisans' shops. You won't find a mall anywhere near this business district. Oakmont also offers a popular walking nature park, a yacht club, and public golf courses near the private country club.

If you're traveling to Oakmont from downtown, it's best to stay on high-speed Route 28 on the other side of the Allegheny, then cross the Hulton Bridge to Oakmont. You can't miss the Hulton Bridge—it's lavender.

Penn Hills

Next to Pittsburgh, Penn Hills is the largest municipality in Allegheny County, some 53,000 residents strong. The community was formerly a cluster of independent coal mining enclaves brought closer together by the completion of I-376 (the Parkway East).

Penn Hills spans 20 square miles as well as a variety of

INSIDERS' TIP

Many local communities sport colorful names. For example, you can drive from Moon (Township) to (the Borough of) Mars in about 40 minutes.

residential styles. You'll find single-family homes on quiet suburban streets as well as large multiunit residential buildings. The community boasts an appealing diversity of residents representing many races, income levels, and styles.

Shopping districts here are long and linear, stretching for miles along both Rodi Road and Frankstown Road, and there are several smaller shopping clusters as well. Penn Hills is a few minutes' drive from the Pennsylvania Turnpike and about 25 minutes from downtown Pittsburgh.

Shadyside

Shadyside often has been compared to Washington's Georgetown neighborhood, and there are similarities. In Shadyside, you'll find some of the city's loveliest and largest homes, including stunning Victorian mansions. You'll also find one of the trendiest and nicest shopping districts along Walnut Street, home to a variety of restaurants and upscale boutiques. Exploring Walnut Street is a treat, as you'll find many unusual and unheralded shops tucked around corners and up stairs. The neighborhood hosts an annual arts festival that packs them in on Walnut Street.

Shadyside has a strong, solid residential component as well. Walnut Street may be the neighborhood's most prominent feature, but the largest portion of Shadyside consists of solid middle-class and working-class homes. The average single-family home price is about $147,000, but you can find condominiums for under $100,000.

The neighborhood is home to Chatham College and Shadyside Hospital, as well as a number of stately churches. Shadyside is an easy bus trip from downtown Pittsburgh, about 5 miles away.

Squirrel Hill

Meet one of the most attractive and diverse neighborhoods in the City of Pittsburgh. Squirrel Hill is an especially large city neighborhood with nearly 30,000 residents. You'll find a broad variety of residential styles here, including many high-rise apartment buildings and sprawling brick mansions along Beechwood Boulevard and in the section of the neighborhood informally called "North of Forbes." The average sales price of a Squirrel Hill home is about $160,000, though the upper end of the range is $500,000 and beyond. Surprisingly, it's also possible to find some homes in the $45-$60,000 range on side streets in Squirrel, especially in the area where the neighborhood borders on Greenfield.

Just as important as the attractive housing is the neighborhood's blend of residents. Squirrel Hill is an important center of Judaism, home to a dozen synagogues and temples as well as the Jewish Community Center. Yet the defining characteristic of life here is ethnic diversity. Walk along the bustling Murray Avenue shopping district and you'll see delicatessens; pizza parlors; a Middle Eastern bakery; and Greek, Chinese, and sushi restaurants. At the hub of the neighborhood, the corner of Murray and Forbes avenues, the Jewish Community Center stands alongside St. Edmund's Academy, which is a Diocese of Pittsburgh elementary school, and across the street from Sixth Presbyterian Church.

The shopping district lacks a major department store as anchor but is just about self-sufficient in every other way, with businesses ranging from convenience stores to movie theaters to couturiers. For recreation, Frick Park is an urban jewel, with miles of hiking and jogging trails, picnic areas, athletic fields, and, believe it or not, a birding stand. For more on Frick Park, see our Parks chapter.

Squirrel Hill is about 5 miles from downtown Pittsburgh, easily accessible from I-376 (the Parkway East). When you visit the neighborhood, check out the former school where a portion of the film *Diabolique* was shot. The movie was bad; Squirrel Hill gets four stars.

INSIDERS' TIP

Two of downtown Pittsburgh's most popular plazas are Mellon Square and Market Square. Many downtown workers eat lunch in the squares. Market Square also hosts performances, rallies . . . and countless pigeons.

Swisshelm Park

Ask Pittsburgh residents about Swisshelm Park and you'll probably evoke a lot of puzzled looks. That's because Swisshelm Park, though within the City of Pittsburgh, is cut off from the rest of the city by sprawling Frick Park. In fact, if you begin from any point in Pittsburgh, you can't drive to Swisshelm Park without first leaving the city.

That isolation has enabled Swisshelm Park to develop as a tight-knit, family-oriented neighborhood of about 1,500 residents. Residential style here is largely single family, with few rental properties available. You'll find primarily suburban-style ranch homes and two-story brick dwellings, with the typical home selling for about $60,000.

The center of recreational and civic life is the Sarah Jackson Black Community Center, with a wide range of outdoor activities offered in Frick Park. Swisshelm Park does not offer any businesses to speak of—a blessing or a curse, depending on your point of view. You'll find plenty of shopping opportunities, however, in adjacent Swissvale and the nearby Edgewood Towne Center mall.

For a great place to raise a family . . . and retain some mystery about your lifestyle . . . try the splendid isolation of Swisshelm Park.

South

Bethel Park

Some key statistics will give you a good feel for this attractive South Hills suburb of Pittsburgh. The average home price is better than $106,000. About 91 percent of the community's high school graduates go on to further education. Four of every five homes are owner occupied.

If you're getting the sense of a family-oriented community of some means, welcome to Bethel Park. The community is less than 10 miles from downtown Pittsburgh, but many residents find all the amenities they need in local shopping malls, such as the massive South Hills Village. While the drive to Pittsburgh is easy, many commuters prefer to utilize park-and-ride lots and the "T" trolley-subway system. For more on this system, see our Getting Around chapter.

Most homes in this community of nearly 38,000 were constructed after World War II. They tend to feature from two to four bedrooms and well-maintained lawns. Bethel Park is adjacent to South Park, a 1,999-acre, Allegheny County-run facility that glitters as one of the jewels of the municipal park system. For more on South Park, see our Parks chapter.

Brookline

Brookline reflects many of the attractive qualities of Pittsburgh's South Hills. A large city neighborhood of nearly 15,000 people, Brookline is less than 4 miles from downtown, which is accessible by both bus and the trolley-subway system known as the "T." It's also on the doorstep of the region's heavily populated southern suburbs.

For many years, the near-exclusive residential style in Brookline was single family, with solid homes well spaced along tree-lined streets surrounding Brookline Boulevard. In recent years, the neighborhood has entertained development of an apartment building, a townhouse development and two senior citizen highrises, diversifying residential life. Prices for homes often range from $20,000 to $120,000.

The neighborhood's business district, though without major anchors, will meet most of your shopping needs. Brookline also boasts two community swimming pools and Seton-LaSalle Catholic High School.

Mount Lebanon

Mount Lebanon is one of Pittsburgh's showcase communities; a home in this South Hills suburb represents the aspirations of many local residents. Most homes in this community of more than 33,000 sell for between $150,000 and $250,000, although you'll find plenty well beyond that range. The typical Mount Lebanon home is freestanding, made of brick, with three to four bedrooms and spacious grounds. Homes are set back from tree-lined streets that are part of Mt. Lebanon's rich history—the community was named for two Cedars of Lebanon trees planted on Bower Hill Road, a main thoroughfare.

Mt. Lebanon's many amenities provide another foundation for the community's reputation. The upscale Galleria Mall anchors the busy business district. For recreation, the community offers 300 acres of parklands, a swimming pool, a tennis center, a nature reserve, an athletic field with artificial surface, an indoor ice skating rink, and a 9-hole golf course.

For all that, it is Mt. Lebanon's education system that is perhaps its most admired feature. Excellent public and private school networks lead to the high school, from which 92 percent of graduates go on to post-secondary education. As you might expect, residents are aware and politically active. It's a great place for a debate . . . as you stroll along quiet, shady streets.

Mt. Washington

Few urban areas can offer the visual excitement that Mt. Washington provides. Located at the top of Mt. Washington (naturally), the neighborhood offers breathtaking views of the city and its rivers below. Grandview Avenue, the neighborhood's main thoroughfare, provides several observation decks and souvenir shops, as most visitors to Pittsburgh include Mt. Washington on their itinerary. If you've enjoyed those sweeping views of Pittsburgh in films and advertisements, chances are they were shot from Mt. Washington.

Because of the view, homes in Mt. Washington can be quite dear. Newer condominiums—some of them actually cut into the mountain—can fetch up to $800,000.

Once past such conversation pieces, however, you'll find a community of stable homes that sell for an average of $58,000. The grand view may be a block or two away, but you'll find an active business district along Shiloh Street and a stable population of about 10,000.

You'll also have an opportunity to utilize one of the most unusual means of transportation—the inclined plane, sort of a trolley car that shuttles passengers up and down the mountainside. The Duquesne and Monongahela inclines are tourist attractions, but residents who work downtown also ride the inclines; they're at work in a few minutes, and they avoid parking hassles. For more on the inclines, see our Getting Here, Getting Around and Attractions chapters.

Peters

Peters has been one of the strong growth areas in Western Pennsylvania. The township is strategically located just across the Allegheny County border in Washington County, thus able to attract residents from Pittsburgh's South Hills as well as those in Washington County and points south and west.

Transformed from a semi-developed community, Peters is now home to more than 14,000 residents who live in spacious homes with large, landscaped lots. Home prices begin at $100,000, with some larger homes selling for $500,000 or more. The average home price is about $200,000.

Most homes—92 percent—are owner occupied, and there is scant commercial development here. With its location along Route 19, residents have access to as many shopping malls as they would ever need.

Peters residents value education, as 93 percent of the township's high school graduates continue their education.

South Side

Frequently, the term "neighborhood in transition" is a euphemism for a community on a downhill slide. South Side is a City of Pittsburgh neighborhood that has been in transition, and the result is one of the most lively neighborhoods you'll find.

Lofty Expectations

Eve Picker has lofty ambitions for downtown Pittsburgh. Literally. The architect-turned city planner-turned developer has taken on the enormous task of introducing residential lofts in the heart of the city. It's a project that other developers have found daunting. The early indications, however, are that the lofts of Picker and her company, No Wall Productions, (412) 362-7985, will bring an exciting new residential component to the city.

While artists' lofts in the city are nothing new, developers who have tried to create residential lofts have been frustrated by the prevailing architecture of downtown. Pittsburgh's older structures, jewels though they be, are architectural Olive Oyls, tall and skinny, not conducive to development of living space with workable dimensions. Conversion of such buildings to marketable living quarters is laborious and risky, so fraught with uncertainties that financial institutions have been reluctant to underwrite downtown loft developments.

Enter Picker, a native of Sydney, Australia, with a master's degree in urban design from Columbia University and just the right mix of experience and determination for the job. Her training as an architect familiarized her with the design principles that helped her envision residential lofts—and convinced her that she didn't want to remain an architect.

"I'm not sure it was architecture so much as it was me," she says. "I'm an entrepreneurial type. I want to work on big projects that affect public spaces, yet at a large firm, I'd be sort of at the bottom of the ladder, not really knowing I contributed.

"I'm impatient and need a lot of things happening at the same time. In development, you're involved and responsible every step of the way. As an architect, you can't do that. You're only responsible for a little piece of it."

She served a stint with the City of Pittsburgh Department of Planning, a position that enabled her to become familiar with virtually every foot of usable space in downtown Pittsburgh, and worked with a neighborhood development corporation, participating in more than a dozen residential developments.

When she found an abandoned former paper products warehouse in downtown's Firstside district along the Monongahela River, she knew she had the right property. Financing remained the final piece of the puzzle. Picker surmounted that obstacle by signing on National City Bank as both her financier and equity partner.

"I was very innocent at the start of the project," Picker says. "To take on a project that may take two years to pull together and then won't pay you a lot, it's scary. I'm edgy still. I think that's why it never happened before. No one wanted to take that leap before. In the end I jumped off the cliff."

After about 18 months of work, the building, renamed 429 Firstside Lofts, was ready. The eight-story structure features commercial space on the ground floor, then one loft on each of the remaining stories. The lofts are marvelous blends of original elements and practical new touches. Picker retained much of the building's original steel, including a number of discolored imperfections. Powder rooms just off the elevators feature the building's original brick walls on one side. To preserve as much living space as possible in the 1,850-square-foot lofts, Picker wall-mounted appliances in the kitchen, as well as the washers and dryers tucked unobtrusively into the principal bathroom. There are no doors from the elevator to the lofts. Step off the elevator and you're in your space.

Eve Picker has lofty ambitions for downtown Pittsburgh.

Photo: John Beale courtesy of Pittsburgh Post-Gazette

Perhaps the neatest touch is the rooftop deck, where residents can gather to relax, dine and enjoy the river traffic along the Mon below.

With most of her funds tied up in the conversion, Picker had a tiny advertising budget to announce the offering of her lofts as condominiums. It was a major concern, but she needn't have worried. Buyers quickly snapped up six of the seven lofts, priced between $155,000 and $195,000. Picker bought the seventh herself and plans to rent it out until what she playfully calls her two "teenage appendages" are on their own and she and her husband need less space.

Her buyers are an eclectic upscale mix—an investment banker, an exhibit designer, a pair of California transplants, an assistant prothonotary. (While greeting local elected officials once, Harry S Truman barked, "What the hell's a prothonotary?" Now we know. It's someone who buys a loft in downtown Pittsburgh.)

Seven lofts don't necessarily a trend portend, and it isn't clear how many such units the market will bear. Nevertheless, even before 429 Firstside Lofts sold out, Picker was well on her way to acquisition of a second downtown building for conversion to residential lofts. Despite the uncertainties, it seems likely that Pittsburgh has found a new residential style, and that Eve Picker has found a calling.

"I love Pittsburgh," she says, "I love its scale. It's a great place to bring up a family. You can drop off your kids at school, go skiing for the day, and be back in time to pick up your kids when school's out.

"I think what I'm doing is important to downtown. I don't approach this from the bottom line—maybe I won't be a great developer because of that. Because I'm an urban designer, I don't approach things the way other developers do. It has to be something I want to do.

"Every building is different. They speak to me and tell me what they want to be."

> One of the principal sources of financial assistance is the Urban Redevelopment Authority of Pittsburgh, (412) 255-6666, a public agency that provides both mortgage and home rehabilitation financing through a variety of programs.
>
> Typically, loans in such programs are originated by local banks and guaranteed by URA. Most programs have income restrictions and other eligibility requirements, and URA can help only in the city proper.

The neighborhood, a long, linear community that stretches for about 30 blocks along the Monongahela River, for many years was characterized by older multistory homes with party walls. Many residents worked at LTV's South Side steel mill, which would become a casualty of Big Steel's decline. The business district along East Carson Street was community serving but sedate.

In the 1980s, young professionals discovered the South Side as a way to beat downtown rents and began renovating older structures for their offices. Trendy taverns, restaurants, galleries, and retail shops sprang up to serve this new younger crowd. South Side Local Development Company initiated a project, with the Urban Redevelopment Authority of Pittsburgh, to create 300 units of riverfront housing. URA also is working to renovate the abandoned LTV site.

All this development has served to create a vibrant neighborhood, as renowned for its nightlife as it is for its family life. The price range for South Side homes is broad, reflecting the varying styles. While the average price is about $47,000, you can acquire an older, party-wall-type home for as little as $20,000. On the other hand, newer or renovated homes sometimes bring $200,000 or more in this up-and-coming neighborhood.

Upper St. Clair

When you see the initials "USC" in western Pennsylvania, don't mistake the acronym for a reference to the University of Southern California or the University of South Carolina. In these parts, USC means Upper St. Clair, an affluent community at the southwestern edge of Allegheny County near the Washington County border.

Why is USC so recognizable? Perhaps it's because of the quality of the township's homes. Prices begin at about $100,000 and rise to $250,000 or more for spacious homes with well-manicured grounds. Most of the homes were built after World War II, and most—93 percent—are owner occupied. You will find some modern apartment complexes, but large family-style homes remain the rule.

Perhaps USC is so prominent for its emphasis on education. An astonishing 98 percent of its high school graduates pursue post-secondary education, a figure that may be unequaled in the region.

Shoppers have access to a clutch of malls along Route 19, the highway that connects Allegheny and Washington counties, and Upper St. Clair is only a few minutes' drive from I-79. The township is about a 20-minute commute from downtown Pittsburgh.

Washington

For years, Pittsburgh area residents have referred to this city 25 miles southwest of Pittsburgh as "Little Washington." While that may seem a logical way of distinguishing it from that city inside the Beltway, you can understand why residents of Pennsylvania's Washington could be miffed. This is a city with a colorful history and a strong modern identity.

Washington was the center of the Whiskey Rebellion, an 18th-century challenge to the federal government's taxing authority, as well as an important stop on the National Road and the Underground Railroad. Today the city is home to Washington & Jefferson College, where the Olin Fine Arts Center stages many cultural events, and 45 places of worship.

Washington is strategically positioned at the junction of two interstate highways—I-70 and I-79—providing easy access to West Virginia and Ohio. Once a center for manufacturing, Washington now relies on the service and professional sectors for employment opportunities.

West

Banksville

Just west of downtown is a neighborhood that combines many elements of City of Pittsburgh life. Banksville offers stately older homes as well as newer dwellings that seem more suburban, with sweeping, manicured lawns and flower beds. While such homes are popular with families, the neighborhood is also home to Crane Village and Hiland Hills, two of Pittsburgh's largest garden apartment complexes, which typically cater to more transient residents. Homes in Banksville generally sell for between $60,000 and $90,000.

The heart of the shopping district is Banksville Road, a strip of shopping plazas that can satisfy most of your shopping needs. Banksville Road also functions as the main thoroughfare. Inbound, it takes you to the Parkway West and downtown; outbound, it leads on to the heavily populated South Hills. Banksville is a taste of the suburbs within the city.

Beaver

"Imagine a rolling English landscape, with the softest of blue skies, dotted at three-mile intervals with quiet little villages, or aggressive little manufacturing towns." That's how Rudyard Kipling described the Beaver Valley in a letter to a friend. Today, the community of Beaver, the county seat of Beaver County about 30 miles southwest of Pittsburgh, retains much of the charm that so enamored Kipling.

With little or no industry in the town itself, Beaver offers broad, shaded streets, lush parks, and views of the nearby Beaver and Ohio rivers. Most residents live in single-family homes and enjoy such amenities as The Gazebo in the heart of town, which features live entertainment during warm weather months.

Stability is the watchword in this community of about 5,500. The town's churches represent nine different denominations. Residents show such pride in their community, and such concern for their neighbors, that the police department and parent-teacher organizations sponsor an annual bicycle registration to discourage theft.

If you doubt the town's commitment to stability, consider that Robert P. Linn has served as mayor continuously since 1946—an achievement that has earned Hizzonor a place in the *Guinness Book of Records*.

Beaver Falls

Among the notables who have called Beaver Falls home is one Joe Willie Namath, one of the National Football League's legendary quarterbacks and partygoers. Sometimes it's hard to imagine Broadway Joe in this quiet, friendly town of about 10,500 located west of Pittsburgh along the Beaver River in Beaver County.

A center of social activities in Beaver Falls is 37th Street Park, where folks gather on park benches and kids enjoy the annual Easter egg hunt around the gazebo. The largest local employers include Republic Steel; Armstrong World Industries, a manufacturer of ceiling tiles; and Geneva College, situated in a popular residential area called College Hill.

Residential style is eclectic, with single-family homes, duplexes, rental properties, and high-rise multiunit buildings all available.

Canonsburg

Is it possible that one small Southwestern Pennsylvania town produced both Perry Como and Bobby Vinton? Indeed it is, and that town is Canonsburg, hard by I-79 in Washington County, about 15 miles southwest of Pittsburgh. The community has changed a bit since the days when

Mr. C. was crooning for the patrons of his barber shop. Single-family homes still honeycomb the hillsides between I-79 and Pennsylvania Route 19, but the town also has seen a number of planned communities.

Most prominent among these is Southpointe, a complex that features industrial, office, residential, and recreational uses. You can admire Southpointe's townhomes and golf course from I-79; if you drive in for a closer look or inquire about residential opportunities, you won't be the first passerby to do so.

Many of the town's 9,500 residents work at local businesses, including Pennsylvania Transformer Technology, Sarris Candies, and the antique shops that dot the main thoroughfare. One of the real attractions of Canonsburg is that location along I-79, about 35 minutes from the West Virginia and Ohio borders.

The city fathers are raising money to underwrite creation of a Perry Como statue to stand before town hall. If you live here, we can't guarantee that you won't break into a chorus of "Bless This House." If it happens, don't say we didn't warn you.

Moon

Moon traces its history to 1788, when it was among Allegheny County's initial group of townships. The origin of its name remains something of a mystery, though some say it derives from the crescent-shaped bend in the Ohio River, which forms Moon's northern border.

In contemporary times, Moon has experienced significant residential and commercial growth, thanks in part to the expansion of Pittsburgh International Airport a few miles away. To meet the needs associated with the airport, Moon offers a variety of recently constructed housing, including both single-family dwellings and luxury multiunit buildings.

The township of about 25,000 residents is home to Allegheny County's Settler's Park as well as the township-operated Robin Hill Park, site of many recreational and cultural activities, and five golf courses. With its location near I-279 (the Parkway West), Moon is within easy reach of both the airport and downtown Pittsburgh.

Sewickley

Once a summer retreat area for Pittsburgh's wealthiest families, Sewickley today is a charming residential community, one of a chain of such towns along the Ohio River in Allegheny County. In Sewickley and neighboring Sewickley Heights, you'll find some of the largest and most expensive homes in the region, but you'll also find lovely and more affordable housing as well.

The commercial district features a village atmosphere and quaint boutiques, art galleries, antique shops, and restaurants. Sewickley's approximately 4,000 residents take great pride in the breadth and quality of the public services the community provides, including careful oversight of renovations to historic older homes.

Sewickley offers five recreational complexes. If you live in Sewickley, you'll be well positioned for convenient travel. It's about 10 minutes from Pittsburgh International Airport, 20 minutes from downtown Pittsburgh, and right on the doorstep of Beaver County.

Westwood

Westwood has such an underdeveloped look to it that many Pittsburgh residents might not be aware there's a neighborhood here. This City of Pittsburgh neighborhood about 3 miles from downtown has a rural flavor to it, with wooded areas and yards that sometimes resemble pastoral fields. One Westwood homeowner with just such a flat, grassy yard leases the field for company picnics.

Homes in Westwood—from grand old Victorians to two-story neocolonials—typically sell for about $52,000 and of-

INSIDERS' TIP

Freedom Corner in the Hill District, so named because many civil rights marches began there, today serves as the starting point for parades.

ten include undeveloped acreage. The community recreational complex offers a swimming pool and tennis courts, and residents enjoy easy access to the shopping malls along I-279 (the Parkway West).

Westwood offers an old-fashioned sense of neighborhood; residents stage block parties and watch their kids play soccer in the streets. Westwood isn't exactly a neighborhood that time forgot, but it is a throwback.

Real Estate

Pittsburgh residents tend to stay put. Nevertheless, you'll find thousands of homes on the market at any given time, with activity peaking in the spring. The region's housing stock is a blend of older homes, many of them rehabilitated, and recently constructed dwellings. Thus, the price range for homes in the area is quite broad, beginning at a few thousand dollars for a "handyman's special" and soaring to $1 million or more at the high end.

No matter the type of home you seek, the prices in Pittsburgh will surprise and please you. According to 1996 data, the average purchase price for homes in the City of Pittsburgh was $63,000, a figure that compares favorably to that of just about every other major urban market. Elsewhere in our six-county coverage area, average home prices range from $65,600 in Armstrong County to $123,900 in Butler County.

Because neighborhoods in the region are numerous and diverse, you might find it helpful to work with a real estate agency to identify some options for you. The real estate sector here is large, active, and sophisticated. Their marketing thrusts include the traditional, such as printed materials, to the innovative, such as television programs and comprehensive web sites.

We've profiled a number of agencies to help point you in the right direction. The list is by no means exhaustive, but our profiles will introduce you to the largest agencies in the area as well as a number of neighborhood specialists. Happy hunting!

Realtors

Albert Anthony Real Estate
528 E. Eighth St., Munhall
• **(412) 461-5209**

Albert Anthony and his wife Judie handle the sale of homes in the East End and the South Hills. They also offer residential property management and commercial appraisals. While the median price range of homes they sell is $79,900 to $129,000, some homes—like large, stately places of residence in Squirrel Hill—may bring as much as $400,000. The Anthonys also are happy to sell marketable homes in their area in lower price ranges.

The couples' office is only about a mile from their own home, and they know the areas they represent personally. They'll be sure to give you personal service, too.

Barnes and Associates Real Estate
102 Lexington Ave., Aspinwall
• **(412) 781-3171**

Barnes and Associates concentrates on homes in Fox Chapel and surrounding communities. They average about 50 sales per year, significant volume with such a small geographic concentration, so you know the agency is highly regarded in the community. The homes they handle range in price from about $50,000 to $250,000 and more, and each deal gets the personal attention of proprietor Maryanne Barnes.

If doing most of the work to sell your own home (and avoiding paying commissions) appeals to you, check out Mary Anne Barnes' brainchild, Real Estate Express. For very modest fees, Mary Anne will provide you with everything you need to sell your own home and you'll have her and her associate's expertise at your fingertips. The best news is that this service could save you anywhere from $6,400 to $44,000, depending on the selling price of your home.

Century 21
6 Sylvan Way, Parsippany, NJ
• **(800) 221-5737**
• **www.century21.com**

One of the largest agencies in the region, Century 21 boasts 26 offices in Southwestern Pennsylvania, each independently owned and operated. Since Century 21 does not have administrative offices locally, you have the option of contacting the regional headquarters in Parsippany or phoning any of the local offices.

The company offers an innovative program called Century 21 Communities, an America

With more than 350 real estate agencies listed in the phone book, it's sometimes difficult to know where to begin when you're in the housing market. Many realtors in the region participate in a cooperative organization known as West Penn Multi List; when you deal with these companies, they'll have a comprehensive list of homes available, rather than the listings of one agency only.

If you'd prefer to get a feel for the market yourself, you can pick up a free copy of *Homes Guide By Realtors,* a twice-monthly publication of the Realtors Association of Metropolitan Pittsburgh (RAMP) that provides a comprehensive list of homes for sale and is available free at many area supermarkets.

Also available at supermarkets are reprints of the Sunday real estate section of the *Tribune-Review,* a Pittsburgh daily newspaper. The section includes both comprehensive listings and feature stories. You also will find it at the *Trib's* web site, tribune-review.com.

While you're at the grocery store picking up all this material, check out a newer publication called *Homes for Sale by Owner.* The twist here is that the owners represented in this bi-weekly publication are marketing their homes without agents. You can buy a photo ad for two weeks for as little as $49. For more information, contact the company at (412) 920-1589.

If selling a home all by yourself seems a little daunting, check out the "Real Estate Express" service offered by Barnes and Associates Real Estate (see their write-up for more).

For some good guidelines on selecting a home, apartment, or builder, try these referral agencies: RAMP, (412) 261-5200; Apartment Association of Metropolitan Pittsburgh, (412) 231-8111; Builders Association of Metropolitan Pittsburgh, (412) 231-8111. RAMP also will provide a free directory of realtors, as well as a spiffier, more informative version priced at $100. While these trade organizations will not recommend specific companies, they will offer good advice on how to evaluate agencies and contractors.

You also can try the Real Estate Hotline of the *Pittsburgh Post-Gazette's* PG Link. If you call (412) 261-1234, you can get round-the-clock general information on closing costs, warranties, negotiations, and market appraisals.

Online site that provides access to information about 700 neighborhoods across North America. Enter a ZIP code and you can find what a community's residents like to drive, read, and watch on television.

Coldwell Banker Real Estate
9576 Perry Highway, McCandless
• **(412) 765-0900**

With 14 offices and 800 agents in Southwestern Pennsylvania, Coldwell Banker tries to make buying and selling homes as convenient as possible for its clients. Dedicated divisions handle mortgages, relocations, and title services, while the company deploys a special unit for homes priced at $350,000 and above.

The company adheres to a 22-point guarantee for sellers and buyers. Among the company's service guarantees: If they don't convey a decision about your loan application the same day it's filed, they'll pay you $250; if they don't meet the scheduled closing date, they'll reduce your interest rate by 1/8 percent. (Certain restrictions apply; call for details.)

Coldwell Banker publishes *The Real Estate News & Buyers Guide,* featuring pictures and descriptions of every home in its inventory. It runs as an insert in a number of local newspapers, or you can subscribe for free by calling the agency.

Dunn Real Estate Services
512 Foreland St., Pittsburgh
• **(412) 322-2000**

Here's a small agency with four agents that specializes in City of Pittsburgh properties, with particular emphasis on 15 Northside neighborhoods that produce 85 percent of the company's business. You'll find an exhaustive knowledge of those 15 neighborhoods at Dunn, as well as familiarity with special financing programs—an important plus for first-time buyers. Because

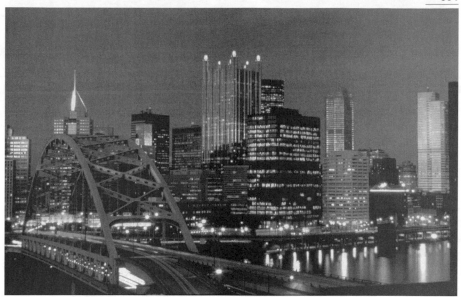

If you want a grand view of the skyline, expect to pay for it.

Photo: Andrew A. Wagner

it's so well known on its turf, the agency can reach special audiences, such as employees of Northside companies, that mass advertising might miss.

Equity Real Estate
2029 Murray Ave., Pittsburgh
• **(412) 422-9200**

Equity is a mid-sized agency specializing in the city's eastern neighborhoods. The company has 40 agents with thorough knowledge of their territory. If you visit Equity, you'll find its ownership and senior management right there on the premises, every day. The agency maintains contacts with a wide variety of lenders to ensure that buyers have access to the best financing packages.

Harris Realty
2214 Murray Ave., Pittsburgh
• **(412) 521-7050**

If you're looking for a home in Pittsburgh's eastern neighborhoods, the folks at Harris are your prospective neighbors. Its three full-time and eight part-time agents are residents of such eastern neighborhoods as Squirrel Hill, Shadyside, Greenfield, and Point Breeze. They know your turf and can help you negotiate it, whether you're in the market for an estate or a fixer-upper. When you phone Harris, your call will be taken by a real, live person, 24 hours a day.

Howard Hanna Real Estate Services
119 Gamma Drive, O'Hara
• **(412) 967-9000, (800) 646-RELO**
• **www.howardhanna.com**

For more than 40 years, Howard Hanna Real Estate Services has been one of Western Pennsylvania's most prominent agencies. It's the largest, family-owned, full-service real estate company in the Pennsylvania, Ohio, and West Virginia tri-state area. It operates 58 offices with approximately 1,100 full-time sales associates. Among the services Howard Hanna provides are appraisals, financing, and relocation and closing services.

With the breadth of the agency's coverage come a number of valuable customer services. These include a "money back guarantee" for the buyer of your home; an advanced equity loan program, which allows the purchaser of your home to borrow against equity from Howard Hanna Real Estate to meet current mortgage payments; and an apartment trade-in program, so that if your home is purchased by an apartment dweller, Howard Hanna Real Estate will assume the renter's lease.

The agency also employs marketing techniques with a technology twist, such as producing the weekly *Real Estate Digest/Showcase of Homes* each Sunday morning on KDKA-TV, and featuring the agency's entire list of homes on its web site.

Getting to the Point, (412) 362-3363, works with corporations, hospitals, and academic institutions to assist them in recruiting candidates who visit the Greater Pittsburgh region and in providing the a smooth transition for those who have already accepted positions here. These services aren't real estate related per se; Getting to the Point has no vested interest in real estate and provides services focused exclusively around the well-being of individuals and families relocating to the area. Services are extensive and include such niceties as tours of the Pittsburgh region; information about schools and pre-schools and basic human resources (bankers, pediatricians, accountants, etc.), contacts for spouses seeking employment, and assistance with finding temporary rental housing. Better yet, employers and potential employers foot the bill. Check out Getting to the Point's web site at www.getting-to-the-point.com

Lavelle Real Estate
2909 Centre Ave., Pittsburgh
• (412) 621-2992

Many companies claim to be family businesses; Lavelle Real Estate walks the walk. Robert R. Lavelle received his broker's license in 1951 and still runs the business. His son and wife are Lavelle Real Estate brokers, while his daughter-in-law serves as office manager, coordinating the activities of five agents.

It's no coincidence that the agency is located in the Hill District, the hub of Pittsburgh's African-American community. "As a minority-owned institution," Robert Lavelle says, "we're trying to help black people own homes. We want to motivate people, to let them see a black business with the accoutrements of success." This is an agency with experience—and a mission.

Northwood Realty Co./
Better Homes and Gardens
4100 Route 8, Allison Park
• (412) 487-3200, (800) 245-6172
(relocation)

Northwood is a full-service firm that operates throughout Southwestern Pennsylvania, with 32 offices and 700 agents. Just as significant, its Better Homes and Gardens affiliation provides it with the opportunity for national and international referrals. If you're planning to move almost anywhere, chances are Northwood has an affiliate there.

The agency has a number of special programs to serve customers. It offers a 30-minute television show each Sunday at 11:30 AM on WPXI-TV to showcase all homes on its current list. To learn the status of any home, you can call (412) 492-1100 around the clock, punch in the home's five-digit code, and hear a tape of an agent describing the unit and its status.

Finally, Northwood maintains an "Elegant Homes" division to market homes priced at $300,000 and above.

Prudential Preferred Realty
9401 McKnight Rd., McCandless
• (412) 367-8028, (412) 261-4800
(relocation)
• www.prudentialpreferred.com

Though owned and operated locally, Prudential Preferred is a franchise of Prudential nationally, providing it with strong relocation services. With in-house capabilities for mortgages, insurance, and settlement services, Prudential Preferred can provide something approaching one-stop shopping for buyers.

Prudential Preferred operates 23 offices with more than 600 sales associates, giving it broad reach throughout Southwestern Pennsylvania. If you purchase a home through Prudential Preferred, the agency will buy your former residence, at a mutually agreeable price, if they can't move it within six months. If you're thinking of real estate as a career, try Prudential Preferred's in-house instructional program, which will prepare you for the appropriate state exams.

Karen L. Smith & Associates
1205 E. Carson St., Pittsburgh
• (412) 488-0100

The South Side is one of Pittsburgh's hottest neighborhoods, offering a compelling mix of restored older homes and new construction along the Monongahela River. Karen L. Smith & Associates specializes in South Side properties as well as other City of Pittsburgh neighborhoods. When proprietor Karen Smith offers advice about South Side housing, she speaks from experience, having acquired and rehabilitated a building in the neighborhood for her own home. The company employs four full-time agents.

Childcare

Few services are as important to families as quality, reliable childcare. As the frequency of dual wage earners within families has increased, the quest for childcare services has become a key determinant in the ability of both parents to continue working, to meet their economic goals, and to provide a supportive and loving environment for their children. Fortunately, the news on this front in Southwestern Pennsylvania is good. There is help as you embark on the search for reliable, safe, and educational care for your children.

For many local residents, childcare goes by the decidedly unscientific names of Grandma and Grandpa. Family roots run deep in this region, with extended families often residing together or in the same neighborhood. For parents living in extended families, the need for professional childcare may not compelling. Yet that same emphasis on families and family values has helped inspire a broad network of professional childcare sources for those parents who live outside extended families

Parents here have many choices. Not only will you find licensed day care centers, but you'll also discover family-run childcare in private homes. Hiring independent baby-sitters, signing up with a Mother's Day Out program, or enlisting the services of an au pair also may work well for your set of circumstances. In addition, there are agencies that can assist you if your child becomes ill and you're unable to take off work to be the primary caregiver.

With the exception of unique childcare arrangements, this chapter will not list, describe, or recommend individual day care establishments. Our purpose is to guide your decision making, explore the standards for what most experts regard as quality care, introduce community resources, and present alternatives. This chapter does contain a list of support groups and organizations that help both parents and other caregivers provide for healthy, happy nurturing.

LOOK FOR:
• Referral Services
• Special Care
• Part-Day and After-School Programs
• Support Organizations

Understanding Quality Childcare

The Pennsylvania Commission for Women has produced a handy Day Care Checklist to guide parents in choosing quality childcare. This two-sided, blue checklist describes the characteristics you should look for in caregivers and staff, signs of safe facilities, health and safety factors, program components, and other indicators of good care. It suggests questions to ask potential providers, such as "May I drop in any time?" and "Is there a parents' group or program?" To get your checklist, write the commission at P.O. Box 1326, Harrisburg, PA 17105, or call (717) 787-8128.

In Pennsylvania, the state Department of Public Welfare is the agency that regulates day care facilities in the following categories:

• Day Care Centers—state-licensed facilities providing care for seven or more children

• Group Day Care Homes—state-licensed facilities providing care for no more than 12 children

• Family Day Care Homes—state-certified family residences with one care giver for four, five or six children unrelated to the care giver

• Nursery Schools—part-time preschool facilities licensed by the Pennsylvania Department of Education

For more information about day care facilities in the Commonwealth, call one of the state's regional toll-free hotlines. In Southwestern Pennsylvania, that number is (800) 222-2149. Parents also may use this line, staffed by the Pennsylvania Department of Public Welfare, to investigate complaints, obtain day care regulations, or ask other questions.

Additionally, MetLife Consumer Education Center has produced a useful pamphlet called "Choosing Childcare." While the booklet does not offer referrals for our region, it does an excellent job of explaining the differences in types of childcare and presents points to cover when you inspect facilities and interview potential caregivers. For your free pamphlet, call (800) METLIFE.

Referral Services

directory of available programs which offer both private and subsidized childcare.

Child Care Partnerships
305 Wood St., Pittsburgh
• **(412) 261-CARE**

A program of the YWCA of Greater Pittsburgh, Child Care Partnerships (CCP) is committed to improving the quality of childcare, providing referral services to parents at every economic level, providing subsidies to eligible parents, and enhancing the childcare system within the region.

If you're a parent searching for childcare, CCP's referral specialists will provide information on regulated (licensed or registered) childcare providers as reported by the Department of Public Welfare. Parents ultimately are responsible for screening and monitoring their childcare providers, but CCP has valuable information to guide parents to the best choices.

CCP also provides consultation and information to businesses interested in helping their employees balance work and family life. Employers contract with CCP for resource and referral services as well as work-site seminars, workshops, and other speaking engagements related to job and life issues.

Finally, Child Care Partnerships houses a Resource Room at its downtown location where childcare providers can borrow training materials, videos, books, and other tools. Training programs for providers—scheduled in the evenings and on Saturdays—also are available.

Childcare Choices
1008 Seventh Ave., Ste. 201, Beaver Falls
• **(800) 322-8504**

Childcare Choices offers information to parents about the location, costs, and eligibility requirements of day-care programs in Beaver County. The office maintains a

National Association for the Education of Young Children (NAEYC)
1509 16th St. NW, Washington, D.C. 20036-1426
• **(800) 424-2460**

Write or call this nonprofit, professional organization to receive a free list of accredited programs in the Pittsburgh area. Day-care facilities that are accredited by this national group have met a stringent set of guidelines that promote the well-being of children. Childcare programs participate in the NAEYC assessment program on a voluntary basis.

The Early Childhood Initiative
1 Smithfield St., Pittsburgh
• **(412) 456-6706**

A public-private partnership, the Early Childhood Initiative is designed to help low-income children up to 5 years of age become successful, productive adults by enrolling them in high-quality early care and education services. The initiative is a United Way agency.

EF Au Pair
1 Memorial Dr., Cambridge, MA 02142
• **(800) 333-6056**

EF Au Pair provides carefully screened young men and women, ages 18 to 26, who will join a family and care for the children during a yearlong cultural exchange program. As live-in companions, au pairs work up to 45 hours per week—no more than 10 hours on any day—providing childcare in exchange for room, board, and a valuable cultural experience. You may contact the home office at the number above or either of EF Au Pair's coordinators in our region: Janet McDermott, (412) 341-3151, and Mimi Wells, (724) 935-0016.

INSIDERS' TIP

When you call Child Care Partnerships, (412) 261-CARE, you'll receive a checklist titled "Choosing Quality Childcare" that can help you make the best choices.

The Children's Center at Magee-Womens Hospital; counselors April Speed and Jan McLay.

Photo: Courtesy of Magee-Womens Hospital

Special Care

The Get Well Room
327 Craft Ave., Pittsburgh
• (412) 641-1267

Located in the city's Oakland medical complex, The Get Well Room is a separate area of The Children's Center of Pittsburgh, comfortably equipped to care for children from 6 months through 12 years of age with mild respiratory or gastrointestinal illnesses. It's affiliated with Magee-Women's Hospital.

Supervised by a pediatric nurse, the staff provides a warm, caring atmosphere for children who cannot attend their regular childcare programs due to illness. The nurse decides how many children can be accepted on any given day.

Children may participate if they have mild fevers (103 degrees or less) or bronchitis, croup, asthma, diarrhea, occasional vomiting, or pain or fever from vaccinations. Children suffering from chicken pox, respiratory distress, continuous vomiting or diarrhea, and those with fevers higher than 103 degrees are not appropriate candidates for The Get Well Room.

If the services of The Get Well Room might help you, you'll need to complete a registration form and have your child's physician complete a health appraisal. Both forms must be on file at The Children's Center before your child can use The Get Well Room. The registration fee is $15 per family.

In addition, fees for services are due when those services are rendered. Some businesses offer their employees assistance in paying for this form of childcare. All medications should be brought in their original, labeled containers. The Get Well Room is open from 7 AM to 5:30 PM Monday through Friday.

The Therapeutic Parents' and Children's Center
330 Blvd. of the Allies, Pittsburgh
• (412) 562-9440

The Therapeutic Parents' and Children's Center, a program of Family Resources, is a therapeutic preschool for children suffering developmental and emotional delays as a result of abuse or neglect. This service intervenes early in children's lives to help keep them on track developmentally and to aid their families in meeting their special needs. Call Family Resources for more information if you feel this type of care is appropriate for your child. Other services of Family Resources are described under "Support Groups," below.

Part-Day and After-School Programs

In many communities in the region, you'll find part-time programs to help you meet your childcare needs. Churches and synagogues offer Mother's Day Out programs for infants to kindergarten-age children. After registering your child, you can arrange a schedule that gives you several hours of childcare at nominal charges, similar in most cases to what you would pay a baby-sitter. To find such respite when you need it, contact churches and synagogues in your community.

In addition, many school districts can direct parents to after-school programs. Check with your school district's administrative office to determine if it offers such a program (see our Education chapter for school district contact information).

Organizations such as the YMCA or YWCA offer after-school or latch-key programs, while some churches also provide mid-week programs for children and youths. Since the Greater Pittsburgh community is so vast, the range of services offered varies considerably. Each YMCA or YWCA, for instance, reflects the social and economic needs of the individual community. Thus, there could be subsidized childcare available in some neighborhoods, and latch-key programs in others.

Regardless of the type of program you consider, do ask a few basic questions, including:

• Are these programs for children of a particular age? Or are various ages combined within the same program?

• What kinds of activities are offered?

• Who supervises the chidren?

• Are the surroundings safe?

• Is there a fee to be involved, or is membership or residency required (in the case of the YWCA, a church, or a school district)?

• Does the program operate during summers, holidays or snow days, or solely on school days?

Armed with these questions, you should turn to

your local telephone directory or yellow pages to begin your search for the care that's appropriate for your child.

Support Organizations

Alliance for Infants and Toddlers, Inc.
2100 Wharton St., Ste. 705, Pittsburgh
• (412) 431-1905

The Alliance provides developmental screening and tracking for children from birth to 3 years of age throughout Allegheny County. Your child may participate if there is parental concern or a history of medical, environmental, or biological factors such as prematurity or a stay in a neonatal intensive care unit.

To be eligible for Infant/Toddler Early Intervention Services, children must be diagnosed with physical or mental conditions which place them at high risk for developmental delays. Services of the Alliance are free and confidential. Call them to arrange an assessment to determine eligibility.

ARC–Allegheny
711 Bingham St., Pittsburgh
• (412) 995-5000

The mission of ARC–Allegheny is to protect the rights of, and promote opportunities for, those with mental retardation and developmental disabilities, and to do so within a family context. The organization's diverse services include early intervention, assessments and therapy for infants and toddlers, family support networks, respite and sitter care, specially designed homes to meet the needs of older adults, employment initiatives, and recreational, vacation and summer camp opportunities.

You'll find more about ARC–Allegheny in our Healthcare chapter. While ARC–Allegheny serves Allegheny County, you'll also find ARC organizations in four other counties within our primary service area. These are:

• ARC–Beaver County, (724) 775-1602 or (800) 272-0567

• ARC–Butler County, (724) 282-1500

• ARC–Washington County, (724) 222-6960

• ARC–Westmoreland County, (724) 837-8159

INSIDERS' TIP

La Leche League, (412) 276-5630, can put you in touch with volunteer groups in your area that are providing support for nursing mothers.

Allegheny Intermediate Unit
1400 Penn Ave., Ste. 201, Pittsburgh
• (412) 394-5700

The Allegheny Intermediate Unit (AIU) is the larg-

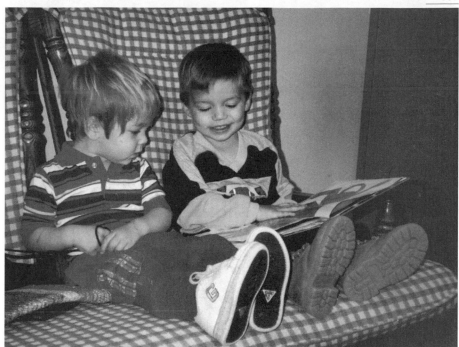

It's never too early for youngsters to learn to read.

Photo: Courtesy of Butler County Chamber of Commerce & Tourism

est of Pennsylvania's 29 intermediate units, which provide curriculum-enhancement services to school districts. Working with school districts throughout Allegheny County, this nonprofit regional education agency administers such initiatives as Head Start, Project DART, and programs for gifted students.

Each school district in Pennsylvania is served by an intermediate unit. See our Education chapter for a description of intermediate units in our region.

Big Brothers and Big Sisters of Greater Pittsburgh
5989 Penn Cir. S., Pittsburgh
• (412) 363-6100

This agency matches caring adults with at-risk children from single-parent households in Allegheny and Washington counties. These one-to-one mentoring relationships help children thrive. Volunteers are welcome, but the selection process is rather rigorous, including a thorough interview, background checks and clearances, and training.

You'll find a similar organization in each county in our primary service area. You can reach them at these numbers:

• Big Brothers Big Sisters of Armstrong County, (724) 763-4181
• Big Brothers Big Sisters of Beaver County, (724) 728-4300
• Big Brothers Big Sisters of Butler County, (724) 287-4733
• Big Brothers Big Sisters of Westmoreland County, (724) 837-6198
• Big Brothers and Big Sisters of Greater Pittsburgh, Washington County Office, (724) 228-9191

Family Communications, Inc.
4802 Fifth Ave., Pittsburgh
• (412) 687-2990

The Mister Rogers' Neighborhood Childcare Partnership is a joint effort of Family Communications, public television stations, and others committed to the education and welfare of children. The partnership offers training and support materials for childcare providers as well as a quarterly newsletter.

Another project, *The Mister Rogers Plan & Play Book*, extends the popular television program to the childcare setting, with over 400 richly illustrated pages of easy-to-do activities. For more about Mister Rogers and his pioneering work with children, see our Worship and Kidstuff chapters.

Family Resources
141 S. Highland Ave., Pittsburgh
• (412) 562-9440

Family Resources is the largest child abuse treatment and prevention agency in Allegheny County. It works to strengthen families and neighborhoods by providing training for professionals as well as crisis intervention for families where abuse has occurred. Licensed as an outpatient mental health facility and provider of enhanced mental health services, Family Resources is a United Way member agency.

The services offered by Family Resources are diverse. They include parent support services such as Parents Anonymous groups, nurturing courses, The Therapeutic Parents' and Children's Center described above, and a 260-acre Family Retreat Center in Warrendale that is available year-round to community organizations, social and religious groups, schools, and businesses. Family Resources can help connect parents with primary health care, substance abuse treatment, housing services and job placement and recreational programs.

In addition, the agency operates the WARMLINE, a telephone service offering parenting information, referrals, and support. You can ask nonmedical questions regarding such topics as discipline, postpartum depression, children's bedwetting, and general parental stress. The WARMLINE is staffed by trained volunteers. It's free and confidential. You can reach it at (412) 641-4546, (800) 641-4546 if you're outside Allegheny County.

Parent & Child Guidance Center
2644 Banksville Rd., Pittsburgh
• (412) 343-7166

This nonprofit organization provides a diversity of mental health, mental retardation, educational outreach, testing, and consultation services for children and families, as well as outpatient clinical treatment and a therapeutic preschool for children ages 3 to 5 with severe social and emotional delays.

One of the center's most heavily utilized programs is called Families In Transition. It offers education for parents and others

dealing with separation, divorce, remarriage, and family alcoholism.

The center also maintains the Parentline, (412) 343-7166, a telephone service for parents and other primary caregivers who wish to discuss their concerns with a professional. There is no charge for Parentline, and callers may remain anonymous if they wish. The line operates five days a week, Monday through Friday, from 9 AM to 6 PM.

Parental Stress Center
1700 E. Carson St., Pittsburgh
• (412) 381-4800

The mission of the Parental Stress Center is to prevent child abuse and neglect through education, counseling and support services. Its Critical Differences Program provides intensive in-home assistance to families under severe stress due to economic, health, social, or environmental pressures.

The center also offers parenting workshops, teen groups, support groups, and other family-related education and training services; center personnel will help you schedule these for weekdays, weekends, and evenings in locations throughout Allegheny County. In addition, the agency's Fathers' Resource Center helps fathers maintain an active role in their children's lives. Services include weekly support groups for dads, anger management programs, and mentoring opportunities. For more information on this program, call (412) 488-DADS.

Parental Stress Center is a United Way member agency. For more on the center, see our Healthcare chapter.

Parents Anonymous
2001 N. Front St., Bldg. 2, Ste. 222,
Harrisburg • (800) 448-4906

If you feel occasional anger and frustration associated with the challenges and pressures of raising children, Parents Anonymous support groups can help you develop coping and management strategies. When you contact the Parents Anonymous state resource office in Harrisburg at the number listed above, they'll put you in touch with support groups in your area. Parents Anonymous is run by various organizations throughout the state.

You also may contact Family Resources, (412)

INSIDERS' TIP

Children's Hospital of Pittsburgh provides dozens of educational classes for parents, many of them free. Call the Community Education line at (412) 692-7105 for class schedules and parenting information.

363-5742, if you're in Allegheny County, or Parent-wise Inc. for Parents Anonymous of Westmore-land County, (800) 544-0227. In Beaver County, Family Enrichment runs the program; call (724) 774-5533. Family First is the host agency in Butler County at (724) 284-4894; and Community Action Southwest sponsors Parents Anonymous in Washington County. Contact them at (724) 447-2053.

Ronald McDonald House
500 Shady Ave., Pittsburgh
- **(412) 362-3400**

Opened in 1979, Ronald McDonald House is a home away from home for families who must travel hundreds, even thousands of miles from their own communities for medical treatment for their children. Located near Children's Hospital, the house is designed to encourage interaction between guests and to help them cope during a trying period.

Safe Sitter
**1500 N. Ritter Ave.,
Indianapolis, IN 46219**
- **(800) 255-4089**

Founded in 1980 by Indianapolis pediatrician Patricia A. Keener, M.D., Safe Sitter is a babysitter training program designed to reach young persons ages 11 to 13 before they begin actively babysitting. In one-day or two-day courses, usually offered at local hospitals, Safe Sitter teaches youths what to expect when dealing with children, how to avoid difficult situations, and how to solve problems if they occur. Students learn such techniques as rescue breathing and accident management, and they're also grounded in the business aspects of babysitting.

The program helps young babysitting entrepreneurs, of course, but it also is a boon to parents, providing them with a pool of well-trained babysitters. Safe Sitter includes more than 550 participating hospitals and teaching sites—including those local hospitals listed below—in the United States and abroad. In fact, St. Clair Hospital in Pittsburgh's South Hills served as the pilot site for the rollout of Safe Sitter's one-day instructional program.

While participating hospitals cannot recommend particular sitters, they can verify that a potential caregiver you might be considering has successfully completed a Safe Sitter course of study. Local participants include:
- Allegheny Valley Hospital, (724) 226-7240
- Canonsburg Hospital, (724) 225-4763
- Brownsville Hospital, (724) 785-1876
- Children's Hospital of Pittsburgh, (412) 692-7105
- Latrobe Area Hospital, (724) 537-1755
- Mercy Hospital of Pittsburgh, (412) 232-8125
- St. Clair Hospital, (412) 344-6600 ext. 2597
- UPMC Health Center, (412) 422-9802
- The Washington Hospital, (724) 223-3840

INSIDERS' TIP
For a listing of the Top 25 largest day care providers in the region, consult The Book of Lists published annually by *The Pittsburgh Business Times*. It's available in most libraries, with a new version published each year.

CHILDCARE

Education

The diversity of local government in southwestern Pennsylvania extends to the area of education. It's an arena that's always important, usually colorful, and sometimes frustrating. Sheer numbers tell a large part of the story here. Of the 501 school districts in the Commonwealth of Pennsylvania, 100 of them serve our six-county principal coverage area. Since many aspects of public education are left to the discretion of local school districts, standardization in any area is rare.

Local residents care deeply about their schools and the quality of education those schools are providing. Media have responded to that keen interest by expanding their coverage of schools and school districts. With at least 100 board meetings to cover every month, to say nothing about day-to-day and ongoing issues, local media must devote a great deal of attention to schools. This, in turn, creates additional interest, which generates even broader coverage. It's a cycle that assures thorough coverage of—and ever-widening interest in—the education scene.

Rather than provide you with profiles of 100 school districts, which we feared would be numbing and counterproductive, we've taken a somewhat different approach in this chapter. In our look at public education, we've tried to explore the most important issues—most notably school choice and standards—and to provide some insight into how local school districts are dealing with these issues. Our treatment is by no means exhaustive; it seems unlikely that any could be.

We've rounded out our look at the education scene with some background on diocesan schools and profiles of other private schools, or independent schools, as they sometimes prefer to be known. You'll find that when it comes to education in Southwestern Pennsylvania, you may have more options than you ever imagined.

Public Schools

Organization

Public education in Pennsylvania is provided by 501 school districts; our six-county coverage area boasts 100 of those school districts, making education here diverse and colorful. Many districts have been formed through consolidation, so that most districts encompass several municipalities or more, though this is not universally the case. Some districts have taken their names from the communities they serve. Carlynton School District in Pittsburgh's western suburbs, for example, spans the municipalities of Carnegie, Rosslyn Farms, and Crafton. On the other hand, on the heels of some mergers, district administrators couldn't find names that incorporated all their communities, so they threw up their hands and went in other directions. When schools in Dormont, Castle Shannon, and Green Tree merged into a single district, they opted for the name Keystone Oaks, a pleasant-sounding appellation with no syllabic echoes of any of the participating communities.

School districts are governed by nine-member elected boards that in turn name superintendents to lead district administration. The Pittsburgh School District, including the City of Pittsburgh and the Borough of Mt. Oliver (a municipality surrounded by the city), is the region's largest, serving more than 40,000 students in 11 high schools, 19 middle schools, 59 elementary schools, five special-use schools, and one adult education school.

Outside of Pittsburgh, the largest district in the region is the sprawling North Allegheny School District, which includes 13 schools and more than 8,300 students. The smallest district in our region is Beaver County's Midland Borough School District, with 365 students and one school. In one of those regional quirks you'll come to love, Midland Borough high school students actually attend East Liverpool High School across the border in Ohio, because there aren't enough students to support a local high school.

Most districts have separate buildings for elementary, middle, and high schools, but you will find a number of junior-senior high schools. Several of the smallest districts teach all their students, irrespective of grade level, in the same building.

Grade Levels and Nomenclature

As most facets of education in Southwestern Pennsylvania, grade levels and nomenclature are far from standard. Districts tend to group their students into three broad grade levels, but you'll find a great deal of variation in how the levels are defined and what they're called. A common structure is kindergarten through grade 5 for elementary school, grades 6 through 8 for middle school, and grades 9 through 12 for high school. (High schools often are referred to generically as "secondary schools.") A variation is K through 6 for elementary school, 7 through 9 for junior high school, and 10 through 12 for high school. A few school districts divide grades 9 through 12 into intermediate and senior high schools, while a few eliminate the middle level entirely. All school districts offer kindergarten classes, and some have preschool programs.

This may not be the most vital aspect of education in our region, but if you're used to a structure that includes middle schools, for example, you might want to seek out a district that offers such schools.

Standards

Academic standards are a matter of state policy-and an issue that generates more discussion locally than any education-related issue other than school choice. In fact, in the Pennsylvania Legislature regularly considers revamping statewide standards.

Currently, the state wants its students to achieve competence and understanding in the following areas: communications; mathematics; science and technology; environment and ecology; citizenship; arts and humanities; career education and work; wellness and fitness; and home economics, which the state describes as "principles of money management, consumer behavior, and child health." This translates into a variety of required courses at the high school level. These include:

- Language arts, integrating reading, composition, listening, speech, literature, and grammar;
- Mathematics, including problem-solving, algebra, and geometry;
- Science, including at least one laboratory science featuring hands-on experiments;
- Social studies, including Pennsylvania, U.S., and world history, as well as civics, economics, geography, and multicultural studies;
- Environmental education;
- The arts, including art, music, dance, and theater;
- Microcomputers and software;
- Information skills;
- Wellness and fitness, incorporating physical education, aerobic fitness, and alcohol, chemical, and tobacco abuse instruction.

If you were graduated from a Pennsylvania high school,

you may be saying, "Gee, I never had all those courses." You probably did, but not as discrete classes. The state gives school districts the option of folding instruction in these areas into other, related courses.

School districts also must offer vocational-technical education, AIDS prevention courses, at least two languages other than English, and an English program geared to students for whom English is not the "dominant language."

Curriculum

In a refrain you'll hear repeated throughout this chapter, curriculum is largely a district prerogative. Since all school districts must assure that their students meet state standards, the academic core at each curriculum is fairly standard. From there, it's a wide-open affair. Electives vary widely. Driver's education, for example, is among the most popular electives but not universally offered. If you're considering locating in a local school district, one question you'll want to ask will be about electives offered.

Curriculum Enrichment

Enhancing and enriching the classroom experience is an area where Pennsylvania school districts shine. Some years ago, the state realized that teachers and administrators would be too burdened with day-to-day matters to give much consideration to curriculum innovations, so they developed 29 new groups reaching every county of the state and charged them with the mission of innovation. The organizations, known as intermediate units, function in specific geographic areas. Our region boasts seven IUs: IU1, serving Washington, Greene, and Fayette counties; IU2, for Pittsburgh and Mt. Oliver; IU3, the state's largest, covering Allegheny County, except Pittsburgh and Mt. Oliver; IU4, including Butler, Lawrence, and Mercer counties; IU7, for Westmoreland County; IU27, covering the Beaver Valley; and IU28, serving Armstrong and Indiana counties.

The impact of the IUs is varied and broad. Their services range from the Head Start program for preschoolers to programs for gifted students. They work with the Governor's Schools of Excellence, six residential summer programs held on college campuses. In Allegheny County, the IU has worked with four schools to establish a distance learning network; at the same time, the Allegheny Intermediate Unit provides educational services to adjudicated students, such as those at the Shuman Center, the county's principal juvenile detention center. IU1, which works largely with rural school districts, has linked 45 schools in a fiber optic network that provides teleconferencing capability; IU1 also is implementing a mobile computer program that will use vans to deliver computer and Internet capability to schools.

The work of the IUs is challenging and exciting—the Allegheny Intermediate Unit applies 1,500 full- and part-time employees to the task. They're an essential element in Pennsylvania's education system. If there were no IUs, we'd have to invent them.

Textbooks

Since textbook selection is a school district prerogative, the region has no standard textbooks. Rather, there are many. While textbook selection has been a flashpoint in some parts of the country, it's generally been less than incendiary here. The only way you can get involved is to work with your school district.

Teachers

All public school teachers in the Commonwealth must be certified by the Pennsylvania Department of Education, which maintains different requirements for different

INSIDERS' TIP

Information on private schools can be hard to come by because the schools are, well, private. For a comprehensive listing, try the Pennsylvania Education Directory. This annual also lists every public school, by district and county, in the Commonwealth, as well as proprietary and trade schools. You can get yours from Applied Arts Publishers, Box 479, Lebanon, PA 17042-0479, (717) 272-9442. Cost is $14 plus tax, with a $2 discount for educators, school districts, and libraries.

Lab work is an integral part of the education process.

teaching levels. Pennsylvania has reciprocal certification agreements with a number of other states, so if you're a teacher relocating to the Keystone State, you'll still have to apply for your certification, but you may not have to worry about any further requirements.

Hiring policies are pretty much the domain of school districts. A few, such as the Pittsburgh School District, impose residency requirements, but most do not. Virtually all public school teachers in our six-county coverage area are represented by unions the two most prominent are the Pennsylvania State Education Association, an affiliate of the National Education Association, and the Pennsylvania Federation of Teachers, an affiliate of the American Federation of Teachers.

One of the practical implications of the broad teacher unionization in Southwestern Pennsylvania is that as contracts expire, negotiations between unions and their school districts become quite public—and sometimes passionate. With 100 school district-teacher union contracts in the region, bargaining is pretty much a constant. Counting down the days to a potential strike or lockout is something of an annual rite of summer here. Fortunately, delays in the start of the school year are averted most of the time.

Special and Gifted Education

While all states require programs for students judged exceptional—often called special education—Pennsylvania is among the minority of states that also requires educational programs for those deemed gifted. The rules for both sets of programs are fairly similar. In each case, the designation "exceptional" or "gifted" is determined through a process called a multidisciplinary review, which may be requested by the school or a parent. In all cases, the schools prefer to consider parents part of the evaluation team and seek parental consent for, and participation in, the review. Where parental consent is withheld, the district may seek a court order for a review, but this is rare.

If the review panel determines that a student needs special programs, these may be provided through the district and specially assembled Individualized Educational Teams, or the students may be referred to one of 11 special services schools in our region, including the Western Pennsylvania School for the Blind and the Western Pennsylvania School for the Deaf. In a related program, preschoolers under the age of 5 may be eligible for a school-district's early intervention services following an evaluation; parents may request that evaluation.

EDUCATION

That gives you some background on the rules, but it doesn't begin to describe the variety of programs for exceptional and gifted students. The state provides overall supervision but expects school districts to develop and fund their own programs. The Pittsburgh School District operates three centers that offer specially designed instruction for exceptional children; other districts offer their services on site. Similarly, in the area of gifted education, the Pittsburgh School District maintains special centers that elementary and middle school students attend one day per week; high school students, on the other hand, typically receive their special programs on site.

While there's no charge to parents for special or gifted education programs, there's no end to the variations in the ways area school districts provide these programs. If you're considering locating here, this is clearly an area you'll want to explore.

Alternative Education

Many districts provide alternative programming for suspended students and others who need support due to behavioral and academic difficulties. These may be site-based programs or schools dedicated to alternative education. The Pittsburgh School District, to cite one important example, offers both types of programming. Its alternative elementary school programs are site-based, while middle school and high school students may be assigned to dedicated buildings. If you have the opportunity to choose your school district, you may want to inquire about its alternative education programs.

School Choice

This has been perhaps the hottest topic in the impassioned debates about education in Southwestern Pennsylvania, usually triggered by the busing plans that several districts employ to achieve racial balance in their schools. Groups rally round the "busing" and "neighborhood schools" flags with vigor and conviction. The issue, however, may be more symbolic than an actual concern, since even the few districts that bus students tend to keep it to a minimum. Thus, the number of students affected by busing is relatively few.

A more far-reaching component of the school choice debate involves the possibility of public financial support for parents who opt to send their children to private schools. Advocates have proposed publicly supported tuition vouchers for students who attend private schools. While this proposal has failed to carry the Pennsylvania Legislature, look for this debate to continue.

For many students and their families, the debate about choice is theoretical, as students in most cases are required to attend the schools designated by the districts in which they reside. There are several opportunities for choice.

Under state law, students may opt to attend public schools outside their district, provided they pay tuition to the schools they attend. Tuition rates are established by the state, based on the cost of education in each district; among Allegheny County school districts, annual tuition rates range from approximately $5,000 to $11,100. You will find a catch here, however. No school district is required to accept students from other districts. So even if you're willing to pay the price for sending your child outside your district, you need the cooperation of the other school district.

Yet another element of choice is provided by the Pittsburgh School District through its "magnet schools" program. Magnets are elementary and secondary schools that focus on particular areas of study. Since one of the goals of the magnet program is to achieve racial balance through voluntary choice, 50 percent of slots at each magnet are reserved for African-American students, 50 percent for students of other races. Some magnet options are sequential, beginning in kindergarten and continuing through middle school and high school. Some give preference to younger siblings of those enrolled in magnet programs, or to students who reside in particular neighborhoods.

At the high school level, the district offers magnets in international studies, creative and performing arts, pre-

INSIDERS' TIP

The Fox Chapel School District and the Keystone Oaks School District have connected their respective buildings with fiber optic networks. They utilize their networks in a variety of ways, including student-produced video news magazines transmitted daily to each school.

engineering, computer science, teaching, law and public service, junior ROTC, public safety, high technology, and vocational-technical training, as well as one called a "Traditional Academy" in a highly structured and disciplined setting. Other magnets are available at the elementary and middle school levels.

Magnets are open to students throughout the city, so long as racial balances are preserved; when there are more applicants than a school can accommodate, slots are awarded by lottery.

Charter Schools

The sentiment for school choice has inspired a new type of educational option in the region— charter schools. In June 1997, Pennsylvania became the 27th state to enact legislation authorizing charter schools, which may be defined as independent public schools that are designed by individuals or groups to fulfill a specific educational mission. Each charter school must be approved and funded by the local school district in which the charter school is located. Any students can opt to attend charter schools in their districts, and no tuition charges are permitted.

In early 1998, school boards reviewed and approved a number of proposed charter schools. As a result, the first charter schools in Southwestern Pennsylvania opened their doors in September 1998. Among these were Manchester Academic Charter School, Urban League of Pittsburgh Charter School, and the Thurgood Marshall Academy. Recently, a new charter school, the Career Connections Charter School, was opened, accommodating ninth graders only in 2000, with plans to add other grades. While the missions of charter schools differ, most plan longer school days and school years than found in traditional schools.

If a charter school sounds like an option you'd like to consider, you'll find several sources of information about them. Locally, Duquesne University has established the Charter Schools Project, (412) 396-4492, which tracks charter school information and has staged conferences about the subject. The U.S. Department of Education Office of Educational Research and Improvement has undertaken a four-year study of charter schools in America and published a first-year report. It's available at several web sites: www.uscharterschools.org. and www.ed.gov/pubs/charter.

Transportation

The groundswell of support for school choice is manifest in the area of transportation as well. Under state law, school districts may provide transportation for their students, or they can elect not to. A number opt out of transportation, forcing students to find their own way to school. Why would they impose this requirement on their students? It might be because state law also mandates that districts providing transportation for their students must provide the same type of transportation for nonpublic school students within their districts. Moreover, students can attend nonpublic schools up to 10 miles beyond a district's borders and still be eligible for free district-provided transportation.

Some public school districts have contested this requirement; the Pittsburgh School District filed and lost court action against the requirement, pointing out that transportation for nonpublic students—by bus, van, and cab—accounts for about 28 percent of its annual transportation budget.

The purpose of the policy, of course, is to make it easier and less expensive for parents to choose private schools for their children. Whether or not you agree with the policy of public financing for certain aspects of private schools, there's no doubt that the state's transportation program has made private schools more accessible to more families.

Home Schooling

The increase in home schooling throughout the Commonwealth is one final ramification of the thrust for school choice. Since 1986, parents, guardians, and legal custodians have been authorized to teach their children at home. In 1988-1989, the statewide total of children so taught was 2,152; by 1996-1997, the total had grown to 17,861. In our six-county service area, 99 of 100 school districts reported at least one student being taught at home. The only exception: Clairton City School District in southern Allegheny County.

Those teaching their children at home must file an annual home education affidavit with their school districts. This notarized document must specify the name of the home education supervisor, an outline by subject area of proposed educational objectives, and evidence of each child's immunization and access to health services. The affidavit also must specify any curriculum materials—including textbooks—to be borrowed from the school district.

In many cases, school districts welcome home-taught children to the fold, opening their extracurricular activities to such students. In other districts, home-taught children will feel like beggars at the feast, with districts grudgingly agreeing to their participation in school activities. If you plan to teach your children at home but want them to enjoy some of the socialization benefits of group schooling, the best approach may be to discuss your plans with district and school administrators. At the very least, you'll get a good idea where you stand.

Athletics

Interscholastic athletics in Pennsylvania is largely the domain of the Pennsylvania Interscholastic Athletic Agency (PIAA)—its administrative unit in our region is the Western Pennsylvania Interscholastic Athletic League (WPIAL). PIAA rules and regulations govern interscholastic sports for 1,300 schools in the Commonwealth—including 130 private schools—and 225,000 students. The PIAA operates and organizes championships in 11 boys' sports and 10 girls' sports.

The roster of interscholastic sports offered varies from district to district, but among the most popular are baseball, basketball, cross country, football, soccer, swimming and diving, tennis, and track and field for boys, and basketball, cross country, field hockey, soccer, softball, swimming and diving, tennis, track and field, and volleyball for girls. You'll also find interscholastic programs in bowling, golf, ice hockey, lacrosse, and rifle. Most districts also maintain active intramural programs.

To assure fair and fun competition, the PIAA classifies its member high schools by enrollment, with categories ranging from Class A for the smallest schools to Class AAAA—Quad A, as it's known—for the largest schools. Classifications may vary from sport to sport. For example, a high school with 175 boys in grades 9 through 12 would play in Class A in baseball but in Class AA in basketball. The PIAA modifies its classification guidelines as enrollment fluctuations dictate. For the most current classifications, playoff schedules and other PIAA news, check out the agency's web site, www.piaa.org.

Keep in mind that if your children want to participate in interscholastic sports, they must maintain certain academic standards. Generally, the WPIAL requires a 1.5 grade point average for sports participation. School districts, however, have the option to impose more stringent standards. The City of Pittsburgh has done that, requiring a 2.0 grade point average of its student-athletes.

Parent Involvement

The fragmentation of government in Southwestern Pennsylvania may be lamentable in some areas, but the great number and diversity of schools and school districts in the region provide unusually rich opportunities for parent involvement in their youngsters' education. Parent-teacher organizations are a traditional model for parent involvement, but there are others that afford a more hands-on approach. Consider the Pittsburgh School District as an example. In the city, each school has a Parent School Community Council that works with administrators on such operational areas as curriculum and other academic programs. In all, these councils involve about 1,400 people in the administrative process.

INSIDERS' TIP

Public schools in our region are supported by the proceeds of wage taxes, real estate taxes, and a number of smaller taxes.

With 100 school districts in the region, voters must elect 900 school board members. You may never have considered public service as an elected official, but Southwestern Pennsylvania provides you with that chance. Many school board members have little prior political experience; they became involved because they wanted to help their children as the youngsters progressed through the system.

If you do consider a run for a school board seat, re-

If you're considering college in the Commonwealth, it will be worth your while to become familiar with the Pennsylvania Higher Education Assistance Agency, the state's most important source of financial aid for college and university students. In 1997, PHEAA's loans, grants and other financial assistance totaled more than $293 million, a stunning amount. What's more, PHEAA offers more than financial aid alone, valuable though its dollars may be. Its Early Awareness Program, for example, introduces middle school students and their families to the benefits of early planning for higher education.

You can reach PHEAA in a number of ways. For loan information, the best number is (800) 692-7392, while for grant information, it's (800) 692-7435. You can write PHEAA at 1200 North Seventh St., Harrisburg, PA 17102-1444, or visit their web site, www.pheaa.org.

member that this is full-fledged politics. The parties nominate their candidates in primary elections, with the winners determined in general elections. While some seats are uncontested, other elections are intense, involving media coverage and debate that may be less than genteel. Electoral politics is not for all tastes, but if you can endure the rough and tumble nature of elections, a school board seat may await you.

Diocesan Schools

Diocesan schools are a powerful and important force in our region. If you considered the Catholic schools of the Diocese of Pittsburgh a school district, they would constitute the fourth largest school district in the Commonwealth. The Diocese of Pittsburgh and the Diocese of Greensburg include all six counties in our principal coverage area. Together, they operate 154 schools—including 13 high schools—that serve more than 40,000 students.

Each diocese is divided into administrative units known as deaneries that include elementary and secondary schools, or elementary schools only. The two deaneries in Washington County, for example, offer elementary schools only, so graduates of those schools will have to travel a bit to continue their education at a diocesan secondary school. Teachers at most—but not all—diocesan high schools are represented by the Federation of Pittsburgh Diocesan Teachers.

The emphasis on academics at diocesan schools is tangible. Diocese of Pittsburgh secondary schools send 96 percent of their graduates on for further education, an impressive statistic. The high schools typically offer extensive honors and advanced placement programs as well as innovative college-in-high school programs that inspire and prepare students for higher education.

Diocesan schools are private, so state mandates for gifted and special education don't apply to them in the same ways as they do to public schools. However, public school districts include students of diocesan schools in some of their programs for exceptional children. In two of its high schools, the Diocese of Pittsburgh also offers a noncollege-directed curriculum for developmentally challenged students, who take most courses in a resource room but share some regular courses with the general student body.

The range of extracurricular activities available to students is broad, including clubs for drama, instrumental and vocal music, and forensics, as well as school newspapers and yearbooks. In athletics, the schools participate with public schools in the Western Pennsylvania Interscholastic Athletic League in such activities as baseball, basketball, bowling, crew, cross country, field hockey, football, golf, ice hockey, lacrosse, soccer, softball, swimming, tennis, track, volleyball, and wrestling. Note that some schools offer a number of these sports as club or intramural activities, rather than as interscholastic sports, and that some diocesan high schools impose more stringent grade requirements than does the WPIAL.

Since diocesan schools are private, they maintain both admissions standards and tuition charges. While admission is generally open, the schools will review placement tests, academic records, and personal interviews. Many schools offer financial aid programs, with need assessment performed by an independent outside agency, as well as work-study programs. In the

EDUCATION

Diocese of Pittsburgh, all students are eligible for support from the Bishop's Education Fund, which offers need-based grants.

The schools welcome parental involvement through such vehicles as school, parent advisory, and development boards, and activity booster organizations—these are particularly supportive of athletic and musical activities. If diocesan schools sound like an option you'd like to explore, you can contact the Diocese of Pittsburgh Education Secretariat at (412) 456-3100 or visit the web site for the Diocese of Greensburg, www.catholicgbg.org, for information on schools. These sources may also be able to refer you to Catholic education contacts in other districts.

Other Private Schools

If you're shopping for a private school, you'll find a rich variety in Southwestern Pennsylvania. The region boasts a wide assortment of college prep schools, religion-focused schools, and those targeted to students with special needs. We've presented profiles of schools that offer high school education—private grade schools would be too numerous to cover effectively—but where such schools offer primary education as well, we've noted that. Unless otherwise noted, the schools charge tuition and are coeducational.

Keep in mind that private schools are just that—private. They operate largely outside the purview of the State Department of Education and so are free to establish their own guidelines and policies in most areas of operation. If you're researching private schools, ask as many questions as you can, as their programs and policies vary widely.

North

Bethel Christian Academy
2438 California Ave., Pittsburgh
• **(412) 321-6333**

Bethel Christian Academy, located on Pittsburgh's North Side, offers kindergarten, elementary, and high school programs that employ Accelerated Christian Education, an individualized learning program that enables students to learn at their own pace. Each classroom is equipped with a computer, and high school students have the opportunity for more extensive classwork on computers. The Pittsburgh-Mt. Oliver Intermediate Unit provides remedial services where needed to Bethel Christian students.

Students compete with other Christian schools in such sports as soccer, volleyball, and basketball. They also bring their own lunches, because Bethel Christian does not provide them. You can opt to pay tuition in 10 monthly installments. Bethel Christian is a day school.

Shadyside Academy
423 Fox Chapel Rd.,
Fox Chapel
• **(412) 968-3000**

Founded in 1883, Shadyside is the region's largest private school, with its junior, middle, and senior schools. The senior school (high school) offers a five-day boarding program, an attractive and unusual asset; 500 students are enrolled in the senior school alone. The campuses span 172 acres, 25 buildings, and 10 athletic fields. (If you're interested in the junior school, it's located in the East End of the City of Pittsburgh in a neighborhood called Park Place.)

Shady Side's emphasis on college preparation is strong; typically 100 percent of graduates attend four-year colleges or universities. Distinguished alumni include Pulitzer Prize-winning author and historian David McCullough and former astronaut Jay Apt, who once served as director of Pittsburgh's Carnegie Museum of Natural History. The school boasts a student-teacher ratio of 9:1. Shady Side provides financial aid—most of it need-based—to more than 15 percent of its students.

Students participate in more than 50 clubs and are invited to become involved in the school's operations through membership on committees for curriculum, admissions, discipline, and independent study. For hands-on environmental study, Shady Side's Maine Coast Semester affords students the chance to live on a working farm for half a school year. Shady Side's varsity athletic teams com-

INSIDERS' TIP

For more on the Pittsburgh Public Schools, see the district's home page, www.pps.pgh.pa.us/. If homeschooling is more your bailiwick, check out www.pahomeschoolers.com/.

EDUCATION

pete in the Western Pennsylvania Interscholastic Athletic League as well as head-to-head with other independent schools.

If you're thinking about applying to the senior school, Shady Side requires both an interview and a campus tour.

Vincentian Academy— Duquesne University
Peebles and McKnight Rds., McCandless
• (412) 635-5200

Vincentian Academy's relationship with Duquesne University is a strong attraction. The academy is linked to Duquesne's computer network, bringing its students access to that resource. Vincentian also is part of Duquesne's Campus Ministries Program to assist in its commitment to values and public service. Perhaps most importantly, Vincentian graduates who enroll at Duquesne University are eligible for both automatic admission and 25 percent tuition scholarships. The academy emphasizes that it expects and encourages its students to enroll at prestigious colleges and universities across the country rather than at Duquesne exclusively. Still, having that admission in the bank can be quite a comfort.

Located in Pittsburgh's North Hills, Vincentian is a day school that participates in the International Baccalaureate, an academic program offered by more than 700 schools worldwide. The IB program strives for a balanced education that facilitates geographic and cultural mobility and promotes international understanding through shared academic experiences. The curriculum includes studies in language, individuals and societies, experimental sciences, mathematics, and a range of electives. One specific advantage of an IB Diploma: a number of colleges and universities grant up to a year's academic credit for students who earn it.

The student-teacher ratio is an appealing 7:1. Vincentian offers financial aid but describes the program as "limited." Students participate in 11 sports and more than two dozen additional extracurricular activities. If someone in your family is interested in Vincentian, take advantage of the school's "shadowing" program, which invites prospective students to spend a day with current students.

East

The Ellis School
6425 Fifth Ave., Pittsburgh
• (412) 661-4880

Founded in 1916, Ellis is an independent school for girls in kindergarten through 12th grade. Its 7-acre campus lies in Pittsburgh's Shadyside neighborhood, just a quick bus trip from all the amenities of Oakland's university complex. Some statistics about Ellis will tell you much about the school. Its student-teacher ratio is 8:1, while its student-computer ratio is 4:1. Of the seniors among the 460 students, each typically is enrolled in at least one advanced placement course.

The academic program at Ellis blends required courses with a diverse menu of electives. All 9th graders, for example, study the Concepts of Physics, which kicks off a three-year science sequence that also includes chemistry and biology. Ninth graders also write at least 10 papers for English class and a research paper in the social sciences. On the other hand, more than 90 percent of students opt for electives in the fine arts. In addition to their class work, students provide volunteer service for more than 60 organizations.

Ellis administers tests to all applicants for admission. These usually are scheduled in December and January, but the school will make special arrangements to accommodate your schedule. More than 15 percent of Ellis students receive financial aid.

Heritage Christian School
200 Elicker Rd., Plum
• (412) 795-3311

A member of the American Association of Christian Schools, Heritage Christian School offers kindergarten through twelfth grade education based on the philosophy that the school is an extension of the Christian home. Textbooks are Bible-based, and the school itself operates from Bible Baptist Church in the eastern suburb of Plum.

The school bases its calendar and certain graduation requirements on the state's public school guidelines, but it also features a number of

INSIDERS' TIP
If you're an early riser, you can learn more about the Pittsburgh School District and Diocese of Pittsburgh schools by listening to radio station KQV-AM, 1410 on the dial, on Sunday mornings. The Diocese airs *Pittsburgh Catholic Schools: Education Plus* at 6 AM, while the Pittsburgh School District airs *Focus: Education* at 7:05 AM. Air times are subject to change.

EDUCATION

variations. Admissions, which are based on an interview, academic performance, and placement testing, always are granted on a probationary basis, giving the school an opportunity to determine how students handle the traditional structure of Heritage Christian, which maintains a dress code and other conduct guidelines more stringent than public schools. Conveniently, the school offers an after-school ride program for those students whose parents are unable to pick them up when the school day ends.

Parents may opt to pay tuition for their children in 10 monthly installments.

The Kiski School
1888 Brett Ln., Saltsburg
• (724) 639-3586

In 1878, ambitious developers constructed a rambling Victorian hotel on the cliffs above the Kiskiminetas River in the Westmoreland County town of Saltsburg to serve pilgrims who flocked to the area for the alleged curative powers of its mineral springs. The "Magic Waters" soon dried up, leaving the hotel for purchase and conversion to the Kiskiminetas School For Boys At Saltsburg. It flourishes still on that site, but today, it's known more simply as The Kiski School.

It's a 350-acre, residential, college preparatory school for 250 boys from grades 9 through 12. The academic schedule is demanding and Kiski doesn't apologize for it, claiming that a rigorous approach "is designed to allow a boy to enter a college equal to his ability and to succeed once he is there." Average class size is 10. Homework averages one hour per class meeting, and just to be sure underclassmen are completing that homework, Kiski conducts a two-hour supervised study period each evening. The school requires three years of language study and a Life Skills course, which includes instruction in computer literacy, health and wellness, and speech.

Kiski is serious about athletics as well. If you don't plan to participate in an interscholastic sport in each of the three athletic seasons, you may arrange an "alternate physical development activity" with the permission of the athletic director or headmaster. You'll find other extracurricular activities—including 30 special interest activities—that aren't quite so mandatory, as well as a summer program of classes and sports.

Among Kiski's most distinguished alumni is Bob Mathias, the first man to win the Olympic decathlon twice (1948 and 1952). An equally impressive achievement: Kiski's headmaster,

John A. "Jack" Pidgeon, has served in that position continuously since 1957. "If I had only one rule for the boys," the Headmaster writes, "I think it would be 'Behave like gentlemen,' which implies a rather complete code of conduct."

The Oakland School
362 McKee Pl., Pittsburgh
• (412) 621-7878

If you're looking for individualized education for your children, you'll find it at The Oakland School, where the average class size is 6. To maintain that class size, this day school limits its total enrollment to 60 students. The school is coeducational and situated in the heart of Oakland's university-medical complex, from which it draws both energy and resources.

The academic program includes studies in communications, mathematics, arts, humanities, science, social studies and computer education, as well as programs in up to six foreign languages, depending upon student interest: Latin, French, Spanish, German, Japanese, and Russian. Students may participate in a wide variety of extracurricular activities and are required to perform community service. A work study program provides students with academic credit for field experience, while a mentor program pairs students with staff advisors. The Oakland School describes its financial aid opportunities as "limited."

Trinity Christian School
299 Ridge Ave., Forest Hills
• (412) 242-8886

Since 1953, Trinity Christian School has been "educating students for a lifetime of learning and service to God," as the school describes its mission. The program is based on the Reformed tradition, but these days school welcomes all. Its 370 students in kindergarten through high school represent nearly 100 churches. More than 90 percent of Trinity Christian graduates seek higher education. The school enhances its curriculum with honors programs in physics, calculus, and advanced mathematics. Facilities include computer and photography labs as well as an art room and soccer and softball fields.

The Winchester Thurston School
555 Morewood Ave., Pittsburgh
• (412) 578-7500

Winchester Thurston boasts two campuses—a campus in Pittsburgh's Shadyside neighborhood for students from kindergarten readiness through grade 12, and a campus in the northern suburb of Allison Park for students in kindergarten through grade 5. In all, the school serves about 600 students with an attractive student-teacher ratio of 9:1, affording each student a great deal of individualized attention.

The school has undergone changes in recent years. From its founding in 1887 through 1991, Winchester Thurston admitted girls only. Beginning in 1991, boys were phased in, so that the school is now fully coeducational. All receive strong preparation for college, as evidenced by the class of 1999. Of graduates that year, 96 percent went on to four-year colleges or universities, while the balance deferred their college plans.

Areas of study include English, social studies, modern and classical languages, science, mathematics, health and physical education, computers, and visual and performing arts. Winchester Thurston encourages students to enhance their classroom instruction by taking advantage of the many cultural amenities of the nearby Oakland university-medical complex, and through participation in extracurricular activities. In addition to athletics, these include more than 30 clubs and activities that focus on interests as diverse as rocketry; poetry; math; world affairs; and the student newspaper, yearbook, and literary magazine. Students also may take advantage of opportunities for international travel, study, and exchanges.

Admission requirements include academic testing, which typically is scheduled in January and February. Financial aid takes the form of need-based grants.

Yeshiva Schools of Pittsburgh
2100 Wightman St., Pittsburgh
• (412) 422-7315

The goal of Yeshiva Schools, located in Pittsburgh's Squirrel Hill neighborhood, is to offer a traditional Jewish education that combines an emphasis on moral values and a comprehensive secular education. Classes range from Tiny Tots through high school, with boys and girls in separate classes and buildings once they reach high school. Total enrollment is 425.

For high school students, the secular curriculum focuses on the development of analytical and communications skills, while the Jewish Studies curriculum includes coursework in Jewish Law and History, Jewish Philosophy, and Bible and Prophets with Commentaries. Students participate in a wide range of community projects, including a weekly hospital visitation program.

Yeshiva is such a magnet for Jewish youths that about 5 percent of its students come from out of town and board with local friends of the Yeshiva. In 2000, Yeshiva Schools of Pittsburgh was awarded the prestigious Blue Ribbon Award of Excellence from the U.S. Department of Education.

West

INSIDERS' TIP
If you want to get involved with education policy for the region, try the Education Policy and Issue Center and the Commission of Workplace Excellence, (412) 281-2000. The groups are a collaborative effort of business, civic, education, and philanthropic leaders dedicated to developing public policy strategies for education and workforce development.

Sewickley Academy
315 Academy Ave., Sewickley
• (412) 741 2230

The facilities at Sewickley Academy are outstanding. Over its 21 acres about 12 miles northwest of downtown Pittsburgh, this day school boasts two libraries; six science labs; three computer labs; four athletic fields; two gyms; studios for music, dance and art; a 635-seat auditorium; an art gallery; three playgrounds; and two tennis courts. That's enough to make a college jealous.

The academy offers an early childhood program as well as lower, middle, and senior schools; total enrollment is around 800 students, with an overall student-teacher ratio of 8:1. In the senior school, the academy supplements its core curriculum with a variety of electives and study abroad options. These include programs in Paris, Munich, and Sydney. On the domestic front, students can opt for a Maine Coast Semester, which focuses on environmental studies.

The academy requires community service and gives seniors the option of undertaking a two-week field project to learn about career opportunities. Prospective students are evaluated on the basis of previous school records, teacher recommendations, an entrance examination, and an interview. Sewickley Academy provides financial aid to about 20 percent of its students.

EDUCATION

Higher Education

LOOK FOR:
• Colleges and
  Universities
  throughout
  Western
  Pennsylvania

It would be hard to imagine a richer selection of educational options than those offered by the colleges and universities of Southwestern Pennsylvania. In our six-county coverage area, there are no fewer than 31 degree-granting institutions with a compelling diversity of academic programs, campus settings, and social and extracurricular opportunities.

You'll find private institutions, institutions owned by the state, and those that are somewhere in between; colleges with large enrollments spread over multiple campuses and colleges with fewer than 1,000 students; schools that focus on the liberal arts and those that emphasize technical disciplines; colleges that pulsate with the rhythm of urban Pittsburgh and those set in idyllic locales. Even in their diversity, colleges and universities are a powerful force in the region.

Most of these institutions have proud histories that span many decades if not centuries. That's not to say, however, that higher education is static. In fact, few sectors have been more dynamic in recent years. As the market for traditional-aged students has become more competitive, colleges and universities have changed accordingly. For many years the region had four institutions that admitted one gender only; three of those now are coed. Our liberal arts colleges have implemented career-related thrusts, and our technical institutes have introduced core curricula in the liberal arts.

A common denominator has been the expansion of services for nontraditional students. What this means for you is an unprecedented range of continuing education courses—both for credit and leisure learning—that the institutions often will deliver to your worksite or neighborhood.

It's an exciting scene, one you'll want to explore. We've profiled the local institutions that offer associate, baccalaureate, or graduate degrees, capturing the highlights of their academic and continuing education programs, campus life, and opportunities for social and educational enrichment. *Peterson's Guide to Colleges in the Middle Atlantic States* is a source for some of our information. Where institutions maintain multiple campuses, we've profiled each campus separately, in case you're targeting schools in specific geographic areas.

Downtown

Duquesne University
600 Forbes Ave., Pittsburgh
• **(412) 396-6000**

Duquesne University opened its doors in 1878 as the Pittsburgh Catholic College of the Holy Ghost, with an enrollment of 40 students.

To say that the university has grown would be an understatement. Today, Duquesne boasts a student enrollment of more than 9,400, and it's one of the most important educational institutions in the region. Its 43-acre campus sits on "The Bluff," a hill overlooking both Downtown Pittsburgh and the Monongahela River. The excitement of Downtown is only a few blocks away, but in the seclusion of The Bluff, Duquesne is very nearly a self-contained community.

Within the university, nine schools of study offer baccalaureate, master's, and doctorate degree programs, many developed as partnerships with local corporations and philanthropists. These include the Bayer School of Natural and Environmental Sciences, developed with the support of the Bayer Corporation, and the A.J. Palumbo School of Business Administration. The Mylan School of Pharmacy features a six-year doctor of pharmacy program, while the Rangos School of Health Sciences offers programs in physical and occupational therapy, physician assistant, and perfusion technology. You'll also find schools of law, education, music, and nursing. The university offers a variety of study-abroad programs through affiliations with institutions in Spain, Colombia, France, and Belgium. In addition, Duquesne confers many graduate degrees (both master's and doctorate) in a multitude of disciplines. More than 78 percent of students receive some form of financial aid.

Continuing education plays an important role at Duquesne. The university's Saturday College program leads to a bachelor's degree in professional studies and a master's degree in leadership and liberal studies. The university customizes leadership training programs for onsite delivery to local corporations, and it participates in the educational consortium that provides programs at the Harrisburg Dixon Center in the state capital.

About 57 percent of the undergraduate students live on campus, where they enjoy computer access in every dorm room. In fact, Duquesne was named one of the nation's 100 "most wired" colleges and universities by Ya-hoo! Internet Life for two consecutive years. Student activities take on a strong communications flavor, as students participate in the campus newspaper, The Duke, and two radio stations. WDSR is a campus-only station, while WDUQ-FM is a National Public Radio affiliate that broadcasts a full schedule of public affairs, jazz, and sports programming to the entire community.

Speaking of sports, Duquesne's varsity basketball teams participate in the NCAA Division I Atlantic 10 Conference, while it's men's football program is a member of NCAA Division I-AA. For a more detailed look at Duquesne basketball, see our Spectator Sports chapter.

Duquesne is a Catholic university—its formal name is Duquesne University of the Holy Ghost. When you study here, you'll find an emphasis on values. Duquesne has stressed that emphasis in a variety of advertising campaigns, perhaps an unusual pitch for a university in a highly competitive market. Duquesne's continued growth demonstrates how well that competitive market has responded.

Point Park College
201 Wood St., Pittsburgh
• (412) 391-4100

If you're looking for a college in the heart of Downtown Pittsburgh, look no further. Despite its name, Point Park College is not located exactly in Point State Park. It is, however, squarely in the center of Pittsburgh's business district, which provides it with energy and excitement.

The college offers its 2,300 full- and part-time students more than 50 academic programs leading to associate and baccalaureate degrees. Point Park is especially known for its programs in performing arts and communications, represented by majors in children's theater, dance, film and video production, journalism and communications, and theater arts. In addition, Point Park awards the master of arts in journalism and communications as well as the master of business administration. Classes at Point Park average 15 to 20 students.

The college's facilities also have the distinctive flavor of communications and performing arts. You'll find seven dance studios, a color television studio, a newsroom, a desktop publishing laboratory, and a radio station. Performing arts students gain practical experience at the landmark Pittsburgh Playhouse of Point Park College, located in Pittsburgh's Oakland neighborhood, about 3 miles from the college. The Playhouse, which the college has owned and run since 1968, typically hosts 15 productions each year.

If your schedule won't allow you to attend weekday classes, consider Point Park's "Saturday Fast" program, where you can earn

INSIDERS' TIP

In today's competitive market, local universities will go to great lengths to accommodate students. How far will they go? In 1997, Duquesne University staged a special commencement ceremony for one graduate, an Orthodox Jewish student who could not participate in the general commencement because it fell on the Jewish Sabbath.

HIGHER EDUCATION

your baccalaureate degree in business or applied corporate communications after two years of Saturday-only classes. The college offers the Saturday Fast program at its downtown campus, at Beaver County Community College, and at a satellite site in Cranberry, Butler County.

About 40 percent of the full-time students reside on campus in a 21-story dormitory that once was a hotel. Point Park sponsors six varsity sports and competes in the Keystone-Empire Collegiate Conference of the National Association of Intercollegiate Athletics. Extracurricular activities include ad, television, environmental, health, and ski clubs, and the Cavalcade literary magazine. About 90 percent of Point Park students receive some form of financial aid.

Robert Morris College
Pittsburgh Center
600 Fifth Ave., Pittsburgh
• **(412) 227-6857**

While we've profiled the main, Moon Township campus of Robert Morris College in the "West" section of this chapter, we'd be remiss if we didn't note RMC's Pittsburgh Center in Downtown Pittsburgh. At its Pittsburgh Center, RMC provides an appealing roster of continuing education programs, including programs for professional and career development; professional designation and certification; prelicensing and relicensing; certificates; supervisory and leadership development; and professional skills-building.

The center is only two blocks from Grant Street, the hub of Pittsburgh's political activity, and a quick walk from such major employment centers as USX Tower, One Oxford Centre, and One Mellon Bank Center. Most courses are offered in the evening, and the college will customize courses for delivery at worksites.

North

Butler County Community College
College Dr., Butler
• **(724) 287-8711**

Chartered in 1966, BCCC was the region's first community college. It serves more than 3,000 enrolled students and a total of 14,000 people who take advantage of the college's many educational opportunities. BCCC awards three degrees—associate of arts, associate of science, and associate of applied science—but its reach extends far beyond degree programs.

The college offers for-credit courses at three community sites: Cranberry Community College Center in Butler County, Lawrence County Area Vocational Technical School in New Castle, and Lenape Area Vocational Technical School in Ford City, Armstrong County. In addition, BCCC provides an extensive schedule of leisure-learn courses in such areas as occupational advancement, public safety, literacy, and computers. Its Business and Industry Training Institute works with local businesses on training and productivity programs, while its Center for Economic Education provides workshops and instructional materials for elementary and secondary economics teachers.

The sprawling, 13-building campus is set on 323 acres of rolling hills with venerable oak trees. Among those buildings are the computer learning center, where students may access terminals, and the student union. The field house features a basketball court that converts to tennis courts, volleyball courts, a batting cage, racquetball courts, and weight lifting apparatus, while outdoor facilities include golfing areas and jogging and walking trails—many available for community use.

BCCC maintains an open admissions policy—all high school graduates and those with diploma equivalents are granted admission. Tuition is three-tiered. The tuition for Butler County residents is half that for residents of other Pennsylvania counties, which in turn is two-thirds of the charge for out-of-state residents. The college offers a diverse financial aid program.

Community College of
Allegheny County
800 Allegheny Ave., Pittsburgh
• **(412) 323-2323**

The reach of the Community College of Allegheny County is hard to overestimate. It's the largest community college in Pennsylvania, with more than 25,000 enrolled students. Among the reasons for CCAC's popularity are its open admissions policy and a tuition schedule that favors local residents. Tuition for Allegheny County residents is half that of tuition for residents of other Pennsylvania counties, and one-third the charge for out-of-state residents. Roughly 40 percent of students receive financial aid.

It's more than attractive tuition that draws students to CCAC, as the college offers over 200 academic programs leading to the associate of arts, the associate of science, and the associate of applied sciences degrees. In addition, stu-

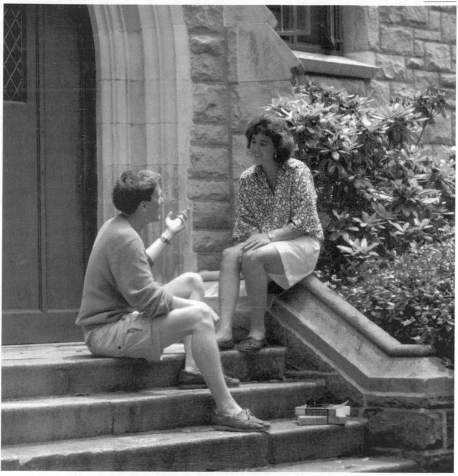

Students chat on the campus of Westminster College, one of the many in Western Pennsylvania's belt of small colleges and universities.

Photo: Rich Smaltz courtesy of Westminster College

dents in CCAC's elementary education program can earn baccalaureate degrees from Indiana University of Pennsylvania while studying at CCAC. The average age of CCAC students is nearly 30, indicating that many are returning to studies after an extended absence.

While the college's academic programs defy easy summary, many are part of the following broad departments: arts and humanities; information sciences; business and accounting; mathematics and science; allied health programs; nursing; social sciences; and engineering technologies. Through the information sciences program, students earn degrees and certificates in office technology and court reporting. Students in allied health programs may specialize in nuclear medicine, radiation therapy,

or diagnostic medical sonography, while nursing students can participate in cooperative education programs with more than 200 area health care agencies.

In a word, CCAC is accessible. It maintains four area campuses, in addition to its North Side administrative offices, for the convenience of students—you'll find profiles of these in the "North," "East," and "South" sections of this chapter. The average class size is 20, and students have access to more than 1,500 microcomputers linked across the campuses by local area network. The campuses together boast more than 1 million square feet of classroom space and more than 200,000 volumes in their libraries. CCAC offers child care centers at each campus as well as intramural and varsity sports.

If you're a Pennsylvania resident or thinking of relocating to the Commonwealth, you'll want to become familiar with the State System of Higher Education, the administrative agency for 14 universities in Pennsylvania. We've profiled the three member universities in our coverage area—California, Indiana, and Slippery Rock. You'll find the other 11 in Bloomsburg, Cheyney, Clarion, East Stroudsburg, Edinboro, Kutztown, Lock Haven, Mansfield, Millersville, Shippensburg, and West Chester,

It's a large system encompassing more than 94,000 students. One of the most important features of the system is the attractive tuition for state residents—generally several thousand dollars lower than what out-of-state students and their families pay. It's no accident that 92 percent of system students are Pennsylvania residents.

While the sports line-up varies from campus to campus, the teams participate in three conferences: the Western Pennsylvania Collegiate Conference, the Pennsylvania Collegiate Athletic Association, and the National Junior College Athletic Association. About the only thing you won't find at any of the sites is on-campus housing.

Among the most impressive and attractive aspects of CCAC is its broad program of continuing education. In addition to programs at its four campuses, the college maintains eight off-campus continuing education centers—in Bethel Park, Braddock, Downtown, Homewood-Brushton, McKeesport, Neville Island, Robinson, and Turtle Creek—where more than 62,000 people participate in continuing education and community service programs. Even more impressive, CCAC delivers continuing education programs—many of them customized corporate training programs—to more than 400 off-campus sites.

Community College of Allegheny County—Allegheny Campus
808 Ridge Ave., Pittsburgh
• (412) 237-2525

Located on the North Side near CCAC's administrative offices, the Allegheny Campus is the largest of the college's four campuses, with more than 8,600 students. The campus is a blend of stately older buildings that trace their roots to the early 19th century and modern structures built in the 1970s. The 52,000-square-foot student services center fea-

tures a theater-auditorium, classrooms, and a cafeteria.

The convenient locations mean you can walk from campus to Downtown or such North Side attractions as Three Rivers Stadium and the National Aviary. Make sure you take a walking tour of the mansions near the campus. One was the home of industrialist Harry Thaw, who gained notoriety by gunning down architect Stanford White in a famous 19th-century love triangle.

Community College of Allegheny County—North Campus
8701 Perry Highway, McCandless
• (412) 366-7000

The North Campus of CCAC serves students in Pittsburgh's northern and western suburbs. The campus serves more than 6,500 students in a 153,000-square-foot building. That's a far cry from the campus' more humble origins—a trailer in the parking lot in what was then North Hills Passavant Hospital.

Grove City College
100 Campus Dr., Grove City
• (724) 458-2100

Grove City College is dedicated to being "a Christian college of liberal arts and sciences," a mission infused in all aspects of study and life at this Butler County college. Though affiliated with the Presbyterian Church (U.S.A.), the college is not narrowly denominational but expects attention to matters of faith from its students. Each student must attend a minimum of 16 chapel services per semester. If you

INSIDERS' TIP

One of the most important sources of financial aid in the Commonwealth is the Pennsylvania Higher Education Assistance Agency (PHEAA), (717) 720-4000. For more information about PHEAA, see our Education chapter.

need any other indications of Grove City's commitment to its vision, consider this: The college eschews all state and federal aid, the better to maintain its independent vision.

Grove City awards the bachelor of arts, the bachelor of science, the bachelor of music, the bachelor of science in electrical engineering, and the bachelor of science in mechanical engineering degrees. The engineering programs are distinctive, offering dual emphases in science and technology and liberal arts. Core courses stress cultural literacy and communications skills, while non-engineering majors must study a language. Coursework is demanding but fulfilling, as about 80 percent of entering freshmen graduate from Grove City.

The lovely campus spans more than 150 acres and 27 buildings just a few minutes from I-79, making it accessible from Pittsburgh some 60 miles to the south. Of the 2,300 students, more than 90 percent reside on campus. The Technological Learning Center includes 121 microcomputers and three big-screen projection systems. Grove City enhances those facilities by providing each freshman with a color notebook-sized computer and printer. For extracurricular activities, the college sponsors more than 100 organizations and special interest groups; for relaxation, students enjoy events at the J. Howard Few Fine Arts Center and bowling, handball, and racquetball at the student union.

Grove City features an extensive intramural sports program and fields 18 intercollegiate teams for men and women.

Grove City is relatively affordable for a private school. Since the college maintains a sizeable endowment, tuition is usually lower than similar schools. About 50 percent of freshmen receive financial aid. Admission to Grove City is quite competitive, which may be due to its popularity, price, and fine reputation. If you or a family member is thinking of applying, the college strongly recommends an interview with its staff. While visiting, check out the Prime Outlets (see Shopping) and the nearby towns (see Daytrips/Weekend Getaways).

Indiana University of Pennsylvania
316 John Sutton Hall, Indiana
• (724) 357-2302

Located about 50 miles northeast of Pittsburgh, Indiana is known as the "Christmas Tree Capital of the World" and the hometown of actor Jimmy Stewart. If it's not as prominent for Indiana University of Pennsylvania, it should be. Founded in 1875 as Indiana Normal School, a small teacher training institution, IUP has evolved into a major university with 14,000 students representing nearly every state and 60 countries. It's the largest university in the State System of Higher Education (which does not include Penn State University).

Duquesne University is just one of the many institutions of higher learning in Pittsburgh.

Photo: Courtesy of Duquesne University

Academic offerings include more than 100 undergraduate majors with a variety of internship and study-abroad programs. At the graduate level, IUP offers more than 40 master's programs and eight doctoral programs. Extensive as those offerings are, the university further enhances them through a variety of creative partnerships. Through a joint initiative with The Western Pennsylvania Hospital in Pittsburgh, IUP provides a program of study in respiratory care that has achieved a 100 percent employment rate for its graduates. In cooperation with Allegheny General Hospital and MCP-Hanemann School of Medicine of Allegheny University of the Health Sciences, IUP offers a pre-professional program for students planning to serve as general practice physicians in the Pittsburgh area.

You'll find academic support services at IUP quite convenient and useful. Campus buildings are connected via a private fiberoptic link, which provides resident students with in-room Internet access and other computer capabilities. The university's Robert E. Cook Honors College is more than a mere designation, as members live together in the same residence hall and form a community.

IUP features a large resident student community—about 4,500 strong—and about 120 student organizations including a newspaper and radio and television stations. The school sponsors an intramural sports program as well as 17 varsity sports, participating in the NCAA Division II Pennsylvania State Athletic Conference. Students living on campus enjoy IUP's unusual in-room video service. Rather than contract with the local cable television provider, IUP developed its own television programming service that blends the customary satellite-delivered fare with more education-oriented programming, such as foreign language channels.

IUP is a bit outside our principal coverage area, but as you can see, it's worthy of inclusion. IUP also runs the Monroeville Graduate and Professional Center in eastern Allegheny County. At the center, IUP offers master's programs in adult and community education, business administration, criminology, elementary education, and industrial and labor relations.

La Roche College
9000 Babcock Blvd., McCandless
• (412) 367-9300

The Sisters of Divine Providence founded La Roche College in Pittsburgh's North Hills in 1963, when the northern suburbs began the great growth spurt that continues to this day. As a result this private, Catholic, liberal arts institution offers a beautiful suburban campus to a growing population base while still providing access to the business and social attractions of Pittsburgh. It's been a formula for success at La Roche.

La Roche awards the bachelor of arts, bachelor of science, and master of science in human resources degrees, as well as bachelor's and master's degrees in nursing. The college's 1,500 students select majors from 35 disciplines covering the humanities, including elementary education, language and literature, international studies, and sociology; the arts, including dance, professional writing, graphic design, and interior design; business, including accounting, finance, and international management; and science, including computer science, biology, chemistry, medical technology, and psychobiology. Students in virtually every major have the opportunity for internships—many with top Pittsburgh employers.

Residence life is one of the neatest aspects of the La Roche experience. The college's 350 resident students live in apartment-style suites that feature two or three bedrooms. Typically four to six students live in each suite. The Kerr Fitness and Sports Center includes a gymnasium, an elevated track, a dance and karate studio, a weight room, and racquetball courts. Other activities include a student newspaper, a drama club, and men's and women's varsity and intramural sports. La Roche belongs to the NCAA Division III Allegheny Mountain Collegiate Conference.

One of the most interesting and satisfying opportunities for students is participation in the La Roche Challenge program, through which honor stu-

INSIDERS' TIP

The intersection of the campuses of Carnegie Mellon University and the University of Pittsburgh is one of the most engaging spots in the city. Along the informal border, you'll find Carnegie Library of Pittsburgh, the Hillman Library, the Frick Fine Arts Building, Phipps Conservatory and Botanical Gardens, and Flagstaff Hill, a great site for lounging and people-watching. Look very carefully and you'll also pick out a brick wall that is the last surviving portion of Forbes Field, former home of the Pittsburgh Pirates.

dents teach pupils at 14 participating Catholic elementary schools. The younger students visit the La Roche campus for 20 classes each year, including instruction in such areas as computer graphics, desktop publishing, ballet, and Native American history. It's a great way to serve the community and get valuable practical experience in return.

Slippery Rock University
Old Main, Slippery Rock
• (724) 738-9000

Founded as a teacher education institution, Slippery Rock has grown into a multipurpose university with roughly 7,800 students and more than 60 degree programs in the four colleges and other departments and graduate studies. The university is in Butler County, about 75 minutes from Pittsburgh along I-79. It's one of 14 institutions in the State System of Higher Education.

If you study biology or geology at Slippery Rock, you'll have the opportunity to travel to the Marine Science Consortium at Wallops Island, Virginia. The consortium is a nonprofit corporation dedicated to research and instruction in the marine sciences, and Slippery Rock is a member of the consortium.

INSIDERS' TIP

In July and August, Saint Vincent College hosts the Pittsburgh Steelers training camp. Most sessions are open to the public, and several are designated as photo days.

The university offers a broad continuing education program that features credit courses, workshops, and seminars. It offers classes at a satellite site in Cranberry, Butler County, and at the St. Francis Hospital School of Nursing in New Castle, Lawrence County. The community also takes advantage of Slippery Rock's conference facilities, which include banquet halls that can accommodate up to 1,000 people and overnight facilities.

One of the most compelling aspects of the university is its campus, spread over more than 600 acres and dotted with woods, streams, and ponds. Moreover, it's near the McKeever Environmental Learning Center, a state-operated facility that provides general environmental education and instruction in environmental education for student-teachers. The college also boasts 11 residence halls, nine auditoriums, 12 athletic fields, and tennis courts. If that's not enough, head to Morrow Field House, where you'll find a gymnasium, a swimming pool, handball courts, a dance studio, and a running track.

About 35 percent of students live on campus, and about 80 percent receive financial aid. Slippery Rock sponsors 22 varsity sports and competes in the NCAA Division II. Students take advantage of the setting and the facilities through such organizations as skiing and hiking clubs and the campus television and radio stations.

Westminster College
S. Market St., New Wilmington
• (724) 946-8761, (800) 942-8033

This Lawrence County liberal arts college is slightly north of our principal coverage area, but you ought to know about it—if only for its convenient location, excellent reputation and nearby tourist attractions. It's about 60 miles from Pittsburgh, primarily via I-79, and only about 85 miles southeast of Cleveland, making it accessible from both major urban centers.

Westminster, however, is decidedly not urban. Its 300-acre campus in the rolling hills of Western Pennsylvania offers tranquillity that you'll appreciate. Affiliated with the Presbyterian Church (U.S.A.), Westminster was founded in 1852 and was among the first colleges to offer equal admissions to women seeking baccalaureate degrees. Today, the college offers 39 academic majors—with internships available in each one—and six preprofessional programs. Among the most interesting majors is Sacred Music, a joint program with Duquesne University through which students take classes on both campuses. Class size typically is smaller than you'll find in many colleges and universities.

Virtually all of Westminster's 1,500 students live on campus, where they take advantage of a broad computer network that provides them with Internet access and other functions from their dorm rooms. One of the most important volunteer activities on campus is service with Habitat for Humanity, which involves about 300 Westminster students in its programs of constructing homes for families in need. If you're looking for a less arduous leisure activity, try some stargazing at the observatory in the Hoyt Science Resource Center. Westminster sponsors an intramural sports program and 16 varsity sports at the NCAA Division II level. There's a proud tradition of sports excellence here. The football team has achieved six national titles and 11 undefeated seasons. When

HIGHER EDUCATION

the football team left the National Association of Intercollegiate Athletics in 1997, it left as the all-time leader in wins.

While Westminster is a college affiliated with the Presbyterian Church, it's known among students and graduates as being less strict in the areas of dorm room inter-visitation and chapel attendance.

New Wilmington and the surrounding areas of Volant, Sharon and Grove City (with the Prime Outlets) surely make this an attractive destination to visit while transporting kids to and from college, or merely checking out the campus. (See our Daytrips/Weekend Getaways and Shopping chapters).

East

Carlow College
3333 Fifth Ave., Pittsburgh
• (412) 578-6000, (800) 333-CARLOW

Carlow College was founded in 1929 by the Sisters of Mercy to help women realize their potential. While Carlow today admits men without actively recruiting them, it remains a Catholic, liberal arts college primarily for women. It's set on a hillside overlooking Pittsburgh's Oakland neighborhood; as you stroll through the quadrangle, you get a satisfying sense of community while knowing that the amenities of Oakland's university-medical complex are just down the hill below.

Carlow confers three baccalaureate degrees—bachelor of arts, bachelor of science, and bachelor of science in nursing—as well as three master's degrees. Undergraduates select from 34 majors. While these are rich in humanities programs including creative writing, English, philosophy, history, social work, and sociology, they also feature such business programs as accounting, business management, and medical marketing, and such science-based programs as chemistry and four biology tracks.

Carlow offers pre-professional programs in dentistry, medicine, optometry, osteopathy, pharmacy, physical therapy, podiatry, law, and veterinary medicine. Whatever your major, Carlow requires study in a core curriculum that represents the humanities, natural sciences, and social sciences, as well as such interesting courses as public speaking and women's studies.

Students participate in more than 20 organizations—when they're not too busy enjoying the many social and cultural opportunities of Oakland. While Carlow offers only one residence hall, students are guaranteed housing. The college sponsors five varsity sports, offers crew as a club sport, and provides a fitness center, swimming pool, and gymnasium. Approximately 92 percent of full-time students receive financial assistance.

One of Carlow's most appealing strengths is its extensive continuing education programs. In addition to maintaining satellite sites in Beaver, Cranberry and Greensburg, the college offers the Carlow Weekend College and the Carlow Accelerated Program. Both enable working students to develop class schedules that accommodate their professional schedules while working toward degrees. Through Carlow Hill College, a continuing education program targeted to the primarily African-American residents of Pittsburgh's Hill District neighborhood, students develop leadership skills and enhanced career possibilities.

Carnegie Mellon University
5000 Forbes Ave., Pittsburgh
• (412) 268-2000

Few degrees are as prestigious as those from Carnegie Mellon, a private university of about 7,500 students with a dual focus on education and research. It was founded in 1900 by industrialist and philanthropist Andrew Carnegie, whose vision was a vocational training school for the children of the city's working class. It was renamed Carnegie Institute of Technology in 1912 and merged with the Mellon Institute in 1967.

An important component of Oakland's university-medical complex, Carnegie Mellon includes four undergraduate colleges (in technology, fine arts, humanities and social sciences, and science) and three graduate schools—the Graduate School of Industrial Administration, the School of Computer Science, and the H. John Heinz III School of Public Policy and Management.

The university is perhaps most prominent for its leadership in the arts and technology, an unusual combination but one that works well at Carnegie Mellon. The university introduced its undergraduate drama degree in 1917; since then, a number of young men and women who later would gain fame as actors, directors, and set and costume designers learned their art and craft at CMU. Among actors who have studied at the university are George Peppard, Holly Hunter, Ted Danson, and Jack Klugman.

In technology, Carnegie Mellon operates the National Robotics Engineering Consortium. Located in Pittsburgh's Lawrenceville neighborhood along the Allegheny River, the consortium develops robots to explore volcanoes and other hazardous environments, and vehicles that can be driven without human operators on board. The work of Carnegie Mellon students and faculty in such fields as computer science, software development, and robotics has resulted in the creation of more than 70 "spinoff" companies.

Carnegie Mellon's strength in technology has important implications for the university's students. About 85 percent of students use computing in their educational activities. Through the university's computing network—called "Andrew" after benefactors Andrew Carnegie and Andrew Mellon—all students have access to personal computing workstations.

The campus spans 103 acres and 66 buildings. Student activities vary from special interest clubs and a newspaper and a radio station to fraternities and sororities. The university sponsors 17 varsity athletic teams—the men's football team participates in the University Athletic Association of NCAA Division III. Fitness and recreation facilities include tennis courts, gymnasiums, racquetball courts, swimming pools, and weight/fitness rooms. In an innovative arrangement, the university, through an affiliated corporation, operates the City of Pittsburgh's Schenley Golf Course, which is adjacent to campus. (For more on the course, see our Golf chapter.) About 75 percent of undergraduate students reside on campus, and about 65 percent receive some form of financial aid.

Chatham College
Woodland Rd., Pittsburgh
• (412) 365-1100

When you're enjoying the freshness and beauty of Chatham's 32-acre wooded campus, surrounded by the converted mansions that serve as the college's residence halls, you'll probably forget that Fifth Avenue, one of the city's busiest thoroughfares, is only a hillside away. That sense of splendid isolation within the bustling city is part of Chatham's charm.

Chatham is the last of the region's exclusively single-gender institutions of higher learning (men are admitted to graduate programs only)—it's been preparing women for personal and professional success since 1869. Its more than 40 baccalaureate degree programs feature small, seminar-style classes and a variety of hands-on learning experiences, including two guaranteed internships in a field related to your

major as well as a mentoring relationship with a leading professional woman.

Chatham also offers master's level programs in physical therapy, occupational therapy, physician assistant studies, teaching, management, and counseling psychology. Chatham graduates receive preferred entry into these programs. Collaborative programs provide a bridge to medical school, engineering, and an environmental and occupational health master's program.

Providing broad and challenging experiences is one of Chatham's key goals, one the college achieves through several innovative programs. One is a senior tutorial, a yearlong independent research project on a topic of each student's choosing. Another is Chatham Abroad, an exciting opportunity for travel through which each student experiences a three-week trip with faculty and classmates to countries such as Egypt, France, Spain, England, Belize, Ireland, Morocco, and Italy. Chatham's Global Focus program provides international events and activities, with a different area of the world highlighted each year.

Of Chatham's roughly 900 students, about 45 percent reside on campus or in college-owned apartments on 5th Avenue. More than 92 percent of students receive some form of financial aid. A fiberoptic network connects everyone on campus and provides each student with Internet access. Chatham sponsors more than 40 student organizations, NCAA Division III teams in six sports, and a variety of club and recreational sports. One of Chatham's most distinguished graduates is Rachel Carson, founder of the modern environmental movement. In her honor, Chatham maintains the Rachel Carson Institute, an advocate for the environment that also produces environmental awareness programs for high school students.

Community College of Allegheny County—Boyce Campus
595 Beatty Rd., Monroeville
• (412) 371-8651, (724) 327-1327

Nearly 6,000 students are enrolled in academic programs at Boyce Campus; sometimes it's hard to imagine how they concentrate on their studies. The campus serving Pittsburgh's eastern suburbs is adjacent to Allegheny County's Boyce Park, which offers the closest downhill skiing slopes to

INSIDERS' TIP

Washington and Jefferson College is the smallest school ever to play in the Rose Bowl. In the 1922 "Granddaddy of Them All," W&J played the University of California to a scoreless tie, using only 11 players in the process.

HIGHER EDUCATION

Pittsburgh. For students who can manage to stay off the slopes—we're only kidding here, as Boyce Campus students are as dedicated as any other students—the campus provides a multipurpose center that includes a gymnasium, a theater, and classrooms. If by some chance you are interested in Boyce Park, you'll find a profile in our Parks chapter.

Electronic Institutes
4634 Browns Hill Rd., Pittsburgh
• **(412) 521-8686, (800) 721-8686**

Electronic Institutes prepares students for employment in fields related to engineering, with programs of study leading to the associate in specialized technology degree in electrical technology or electronic and computer technology. As befitting such a focused program, the academic schedule is fairly rigorous, with classes in session about 48 weeks of the year. Instructors take attendance each day, further emphasizing the seriousness of the mission here.

Electronic Institutes is set on Browns Hill Road, a steep hill overlooking the Monongahela River that connects Pittsburgh to the Homestead High Level Bridge and the suburb of Homestead just across the river. While classrooms and laboratories offer a wide variety of electronics equipment for hands-on training, the institution does not offer residences, so students must find their own housing. Electronic Institutes provides assistance in that search, as well as placement services whenever graduates require them. Electronic Institutes offers a number of financial aid programs.

Penn State McKeesport
University Dr., McKeesport
• **(412) 675-9000**

A regional campus of the Pennsylvania State University, Penn State McKeesport offers the first two years of more than 160 baccalaureate degree programs. Those are far from the only academic options here, as students also pursue associate degrees in five programs and master's degrees in adult education and counselor edu-

Designed by Charles Klauder, the Cathedral of Learning is the centerpiece of the University of Pittsburgh campus in Oakland.

Photo: Jeff Greenberg

cation. Students in the business administration and liberal arts associate degree programs have the opportunity to attend weekend and evening classes to better accommodate their schedules.

Founded in 1948, the college is about 10 miles southeast of Pittsburgh. Of the nearly 1,000 students, about 200 reside on campus. For those who commute, Penn State McKeesport maintains plenty of free parking, an important perk. Students participate in such activities as theater production and the campus radio station. Through community outreach services such as the Penn State Educational Partnership Program and the Educational Opportunity Program, student tutors assist middle school and high school pupils in after-school study programs, a nice way of blending education and community service.

The student-faculty ratio is 16-1, while the student-computer ratio is 8-1, helping assure that students get the attention and support they need. Students participate in an intramural sports program as well as two varsity sports—men's basketball and women's volleyball. The teams compete in the Western Pennsylvania Collegiate Conference and the Penn State Commonwealth Campus Athletic Conference. About 80 percent of students receive some form of financial aid.

Penn State New Kensington
3550 Seventh Street Rd., Upper Burrell
• (724) 339-5466

Like the Penn State campuses in McKeesport and Beaver, Penn State New Kensington is part of the Pennsylvania State Commonwealth College and draws on its considerable resources. Students at the 72-acre Penn State New Kensington, founded in 1958 and located in Westmoreland County about 20 miles from Pittsburgh, can complete the first two years of almost any of Penn State's 160 baccalaureate degree programs. Seventy-two percent of Penn State New Kensington students are enrolled in such programs.

There are, however, other options, including four-year programs in nursing and electromechanical engineering technology that can be completed on site. In addition, the college offers associate degree programs in business administration, allied health, engineering technology, liberal arts, and sciences. Class size is comfortable—the student-faculty ratio is 18-1. When they're not studying, students relax at the gymnasium, racquetball courts, and fitness center, or broaden their experience through the Outdoor Adventure Club, the Multicultural Club, and such community projects as homebuilding with Habitat for Humanity.

Penn State New Kensington offers an intramural sports program as well as two varsity teams—men's basketball and women's volleyball—that compete in the Western Pennsylvania Collegiate Conference and the Penn State Commonwealth Athletic Conference. You won't find on-campus housing; many students rent apartments in a building adjacent to campus. About 80 percent of students receive some form of financial aid.

INSIDERS' TIP

Financial aid at area colleges and universities can take a number of forms—scholarships, grants, loans, part-time employment, or a combination of these tools.

Pittsburgh Institute of Aeronautics
5 Allegheny County Airport, West Mifflin
• (412) 462-9011, (800) 444-1440

Pittsburgh Institute of Aeronautics was founded in 1927 by Glen Curtiss and Orville Wright—yes, that Orville Wright—so you know the history of the institute is solid. You may not be flying solo over Kitty Hawk, but you will have the chance to study for an associate degree in specialized technology in one of two programs. The Aviation Maintenance Technician Program leads to a test for the airframe and powerplant license. The Avionics Technician Program (AVT) program will prepare you for the FCC General Radiotelephone license.

You can complete the programs in 21 months, making them especially attractive. For the first six weeks, you'll study such basics as English, algebra and physics. After that, it's all hands-on work with airplanes, jets, and helicopters, as well as work in the shop and the lab. You can begin your classes at one of four times during the year. Graduates interested in pursuing baccalaureate degrees can receive advanced standing credits at any of the 12 colleges and universities with which PIA maintains cooperative agreements. Two of those cooperating institutions are in Pittsburgh: Community College of Allegheny County and Point Park College.

PIA does not offer its 225 students housing or financial aid, though it gladly accepts grants, scholarships and private funding you receive from other sources. PIA claims an outstanding placement record, indicating that its graduates typically receive from four to six job offers. Prepare for takeoff!

Pittsburgh Institute of Mortuary Science
5808 Baum Blvd., Pittsburgh
• (412) 362-8500

This is the region's only degree-granting institution for mortuary science, so it has a comparatively large enrollment—about 150 students. The institute welcomes about 50 new students each January, May and September; the trimester approach means that most students can find a convenient time to launch their studies.

Located in Pittsburgh's Shadyside neighborhood, the institute awards the associate in specialized business degree, which usually leads to a career in funeral service management, and the associate in specialized technology degree, which focuses more on the technical aspects of mortuary science. In addition, the institute maintains cooperative programs with four colleges and universities—Point Park College, California University of Pennsylvania, Thiel College, and Gannon University—that enable its graduates to earn bachelor of science degrees at the campuses of the cooperating institutions.

In addition to the technological aspects of mortuary science, students learn about the human and historical components of the business through courses like world religions, ethics, gerontology, communication skills, and psychology of grief and counseling. The institute offers financial assistance but no on-campus housing.

Pittsburgh Theological Seminary
616 N. Highland Ave., Pittsburgh
• (412) 362-5610

The seminary was founded in 1794 in a log cabin with six students and one teacher. For more than 200 years, it has pursued the same vision: nurturing men and women in their faith, while preparing them for pastoral ministry and Christian lay leadership. The seminary is affiliated with the Presbyterian Church (U.S.A.), but its community is ecumenical, with over 20 denominations represented in the student body.

Located in Pittsburgh's East Liberty neighborhood and boasting 13 acres of green grounds, the seminary confers the master of divinity, master of arts, master of sacred theology, and doctor of ministry degrees. Joint degree programs with local colleges and universities allow students to earn a master of divinity degree from the seminary and a master's degree in law, social work, public health, business, or sacred music from the collaborating institution. Similarly, a Ph.D. program from the University of Pittsburgh is available to seminary students. The seminary offers an evening program that enables master of divinity students to complete their work in six years.

Students can take advantage of a number of continuing education programs as well as the Metro-Urban Institute, which provides field education experiences. The seminary provides both dorm rooms and unfurnished apartments (pets aren't permitted in either) as well as childcare services during regularly scheduled daytime class hours. The student association arranges recreation and athletic events, utilizing the seminary's tennis courts. Students also have limited access to the gym and swimming pool at Peabody High School, just across North Highland Avenue, and they enjoy a weekly vol-leyball game at a local church. Financial aid is available.

The purposes of the seminary clearly are serious, but you'll also appreciate the zest for life here as embodied in the warning signs along campus drives. The signs say, "Thou Shalt Not Park Here."

Reformed Presbyterian Theological Seminary
7418 Penn Ave., Pittsburgh
• (412) 731-8690

If you drive along Penn Avenue in Pittsburgh's Point Breeze neighborhood, you might mistake this campus and its attractive grounds for the estate of a wealthy industrialist. It may look that way, but there's serious work going on here, as the seminary's primary purpose is to train ministers of the gospel for church leadership. The student body is small, numbering about 100 students, yet those students represent more than 20 denominations.

The seminary was founded in 1810 and boasts a colorful history. In its early days, the Synod of the Reformed Presbyterian Church elected a professor of theology; whenever he moved to a different congregation, his students moved with him. Thus, the seminary had five different locations between 1810 and 1856.

Today, the seminary awards the master of divinity degree with emphasis in biblical studies, systematic theology, church history, and pastoral theology. The institution stresses the importance of local churches, offering practica in different areas of ministry and requiring a local church recommendation for admission to the seminary.

Technology plays an important role in scholarship at the seminary. A climatized rare book room houses more than 1,000 volumes, while computer terminals feature Hebrew and Greek characters for display and study of ancient texts.

Saint Vincent College
300 Fraser Purchase Rd., Latrobe
• (724) 537-4540

Saint Vincent is a Catholic, Benedictine liberal arts college in Westmoreland County, about 35 miles east of Pittsburgh. About 25 percent of the faculty are Benedictine Monks, infusing the campus with a zest for life and learning. At Saint Vincent, you'll find plenty of opportunity for both.

The college offers baccalaureate degrees in more than 50 disciplines, spanning a wide range of humanities, business, and science programs. You'll find a number of appealing concentrations in the arts, business administration and family and consumer sciences tracks, as well as preparatory programs in law, medicine, dental medicine, engineering, health professions, chiropractic, optometry, podiatry, theology, and veterinary medicine. Through cooperative programs with Seton Hill College and Duquesne University, Saint Vincent students may pursue additional programs, including occupational therapy, pharmacy, and physical therapy, leading to graduate degrees at Duquesne. The college offers study abroad through its relationship with Fu Jen Catholic University of Taiwan.

Of Saint Vincent's 1,200 students, about 875 reside on the 400-acre campus. The campus features a number of neat structures. These include the central commons building, which offers an amphitheater, a planetarium, and a robotics lab, and the Instructional Technology Resource Center, where students go on-line. You can participate in the campus radio and television stations, provide community service through the Campus Ministry Program, or participate in six men's varsity sports or five women's varsity sports. The college competes in the National Association of Intercollegiate Athletics. Saint Vincent provides financial assistance to more than 90 percent of the students who apply for it.

You'll come to appreciate the college's productive relationship with Seton Hill College, which is less than 10 miles west along Pa. 30. For most of their respective histories, when Saint Vincent admitted only men and Seton Hill only women, the two institutions developed a "brother-sister" relationship that featured cross registration for courses and joint social functions. Today, both schools are coeducational, but their productive relationship remains. A free shuttle bus operates between the two campuses.

Seton Hill College
Seton Hill Dr., Greensburg
• (724) 834-2200, (800) 826-6234

The word "community" is used rather loosely these days, but when you visit Seton Hill College, you'll know at once that you've arrived at a community. Founded in 1918 by the Sisters of Charity, Seton Hill is a Catholic liberal arts college with a lovely 200-acre campus high atop a Greensburg hill, about 35 miles east of Pittsburgh. For most of its years a women's college, Seton Hill now is fully coeducational with a faculty that features members of the Sisters of Charity and lay persons. The

campus includes both retirement quarters and a cemetery for the sisters—both of them not far from tennis courts and an exercise course for the college's roughly 1,100 students. The campus is dotted with intriguing pipe sculptures produced by Josefa Filkosky, a member of the Art Department faculty. You won't find many colleges with a stronger commitment to a mission and a community.

Undergrads choose from more than 40 areas of study, including physician assistant, art therapy, biology, psychology, education, management, and visual and performing arts. Class size typically is comfortable, with a student-faculty ratio of 13-1. Honors programs, independent study and seminar work are available to students, and study in most majors includes internships. At the graduate level, Seton Hill awards the master of arts degree in elementary education, special education, and art therapy. In addition, the college offers an innovative program in which students may earn a bachelor of arts degree, certification in elementary education, and a master's in elementary education in five years—all for the price of a bachelor's degree.

Seton Hill's Accelerated Saturday Degree Program is designed for students who wish to pursue degrees while continuing to work full time. Through the program, students can obtain their degrees in management, accounting, general studies or human services within the traditional four years while taking classes on Saturdays only.

Students participate in the campus newspaper and literary magazine as well as intramural and varsity sports. Seton Hill sponsors varsity teams in basketball, cross country, equestrian, soccer, softball, tennis, and volleyball. For leisure, you'll find a gymnasium, a swimming pool, volleyball and badminton courts, softball and soccer fields, and a fitness trail that winds through the surrounding hills. The college also provides van transportation for trips to local and Pittsburgh shopping districts, while students plan regular excursions to New York City and Washington, DC.

Seton Hill awards merit-based scholarships in theater, art, music, biology, chemistry, and mathematics. Through the Seton Hill College Presidential Scholarship program, students who graduate in the top 30 percent of their high school class are eligible for awards up to $6,320 annually. When you're checking out the facilities, make sure you stop in Reeves Memorial Library to enjoy the unusual sculpture of a student, head down on the table, weary or asleep from studying.

HIGHER EDUCATION

As befitting a college where community is so important, Seton Hill provides important services to the broader community. These include plays staged by the theater department in Reeves Theatre, exhibitions of student art in Harlan Gallery, and the Lynch Lecture Series, which brings nationally prominent speakers and performers to campus. The college is home to the National Catholic Center for Holocaust Education as well as the National Education Center for Women in Business, which serves as a nationwide clearinghouse for information and research on women's business ownership while offering consulting services and classes in entrepreneurship.

University of Pittsburgh
5th Ave. at Bigelow Blvd., Pittsburgh
• (412) 624-4141

The importance of the University of Pittsburgh would be hard to overestimate. It serves approximately 32,000 undergraduate and graduate students. If you don't find that figure impressive, consider it another way: roughly 5.5 percent of all students enrolled in institutions of higher learning in Pennsylvania are enrolled at the University of Pittsburgh.

The school was founded in 1787 as The Pittsburgh Academy, and it has remained close to the community it serves. Its signature building, the 42-story Cathedral of Learning, was financed in the 1920s largely through the contributions of area residents, who "bought" bricks for a nickel apiece. The university has produced 180,000 graduates—many are among the region's business, professional, and civic leaders.

When you're speaking about the university, it's important to discuss both education and research, as Pitt is a leader in each. In education, the university offers 367 distinct degree programs as well as other dual, joint, and cooperative degree programs. It offers graduate programs in arts and sciences, business, dental medicine, education, engineering, health and rehabilitation sciences, information sciences, law, medicine, nursing, pharmacy, public and international affairs, public health, and social work. The College of General Studies offers undergraduate programs on a part-time basis for students with full-time jobs or other commitments, while the Honors College provides attractive seminar-style classes for high-achieving students. The university maintains regional campuses in Bradford, Greensburg, Johnstown, and Titusville.

In the area of research, Pitt is a member of the prestigious Association of American Universities, a consortium of the 62 leading research universities in North America. Its faculty has pioneered the way in such discoveries as silver-sheathed superconducting wire and development of a method to decontaminate chemical weapons. Among the university's most prominent research centers are the University Center for International Studies, the Center for Biotechnology and Bioengineering at the Pittsburgh Technology Center, the University Center for Social and Urban Research, the Thomas E. Starzl Transplantation Institute, and the University of Pittsburgh Cancer Institute. In addition, Pitt's six schools of the health sciences work closely with UPMC Health System, the region's largest network of hospitals, clinics, and research centers. For more on UPMC Health System, see our Healthcare chapter.

You won't want for academic support here, as Pitt's libraries house approximately 4 million volumes and subscribe to about 25,000 journals and periodicals. All dormitories are equipped with personal computing facilities, and you'll have access to portable laptop computers at Hillman Library, the university's principal library.

The split-level campus dominates the Oakland neighborhood, spanning 90 buildings and 132 acres. On the lower level, on and around 5th and Forbes avenues, you'll find the Cathedral of Learning and its Nationality Classrooms, 24 authentically designed rooms depicting the ethnic art and culture of their respective lands. For more on the Nationality Classrooms, see our Attractions chapter. Nearby, you'll see a trio of buildings both historic and functional. The Center for American Music is housed at the Stephen Foster Memorial, a tribute to the great Pittsburgh-born composer. Heinz Memorial Chapel, an interfaith chapel built in the French Gothic style, features magnificent stained glass windows that soar skyward and is a popular venue for weddings; better make your reservation before you pop the question, as the waiting list typically is lengthy. The William Pitt Union, the center of student life, opened in 1898 as the grand Hotel Schenley, a favorite stopping place for visiting dignitaries and actors.

On the upper campus, you'll find such amenities as the venerable sports arena—Fitzgerald Fieldhouse—the university's principal gymnasium, swimming pool, and other student and community athletic facilities, and the residences of campus fraternities and sororities.

Student life is as varied as you would expect. While many students are commuters, about 5,000 live on campus, and many others rent apartments off campus. Tuition for state residents is about half that for out-of-staters. About 70 percent of undergraduates receive financial aid. The university sponsors more than 400 student organizations, including a campus radio station and *The Pitt News,* a newspaper published five times each week. You'll want to scan the newspaper for coupons good at Oakland businesses and ads for sales and housing availabilities.

The university sponsors a full range of intramural sports and 19 varsity sports for men and women, who compete in the Big East Conference. For more on varsity football and basketball at Pitt, see our Spectator Sports chapter.

This is a vital urban campus, where social and cultural opportunities abound. Rare is the day when you can't find at least several appealing lectures or performances on campus. On the other hand, if you'd prefer to spend your noon hour sunning on the Cathedral lawn, that's part of the Pitt charm, too. And if you want to take classes in the Cathedral of Learning but not for degree status, investigate one of the many courses through Pitt's Informal Program (a non-credit division), with classes in everything from how to become a writer to learning more about Pittsburgh's history and architecture.

University of Pittsburgh at Greensburg
1150 Mt. Pleasant Rd., Greensburg
• (724) 836-9942

This 205-acre regional campus of the University of Pittsburgh was built on the former private estate of Commander Charles McKenna Lynch. It's only 3 miles from downtown Pittsburgh, but it will give you an appealing sense of satisfaction and community. The university serves 1,500 students through 17 four-year programs leading to baccalaureate degrees and a number of pre-professional programs completed at the university's main campus in Pittsburgh.

Majors include accounting, administration of justice, anthropology, biological sciences, environmental science, information science, management, and political science, and you also may design your own major. All students must complete general core requirements that include courses in communications, mathematics, and critical reasoning, as well as five courses each in humanities, social sciences, and natural sciences. If you can't

attend class every day for personal or professional reasons, try the University External Studies Program. You'll attend three on-campus workshops per term and complete the balance of your studying at home.

About 45 percent of full-time students live on campus, where they enjoy the McKenna Computer Center; Chambers Hall, which features a gymnasium, a running track, and racquetball courts; and Millstein Library, which provides access to the Internet as well as the University of Pittsburgh Digital Library. A member of the NCAA Division III Allegheny Mountain Collegiate Conference, the university sponsors seven varsity sports as well as intramural sports. The financial aid program is extensive and varied, with all awards based on need.

Westmoreland County Community College
400 Armburst Rd., Youngwood
• (724) 925-4000

One of the most appealing aspects of WCCC is its reach. In addition to the main campus about 6 miles south of Greensburg and 35 miles east of Pittsburgh, the college maintains Westmoreland County campuses in Belle Vernon, Latrobe, New Kensington, and Penn Township, to accommodate its 5,770 full- and part-time students. In addition, WCCC uses distance learning technology to teach certain courses simultaneously at several or all campuses, minimizing students' travel requirements, and it offers telecourses for students who can't make it to campus.

Academic programs prepare students for careers or transfer to baccalaureate degree programs at four-year institutions. The college awards the associate in arts degree and the associate in applied science degree, with nearly 50 majors available. Principal programs include accounting, allied health, business, computer information systems, engineering science and industrial technology, horticulture, hospitality management, human services, liberal arts, and science, media technology, and office administration. Study in certain specialties within those departments leads to a certificate or diploma.

The main campus in Youngwood spans 80 acres and four buildings. Students have access to more than 500 computers with Internet access. For relaxation, the college provides

INSIDERS' TIP

Most colleges and universities offer a full range of non-credit courses—sometimes tuition-free for seniors—so you can enjoy your favorite hobby or interest in a classroom near you.

a gymnasium, racquetball courts, a health fitness center, and an indoor track. Area employers take advantage of the classrooms, laboratories, and offices in the Business and Industry Center at the Youngwood campus.

If you're a Westmoreland County resident, you'll like the tuition schedule—you'll pay half what nonresidents pay. WCCC offers a variety of financial aid programs, including many scholarships endowed by local businesses and foundations.

South

California University of Pennsylvania
Third St., California
• **(724) 938-4000**

Nestled in a bend of the Monongahela River about 30 miles from Pittsburgh, California University is an important member of the State System of Higher Education and one of the key institutions of Washington County. The university awards associate, baccalaureate and master's degrees in more than 100 academic programs offered through the College of Education and Human Services, the College of Liberal Arts, the Eberly College of Science and Technology and the School of Graduate Studies and Research. Continuing education students will find a rich selection of courses in the Lifelong Learning program and at the university's satellite site at Southpointe Technology Park in Canonsburg.

California serves nearly 5,800 students on its 80-acre campus, which includes six residence halls that house 1,500 students. One of the most inviting features on campus is the 104-acre Roadman Park, which includes athletic fields and courts, running facilities, and a stadium. You won't have to worry about academic support here, as the university boasts more than 1,800 computers—more than one-third of them available to students for e-mail and Internet access and other functions. The student-faculty ratio is 21:1.

Students participate in more than 130 organizations, including the *California Times* newspaper, the *Flipside* magazine, a radio station, and a television station. The university sponsors a program of intramural sports and 13 varsity sports, participating in the NCAA Division II Pennsylvania State Athletic Conference. In 1996–97, the women's softball team captured the NCAA Division II national championship. If you're a Trekkie, you'll get a kick out of the athletic teams' nickname—the Vulcans. More

than 75 percent of students receive some form of financial aid.

Community College of Allegheny County—South Campus
1750 Clairton Rd., West Mifflin
• **(412) 469-1100**

The South Campus of CCAC serves Pittsburgh's southern suburbs on a 200-acre site near Century III Mall. Its six-story principal building features a learning assistance center, a community library, a theater, a student dining area, and classrooms. In addition, the campus boasts a learning resource center that offers computer labs and an allied health/nursing complex, and a gymnasium-fitness center. Nearly 6,600 students are enrolled.

Washington and Jefferson College
60 S. Lincoln St., Washington
• **(724) 223-6078**

"Two great presidents . . . one great college" is a tag line W&J frequently uses as a quick introduction to the institution. As you learn a little about W&J, you'll probably agree. It was founded in 1781, making it the oldest college west of the Allegheny Mountains, and has maintained its focus on liberal arts and small classes for more than 200 years. With a student-faculty ratio of 12:1, W&J offers its 1,117 students plenty of individualized attention in its classes.

The college offers baccalaureate degrees in a broad variety of majors. The humanities—including programs in art, art education, education, French, German, Spanish, history, sociology, and political science—are well represented. You also can major in business-focused disciplines such as business administration and entrepreneurial studies and science-based areas including biology (the most popular major), biochemistry, chemistry, environmental science, and neuroscience. The college offers preparatory programs in law, medicine, dental medicine, optometry, physical therapy, podiatry, and veterinary medicine. Through exchange programs, W&J students may study abroad at the University of London and The College of Higher Studies in Colombia.

One of the highlights of the academic calendar is the break between terms, which W&J has formalized as "January Intersession," when students are encouraged to broaden their experiences. Many do just that. During Intersession 1997, nearly 100 students traveled to such destinations as Egypt, Greece, East Africa, and Australia for study trips led by W&J faculty. Other students contributed to the 4,200 hours of com-

Slippery Rock University offers 60 degree programs.

Waynesburg College
51 West College St.,
Waynesburg
• (724) 852-3289,
(800) 225-7393

While Waynesburg College is southwest of our principal coverage area, it's an important institution in our region that you should know about. Moreover, it's just off I-79 in Greene County, about 50 miles from Pittsburgh, so accessibility is no problem.

This private college, founded in 1849, is affiliated with the Presbyterian Church (U.S.A.) and serves more than 1,200 students on a campus just two blocks from the Waynesburg business district. Degrees offered include master of business administration (offering a criminal justice track), bachelor of arts, bachelor of science, bachelor of science in business administration, bachelor of science in nursing, associate in business administration, and associate in general studies. Within those degree programs are several innovative initiatives.

Waynesburg offers a program in marine biology that features an academic year at Florida Institute of Technology in Melbourne, Florida. The college cooperates with several university schools of engineering to provide joint programs in chemical, electrical, and mechanical engineering, among other engineering-related disciplines, and offers similar joint programs in medical technology.

Community service is important here—the college requires 30 hours of such service from each student—and includes such activities as building homes with Habitat for Humanity and teaching computer skills aboard the college's mobile technology van. As further service to the community, Waynesburg maintains a center for education and technology to provide training and programming for local businesses as well as an adult continuing education center in Pittsburgh's South Hills.

If you're studying communications, you'll enjoy the extracurricular opportunities at Waynesburg. They include a campus radio station, television studio, newspaper, yearbook,

munity service that the college's faculty, staff and students log annually.

The 43-acre campus is located in the City of Washington, an easy 25-mile drive south from Pittsburgh along I-79. Ohio and West Virginia are about 30 minutes from the W&J campus via interstate highways. About 82 percent of students live on campus, where the college is completing the wiring of dorm rooms for cable television and data. The Student Resource Center and a related teaching lab offer 70 computers for student access. About 70 percent of students receive some sort of financial aid.

W&J belongs to the Presidents' Athletic Conference and the NCAA Division III, sponsoring 11 men's and nine women's varsity sports as well as a diverse intramural sports program. If you spend time on campus, you'll also get to know the Olin Fine Arts Center, which includes both an art gallery and a hall for performing arts.

and poetry magazine. The college is a member of the NCAA Division III and competes in seven men's and seven women's varsity sports.

More than 80 percent of Waynesburg students receive financial aid in a typical year.

West

Community College of Beaver County
1 Campus Dr., Monaca
• (724) 775-8561

When CCBC moved from its temporary headquarters in 1971, the college's leadership was looking for a location that would be convenient for most Beaver County residents. They found it here, within four miles of the geographic center of the county. The distance from the 75-acre campus to the most remote point in the county is 17 miles, meaning that no Beaver County resident has more than a 30-minute drive to get here.

The college offers 39 programs of study leading to associate degrees. These include programs in allied health, nursing, and aviation sciences. The Aviation Sciences Center features a functioning air traffic control tower at Beaver County Airport, operated by students and college faculty who are professionals in the field. The program is so progressive that the Federal Aeronautics Administration has established an Aviation Education Resource Center on site and has an agreement with CCBC for direct hire of the college's air traffic control graduates.

The college's open admissions policy works particularly well for older students returning to classes after some time away; the average student age here is 26. You'll find three levels of tuition, with Beaver County residents offered the lowest tuition, followed by tuition for residents of other Pennsylvania counties and then for out-of-state residents. CCBC provides support to students with families through the Campus Child Care Center. The Library Resource Center offers multimedia retrieval capability among its research tools. All of the college's roughly 1,150 full-time students are commuters, as there are no on-campus housing facilities.

CCBC offers varsity athletics in baseball, basketball, golf, softball, tennis and volleyball, participating in the National Junior College Athletic Association. The campus also is

home to the Beaver County Hall of Fame, where such sports legends as Joe Namath, Mike Ditka, and Tony Dorsett—all reared in Beaver County—are enshrined.

Geneva College
3200 College Ave., Beaver Falls
• (724) 846-5100, (800) 847-8255

Set on 55 scenic acres overlooking the Beaver River, Geneva College is an institution with a mission: to educate students through biblically based programs anchored by the historic evangelical and reformed Christian faith. It's a mission that informs all of Geneva's programs.

Degrees offered by the college include bachelor of arts; bachelor of cience in education, business administration, and engineering; and associate in business administration, engineering, and biblical studies. Geneva also provides pre-professional programs in cardiovascular technology, criminal justice, medical technology, and nursing.

While the college's mission is rooted in Christianity, that doesn't mean Geneva subordinates vocational preparation. A number of the college's most innovative programs include strong practical components. It offers a dual-degree program in aviation/business administration, in cooperation with the Community College of Beaver County, that leads to an associate degree in aerospace management, air traffic control, or professional piloting, as well as appropriate Federal Aviation Administration licenses and certification. Biology majors studying for a B.S. may spend one of their four years at Virginia's Fairfax Hospital. For study in other medical disciplines, Geneva maintains affiliations with the University Hospitals of Cleveland, St. Joseph's Hospital in Lancaster, and St. Vincent Health Center in Erie.

Students in all programs have broad access to the tools of technology. To cite one example, Northwood Hall, site of business and psychology classes, offers more than 100 computers for student use. The college estimates that more than 90 percent of its students receive some form of financial aid. One of the more innovative methods of helping students is an honor scholarship presented—regardless of need—to each student in an academic program who meets certain academic standards.

The student center is the heart of campus life for

HIGHER EDUCATION

the more than 1,750 Geneva students, more than half of whom are commuters. Activities include a student newspaper, cable television and FM radio stations, a yearbook, a literary magazine, a marching band, and an a cappella choir. Geneva participates in a variety of intramural and varsity sports, the latter as a member of the National Association of Intercollegiate Athletics.

Penn State Beaver
Broadhead Rd., Monaca
• **(724) 773-3500**

One of 12 campuses that form Penn State Commonwealth College, Penn State Beaver is a 100-acre campus set in the heart of Beaver County, about 30 miles northwest of Pittsburgh and 15 miles from Pittsburgh International Airport. For its 825 students, the college offers the first two years of more than 180 Penn State baccalaureate degree programs. In addition, the college offers four associate degree programs—liberal arts, science, electrical engineering technology, and hotel, restaurant, and institutional management. In one component of the hotel, restaurant, and institutional management program, students operate a dinner cafe one day a week as part of a field practicum. Penn State Beaver also offers professional certificate programs and graduate-level courses for teachers, with evening class schedules available for these programs.

Student life is full and varied, especially for those residing in the college's two residence halls. Among the most popular student activities is participation in the Masquers, which has brought live theatre to preschool and elementary school children since 1969. Students also participate in five intercollegiate sports, a variety of intramural sports, and the campus radio station, WBVR.

As the Masquers demonstrate, Penn State Beaver strives to be a force in the community, providing students with the opportunity to network and form useful contacts. Since 1976, the Brodhead Cultural Center on campus has staged free or low-cost concerts and theatrical productions in the 700-seat, open-air J.P. Giusti Amphitheater. The campus sponsors an annual celebration of the birthday of the Rev. Martin Luther King Jr. with a program and a guest speaker.

The college's adult literacy program provides educationally disadvantaged adults with tutoring in reading, math, civic literacy, family support, and English as a foreign language, while its partnership with the Aliquippa School District enriches the lives of disadvantaged youths and their families by providing academic and life skills support.

Robert Morris College
881 Narrows Run Rd., Moon
• **(412) 262-8206, (800) 762-0097**

Robert Morris College is named for one of the key financiers of the Revolutionary War; most campus buildings bear the names of America's early heroes and patriots. The pleasant campus is spread over 230 sloping acres about 5 miles from Pittsburgh International Airport. It's a convenient location for visitors.

Once you start to talk about academics at RMC, you'll leave the 18th century pretty quickly, as this private college means business—literally. RMC focuses on business education at the undergraduate, graduate, and continuing education levels. Its productive relationships with many local businesses help graduates find jobs and advance in their careers. More than 18,000 RMC alumni live and work in the region. The college's Sewall Center for Leadership, a meeting, convocation, an athletic center, is a popular site for corporate training programs.

You can pick from more than 30 majors leading to the bachelor of arts, bachelor of science and bachelor of science in business administration degrees. Among the undergraduate majors you won't find at many institutions are sport management, tourism management, and aviation management. The college awards associate degrees in business administration and computer and information systems; in a joint program with Allegheny General Hospital and Pittsburgh's Ohio Valley General Hospital, students may earn an associate in science degree from the college and a certificate in radiologic technology from one of the hospitals. At the graduate level, RMC offers 11 programs of study leading to the master of science, master of science in business administration and master of business administration degrees. For students with busy professional schedules, the college offers The One-Day-A-Week Program, which enables students to take the bulk of their classes on Saturdays. The program is available at both the Moon campus and the Pittsburgh Center.

For years, businesses have lamented the poor communications skills of their employees. RMC has come to the rescue with an innovative Communications Skills Core program for all students in bachelor degree programs. The communications requirement includes five courses in the first several years of study and four courses during the upperclass years. The courses focus on five key areas: communication principles; skills and strategies; written, oral, and nonverbal language; collaborative, interpersonal, and intercultural skills; support technologies; and affective behaviors.

RMC's 5,000 full-time and part-time students enjoy access to the Academic Media Center, which features photography and audio production facilities as well as a crackerjack television production studio, one of the finest campus studios you'll find. TV production here is no academic exercise, as RMC students program a channel for the local cable television operator, which provides in-room cable services to the college's 900 resident students. RMC competes in the NCAA Division I Northeast Conference in all its varsity sports but football, which is a Division II program. (For a more detailed look at RMC basketball, see our Spectator Sports chapter.) The college offers 10 intramural sports. More than 70 percent of RMC students receive financial aid.

RMC offers extensive continuing education programs through its Pittsburgh Center in Downtown Pittsburgh. For a profile of the Pittsburgh Center, see the Downtown section of this chapter.

Trinity Episcopal School for Ministry
311 Eleventh St., Ambridge
• (724) 266-3838, (800) 874-8754

"Serving Jesus Christ within the Episcopal Church, while welcoming committed Christians from all traditions." That's how Trinity Episcopal School for Ministry describes its mission, which it pursues in a variety of ways. Located in Beaver County, Trinity is a graduate school for religious study offering the doctor of ministry, master of divinity, master of divinity/master of arts in professional psychology, master of arts in religion, and master of arts in mission and evangelism degrees.

Trinity is set on a city block in the heart of Ambridge, symbolizing its role in the community. The school emphasizes field education opportunities, which include preaching, leading small groups, service as hospital chaplains, and work with missions for the homeless. Through the Trinity Episcopal Extension Ministries program, students may earn up to 24 credits prior to enrollment through home study supplemented by some time on campus. TEEM also is available to students in seven other cities.

While the school advises students to expect a demanding academic schedule, it provides plenty of support, including weekly meetings with advisee groups comprised of both professionals and students and two quiet days each term, when students get a break from their studies to reflect and worship. Married couples are welcome here—consistent with the school's belief that husbands and wives should minister as partners—but school-provided housing is limited.

When you're here, check out the mural that covers the entire back wall of the library building. Painted by students, it blends biblical themes and representations of local settings.

Proprietary Schools

In addition to degree-granting institutions, Southwestern Pennsylvania offers a large and eclectic group of for-profit trade schools, many of which award certificates in specialized trades. Business schools and beauty academies probably are the largest groups, but you'll also find schools for massage, pet grooming, gunsmithing, floral arrangement and care, truck driving and diesel technology, lethal weapons training . . . well, you get the idea.

These schools are so numerous—easily more than 100 in our principal coverage area—that they defy easy summary or description. To our knowledge, no one has tried. For a statewide list of private licensed/registered schools, a good resource is the *Pennsylvania Education Directory*, an annual published by Applied Arts Publishers, Box 479, Lebanon, PA 17042-0479, (717) 272-9442. Cost is $14 plus tax, with a $2 discount for educators, libraries, and school districts. You'll get names, phone numbers, and addresses, but no descriptions.

Healthcare

Southwestern Pennsylvania has many attractions, yet its healthcare sector may be one of its most abiding strengths. The region is a center for medical treatment and research, bringing local residents high quality health care and the promise that they will be the beneficiaries of cutting-edge developments. In addition, the region's reputation as a leader in healthcare serves as a magnet for medical professionals, who in turn contribute to the strength of the sector, creating a cycle of growth.

The center of the region's healthcare sector is Oakland's medical complex, which derives much of its energy and personnel from the University of Pittsburgh Medical Center (UPMC). Community medicine is well represented in the region, too, both by independent hospitals throughout our six-county coverage area and by providers affiliated with Pittsburgh-based health systems.

One could chart the history of healthcare here through its pioneers and milestones, such as Dr. Jonas Salk's development of his polio vaccine, Dr. Thomas Starzl's trailblazing work in organ transplantation; even in the development of the Mr. Yuk poison prevention program, an initiative that has saved an inestimable number of lives. Most recently, holistic medical alternatives have begun to be offered along with allopathic medicine at several UPMC hospitals, West Penn Allegheny Health System, and at doctors' offices throughout the area. You'll also find holistic practitioners, such as licensed acupuncturists and qualifiers practitioners of herbology and homeopathy, practicing in offices of their own. Just as Salk and Starzl were pioneers in saving lives, the holistic practitioners in the area are pioneers in saving the *quality* of lives.

No history of Pittsburgh healthcare would be complete without mentioning the contributions of Pittsburgh's workers and labor unions. When Pittsburgh was the industrial heart of America, it was laborers, unions, and their companies that advanced the notion of employer-provided health insurance. There may be no single person to credit for this, but it's an important contribution nonetheless.

In our look at the region's healthcare system, you'll find profiles of holistic health practices, hospitals, rehabilitation centers, and health insurance providers. We've also provided descriptions of organizations that can serve as valuable resources—and sources of referrals—for you. Finally, we've presented descriptions of some special services providers. You might not need them now, but it's sure comforting to know they're here.

LOOK FOR:
- **Wellness**
- **Hospitals**
- **Rehabilitation Centers**
- **Health Maintenance Organizations**
- **Resources & Referrals**
- **Special Services**

Wellness

Unless you're experiencing a life-threatening emergency, you can call one of the referral sources listed in our Resources section to find the name of a physician, or confidently visit one of the practitioners listed below. In some cases, both acute and chronic, working with a holistic practitioner can heal your illness; in almost all others, you can improve your quality of life.

While the modalities holistic practitioners use vary widely, one thing you'll find in common among these trained professionals is that they all ask you questions about you and your life, not just questions about your symptoms of illness. They do this because they take into account the gestalt of who you are when they're treating you—that's the nature of the "holistic" approach. In addition, most holistic practitioners strive to create a comfortable and nurturing healing environment.

Some of the most commonly used holistic modalities are acupuncture, chiropractic, massage, homeopathy, and herbology. Acupuncture—which involves the insertion of needles about the thickness of a strand of hair into particular, superficial points on the body—is useful in treating a range of symptoms, as well as the root causes of illness, including pain, headaches, hormonal imbalances, systemic weakness related to various diseases, addictions, and acute and chronic viral illnesses. In chiropractic, the spine is manipulated, with the goal of relieving pain and freeing the body's energy for health and well-being. While there are many types of massage, most are pleasant, pain-relieving, and relaxing; discuss your goals with the massage practitioner you contact to make sure the type of massage she or he does will help you achieve what you desire.

Homeopathy and herbology, often confused by new holistic health patients, are distinct sciences. Used widely in European countries, homeopathy works on the principle of "like produces like" and uses remedies containing only the "energy imprint" of the physical substances from which they were produced. These remedies address physical, mental, and emotional symptoms and can be used to bring the body back to balance during either acute or chronic illness—or simply to strengthen an individual's constitution. Herbology uses either Western or Chinese herbs in single or combination form to effect changes in the same way that pharmaceutical drugs do. Some traditional drugs are even made from herbs. For instance, the heart medication digitalis is made from foxglove, a plant originally found in the wild. In any case, many of the holistic modalities you may try have been used successfully for thousands of years—that's longer than any clinical trial we know of.

The list we give below is by no means exhaustive. Out of the many practitioners in the area, we've selected the people we or our trusted friends personally know are top-notch. If you're looking for a type of practitioner we haven't described here, call the Nuin Center at (412) 661-6108 or pick up a copy of *Point of Light* magazine at one of Pittsburgh's health food stores.

The Nuin Center is a Highland Park professional building and group meeting location center once part of the Mellon estate. The majority of the tenants are healing arts practitioners, as the intention of the center's founders was to create a space supportive of the healing arts. *Point of Light* is a free, quarterly magazine that covers healing arts and "New Age" happenings from a popular perspective. Many reputable practitioners advertise in the magazine.

North

Acu-Care: The Acupuncture Center of Pittsburgh
7500 Brooktree Rd., Ste. G102, Wexford
• **(724) 452-9334, (724) 933-4646**

Sharon Tillotson-Gallagher, R.ac. implements the Japanese style of acupuncture in her practice. As compared to traditional Chinese acupuncture, this style often uses fewer needles inserted even more superficially than in the Chinese style. While Sharon treats people of all ages and genders, she says her average patient is a woman aged 20 to 80 who has a relatively healthy lifestyle and diet and is seeking either preventative care or care that will help her maximize her health. Sharon describes her specialties as preventative care and women's health issues; although she has treated severely ill patients, this is not her focus. Representative conditions that she has treated successfully are amenorrhea and dysmenorrhea, PMS, infertility, recurring headaches, allergies, arthritis, sports-related injuries, and addiction to cigarettes. It takes about twenty minutes to reach her office from downtown Pittsburgh.

East

Stephanie Amada
1824 Murray Ave., Ste. 204, Pittsburgh
• **(412) 422-2188**

Stephanie specializes in aromatherapeutic massages, shiatsu, and Swedish deep tissue massage. Trained in massage at the Pittsburgh School of Massage Therapy, she completed Perdu University's international training program in essential oils, has a certification in aromatherapy from Aveda, and is currently completing a second such certification through the Pittsburgh Aromatherapy Institute. She has her own line of essential oil blends called Terraroma.

Stephanie Schmidt with daughter Abigail at Magee-Womens Hospital's Neonatal Intensive Care Unit.

Photo: Courtesy of Magee-Womens Hospital

Stephanie has given talks about massage at the University of Pittsburgh Medical School and she teaches massage and aromatherapy at the Career Training Academy's Monroeville and New Kensington sites. She belongs to the International Massage Association and the Natural Oils Research Association. She shares an office with Rhetta Flagg.

Acupuncture Energetics, Wellspring Valley Center
Donegal Lake Access Rd., Stahlstown
• (724) 593-6237

Acupuncture Energetics forms the cornerstone of the Wellspring Valley Center, which was founded by Christine Simmons, R.ac. Christine holds a master's degree in acupuncture and Chinese medicine from the Traditional Acupuncture Institute in Columbia, Maryland. To assist her clients in achieving greater health, along with acupuncture, Christine often uses Chinese and Western herbs, Jin Shin acupressure process, polarity therapy, movement therapy, and the Feldenkrais and Alexander techniques. One of Christine's specialties is helping clients access and recognize their emotions, with the goal of transforming emotional blocks that contribute to reduced mental and physical health. She treats clients of all ages with both acute and chronic illnesses, as well as those who are seeking preventative medical treatment, and describes the purpose of her work as being "to help people help themselves as they travel their personal journey to wholeness and self-knowledge."

Although it will take you at least 45 minutes to travel from Pittsburgh to see Christine, it's worth it. She's an experienced and talented practitioner, and you'll enjoy the lush country setting across from Donegal Lake, where Christine lives and works.

Alan Berman, D.C.
4354 Murray Ave., Pittsburgh
• (412) 422-7005

Alan is a graduate of the Sherman College of Chiropractic and uses various techniques in his adjustments, including diversified and cervical specific. He has been in practice in the same location for 21 years, and he accepts a wide range of insurances. Massage, various forms of physical therapy, and consultations with a nutritional counselor are also available through his office.

Julie Ann Caryl, D.C. and Pamela Huston, D.C.
3 Parkway Center East,
2020 Ardmore Blvd., Forest Hills
• (412) 273-3600

Julie and Pam are graduates of the Palmer College of Chiropractic and are certified in applied kinesiology and the Nambudripad Allergy Elimination Technique (NAET). Applied kinesiology is a system that evaluates structural, chemical, and mental aspects. It employs muscle testing with other standard methods of diagnosis. Nutrition, chiropractic adjustments, acupressure, exercise, and education are used therapeutically to help restore wellness.

NAET diagnosis and treatment of allergies integrates methods from the disciplines of kinesiology, chiropractic, acupressure, and nutritional science. In addition to the standard applications of chiropractic, Julie and Pam help clients with problems with environmental sensitivities, allergies, and a myriad of acute and chronic health problems. It's likely your insurance will reimburse you for treatment with the doctors, who offer comprehensive 30-minute and one-hour sessions.

> **INSIDERS' TIP**
>
> **Among its many medical firsts, Pittsburgh was the site of the first hospital-based helicopter in the Northeast—Life Flight.**

The doctors are members of the Pennsylvania Chiropractic Association, the Human Ecology Action League, The Center for Science in the Public Interest, and the Physicians Committee for Responsible Medicine. You'll start feeling more relaxed as soon as you sit down next to the burbling meditation fountain in their waiting room and have a cup of tea.

The Center for Pain Treatment
1312 E. Carson St., Pittsburgh
• (412) 431-9180

A chiropractor, Kathleen C. Clarkin, and four board-certified trigger point myotherapists—Tassos Spanos, Mark Spanos, Nancy Shapiro, and Richard Finn—comprise the Center for Pain Treatment. In addition to their certification, all the myotherapists have personally studied with Dr. Janet Travell, the originator of trigger point myotherapy and White House physician to presidents Kennedy and Johnson.

To understand how trigger point myotherapy works, it's useful to know that a trigger point is a self-sustaining irritable spot in a muscle. This irritable spot gradually causes the affected muscle to become tighter and shorter, limiting the function and motion of the muscle and causing weakness and/or pain. Most of the time, the trigger point, which is at the site of a trauma to a muscle, refers pain to another area of the body, just like a hole in a roof may cause a leak in a distant area of the ceiling. Using various massage-like techniques, a trigger point myotherapist stretches the muscle, unwinding the trigger point and thus easing the patient's pain.

Trigger point myotherapy is useful in treating a wide variety of pain syndromes, including carpal tunnel, TMJ, migraines, sciatic, tendonitis, arthritis, and both fibromyalgia and myofascial pain syndrome (which is often misdiagnosed as fibromyalgia). The therapy is also useful in improving the performance of athletes and musicians, and in cases where muscle weakness or distortion, rather than pain, is present. (Cases like the latter might include people recovering from strokes, for instance.) There's a good chance your insurance carrier will reimburse you for your sessions, as long as treatment is supervised by the chiropractor on staff.

Donna Davis, R.N.
7424 Washington, Ave., Swissvale
• (412) 271-7050

Donna implements a wide variety of massage techniques in her practice. She does traditional Swedish massage, Paul St. John Neuromuscular Therapy, the Ingram method of foot reflexology, therapeutic touch, and the Upledger form of cranial sacral therapy. She also uses Sat Nam Rasayan, a yogic form of healing that allows both practitioner and patient to be in a relaxed, neutral frame of mind.

Although the state of Pennsylvania does not require massage therapists to be certified, Donna has successfully completed the national certification test for massage. She's a member of the American Massage Therapy Association as well as the International Association of Healthcare Practitioners. We find her to be a particularly compassionate practitioner.

Francine Fettman, Ph.D.
4721 McKnight Rd., Pittsburgh
• (412) 364-4291

Dr. Fettman is a cognitive behavioral therapist who incorporates EMDR (Eye Movement Desensitization and Reprocessing) in her work. She describes EMDR as a technique that uses a client's own bilateral stimulation (usually in the form of eye movement) to facilitate the processing of disturbing and traumatic events. Her areas of specialty include the treatment of trauma, abuse, stress, and some anxiety disorders. She has a Ph.D. in developmental psychology from the University of Pittsburgh and she is certified in the practice of EMDR.

HEALTHCARE

Rhetta Flagg
1824 Murray Ave., Ste. 204, Pittsburgh
• (412) 422-2188

Rhetta specializes in cranial sacral therapy and neuromuscular technique (a particular type of very deep massage incorporating trigger points). She has been doing trigger point work for over 14 years and is an instructor in neuromuscular technique. She's the state chapter president of the American Massage Therapy Association. She was trained through the Pittsburgh School of Massage Therapy and the Chicago School of Massage. She shares an office with Stephanie Amada.

Joyce Gelles, D.C.
Murry Ridge Professional Center,
5290 Logans Ferry Rd., Ste. B, Pittsburgh
• (724) 325-4554

Joyce began her practice in 1980, shortly after she graduated from Palmer College of Chiropractic. She offers gentle chiropractic treatment for all ages, implementing multiple low force techniques, Sacro Cranial, acupressure, myofascial release, micromanipulation, neuroemotional technique, and Nambudripad Allergy Elimination Technique. She accepts insurances, but is not part of any HMO groups.

EarthWalk: The Center for Personal and Planetary Evolution
5655 Bryant St., Pittsburgh
• (412) 361-2300

The founders of EarthWalk, Pauline Dishler and Deb Schnitta, offer private sessions, as well as courses in growth and self-awareness through meditation. In private sessions, their approach focuses on supporting the body to return to balance from illness or stress. Frequently, their clients seek assistance with chronic or complex physical or life issues.

Pauline has studied with Barbara Brennan, one of the founders of mind-body medicine. She has also continued with postgraduate studies in advanced energy training. She's a registered nurse with a masters in education, and offers a solid bridge between traditional and complementary medicine.

Deb has studied with Rosalyn Bruyere, one of the leading healers in the world. Also a registered nurse, she has completed extensive postgraduate training in advanced energy training. She has pioneered an advanced energy training to assist others in working with the human body at the level of cellular illness.

No two sessions with Pauline or Deb are alike. The energy work they do, however, is gentle and pleasing to most clients. Often clients report feeling supported in a state of love that is beyond the human personality. Both Pauline and Deb are mentioned in Diane Goldner's book *Infinite Grace* as two of the pre-eminent healers in the country.

Through EarthWalk, they offer courses intended for those seeking a spiritual approach to shifting life issues, which are a cornerstone of spiritual development in Pittsburgh. A wide range of courses is available from introductory meditation to learning to work with illness at the level of the body's cells.

Mandala
211 S. Craig St., Pittsburgh
• (412) 682-2703

Mandala has long been known in Pittsburgh as a bookstore where topics like Eastern spirituality, metaphysical teachings, and holistic healthcare sell well. The store's move to Oakland from Squirrel Hill has brought with it an expansion as well as a beautiful and much larger location: On its second floor, massage therapists and energy workers practice in richly decorated offices, and Mandala hopes soon to include practitioners of other holistic modalities as well.

One of Mandala's co-owners, Steve Sciulli, along with his wife Ami, form Life in Balance, a sought-after ensemble that plays Japanese Shakuhachi flutes, quartz crystal bowls, and Tibetan singing bowls, creating a vibrational environment for deep relaxation. Life in Balance has several CDs on the market, and it's a special treat when Life in Balance is in town offering Tuesday evening performances at Mandala. Go and see how deeply you can relax; deep relaxation offers a special opportunity for healing.

Pittsburgh Aromatherapy Institute
21 West St., New York
• (412) 579-7005

The Aromatherapy Institute holds classes in both New York City and Pittsburgh. When the master teacher and director of the school, Patricia Betty, travels to Pittsburgh to teach courses, she offers private massages, facials, and essential oils consultations.

Pat is the owner of E-Scentially Yours, an aromatherapy practice and retail source in New York, and the author of *Aromatherapy: A Personal Journey through Your Senses* and *Essential Beauty*. She opened New York City's first aromatherapy business in 1980. In addition, she is on the staff at the New York Botanical

HEALTHCARE

Garden and the Seminar Center. She has been featured in print publications such as *New York New York, New York Newsday, Japanese Cosmopolitan*, and on television networks FX, NBC, and CNN, as well as online at citysearch.com.

Squirrel Hill Family Wellness Center
1926 Murray Ave., Squirrel Hill
• (412) 422-LIFE

Franne Berez, M.D., N.D. founded the Squirrel Hill Family Wellness Center in 1988. She is a Board Certified Family Practitioner with a special interest in holistic medicine for women and children, although she treats patients of all ages and genders. Complete evaluation includes a standard western medical interview, lab evaluation, hospital testing with referral to appropriate medical specialists if needed, and psychosocial evaluation. These conventional medical practices are combined with time-honored methods of naturopathic, homeopathic, and traditional Chinese diagnosis; in fact, most patients coming to see Franne seek her expertise in homeopathy.

And don't worry if doctor's offices usually set your teeth on edge. You won't even see the exam room until the last few minutes of your interview with the doctor, and forget the paper gown. You'll tell Franne about what ails you while you sit in a rocking chair in her casually decorated office. You might even still be sipping the last bit of that tea you made for yourself in the waiting room.

Mary Magan, L.Ac., who recently joined the center as a nationally certified acupuncturist and herbalist, takes a similar approach to her patient interviews. Treatments with Mary, whom we find exceptionally gentle, often include acupuncture, herbology, homeopathy, nutritional counseling, massage, or electrical therapy.

UPMC Shadyside, The Center for Complementary Medicine
5230 Centre Ave., Pittsburgh
• (412) 623-3023

Interestingly enough, when it originally opened its doors in the early 19th century, Shadyside was an independent, homeopathic hospital. While that ceased to be its identity a long time ago, Shadyside was one of the first hospitals in the country to offer such programs as medical hypnosis, pain management utilizing therapeutic touch and biofeedback, and therapeutic touch for inpatients. When national demand pushed doctors and hospitals to consider how complementary medicine could interface with conventional, allopathic medicine, the hospital was a natural site for innovation.

In 1999, UPMC Shadyside's Center for Complementary Medicine was chosen by *New Age* magazine as one of the top six complementary medicine centers in the country. The center's mission is to work in cooperation with physicians treating patients with all kinds of health conditions and to individually tailor programs for patients that suit not only their presenting conditions, but that also take into consideration what suits their personality types and spiritual and emotional needs.

The center offers acupuncture, traditional Chinese medicine, botanical medicine, naturopathic counseling, EMDR, medical hypnosis, relaxation therapy and guided imagery, body-centered psychotherapy, reflexology, shiatsu, therapeutic massage and touch, and comprehensive holistic evaluations by physicians. Soon, the center will also offer chiropractic care and biofeedback.

Whole Health Resources
2015 Murray Ave., Squirrel Hill
• (412) 421-7760

Whole Health Resources is synonymous with the work of Deborah Barr, who founded this center for holistic health counseling in 1985. Deborah—who has many years of training in meditation, yoga, whole foods nutrition, and spiritual development—provides counseling sessions relating to holistic health, macrobiotics and others forms of nutrition, natural weight loss, and attitudinal healing. She frequently gives personal development workshops and provides corporate and personal wellness coaching. She also offers shiatsu massage, foot reflexology, acupressure facial massage, and whole foods cooking instruction. Deborah's clients, each of whom participate in a wellness program they've designed with her, regularly report improvements in their health, such as stable blood sugar levels, better sleep quality, and more balanced energy. We find Deborah's positive attitude rubs off—a nice bonus.

Two other practitioners share Deborah's light-filled offices: Tory Butterworth, Ph.D., a body-centered psychotherapist, and Betsy Reiling, MPh., a homeopath. Tory holds a doctorate in psychology and has done additional training to qualify her to do body-centered psychotherapy. This form of psychotherapy works best when pursued on an extended care basis, as it addresses long-term patterns on both the mind and body levels. Tory offers free initial sessions so clients may ascertain whether the work is a good fit for them without incurring expense. Betsy, who practices classical homeopathy, has over 1,000 hours of formal training with homeopaths from all over the world. The focus of her practice is on helping clients overcome physical, mental, and emotional obstacles so they have the freedom to pursue their dreams. She also notes that she is happy to work with other practitioners her patients may be seeing, including medical doctors.

Classes in tai chi, yoga, aromatherapy, and other forms of personal and professional development are held at Whole Health Resources on a regular basis. One-on-one yoga therapy sessions are available by appointment.

Hospitals

Southwestern Pennsylvania is justifiably renowned for its leadership in medical research and treatment, and its many teaching, community, general, and specialized hospitals form the core of the health sector. In recent years, however, the region's medical group has experienced considerable volatility, as hospitals have in some cases merged to form networks and absorb physicians' practice groups, restructured to create for-profit arms in other cases, and downsized in still other cases. The result has been a new look for the health sector here; while many of the players remain the same, the names and services may have changed.

The two largest networks are UPMC Health Center, which encompasses 14 hospitals and a number of other units, and the West Penn Allegheny System, which includes seven hospitals, a hospice, and a nursing center. Smaller networks include St. Francis Health System, Pittsburgh Mercy Health System, and Heritage Valley Health System.

The implications for healthcare consumers are not yet clear. According to the Hospital Council of Western Pennsylvania, the number of staffed hospital beds in Western Pennsylvania declined 2.6 percent in 1997, while the number of full-time equivalent hospital employees dropped 2.9 percent during the same period. On the other hand, the number of inpatient surgical operations increased by 3.2 percent. It probably will be years before we fully understand the ramifications of the reshuffling in the medical sector.

In our descriptions of area hospitals, we've noted where facilities are part of a network. Where a network or system operates multiple hospitals, we've listed each hospital in its proper geographic section, while noting its affiliation with the network. If a network or system provides services apart from its hospitals, we've described those under the system or network header. Keep in mind that the sector continues to be volatile, experiencing at least several consolidations each year.

Downtown

Mercy Hospital of Pittsburgh
1400 Locust St., Pittsburgh
• **(412) 232-8111**

The flagship of Pittsburgh Mercy Health System, this tertiary and teaching hospital is located in uptown Pittsburgh near Duquesne University. The 500-bed facility groups its special services into five "Centers of Excellence": Mercy Heart Institute, Mercy Cancer Institute, Mercy Women's Health Center, Mercy Children's Medical Center, and Mercy Trauma and Burn Centers.

Mercy Heart Institute cares for approximately 10,000 patients annually, while the Mercy Cancer Institute was the region's first to offer radiation therapy in the 1950s. Mercy offers Pittsburgh's only Level 1 Regional Resource Trauma Center and Burn Center, which features a trauma team available round the clock.

Key components of the Mercy Children's Medical Center include units for neonatal intensive care, 24-hour pediatric emergencies and pediatric trauma intensive care, and ambulatory and short-stay pediatric care, as well as a newborn nursery. The Children's Medical Center also offers a program that meets the changing medical needs of women and children as they advance through life.

Mercy's community outreach includes the Parish Nurse and Health Ministries Program, which places nurses in inner city parishes in the Diocese of Pittsburgh, a pediatric clinic at the downtown Salvation Army, and Operation Safety Net, which meets the medical needs of Pittsburgh's homeless. Through Operation Safety Net, a collaborative effort with a number of human services organizations, teams of healthcare providers travel the streets of Pittsburgh to meet the homeless on their turf and render medical care.

Pittsburgh Mercy Health System
1400 Locust St., Pittsburgh
• **(412) 232-8111**

Mercy Health System boasts one of the richest traditions in the region's healthcare sector, tracing its roots to the 1847 founding of its predecessor hospital by seven Sisters of Mercy from Carlow, Ireland. System executives describe the organization as a "Catholic system of health care." In addition to Mercy Hospital of Pittsburgh and Mercy Providence Hospital, both described in this section, the system includes a 150-bed skilled nursing facility, a 26-bed personal care residence, and a network of primary care physicians.

The system also operates Mercy Behavioral Health, a network of community-based mental health, mental retardation, drug and alcohol services, and an outpatient physical rehabilitation facility in partnership with St. Clair Health System.

St. Francis Central Hospital
1200 Centre Ave., Pittsburgh
• **(412) 562-3000**

This 202-bed acute care hospital, located near the Mellon Arena, is part of the St. Francis Health System. It offers a 19-bed skilled nursing unit and a Department of Oral Surgery that provides mouth, teeth, jaw, and facial treatment for adults and children. Other facets of the hospital are The Heart and Lung Institute, colo-rectal diagnosis and treatment, a podiatry department, and an addiction services unit. The hospital maintains community primary care centers in Pleasant Hills, Robinson, and the Pittsburgh neighborhoods of Brookline and Mt. Washington.

North

West Penn Allegheny Health System Armstrong County Memorial Hospital
One Nolte Dr., Kittanning
• **(724) 543-8500**

As a community hospital, Armstrong County Memorial emphasizes outreach and education programs, featuring classes on 10 different topics including breastfeeding, CPR, babysitters emergency care, osteoporosis education, and a safe driving course for seniors. The hospital operates primary care centers in the communities of Elderton, Leechburg, and Sarver, and will provide you with physician referrals if you call (724) 543-8473.

At its main campus, the 215-bed hospital offers magnetic resonance imaging, psychiatric care, home health services, the Richard G. Laube Cancer Center, physical and occupational therapy, and programs in rehabilitation therapy

and aquatic therapy. You'll find programs in cardiac rehabilitation, organ and tissue donation, sentinel nod biopsy, Stereo TacTic, breast biopsy, brachytheraty (prostate seeding program), and pre- and post-natal care, as well as a sleep disorders lab and a wound care clinic. You can get your annual flu shots at Armstrong County Memorial and attend the annual health fair that the hospital sponsors.

Butler Health System-Butler Memorial Hospital
911 E. Brady St., Butler
• **(724) 283-6666**

Butler Health System describes itself as a community-based system of health care services that provides multiple facets of health care, including prevention, treatment, and expanded outpatient services. What that means for you is a variety of useful and timely programs and services. The system centers around Butler Memorial Hospital, a 308-bed facility with more than a century of experience. An acute care hospital, Butler Memorial offers inpatient and outpatient services, as well as skilled nursing beds.

Among the services the hospital offers are a heart center, including open-heart surgery; a center for sleep disorders; a women's health center; a round-the-clock emergency department; CAT scanning and magnetic resonance imaging; and pain management programs. The hospital also offers prenatal care and delivery services, post-partum care, pediatric assessment, and home visits. Its birthing suites allow for labor, delivery, and recovery—all in the same room. The hospital also sponsors the Butler Regional Recovery Program for drug and alcohol abuse treatment, with community centers in Butler, Cranberry, and Natrona Heights.

Butler Health System provides outpatient lab and X-ray services at several community locations, including the Butler Mall and locations in the East Brady, Slippery Rock, Zelienople, and Saxonburg communities. As part of its education program, the hospital offers classes in babysitting, diabetes care, personal stress management, and smoking cessation.

Mercy Providence Hospital
1004 Arch St., Pittsburgh
• **(412) 323-5600**

Mercy Providence Hospital, part of Pittsburgh Mercy Health System, is a 144-bed community hospital on Pittsburgh's North Side. Its surgical facilities include five suites and a specially designed urology room. Surgical specialties include total joint replacement and cataract surgery. Two-thirds of all procedures are completed on an outpatient basis.

Most of the hospital's outpatient services are centralized in the Arthur J. Rooney Diagnostic and Treatment Center, which provides diagnostic imaging and cardiology services and houses a 24-hour emergency department and a 24-hour psychiatric evaluation and referral center.

St. Francis Hospital, Cranberry
One St. Francis Way, Cranberry
• **(724) 772-5300**

Part of the St. Francis Health System, St. Francis Cranberry is only a half-mile from I-79, providing easy access for residents of Butler and Beaver counties and the North Hills of Allegheny County. It offers round-the-clock emergency care, enhanced by an on-site helicopter to transport critically ill patients. Located on the campus are: St. Francis Hospital North; St. Francis Regional Cancer Center; St. Francis Medical Office Building North, which provides laboratory and radiology services, including CAT scans, magnetic resonance imaging, X-rays, ultrasound, and mammography; and St. Francis Nursing Center North, which offers skilled and intermediate nursing care as well as physical and occupational therapy.

Suburban General Hospital
110 S. Jackson Ave., Bellevue
• **(412) 734-6000**

Part of the West Penn Allegheny Health System, Suburban General provides important services to residents of the Pittsburgh suburbs known as the North Boroughs. The 195-bed community hospital offers care in more than 30 medical specialties. These include general medical and surgical services, outpatient services, critical care, physical rehabilitation, kidney dialysis, cosmetic surgery, and occupational medicine. In addition, the hospital features an emergency department and a physical rehabilitation unit.

Suburban General provides a free health education club for those over 55 years of age. It's called the Senior Advantage Club, and it holds monthly health education programs and provides free flu shots, blood pressure readings, and a variety of health screenings. The hospital also sponsors a wide range of health education programs and support groups.

UPMC Passavant
9100 Babcock Blvd., McCandless
• **(412) 367-6700**

Located 12 miles north of Pittsburgh, UPMC Passavant is a 260-bed facility serving northern Allegheny County and southwestern Butler County. Founded in 1849, Passavant offers medical specialties in cancer and cardiac care, emergency medicine, obstetrics and gynecology, and orthopedics. The hospital features a chest pain center; subacute care units; surgical services; physical and occupational therapy departments; and centers for sleep, pain management, and speech, voice, and swallowing disorders.

UPMC St. Margaret
815 Freeport Rd., Pittsburgh
• **(412) 784-4000**

UPMC St. Margaret provides 250 acute care beds and has more than 500 physicians on staff offering medical specialties in arthritis, rehabilitation, orthopedics, family practice, gerontology, and occupational health. The hospital was founded in 1898, merged with UPMC in 1997, and serves as a valuable resource for more than 200,000 residents of Pittsburgh's northern and eastern suburbs. St. Margaret reaches into the community through such programs as paramedic response teams to assist local volunteer units, athletic training services for schools, and a variety of health screening programs.

One quirk about the hospital's location: While it's surrounded by suburban municipalities, it is part of the City of Pittsburgh.

VA Medical Center
325 New Castle Rd., Butler
• **(724) 287-4781, (800) 362-8262**

Approximately 35 miles north of Pittsburgh, this U.S. Department of Veterans Affairs center provides a wide range of primary medical services, including outpatient care, preventive services, and acute hospitalization. Special programs include geriatric/extended care, physical rehabilitation, substance abuse treatment, and mental health care. The center offers home-based primary care, a program for homeless veterans, and an outpatient facility in the Butler County community of West Middlesex. While affiliated with the VA Pittsburgh Healthcare System, the Butler facility is administered separately.

INSIDERS' TIP

The University of Pittsburgh Medical Center includes 40 buildings in a "superblock" in Oakland bounded by Fifth Avenue and DeSoto, Terrace, and Darragh streets. It's one of the world's most concentrated medical complexes.

HEALTHCARE

Brad Magill: Answering the Emergency Call for Emergency Communications

Western Pennsylvania has a proud medical history. It was here that Dr. Jonas Salk developed and implemented his polio vaccine, here that Dr. Thomas Starzl performed his pioneering work in transplant surgery. When it came to emergency communications, however, Allegheny County was until recently the sick man of Southwestern Pennsylvania.

Put most simply, the problem was a multiplicity of unintegrated systems across the county's 130 municipalities. The county's checkerboard of municipal fiefdoms can be quite charming, creating distinctive communities with their own attractions and flavor. In emergency communications, that lack of coordination was anachronistic and dangerous—anachronistic because every county adjacent to Allegheny County already boasted a fully functioning 911 communications system, dangerous because residents had many emergency numbers to remember and dispatchers often couldn't tell which calls emanated from their service areas. As recently as the start of 1998, the local white pages listed more than 150 emergency numbers—including ambulance, police, and fire departments—across Allegheny County.

Enter J. Brad Magill, who had operated Butler County's 911 system for 17 years. Magill, deputy chief of the Division of Emergency Services, was charged by the county with creating a unified 911 system out of the crazy quilt of existing mechanisms. Magill got some sense of the difficulty of the task at early planning meetings, when he was lobbied by numerous municipal representatives to designate their towns as 911 centers.

"They wanted 41 centers," Magill recalls, "and I was able to get it down to six. People told me I did a helluva job. Now, as I look back on it, I'm disappointed I didn't push for one center."

Five of the centers are known by their regional locations—Eastern Regional, Mon Valley, South Hills, Southwest Regional, and Northwest Regional. The sixth center, serving many of the county's northern communities, is called NEWCOM, a bizarre quirk that resulted when a temporary name jotted down on preliminary paperwork somehow stuck. The City of Pittsburgh constitutes an unofficial seventh center, though the city is a full participant in the system.

Even then, Magill's work wasn't done, as the county was sued by 16 municipalities who stubbornly resisted the consolidation. Once those obstacles were surmounted, Magill was ready to purchase and install the equipment to complete the coordinated system. The equipment will provide dispatchers with the name and address of each caller, facilitating speedy response, although Magill says his dispatchers still plan to question callers to glean as much useful information as they can.

Magill is quick to point out that the system is not foolproof. If you call

911 from an Allegheny County institution with multiple phones and addresses, for example, the system can relay only the institution's principal address, a problem with calls from, say, college campuses. Cell phone calls represent an ongoing frustration for all 911 systems, as current technology cannot convey the address of call origination.

"Cellular phones drive us crazy," Magill says. "The first question we ask when someone on a cell phone calls about an accident is, 'Where are you?' The answer is, 'I don't know', or 'I'm on the Parkway or Route 8.' The second question we ask is, 'Are there any injuries?' The answer usually is, 'I don't know, I didn't stop.'

"If you're on a cell phone and you don't know where you are and you haven't stopped, keep on going. Someone else [with better information] will call us."

Addresses on the border between two communities—whether within Allegheny County or adjacent to it—still will be troublesome, although Magill expects much more active dispatcher collaboration in the new system. Moreover, since address changes must be manually entered, the system will be no stronger than the companion mechanism that captures and enters address changes.

"We have almost 1 million phone addresses, and 8,000 of them change every day," Magill laments. "Businesses open and close, people move in and out. That means that every day, there are 8,000 opportunities to mess up the database. I believe there are 10,000 errors in our database and probably another 5 percent we don't know about."

Technological advances help all regional 911 systems overcome those problems. In any case, the flaws seem minor in light of the achievement. Thanks to Magill, all you'll have to do if you're in trouble in Allegheny county is dial 911.

VA Pittsburgh Healthcare System
1010 Delafield Rd., Aspinwall
• **(412) 688-6000**
7180 Highland Dr., Pittsburgh
• **(412) 365-4900, (800) 647-6220**
University Dr., Pittsburgh
• **(412) 688-6000, (800) 309-8398**

While the U.S. Department of Veterans Affairs VA Pittsburgh Healthcare System operates three facilities in the Pittsburgh area, we'll address them as a single unit, since that's the way system administrators regard it. Together, the three divisions comprise a major medical/surgical tertiary care facility with programs in orthopedics, same-day surgery, rehabilitation, radiation therapy, mental health, and substance abuse. The system features a liver transplant center, a regional cardiac surgery center, and an oncology network center. For your initial contact with the system, try the Aspinwall Division at the number listed above.

East

Life Care
225 Penn Ave., Wilkinsburg
• **(412) 247-2424**

This 155-bed facility, part of the Allegheny University Hospitals system, is located just across the City of Pittsburgh border and specializes in extended acute care, a specialized treatment program targeted to acutely ill patients who face a prolonged hospital stay due to complex medical problems. The emphasis is on intensive nursing attention and frequent physician care as part of a multidisciplinary approach. The hospital estimates that it can provide such care for 60 to 75 percent of the cost of a traditional hospital stay.

The program includes a high-observation unit as well as a therapeutic apartment used by patients prior to discharge to help them adjust to life at home. AUH Forbes Metropolitan also offers a skilled nursing unit, inpatient rehabilitation services, and geriatric psychiatry.

Forbes Regional Hospital
2570 Haymaker Rd., Monroeville
• **(412) 858-2000**

This 347-bed hospital serves Pittsburgh's eastern suburbs with a broad variety of specialties. These include obstetrics and gynecology; pediatrics; mental health; oncology; emergency medicine; and cardiology and diagnostic imaging, including magnetic resonance imaging and cardiac catheterization. The hospital's campus also includes the Forbes Family Health Center and the InterCommunity Cancer Center, which provides outpatient radiation therapy and

HEALTHCARE

chemotherapy as part of the hospital's cancer care services.

The facility's extensive obstetrics services include classes in Lamaze, prenatal care, breastfeeding, infant/child CPR, understanding puberty, and sibling relationships. At the Forbes LifeStyle Center, you'll find programs in wellness, weight loss, diabetes management, and cardiac rehabilitation.

Children's Hospital of Pittsburgh
3705 Fifth Ave., Pittsburgh
• (412) 692-5325

Children's Hospital has a legendary history. Dr. Jonas Salk developed and introduced his polio vaccine here. Children's personnel developed the "Mr. Yuk" poison prevention campaign in 1971—a program still saving lives today. More recently, Children's developed one of the world's largest pediatric transplantation centers in association with the University of Pittsburgh and Dr. Thomas Starzl.

Part of Oakland's medical complex, Children's is the only freestanding hospital in the region dedicated solely to the care of infants, children, and young adults. This 235-bed facility and its approximately 600 physicians pursue a three-part mission that encompasses patient care, biomedical research, and education. Children's offers services in cardiology, cardiothoracic surgery, diabetes, hematology/ oncology, neurosurgery, organ and tissue transplantation, orthopedics, otolaryngology, and pediatric surgery. The hospital maintains centers for pediatric trauma and pediatric emergency care, treating more than 150 children each day in these units.

With its $12 million annual research budget, Children's focuses on such conditions as juvenile diabetes and the causes and treatment of otitis media (inner ear disease) in infants and children. Special services include a child abuse investigation unit, summer camping programs that focus on quality of life after transplantation and heart disease, and community education classes in positive parenting and injury prevention.

The hospital functions as a regional referral center, serving roughly 5.5 million children in the tri-state area. It also operates three regional facilities: Children's South in Bethel Park, Children's North in Sewickley, and Children's East in Monroeville. The regional facilities offer a wide variety of outpatient services as well as same-day surgical services. For directions to any of the Children's facilities, call the Direction Hot Line, (412) 692-8088.

Citizens General Hospital
651 Fourth Ave., New Kensington
• (724) 337-5000

Since 1912, Citizens General has been serving residents of the Allegheny and Kiski valleys. Its medical staff numbers nearly 200 physicians operating in more than 35 specialties. Among the hospital's most important services are a Radiology Department that assists in the early detection of breast cancer, a Heart Station with advanced diagnostic capabilities, and a Rehabilitation Services Department that offers a far-reaching sports medicine program. In addition, Citizens offers a senior behavioral health center geared specifically toward seniors experiencing mental illness.

The Citizens General HealthPlace program offers screenings and seminars, including sessions on diabetes management, relaxation and massage techniques, urinary incontinence, hypertension, breast cancer awareness, and insurance counseling. The hospital provides rehabilitation at a community-based site in Plum.

Latrobe Area Hospital
121 W. 2nd Ave., Latrobe
• (724) 537-1000

Latrobe Area Hospital is a 260-bed community teaching hospital that serves primarily Westmoreland County. The facility provides an array of basic and specialized health care services, including general medical and surgical services, round-the-clock emergency care, gynecology and obstetrics, pediatrics, coronary and intensive care, and home health care. The hospital also offers cardiovascular diagnostic and rehabilitation care as well as a wide range of outpatient services, including arthritis care and physical, occupational, and speech therapy. The hospital's cancer program features a radiation oncology center.

In keeping with its community-serving mission, Latrobe Area Hospital sponsors a variety of education and wellness programs as well as seven satellite centers. The satellites—located in Blairsville, Hannastown, Latrobe, Ligonier, Mt. Pleasant, Norvelt, Saltsburg, and Greensburg— offer diagnostic, mental health, and home health services. Not all satellite centers offer all services.

Magee-Womens Hospital
300 Halket St., Pittsburgh
• (412) 641-4747 • www.magee.edu

Since the opening of Magee-Womens Hospital in 1911, women have been at the center of the institution's mission: providing excellence and innovation in clinical care, education, research, and the health of women and infants. The hospital's impact on the region has been, and continues to be, far reaching. Rare is the Pittsburgh-area family that hasn't selected Magee for a birth or some aspect of neonatal care.

The hospital calls its philosophy "Womancare," and a review of Magee's services leaves no doubt that the name is appropriate. Highlights of Magee's services include the latest in infertility treatment; a maternal-fetal medicine program for high-risk mothers and infants; a comprehensive array of educational programs to prepare parents and siblings; and an obstetrics program that boasts the region's newest labor, delivery, and recovery suites, plus private post-partum rooms in a totally family-centered environment.

Magee is a nationally designated Center of Excellence in Women's Health and one of the top recipients for National Institutes of Health funding for women's and infants' health research. In addition, Magee believes in empowering women with education and resources to give them the confidence they need to take an active role in their healthcare decisions. Testifying to Magee's excellence in this area, the Magee/University of Pittsburgh Cancer Institute Breast Program was rated as one of the top 10 breast programs in the country by *SELF* magazine and encompasses the most up-to-date, research-driven care for the prevention and treatment of breast cancer. Magee also makes itself a part of the Greater Pittsburgh community. Five Womancare Centers located throughout Allegheny County act as sites for Magee's educational programs and offer mammography, ultrasound, bone density screenings, specialty physician services, and Ob/Gyn practices. In addition, Magee has seven Neighborhood Health Centers that provide prenatal and primary care to patients.St. Francis Health System

4401 Penn Ave., Pittsburgh C (412) 622-4343
St. Francis Health System provides a full range of care through an integrated delivery system, part of its mission of creating a faith-based health alliance including hospitals and universities. The three hospitals profiled in this section—St. Francis Central Hospital, St. Francis Medical Center, and St. Francis Cranberry—total 1,305 beds. The system also operates St. Francis Hospital of New Castle, in addition to

INSIDERS' TIP

Allegheny County's 911 system is supported in part by a charge on telephones. If you live in the City of Pittsburgh, you pay 74 cents per month. Elsewhere in the county, the charge is $1.

nursing centers in Cranberry and the Highland Park neighborhood of Pittsburgh.

St. Francis Medical Center
400 45th St., Pittsburgh
• (412) 622-4343

This 529-bed regional referral teaching hospital, set in Pittsburgh's Lawrenceville neighborhood, is the flagship of the St. Francis Health System. St. Francis offers a broad variety of medical specialties including orthopedics, stroke treatment, magnetic resonance imaging, the Greater Pittsburgh Sleep Center, and maternity services that feature five labor/delivery/recovery suites and nine post-partum suites.

At the 24-bed Center for Critical Care, physicians evaluate and treat acute or life-threatening illnesses—heart attack, stroke, cancer—and the team provides transport by helicopter. The Center for Cancer Care offers a full range of oncology services, including chemotherapy and radiation therapy. Other medical centers within the hospital specialize in rehabilitation, laser surgery, and ophthalmology.

St. Francis is highly regarded for its psychiatric and addiction services, which the hospital has provided since the 19th century. In treating chemically dependent patients, the hospital provides a continuum of care that includes inpatient and ambulatory detoxification, group and family outpatient therapy in seven community centers, and outpatient methadone maintenance. St. Francis' psychiatric services are similarly broad, addressing eating disorders, depression, anxiety, psychosomatic disorders, and emotional problems of the elderly.

As a teaching institution, St. Francis offers what it bills as the shortest diploma program in the tri-state area for the education of registered nurses. It also conducts accredited schools for practical nurses, respiratory care practitioners, and nurse anesthetists. Physicians may study in seven graduate medical education programs.

UPMC Braddock
400 Holland Ave., Braddock
• (412) 636-5000

This 217-bed hospital serves the Turtle Creek and Mon valleys with 225 community-based physicians. Medical specialties include chemical dependency/detoxification, emergency medicine, orthopedics, coronary and medical/surgical intensive care, and same-day surgery. The hospital features three units dedicated to the needs of patients coping with mental illness, as well as a 30-bed progressive care center that functions as a long-term care facility.

UPMC Health System
3811 O'Hara St., Pittsburgh
• (412) 647-2345

UPMC Health System, affiliated with the University of Pittsburgh schools of the health sciences, strives to be an integrated system for health care in Western Pennsylvania, offering a full range of healthcare services. At its Oakland campus, UPMC operates UPMC Presbyterian, UPMC Montefiore, Eye and Ear Hospital, Western Psychiatric Institute and Clinic, and the University of Pittsburgh Cancer Institute. In all, these hospitals provide 1,221 beds and form the core of Oakland's medical complex.

Two of UPMC's hospitals—UPMC Presbyterian and UPMC Shadyside—are tertiary care facilities, and there are nine community hospitals: UPMC Beaver Valley, UPMC Braddock, UPMC Passavant, UPMC South Side, UPMC St. Margaret, UPMC McKeesport, UPMC Bedford Memorial, UPMC Horizon, and Lee Regional. All those within our six-county coverage area are profiled in this Hospitals section.

At the hospitals on UPMC's Oakland campus, medical specialties include cardiology, human genetics, sports medicine and orthopedics, geriatrics, occupational and environmental medicine, AIDS treatment and immunology, trauma and emergency medicine, ophthalmology and otolaryngology, neurosurgery, cardiothoracic surgery, psychiatry (including inpatient care), and critical care medicine. The complex also includes the renowned Thomas E. Starzl Transplantation Institute, named for Pittsburgh's pioneering organ transplant surgeon.

UPMC's Physician Division manages practices encompassing more than 3,000 primary care physicians and physician specialists, while its Insurance Division offers managed care products. Through its Diversified Services Division, UPMC provides rehabilitation and in-home services, a mail-order pharmacy, durable medical services, technology transfer ventures, international health care initiatives, and retirement living options.

UPMC Shadyside
5230 Centre Ave., Pittsburgh
• (412) 623-2121

This 486-bed hospital in Pittsburgh's Shadyside neighborhood traces its roots to 1866 and merged with UPMC Health System in 1997. Its specialty areas include primary care, cardiology, cardiovascular surgery, oncology, women's health services, neuroscience, orthopedics, geriatric services, endocrinology, gastroenterology, sinus surgery, diagnostic imaging, rehabilitation, and obstetrics and gynecology services. The medical staff includes more than 600 primary care physicians and specialists. Getting back to its roots as a homeopathic hospital, Shadyside recently opened the Center for Complementary Medicine. For more information on the Center and the modalities it offers, refer to our Wellness section in this chapter.

The Western Pennsylvania Hospital
4800 Friendship Ave., Pittsburgh
• (412) 578-5000

One of the flagship hospitals of the Western Penn Allegheny Health System, West Penn is a 512-bed tertiary care medical center, founded in 1848 and set in Pittsburgh's Bloomfield neighborhood. Services provided by the 900-member medical staff include sophisticated treatments for cancer, cardiovascular disease, high-risk pregnancies, and diabetes, as well as an innovative, aggressive approach to burn care. The hospital's bone marrow transplantation program is one of the top 20 in the nation, and its burn trauma center was the first in the region to successfully pass the rigorous verification procedures of the American Burn Association and the American College of Surgeons Committee on Trauma. West Penn also has a breast diagnostic imaging center, an infant apnea center, and an outpatient rehabilitation center.

In addition, the hospital was one of the first in the region to have a dedicated patient-focused care unit, and in July 1995, the hospital opened the nine-story Patient Care Tower, specially designed around the patient-focused care concept.

Westmoreland Health System
532 W. Pittsburgh St., Greensburg
• (724) 832-4000

In addition to operating Westmoreland Regional Hospital, Westmoreland Health System provides a number of additional services for Westmoreland County residents. These include The SurgiCenter at Ligonier, specializing in outpatient ophthalmic plastic laser surgery as well as pain management, and MedCare Equipment Co., which offers medical supplies for purchase or rent. Other system units are Westmoreland Regional Hospital Foundation and CareGivers of Southwestern PA, which offers homemaker, live-in, and home health aide services.

Westmoreland Regional Hospital
532 W. Pittsburgh St., Greensburg
• **(724) 832-4000**

A 356-bed hospital, Westmoreland Regional is the flagship of Westmoreland Health System. It offers a Community Comprehensive Cancer Care Center—which features surgery, chemotherapy, radiation therapy, free screenings, and a patient transportation program—and the Heartcenter, which includes a cardiac catheterization laboratory and open heart surgery.

The Westmoreland for Women program offers a wide range of gynecological services and classes for pregnant women and those considering pregnancy. These include sessions in personal birthing plans, lactation, infant/child CPR, and sibling and grandparent education. As part of its obstetrics program, the hospital provides labor/delivery/recovery suites. Other services include rehabilitation, diabetes treatment, home health care and hospice, and a sleep disorders center.

South

Canonsburg General Hospital
100 Medical Blvd., North Strabane
• **(724) 745-6100**

If you're scheduled for surgery at this Washington County facility, you have the option of enrolling in the hospital's Custom Care Program, an initiative that prepares patients for surgery and rehabilitation through education and one-on-one relationships with staff. Nurses will visit your home to explain the surgery process and help you fill out the necessary paperwork, and you'll also get a visit from a physical therapist, who will discuss medication and rehabilitation and possibly conduct a home safety evaluation.

The 120-bed hospital, part of the West Penn Allegheny Health System, features a subacute/skilled care unit(for patients no longer in need of acute care but not quite ready to return home), an emergency department, rehabilitation and laboratory services, medical imaging, and a mammography center.

Canonsburg General offers a number of innovative community programs. Project Healthy Children, an early detection and pre-

vention initiative, offers health fairs, baby sitting training, and shadowing/mentoring programs. Lifeline provides nearly 200 chronically ill senior citizens with the ability to communicate from their homes directly with the hospital's emergency department. Through the Watchful Shepherd program, children at risk for abuse—those referred to the hospital by county authorities or court order—are equipped with push-button devices that activate alarm signals in the hospital's emergency department. Nurses answering the alarms speak directly to the children to assess the situation and can dispatch police to the home.

Jefferson Hospital
Coal Valley Rd., Jefferson
• **(412) 469-5000**

The largest component of the Jefferson Hospital is a 392-bed facility that boasts a medical staff of more than 400 physicians in 37 specialties. Jefferson offers a wide variety of emergency, inpatient, diagnostic, rehabilitative, and therapeutic services. Among its special initiatives are an occupational medicine program, a sleep lab, drug and alcohol detoxification, speech pathology, and a sports medicine program. One of the most consumer-friendly aspects of the hospital is its spacious parking lot, which features nominal rates and security guards.

St. Clair Hospital
1000 Bower Hill Rd., Mt. Lebanon
• **(412) 561-4900**

St. Clair Hospital is a 308-bed, general acute care community hospital that principally serves 13 communities in the South Hills. Medical services include family practice, obstetrics/gynecology, pediatrics, psychiatry, surgery, anesthesiology, emergency medicine, medical imaging, and laboratory functions. The hospital operates a fertility center and a heart center that offers patients the convenience of testing, treatment, recovery, and rehabilitation, all at the same hospital.

St. Clair reaches out to the community through a variety of educational and support programs, many at no cost. These include Feminine Focus, the Cancer Support Group, Maternity Education, and Changes and Choices for Older Adults and Their Caregivers. You can get a complete guide to the hospital's community programs through its

INSIDERS' TIP
Mercy Hospital, now part of the Mercy Health System, was the first hospital west of the Alleghenies.

HEALTHCARE

Public Relations Department, (412) 344-6600, extension 1025.

Monongahela Valley Hospital
Country Club Rd., Monongahela
• (724) 258-1000

Mon Valley Hospital was formed in 1972 through the merger of Charleroi-Monessen Hospital and Memorial Hospital in Monongahela, both of which traced their roots to the turn of the century. Thus, this facility has an outstanding track record of service to Mon Valley residents.

The 277-bed facility boasts a 180-member medical staff representing more than 40 specialties. Among the services offered are obstetrics/gynecology, psychiatric, critical and cardiac care, rehabilitation, emergency medicine, occupational health, and drug and addictive disease treatment. Mon Valley provides comprehensive oncology services, including a Regional Cancer Treatment Center, and it features a SameDay Surgery Center. The campus also includes an education conference center complex.

UPMC South Side
2000 Mary St., Pittsburgh
• (412) 488-5550

Part of the UPMC network since 1996, this hospital was founded in 1889 and today boasts 216 beds and a variety of medical specialties. These include acute medical/surgical services; rehabilitation; physical, occupational, and speech therapy; geriatric services; emergency and occupational medicine; and subacute care. The facility on Pittsburgh's South Side also offers an inpatient psychiatric unit, a cardiac catheterization laboratory, a sleep laboratory, and a peripheral vascular lab.

The Washington Hospital
155 Wilson Ave., Washington
• (724) 225-7000

The Washington Hospital and its School of Nursing have provided valuable services to Washington and Greene county residents since 1897. The 258-bed facility, the largest employer in Washington County, offers cardiac care, obstetrics and women's services, occupational medicine and rehabilitation, home health and hospice services, emergency care, mental health treatment, sleep disorder care, and a wellness center.

In addition, you'll find a children's therapy center, a cancer care center, and a reentry program that helps patients return to everyday living. Washington Hospital operates 20 satellite facilities in the region.

West

The Medical Center, Beaver
1000 Dutch Ridge Rd., Beaver
• (724) 728-7000

Part of Heritage Valley Health System, The Medical Center is a 407-bed facility that traces its roots to 1894. The hospital offers emergency treatment, maternity and child care services as well as cancer and cardiology treatment, including open heart surgery. Other services include home care, occupational medicine, plastic and reconstructive surgery, psychiatry, rehabilitation, and rheumatology care.

Pittsburgh's Ohio Valley General Hospital
Heckel Rd., Kennedy
• (412) 777-6161

This 103-bed hospital was founded in 1906 as McKees Rocks General Hospital, so its record of service to the community spans nearly a century. Ohio Valley's services include emergency and primary care, specialty medicine, cancer care, cardiology, cardiac rehabilitation, critical care, general and specialty surgery, respiratory therapy, rehabilitation, obstetrics and gynecology, home care, lithotripsy, and such diagnostic services as magnetic resonance imaging and SPECT imaging.

The hospital also offers a number of special services, including the Wound Care Center, for treatment of chronic, nonhealing wounds; the Cataract & Eye Surgery Center; the Sleep Evaluation Center; and a health and wellness program for those over 50. Ohio Valley operates a school of nursing, which offers a 22-month diploma program with 36 credits from Carlow College, and a school of radiography, leading to a certificate and an associate degree from Robert Morris College.

To fulfill its mission of service to the community, Ohio Valley maintains a speakers' bureau and community education programs.

Sewickley Valley Hospital
720 Blackburn Rd., Sewickley
• (412) 741-6600

Sewickley Valley Hospital, a component of

INSIDERS' TIP
The electron microscope was invented in Pittsburgh.

Magee-Womens Hospital delivers thousands of babies each year and remains a leader in women's healthcare.

Photo: John McCaulley

Heritage Valley Health System, offers 208 beds and a variety of services that include cardiology, diagnostic radiology, orthopedic surgery, rehabilitation, peripheral vascular surgery, ophthalmology, oncology, psychiatry, and transitional care.

UPMC Beaver Valley
2500 Hospital Dr., Aliquippa
• **(724) 857-1212**

UPMC Beaver Valley features 183 beds and medical specialties in home health and hospice care, skilled nursing, emergency medicine, psychiatry, cardiac catheterization, and occupational medicine. It offers cancer treatment in conjunction with the University of Pittsburgh Cancer Institute and maintains a cardiopulmonary physiology lab for diagnosis of heart and lung disease.

Rehabilitation Centers

While a number of area hospitals offer rehabilitation services, Southwestern Pennsylvania also boasts facilities that focus on rehabilitation. The organizations described below span the full range of services, including physical rehabilitation and rehabilitation from alcohol, drug, and chemical dependency.

Eagle Physical Therapy
201 Smith Dr., Ste. B, Cranberry
• **(724) 772-4700**

Eagle provides a full range of outpatient physical rehabilitation services at 12 area offices north and west of Pittsburgh, including: Allison Park, Moon, Robinson, Murrysville, Westview, Bridgeville, and Wexford in Allegheny County; Butler, Mars, and Zelienople in Butler County; Baden in Beaver County; and Uniontown in Fayette County. Treatment covers such conditions as athletic joint and spinal injuries, hand therapy, arthritis, pediatric rehabilitation, osteoporosis, TMJ, headaches, foot and ankle sprains, women's health, and neurological disorders. Eagle also offers occupational and speech-language therapy.

You'll need a doctor's prescription before utilizing any of the services of this for-profit company. Insurance plans typically cover—in full or in part—many of Eagle's services.

Gateway Rehabilitation Center
Moffett Run Rd., Center Twp.
• **(412) 766-8700**

A nonprofit agency, Gateway offers both inpatient and outpatient chemical dependency treatment programs—for adults and adolescents—at nine southwestern Pennsylvania locations: Ambridge, Beaver Falls, Center Township,

HEALTHCARE

Cranberry, Fox Chapel, Greensburg, Green Tree, Monroeville, and Peters. Gateway provides specialized programs for women, youths and young adults, residents of public housing communities, and referrals from the Pennsylvania Department of Corrections. Gateway recently opened a dual disorders treatment program at its Center Township facility for adults with concurrent chemical dependency and mental health problems.

Gateway offers comprehensive community and school-based prevention services through its VISION Prevention Program. The center also provides employee assistance program services, training, and professional conferences.

A special touch: when clients have achieved six months' sobriety, they're invited to participate as Gateway volunteers.

UPMC Rehabilitation Hospital
1405 Shady Ave., Pittsburgh
• **(412) 420-2345**

This 85-bed facility in Pittsburgh's Squirrel Hill neighborhood helps area residents with brain injuries, spinal cord injury and disease, stroke, and orthopedic injuries recover, live with their conditions, and work toward independence. The hospital offers acute inpatient and outpatient services. Individual patient treatment programs include behavioral medicine; nutrition services; occupational, physical, and speech-language therapy; and vocational/community reentry services. The hospital also offers an arthritis swim program open to both outpatients and members of the community at large.

The Watson Institute
301 Camp Meeting Rd., Sewickley
• **(800) 922-4226**

The Watson Institute provides comprehensive special education programs for children ages 3 to 12 who have developmental disabilities, including autism (The Watson Institute's specialty), cerebral palsy, muscular dystrophy, neurological impairments, and pervasive developmental disorders.

Health Maintenance Organizations

HMOs have become a vital aspect of daily life. Many Southwestern Pennsylvanians—whether self employed or employed by firms large or small—now have the option to receive medical insurance from HMOs. They've become

so important, if not downright omnipresent, that a local nonprofit organization, The Pittsburgh Business Group on Health, has begun publishing regular statistical reports on certain aspects of HMOs. Those reports are described in our "Resources & Referrals" section below. In the following section, we'll introduce you to the primary players. The category "commercial enrollees" includes enrollees not receiving Medicare or Medicaid assistance. Our descriptions are adapted from the *Pittsburgh Business Times 1998 Book of Lists*, (412) 481-6397.

Keystone Health Plan West
120 Fifth Ave., Pittsburgh
• **(412) 544-7000**

Keystone Health Plan West is operated by Highmark Blue Cross Blue Shield, the region's largest health insurer. The plan operates in 29 counties and has 2.5 million members in Western Pennsylvania alone.

HealthAmerica Pennsylvania
5 Gateway Center, Pittsburgh
• **(412) 553-7300, (800) 735-2202**
• **www.healthamerica.cvty.com**

HealthAmerica and HealthAssurance, headquartered in Pittsburgh and Harrisburg, Pennsylvania, provide managed health care products and services including HMO, POS, PPO, and Medicare + Choice to 6,300 employers and more than 500,000 members in Pennsylvania and Ohio. In 1999, HealthAmerica was ranked by *Newsweek* magazine as the best health plan in Pennsylvania, and the best in the nation for women's and child and adolescent care.

Med Plus Three Rivers Health Plans
300 Oxford Dr., Monroeville
• **(800) 400-4003**

Nearly 100 hospitals and close to 5,000 doctors participate in the company's programs, which serve Medicaid and CHIP program recipients only. (CHIP is a health plan for uninsured children and youth 18 and younger.)

UPMC Health Plan
112 Washington Pl., Pittsburgh
• **(412) 454-7500**

Owned by UPMC Health System, UPMC Health Plan serves nearly 40,000 commercial enrollees. In our principal coverage area, the plan features 15 participating hospitals, 443 participating primary care physicians, and 515 participating physician specialists. One notable feature of UPMC Health Plan is that if your doctor orders something, you've got it. There are

HEALTHCARE

no administrators policing doctors' decisions in this plan.

UPMC Health Plan Best Health Care
P.O. Box 8440, Edgewood 15218-0440
• (800) 286-4242
This program, which operates in Allegheny, Armstrong, Beaver, Washington, and Westmoreland counties, serves nearly 27,000 Medicaid recipients.

Aetna US Health Care
5313 Campbell's Run Rd., Robinson
• (412) 788-0500, (800) 233-3105
A total of 52 hospitals, 1500 primary care physicians, and 2,600 physician specialists in the region participate in Aetna US Health Care plans. The plan boasts 120,000 commercial enrollees and 30,000 Medicare enrollees in the Western Pennsylvania region.

Resources & Referrals

Western Pennsylvania's presents a rich variety of healthcare opportunities—so rich, in fact, that determining the best opportunities for you and your family can be challenging. A number of organizations are dedicated to helping you navigate the healthcare system. Consider these organizations valuable resources for referrals and pertinent information.

Allegheny County Medical Society
713 Ridge Ave., Pittsburgh
• (412) 321-5030
When you're looking for a physician, the Allegheny County Medical Society can provide you with information that will help in your selection. The society will not make specific recommendations, of course, but it will provide information on office location; hospital privileges; specialties and subspecialties; and board certification and education, including undergraduate, medical school, and residency credentials.

There's no charge for the information, but the service has limitations. You can request information for up to three physicians per call. The society does not provide information on specific procedures performed or disciplinary actions. Finally, while the society includes more than 3,000 member

physicians, it has no information to offer you about nonmember physicians.

Consumer Health Coalition
650 Smithfield St., Pittsburgh
• (412) 456-2216
The coalition focuses on educating the public about children's health and managed care issues—and on important policy changes in these areas. The group holds information meetings, distributes a free quarterly newsletter, and works with policy makers to convey public input. When you call them, they'll be happy to provide information and referrals.

Contact HelpLine
P.O. Box 111294, Pittsburgh
• (412) 578-2450, (412) 255-1155
Imagine a friend you could call round the clock, seven days a week, for advice on any medical or emotional problem that was troubling you. You don't have to imagine it, because you have just that friend in HelpLine. Operating with Contact Pittsburgh, HelpLine is an information and referral center staffed all day, every day, by phone counselors who will listen as you describe your situation, then refer you to community resources.

HelpLine is affiliated with a number of self-help and support networks. While their service area generally is Allegheny County, they won't let you down if you call them from another county. If they can't offer immediate assistance, they'll refer you to a sister information and referral center that operates with a nationwide scope.

HelpLine also publishes "Where To Turn," a directory of health and human services in Allegheny County, a guide that first appeared in 1908. While HelpLine's phone counseling and referrals are free of charge, there is a cost for the directory. HelpLine is a partnership of Contact Pittsburgh and United Way of Allegheny County.

The Hospital Council of Western Pennsylvania
500 Commonwealth Dr., Warrendale
• (724) 776-6400
The council includes most of the hospitals in Western Pennsylvania, and most of its services are targeted to member hospitals. Nevertheless, council staff are knowledgeable about most healthcare providers,

INSIDERS' TIP
If you're interested in keeping up with regional healthcare trends, try a subscription to *Hospital News*, (412) 395-1775, priced at $28 annually. While this monthly tabloid is targeted to medical professionals, many of its features are of interest—and comprehensible—to the rest of us.

HEALTHCARE

services, and institutions in the region, and they'll be happy to point you in the right direction when you call. They will not, however, recommend specific physicians or providers.

Pittsburgh Business Group on Health
c/o Greater Pittsburgh Chamber of Commerce, 4256 Sixth Ave., Pittsburgh
• **(724) 251-0230**

The Pittsburgh Business Group on Health (PBGH) is a nonprofit organization promoting the delivery of quality, cost-effective, value-based healthcare in Southwestern Pennsylvania. Members include large and mid-sized employers who combined provide health care benefits to over 400,000 employees, retirees, and dependents in the region.

While many PBGH services are targeted to its members, the organization performs several important functions of considerable interest and value to consumers. Perhaps the most significant of these is an annual report called Western Pennsylvania HMO Performance Scorecard that provides information about local HMOs in many key categories. For example, the Scorecard will tell you the percentage of participants in each HMO who benefited from such services as mammography screening, pap smears, prenatal care, immunizations, retinal screening, and a number of other procedures. This information can help you determine which HMO might work best for you. There is charge for the Scorecard. You can get yours by contacting PBGH at the address or phone number above.

Rx Council of Western Pennsylvania
1709 Blvd. of the Allies, Pittsburgh
• **(412) 471-9570**

The council offers a valuable and unusual service by providing emergency prescription assistance to low-income Allegheny County residents. A nonprofit organization, the council focuses on those in danger of falling through the cracks—people who can't afford to pay for their prescriptions but are not eligible for assistance from other programs.

The council offers two companion programs. First, it issues emergency vouchers to cover the cost of a monthly supply of a prescribed medication. Prescriptions can be filled at any pharmacy, which may enhance the benefits by offering its medications at a discount. Through the second program, the council helps its clients apply to the pharmaceutical industry's indigent programs, which provide a complimentary six-month supply of prescribed medicines. The council also acts as an advocate for admission of eligible clients

into programs that could provide more comprehensive health care coverage.

The council maintains income eligibility guidelines for its programs.

Special Kids Network
5320 N. Pioneer Rd., Gibsonia
• **(800) 986-4550**

If you have a child with a chronic or disabling health condition, Special Kids Network can help you find the services you need. A service of the Pennsylvania Department of Health, it's a statewide network with six regional offices throughout the Commonwealth. Trained telephone counselors will provide referrals from a statewide database grouped into six broad categories: education/training, health care products/services, recreation/leisure, social service/counseling, support/advocacy, and therapy. The database includes more than 5,300 agencies.

Special Services

With its active and multifaceted healthcare field, Southwestern Pennsylvania is blessed with a broad variety of special services providers. For example, you'll find support groups for most ailments and many hospital-based community outreach programs. While it would be impossible to profile all of the region's special services providers, we've described some below that stand out because of the broad applicability of their services.

The Alliance for Infants & Toddlers
2100 Wharton St., Pittsburgh
• **(412) 431-1905**

Do you have questions about the way your child plays, learns, moves, or talks? The Alliance for Infants & Toddlers coordinates early intervention services for children from birth to their third birthday. The various early intervention supports and services are designed to build and enhance the natural learning that occurs in a child's life. Services include developmental screening and assessment, family support, and resources coordination. All services are provided in the home, daycare, or other community setting identified by the family. Services are provided at no cost to the family.

Forbes Hospice
6655 Frankstown Ave., Pittsburgh
• **(412) 665-3301**

Forbes Hospice opened in 1979 as the first of its kind in the state, offering both inpatient and

Womancare Birth Center—mother Makeshelia Berry and baby Ondrea Berry.

Photo: Courtesy of Magee-Womens Hospital

home-care services. The hospice provides for the physical, emotional, and spiritual needs of patients with terminal illnesses and their families. Through its eight-bed unit, an extensive home-care program, and bereavement counseling services, the hospice supports death with dignity, removing the stigma and isolation that often accompanies a terminal illness. Forbes Hospice has been a model for both its innovative care protocols and for reimbursement reform.

ARC-Allegheny
711 Bingham St., Pittsburgh
• (412) 995-5000

The mission of ARC-Allegheny is to promote opportunities for, and protect the rights of, people with retardation and developmental disabilities. In ARC's Children's Division, 600 infants and toddlers each year receive assessment and therapy through early intervention. The agency's Senior Project includes three homes specially designed for older adults.

Other programs include Parent to Parent, which links families whose children may have similar circumstances or needs; integrated camping and recreational opportunities for children and adults; ESPRIT, which offers families raising at-risk children instruction in housekeeping skills; medical appointment scheduling; toy selection; and Time-Out, which provides respite care for families. ARC's Parc-Way Supported Employment program employs 238 workers at four facilities and has placed more than 100 adults with retardation on the payrolls of local businesses.

Burger King Cancer Caring Center
4117 Liberty Ave., Pittsburgh
• (412) 622-1212
• trfn.clpgh.org/cancercaring

The center is a nonprofit organization dedicated to helping people diagnosed with cancer—as well as their families and friends—cope with the emotional impact of the disease. This is not a medical treatment facility; its services help those undergoing treatment cope with the emotional impact of cancer.

Services—all free of charge—include a telephone helpline, professional guidance from social workers, and support groups targeted to children, young adults, women with breast cancer, families of those with cancer, and survivors of those claimed by the disease. The center provides a newsletter, a resource library and community resource referrals, as well as workshops in nutrition, exercise, music therapy, and journaling. The center is funded by Southwestern Pennsylvania Burger King franchisees and their corporate partners, Heinz USA and Coca-Cola Foundation.

HEALTHCARE

Child's Way
5425 Baum Blvd., Pittsburgh
• **(412) 365-6065**

A joint program of The Children's Home of Pittsburgh and The Rehabilitation Institute, Child's Way is an outpatient day facility that supports the prescribed care needs of medically complex children. When children are here, they enjoy socialization and interaction with other youngsters while receiving care from pediatric nurses, therapists, development specialists, and caregivers. In addition, Child's Way pioneered the first pediatric extended care center in Pennsylvania.

The two sponsoring organizations founded Child's Way after watching families struggle to meet the needs of medically fragile children. In such situations, one parent often is forced to sacrifice employment to care for their child, aggravating the financial strain. One of the goals of Child's Way is to enable parents to return to work or school, knowing that their children are well cared for at Child's Way.

Donated Dental Services
901 West St., Wilkinsburg
• **(412) 243-4866**

DDS provides complimentary dental services to people who are disabled, elderly, or what the program calls "medically compromised." That includes those who have a permanent disability and can neither afford dental care nor receive it through other programs. Services also may be provided for those who are Medicaid eligible but with dental needs not covered by any current provider. The condition must be severe enough to prohibit or significantly limit gainful employment. Due to the overwhelming need, no one may receive program services more than once.

DDS is a program of the Foundation of Dentistry for the Handicapped, with funding from the Mellon Foundation and support from the Pennsylvania Dental Association and Eastern Area Adult Services. More than 350 Western Pennsylvania dentists, as well as many specialists and laboratories, contribute their services to DDS.

Family House and The Inn at Montefiore Hospital
233 McKee Pl., Pittsburgh
• **(412) 578-8600**
514 N. Neville St., Pittsburgh
• **(412) 578-3640**
3459 Fifth Ave., Pittsburgh
• **(412) 647-7777, (412) 647-8777**

While Pittsburgh was growing as a medical center—and particularly prominent for its treatment of children—it became apparent that something was lacking in services offered. Families who journeyed to town for medical care for their relations often could not locate economical lodgings that also were convenient to Oakland's medical complex. Family House was one of several local organizations that stepped into that breach.

Family House maintains the three facilities listed above for minor and adult patients and their families who travel to Pittsburgh for evaluation or treatment of serious illnesses. Patients and their families may stay at The Inn or at either Family House location—they're both within walking distance of Oakland's medical center, but UPMC also provides courtesy shuttle service.

The facilities feature both single and double rooms as well as suites for four to six people. All rooms have private telephone lines. You'll find communal kitchens, private bathrooms, television lounges, and laundry facilities. Guests at Family House residences are responsible for fees, but these are well below the market rate for commercial lodging.

HealthPlace
120 Fifth Avenue Pl., Pittsburgh
• **(412) 544-7392**

If you've ever imagined a shopping mall where every service or product you could buy was designed to improve your health, then you've imagined HealthPlace. A division of Highmark Blue Cross Blue Shield, HealthPlace shapes the idea of prevention into a bright, fun environment, with a variety of stations that provide many benefits. You'll find a site for cholesterol, blood pressure, and skin cancer screening; a site for lifestyle change programs; and stations that offer referrals, counseling, and information.

Physicians often prescribe HealthPlace so patients can learn more about their conditions and diagnoses. HealthPlace also sponsors programs in smoking cessation, relaxation, CPR, yoga, and tai chi, among other topics. In addition to the center in downtown Pittsburgh, you'll find HealthPlace at 11 other locations in Western Pennsylvania.

HomeHelp
903 West St., 2nd fl., Pittsburgh
• **(412) 247-4000**

This is a nonprofit agency that provides home care throughout Allegheny County and the surrounding areas. It's sponsored by a multi-denominational group that includes Baptist Homes of Western Pennsylvania, the Jewish Association on Aging, and Presbyterian SeniorCare. The agency offers skilled nursing care, rehabilitation, and medical-social services, all of which generally are covered by health insurance programs. Other services include household chores, live-in companions, and sleepover services, all of which are on a self-pay basis.

Jewish Association on Aging
200 JHF Dr., Pittsburgh
• **(412) 422-5600**

Among the many valuable services provided by the association is the Sivitz Jewish Hospice, which is staffed by professionals and volunteers who are specially trained to understand Jewish values and traditions. Other services include adult day services; kosher meals for delivery to homebound adults; and personal care, assisted living, and nursing/rehabilitation centers.

John J. Kane Regional Centers
955 Rivermont Dr., Pittsburgh
• **(412) 422-6800**
100 Ninth St., McKeesport
• **(412) 675-8600**
110 McIntyre Rd., Ross
• **(412) 369-2000**
300 Kane Blvd., Scott
• **(412) 429-3000**

The Kane regional centers are skilled nursing facilities offering 360 beds per facility. While the region boasts other providers of skilled nursing services, the Kanes have a distinguished and unusual history. Formerly operated by Allegheny County as a broad health care provider for the indigent elderly, the Kanes were turned over to a private operator in the 1990s and have broadened their mission.

They offer a variety of rehabilitation services including physical, occupational, and speech therapy, as well as dietary services for those with special needs. Physicians and other medical specialists are brought to the centers to care for patients' needs.

The Kane environment offers large activity rooms, intimate sitting areas, outdoor barbecue courts, acres of landscaped grounds, nonsectarian chapels, and onsite barber/beauty shops. Accepted methods of payment include medical assistance, medical assistance pending, third-party insurance, private payment, and contracts with HMOs on a case-by-case basis. Evening and weekend admissions are common to help families manage their busy schedules.

William and Mildred Orr Compassionate Care Center
6023 Harvard St., Pittsburgh
• **(412) 362-3550**

With hospitals discharging patients more quickly than ever, elderly patients and those at risk of homelessness can be placed in a precarious position upon their discharge, sometimes lacking residences and caregivers to help them through their recuperation. The Orr Compassionate Care Center has stepped into that breach by providing post-hospitalization respite care for the elderly, the frail, and the homeless.

The 14-bed facility in Pittsburgh's East Liberty neighborhood is a Christian ministry that not only provides three meals a day, laundry service, case management, and pastoral care to residents, but it also helps them work toward self-sufficiency for their eventual release from the center. Physicians, social workers, and clergy typically refer prospective residents to the center. Because the facility is not a medical center, residents must provide and administer their own medication, make arrangements for any nursing care or therapy, and provide detailed information about their medical histories. Most stays at the center range from a few days to three weeks.

Parental Stress Center
1700 E. Carson St., Pittsburgh
• **(412) 381-4800**

The Parental Stress Center provides solution-focused family education, counseling, and support in Southwestern Pennsylvania and beyond. Locally, intensive in-home service is combined with neighborhood-based parenting education and support to provide the necessary assistance to families. The agency operates seven days a week.

Specific populations are served, including birth families, foster and adoptive families, grandparents and other caregivers, non-custodial parents (especially fathers), and teens. Special programs include Family Unification Services, Community Visitation Network, Critical Differences (support, information, referral), Father's Resource Center, Parenting Education, Training and Support, and Grandparents as Parents.

No family is denied service due to difficulty with payment. Private donations cover these costs. Also, anyone may make a referral, and self-referral is acceptable as well.

If you're interested in furthering the work of this nonprofit agency, they'll welcome you as a volunteer.

The Pittsburgh Poison Center at Children's Hospital of Pittsburgh
3705 Fifth Ave., Pittsburgh
• **(412) 681-6669**

If you have kids, chances are you're pretty familiar with Mr. Yuk, that nasty-looking green-faced guy whose face you've slapped on dozens of potentially dangerous household products. Mr. Yuk—and the accompanying Poison Prevention Program—were developed here in 1971 and now constitute the largest poison prevention program in the nation, spanning 22 states and the United Kingdom.

Beyond its prevention program, the center is staffed by registered nurses—available round the clock—who also are clinical toxicologists and certified specialists in poison information. When you need advice about a substance or treatment, call the hotline at (412) 681-6669. They'll tap a database that provides instant access to treatment protocols on thousands of chemicals, medicines, plants, and everyday household products. The center is funded by government monies and private contributions.

Pittsburgh Specialty Hospital
215 S. Negley Ave., Pittsburgh
• (412) 661-0814, (800) 241-7700

Located in Pittsburgh's East End, Pittsburgh Specialty Hospital (formerly the Podiatry Hospital has expanded its services to now include podiatry, pain management, and plastic and reconstructive surgery. For the past 22 years, Pittsburgh Specialty Hospital has provided comprehensive foot and ankle care. Of its services, 90 percent are performed on an outpatient basis in a well-staffed, comfortable environment. Within the hospital, the outpatient department provides quality non-surgical evaluation and treatment of ankle and foot problems.

The Pain Management program offers a multi-disciplinary approach to the evaluation and treatment of chronic neck and back pain, fibromyalgia, reflex sympathetic dystropy, and migraines. Patients are evaluated by a board-certified anesthesiologist, chiropractor, and physical therapist working as a team to provide the maximum pain relief and return to a normal lifestyle.

To maximize your comfort, the hospital invites you to spend the night before and after any scheduled surgery as its guest, at no charge to you.

Ronald McDonald House Charities of Pittsburgh
500 Shady Ave., Pittsburgh
• (412) 362-3400

Ronald McDonald House Charities of Pittsburgh meets the lodging needs of people traveling to Pittsburgh for medical treatment of family members. This organization, however, spe-

cializes in the needs of parents, and it achieves this goal through three important services.

First, the organization developed and maintains The Ronald McDonald House of Pittsburgh, a short-term facility for the families of children being treated in the city. The facility offers each resident family a room of their own, a kitchen, laundry facilities, and toys for their children. The group living arrangements help families interact and cope.

In 1994, The Ronald McDonald House expanded its services by opening a second house to provide long-term housing. Finally, the organization established a grants program that awards funds to other nonprofit groups. The organization is funded by individual and corporate donations, as well as fundraisers. Guests at the organization's houses pay a small fee, but the organization pledges to help all, regardless of anyone's ability to pay.

Transitional Infant Care Hospital
5618 Kentucky Ave., Pittsburgh
• (412) 441-0700

Operated by The Children's Home of Pittsburgh, Transitional Infant Care Hospital is a pioneer in providing medical and nursing care for infants who have progressed from natal intensive care units but may not be ready for home just yet. TIC patients, all of whom must be medically stable, typically are premature infants, at-risk babies with congenital anomalies, and babies under the care of hospices. Your physician may refer you to TIC, but you're also welcome to contact the hospital yourself.

Families benefit from TIC's care by developing hands-on ability to deal with complicated treatment regimens, by learning to recognize potential problems at their earliest stages. In addition, TIC will work with you to create a care schedule that is feasible for you to manage. The hospital develops a care team for each infant that includes a physician, a primary care nurse, a medical social worker, and an infant development specialist. TIC offers transitional ventilator services and an infant massage program; they're happy to teach parents massage techniques.

If you or your physician is considering TIC, they ask that you take a pre-admission tour. You'll find softly playing music, a nursery, "nesting rooms" where families can care for their infants privately, a rocking chair beside each crib, cameras so that you may take pictures of your child, and hand-made baby quilts in each room—a gift from TIC's volunteers when you're ready to take your baby home.

HEALTHCARE

Media

As we've indicated in other chapters, Pittsburgh is a city of divergent cultures, many different interests, and great loyalty. Thus, it's no surprise that the media serving its populace is just as varied in its commitment to disseminating news, information, and entertainment.

Pittsburgh used to be a two-newspaper town, with the *Pittsburgh Post-Gazette* and *The Pittsburgh Press* both publishing from Downtown offices. Following a lengthy strike in the early '90s by non-reporting staff of both papers, the *Press* fell by the way side, leaving the city with only the *Pittsburgh Post-Gazette*. But others saw the void and quickly filled it. So when you read the following listings you'll see that, once again, Pittsburgh is a two-paper place.

Because we're so neighborhood oriented, you'll find a plethora of weekly community newspapers, most of which publish on Wednesdays. And rest assured, we're wired. Many of the newspaper, radio, and television listings offer websites where you can find out plenty of information online.

As of this writing, Greater Pittsburgh ranks 20th in terms of national television market size, as measured by Nielsen. Arbitron puts our radio market ranking at 22nd nationwide. Regarding radio, there are so many choices on the dial that we don't give individual write-ups to the stations, but have provided a thorough list to guide your listening choices. Note that if you're a fan of National Public Radio, you can tune into WDUQ, a radio station broadcast from Duquesne University at 90.5 on the FM dial.

Also worth mentioning is that we have local affiliate television stations for all major networks, not to mention the first public educational station in the nation (WQED). You may be surprised to learn that a young Fred Rogers left a promising career at NBC in New York City to pioneer educational television in Pittsburgh at WQED.

Of course, with pride and achievement comes controversy. For many years, Pittsburgh enjoyed two public, educational TV stations, with WQED and its sister station WQEX. While they were under the same umbrella organization, they broadcast mostly different material. But when financial woes caught up with the stations, WQED sought to unload the smaller, struggling entity. In fact, in November 1997, it no longer broadcast separate material but merely simulcast on WQEX whatever was on WQED airwaves.

Things looked promising when the FCC approved the elimination of WQEX and the transfer of its educational license and channel 16 dial position to Christian broadcaster WPCB. Paxton Communications was to buy Channel 40 (WPCB), and that money would have been split between WQED and Cornerstone Television, which operates WPCB. The sale would have allowed WQED to pay down substantial debts.

Somehow former presidential candidate Senator John McCain got involved, urging the FCC to make a faster decision. A group called Save Pittsburgh Public Television waged a campaign against the proposed sale, and by the looks of the editorial pages, many residents had strong opinions also, calling some of the maneuvers strong-arming without any interest in the public good.

LOOK FOR:
- **Newspapers**
- **Magazines**
- **Television Stations**
- **Radio Stations**

The three-way deal fell through in January 2000 when Cornerstone Television abruptly pulled out of the license-swapping agreement with WQED and Paxton Communications. Its reason was simple—the FCC had restrictions and a drastically different idea of what constituted educational programming. The religious broadcasting network would have had to alter its programming and mission. This sent all groups back to the drawing board, and at this writing, it's unclear what the future will hold for any of these interests, and certainly the fate of WQEX-TV.

Now that you have some background, we believe you'll enjoy perusing the list, and most likely, you'll find a media outlet to bring you news, commentary, listings, or entertainment you need to fill your disposable time. We'll start with a rundown of metro and community daily newspapers. Next, we'll turn our attention to magazines and specialty publications in our region, followed by television and radio outlets. For sure, you won't be without information!

Metropolitan Newspapers

Pittsburgh Post-Gazette
34 Blvd. of the Allies, Pittsburgh
* **(412) 263-1100**
* **www.post-gazette.com**

William and John Block serve as the publishers of this daily newspaper, founded in 1786. A decade ago, Pittsburgh was a two-newspaper town with the *Pittsburgh Post-Gazette* published in the morning and *The Pittsburgh Press* published every afternoon. As odd as it may sound, both papers were housed in the same building and shared some combined services and support staffs under a joint operating agreement. Editorial functions, however, were always kept on separate floors, and indeed the two papers were competitors.

In May 1992, a strike by non-reporting staff effectively halted operations for both papers. The *Pittsburgh Post-Gazette* introduced a town crier who stood on particular Downtown street corners to essentially shout the news to passers by. A fax service was also popular for those who simply needed their daily fix of headlines and top stories in print.

The strike lasted eight months, and culminated in the disbanding of *The Pittsburgh Press,* which was a Scripps-Howard paper. The *Pittsburgh Post-Gazette* bought the *Press,* and incorporated numerous reporters and support personnel into its staff. Today, the paper is considered by many to be more liberal in its editorial views than its main rival, the *Tribune-Review.* Well-known syndicated columnists as well as a few local favorites are found within the pages of the *Pittsburgh Post-Gazette,* sometimes known by its initials "the PG" for short.

Readers will come to look for particular sections they may deem their favorites each week, such as Health on Tuesdays or Homes on Saturdays. Each Monday, read the financial advice of Jane Bryant Quinn, and Tuesday through Saturday the personal finance column of Bill Flanagan, who doubles as the money editor at KDKA-TV. If you want to know who was "Seen" around town, read Monday's magazine section. Other *Post-Gazette* columnists include Tony Norman, Bryan O'Neill, and Sally Kalson for general commentary, and others covering television, radio, and restaurant beats. And since the two advice columnists are popular, the paper alternates using Ann Landers and Dear Abby. The *Post-Gazette* on Sunday features the "Parade" magazine supplement.

Tribune-Review
655 Rodi Rd., Pittsburgh
* **(412) 380-5600**
* **www.pittsburghlive.com**

This daily paper, once known more commonly as the *Greensburg Tribune-Review,* gained great ground during the newspaper strike in 1992. With both Pittsburgh dailies out of commission, Richard Mellon Scaife, conservative owner of the paper, began publishing more Pittsburgh news that year. The new paper was known as the *Pittsburgh Tribune-Review,* and it continued after the strike ended. Thus, if you hear someone speak of "the Trib," you'll know they mean the *Tribune-Review* and some of the history associated with this paper. Scaife bought several smaller newspapers in 1997, incorporating them into his publishing umbrella. Among them were the *North Hills News Record,* the *Valley News Dispatch,* and the *Leader Times* in Kittanning.

Founded in 1889, the *Tribune-Review* is known to

INSIDERS' TIP

Two large communities have their own magazines that are distributed to residents. *Mt. Lebanon Magazine* is located in the South Hills, while *Gateway to Monroeville* features news of Monroeville and Pitcairn.

have a more conservative slant than the more liberal *Post-Gazette*. The address given above is for Pittsburgh operations, yet a sizeable staff exists at Cabin Hill Drive in Greensburg. You can reach that office at (724) 834-1151.

Each Friday, the Trib publishes "the Ticket," filled with the weekend entertainment offerings. It's in every paper, but you can sometimes find the supplement by itself at stores and movie theaters, free of charge. On Sundays, you'll read the supplements "USA Weekend," "Focus," and "Access: America's Guide to the Internet." Syndicated national columnists in the *Trib* include Martha Stewart, Cherie Bennett, and Ann Landers. Ed Blank writes about entertainment, and Jack Markowitz, the retired business editor, keeps an eye on the business scene. Other local columns are written by Dimitri Vassilaros, Lynne Glover, Eric Heyl, and Mike Seate, and you can find them on the paper's website as well. And if you're a fan of love in the afternoon, keep tabs on plot movement with the "Soap Scene" column.

Other Daily Newspapers

Beaver County Times
400 Fair Ave., Beaver
• **(724) 775-3200**
• **www.timesonline.com**

A daily paper serving all areas in Beaver County and the western suburbs of Allegheny County, the *Beaver County Times* was founded in 1946, making it a younger paper than many of its peers. F. Wallace Gordon publishes the newspaper.

Butler Eagle
P.O. Box 271, Butler
• **(724) 282-8000**
• **www.butlereagle.com**

As a daily newspaper founded in 1869, this newspaper serves Butler County readers including the areas of Cranberry Township and Slippery Rock. Vernon Wise, Jr. is the current publisher.

Latrobe Bulletin
1211 Ligonier St., Latrobe
• **(724) 537-3351**

Published Monday through Saturday, this

newspaper was founded in 1873 to serve eastern Westmoreland County communities. Thomas Whiteman serves as publisher.

Observer-Reporter
122 S. Main St., Washington
• **(724) 222-2200**
• **www.observer-reporter.com**

Founded in 1808, this daily paper serves the communities surrounding the city of Washington, including Canonsburg, Waynesburg, Peters Township, Monessen, McMurray, and parts of Greene County. John and William Northrop are the current publishers.

The Daily News
409 Walnut St.,
McKeesport • (412) 664-9161
• **www.dailynewsmckeesport.com**

Published Monday through Saturday, this paper is also known as the *McKeesport Daily News*. It primarily covers this town as well as the surrounding communities of Clairton, Duquesne, Homestead, Munhall, West Mifflin, and White Oak. Patricia Mansfield Miles serves as the publisher. The paper was founded in 1884.

Valley News Dispatch
210 Fourth Ave., Tarentum
• **(724) 224-4321**
• **www.triblive.com**

Founded in 1891, this daily newspaper serves the areas of Armstrong County as well as parts of Butler and Westmoreland Counties. Richard Mellon Scaife, publisher of the *Tribune-Review,* purchased the paper in 1997 along with several other newspapers in outlying communities.

Alternative Weekly Newspapers

City Paper
650 Smithfield St., Pittsburgh
• **(412) 316-3342**
• **www.pghcitypaper.com**

Billed as a locally owned news and entertainment weekly, the *City Paper* is managed by Steel City Media and was founded by Brad Witherell. Since its start in 1991, it has covered a wide range of off-beat news from local vocals to the current buzz on the street,

---

INSIDERS' TIP

Each fall, WQED offers a day where children and families can tour the studios where *Mister Rogers' Neighborhood* is taped. While it's usually a Saturday in October, call (412) 622-1300 for the exact day and times.

newly released movies, the arts scene, dining, and nightlife. Each issue features an in-depth cover story. While you can subscribe to the paper for a fee, why bother? It's given away, free of charge, at many locations and outdoor boxes, especially at music and bookstores as well as some movie theaters.

InPgh Weekly
2000 E. Carson St., Pittsburgh
• **(412) 488-1212**

Launched in 1984, this weekly entertainment tabloid forced larger metropolitan newspapers like the *Pittsburgh Post-Gazette* and the *Tribune-Review* to beef up their weekend arts and entertainment coverage. In each issue of *InPgh Weekly,* you'll find features and regular coverage of music, theater, books, exhibits, food, film, and much more. It takes subscriptions, but here too, you'll find *InPgh Weekly* at many music or bookstores, movie theaters, and the like, free of charge.

New Pittsburgh Courier
315 E. Carson St., Pittsburgh
• **(412) 481-8302**

Founded in 1910, this newspaper is published twice weekly for the African-American community with relevant issues and prominent Pittsburghers. Rod Doss serves as the current editor and publisher. The paper's editorial offices are on the city's South Side.

Pittsburgh Business Times
2313 E. Carson St., Pittsburgh
• **(412) 481-6397**
• **www.amcity.com/pittsburgh**

Published weekly for the business community, the *Pittsburgh Business Times* covers regional issues of interest to executives and industry leaders as well as Pittsburgh business headlines. The paper often profiles business trends and prominent people, and it offers a diet of popular columnists. The publisher is Alan Robertson with offices on the city's South Side. The paper is affiliated with American City Business Journals Inc. The *Business Times,* as it's frequently referred to, also publishes the *Employment Paper,* distributed through the mail, at libraries and various other locations with information for job seekers.

Pittsburgh Parent
P.O. Box 374, Bakerstown
• **(724) 443-1877**
• **family.go.com/Local/pitt/**

If you're a parent or soon will be one, this is the resource for you. In fact, since *Pittsburgh Parent* is distributed free of charge to over 500

Post-Gazette *boxes are easy to find.*

Photo: Courtesy of Pittsburgh Post-Gazette

locations in Allegheny, Beaver, Butler and Westmoreland Counties, teachers and many other professionals read it as well. Each issue features an in-depth cover story, while the rest of the editorial comes largely from wire services or public relations material. Look for the annual "Around & About Pittsburgh Guide," and each issue be sure to peruse the calendar of events and fun activities for families.

Major Weekly Newspapers

Gateway Publications
610 Beatty Rd., Monroeville
• **(412) 856-7400**
• **www.ghplus.com**

Several community newspapers are published by Gateway Publications and come out on Wednesdays. The company is headquartered in Monroeville, but there are local offices for many of the papers outside the eastern suburbs. We'll list here the newspapers, and note the communities where they are not obvious in the publication's title.

Gateway Publications include the *Bridgeville Area News, Coraopolis Record, Cranberry Journal, Moon Record, Murrysville Area Star, North Journal* (covering Pine, Richland, Marshall, Franklin Park, and Bradford Woods communities), *Norwin Star, Oakmont Advance Leader, Penn Hills Progress, Plum Advance Leader, Sewickley Herald, Signal Item* (covering Carnegie, Collier, Crafton, Green Tree, Heidelberg, Ingram, Rosslyn Farms, Scott Township, and Pennsbury Village), *South Hills Record, Times Express* (covering Monroeville and Pitcairn), and *Woodland Progress* (covering Wilkins Township, Churchill, Forest Hills, Turtle Creek, Chalfant, Wilkinsburg, Edgewood, and Swissvale).

Suburban Gazette
421 Locust St., McKees Rocks
• **(412) 331-2645**
Founded in 1892, this community newspaper covers the areas of Robinson and Kennedy Townships and nearby Ingram—all of which make up the Montour School District. Virginia Schramm is the current publisher of this paper that comes out in tabloid format on Wednesdays.

The Jewish Chronicle
5600 Baum Blvd., Pittsburgh
• **(412) 687-1000**
Published on Thursdays by the Pittsburgh Jewish Publication and Education Foundation, this weekly paper is printed in tabloid form. Founded in 1962, it features news relating to Pittsburgh's Jewish community.

The Mount Pleasant Journal
23-33 S. Church St., Mount Pleasant
• **(724) 547-5722**
• **www.lgoffice@scottdale.com**
This weekly newspaper covers the Westmoreland County community of Mount Pleasant and surrounding neighborhoods. The paper was founded in 1873, and its current publisher is Joseph Soforic.

The Pittsburgh Catholic
135 First Ave., Pittsburgh
• **(412) 471-1252**
Founded in 1844, this paper relates news of importance to the Catholic community. Thus, Bishop Donald Wuerl serves as the current publisher for the Diocese of Pittsburgh. Parishioners usually obtain a copy of the paper at church each Sunday so the paper is published at the end of each week.

Magazines

Pittsburgh Magazine
4802 Fifth Ave., Pittsburgh
• **(412) 622-1360**
• **www.wqed.org**
Pittsburgh Magazine is a division of WQED Pittsburgh, home to the city's public television and radio stations. Those who become members of WQED during pledge drives or mail solicitations automatically receive a subscription to *Pittsburgh Magazine*. This monthly magazine features all things Pittsburgh including dining listings and a schedule of upcoming programming on both WQED-TV and WQED-FM. Look for the magazine to name its Pittsburgher of the Year each December. Past recipients have included Fred Rogers and Mario Lemieux. Each summer the magazine publishes its annual City Guide edition. The 1999 edition featured "101 Things We Love About Our Town." *Pittsburgh Magazine* is distributed by mail and is also available for sale on newsstands.

Pittsburgh Prospects
4802 Fifth Ave., Pittsburgh
• **(412) 622-1360**
• **www.wqed.org**
Pittsburgh Prospects is a magazine of regional development in Southwestern Pennsylvania, spotlighting companies that make up the area's new economy. The magazine's mission is to address what needs to be done to further economic expansion and growth in the Pittsburgh area. It's distributed by subscription and newsstand sales. *Pittsburgh Prospects* is published approximately six times a year through a partnership between the Pittsburgh Regional Alliance and *Pittsburgh Magazine,* a division of WQED Pittsburgh.

Television Stations

Fox Sports Pittsburgh
Two Allegheny Center, Pittsburgh
• **(412) 322-9500**
The channel you receive Fox Sports broadcasts on will vary according to the cable or satellite system you use, but for all things sports-related, you'll want to tune in here.

KDKA-TV
One Gateway Center, Pittsburgh
- **(412) 392-2200**
- **www.kdka.com**

Airing on Channel 2, KDKA-TV is the Pittsburgh CBS affiliate with offices and studios in Downtown Pittsburgh. With newscasts in the morning, at noon, at 5 and 6 PM, and wrapping up the day with the 11 o'clock news, KDKA's coverage is comprehensive in all areas, including sports, weather, and consumer and investigative reporting.

The station plays up its "Hometown Advantage," stemming from the fact that many reporters and anchors hailed from Pittsburgh. Locally produced programs include the *Lynn Hayes-Freeland Show,* focusing on African American issues each Sunday morning, and Bill Flanagan's *Sunday Business Page.* Community initiatives have included raising funds for Pittsburgh's Children's Hospital and the KD Turkey Fund each Thanksgiving.

WTAE-TV
400 Ardmore Blvd., Pittsburgh
- **(412) 242-4300**
- **www.thepittsburghchannel.com**

This television station is the local ABC affiliate with offices and studios just off the Parkway East in Wilkinsburg. "DeNardo Weather" is short for the forecasts brought to viewers by WTAE's chief meteorologist Joe DeNardo. Two hours of local news each morning leads into *Good Morning America.* WTAE-TV also offers noon, 5, and 6 o'clock broadcasts and a wrap-up of the day's events at 11 PM. It offers a full range of quality reporting on sports, consumer, and investigative issues.

WTAE-TV airs *Inside Pittsburgh* each Sunday, and throughout the year the station has done many specials for families and children. This initiative is called "Success By Six," and it features locally produced programs as well as public service announcements, some featuring local child psychologist and State Senator Timothy F. Murphy, Ph.D. For many years, the station has been involved with a program called Project Bundle-Up, which provides coats and warm clothing for needy families. The station hosts an auction to raise funds. In addition, WTAE-TV has been aligned with the Race For The Cure, a charity run/walk to raise awareness and funds for breast cancer research. The station has been the media partner for this event since its inception in 1993.

WPXI-TV & PCNC
11 Television Hill, Pittsburgh
- **(412) 237-1100**
- **www.realpittsburgh.com/partners/wpxi/**

This NBC affiliate has its offices and studios high atop a hill on the city's North Side. Known for its reports aboard Chopper 11, this station also gives you Carnegie Science weather, for there is a weather station set up in the Carnegie Science Center, also on the North Side. On Channel 11, watch for health tips and the medical beat covered by Dr. Mike Rosen, a medical doctor now on the station's reporting staff.

Channel 11 also works closely with its cable channel, PCNC (the Pittsburgh Cable News Channel). WPXI-TV news is rebroadcast on PCNC throughout the day, but also look for original television talks shows on the cable channel each morning at 10 AM with Fred Honsberger, and at 9 PM with John McIntire hosting *NightTalk.*

WQED-TV
4802 Fifth Ave., Pittsburgh
- **(412) 622-1300**
- **www.wqed.org**

WQED-TV is Pittsburgh's affiliate for the public broadcasting system (PBS). It airs locally on Channel 13 (though this will vary on each cable system). At the time of this writing, the station simulcasts over WQEX-TV, a sister station on channel 16. However, the station is currently trying to sell WQEX-TV, and indeed had buyers lined up and deals that fell through. So literally, stay tuned to discover what happens in the arena of Pittsburgh's public broadcasting.

The best-known program produced here at WQED is undoubtedly *Mister Rogers' Neighborhood,* seen around the country. *On Q* made its debut as a televised magazine show five nights each week at 7:30 PM beginning in January 2000. The half-hour program covers area business, politics, and current happenings with guests and special reporters appearing alongside the hosts.

WPCB-TV
One Signal Hill Dr., Wall
- **(412) 824-3930**

Founded by the late Rev. R. Russell Bixler in the 1970s, WPCB-TV is a Christian-based broadcasting station owned by Bixler's company, Cornerstone Television. This station and Bixler's mission survived during a time period when many televan-

INSIDERS' TIP

KDKA was the first radio station in the United States.

gelists fell to scandals. Yet Bixler and his wife built the station into a small network with four broadcast facilities—WPCB in Wall, WKBS in Altoona, and low-powered stations in Hermitage and Brookville, as well as a 24-hour satellite channel, and 163 affiliate stations. Bixler's programming often reflected his literal interpretations of the Bible, but it also pioneered contemporary programming such as a Christian music video program called *Lightmusic.* Cornerstone Television was to have purchased WQEX-TV in a somewhat complicated three-way agreement, but pulled out of the deal at the last minute because FCC regulations would have forced the station to change its programming to more education and less religion.

WPGH-TV and WCWB-TV
750 Ivory Ave., Pittsburgh
• (412) 931-5300

These smaller stations operate together. WPGH-TV is a Fox affiliate that also produces 10 o'clock local news each evening on Channel 53 (that number, of course, varies according to your cable system). On Sunday mornings, there's also *Focus On Pittsburgh,* a locally produced program.

WCWB-TV airs on Channel 22, and it's the Warner Brothers affiliate owned by Pittsburgher Eddie Edwards (who formerly had the call letters WPTT-TV). WB as it's known for short produces *Eddie's Digest, Inside/Outside Pittsburgh,* and scouting programs that are locally produced.

UPN
100 1st Ave., Suite 300, Pittsburgh
• (412) 552-1900

Only a local sales and marketing office exists here for UPN. Channel 19 airs UPN programming as well as syndicated shows such as *Jenny Jones* and *Divorce Court.*

Radio Stations

There are numerous radio stations throughout our six-county coverage area. Here, we present the major stations with a brief description of the programming each offers:

News & Talk
KDKA 1020 AM www.kdkaradio.com
KQV 1410 AM www.kqv.com
WPTT 1360 AM www.wshh.com

Sports
WEAE ESPN   1250 AM
www.wtaeradio.com

Rock
WDVE   102.5 FM www.dve.com
WXDX   106.7 FM
www.wxdx.com
WRRK   97 FM
WAMO   106.7 FM/860 AM
www.wamo.com

Contemporary/Soft Rock
WBZZ   93.7 FM
www.b94fm.com
WSHH   99.7 FM
www.wshh.com
WPHH   96.1 FM
WLTJ 92.9 FM

Oldies
WWSW   94.5 FM/970AM
www.3wsradio.com
WJPA 95.3 FM www.wjpa.com

Country
WDSY   107.9 FM
www.y108.com

Classical
WQED   89.3 FM
www.wqed.org/fm

Jazz
WDUQ   90.5 FM
WJJJ 104.7 FM

Christian
WORD   101.5 FM
www.wordfm.com
WPIT 730 AM
WWNL   1080 AM
WPGR   1510 AM
WGBN   1150 AM

Music/News/Sports/Talk
WISR 680 AM www.wisr680.com

Senior Scene

If you're looking for a town with a vital senior citizens community, with diverse programs and services for older residents, wonderful and meaningful volunteer opportunities, and government and nonprofit organizations that understand the needs of seniors, then you've come to the right place in Pittsburgh. You may not consider Pittsburgh a vibrant retirement community just yet, but we'll give you plenty of reasons to change your mind.

The fact is that family and neighborhoods are so important to most local residents that many not only live and work their entire careers here, but they also choose to retire close to their roots. Statistics tell a key part of the story. For example, of the more than 1.3 million people in Allegheny County, better than 23 percent are 60 or older, giving Allegheny the second highest percentage of seniors among America's counties.

With seniors comprising such an important part of the population, both the private and public sectors are attuned to their contributions and particular needs and concerns. You'll find a wide variety of senior recreational centers, residential communities, support organizations—even opportunities to use your experience and expertise to contribute to the region's businesses. The senior scene is vigorous in Pittsburgh.

Government in Pittsburgh, at both the municipal and county level, is active in sponsorship of programs tailored to seniors. Some government-offered services may be restricted to residents of the offering municipality or county. Even where such services are open to all, you're probably more likely to take advantage of opportunities close to your home.

Therefore, to help you best utilize Senior Scene, we've organized our material in two ways. The first section is a county-by-county look at programs, services, and opportunities for seniors; in this section, the City of Pittsburgh is grouped with Allegheny County, as the two entities share administrative responsibility for many services.

Following that, the second section features unrestricted services and opportunities, as well as those where some travel might be expected.

Have fun exploring Pittsburgh's Senior Scene. You'll find it a rewarding journey.

Pittsburgh & Allegheny County

The extensive services and programs for seniors in Pittsburgh and Allegheny County are coordinated by two agencies: Allegheny County Department of Aging, (412) 350-5460, and the City of Pittsburgh Department of Parks, (412) 422-6570, popularly known as Citiparks.

Nineteen other agencies, including nonprofit groups and church-related organizations, assist in the administration of programs in the city and county, with services distributed geographically to every community in the county. Want to know the location of the senior center nearest you, or the most active support group in your neighborhood? The best way is to call the county's Department of Aging for its annual directory of services. It's free of charge, and it will give you all the information you need to make those first phone calls.

Seventy-seven senior centers are located throughout Allegheny County, including some twenty-three centers within the city of Pittsburgh. The centers offer hot meals each weekday—most of them once per day—as well as recreation and socialization opportunities. And don't expect that recreation to be sedentary only. In addition to such standards as bingo, cards, and movies, the centers offer dancing, exercise, crafts, and classes in languages, music, and art appreciation. Up for something a little wilder? The South Side center in Pittsburgh offers basketball—on a regulation court—as one of its senior activities.

Transportation opportunities in Pittsburgh and Allegheny County are far reaching. Older Persons Transportation (OPT) will deliver you to medical appointments, grocery shopping, and senior centers, weekdays from 6 AM to 6 PM. Service is door to door, and the cost is nominal.

Even broader is the service provided by Access, a shared-ride service that will take you anywhere in the county. Call Access at (412) 562-5353 to set up an account with them; about two weeks thereafter, Access will put you in touch with your local carrier, which is likely to be a local taxi service. Access operates from 6 AM through midnight, seven days a week, with advance reservations required. You'll pay for your rides with tickets purchased from Access, but if you're 65 or older, you'll pay only 15 percent of the regular charge.

Armstrong County

In Armstrong County, adjacent to Allegheny County about 25 miles north of Pittsburgh, the Armstrong County Agency on Aging is the principal provider of services and programs for seniors. To qualify for some services, you must be formally assessed by the agency. Give them a call, toll free, at (800) 368-1066, or (724) 548-3290, if you don't mind paying for the call. They'll help you determine which services fit your needs.

The county operates 11 seniors centers in all its major population points—Apollo, Brady's Bend, Dayton, Elderton, Ford City, Freeport, Kittanning, Leechburg, Parker, Rural Valley, and Worthington. General hours are from 9 AM to 2 PM Monday through Friday, with hot meals served at noon. Reservations for lunch must be made one day in advance. If you're unable to cook for yourself, the county will deliver meals to you, once your eligibility for the program has been certified.

In addition to providing opportunities to socialize, the centers offer valuable services, including blood pressure and general health checks under the supervision of registered nurses. For fun, try the craft outlets located at the Ford City and Kittanning centers.

And if you'd like to visit more than one center, don't worry about transportation. The centers provide complimentary rides between all facilities for center programs and activities.

From time to time, we all encounter household chores that we just can't handle. The county is ready to help with those chores, as well as light housekeeping, errands, and laundry. If you have legal questions, the county also will provide legal counseling and representation in such areas as wills and power of attorney.

Beaver County

The Beaver County Office on Aging, (724) 728-7707, provides services and programs for senior citizens in Beaver County, a picturesque 20-minute drive from Pittsburgh along the Ohio River through attractive riverfront communities. The office operates five senior centers, in Aliquippa, Baden, Beaver Falls, Midland, and Monaca. The centers serve hot lunches and welcome spouses to join in. To participate, make your meal reservations one week in advance. Once approved by a caseworker, you also may order home-delivered meals Monday through Friday and take advantage of county-provided assistance with household chores.

INSIDERS' TIP

The list of residence options in this chapter is by no means exhaustive. Get on the web and check out www.seniorhousing.net. This site, a link of www.rent.net, allows you to search for retirement community listings in any geographic area within the United States, with regional and city searches as options. A search for "Pittsburgh and surrounding communities" yielded 213 listings when we tried it. The site also lists great explanations of the terms used to describe senior residence options.

If you're 65 or older, transportation is a snap in Beaver County, as you may ride Beaver County Transit Authority buses free from 9 AM to 3:30 PM If you're more than a quarter-mile from public transportation, you may arrange door-to-door, shared-ride transportation with Demand and Response Transit (DART) buses.

The county also sponsors varied activities for seniors; many of these are important but others are just plain fun. To make sure seniors are aware of all appropriate events, the county produces a quarterly newsletter called Kenn-Age News featuring articles of interest to seniors, as well as a weekly radio show, "Spotlight on Senior Citizens," which airs Sundays on WBVP-AM, 1230 on the dial.

For fun, join other seniors at the Beaver Valley Mall the second Wednesday of every month. Beginning at 10 AM, "Day at the Mall" features refreshments, prizes, entertainment, blood pressure screening, and store discounts.

And if gardening is your thing, you'll love the county's "Mini Gardens" program, operated in conjunction with the Pennsylvania State University, which reserves gardening lots for senior citizens each spring.

Butler County

If you're a senior citizen in Butler County, about 25 miles north of Pittsburgh, you'll have every opportunity to tune in to county happenings. The Butler County Area Agency on Aging, (724) 282-3008, provides a number of useful communications vehicles to ensure that you're aware of local happenings.

The Voice of Senior Citizens radio shows airs every Sunday at 7:05 AM on WISR-AM, 680 on the dial, while subscribers of Armstrong Cable can catch Seniors Today on Channel 10 for a look at events and timely features. The agency also produces and distributes a monthly newsletter called Senior Express.

The agency maintains 10 seniors centers—in Bruin, the city of Butler, Chicora, Cranberry, Evans City, Mars, Mt. Chestnut, Saxonburg, Slippery Rock, and Zelienople—which serve hot meals daily. Don't forget to make your meal reservations at least one day in advance.

The agency also offers home delivery of meals to those who qualify, as well as a referral service for caretaking and home chores. Perhaps the most comprehensive of agency services is transportation, provided by the Butler Area & Rural Transit (724) 282-6060. Known locally, as B.A.R.T., the shared-ride service will transport those 60 and older from their homes to senior centers, medical appointments, shopping malls, and grocery stores. You can ride anywhere in the county at no charge.

Washington County

The hub for senior services and programs in Washington County, which lies about 20 miles southwest of Pittsburgh, is Aging Services of Washington, Greene, and Fayette Counties, (724) 228-6856. The agency has more than three decades' experience in helping seniors and serves more than 5,000 residents each month.

You can choose from nine Senior Community Centers that feature recreation, socialization, and educational programs. Each center provides a free hot lunch each weekday and will deliver meals Monday through Friday for those unable to cook for themselves. The centers are located in Avella, Bentleyville, Burgettstown, Canonsburg, Claysville, McDonald, and Vestaburg, with two centers in the city of Washington.

Seniors in need of home support services, including laundry, shopping, and cleaning, will find agency workers ready and willing to help.

INSIDERS' TIP
Tickets to the Westmoreland Symphony Orchestra and other performances sometimes are available free of charge from the Westmoreland County Area Agency on Aging.

Westmoreland County

The Westmoreland County Area Agency on Aging, (800) 442-8000 or (724) 830-4444, likes to describe life as

Each year, seniors participate in the Senior Festival held in PPG Plaza, Downtown.

Photo: Courtesy of RSVP of Allegheny County

an orienteering event, in which contestants navigate unfamiliar terrain using a map and a compass. The agency thinks of itself as the compass, helping senior citizens reach their destinations.

The nerve center for the agency's services to senior citizens is the network of senior centers it operates. A total of 13 such centers dot this county to the east of Pittsburgh. They're located in Avonmore, East Vandergrift, Greensburg, Herminie, Jeannette, Latrobe, Laughlintown, Laurel Valley, Monessen, New Alexandria, New Kensington, New Florence, and West Newton.

As do senior centers throughout the Pittsburgh area, Westmoreland's centers offer hot meals as well as the opportunity for home delivery of those meals. Centers in Westmoreland also emphasize health and wellness through a variety of neat and unusual classes, exercise, tai chi, and aquaerobics among them.

For transportation to key activities, you'll find two types of subsidized services available. If you're 60 or older, you're eligible to use Priority Transportation, funded through the county, for rides to medical appointments, seniors centers, senior center-based shopping, adult day care, and the county's vision center only. You'll receive a 95 percent discount on the cost of your taxi or van trip. If you're 60 or older, you'll receive the same discount and be able to travel to many more destinations in your area, using a shared-ride service funded through the state. You may also ride Westmoreland county buses for free. Now you're all set for life's orienteering!

Other Services & Opportunities

Publications

With senior citizens comprising such an important force in Pittsburgh, it could be difficult to keep up with all the services, programs, and opportunities available. Fortunately, the private and public sectors have teamed to produce a number of publications to help you identify just the right opportunities for you.

Volunteers of the Retired Senior Volunteer Program prepare Meals On Wheels lunches.

Photo: Courtesy of RSVP of Allegheny County

Particularly useful is *Pittsburgh Senior News,* (412) 367-2522, a tabloid that can keep you current with activities because of its monthly publication schedule. The newspaper blends information about activities and services with cultural and entertainment news, as well as feature stories by and about senior citizens. Pay close attention to the advertisements, which often bring news of discounts and bargains for seniors.

The newspaper also offers up-to-date information about current activity schedules for local chapters of the American Association of Retired Persons (AARP)—a valuable tool, as Pittsburgh offers more than 100 AARP chapters. Subscription rate for the publication is $15, but seniors may get it for $12. You can pick it up for free at scores of distribution points, many of them located at newspaper honor boxes.

The *Resource Guide for Older Adults and Their Families* takes a somewhat different, but equally effective, approach. This publication comes out every two years and focuses on well-detailed listings of services and programs. The guide cannot deal with current events, of course, but it provides a broad look at opportunities for seniors that are unlikely to change.

Categories covered include community outreach and referral services; crisis, mental health, and caregiver services; Medicare, Medicaid, and medical insurance; medical and health care services; and housing options. The outreach section, in particular, is as good as any you're likely to find, offering both familiar and more obscure service providers.

The guide is published under the auspices of Older Adult Service and Information System (OASIS), a public-private partnership headquartered in Kaufmanns department store in downtown Pittsburgh. You can order your free copy from OASIS, (412) 232-9583, or (800) 921-9443.

A second helpful publication is the *Senior Citizens Guide to Pittsburgh,* which is produced by Spindle Publications headquartered in suburban Pittsburgh. As an annual, this guide, too, is limited in the current information it can convey. Instead, the publication focuses on interesting travel features and "how-to" pieces, as well as service directories.

Two of the best directories offered are the listing of senior citizens centers and the guide to volunteer organizations. If one of your goals is to remain active in the community, you'll find plenty of opportunities in this publication. The publication, begun in 1987, is available free at

SENIOR SCENE

any of the area agencies on aging described in this chapter. You also may contact Spindle Publishing, (412) 531-9742; they'll be happy to mail you one copy for free, but if you require multiple copies you're responsible for postage.

Volunteer Programs

Volunteerism is alive and well in Pittsburgh, at least in part because of the leadership of senior citizens. Seniors provide valuable assistance to both nonprofit and for-profit organizations, which are happy to rely on the experience and expertise that would otherwise be hard to acquire. When seniors volunteer, they—and the organizations they assist—are sharper for it.

One of the most fertile and rewarding volunteer opportunities is helping fellow senior citizens in need. Preserve, The Volunteer Support Network for Seniors, (412) 456-6887, offers just such opportunities by pairing volunteers with seniors who might benefit from a friendly phone call. New Heritage Volunteer Program, (412) 464-1300, offers similar opportunities; its senior volunteers often serve meals at senior centers.

Reach Out Pittsburgh, (412) 422-6402, goes one step beyond by dispatching teams of volunteers out into the neighborhoods to inform seniors about the rich variety of services available to them. Many of the volunteers are seniors, who can speak first hand about their experiences. Volunteers hit the streets twice a year.

More comprehensive still are the check-in services offered by Interfaith Volunteer Caregivers of Southwestern Pennsylvania, (412) 687-6712. Volunteers call on seniors in need and help out with shopping, transportation, and completion of Social Security and Medicare forms. Interfaith Volunteer Caregivers also offer errand, "friendly visiting," and "telephone reassurance" services.

Hospice Preferred Choice, (412) 271-2273, works with home care patients. Volunteers provide companionship as well as respite for caregivers.

Perhaps working with children would give you the most satisfaction. If so, try the Foster Grandparents Program, (412) 263-3163, which operates in Allegheny, Beaver, Butler, and Washington counties. Through the program, low-income volunteers 60 and older spend 20 hours each week with disabled or special-needs children. You'll receive a tax-exempt stipend—and immeasurable satisfaction—for your efforts.

At the University of Pittsburgh, in the Generations Together program, (412) 648-7150, senior volunteers mentor and tutor youths. A special Generations Together feature matches seniors who have been professional artists with kids eager to learn artistic skills. A similar program in Westmoreland County, Generations Together, (800) 442-8000, utilizes senior volunteers to counsel abused and neglected children. There's an added benefit—volunteers are paid at minimum wage rates for their valuable efforts.

If using your experience to help consumers is your primary concern, try the Better Business Bureau of Southwestern Pennsylvania at (412) 456-2700 and ask for the volunteer coordinator. BBB is well known for helping consumers answers questions about, and resolve complaints

Miles to Go

When Horace Miles retired from his multifaceted career, he expected to enjoy a leisurely retirement. Some retirement. Today, Miles is a very active member of the Pittsburgh chapter of the Service Corps of Retired Executives (SCORE), a volunteer agency that mentors young companies across the entire business spectrum. The Pittsburgh chapter of SCORE, formed in 1964, was among the nation's first. Its membership numbers 60 strong, all of them retired and all on the prowl for young companies they can counsel in such key areas as personnel, financing, marketing, and other operational challenges. SCORE is sponsored by the Small Business Administration, which propelled Miles into his leadership role.

"The former district director of SBA suggested that I consider this as a way to keep my skills up," Miles recalls. "I found it appealing because to me, the most interesting thing is doing something new, learning something new. I'm working harder now than I ever did."

Miles' varied career helped prepare him for his "retirement," providing him with diverse expertise in all facets of management and business development. With undergraduate degrees in math and physics, he entered the computer field in the late 1950s. In the infant computer industry, Miles' expertise was in demand. He worked for a bank and later founded an international consulting company that coordinated computer services for clients in Canada, Italy, and France.

He has sold computer peripherals in the Far East and highly technical fabricating equipment for the glass industry. His broad experience has given him firm ideas about what separates successful businesses from mere wannabes.

"The thing that always has interested me is business," Miles says. "It's the toughest thing you'll ever do, and it's becoming more of a challenge. But in a sense, business problems are business problems are business problems. It's formulaic in that sense. From that standpoint, when you work with young companies, you can find out what's needed, they can feed back, and you find out where the cracks are."

The companies that Miles has mentored reflect the breadth of his career:

• A pet-sitting business that was expanding and considering new hires. Miles' advice: Use contractors rather than full-time employees, to avoid the expense of benefits packages and the like.

• A plasma physicist in the business of producing robots for semiconductor manufacturing. "He had some technical problems in making his product, but what he really needed was an inventory system, and to make sure he was ordering his parts in an economical manner."

• A singer/songwriter who wanted to reach a broader, more

Horace Miles counsels young Pittsburgh businesses through the Service Corps of Retired Executives.

Photo: Ric Evans

lucrative market. "I don't feel qualified to comment on whether his songs are good or bad, but I do have some friends who have listened to his work and essentially blessed it. My role is to see how he might market his work while retaining control over it."

Success stories are not uncommon for SCORE. Perhaps its most amazing rags-to-riches tale is that of Riverside Design Group, a producer of high-design giftware, including private-label products for corporate clients. Aided by a SCORE counseling team, Riverside Design streamlined its planned product lines and now sells to more than 400 museums, giftware retailers, restaurants, and catalogues.

Miles does not commit all his hard-earned leisure time to SCORE. In his idle moments, he produces videos with musical themes, tinkers with magic, fences, and serves on the boards of two nonprofit organizations. But even his recreational activities benefit SCORE. In the workshop staged for all potential SCORE clients, for example, Miles works in several of his magic tricks.

While the organization includes women and minority volunteers, one of the chapter's goals for the future is to further diversify its membership. Because there are comparatively few minorities who are both retired and former executives, this one may take more than sleight of hand.

If you're looking for a way to contribute your years of expertise to young businesses, call SCORE and Horace Miles at (412) 395-6560, or visit them at their headquarters in the Federal Building, 1000 Liberty Avenue, in downtown Pittsburgh, or at their McKeesport or Beaver outreach centers. If you volunteer with SCORE, you'll get your transportation costs reimbursed . . . and a large measure of satisfaction.

"Business is a blood sport," Horace Miles says. "It's difficult to create and sustain a business. The satisfaction in this work is helping a company grow and seeing it progress over a number of years. The frustration is that a lot of companies we see either don't have the wherewithal or they don't really understand what needs to be done. So you don't see them again.

"It doesn't mean they aren't good entrepreneurs, it's just that this isn't a good idea. If you save people from going down that road, that's satisfying, too."

Questions about programs and services for seniors? Often, the best places to look for answers are the area agencies on aging, which administer state programs and supplement them with local initiatives. You'll find them at these numbers:

Allegheny County Department of Aging ...... (412) 350-5460, (800) 344-4319
City of Pittsburgh Citiparks .... (412) 422-6570
Armstrong County Agency on Aging .... (800) 368-1066
Beaver County Office on Aging .... (724) 728-7707
Butler County Area Agency on Aging .... (888) 367-2434
Aging Services of Washington County .... (800) 342-8980
Westmoreland County Area Agency on Aging .... (724) 830-4444

Other frequently called numbers include:

Eldercare Locator .... (800) 677-1116
Elderlink .... (412) 422-0400
South Hills Health System Senior Services .... (412) 469-7099
Contact Helpline .... (412) 578-2450

With more than 2.4 million of its citizens age 60 or over, the Commonwealth of Pennsylvania has a significant stake in the well being of senior citizens. The state reaches out to seniors in a variety of ways—by providing funding for 52 area agencies on aging across the Commonwealth, by dedicating proceeds from the Pennsylvania Lottery exclusively to programs for seniors, and by operating a number of major programs on a statewide basis. In all, the state funds or administers more than 50 programs or benefits for seniors.

Among the most far-reaching programs are Pharmaceutical Assistant Contract for the Elderly (PACE), which helps to pay for prescribed medicines, and rent and property tax rebates, which can amount to as much as $500 per year. Both programs are targeted to those 65 and older who meet income eligibility guidelines.

To enroll in PACE or for rent and property tax rebates, pick up your application at any area agency on aging, pharmacy, senior community center, legislator's office, or contact the Pennsylvania Department of Aging in Harrisburg. The toll-free number for PACE is (800) 225-7223.

against, local businesses. Senior volunteers perform many of these key functions. You'll play an important role in telephone answering, complaint handling, mediation and arbitration, data entry, and public speaking. Check out the BBB's web site, www.pittsburgh.bbb.org, to learn more about these opportunities.

For broader volunteer opportunities, several agencies will do the job. Since 1972, the Southwestern Pennsylvania Chapter of the American Red Cross has sponsored the Retired and Senior Volunteer Program of Allegheny County (RSVP), (412) 263-3184, a program that matches volunteers with such nonprofit organizations as arts and cultural groups, hospitals and schools, and consumer agencies.

The program is large and diverse. More than 1,000 volunteers participate in at least 117 organizations, contributing meaningful volunteer service and enriching their own lives as well. RSVP also hosts an annual awards dinner to recognize outstanding volunteers. If you're 55 or older, respond to RSVP. It may kick-start you on a new career.

Pittsburgh Cares, (412) 471-2114, offers a similar broad range of opportunities for its 1,450 volunteers, which continue to increase in number. The agency schedules more than two dozen monthly events, ranging from delivering holiday meals to the homebound to craftmaking with mentally challenged people. Pittsburgh Cares works with more than 80 community service agencies, an indication of how deeply the roots of volunteerism grow in Pittsburgh. Yet another Pittsburgh trademark: the agency encourages families to volunteer together. Check out this organization on the web at www.pgh.cares.org.

Retirement Communities

We're living longer, we're enjoying our mature years more, and we're looking for more residential options that are tailored for our needs and desires. In Pittsburgh, with its sizable population of seniors, you'll find just those options in an appealing variety of retirement communities.

The number of such communities has mushroomed in Pittsburgh in recent years, although not quite as fast as the number of people who want to live in them. This has resulted in waiting lists at a number of the most popular communities. We haven't noted which communities have waiting lists, since that's so changeable, but it is something you should be aware of as you check out these listings.

Nevertheless, such a rich variety is available today that you'll want to carefully consider your preferences before

INSIDERS' TIP

The State of Pennsylvania offers "ombudsman" services to answer your questions and provide information about your rights as a consumer. To reach the ombudsman's office, call (717) 783-7247, or contact any county area agency on aging. Also, see the web site: www.aging.state.pa.us

ACCESS provides rides to more than two million riders every year.

Photo: Roy Engelbrecht courtesy of Port Authority of Allegheny County

making a selection. Do you prefer communities away from the city center, tucked into the rolling hills of Western Pennsylvania? Or would you be most happy in an urban setting, close to all the city's opportunities? You'll find both types in Pittsburgh and environs.

You'll also want to carefully consider the services, amenities, and pricing options. At some communities, residents pay a monthly rental fee. In other communities, you can own your home by making a sizable up-front payment, which in some cases is partially refundable when the unit is turned over. Condominiums also can be an option.

Make sure that you inquire about the common or community fee, which typically is assessed monthly. Services and amenities that come with such fees can vary widely. These can range from the most basic, such as meals and laundry, to the most lavish, such as use of a nearby golf course.

If you're selecting a retirement community, probably the best initial advice anyone can give you is this: take your time. Do your homework. Make a day out of visiting a prospective new home, taking the tour that each will gladly offer you, and asking a lot of questions to make sure the community fits your needs. Your patient research will result in the best match for you.

North

LAS/Crown Pointe
100 Newhaven Ln., Butler
• (724) 282-7710, (800) 741-0623

LAS/Crown Pointe is located on a former dairy farm about 25 miles north of Pittsburgh. You won't find any bovine types around now, of course, but the former use of the site gives you some idea of the placid setting.

At LAS/Crown Pointe, you have three different options for living arrangements. If you prefer to buy your residence, your purchase price will be a little over $100,000. If renting is more your style, your payments will range from around $400 to a little over $2,000 per month. And you also can opt for a leasing contract.

You'll enjoy restaurant-style dining, fitness and wellness programs, a full schedule of recreational and social activities, and the opportunity for a continuum of care if needed.

The homes are attractively designed, featuring two or three bedrooms, cathedral ceilings, and air conditioning. LAS/Crown Pointe is royally appointed, indeed. The complex is operated by Lutheran Affiliated Services, which also operates LAS/Crown Pointe retirement communities in Zelienople and Greensburg, both described below.

LAS/Passavant Retirement Community
401 South Main St., Zelienople
• **(724) 452-5400, (800) 741-0623**

The second of the three Pittsburgh retirement communities operated by Lutheran Affiliated Services, this community is set in a rustic locale about 35 miles north of Pittsburgh.

Living options include cottages and apartments, with monthly fees ranging from a little over $1,000 to a little over $2,000. You'll get quite a bit for your monthly fee, including utilities, cable TV service, social services, and two meals per day. For an additional fee, you can take advantage of laundry service and visits to doctors and the beauty and barber shops.

One of the most appealing opportunities at all three LAS communities is the emphasis on leisure learning. At Zelienople, classes range from horseback riding to safe driving, while activities include such fun events as hayrides, bonfires, softball, and line dancing.

And if you're an angler, here's one just for you: the community sponsors regular fishing outings at nearby Moraine State Park. You might just want to cast your lot right here.

Sherwood Oaks
100 Norman Dr., Mars
• **(724) 776-8100, (800) 642-2217**

Yes, it really is located in Mars, and Sherwood Oaks does resemble a heavenly body. Set on 84 pastoral acres 23 miles north of downtown Pittsburgh, Sherwood Oaks boasts its own lake, with the shore dotted by the townhomes that comprise the community. Choose from eight different floor plans for your townhome.

Sherwood Oaks involves committing a one-time entrance fee around the price of a nice home, in addition to monthly service fees. Make sure to ask about the three refund options for your entrance fee—you may be able to get a substantial percentage back.

You'll want to take advantage of the indoor pool and hot tub; boating and fishing on the lake; the woodworking shop; the hair styling salon; and the croquet, boccie, shuffleboard, horseshoe, badminton, and putting facilities. For a good read, check a book out of the community library. For your medical needs, a health care center is available on site, and the community is affiliated

with the nearby North Hills Passavant Health Corporation. Assisted living services and skilled nursing care are available where needed.

Sherwood Oaks is near two major highways—the Pennsylvania Turnpike and Interstate 79—so visitors have easy access. When they come, put them up at the community's guest lodge.

East

Canterbury Place
310 Fisk St., Pittsburgh
• **(412) 622-9000**

Been an urban type all your life and can't bear to leave the throb and throngs of the city? Then Canterbury Place may be your place. The facility offers a continuum of care, including independent living, assisted living, personal care, nursing care, and Alzheimer's care, all contained within a stately brick building about two miles from downtown—and even closer to the medical center complex in Oakland. In fact, Canterbury Place is affiliated with the University of Pittsburgh Medical Center, providing access to first-rate medical care. Living options include semiprivate, studio, and one- and two-bedroom apartments.

The staff plans meals and activities far in advance, so you'll always have a good idea of coming attractions. While you'll be close to all of Pittsburgh's entertainment spots, the events calendar at Canterbury Place might persuade you to stay at home. Featured are cocktail hours, concerts, bingo, video biographies, and films.

And if you want to invite friends to join in, feel free. You can use The Chalfant Room, an on-site private dining room, free of charge.

Clover Commons
600 Cloverview Circle, Plum
• **(412) 793-2333**

If you prefer a variety of homes from which to choose, Clover Commons may be the community for you. Designed by builder Myles Sampson, the site about 15 miles east of downtown Pittsburgh along Route 286 offers dozens of floor plans, with homes build to your specs starting at $69,000. In addition to accessibility from Route 376 (get into the habit of calling it "The

INSIDERS' TIP
Want to know what you're entitled to in Pennsylvania now that you've reached retirement age? Feel you've been done wrong? Check out the Pennsylvania Department of Aging's "Benefits and Rights for Older Pennsylvanians."

Parkway East"), Clover Commons is within hailing distance of the Pennsylvania Turnpike.

Sampson and his associates built this community with active and enjoyable lifestyles in mind. Thus, you'll find a heated swimming pool; cabana; a pool table; and shuffleboard, horseshoe, and boccie facilities.

You can ride the community minibus, bike and walk with friends . . . in fact, you'll enjoy all the advantages of neighborhood living, because Clover Commons and its handsome homes are a neighborhood.

When you visit Clover Commons, make sure you take a few minutes to inspect its two sister retirement communities—Cloverleaf Estates in Delmont and The Village of Clover Ridge in Murrysville. They're a few minutes' drive from Clover Commons and offer substantially the same living and recreational options.

Longwood at Oakmont
500 Rt. 909, Verona
• (412) 826-5700

How popular is Longwood at Oakmont? Consider that residents have come from 13 states to retire there. Pretty impressive for a region where people tend to stay put. Longwood is located just a chip shot from Oakmont Country Club, the site of many major Professional Golf Association tour events. That may account in part for Longwood's popularity, but there are many other attractions.

You'll have plenty of residence options at Longwood, beginning with a studio apartment and reaching all the way to an elegant three-bedroom country home. Entrance fees, which are 90 percent refundable, range from $87,100 to $341,000, while the monthly maintenance fee goes from $1,691 to $2,793. Add $840 to the monthly fee for a second occupant.

Longwood calls itself a continuing retirement care community, meaning that should the need arise, you can take advantage of unlimited nursing care days at the on-site health center at no additional cost.

The range of services is breathtaking. Airport transportation, newspaper, grocery, and pharmacy delivery, guest accommodations—all are available to residents at no extra cost. The clubhouse offers swimming and a Jacuzzi, and you'll also enjoy movies, lectures, musical programs, and food festivals, to name just a few of the regular activities.

INSIDERS' TIP

Each year in late summer, Allegheny County sponsors a three-day Seniors Festival, featuring dozens of booths that showcase the talents of seniors.

And if you're looking to join the Senior Tour, where better to go?

South

Asbury Heights
700 Bower Hill Rd., Mt. Lebanon
• (412) 571-5188

The variety of living options is one of the most important features of Asbury Heights, which is operated by United Methodist Services for the Aging. The community offers townhomes and a multitude of styles of apartments, suites, and residential rooms, all set on a 27-acre campus only minutes from downtown Pittsburgh.

With that diversity of residential options, you'll want to spend some time reviewing the pricing plans. Asbury Heights will be happy to provide them.

The pleasant campus is ideal for outdoor activities, including walking, gardening, shuffleboard, horseshoes, and putting. For shopping and personal services, try the on-site skylight mall, with banking and postal facilities, a beauty parlor and barber shop, and an ice cream parlor, and country store.

One of Asbury Heights' most unusual features is its elevation. Located at one of the highest points in Allegheny County, the community offers commanding views of western Pennsylvania's rolling hills. At Asbury Heights, you'll be on top of the world.

Asbury Heights includes facilities for assisted living; nursing care; and a dedicated facility for Alzheimer's care, which is decorated beautifully. In addition to on-site doctors, the community provides regular visits from a dentist, a podiatrist, and an ophthalmologist. Moreover, a social worker is assigned to each resident of the community, just to check on your well being.

Fair Oaks of Pittsburgh
2200 West Liberty Ave., Pittsburgh
• (412) 344-9915

Want the best of urban and suburban retirement? Try Fair Oaks of Pittsburgh. The community is situated on 15 hilly acres in Pittsburgh's South Hills, isolated enough to provide privacy but only a mile from all the attractions and opportunities of downtown Pittsburgh.

Fair Oaks features 80 efficiency and apartment units that offer independent living as well as assisted living and personal care, assuring a continuum of care. Two entrance plans are available: the management plan, which offers you the option of making a small down payment ($3,000) and then paying a monthly rental fee; and the endowment plan, which requires a large down payment up front, but offers a low monthly payment.

You can shop at the Fair Oaks Country Store or pamper yourself at the on-site beauty shop. You won't have to worry much about how to spend your time, as the Fair Oaks staff plans its recreational activities well in advance, providing a monthly activities calendar. A calendar we sampled featured a trip to a local restaurant, a current events lecture, sessions of bingo and Scrabble, and on-site concerts by a clarinetist, an orchestra, and a barbershop quartet. The Fair Oaks folks will have you singing "Sweet Adeline" in no time.

Friendship Village
1290 Boyce Rd., Upper St. Clair
• (724) 941-3100
• www.friendshipvillagepa.com

For a retirement community with a track record, try the friendly folks at Friendship Village. The community is operated by Life Care Services Corporation, a nonprofit company with more than 30 years' experience operating over 100 retirement communities. Those communities serve over 20,000 residents across the country, so the extended Life Care community is a large one, indeed.

Set on 70 acres in the lovely suburb of Upper St. Clair, about 15 miles south of Pittsburgh, Friendship Village offers one-, two-, and three-bedroom apartments, which residents appoint with their own furnishings. The village offers 14 different apartment styles as well as private carriage homes. Entrance fees range from $65,200 to $378,750—90 percent of it refundable. Monthly service fees range from $1,040 to $2,652. Additional fees apply for a second person.

If golf is your game, you'll become more than familiar with the nine-hole Frosty Valley Golf Course next door to Friendship Village; rounds are complementary for residents. Amenities include laundry, housekeeping and maintenance service, and a village store and bank, while recreational facilities

are an exercise room, a woodworking shop, a library, studios for crafts and the arts, and landscaped walking paths. You can putter about your own garden or relax with friends in the Pub.

Friendship Village guarantees lifetime nursing care, should the need arise, at its on-site Health Center. Sounds to us like a friendly village.

Residence at Country Meadows
3580 Washington Pike, Bridgeville
• (412) 257-4581

When George M. Leader was governor of Pennsylvania in the late 1950s, he appointed the first commissioner on aging and inspired other legislation designed to improve conditions for seniors. This was more than a passing political fancy for Leader. Today, his family operates the Residence at Country Meadows, one of eight such retirement communities in Pennsylvania developed and operated by the Leader family.

At the community only a few miles from downtown Pittsburgh, residents enjoy a variety of accommodations and care options, including, respectively, apartments, efficiencies, and rooms, and independent living, assisted living, and nursing care arrangements. Monthly rentals start at $1,370.

The Residence has developed a "Total Wellness Program" that includes exercise classes as well as social opportunities. Through its continuum of care philosophy, the complex also offers assisted living, a nursing and rehabilitation center, and an Alzheimer's' residence.

Three cheers for the Gov.!

Vanadium Woods Village
50 Vanadium Rd., Bridgeville
• (412) 221-2900

Vanadium Woods offers the best of city and suburban life. It's nestled in a secluded tree-lined development, yet it's only minutes from the large shopping malls of Pittsburgh's South Hills. The community is part of a growing network of retirement communities being developed by the Retirement Villages of St. Margaret.

The recently built, three-story Vanadium Woods is reminiscent of a grand hotel, offering a beautiful atrium and many attractive lounges, plus a library, chapel, barber shop, activity centers, and many other amenities. Two of residents' favorite activities are on-site performances and trips to the Pittsburgh Sym-

INSIDERS' TIP
Have a disability? Need a special parking placard or plate? Contact the Pennsylvania Department of Transportation, toll free, at (800) 932-4600.

phony. Apartment rentals range from $1,221 to $2,175 (add $395 for double occupancy), and include just about everything you could think of: common fee, three meals per day, repairs and maintenance, cable TV, housekeeping, transportation, educational and wellness classes—even light bulbs and toilet paper.

It's all part of what the folks at Vanadium

INSIDERS' TIP

Seniors dine inexpensively and stylishly by taking advantage of "Early Bird" discounted dinners at many Pittsburgh restaurants.

Woods call "management from the heart," a philosophy that extends to such niceties as published weekly menus and van schedules. Community managers say they like to provide a "pampered retirement lifestyle" for their residents. Hey, don't feel guilty about it. You deserve it.

West

Leo Meyer Manor
1015 Church Ave., McKees Rocks
• (412) 331-8000

Leo Meyer Manor, a retirement community sponsored by Christian Housing, operates on a firm philosophy. "We believe," they say, "that people who need other people are the happiest people." No, Barbara Streisand doesn't live there, but a lot of friendly folks do.

The community is a high-rise building in the suburb of McKees Rocks, about five miles down the Ohio River from downtown Pittsburgh. Residences at Leo Meyer are efficiency apartments that include kitchens. The monthly fee, which equals 30 percent of your income plus $308, includes meals, laundry and cleaning service, utilities and maintenance.

If the need arises, medical services can be obtained from a nearby family health clinic. There's also a UPMC-affiliated hospital in McKees Rocks for more serious concerns.

SENIOR SCENE

Worship

Immigrants who settled in Southwestern Pennsylvania for the purpose of prosperity brought with them riches of another kind—adherence to their spiritual past. As a result, our region is as diverse in its religious make-up as it is in its ethnicity.

Many of the churches and synagogues in which Pittsburghers worship tell their stories better than any words could. For instance, the stained-glass windows inside St. John The Baptist, a Ukrainian Catholic church on the South Side, chronicle immigrant life, including the life of the church. The Strip District's St. Patrick-St. Stanislaus Parish, more commonly referred to as Old St. Patrick's, was founded by Irish immigrants in 1808. Here, you'll find a set of 28 marble stairs, a replica of the holy stairs that Jesus had to climb to reach the court of Pontius Pilate. To comply with local custom, you may ascend these stairs only on your knees.

Family heritage is largely responsible for the strength and continuity of religion in Greater Pittsburgh. Because many extended families remain in the region, it's not uncommon for them to remain in their churches of origin as well. Some church congregations boast three or four generations of Pittsburgh families in their membership, a sturdy and natural conveyor belt for traditions and beliefs. Whether it's making pierogies (potato dumplings) in the church kitchen, teaching children the art of pysanky (hand-painting Easter eggs), or simply preserving historic houses of worship, such cherished rituals make churches, synagogues and other congregations pivotal players in their respective communities.

Most smaller communities have newspapers which may list worship services as well as church-sponsored social and educational events. Sampling these opportunities is a great way to get to know parishioners, and ultimately, find a church home.

Christian Associates of Southwest Pennsylvania, (412) 688-9070, offers information about churches and denominations in nine regional counties. The nonprofit organization encompasses 23 Christian faith traditions, representing the diversity you'll find here.

Strength in Diversity

Of the many religions represented in Southwestern Pennsylvania, Catholicism has the most adherents. Second in number are the Presbyterian denominations. In fact, there are more Presbyterian churches here than anywhere else in the country, perhaps due to the influence of the Scotch-Irish immigrants who brought their religious fervor with them. Lutherans, Methodists, Episcopalians, Baptists, Charismatics, and Unitarians also thrive here, as do Christian and Missionary Alliance, Church of the Brethren, United Church of Christ, Assembly of God, and Greek and Russian Orthodox congregations.

INSIDERS' TIP

If you're looking for listings of worship opportunities, check out the Saturday editions of the daily newspapers, or your own community weekly paper.

Monroeville's Old Stone Church, founded in 1834, as home to Cross Roads Presbyterian Church, is now a historic landmark and the site of special services.

Photo: Sharon A. McIndoe courtesy Monroeville Historical Society

WORSHIP

Pittsburgh's Squirrel Hill neighborhood is the hub of the Jewish community, and the hub of the hub is the Jewish Community Center; (412) 521-8010. You'll also find synagogues throughout the suburbs and outlying counties. African Methodist Episcopal churches dot the Hill District, the heart of the region's African-American community, as well as suburban communities just beyond the city. While they make up a small percentage of the religious population on this side of the state, the Amish also are represented in Western Pennsylvania, particularly in Lawrence and Mercer counties somewhat north of our principal coverage area. (See our Daytrips & Weekend Getaways chapter for more information on the Amish).

In Pittsburgh's eastern suburbs of Monroeville and Penn Hills, many more congregations make their home. There are followers of the Baha'i, Hindu, Sikh, Zer and Islamic traditions. Indeed, the SV Temple, just off Interstate 376 (the Parkway East) in Penn Hills, is said to be the first authentic Hindu structure in America. The Muslim Community Center of Greater Pittsburgh, in Monroeville, offers both a mosque and a social hall. The center conducts services five times daily and offers special services during holy periods. All are welcome at the center, as it maintains no membership as such.

The region also boasts a healthy number of independent congregations and churches that attract residents and visitors with their unique missions and spiritual focus. The Western Pennsylvania division of the Salvation Army, to name only one, is comprised of many corps where worshippers can participate.

Finally, you may be seeking a setting for that once-in-a-lifetime service, such as a wedding. For these events, nondenominational churches are available, including Heinz Chapel on the University of Pittsburgh campus, as well as the Old Stone Church in Monroeville (maintained by the Monroeville Historical Society). Contact campus personnel—or municipal officials where appropriate—to determine how you may use historic or prominent churches for your special event.

Where Two or Three Are Gathered . . .

As diverse as worship is here, it's reassuring to note that organized religious bodies regularly collaborate on worthy causes. Examples of this include interfaith efforts to combat racism, churches joining together to raise funds for the hungry, and multidenominational support for the erection of domestic violence shelters.

Interfaith consortiums, such as the Monroeville Interfaith Ministerium, bring church leaders together to promote unity and work for the good of the community. Congregations within such groups wholeheartedly support each other's efforts. While one church might sponsor a food pantry, another might provide a clothing ministry; church leaders routinely encourage their parishioners to support the efforts of other congregations.

Unique Ministries

If you look through any local newspaper's worship listings, you'll discover services that are taped for radio broadcast or televised for home-bound viewers. Some of these services are signed for the hearing-impaired. Cornerstone Television, incorporated in the 1970s as a nonprofit organization, is a television ministry that provides religious and inspirational programming throughout much of Pennsylvania. From its headquarters midway between Greensburg and Pittsburgh, its signal reaches such distant points as Altoona and Jefferson, Perry, Lawrence, and Mercer counties. To enhance Cornerstone's programming, volunteers staff telephone prayer lines as a form of outreach. You'll find more about Cornerstone in our Media chapter.

Another unusual ministry is that of Fred Rogers, highly acclaimed host of public television's Mister Rogers' Neighborhood, which is produced in Pittsburgh at WQED-TV and broadcast nationally. Some may find it surprising to learn that he's an ordained Presbyterian pastor. Indeed, Mr. Rogers attended the Pittsburgh Theological Seminary, took graduate courses in child development at the University of Pittsburgh and worked with Pittsburgh's Arsenal Family and Children's Center. When he was ordained in 1963, he was given the special charge of ministering to children through television. He does it by creating a sanctuary of truth and honesty where his young viewers are accepted just as they are—a founding principle of many faiths. (See our Kidstuff chapter for a profile of Fred Rogers and his work with children.)

You'll find yet another unique ministry in the most unlikely of places—the suburban shopping mall. Among so many secular storefronts, it may seem strange to find the Monroeville Mall Ministry, but this volunteer-staffed "talk shop" has been a permanent part of the mall since the complex was built in the early 1970s.

Much of this group's ministry involves simply listening, even about mundane matters such as finding the right store. For all that, a surprising number of shoppers stop by to confide their worries, their personal or family problems and their need for assistance. Volunteers are equipped with referral information but do not proselytize. Their mission is to maintain a presence and to help their fellow Pittsburghers in need.

Values and Spirituality

To describe the region's stately churches, diversity of faiths and unusual ministries, useful though that may be, does not quite get to the heart of religion in Southwestern Pennsylvania. Just as the immigrants who settled here built churches to resemble those they had left behind, they also constructed a system of values based on those of the Old World. Many of the churches are gone; the values remain as the foundation of modern Pittsburgh.

The strength of religious beliefs in Southwestern Pennsylvania infuses our region with spirituality that is an important component of our personal and professional lives.

INSIDERS' TIP

To learn more about the architectural beauty of Pittsburgh churches and synagogues, along with their ethnic traditions, rent a copy of *Holy Pittsburgh* at your local library. Produced by public television station WQED, this video is a wonderful overview of the region's religious heritage.

The Millennium Creche lights up the holiday night.

WORSHIP

Religion and commerce here are intertwined. Clergy have served as elected officials, labor leaders, chiefs of important civic organizations. Their impact goes well beyond their immediate roles, as our clergy often serve as directors for nonprofit organizations and public corporations, bringing a set of values and a spiritual outlook to the world of commerce and public service.

Of the degree-granting institutions and hospitals that we profile in our Healthcare and Higher Education chapters, many are administered by, or affiliated with, religious orders. The Catholic Diocese of Pittsburgh operates an elementary and secondary school network that, were it a public school district, would be the fourth largest in the state. Is it any wonder, then, that our hospitals play a key role in providing services to the homeless and other populations in need?

Usually, the interrelationship of religion and commerce works to the benefit of each. Some years ago during the death throes of Big Steel, when bitter disputes between labor and management were common and costly, the warring sides in one impasse were encouraged to meet over breakfast and prayers. The results were so successful that prayer breakfasts became commonplace, though even they could only postpone the inevitable.

Just as in all relationships, the union of religion and the workaday world has its rough patches. We see evidence of this nearly every year at Christmas time with the attempts by groups or citizens to erect creches on government property. Predictably, some groups have been opposed to these actions. In 1999, however, the Pittsburgh Creche Project erected what the group hopes will become a permanent fixture in the city.

Following the example set in St. Peter's Square, the focal point of the Vatican in Rome, the Christian Leaders Fellowship, in conjunction with the Diocese of Pittsburgh, had a plan. They commissioned the Vatican artist Pietro Simonelli to create the figures of Jesus, Mary and Joseph, the Magi and shepherds, various animals, as well as the design for the stable. USAirways even flew some of the figures in from Italy (though no one can confirm that they flew first class!).

Never before has the scene been reproduced. But in 1999, the nativity adorned the USX Plaza on Grant Street for the month-long holiday season. Perhaps the most amazing feat was the army of volunteers that supported the project. From local nuns who sewed garments for the figures, to foundation and corporate support, as well as the Christian Leaders Fellowship, the effort to prevail was truly ecumenical.

Ultimately, worship in Pittsburgh has a complex, multifaceted relationship with the secular world around it. You may not understand this relationship right away—few of us grasp it completely—but you can see a powerful symbol of it whenever you're traveling on Interstate 279 just north of the Allegheny River. It was in the 1970s that this spur of I-279 was conceived as a way of linking the city and its northern suburbs in a manner that might inspire growth throughout the corridor. The problem: the East Street Valley, through which I-279 would pass, was home to a number of residences as well as St. Boniface Church, which served a congregation established in 1884.

Pittsburghers stubbornly resisted the razing of the church. In a compromise that was years in the making, valley residents were relocated and their former homes plowed under; St. Boniface was permitted to remain. Since then, the road has indeed sparked development throughout northern Allegheny County and Butler County. St. Boniface continues to serve parishioners. Regard it as an eerie and solitary reminder of spirituality's prominent place in the heart of Pittsburgh as you tool along that high-speed highway to tomorrow.

INSIDERS' TIP

Those wishing to make tax-deductible gifts to the Pittsburgh Creche Project may send a check designated "Creche Project" to the Diocese of Pittsburgh, 111 Boulevard of the Allies, Pittsburgh, PA 15222.

WORSHIP

Index